BRITISH POLICY TOWARDS
WEST AFRICA

Select Documents, 1875–1914

BRITISH POLICY
TOWARDS
WEST AFRICA

Select Documents
1875–1914

With Statistical Appendices, 1800–1914

C. W. NEWBURY

OXFORD
AT THE CLARENDON PRESS
1971

Oxford University Press, Ely House, London W. 1

GLASGOW NEW YORK TORONTO MELBOURNE WELLINGTON
CAPE TOWN SALISBURY IBADAN NAIROBI DAR ES SALAAM LUSAKA ADDIS ABABA
BOMBAY CALCUTTA MADRAS KARACHI LAHORE DACCA
KUALA LUMPUR SINGAPORE HONG KONG TOKYO

PRINTED IN GREAT BRITAIN
AT THE UNIVERSITY PRESS, OXFORD
BY VIVIAN RIDLER
PRINTER TO THE UNIVERSITY

PREFACE

THIS second volume of official documents continues the survey of British relations with West African societies during the period of international partition, expansion into the interior, and the consolidation of the four colonial states formed under British rule before 1914. Certain limitations are imposed on the selection of primary materials from British sources: international partition, for example, is treated less from the point of view of European diplomatic history and more from the standpoint of officials and traders anxious to preserve and expand revenue, trade, and territory. The details of military campaigns and punitive expeditions which accompanied British expansion have been illustrated more briefly than the increasing use of force might require in a study of the origins of colonial control. On the other hand, it has been necessary to concede a large place to the embryonic developmental goals set by British administration in the fields of commerce, agriculture, mining, and public works.

The statistical appendices surveying British trade with West Africa as a whole cover, as far as sources allow, the chronological period of Volumes I and II. They include the less reliable statistics of finance and trade compiled by the colonial governments of the British territories on the coast and an indication of public loan expenditure before 1914.

The same editorial conventions have been followed as in Volume I, by noting 'A' (Additional), or 'D' (Deleted) sections in amended drafts of dispatches. Primary printed texts have been checked against manuscript documents, where these have survived.

In addition to the editions of basic sources listed in Volume I, selections concerning British relations with the Gold Coast in the later nineteenth century may be usefully supplemented by G. E. Metcalfe, *Great Britain and Ghana: Documents of Ghana History* (University of Ghana, 1964). Other sources for the partition period are to be found in Sir E. Hertslet, *The Map of Africa by Treaty* (London, 1894 and 1909), and in the neglected and more complete treaty series compiled by the Colonial Office in *African* no. 411 (1642–1891) and *African* no. 1010 (1892–1908).

C. W. N.

Institute of Commonwealth Studies, Oxford
October 1970

CONTENTS

LIST OF MAPS

LIST OF SELECT DOCUMENTS
1875–1914
WITH STATISTICAL APPENDICES
1800–1914

I. RELATIONS WITH AFRICAN SOCIETIES
A. SENEGAL, GAMBIA

C. Gold Coast

D. Dahomey, Nigeria

II. EXPANSION AND INTERNATIONAL PARTITION

III. JURISDICTION AND ADMINISTRATION

A. COLONIES AND PROTECTORATES

B. FINANCE AND PUBLIC INVESTMENT

C. Defence: West African Frontier Force

IV. ECONOMIC DEVELOPMENT

A. TRADE AND TARIFFS

V. STATISTICAL APPENDICES: 1800–1914

I

RELATIONS WITH AFRICAN SOCIETIES

Introductory Note

THE methods of regulating relations with African authorities which had evolved from the abolition of the slave trade were continued, after 1875, in order to preserve British trading interests in areas outside administrative control. So long as the undesirability of acquiring West African territory remained a principle of general policy, the main methods were diplomatic missions to the interior, treaties of trade and friendship, stipends, and the use of force. Gradually, the purpose of treaties changed: from about 1884 they were made to keep out foreign rivals, as much as to guarantee open markets; and the use of armed expeditions to resolve conflicts of jurisdiction became more frequent.

The change is readily seen in the most important sphere of British commercial interest—on the Lower Niger and in the Delta—where consular and naval officers attempted to bring order into the palm-oil markets by treaty, arbitration, commercial regulation, bombardments, and removal of chiefs. After 1879, the National African (Royal Niger) Company was encouraged to pursue its own policy of regulating the conditions of trade in the river markets south of the Benue, independently of consular jurisdiction at Bonny and Fernando Po. Elsewhere along the Slave Coast, relations with Dahomey ceased to be of much interest to the Foreign Office or the Colonial Office, following the naval blockade of 1876. But Lagos relations with the Yoruba interior were still considered to be commercially important, and a series of missions, 1879–93, kept open communications between rival African authorities, committing the British Government to further intervention.

In the two northern colonies, Sierra Leone and the Gambia, there was little departure from the well-established methods of treaty and patrol before 1887. In Sierra Leone the policy of paying stipends to chiefs in clientage relations with Freetown was revived in 1875 and brought up to date by Governor Rowe in 1880. But whenever treaties and the reference of internal disputes to Freetown broke down, a growing number of military reprisals were made to keep order in adjacent coastal markets. Expeditions to Bagru and the Sherbro in 1875 were extended into the Scarcies, the Jong river, and to Yoni in 1887. This latter action raised the question of maintaining a permanent police militia and led to the formation of the Sierra Leone Frontier Police in 1890. Along the Gambia the spasmodic destructive wars between Islamized Marabouts and Soninki factions continued unabated. Despite the negative policy of non-interference, there were some notable attempts at diplomacy, treaty-making, and establishing stipendiary relations with Marabout adventurers on the upper river. Communications were kept open with the leaders of the important Fula confederation in Bondu, Futa Jallon, and the Casamance. The Colonial Office under Carnarvon did not permit Acting Administrator Cooper to consolidate these negotiations and arrange a general settlement with African authorities above MacCarthy Island. But other evidence indicates that channels of information were preserved with the Senegal–Gambia interior (A. 4); and from 1877, with official approval, armed patrols by Gouldsbury and others frequented the lower river, without territorial expansion. Both Gouldsbury and Governor Rowe revived the older policy of trying to inflict fines and making payment of stipends.

The year 1887 saw the commencement, first on the Gambia and then in Sierra Leone and the Lagos interior, of a more active policy of treaty-making, in response to French advances in West Africa (A. 9, B. 23, D. 14). The formal definition of the British sphere of influence on the Gambia in 1889 led to a series of expeditions to settle questions of taxation and Soninki–Marabout feuds. Similarly, in the Sierra Leone interior treaties multiplied after 1887, when it was decided to introduce a clause to forestall foreign powers. The employment of diplomatic missions to the Futa Jallon and to Almamy Samori reflected international rivalry, as much as traditional concern for trade routes. Arrears of stipends promised to the Almamy of Timbo under earlier treaties were made up; and relations with Samori were encouraged, so long as the War Office regarded him as a potential ally against the French, rather than a source of danger to authorities within the British sphere of interest in Sierra Leone (B. 18). At Lagos in 1887 pre-emptive treaties of trade and friendship with Ife, Ilaro, and Oyo were authorized to secure western Yoruba as a British sphere; and in 1890 an attempt was made to settle the outstanding dispute in the interior between Ilorin and Ibadan. On the Gold Coast, by contrast, the future of British relations with the Fanti, after 1874, was dominated by unanswered questions about Ashanti. Lacking a regular administration by district commissioners outside the towns, the 'protected' areas adjacent to the coast were somewhat arbitrarily controlled by the use of fines and the deposition of minor chiefs. The policy of paying stipends was not applied, and the abortive taxation policy of the 1850s remained in suspense. There were a few punitive expeditions, such as the savage action against Tavievi in 1888 (C. 9). North of the Prah river, missions to Kumasi by Lonsdale, Barrow, and Ferguson discussed the familiar problems of trade, roads, and refugees which the war of 1873–4 had not settled. The deeper issue, after the war, was the integrity of the Ashanti confederation and its relations with neighbouring states—Adansi, Gyaman, Attabubu. The possible disintegration of the kingdom was envisaged in the Colonial Office. But the accession of Prempeh (Kwaku Dua III) in 1888 ruled out tentative proposals for British protection. As in the other West African settlements, the method of establishing claims to the interior by treaty was commenced in 1892 (C. 15).

By the early 1890s, therefore, the nature of British relations with African societies in the forest zone and the near savannah had begun to change from clientage to formal control, precipitated by international rivalry in the West African markets and implemented by treaties of a new type and by the increasing use of force. In the Gambia this meant little more than the removal of the last of the Marabout war-lords, Fodi Silla and Fodi Kabba, in 1894 and 1901. In Sierra Leone, by 1893, the area demarcated by international treaty began to be organized as a formal protectorate (B. 28). On the Gold Coast, in 1893, the crisis with Ashanti over Attabubu, which was taken under British protection, allowed Governors Griffith and Hodgson to prepare and justify plans for territorial expansion. The final step was delayed by Lord Ripon in 1894. But after the rejection of Governor Maxwell's project for stipendiary status for Ashanti chiefs, the old topics of sacrifices, slaves, missionaries, and the indemnity of 1874 provided pretexts for the ultimatum of 1895 (C. 22). The conquest of Ashanti in 1895–6 opened the way for the protection of neighbouring states and formal administration of the annexed colony. On the Lower Niger the use of force was well established as a means of establishing paramountcy, with the deposition of Nana of Benin in 1894 and the crushing of the Akassa rising by the Niger Company in 1895. In the Lagos interior the decisive military action against Ijebu in 1893 marked a complete break with past policy since the days of Glover. Carter's mission to the interior consolidated treaty relations with Oyo, Abeokuta, and Ibadan; the boundary with Ilorin was roughly positioned. The bombardment of Oyo in 1895 drove home the change from diplomacy to conquest, although the administrative control of western Yoruba was very incompletely defined. But after 1895 British policies of trade and arbitration in the Yoruba states were supervised by resident commissioners, travelling commissioners, and visiting governors. In the east, determination to incorporate Benin within the administration of the Niger Protectorate resulted in the expedition of 1897. To the north, relations with the Hausa–Fulani states were left to the Royal Niger Company. The Akassa rising delayed the campaign projected by Sir George Goldie for the occupation of Bida and Ilorin in 1897. As yet, no action was intended against Sokoto or Gwandu. But after the formation of the West African Frontier Force, Lugard completed the extension of British rule by conquest, beginning with Kontogora and Yola in 1901 and followed by the storming of Kano and the capture of Sokoto in 1903. Limited actions after the 'Satiru' rising of 1906 did not basically alter this paramountcy, established by force and consolidated by Governors Girouard, Bell, and Lugard himself.

A. SENEGAL, GAMBIA

I

ACTING ADMINISTRATOR H. T. M. COOPER TO GOVERNOR C. H. KORTRIGHT: SONINKI-MARABOUT WARS, 30 MARCH 1875[1]

I HAVE the honour to report, that having received information from the Manager of McCarthy Island that Baccary Sardah, King of Bundoo, was in the vicinity of Yarbutenda, our highest trading port on the river, I accordingly proceeded in the Colonial steamer 'St. Mary', to have an interview with him.

I left Bathurst on the 16th February, the Honourable W. H. Berkeley accompanying me, and after visiting various places on my way up, I arrived at Yarbutenda on the evening of the 19th, having run a distance of 330 miles.

On the 20th, I had an interview with the King, who was with his army (mustering about 18,000 men) a few miles off. He expressed his regret at not having met your Excellency; I informed him, however, that it was unavoidable. I then made a proposition to him so that a Conference could be held and matters so arranged on a secure basis that there would be peace throughout the river henceforth. He fell into my views, which were, that Mahmoud ⁿDerry Bar, the great Marabout Chief, Moloh, the great Foulah King, myself, and himself, should meet at a certain rendezvous and discuss the subject. The place named was Contafarra, a town midway between McCarthy Island and Yarbutenda (the latter distant from the former 150 miles). I named the 20th of March for the day of the Conference.

[Cooper met the King of Bondu, Bokari Sardu, again at Yarbutenda on 22 March; he requested military aid in the form of a blockhouse and an increased subsidy; Cooper later visited Mahmud NDari Bar in Baddibu, but could obtain no joint meeting between the chiefs.]

[1] *Parl. Papers*, 1876, lii [C. 1409], pp. 32–4. *Capt. H. T. M. Cooper* of the Royal Marines had seen active service in China, San Juan, British Columbia, and was Acting Administrator of the Gambia, 1872–6. This policy of building up an alliance of Gambia chiefs was not approved: Carnarvon to Kortright, 18 June 1875, C.O. 87/107; but local officials persisted in the practice.

2

ACTING ADMINISTRATOR H. T. M. COOPER TO LORD CARNARVON: SONINKI-MARABOUT WARS, 20 JUNE 1875[1]

As a length of time will elapse before I can receive advice from Sierra Leone as to how the present urgent matter is to be tided over, I earnestly request your Lordship's instructions as soon as convenient. The Marabouts in Lower Combo have succeeded in destroying the last remaining stronghold of the Sonninkees (viz., Busumballa), but as the latter have taken refuge in a town by name of Lamin, and which is about 400 yards from the British ground, and a place called Albert Town, yet I do not feel myself justified in enforcing them to remove (the two Sonninkee Kings being there) as they state that the arrangement made with the Marabouts as regards neutral ground (copies enclosed) by Governor Kortright was not agreed to by them, and, therefore, the ground is still in their possession.

The town of Lamin has been in existence for some years, and has been taken and retaken by the hostile parties, lastly by the Sonninkees, who now hold it.

The Marabouts have as yet acted straight forwardly to us, but some renegades employed by them are quite ready in the event of their capturing the town of Lamin to push on to our ground in pursuit of the refugees. Besides this, the refugees that have been collecting on our territory are ready to run to the assistance of their friends, in the event of an attack being made on the town of Lamin, and I have, therefore, ordered the available police (thirty-eight) to the frontier line to disarm all those running on to our ground, or from our ground to join the hostile parties (copy of Proclamation inclosed).[2] This with my small force is attended with risk, and if a man is wounded or shot it might implicate me, as I have the whole responsibility on myself. I therefore ask permission to demand the evacuation of the town of Lamin, or the destruction of the same, this being the only course open to me, as I have already had interviews with both Marabouts and Sonninkees, and offered the latter ground on our ceded mile in Barra (on the opposite side of [the] river), and which they refused; on the other hand, if some decided course is not taken when the attack is made shots must enter our ground and probably kill our subjects, stockades having been erected ten yards

---

[1] C.O. 87/107. For the significance of this Marabout advance for the history of the Gambia basin, see J. M. Gray, *A History of the Gambia* (Cambridge, 1940), p. 455.
[2] Encl. Proclamation, 10 June 1875. See also *Parl. Papers*, 1876, lii [C. 1409], p. 43.

from our line in order to cover the retreat of runaways should the town of Lamin be broken.

My force being, as I have said before, so small, it is necessary that a decisive move be made; I will carry it out to the best of my ability, and I think successfully, but if the matter is delayed, trouble may arise. The Marabouts intend soon to attack, but I have sufficient influence over them to put them off for a time, unless they are annoyed by the opposite parties.

3

LORD CARNARVON TO THE OFFICER ADMINISTERING THE GOVERNMENT: SONINKI–MARABOUT WARS, 9 JULY 1875[1]

I HAVE received your despatch of the 20th ultimo, reporting that the Marabouts had destroyed the last stronghold of the Sonninkees in Lower Combo, and that the latter had taken refuge in a town called Lamin, close to the British frontier, and requesting instructions for your guidance under the circumstances.

2. I hope that before this time you will have had the advantage of the presence and advice of the new administrator, Dr. Rowe, and that the position of affairs may have assumed a less critical aspect.

3. I am not, however, prepared in any case, without much fuller explanation of the reasons which induce you to propose such a course, to authorize you to demand the evacuation or destruction of the town of Lamin, or to make as you propose, any 'decisive move'.

4. Even if I were fully satisfied that such a proceeding was in itself right, I should hesitate to sanction your undertaking it with the small force at your command, as any unsuccessful action might produce disastrous and even irretrievable results.

5. I have therefore to urge upon you the imperative necessity of using the utmost caution and circumspection in your dealings with the natives, and of making every endeavour by negotiation and remonstrance to preserve peace.

6. I have requested the Lords Commissioners of the Admiralty to make arrangements for despatching a man-of-war at once to Bathurst, but you will understand that she is sent for the purpose of affording the Colonial Government moral countenance and support, and is not to be brought into action except to secure the safety of the lives and property of British subjects.

---

[1] *Parl. Papers*, 1876, lii [C. 1409], pp. 44–5; and Minutes in C.O. 87/107 which suggest that these disturbances were accepted as additional reasons for an exchange of territories with France. Herbert to F.O., 8 July 1875, C.O. 87/108.

4

ACTING ADMINISTRATOR H. T. M. COOPER TO BOKARI SARDU, KING OF BONDU: DIPLOMATIC RELATIONS, 13 MAY 1876[1]

MY GOOD FRIEND,

As an opportunity occurs I write a few lines to you unofficially and send it by one Mustapha who is about to journey to Segou Sekora[2]— he is a personal friend of mine and understands English well.

As all idea of the transfer of the Gambia to France is for the present at an end, it now becomes necessary to make the country more good than it has ever been—to effect this, I have proposed, as have also some of the people in England, to open up trade with the interior by Segou and Timbuctoo, but as I should like to become acquainted with all the Kings and Chiefs on the route and also make arrangements as regards the protection and assistance to traders and others forming the caravans which I hope will eventually be found passing to and fro from the Headwaters of the Gambia to the Niger. I therefore if able to leave this Settlement in the beginning of July, intend to visit your Capital. I hope you will find me a few Horses & Mules for my journey. From your Capital I shall pass to Kasso and visit your father-in-law, King Samballa,[3] and from thence through Guemakoro,[4] Marcoia, Yamina and on to Segou to visit King Amade Seyhou.

If I succeed in all this, trade for both parties will be greatly increased, and I know you as a sensible King will agree with me in this.

My object is to make as quick a trip as possible, so as to return before the bad months of September & October. Therefore, it solely remains with you men of power to afford me all the help you can.

Wishing you all health and prosperity,

Ever your true friend [no signature].

---

[1] Archives Nationales, Section Outre-Mer, Sénégal, IV. 45/c. The original (with Gambia Government seal) must have come into French hands in 1877 or 1878. It was forwarded to Paris by Governor Brière de l'Isle, 8 May 1880, in support of his arguments for a French advance to the Upper Senegal-Niger.

[2] Segu-Sikoro, capital of the loose federation of states left by El-hadj Umar.

[3] Samballa was an ally of the French in an anti-Tukolor alliance on the middle Senegal.

[4] Guémoukoura—on the salt and gold route to Yamina, across the path of French military operations in 1879-80.

5

ADMINISTRATOR V. S. GOULDSBURY TO ACTING GOVERNOR H. J. HUGGINS: USE OF THE GUNBOAT, 14 APRIL 1877[1]

[He has toured the Gambia river as far as Parang to investigate cases of theft and assault; chiefs have been fined, or cautioned to refer disputes to Bathurst for settlement.]

... On the evening of [8 April] I landed at Baragally, and had an interview with the chief and principal people. I thought it advisable to make some demonstration of power at this place, as it was here that Captain Cooper was insulted on the occasion of his last visit. I therefore requested Captain Heron [of H.M.S. *Seagull*] to have all his available boats manned and brought close to the landing place, and accompanied by him and some of his officers with a detachment of police, I landed and awaited the Chief's arrival. After some little delay the Chief made his appearance, and we had a long 'palaver', during which I pointed out the advantages of being on friendly terms with us, and impressed upon these people the folly of ever exhibiting a hostile spirit, or harbouring any enmity towards us. I spoke at considerable length, and was listened to in a most respectful and attentive manner. The Chief in his reply stated that all I said was true, and that he and his people were most desirous to keep friends with the English, and that they would always do whatever I directed. He thanked me for all the good advice which I had given him, and assured me that there would be no trouble for the future. I may here state that the young man who was Chief in Captain Cooper's time has been deposed, and an older man has been elected in his place. By permission of Captain Heron I invited the Chief and any others who chose, to come aboard the 'Seagull' and inspect her armaments, and one headman and about a dozen of his followers took advantage of the offer, the Chief excusing himself on the plea of its being late. Those who came on board were shown the offensive equipment of the ship, and the headman was permitted to fire off one of the cannon. A rocket was also fired and gave rise to much wonderment. Altogether, I think that what these natives witnessed on board will have the happy effect of keeping the Baragally people in awe for some time to come. Leaving Baragally on the morning of the 9th instant, we arrived back at Bathurst early on the following day.

[1] *Parl. Papers*, 1877, lx [C. 1827], pp. 36–7. *Surgeon-Major V. S. Gouldsbury* was Administrator of the Gambia, 1877–84, but is better known for his exploration in 1881 of the Gambia–Futa Jallon–Sierra Leone region. *H. J. Huggins*, Chief Justice of Sierra Leone, was interim Administrator before the arrival of (Sir) Samuel Rowe in 1877.

Gouldsbury's policy was approved in Carnarvon to Huggins, 31 May 1877, C.O. 87/110. He made other patrols with armed police in 1877 to protect trade routes from attack: Gouldsbury to Rowe, 30 October 1877, C.O. 87/110.

12. In order to make the natives aware of the presence of the gunboat in the river, I requested Captain Heron to have a cannon fired at several points along our route, and I have been since told that the report of these guns was heard at a distance of 20 miles.

13. I am convinced that the appearance at this juncture of an armed vessel in the river has been of much service in inculcating respect and obedience to us on the part of the natives, and that this manifestation of power, and of the capacity for the infliction of punishment, has strongly tended to weaken, if not destroy, the arrogant and troublesome spirit which appeared to exist.

14. With reference to the outrages already alluded to, I have to state that in my opinion they were, if not occasioned, at least contributed to, by the conduct of the traders themselves.

15. I am glad to be able to report that none of the officers or crew of the 'Seagull' suffered from the trip up to McCarthy Island, the health of the ship being unusually good . . .

6

ADMINISTRATOR V. S. GOULDSBURY TO GOVERNOR SIR SAMUEL ROWE: STIPENDIARY CHIEFS, 29 AUGUST 1879[1]

[Gouldsbury has visited Baddibu to make peace between Momodu N'Dare Ba and his lieutenant, Bairam Sisi. The former has been fined $2,470 (£500).]

. . . IN the meantime I beg to recommend that a temporary and provisional subsidy be granted to Beram Ceesay, as he has more than half of the trading stations in Baddiboo in his possession and he protects and encourages trade.

35. Under treaty engagements Mahmood 'Dare Bah bound himself to protect and foster trade in Baddiboo and the neighbouring countries, but his power is limited now, as half his kingdom has been wrested from him, and even in the portion he has as yet been able to retain, his power and influence are much circumscribed.

36. Under the treaty mentioned he receives from this Government a subsidy of £100 per annum, and does so on the conditions of his capacity to carry out, and the fulfilment of, certain engagements. For more than two years these conditions have not subsisted, at least in their entirety; and it becomes a question whether a new (even if temporary) arrangement should not be enacted into, by which the subsidy of £100 a year would be divided between Mahmood

[1] C.O. 87/114. Encl. in Rowe to Hicks Beach, 5 September 1879. The C.O. approved Rowe's instructions to pay Bairam Sisi a stipend to encourage the end of the war in Baddibu.

'Dare Bah and Beram Ceesay, or as an alternative arrangement, whether Beram Ceesay should not receive a subsidy equivalent in amount to that enjoyed by Mahmood 'Dare Bah. . . .

7

A. W. L. HEMMING: MINUTE, FODI KABBA, 1 JANUARY 1880[1]

WE certainly cannot accept any cession of the Jolah country. Even if there were no risk of involving ourselves in hostilities with Fodey Cabbah—and we cannot tell what more powerful chief or tribe might take up his quarrel—the present settlement at the Gambia is quite troublesome enough without any extension of its limits.

Nor can we, I think, interfere actively to stop his incursions. If we attempt to put down slave-hunting in Africa we shall indeed have our hands full.

I would reply that one of the Jolahs should be informed that H.M. is not prepared to accept the cession of their territory or take them under Her protection, but that she regrets that they should be exposed to the attacks of Fodey Cabbah, & Her officers will be instructed to use their good offices to induce him to desist from molesting them & suggest to Dr. Rowe that the Adm[inistrator] should visit the Jolah country in the colonial steamer & endeavour to see Fodey Cabbah & inform him that H.M. views his proceedings with displeasure & try to make an agreement with him to leave the Jolahs alone.

8

ACTING ADMINISTRATOR G. T. CARTER TO CHIEF SAID MATTI: PEACE WITH BADDIBU CHIEFS, 24 JANUARY 1887[2]

I AM glad to be able to inform you that the Queen has been pleased to approve of my entering into a treaty with you on the lines of the conditions which I have already communicated to you, and to which you have signified your agreement.

2. I propose therefore on Saturday next to visit Suwarra Cunda

[1] C.O. 87/114. On Gouldsbury to Rowe, 17 November 1879. For the career of this Marabout chief see Gray, *History of the Gambia*, pp. 452-3. Hemming's note was incorporated in Hicks Beach to Rowe (draft), 26 January 1880.

[2] C.O. 879/26, no. 341. Encl. in Hay to Holland, 13 February 1887. The treaty was signed, 11 February 1887, recognizing Matti as stipendiary chief for the protection of British subjects. It was followed by a round of treaty-making later in the year by Samuel Rowe in Jola (15 September), Fogni (17 September), Kiang (19 September), Jarra (11 October), for peace, access for trade, reference of disputes to Bathurst—and the exclusion of foreign powers.

Creek in a man-of-war, so that a meeting might take place, and a formal treaty be entered into between you and this Government.

3. You will be required to protect British and other legitimate traders at all your ports, to guarantee to levy none but the usual customs, or to permit any to be levied by your subordinates, to cease all warlike operations against Mahmood ᴺDerry Bah and Beram Ceasey, and to guarantee not to engage in any hostilities in Baddiboo, without consulting the Governor at Bathurst. To respect the life of Mahmoud ᴺDerry Bah, and in conjunction with Beram Ceasey to make suitable provision for him so long as he remains quiet and resigns himself to the changed conditions of affairs in Baddiboo. To refrain from molesting or demanding customs from the peaceable settlers on the borders of the Ceded Mile, who have never recognized the authority of the Chiefs of Baddiboo. Much trouble has already been caused in this district by your messengers falsely representing that I had given certain towns to you, viz., Backendick, Kotu, ᴺBullet and Aljahmoodoo, whereas I distinctly stated that they were not mine to give, and that they were merely outside British territory.

4. Lastly, you will be required to leave Beram Ceasey in peaceable possession of the towns he has acquired, and to recognize him as the Chief of that portion of Baddiboo over which he now exercises jurisdiction.

5. In the event of your formally accepting these terms, and so long as you respect them, Her Majesty will honour you by regarding you as an ally, and bestowing a stipend of 100 *l.* a year upon you.

6. You will, I trust, therefore be in a position to state definitely whether you are prepared faithfully to adhere to these terms, as soon as possible after my arrival on Saturday next.

9

R. H. MEADE TO SIR SAMUEL ROWE: GAMBIA TREATIES, 14 APRIL 1887[1]

I AM directed by Sir H. Holland to acquaint you that he has under his consideration, in connexion with your approaching visit to the Gambia, the question of the position of the settlement with respect to the Native territories lying immediately to the north and south of its present limits.

As you are aware, France exercises a protectorate and influence over the countries bordering the Saloum river on the north and the Casamance river on the south.

But between these French territories and the boundaries of British

[1] C.O. 879/26, no. 341. (*Sir*) *R. H. Meade* was Assistant Under-Secretary, 1871–92, and Permanent Under-Secretary, 1892–7, in the C.O.

jurisdiction there are considerable spaces of country over which neither power has at present exercised any authority.

In the interests of British trade and influence on the Gambia it is very undesirable that the French should obtain possession of these districts, as, with the forward action which they are constantly taking in West Africa, it appears not improbable they may attempt to do.

The territories in question are the Barra country, within the 'Ceded Mile' on the north bank of the rivers, and Foreign Combo and Fagni on the south.

Sir H. Holland is not prepared to recommend to Her Majesty's Government that any steps should be taken to assume or exercise a protectorate over these districts, or to annex them in any way to the Gambia settlement.

But he considers it expedient that, if possible, they should be brought within the influence of Great Britain, and I am accordingly to instruct you to endeavour to negotiate with the Chiefs, during your visit to the Gambia, treaties of friendship, including a provision that they will not cede their territories to any other power, or enter into any arrangement with a foreign Government, except through Her Majesty's Government, or with their consent.

It will also be desirable that the Chiefs should agree, if they are willing to do so, to grant protection and facilities to British traders, and to refer any quarrels which may occur among themselves to the arbitration of the Government of Bathurst.

Should you find it necessary, Sir H. Holland will not object to your granting to the Chiefs moderate stipends for the purpose of securing their observance of the treaties, but you will, of course, bear in mind that the finances of the Gambia will not allow of any large outlay on this account.

10

ADMINISTRATOR R. B. LLEWELYN TO LORD KNUTSFORD: GAMBIA CHIEFS, 15 DECEMBER 1891[1]

I HAVE the honour to report that I left Bathurst on the 3rd instant in the steam launch 'Lily' and visited the undermentioned places on the north bank of the river:

(1) Cowar in Saloum just beyond Ballangar, 100 miles from Bathurst;

[1] C.O. 879/36, no. 425. (*Sir*) *R. B. Llewelyn* had been a C.O. clerk; he had served in the West Indies and was Administrator of the Gambia, 1891-9. For the campaign against Fodi Kabba, see Gray, *History of the Gambia*, pp. 466-7, 470-2. The destruction of Toniataba and other towns, 1892-4, led to the complete annexation of Kombo.

(2) Salikaine Creek, and up the Creek to the town;

(3) Suara Creek, and up the Creek to the town,

principally with the object of ascertaining what 'Customs', which word covers all sorts of taxes, were still being demanded in those places by certain persons who continued to act, as alleged, on the authority given to them by the French Government prior to the agreement of the 10th August 1889, by which the boundary line of French influence on the Gambia was determined to be 10 kilometres from the banks of the river.

2. At all the foregoing places I was informed by the Alcaides[1] the 'Customs' are still ordered to be collected for the Chiefs placed over those districts by the French Authorities, although the Chiefs are domiciled outside the English line and live entirely under French Protection; and it is this matter which I now beg to lay before your Lordship, as I think the time has arrived for the practice to cease.

3. The king of Saloum, who lives on the River Saloum, within a mile or two of the French town of Kaolakh, three days' journey from the Gambia, still sends and demands 'Customs' at Cowar and elsewhere near by.

4. NJie Bah, who lives at Nioro, and acts, I was informed, as he alleges, under the orders of the French Commandant stationed there, still demands 'Customs' at Salikaine and 'Suarakunda'.

5. There is also a Chief named Hamar Khojia or Amar Kodia, who lives at Kutango under French protection a long way up the Suara Creek, over the English line, but he still demands 'Customs' in Jukardu, which is on the banks of the Gambia at the mouth of the Suara Creek.

6. Lastly, N'Dari Kanni, who lives at Kataba, a town within the English line a little to the north-west of Devil's Point, demands 'Customs' at Ballangar on the banks of the river and at other places near by. It was at Kataba that the Boundary Commission a year ago found the French flag flying, and N'Dari Kanni alleges he is acting under orders from Nioro.

7. I respectfully submit to your Lordship that it is very desirable that the French Authorities in Senegal should receive instructions from Paris that they are to notify the Chiefs above mentioned, and all others to whom they have given the right to collect 'Customs' in territory on the banks of the Gambia now within the English line, that, as the boundaries have now been determined and the maps issued, that all such rights are cancelled.

8. On the part of Her Majesty's Government, I beg to be authorised to inform the Chiefs and Kings of the places, now under treaty with this Government, which have been ascertained to be outside the line,

---

[1] *Sic*, Alkali, a village chief in Muslim Gambia.

of the change that has taken place and the necessity for cancelling the treaties.

9. I append a list of the towns in Fogni and Jarra, which, as far as I can ascertain, specifies all the places within [outside?] the Government of the Gambia affected by the Treaty of the 10th August 1889.[1]

II

ADMINISTRATOR R. B. LLEWELYN TO THE MARQUIS OF RIPON: KOMBO, 20 MARCH 1894[2]

I HAVE the honour to report to your Lordship that directly Fodey Silah was driven out of Gunjar on the 9th instant, the people in the several towns which had been under his sway began to arrive in Bathurst and offered to submit to the English, so it then became necessary to initiate as quickly as possible some form of government in a conquered country without any headman.

2. As reported to your Lordship in my telegrams, noted in the margin, the Executive Council considered that on account of its proximity to Bathurst, the conquered country should be annexed and form part of the Colony.

3. The question however, was, I admit, rather too important to be decided upon at once, and as it was very necessary to take some immediate action (for the headmen, with their followers, of twenty towns were stopping here to hear the decision of Her Majesty's Government) I held a public palaver in M'Carthy Square at 4 p.m. on the 19th instant without waiting for your Lordship's reply, with the headmen of the towns named in the annexed schedule which represent all the towns in Foreign Combo except Gunjur, Brekama, and Busamballa, where Fodi Silah himself was Chief.

4. In order to make some little impression upon the natives, I asked for a guard of honour of sailors, marines, and West Indian soldiers and invited the public to attend, which they did in considerable number, and the Admiral with his staff, all the Members of Council, Heads of Departments, &c., were present too.

5. I then asked first if the headmen I saw assembled before me acknowledged themselves conquered, and submitted to Her Majesty the Queen, to which they responded by all taking off their caps, bowing their heads to the ground, and remained uncovered during the whole of the palaver.

[1] See below II. 37.
[2] C.O. 879/40, no. 463. This action was approved in C.O. to Llewelyn, 27 April 1894, C.O. 87/145. Fodi Silla as leader of the Kombo Muslims had made a treaty in 1874. Following his defeat in 1894 he was deported to St. Louis.

6. I then told them that, as the Queen has conquered their country, I was now their Chief and they would be governed by English law, and not the law of the Koran.

7. I informed them that, as their Chief, I was entitled to receive customs from the people, but I could not tell them at that meeting what they would have to pay, but possibly a land rent as their neighbours in British Combo did. This did not surprise them at all for they all know the law and practice in the Colony.

8. I explained to them with firmness that the old religious feuds between the Marabouts and Soninkeys would not be allowed to be resuscitated, and they must live peaceably together as elsewhere in the Protectorate, as the English law made no distinction in dealing with persons of different religions.

9. I announced that I allowed the descendants of the old Soninkey inhabitants of the towns of Brekama and Busamballa to return there and they were not to be molested on any consideration and that Busamballa, from its central position, would be my chief town.

10. I introduced Mr. Sitwell[1] to them as the officer I had appointed to travel through the country to see that the details of my orders were carried out, and read out to them the principal orders, of which the attached is a copy.

11. I told them clearly that all the roads were to be open free to all people and they were not on any consideration to stop or interfere in any way with the Jolahs who were passing through the country, but I did not allude to the slave trade, as I thought it better to postpone dealing with this until matters were more settled.

12. At the end of the meeting I told them all to go to their homes, settle down quietly and receive Mr. Sitwell with attention and respect, which they promised to do, and then all shook hands with me and the meeting broke up.

13. Mr. Sitwell, whom I have transferred to Combo from his district higher up the river on the south bank, left this morning with an escort of 25 soldiers (part of the regular garrison of Bathurst) to travel through the whole country which I hope he will thoroughly and successfully accomplish in about three or four weeks.

14. With the information before me which he will collect I shall be able to submit to your Lordship further details and suggestions for the future government of the country.

---

[1] *F. C. Sitwell* one of the first Travelling Commissioners in the Gambia Protectorate (murdered at Sankandi, 1901).

12

ADMINISTRATOR SIR G. C. DENTON TO JOSEPH CHAMBERLAIN: FODI KABBA (TELEGRAM), 21 JANUARY 1901[1]

WITH regard to Fodi Kabba, Ballay[2] has been consulting with his Government, but he says that in any case he cannot take action for six weeks. Consider that most important Fodi Kabba should be crushed and am sure that results will fully justify delay. Brake says that unnecessary to retain men of West India Regiment, and that we can do our part with the Central Africans if the 'Dwarf' goes to Vintang Creek without landing men. Have I authority to agree to delay, and do you approve of West India Regiment being sent away on termination of river operations? I am now proceeding up the river with forces to deal with Sandu and Wuli. The Musa Mollo matter urgently requires settlement:[3] if I can make arrangements with him involving substantial stipend have I authority to promise £200 per annum?

B. GUINEA, SIERRA LEONE

I

R. H. MEADE: MINUTE, SHERBRO CHIEFS, 3 AUGUST 1875[4]

I HAVE gone through these several subjects with Mr. Kortright seriatim.

1. It will clearly be desirable to get possession of Mongeri [Creek] so far as to allow us to place customs officers on it & collect duties. We do not want to increase our responsibilities in other matters or to

---

[1] C.O. 879/66, no. 643. In March French forces captured Medina and killed Fodi Kabba. The punitive expedition agreed to by Chamberlain had been delayed by other colonial wars in Ashanti and South Africa: Chamberlain to Griffith, 16 November 1900. *Sir George Denton* had been Administrator of Lagos for periods, 1889–1900, and was Administrator and Governor of the Gambia, 1900–11.

[2] *N. E. Ballay*, Governor of Senegal and Governor-General of French West Africa, 1899–1902.

[3] *Sic*, Musa Mollah's territory lay either side of the international boundary. By agreement with Denton, 7 June 1901, he came under British protection and resided in British Gambia. See Gray, *History of the Gambia*, p. 479.

[4] C.O. 267/238: on Kortright to C.O., 28 April 1875. Governor Kortright was in London at this date; his dispatches recommending implementation of Governor Kennedy's plan to pay stipends to Sherbo chiefs (approved by Lord Granville in 1869) are in *Parl. Papers*, 1875, lii [C. 1343], pp. 15–36. Encl. peace treaty with Sisi Hanmoh and others, 19 April 1875.

govern more than at present. Mr. K[ortright] agrees in this and thinks that Dr. Rowe might be instructed to open negotiations with Chief Caulker with this object. (He is described as a civilized black man i.e. he dresses in the European fashion & can sit down to table & can eat clean.) Mr. K[ortright] thinks for a yearly stipend there will be no difficulty in getting what we want.[1]

2. I should approve the removal from Bonthe to Bendoo which should be carried out with as little delay as possible. Mr. K[ortright] thinks that the sum he mentions £3,000 (which includes the gaol) will be more than sufficient to do what is necessary.

3. As surplus revenue from Sherbro is annually paid into the Sierra Leone Treasury, the proper arrangement in ordinary circs. would be to make S. Leone provide these necessary funds, but this is impossible—they have no balance and we have lately increased taxation considerably.

I would therefore propose that Dr. Rowe consider whether a small additional duty should be levied in the Sherbro for the express purpose of providing the requisite funds—such duty to be discontinued when the amount has been raised. . . .

2

GOVERNOR SAMUEL ROWE TO
LORD CARNARVON: SHERBRO CHIEFS,
13 MAY 1876[2]

[Enclosing lists of chiefs who have signed agreements and plans of their territories.]

. . . 11. IT might be suggested, My Lord, that as the districts represented by these Chiefs are all outside British territory, their state does not concern us except in so far as it may jeopardize the security of those living on the land under our rule: but in the present state of the Exchequer of Sierra Leone, with an expenditure which cannot be readily reduced, and a revenue dependent almost entirely on the Customs duties; remembering that the greater part of this revenue is collected on goods which are carried beyond our limits to be exchanged there for produce which has been brought from countries still more distant; and that the articles furnished by the British possessions for export may be put down as nearly nil, Your Lordship will at once

[1] Rowe made three treaties with R. C. B. Caulker and George Stephen Caulker and their clans, as chiefs of Bumpe, Ribi, and Cockboro creeks, 21 and 30 December 1875, to consolidate this extension.
[2] C.O. 267/329: encl. treaties with Sisi Hanmoh, Tom Cabby Smith, chiefs of Small Boom and Imperi, 8 May 1876. (*Sir*) *Samuel Rowe* was an army surgeon, Administrator of the Gambia, 1875–6, Governor of the Gold Coast, 1881–4, and Governor of the West African Settlements, 1876–81, 1884–8.

recognise how necessary it is to Sierra Leone that the trade routes to the inland Country should be free, if it be hoped to secure any relation between income and expenditure of the Settlement as derived from existing taxation.

3

GOVERNOR SAMUEL ROWE TO SCARCIES CHIEFS: TREATIES, 25 FEBRUARY 1879[1]

MY FRIENDS,

You, I have no doubt, remember my visit to the Scarcies River in June 1876, when I met you and your brother chiefs at Massammah, when Gambia town was all broken down and the war troubling you on both sides.

2. You will remember also that at that time you and your brother Chiefs signed an agreement in which you offered to Her Majesty the Queen of England the sovereignty of certain parts of your territory, if she should think it desirable to acquire it.[2]

3. At my frequent interviews with you since that time this agreement has often been mentioned by you, and I have always told you that it had not been forgotten, and that you must be patient.

4. I have now the pleasure to tell you that I have received Her Majesty's instructions to notify you that she ratifies the treaty made at Massammah, Great Scarcies River on the 10 June 1876, and accepts the cession of territory which you then offered . . .

4

GOVERNOR SIR SAMUEL ROWE TO SIR MICHAEL HICKS BEACH: CHIEFS' STIPENDS, 24 APRIL 1880[3]

. . . 3. I HAVE succeeded in compiling what I believe to be a complete list with reference to the Treaty or authority under which they are paid; and returns showing the arrears of stipends due to each chief

---

[1] C.O. 879/15, no. 175.

[2] Treaty, 10 June 1876, with Alimamy Sattan Lahai, Bey Farimah, Bey Incah, Bey Sherbro, Bey Mauro (and for two absent chiefs). The chiefs later denied such a cession in a letter to Rowe, 17 March 1879, claiming they had signed only a peace treaty with the Susu. Encl. in Rowe to Beach, 9 July 1879: C.O. 267/338. In the C.O. Hemming took the view the treaty should be upheld: Minute, 2 August 1879; and it had been confirmed locally by proclamation, 25 February 1879.

[3] C.O. 267/340. This policy was approved. For 1879, stipends were evaluated at £837. 1s., and arrears due at 31 December 1879, £1,685, Streeten to Kimberley: C.O. 267/341.

at the end of each year 1876–7–8–9 and consecutive returns proving the accuracy of these statements.

4. In the Estimates for the years 1880, 1879, 1878, the amount of these stipends due for the year was put at £822. 1. 8, and this was considered as the whole sum due for the coming year although £837. 1. 8. would appear to be due by the Books.

5. The sum of £15. o. o. annually due to the Alimamy Mormoh Sankoh is considered forfeited. It would not be paid to any successor of that Chief excepting on receipt of some satisfactory explanation which in the opinion of the Governor would entitle the successor of Alimamy Mormoh Sankoh to a resumption of stipend.

6. The amounts of these outstanding stipends for which provision was made among the liabilities of previous years in the Estimates of 1878–1880 are also less than the amounts which would be thought outstanding on looking at the gross return as the amounts due for stipends considered forfeited and those amounts due for long arrears . . . were deducted from the amount which it seemed likely would be outstanding on the gross account at the close of the year.

7. I have been wishful to arrange that all these stipends should in future be made payable for the period from 1st January to 31 December. This would be a convenience in the Accounts.

8. I believe also it will be a convenience to the chiefs and tend to prevent requests for payment of an advance a practice to which I have always objected.

9. Such an arrangement would also be desirable with a view to bringing together the Chiefs from different Districts at the same time in Freetown in the early part of the year, a time favourable for travel . . .

5

ACTING GOVERNOR W. W. STREETEN TO LORD KIMBERLEY: KOYA WAR, 16 SEPTEMBER 1880[1]

I HAVE the pleasure in informing your Lordship that Chiefs Lahie Bundoo & Gbannah Sehrey—the principal combatants in the late

---

[1] C.O. 267/341. Agreement, 17 September 1880, encl. in Streeten to Kimberley, 18 September 1880, signed by: Almamy Lahai (Bundu), Gbennah Sehrey (Koya), Seku Kamara (Porto Loko), Bokari Bomboli (Koya), Bome Rufa (Koya), Bey Mauro (Bulom), Alimami Fenda, Sankassi Modo (Bulom), Kanray Mahoi (Ribi), Santiggy Nonkoh Lahai (Porto Loko), Santiggy Ansumana Yeamy (Porto Loko), Sori Kamara (Porto Loko), Santiggy Dibbea (Porto Loko), Maliggy Langley (Porto Loko), Lama, Pa King (Koya), Ansumanna (Koya), Sadu Bonkay (Koya), Santiggy Malanko (Koya), Fodey Kamara (Koya), Gballoo Modu (Koya), Santiggy Momo (Koya), Sulimani Bundu (Koya), Touray Bundu, Thompson, Santiggy Kabba (Loko Marsama), Ansumana Foray, Musa (Bulom), Hannah Modu Kroo, Foday Yarneh, Canray Lenkey (Ribi), Tuah Bendu (Ribi), Bokari Sehrey, Sogo Felleh. Fines were paid by Alimamy Bundu Gbennah Sehrey: Minutes, 14 September 1880.

Quiah War—together with the Queens of Quiah and all the principal surrounding Kings and Chiefs have arrived here . . . with the object of being allowed to enter into a general agreement for peace.

2. Chiefs Lahie Bundoo and Gbannah Sehrey have I believe made all the restitution in their power and have expressed the greatest contribution for their past behaviour.

3. I will not trouble your Lordship with the means by which this result has been attained except to observe that I have been greatly assisted in my efforts to bring about peace by Bey Mauro King of the North Bulloms and Alimami Sannassi Chief of Medina Bullom Shore with whose names Your Lordship will be familiar.

4. I receive the whole party—about 300 in number—tomorrow to sign an Agreement with the usual formalities and I trust I am not too sanguine in thinking that there will be no more Quiah disturbances for a long time to come.

6

A MESSAGE FROM SAMORI TO GOVERNOR W. W. STREETEN, 28 SEPTEMBER 1880[1]

STATES, the King sends me with 44 others as the road is so dangerous to accompany the Governor's messengers and see them safe to Freetown. The King gave me no letter but 2 Gold rings as a token of his respect to the Governor and directs me to say to the Governor that he is pleased and thankful to God that the Governor of Sierra Leone sent messengers to see him with letter and presents and thus takes notice of him which never had taken place before in their ancestors' lifetime, and that he hopes this friendship will continue for ever.

The long detention of the messengers is in consequence of the unsettled state of the country and for the Governor's sake every possible care and respect have been taken and shown to them. That he never thought before that the Governor will ever send someone to see him and he thanked God for this notice the Governor of Sierra Leone has taken of him and when he heard the news that the Governor's messengers of Sierra Leone are on the way coming to see him he sent for all his people and informed them that the Governor of Sierra Leone was coming, because his messengers represent him and they received him as such and thanked the Governor for the presents he sent to him and he has not much to say but look[s] to the Governor

[1] C.O. 267/341. 'Foday Alhassannah Suroomadee' representative of 'Sarmadoo' (Samori), Chief of 'Baliyah' (Beyla?): Statement, encl. in Streeten to Kimberley, 3 October 1880. Streeten also forwarded a 'Memorandum of Information' on the trade of Dinguiray and Beyla, 16 October 1880.

as his own friend; whilst the messengers were near his town he sent 1500 of his fighting men to meet [them] on the way, and caused them to fire off 1000 of their guns in honour of the Governor, and sent me with full authority to treat with the Governor in every matter he requires.

7

ADMINISTRATOR V. S. GOULDSBURY: REPORT OF THE FUTA JALLON EXPEDITION, JUNE 1881[1]

[29 March 1881]

. . . HAVING entered the King's yard, I found the potentate himself seated amongst his chiefs and officers, and, the usual salutations having been gone through and compliments exchanged, I was at leisure to observe the King and his surroundings. I found Almamy (King) Ibrahema Soriah to be a man of about 60 years of age, rather tall and slight (as most Foulahs are), and of a pleasing and fairly intelligent countenance. His demeanour throughout our interview was calm and dignified, and yet friendly; and he and his chiefs manifested much pleasure at my arrival. Close to and a little behind the Almamy sat his prime minister or chief adviser, a tall, handsome, old man, with a face expressive of intelligence, wisdom, and determination, and, withal, a face full of kindness and good nature.

On either side of the King his chiefs and retainers were ranged in the form of a semi-circle, and all wore the ordinary Mohammedan costume, the Almamy, as far as dress was concerned, being undistinguishable from his chiefs.

I and my officers having taken seats, I acquainted the Almamy with the objects and reason of my visit to his country, and told him from whence I came, and whither I was going, besides relating something of our journey; and I then conveyed to him Her Majesty's message of peace and friendship, and informed him of Her wishes for the welfare of his country, and Her desire for the maintenance and cultivation of friendly relations between Futa Jallon and the British settlements on the coast.

In reply, the Almamy expressed his great pleasure at my visit, and requested me to convey his best and most grateful thanks to Her Majesty the Queen of England for Her kind message, and for sending

[1] *Parl. Papers*, 1881, lxv [C. 3065], pp. 30–4. Gouldsbury was accompanied by Lieut. Dumbleton, R.E., and Surgeon Browning, R.N., 20 Bathurst armed police, and 87 carriers. He had been instructed to arrange for treaties of trade and friendship, but to make no territorial acquisitions. The expedition had been suggested by Rowe, as a way of putting Gambia's surplus balance for 1880 to good use.

such a high officer as a Governor to be its bearer. He said that he liked the English better than any other nation, and that his greatest wish was to be always friends with them. Both he and his chiefs expressed much surprise at the long distances we had traversed, and the speed with which we travelled; and the King finished with a compliment as to the white man's energy, endurance, and courage. At half-past two o'clock the interview came to an end, and I and my officers took leave of the King and returned to our quarters.

A portion of the remainder of the day following was occupied in getting out and arranging the presents for the King, and in receiving the visits of those who came to see me; and on the 30th [March 1881] at 8 a.m., I repaired to the King's yard, where, by previous arrangement, the King and his principal people were assembled to meet me.

At this interview I reiterated Her Majesty's message, and expatiated on the advantages of peaceful trade and industry; and, having informed the Almamy that I was deputed on behalf of Her Majesty to conclude a treaty of peace and commerce with him, I proceeded to read and explain, clause by clause, the provisions of the treaty that had been prepared for his acceptance and ratification.

After everything had been fully explained, and the import and meaning of every clause had been made clear, I asked the King if he was willing to accept and abide by the terms and provisions of the treaty, and to signify his assent by affixing his signature to the instrument. His reply was that he was willing to conclude the treaty with me, and that he was very glad to be friends with the English, as the Foulahs liked the English, and preferred their goods to those of any other nation.

He went on to say that some Frenchmen went up to Timbo a few years ago,[1] and tried to induce him to make a treaty with them, and to sell them some land to erect buildings on, but that, although they offered him much money, and tried to dazzle him by the project of a railway through his country, and the promise that the French merchants would buy everything that was to be sold in the land, and would purchase at a good price even cow dung, still, charmed they never so wisely, he would have none of them, and they had to go away baulked of their object, the aim of which he believed to be that of conquest and annexation.

Before he would sign the treaty I wished to conclude with him he said that he had a statement to make and some questions to ask respecting a treaty made with him 10 years ago by Mr. Blyden.[2] He thereupon related all the circumstances connected with the treaty he

---

[1] Probably the private adventurer, Aimé Olivier (Comte de Sanderval). See his *De l'Atlantique au Niger par le Foutah-Djallon* (Paris, 2nd edn., 1883).

[2] Blyden, 'Report on the Timbo Expedition, 1873': C.O. 267/320. The Treaty of 4 March 1873 promised the Alimamy £100 a year stipend.

alluded to, and after I had replied to his questions as best I could, he professed his readiness to sign the treaty[1] I had been commissioned to conclude with him; whereupon the necessary signatures were affixed to the instrument, which was in duplicate, one copy being drawn up in English, and the other in Arabic, the latter of which was handed over to the King. . . .

General Remarks

. . . In the first place, as to the facilities for transport offered by the River Gambia, I am bound to confess some disappointment with regard to that portion of the river which lies above Barraconda, it being in the dry season not navigable for vessels of over a few feet draught, and in the rains hardly navigable on account of the rapidly running stream which must pour down its channel. No doubt, if such a river as the Gambia ran through a thickly populated country, whose inhabitants were peaceful and industrious, and had the wants of civilization, or at least others than the few comprised within the West African's desires, that portion of it lying between Yarbutenda and Bady might be utilized as a highway for trade by means of specially constructed steam vessels, and by the removal of obstructions, and the constant dredging of the shallow spots; but such a combination of conditions as above described does not exist in this country, and it would be, I think, but an idle dream to hope that even the lapse of some centuries would bring about such a happy concourse of circumstances.

A great deal has been spoken, and a good deal has been written, in an exaggerated strain as to the capabilities and resources of the West Coast of Africa, and the interior thereof, and the possibility, and indeed probability, of the country becoming a sort of second India, and the last hope of the British manufacturer in his struggle with the competition which presses him so sorely on every side; but those who have indulged in such vaticinations have founded their would-be oracular utterances on the baseless fabric of vague and self-satisfied conjecture, which conjecture happens to be erroneous to the last degree.

Fortunately for the British manufacturer and merchant, their fortunes are not dependent on the El Dorado of West African commerce, and therefore any hope based on that fiction of the future, to wit, the event of Africa becoming England's mart for manufactured goods, is not likely to end in despair.

I think the fact has never been sufficiently recognised that Africa, and especially the west coast of the continent, is but very meagrely populated, and that where there is an extremely sparse population, without prospect or chance of addition by immigration, no great

[1] Treaty of trade and friendship, 30 March 1881.

increase or expansion of trade can arise, even under what otherwise might be the most favourable circumstances . . .

[There is consequently little hope for prosperous trade with the area between Yarbutenda and the Futa Jallon.]

8

AGREEMENT WITH SHERBRO AND MENDE CHIEFS, 16 NOVEMBER 1881[1]

WE, the undersigned Chiefs of Ticonkoh, Bompeh, Looboo, Boom, Bullom, and Kittam, also of Small Boom, Imperreh, and other places in the Sherbro and Mendi districts, having assembled at Bonthe, Sherbro, by the kind invitation of his Excellency . . . for the purpose of inquiring into some serious disputes which would have disturbed the peace and unity which was established by the Government of Sierra Leone in our countries, in February 1880, and ratified by us by an agreement signed by us and dated 6th February 1880. Now we, the undersigned, do by this document confirm in every particular the above-mentioned agreement, and we now repeat the promises contained therein to his Excellency Arthur Elibank Havelock, C.M.G., and in addition to which,

We do hereby solemnly promise that on our return to our several countries we will unite together as requested by His Excellency, the Governor-in-Chief, to do our best to put a stop to the war now going on in the interior between Dowah Mackiah on one side and Mendigrah on the other side, as that war has been and is the cause of our countries being in an unsettled state.

We, Chiefs of Ticonkoh, Bompeh, Looboo, Boom, and Bullom, will do all in our power to prevent any war from being taken to the Kittam River by Foro Cojo, a subject of Bargbor, king of the Upper Boom, and should the said Foro Cojo insist [on] making or inciting war, the matter will be reported by us to the Governor of Sierra Leone, and by his authority the whole of us will unite together to punish that country of Bargbor (Upper Boom).

We have heard with great regret of the bad conduct of one of our fellow Chiefs, Tehbeh, of Higgimah, who having signed the agreement of February 1880, has wilfully violated his promise by attempting to prepare a war for the Kittam, and has thus made himself an enemy of the Queen's Government and of ourselves; and we promise on our own return to point out this bad conduct of his to him, and direct him to come down in person to see the Governor or the Commandant at Bonthe, Sherbro, to explain this conduct of his and to apologize for the same; and if he neglects to obey our direction, we will

[1] *Parl. Papers*, 1883, xlvii [C. 3597], pp. 21–2.

treat him and his head Chief Nallow, of Looboo, as our common enemy, and we will do our best to carry out the promise in paragraph 4, of the agreement of 6th February 1880.

We, the Chiefs of Bullom, Kittam, Imperreh, and Small Boom, who were not present when the agreement of February 1880, was entered into in Freetown, Sierra Leone, which agreement we have heard distinctly read and explained on the 15th instant, do hereby acknowledge ourselves parties to the terms of the agreement, and we promise to adhere to all therein stated and now promised in this present agreement...

Markavoreh, Chief of Ticonkoh; Larsannah, Speaker; Cormovah, representative of Seppeh, Chief of Yengehmah, Bompeh; Goolbroh, Chief of Bompeh; Charley, Chief of Yengehmah; Granjah, Chief of Gangarmah; Gbannah Yandayah, successor of Mendi Massa, Chief of Morfuai; George Thorpe, Chief of Gpaitaimah; Nallow, Regent Chief of Looboo; Gumboo Coco, Speaker; Thomas B. Bongo, Chief of Moh Bongo; Bannah Bango, a Chief of Moh Bongo; Bargbor, Chief of the Upper Boom; Kong Gramgbatoo, Speaker; Brimah Jah, a gentleman of Jimmy, Upper Boom; Kah Gbantah, Chief of the Middle Boom; Bar Yormah, Speaker; Toontoo, Warrior; Wotah, representative of Carpoo, Chief of Bendoo; Humper Dow, Chief of Tarmah; Kong Gbargo, Regent Chief of Tormah, Lower Boom; Saisai Gbaryahcoh, Speaker; Gberry, Chief of Bongeh; Gboangoh, Chief of Tahneenehoo, Mabanta; W. E. Tucker, Chief of Bullom and Sherbar Sherbro; Gpow, Chief of Talliah, Small Boom; Beah Boom, Chief of Gbamgbaiah, Imperreh; Kah Tehpheh, Chief of Imperreh; Mahgbeetie, a Chief of Imperreh; Canray Bassie, Chief of Sang, Bargroo; Joseph Zorokong, for his father Brimah Zorokong, Head Chief of the Kittam; Fah Woondoo, Chief of the Kittam; Foray Gograh, Chief of the Kittam, Bah Chalon, Chief of Manor; Kong Dick, Chief of Gbamany, Boom...

9

THE EARL OF KIMBERLEY: MINUTE,
TREATY WITH FUTA JALLON,
12 FEBRUARY 1882[1]

1. HAVING made the Treaty [in 1873] and agreed to pay the stipend I think it would be discreditable to our good faith and must lower

---

[1] C.O. 267/348. On Havelock to Kimberley, 13 January 1882, informing that he has invited the new Alimamy Ahmadu to collect arrears. Messengers visited Freetown in December 1882 and were given £425; arrears of £575 had been paid to Ibrahima Suri's envoys in February 1881, making a total of £1,000 for the ten years 1873–83. C.O. 267/351, Havelock to Kimberley, 2 January 1883.

Later, Havelock reported news of Bayol's French mission to Timbo. Kimberley

us in the eyes of the natives who were evidently well aware of and displeased at our neglect not to fulfil our engagements, whether pressed to do so or not by the King.

2. I think the Treaty is a useful one. The only use which these Settlements on the West Coast is [sic] to us is to open trade and communications with the interior. Wherever the French can get a footing, they endeavour to exclude all trade but their own. It is our direct interest by all peaceful means to counteract their policy. Approve Mr. Havelock. Tell him to take care that the stipend is punctually paid in future—and to F.O. as proposed.

10

GOVERNOR A. E. HAVELOCK TO THE EARL OF KIMBERLEY: JONG RIVER CHIEFS, 29 JULY 1882[1]

WITH reference to my Despatch of the 5th June 1882, reporting my expedition to Mattroo on the Jong River, I have the honour to transmit a copy of a letter from the Acting Commandant of Sherbro, informing me that the principal Chiefs of the Jong River Country had come to Bonthe for the purpose of expressing their regret for what had taken place at Mattroo, and of asking my forgiveness.

2. The Acting Commandant transmits with his letter[2] a document (of which I attach a copy, conveying the regret of the Chiefs, and their desire for pardon, and concluding with a request that the Government would take them and their country under its protection. This document is signed by the Chiefs.

3. I have desired the Commandant to inform the Chiefs, in reply, that I was glad to receive the spontaneous expression of their regret and of their acknowledgement of their wrong-doing, but that I considered that their apology would have been more complete had they brought with them Dooli Seemo whom, as your Lordship will observe, they denounce as one of the prime movers of the disturbance. Lahsurru, the person mentioned by the Chiefs as being another of the originators of the recent trouble in their country, is, as your Lordship is aware, in detention in Freetown gaol. I added that I would consider their appeal for pardon, and that their request for protection would be also a matter for consideration.

(Minute, 7 March) shared Herbert's feelings of 'jealousy' and fears of exclusion, as in the Melakori. Havelock to Kimberley, 3 February 1882, and minutes.
    [1] *Parl. Papers*, 1882, xlvi [C. 3420], p. 16. (*Sir*) *A. E. Havelock* was Governor of the West African Settlements, 1881–4.
    [2] Acting Commandant Laborde to Freetown Secretariat, 17 July 1882. Signatories of the petition were: Betsy Gay, Humper Femah, Farmah, Humper Congo, Stephen Cleavland.

4. It seems probable that the Jong River country might be held to be included in the territory ceded under General Turner's Treaty of 1825.

11

ADMINISTRATOR F. F. PINKETT TO LORD DERBY: EXPEDITION TO THE SHERBRO, 19 MAY 1883[1]

In continuation of my Despatch of the 16th instant, I have the honour to report that, leaving Freetown with 60 policemen under the command of Captain Jackson, R.A., the Inspector General, on the evening of the 16th instant, we arrived at Bonthe at about 11.20 on the morning of the 17th. Landing the police at once, we were enabled to start the steamer back to Freetown by a little after 1 p.m. She returned last evening, the 18th, at about 7.45, with 60 soldiers of the 2nd West India Regiment.

2. On arriving here I made all the inquiries possible and it appears that it was the warriors of Chiefs Kartegbeh of Ghendemah and Beah Boom Gbambiah who made the raid upon Mosaipeh, which is on the mainland by the waterside between Mamayah and Bendoo. They carried off some 30 people, of these the greater portion were fugitives who had taken refuge there from the plunderers up the rivers. I have written to the Chiefs from whom these people came, and have demanded a return of the captives and satisfaction, and if I do not receive ample amends by Sunday evening, I shall start on Monday and punish them.

3. Gpow, the war-Chief, whose people I drove away from Whymah, Hahoon, and Semabue, is an ally of these people, and it seems clear that he intends to defy the Government. As far as I can learn he has twice attempted to go to Barmany where our police are, but his people would not risk it. He has also, I understand, since received an accession of warriors and wishes to divide them, part to go to Barmany and part to Bendoo. As under any circumstances he has not submitted himself even for the outrage on the pay-boat, I have determined to finish at once and for all with his fortress of Talliah. From the best information I can get he has about 1,000 to 1,500 men there, and therefore on further consideration, and remembering the Despatch of your Lordship's predecessor of the 14th July 1882, concerning the expedition to the Jong river undertaken by Governor Havelock, I have thought it better to get further military assistance than what I had first considered sufficient. This place of Talliah has

[1] *Parl. Papers*, 1883, xlvii [C. 3765], pp. 20–1. *F. F. Pinkett*, Acting Chief Justice and Acting Governor, 1883, 1884–5.

been Gpow's stronghold for some years, and I am surprised that it has been allowed so long to continue a menace to the whole country around. He has five towns, a centre one and four round it, like a five of cards. All these are fenced, and the outside ones not a hundred yards from the middle one. From the waterside it is distant about half an hour to an hour's walk. Though of course Gpow may abandon the place at the first view of our soldiers and police, still I do not think your Lordship will consider me wrong in being unwilling to attack it with the present force at my disposal, for seeing how disaffected the immediate neighbourhood is, I cannot leave Bonthe unprotected. Under these circumstances I have determined to send for 60 more soldiers. The steamer will leave for them tomorrow and return on Tuesday. This will not interfere with the progress of affairs here as the work to be done on Monday and Tuesday can be accomplished without the aid of the Colonial steamer, as M. Vohsen, the manager in Freetown of the Senegal and West Coast of Africa Company (French), before I left most liberally gave orders that the steam launch belonging to their branch firm here was to be placed at the disposal of the Government free of all charges.

4. The presence of the troops here will undoubtedly effect much good, and I have no doubt the destruction of this much dreaded fortress will cause such a pacification of the country that we shall have some quiet for the future . . .

12

AGREEMENT BETWEEN THE GALLINAS CHIEFS, 1 MAY 1885[1]

. . . WHEREAS war has lately been carried on in the Gallinas country, and has spread to the districts bordering it, and has resulted in great suffering to us and to others of the people inhabiting these districts. And whereas we the undersigned chiefs, headmen and others having authority in these lands are desirous of putting a stop to our own sufferings and to the miseries which our people are now undergoing in consequence of the many privations to which they are subject. And whereas His Excellency Sir Samuel Rowe, K.C.M.G., Governor of the West Africa Settlements has visited the town of Bandasumah in the Barrie country, Now we the undersigned desiring to take advantage of his presence do state as follows:

1. We humbly and respectfully beg to offer to the Queen of England, our thanks for having sent Sir Samuel Rowe back again to govern Her possessions which are near to us, and for the interest which Her Majesty has shown in our welfare in so doing.

Desiring to record our sincere wish for a settlement of all the difficulties that now exist between us and the Chiefs and headmen in and on the other side of the Gallinas country, and between ourselves and all those who have become mixed up and who are opposed to us in this war, we solemnly pledge ourselves to abide by any decision which Governor Rowe may come to if he will consent to arbitrate between us and our enemies in our present difficulties. We faithfully promise to visit him at any place which he may select for our meeting to discuss this matter, and to come to that place when summoned by him with all promptitude, transporting ourselves as far as we can, and making use of such conveyance as he may be pleased to provide for us with a view to our reaching the place of meeting which he may select, wherever it may be. With a view to the peace and prosperity of the districts in which we reside or over which we have authority, and in accordance with his advice we faithfully promise to try to remain at peace with each other and not to attack our neighbours. We agree to refer to Sir Samuel Rowe or any other Governor of the West Africa Settlements for the time being, any matter which we cannot decide among ourselves, and if any one of us who is a party to this Agreement shall refuse to refer such matter to the said Governor or to abide by his decision, we the other Chiefs, parties hereto, bind ourselves to unite with the said Governor in punishing him, should the Governor decide that such a course is necessary.

2. We promise that trade routes to our country shall be open to all comers; that we will not prevent any of the people residing inland of this from coming down to our towns and carrying their produce to the sea-board, or the traders on the coast (whether British subjects or others) from passing up to the interior from the sea-board with their merchandize and returning from there to the sea-board with such produce as they may have collected. We bind ourselves to assist them by every lawful means in our power in their traffic to and fro. Their persons and property shall be inviolate, and they may freely carry on trade in every part of our territories and may have houses and factories therein.

3. No Porroh or country law or tax of any kind may be enforced against the subjects of Her Majesty; but if they wrong or injure the subjects and people of the aforesaid Chiefs, the Governor of the West Africa Settlements will be informed by us of the circumstance, and we will be satisfied with whatever decision he may come to in every such case.

4. We agree to permit all ministers of the Christian religion to reside and exercise their calling within our territories, and we guarantee them free protection.

5. We agree and promise to refrain from entering into any correspondence, Agreement, or Treaty with any foreign nation or power

except with the knowledge and sanction of the Governor of the West Africa Settlements for the time being.

6. And as the whole country is at present overrun by bands of fighting men who in the first instance were brought down by different parties in this quarrel, but who now are, in many cases, quite independent of those who first employed them, we beg His Excellency Sir Samuel Rowe to use his influence to cause these fighting men to return to their own country, and we promise to use our best endeavours in future to abstain from sending these strangers to fight for us in our quarrels. . . .

Nyarroh, Queen of Bandasumah; (Signed in Arabic) Bocarry Governor, formerly Governor of the Upper Gallinas and Chief of Sembehoo; Saidoo, Chief of Gonagoo, Malachi, Chief of Potahun, Momo Foreeka, Chief of Pasamboo; Bocarry Sahoon, Chief of Sahoon; Sembey Perewah, Chief of Bahama; Saray (Ceery), Chief of Jeehoomah; Robert Raymond, Brother of Queen Nyarroh; Bannah Sassy, Kroobah of Chief Bocarry Governor; Jeahmah, Chief of Juru and brother of Mendigrah; In the presence of Samuel Rowe, Governor-in-Chief, West Africa Settlements; A. M. Festing, Major, Edmund Peel, Officers on Special Service; John J. Crooks, Deputy Commissary, Private Secretary; J. C. Ernest Parkes, Clerk, Colonial Secretariat, and in the presence of us Henry Tucker and James Tucker (brothers) nephews of W. E. Tucker, Chief of the Tucker land in British Sherbro, who speak English fluently and the Mendi language, who have fully explained this document to the Native Chiefs signatories of the same. H. N. Tucker. James Tucker. We the undersigned do solemnly and sincerely declare that we have read over and explained and interpreted in the Mendi language the above Agreement to the signatories thereof, and that they fully understood the same. (Signed in Arabic) Sannokoh Madder, George Easmon.

13

ALIMAMY BOKARI TO GOVERNOR SIR SAMUEL ROWE: WAR IN THE SCARCIES, 13 JUNE 1885[1]

MY GOOD FRIEND,

My heart leapt for joy when heard of your safe arrival once more in Sierra Leone, but you still meet me a rejected king, still hard upon the same old story, which you have tried some time ago that we should come upon terms of peace with my rebellious subject, which they would not yield to all advise, thus a continual war is amongst us.

[1] *Parl. Papers*, 1886, xlvii [C. 4642], p. 41. *Alimamy Bokari*, chief in Moria and Forekaria. For his career, see Christopher Fyfe, *A History of Sierra Leone* (Oxford, 1962), pp. 340–1, 410, 432.

My heart is solely fixed on you only, black man war is so critical that we cannot come on friendly terms with each other on one day as civilised people.

I am trying to see that the war comes to an end, which the people called Soefars[1] has sent me a message that they are coming to make peace betwixt me and my subjects.

Which moves me to acquaint you of their present object; as to you, I have all confidence; you might have long ago settle this dispute if Providence allow, but my people will not yield; all my brother chiefs have tried that they should come on friendly terms, but of no avail, so nothing but continual war is raging amongst us to these many years.

As the Soefars have promised to come and put an end to the Moriah war which moves me to send my son Quaya Mordoo to acquaint you of the same, and to tell you of all my troubles, although it is falsely rumoured that the Soefars have another object in view, which I did not yet believe such report.

Pardon me to crave your kind generosity, if it please your Excellency, to favour me with a few presents in this my helpless condition . . .

14

GOVERNOR SIR SAMUEL ROWE TO ALIMAMY BOKARI: WAR IN THE SCARCIES, 24 JUNE 1885[2]

ALIMAMY BOKHARIE,

I have received the letter you have sent me by your son.

I am sorry when I came back, after so long an absence, to find your country is still in trouble.

I may tell you that your nephew Quia Foday Dowdah has already sent messengers to me to tell me of this, and to ask me to help him.

Now, I should be willing to help in every right way to put peace between you if I had time, but my time is much taken up just now by the many disturbances in the country round. Your dispute with your people adds to them; and many difficulties result from it, and some of them will continue, I fear, until it is settled. I am afraid you will not find the coming of the Sofas helps you. You would have been wise to seek the advice and assistance of that European Government which has authority over the rivers of your country and with which you are in treating [treaty?], in place of sending to the Sofas.

---

[1] *Sic*, the Sofa troops of Samori.
[2] *Parl. Papers*, 1886, xlvii [C. 4642], p. 41

15

GOVERNOR SIR SAMUEL ROWE TO
F. A. STANLEY: SAMORI, 12 OCTOBER 1885[1]

IN reference to my Despatch, No. 106, dated 1st July 1885, reporting the movement towards the sea coast of the influential Chief, Almamy Sahmadoo, I have the honour to report that information has reached me to the effect that Sahmadoo has recalled his forces from Samayah, as he anticipates a conflict with the French in the neighbourhood of Bamakoo.

2. It is further reported that the French Government intends to dispatch an augmented force to the Niger with a view to punish Sahmadoo for his interference with the French column.

3. It would appear from the Senegal newspaper of the 16th of August that an engagement took place between Sahmadoo's forces and the French soldiers who occupied the fort of Niagassola, that Sahmadoo's forces attacked this place, but that they did not succeed in taking it, and that they lost in the attack about 2,000 men.

4. From the same newspaper, I learn, however, that had it not been for the advent of a Tornado which filled the marsh, and so put a wide sheet of water between the French fort and the horsemen of Sahmadoo, not one of the French soldiers would have escaped.

5. It would appear to me much to be desired that Shamadoo should be persuaded to keep away from the French line of advance, and concentrate his attention on a work that seems congenial to him, viz.: the opening of trade routes between the sea coast of this settlement and the countries over which he has authority.

6. I am of opinion that it is much to the interest of the trade of Sierra Leone to promote friendly relations with him; he has so far shown himself apparently willing to take advice in the matter of his conduct towards those tribes neighbouring the Settlement, who are considered to be in more or less intimate friendly political arrangements with this Government; and it would be certainly a matter of regret that his so far satisfactory action should be diverted into other channels, especially into those in which no conceivable good can possibly result.

7. The attacks which Sahmadoo may make on detached bodies of French forces will perhaps retard, for a very little, the opening of the trade route from the French possessions on the Senegal to the Upper Niger; they will not for a moment replace French influence by one in

[1] C.O. 879/23, no. 318. *F. A. Stanley* (later Lord Stanley and 16th Earl of Derby), Secretary of State for Colonies, 1885–6. For other versions of this disastrous campaign by Colonel Combes against Samori, see A. S. Kanya-Forstner, *The Conquest of the Western Sudan. A Study in French Military Imperialism* (Cambridge, 1969), pp. 119–20. The newspaper story here is not supported by the official reports.

any way more favourable to the development of the resources of the country. On the other hand, such chastisement as the French Government may reasonably be expected to inflict on Sahmadoo, will probably disturb and lower his influence.

8. So far as I can learn it is for the advantage of peace and civilization, and especially for the interest of the trade of this place that his power in the districts which lie on the inland of this Settlement, between it and the basin of the Niger, should be in no way lessened, and I believe it would be an undoubted gain if it could be exercised under English influences.

16

GOVERNOR SIR SAMUEL ROWE TO LORD GRANVILLE: YONI RAIDS, 17 MARCH 1886[1]

[The Yoni have raided Songo Town and neighbouring villages; the Mende have been restrained from retaliation; Major Festing has visited the Yoni chiefs; a meeting to discuss peace terms might be arranged.]

. . . IT is necessary to consider the question of our present relation with the Yonnies as having two aspects; these are essentially distinct, though they are intimately connected. One is, the relative positions of the tribes to each other, and the consequences which this position entails on our border population and on the trade of Freetown; the other is that which concerns only the relation of the Government with the Yonnies consequent on their attack on Songotown and the neighbouring villages in ceded Quiah. Up to the present time their attacks on Rotifunk and towns in the neighbourhood have not been considered in the same light as an attack on Songotown.

23. The present state of affairs between the Yonnies and the other Native tribes with whom they are at feud is that, for the moment, there is a suspension of hostilities; but this is not the result of any arrangement between themselves; both parties are desisting from action in the hope that this Government will arbitrate between them, and while waiting for this, the lawless bands from either side are as likely to attack on any one day as on another.

24. The present state of the matter between the Yonnies and this Government is that the Yonnie Chiefs expressed to Major Festing at Makeni on the 11th February, as I had the honour to report in the enclosures to my Despatch dated 14th February, their regret for

---

[1] *Parl. Papers*, 1886, xlvii [C.4840], pp. 32–4. Rowe obtained a peace treaty with Yoni, Masimera, Koya, Sherbro chiefs at Freetown, 10 May 1886, with the usual condition for referring disputes to arbitration by the Governor of Sierra Leone. Ibid., pp. 60 2.

what had occurred, their willingness to accompany him to Freetown, and to repeat here these assurances of regret. They said it was their intention to, at the same time, ask me to arrange the difficulties between themselves and their neighbours. They were not ready to accompany Major Festing to this place at the time he left, and they have not yet come to Freetown, nor, so far as I am aware, have they proceeded beyond the waterside towns of Rokelle and Mamalaghi. It is quite possible that they have fallen under the hands of the arch schemer and mischief maker Bey Simmerah. The members of the peace mission from the Bullom whom I sent to accompany Major Festing when he returned to Mamalaghi on the 19th January, are still with the Yonnie Chiefs; at least they have not returned to their homes or to Freetown.

25. I do not think it likely that the Yonnies will for some time again cross our border at Songotown or along the Quiah line, but their raids into the Quiah are only in abeyance, pending that settlement of difficulties between themselves and their neighbours which they hope I will undertake, and they are influenced also doubtless by the report that the Quiahs have given their country to the Queen. The Yonnies could be well pleased that the riverside villages of Mafengbe and Makamboray should pass under British authority or should at least be so far under British protection that they can have free access to the Ribbee river at these places, as the Tyamamendis have to the Bompeh at Sennehoo. As to Rotifunk, and the villages along the border of the Bompeh district, if this feud be not arranged shortly the Yonnies will attack them again as they have done before; indeed they are now anxious to retaliate for the attack made on them by a war party from Ribbee and Bompeh, which I had the honour to report in my telegram of the 15th January.

The peaceful section of the Yonnie clan have no personal objection to the punishment by this Government of the marauders who attacked Songotown, but it is more than the life is worth of anyone amongst them, whether Chief or private individual, to take any action, open or treacherous, which would have for its results the handing over of any of the marauders to this Government.

I think it possible that in a public assembly such as I have described, supported by such a force as I have referred to, some surrender of one or other of those who directed or took part in this attack may perhaps be obtained, but any proposal for such action would need to be made with great caution.

The trade on the Rokelle river is not, I think, much affected by this disturbance, but agriculture in the border district is entirely at a standstill. Petty traders on the frontier line between Cockboro and Ribbee have been plundered, and trading operations on the Ribbee are confined to the mouth of that river.

I see no prospect of a satisfactory settlement of the troubles which have prevailed between the Ribbee, Quiah, and Bompeh districts since 1882, excepting the plan I have above sketched.

A military expedition to the Yonnie district may inflict such punishment as may be thought fitting. This might be considered to settle this affair so far as regarded the crossing of the border by the Yonnies, but I do not see that it would tend to improve trade or to put a stop to the feud between the Yonnies and our border tribes, which has led to the plunder of trading factories and to the kidnapping and killing of British subjects, and which will if not settled, lead at no far distant date to similar results . . .

[A gathering of chiefs would cost between £1,500 and £3,000; the Colonial treasury could not meet such a cost at present.]

17

SIR SAMUEL ROWE: MINUTE,
CHIEFS' STIPENDS, 29 NOVEMBER 1886[1]

HAVING regard to financial and political position, I would give the Manoh river Chiefs 50 l., the stipend for 1886–7, and state that the stipends for 1884–5, 1885–6, are forfeited, as are the stipends of South-eastern Krim, Gbemnah, and Gallinas for the same period, and that no stipends will be paid for 1887 unless on the clear showing of the Governor that he is satisfied with the behaviour, both locally and generally, of the Chiefs to whom payment is made. The result will be that the Manoh river Chiefs will use their influence with the Eastern Kittam, Gallinas, and Sulymah to keep peace in the whole country. If we pay the arrears to the Manoh river Chiefs they will have no reason to try to prevent quarrels among the others, and to a certain extent it is an advantage to the Manoh Chiefs that the Sulymah and Gallinas routes to the seaside should be unsafe.

18

R. THOMPSON (SECRETARY TO THE WAR
OFFICE) TO THE FOREIGN OFFICE:
SAMORI, 17 DECEMBER 1886[2]

I AM directed by the Secretary of State to return to you the enclosed letter from the Colonial Office and Despatches from the Officer Administering the Government of Sierra Leone, on the subject of the treaty said to have been concluded between France and the Almamy Samadu.

[1] *Parl. Papers*, 1887, lx [C. 5236], p. 12.   [2] C.O. 879/23, no. 381.

There is, in Mr. Secretary Smith's opinion, no doubt that a treaty has been concluded between Samadu and the French Government.[1]

Whether that treaty does, as stated in the French newspapers, confer special commercial privileges upon France, or whether it is merely an agreement as here stated, that Samadu will place no obstacle in the way of the French advancing to Segou, and that the French will not carry on war-like operations within the territory subject to Samadu, our present information fails to inform us. But that Samadu is anxious to be on good terms with the French is proved by his having sent his son to France.

The rule of this powerful potentate has already been extended into the territories trading with Sierra Leone, and under British influence, and he is constantly bringing new districts under his sway. Up to the present time the judicious action of the Governor of the West African Settlements has kept us on friendly terms with him, but Samadu's policy has always been to take advantage of the quarrels of neighbouring tribes, to intervene by force of arms in favour of one of the combatants, and finally subjugate the territories of both.

If matters continue as at present, it is impossible to say how soon the quarrels of the tribes lying directly behind our West African Coast possessions may bring them under subjection to Samadu, and the Secretary of State cannot but view with apprehension the nearer approach of this great military chieftain to the Settlement of Sierra Leone.

That settlement possesses a military value of the very highest nature, in view of the possibility of the passage through the Mediterranean being barred to our troop ships and our commerce. It is the most important coaling station and harbour refuge between the British Isles and the Cape of Good Hope, and is for that reason being placed in a state of defence against attack by sea. Were we to become involved in war with France, the contingency above mentioned, which would bring Sierra Leone into the first rank among our harbours, would occur, and it is of the utmost importance that it should not be in the power of France to turn against us at such a time a native ruler, who undoubtedly possesses sufficient troops to overrun the entire Colony, and to cause considerable anxiety as to the safety of the town and harbour of Sierra Leone.

Mr. Smith therefore considers that our Imperial interests demand that we should establish the most friendly relations with Samadu, and that at the same time we should endeavour to create a barrier to his further progress towards the coast, by forming a confederation of the friendly tribes, such as was formed on the Gold Coast by Sir Charles McCarthy as a barrier against the Ashantee power.

[1] Treaty officially dated 23 March 1887 (ratified in Paris, 2 October 1887), placing Samori's states under French protection. For its significance, see Kanya-Forstner, *Conquest of Western Sudan*, pp. 147-8, 150.

The first step towards this would, in Mr. Smith's opinion, be the despatch of a friendly mission to Samadu, which he has reason to believe, if sent without delay, might return to Sierra Leone by the end of May. The next step would be to send emissaries to the kings and chiefs of the country mentioned in Administrator Hay's despatch, with a view to inducing them to accept our friendly arbitration in their quarrels, to agree not to cede their countries to any other foreign power, and to unite together against any native enemy.

Mr. Smith therefore desires me to express his hope that as Sir Samuel Rowe is now in London his consideration of the matter may not be deferred till his return to Sierra Leone as proposed by Mr. Stanhope, but that steps may be taken for the despatch of a mission to Samadu during the present winter. Major Festing, whose knowledge of the countries inland of Sierra Leone is exceptional, being also in London, advantage might be taken of his experience.[1]

Mr. Smith would at the same time suggest for the consideration of the Secretary of State for Foreign Affairs whether it might not be possible to agree with the French upon a boundary situated about the eleventh parallel of north latitude, which should limit the extent of French influence in a southern direction, we agreeing not to extend our influence northwards beyond that limit. He considers it of the highest importance that we should prevent further extension of French influence in the direction of Sierra Leone, in consideration of the evil effect which such influence would have in the event of our relations with France becoming otherwise than friendly.

19

ADMINISTRATOR J. S. HAY TO SIR HENRY HOLLAND: YONI RAIDS, 26 FEBRUARY 1887[2]

IN continuation of my despatch of the 19th instant, reporting that I had instructed Mr. Revington to attend the peace meeting between the Mendies and Yonnies, I have the honour to transmit a copy of a communication received from him which discloses the fact that before the proposed peace meeting could be held the Yonnies, headed by

---

[1] The Colonial Office agreed in February 1887 to pay £480 from Imperial funds (later the sum was raised to £1,500) for the expedition. Festing's cursory instructions were sent to him, 4 March 1887; he returned from Boumba in April and left in his report of 26 May 1887 a remarkable account of Samori's forces and interior trade. He was ordered to make a second expedition, 16 January 1888, but died at Sininkoro with only the promise of a treaty in August. For the diary of his mission, C.O. 879/29, no. 366.

[2] *Parl. Papers*, 1887, lx [C. 5236], pp. 66-7. This and other correspondence were referred to Sir Samuel Rowe.

Kondoh, Kongoh, and Kallowah, the same persons who led the raid on Songo town in 1885, attacked the town of Macourie, about eight miles from Sennehoo, within the recognised limits of the territory made over to this Government by General Turner's Treaty of 1825, and confirmed by an agreement signed by Chief T. N. Caulker and others on the 19th of December 1881. I should state that although this Government has not exercised active jurisdiction in the district yet police have been stationed at Sennehoo since the year 1882.

2. In connexion with this subject, I beg most respectfully to point out that our position at present is rather an anomalous one, and that the Chiefs who exercise active control over these districts are in little better case, for whilst we take no active steps to protect them yet we will not permit them to protect themselves as they may think best by force of arms, lest their opponents should suppose that these Chiefs are receiving our tacit support.

3. The case now reported is, I conceive, one in point. The Yonnies complained that they had been attacked by the Mendies and asked that the Bompeh and Ribbie Chiefs should be warned not to unite with their enemies, in compliance with which request I sent Mr. Revington as reported by my despatch of the 17th ultimo. The Bompeh and Ribbie Chiefs not only gave an assurance in accordance with my wishes, but even went so far as to use their influence to bring about a better feeling between the contending parties, when suddenly the Yonnies, leaving for a time the Upper Mendies, swooped down and attacked Macourie.

4. The Bompeh and Ribbie Chiefs are naturally anxious to make reprisals for this act of treachery on the part of the Yonnies and look to us for support which is withheld, whilst in the interests of peace we advise them not to take the offensive.

5. I thus venture, Sir, most respectfully to bring to your notice the actual position of affairs, to enable you to form an estimate of how essential it is to the well-being of this Settlement and the prestige of this Government that some steps should be taken for the better protection of those who are admitted to be within our jurisdiction.

6. In view of the moral effect it would have had, I would at once have endeavoured to meet the present emergency by detailing as many police constables as possible from here for *police duties* in the disturbed districts, but having regard to Lord Derby's Despatch of the 28th November 1884, I felt that I might possibly, Sir, be pursuing a course Her Majesty's Government might not approve.

In these circumstances and pending instructions, I have confined myself to requesting Mr. Revington to remain in the disturbed districts for a time to prevent, if possible, by negotiation any recurrence of incidents such as I now report, and transmit a copy of memorandum to him on the subject.

7. Mr. Lawson, Government Interpreter, has supplied me with a report embodying his views in this matter, a copy of which I forward, and it will be observed that he is of opinion that at present there is no prospect of making peace between the Yonnies and the Mendies who are beyond our control, but observes that the Chiefs within our jurisdiction should be warned to protect their towns, which I have no doubt they will do without much advice from this Government. The difficulty I think will be more in preventing them making reprisals than in their failing to protect themselves. At the same time I would point out the expense to which the Chiefs would be put by the constant engagement of warboys to defend their towns, and which they are quite unable to meet.

8. In conclusion I venture to hope that Her Majesty's Government may be pleased to consider the situation of affairs to which I have felt it my duty to direct attention, and in the meanwhile it will be my endeavour to localise as much as possible the present disturbance and prevent its area being extended.

20

SIR SAMUEL ROWE: MINUTE, YONI RAIDS, 13 MARCH 1887[1]

I T appears to me that the position of Selah and Condor, Coongor, and Kallowah in the Yonnie raid on Songo Town on November 24th, 1885, has not been clearly put before Captain Hay.

Possibly a reference to the raid on Sherbro in 1875, which was punished by the Bagroo expedition, may help me to make my meaning clearer.

In 1875 John Caulker persuaded certain Mendi Chiefs to assist him to make a raid on his own people, and in the course of this raid the war party invaded British territory and there committed murder. For this Caulker (who instigated the attack) was hanged. Kinigbo and Vannah, who led the fighting party, were also hanged.

In the case of the Yonnie raid of 1885, Selah (who is stated to have been born in Bompeh or Ribbee) went to the Yonnies and, in revenge for injuries stated to have been received at the hands of Canray Mahoi, persuaded certain Yonnie Chiefs to espouse his cause, and to sanction an attack on the Ribbee district.

In the course of these attacks the raid on Songo Town occurred, and Coongor, Condor, and Kallowah led the attacking party.

Surely this Selah is not to be allowed to come back to districts under British control, and the fighting leaders Coongor, Condor, and

Kallowah to come to a peace meeting within the border, or, failing their willingness to do this, to Freetown.

The Government might or might not think it worth while to send a military expedition to punish this raid at the time; we have surely not arrived at a position in which we are to parley with those bandits and condone the offence of this renegade Selah.

I submit that, whatever may be the willingness of Her Majesty to admit the excuse put forward by the Yonnie Chiefs in February 1886, she cannot forgive the instigator and leaders of the raid, excepting after their full submission, and possibly after years of punishment, perhaps not then.

There is no hope for peaceful relations between the Yonnies and the border tribes of the Colony but by its being clearly understood that there can be no satisfactory friendship between the Yonnies and Her Majesty's Government so long as Selah, Condor, Coongor and Kallowah are not given up.

The Secretary of State may think it desirable to work towards this end by exercising moral influence only, on the Yonnies and their neighbours, in preference to sanctioning a military expedition to punish them, but I cannot think that he will approve that these fellows be treated with on terms of equality.

The then Secretary of State was pleased to approve the punishment inflicted on the principals in the Bargroo raid in 1875. In 1885 the then Secretary of State approved that the sentence of death pronounced against Doogbah and Kdanbay Yenkain, the men who perpetrated the raids at Sherbro, should be carried out publicly.

The Yonnie raiders have committed the same crimes as those for which the penalty of death was inflicted in the case above referred to. The fact that they have not been caught does not entitle them to be treated in any way differently.

It may suit us to accept the statement of Yonnie Chiefs that this raid was not in any way an act of the Yonnie tribe against the English Colony, but we shall never have any peace if we condescend to parley with the instigator and the actual leaders of an attack on well-known British villages. It is also to be remembered that there are Yonnies, whom these fellows led, already imprisoned in Her Majesty's gaol at the Gambia, for having committed the offences in which these men took part.

21

SIR H. T. HOLLAND TO ADMINISTRATOR J. S. HAY: SIERRA LEONE INTERIOR, 5 AUGUST 1887[1]

I HAVE the honour to acknowledge the receipt of Sir Samuel Rowe's despatch, No. 9, of the 13th of June, transmitting Major Festing's report of his recent journey into the interior as far as Bumban, in the Biriwah-Limbah country.

I have read this report, and Sir Samuel Rowe's remarks upon it, with much interest. Major Festing's proceedings meet with my full approval; and I desire to express my appreciation of the completeness with which he has carried out his difficult and dangerous mission, and of the pains which he has evidently taken to ensure the accuracy of his information.

I concur generally in the opinion expressed in the 11th paragraph of Sir Samuel Rowe's despatch as to the importance of surrounding Sierra Leone by tribes amenable to the influence of the British Government, and I shall be glad to receive from him any further suggestions relating to the manner in which this object may be attained.

When the new scheme of finance and administration, which has been sanctioned, is brought into operation, there will be two travelling Commissioners, a principal part of whose duty it will be to visit the border tribes, with the object of bringing them under British influence and control without the exercise of direct authority, and helping them to organise themselves for protection and defence.

22

AGREEMENT WITH CHIEFS: OPEN ROADS, 19 DECEMBER 1887[2]

WE, the undersigned Chiefs of the Yonni, Masimera, Marampa, Bompeh, Ribbi, Kwaia, and Port Lokko districts having assembled together at the town of Mamaligi on the borders of the Masimera district, after the destruction of the Yonni Bankars or walled towns

[1] C.O. 879/23, no. 318. *Sir Henry T. Holland* (Baron Knutsford, 1888), was Assistant Under-Secretary in the C.O., 1870–4, and Secretary of State for Colonies, 1887–92.
[2] *Parl. Papers*, 1888, lxxv [C. 5358], p. 7273. The Yoni stronghold was captured by an expedition led by Sir Francis de Winton in November 1887. In the C.O. it was doubted whether much had been achieved, unless military action was supplemented by 'a system of permanent quasi-military police stationed in block-houses at different points. But where is the money to come from?' Knutsford, Minute, 13 July 1888, C.O. 267/370

of Robari, Makundu, Roniette, Robang, Makalcomp, and Mamaligi
by the expeditionary force under Colonel Sir Francis de Winton,
K.C.M.G., R.A., feeling the power of the great Queen of England,
and the punishment which has justly been administered to the Yonni
tribe, and through them to the whole country, agree to, and witness
the agreement of, the several Chiefs, parties hereto, to the following
conditions imposed by the said Sir Francis de Winton, K.C.M.G.,
R.A., for and on behalf of Her Majesty the Queen.

I. That Chief Sorie Kessebeh, of Rotifonk, shall keep open the
road between Rotifonk and Robari, and once in every two months
furnish 50 carriers to carry provisions from Mafengbeh to Robari for
the English troops so long as they remain there.

II. That Chief Canray Mahoi shall keep the road between
Mafengbeh and Robari open and in good order, and once in every two
months he shall furnish 50 carriers, if required by the Government,
for taking provisions from Mafengbeh to Robari; he, the said Canray
Mahoi, having charge of the country as far as Mafuluma.

III. That the Kwaia people shall keep the roads between the towns
of Mamaligi and Robari open and in good order, the country in a line
bounded by the Rosolo creek to Matenefora, and *via* Warima to
Robari; the Ribbi river being the boundary between the Kwaia and
Ribbi districts, the ancient boundaries between the Bompeh, Ribbi,
and Kwaia districts remaining the same as heretofore.

IV. That inasmuch as some of the Masimera people took part in the
fighting against the English at Robari and hid the Yonni Chiefs who
took refuge in their country, Bey Simmerah and the Masimerah
people shall pay a fine of 200 *l.* (two hundred pounds) for their par-
ticipation in the war against the English, this fine being paid in kind
of rice at the current market value, or in cattle at Rokell within three
months from the date hereof. It is further understood that Bey
Simmerah shall be taken to Freetown, and shall remain in that place
until the fine is paid.

V. That Bey Cobolo and the Marampa people, for their partici-
pation in the war against the English in giving refuge to fugitive
Yonnie, shall pay a fine of 100 *l.* (one hundred pounds), it being
understood that one half of this fine shall be remitted should the
Yonni insurgent Chiefs be captured and delivered up to the Governor
of Sierra Leone through their instrumentality.

VI. And we, the said Chiefs, parties hereto, being convinced that
it would tend greatly to the maintenance of peace if a paramount
Chief, or Bey Sherbro, were elected over Yonni clan, have nominated
Pa Sey Massah, whose name we beg to submit for the approval of his
excellency the Governor-in-Chief on the West African Settlements
for this appointment, and we promise to support his authority in
every possible way should it meet with approval . . .

Sey Massah of Warimah; Sey Bannah of Warimah; Cappa Soker
Kree of Rokon; Alimamy Ceasay Loll of Rokell; Pa Suba of Magbelli;
Amarah Sauner, of Magbelli; Sorie Kessebeh, for Mayonto, of Rotu-
fonk; Sorie Wongo of Rotufonk; Canray Mahoi of Ribbi; Bannah
Bome of Ribbi; W. T. G. Lawson of Kwaia; Santiggy Ballamodu,
for Alimamy Lahai Bundu, of Forodugo; Banna Serrey of Magbaini;
Alikarlie Morobah Bangoorah, of Port Lokko; Comboh Camarah, of
Port Lokko; signed in the presence of J. C. Ernest Parkes. M. Wakka.

23

GOVERNOR J. S. HAY TO LORD KNUTSFORD:
SIERRA LEONE TREATIES, 5 NOVEMBER 1888[1]

In a Despatch, No. 370, dated October 8, 1886 (African, No. 318,
page 24),[2] which I had the honour to address to your Lordship's
predecessor, I ventured to advocate a scheme of entering into short
treaties with the principal Kings and Chiefs ruling the districts
around the Settlement, in which a clause should be inserted promising
that they would neither cede nor sell their respective lands to any
other European Power without the consent of Her Majesty's Government. This suggestion, from a confidential communication addressed
by the Under Secretary of State for War to the Under Secretary of
State for Foreign Affairs (African, No. 318, page 36), apparently met
with the concurrence of the former, and is similar to the subsequent
suggestion of the late Sir S. Rowe conveyed to your Lordship in the
11th paragraph of his Despatch, No. 9, dated Bathurst, June 13, 1887
(African, No. 318, page 60), with which your Lordship in Despatch,
No. 122, of the 5th August 1887 (African, No. 318, page 83) was pleased
to express your concurrence, and requested him to furnish any further
suggestions relating to the manner in which the object might be
attained.

2. As I am about to place before your Lordship the scheme which
I propose, with your approval, to adopt for the better maintenance
of peace and order in the districts in the near neighbourhood of the
Settlement, the present seems to be a desirable one to revert to the

---

[1] C.O. 879/31, no. 377.
[2] C.O. 879/23, no. 318. This policy was approved in C.O. minutes: C.O. 267/372,
and became the basis for treaties collected by Hay and Administrator S. F. Foster
in the Sierra Leone interior, 1889–91. Some fifty-two of these are listed and printed
in the Confidential Print, African 411, *Collection of Treaties with Native Chiefs &c.*
on the West Coast of Africa, C.O. 879/35. Most are in the form of nos. 25 and 26,
below. The policy was agreed by F.O. to C.O., 9 February 1889; Knutsford to
Hay, 15 February 1889 (draft): C.O. 267/376, and confirmed later in Knutsford
to the Officer Administering Sierra Leone, 1 January 1890: C.O. 879/32, no. 387;
and in Hay to Commissioners Alldridge and Garrett, 20 and 24 February 1890,
ibid.

subject, with a view to obtain your Lordship's sanction to my pursuing a course which I feel I cannot too strongly advocate.

3. The scheme I propose is a simple one. Already we have treaties of friendship and alliance with many of the tribes in the vicinity of the Settlement, and have frequently had offers of the cession of their lands which we have most persistently refused. As recent events have, however, taught us that other nations are not inclined to adopt a similar policy, and may even in face of our treaties of friendship obtain the cession of countries which we cannot afford to lose; and as the proposed outposts, whilst strengthening our position and influence with the interior tribes should, if practicable, have a belt of territory beyond them which we would be certain could not be so ceded, I venture to suggest that I may be permitted to enter into arrangements with the Chiefs in the districts around, that they will neither cede nor sell their lands to any Foreign Power without the consent of Her Majesty's Government.

4. I do not anticipate that there will be any difficulty in effecting this so far as the Chiefs are concerned, and I do not think that any increased expenditure would be incurred as we might utilize the vote for presents, to meet any attendant expense.

5. I beg to attach the draft of the form of treaty which I propose to adopt, should your Lordship be pleased to sanction the proposal.

24

GOVERNOR J. S. HAY TO
LORD KNUTSFORD: EXPEDITION AGAINST
MAKIAH, 20 JANUARY 1889[1]

. . . As already reported, all Mackiah's towns have been taken and burnt, and a large number of captives have been liberated and returned to their homes. He himself is seeking a refuge with Chief Niagwah of Gorpendeh, and the country has been cleared of his war boys.

4. Since energetic action has been taken, I have found the Chiefs with whom I have come in contact only anxious to carry out every order, and the political influence obtained is, I conceive, of considerable value. Not only did Chief Mackavoreh of Tikonko and Dameahwah, one of the principal Bompeh Mendi Chiefs, visit me and express there desire to meet my wishes, but a message from the Tiama Mendi Chief was also received to the same effect. The importance to this Colony of keeping up communication with the interior tribes, and opening up the roads leading to their trading centres, cannot be overrated, and the Chiefs in question have promised to do what they can to foster trade and protect traders.

[1] *Parl. Papers*, 1889 lvi [C. 5740], pp. 88–9.

5. The road that I suggested should be opened connecting the heads of the navigable rivers, extending from Kambia on the Great Scarcies to a point on the Manoh River, our eastern boundary, is already nearly completed. That portion between Bandajuma on the Kittam to Mattru on the Jong River I have passed over myself, and progress is being made with the remainder. In connexion with this subject I would desire to direct your Lordship's notice to the estimate of the cost of making the road in question. By my Despatch, of the 7th November last, I had the honour to point out that the approximate cost has been fixed at 2,000 *l.* I am happy to say that up to the present the work has entailed no cost to Government, and I trust to be able to complete the undertaking without any expenditure of public money.

6. Such are the immediate results of the recent expedition, and I trust that in the no distant future peace and order will be fully restored in the disturbed districts. It is not to be expected that the inhabitants will at once settle down to peaceful avocations, and some time will elapse before they do so, they being naturally of a credulous disposition and disposed to believe every flying rumour that reaches them of impending attack; it is however to be confidently expected that with careful supervision of the Chiefs the people will gradually regain confidence and return to the towns and villages . . .

[He has placed the area from the left bank of the Bum river to the Manoh under Captain C. Crawford in charge of police posts.]

25

TREATY WITH THE LIMBA, 21 OCTOBER 1889[1]

. . . 1. THAT the said Bomboh Lahai will keep all the roads leading through his country from the interior to Kambia on the Great Skarcies River free and in good order for traders to pass to and fro and also protect all British subjects who may settle in his country for the purpose of trade.

2. That there shall be peace between the subjects of the Queen of England and the subjects of Bomboh Lahai, and should any difference or dispute accidentally arise between them, it shall be referred to the Governor of Sierra Leone for the time being, whose decisions shall be final and binding.

3. That British subjects shall have free access to all parts of the Tonkoh Limbah country and shall have the right to build their houses and possess property according to the laws in force in that country;

[1] C.O. 267/378; and in Foster to Knutsford, 31 October 1889. Signatories were: Major Sydney Foster, Alimamy Bomboh Lahai III, witnesses, and translators.

that they shall have full liberty to carry on such trade or manufacture as may be approved by the Governor of Sierra Leone; and should any differences arise between them and the aforesaid British subjects and him the said Almamy Bomboh Lahai as to the duties or customs to be paid to him the said Almamy or the headman of the towns in his country by such British subjects or as to any other matter, that the dispute shall be referred to the Governor of Sierra Leone whose decision in the matter shall be binding and final; and that he the said Almamy Bomboh Lahai will not extend the rights thus guaranteed to British subjects to any other persons without the knowledge and consent of the Governor of Sierra Leone.

4. That he the said Almamy Bomboh Lahai will not enter into any war or commit any act of aggression on any of the Chiefs his neighbours, by which the trade of the country with Sierra Leone will be interrupted, or the safety of the persons and property of the subjects of the Queen of England shall be lost, compromised or endangered.

5. That the said Almamy Bomboh Lahai will at no time whatever cede any of his territory to any other Power, or enter into any agreement, Treaty or arrangement with any Foreign Government except through and with the consent of the Government of Her Majesty the Queen of England &c. &c.; and so long as the provisions of this Treaty are faithfully carried out, he the said Almamy Bomboh Lahai, his successors shall receive £10 (Ten pounds) sterling on the (21st.) Twenty first day of October in every year from the Colonial Government of Sierra Leone . . .

26

TREATY WITH TEMNE AND MENDE CHIEFS, 30 MARCH 1891[1]

WHEREAS the upper portion of the Timmani and Mendi countries have for some time past been divided by an unfortunate disturbance which His Excellency Sir James Hay, K.C.M.G. Governor of the Colony of Sierra Leone has come to settle we the undersigned Chiefs and Headmen at present assembled at Yeleh in Bongkawlenken do hereby promise:

1. That the war which has so long continued between us shall at once cease and that we will use our utmost endeavour to maintain and promote peace.

2. That should any of our boys without knowledge seize or take the persons or property of any of our subjects and the facts are brought to

---

[1] C.O. 267/388. Signatories were: chiefs of Mayappa, Matotoka, Mabome, Mabang, Yela, Foundo, Macrubeh, Taiama, Gondama, Ketumo, Manoquay, Hay, Garrett, Lendy, Lewis, Parkes, and witnesses.

our knowledge we will use every effort to obtain the restoration of the persons and property so taken.

3. That should any of us signatories hereto commence hostilities against any of our fellow Chiefs signatories hereto, we will at once report the circumstances to the Officer of the Government nearest to us and assist him to arrest the party who has so broken his word to be dealt with as the Governor shall see fit.

4. And we the Chiefs and Headmen of Taiama, Gondamah, Jag-baimah, Ketumah and the other Mendi towns do hereby promise that in as much as Murray Goorah who has been engaged fighting in these hostilities has not attended this peace meeting in response to the invitation of His Excellency the Governor but has run away to the Connoh Country we will not permit him to return to any of our towns but should he do so we will report the fact to the nearest Police Officer for such action as His Excellency the Governor may direct.

5. And we the Chiefs and Headmen of the Timmani Country do promise that we will leave our palaver with Murray Goorah entirely in the hands of His Excellency the Governor for such action as he may think fit; that we will carry no war against him and should he wage war against us we will at once complain to the nearest officer for such action as may seem desirable to the Officer Administering the Government of Sierra Leone.

6. And whereas His Excellency the Governor has advised us that it will be to our best interests to farm our lands and maintain peace we all place ourselves unreservedly in the hands of Her Majesty the Queen and pray that she may extend to us that protection which will ensure these results as we are confident that our tribal differences and disturbances can never be put an end to nor peace maintained except-ing by the frequent advice and intervention of Her Officers . . .

27

T. V. LISTER TO COLONIAL OFFICE: SAMORI, 25 JULY 1893[1]

. . . I AM, however, to observe that Lord Rosebery is struck with the fact, which is apparent from the reports of the British Commanding Officer, and from those of Captain Lendy,[2] that it will be difficult for the Government of Sierra Leone to perform its obligations unless

---

[1] C.O. 879/37, no. 447.

[2] Inspector-General of Police sent by Sir F. Fleming to report on the French occupation of Heremakuno. For an account of the clash between British and French columns at Waima, see Fyfe, *History of Sierra Leone*, pp. 517–21. The C.O. (misled by reports from Col. Ellis to the War Office) agreed to the expedition against the advice of Fleming, and persuaded the Treasury to sanction £1,500 to pay for it. In the meantime the proclamation of a Protectorate was postponed.

some measures are taken to show its power in the interior and on the frontier. According to Captain Lendy, Bilali's force, which retired before the French, is still on British soil ravaging Kouranko and Kuniki, and the harassed natives are looking for help from the French, seeing little hope of effective protection from the British authorities. In this state of things there is considerable peril. No agreement signed in London or Paris will of itself suffice to prevent the possibility of frontier difficulties, when the natives, unable to appreciate a paper agreement, are looking for immediate protection to a strong hand. The Sofas are a curse to the country; and if they are harboured within the British Colony when otherwise they might be driven within their own borders by the French, the rule of Great Britain will be looked upon not as a blessing but a curse by the inhabitants. It is therefore essential that active steps should be taken to give within the recognised frontier peace and security. His Lordship would be glad— as this subject may, on the arrival of the French officers, be an awkward element in the discussions which will then be renewed at Paris— to learn beforehand the views of the Marquess of Ripon as to the extent to which assurances may be given that it is the intention of Great Britain to ensure in future respect for her territorial authority.

28

R. H. MEADE: MINUTE, PROTECTORATE, 19 SEPTEMBER 1893[1]

WE have already in our letter to the F.O. of August 18, '93 said that this territory 'may perhaps be regarded as country under the Protection of Her Majesty over which the Govt. of S. Leone by direction of H.M.G. exercises as much control as circumstances permit'. The active steps we are continually taking are inconsistent with anything less than a Protectorate, & I think it must now be definitely admitted that everything within the boundary is under British protection. The impending expedition against the Sofas is pretty complete proof of it.

The only question on this is one of policy—viz whether we should formally proclaim a Protectorate as suggested by the O[fficer] A[dministering] the G[overnment]: or go on as we are doing exercising the functions of protection [D & telling the natives whenever necessary that they are under the protection of H.M.] [A as far as convenience and circs. permit.]

I incline to the latter for the French already regard the territory as British, & would not understand the object of the new departure. But consult F.O.

[1] C.O. 267/403: on Crooks to Ripon, 24 August 1893. Ripon agreed to the second alternative: Minute, 23 September 1893.

C. GOLD COAST

I

GOVERNOR H. T. USSHER: MEMORANDUM, SLAVE-DEALING, [JANUARY 1880][1]

WITH reference to the subject of slave-dealing, and breach of Slavery Laws in this Settlement, I will instance four cases, referring to powerful and important interior and frontier Kings.

1. Enimill Quow, King of Wassaw, fined 100 oz., deposed and exiled to Lagos by Governor Freeling in 1877, vide Despatch Gold Coast No. 89, of 5th April 1877.[2]

2. A case in which the late Quow Daddie, King of Aquapim, was found guilty by me of aiding and abetting slavery, and of gross extortion under pretence of carrying out the wishes of the Government. He fined a Chief an enormous sum for attempting to commit a prohibited offence, that of body carrying. The Chief had to sell all his family and goods, and in despair came to me for help. Quow Daddie died at that time, and escaped punishment; but the principal in the sale was heavily fined, and some of the money restored.

3. The complaints against King Attah of Eastern Akim are too numerous to mention. They include dealing in slaves and pawns and habitually selling them, and causing them to be sold. In considerable tyranny, such as prohibiting the breeding of goats, sheep, and pigs and the planting of yams, &c. on the plea of fetish. On the same ground he only allows two or three day's work in the week. These matters will be deposed to at the proper time by the Basel missionaries, whom he detests and annoys.

The most recent case is that of a British policeman swearing the King's great oath on Buabeng, a powerful Chief. The King's fine for this amounting to 240 l. Buabeng had to sell 30 persons. Mr. Buck, Basel missionary, testifies to this.

There are many smaller cases against him. I have ordered him firmly but civilly to come to Christiansborg and explain his proceedings, and to bring Buabeng with him. Plenty of additional evidence will follow when he is out of his country. Should he be guilty, there is but one way, at the distance he is from us, to treat him, and that

---

[1] C.O. 96/130. Encl. in Ussher to Hicks Beach, 21 January 1880. For the financial reasons which prevented implementation of the stipend policy (inability to raise taxation), see C.O. 879/31, no. 379; and for the failure to apply the Native Jurisdiction Ordinance, see G. E. Metcalfe, *Great Britain and Ghana: Documents of Ghana History 1807–1957* (London, 1964), no. 328, pp. 399–400. H. T. Ussher had served under Governor Glover at Lagos and was Governor of the Gold Coast, 1879–80.

[2] C.O. 96/121.

is a heavy fine and deposition, with exile to Lagos, in the same manner as Governor Freeling dealt with Enimill Quow.

4. A gross case is that of Acquasie Baidoo, Chief of Denkera-Tchuful, a powerful and also a border country. He is detaining, in defiance of my orders, a number of followers of the Queen of Djuabin. I have warrants, but no officers yet to serve them with a suitable force.

5. There are also slave cases frequently enough close to our courts. One was dealt with some time since at Elmina, and a fine of 100 l. imposed, with alternative of imprisonment.

2

COMMANDER J. W. BRACKENBURY TO COMMODORE F. W. RICHARDS: ASHANTI, 18 FEBRUARY 1881[1]

. . . I HAVE the honour to report that messengers from the King of Ashanti were received this morning; these messengers state that the King never intended to threaten war on Assin if the fugitive prince were not given up, but that this was entirely a fabrication on the part of the first envoys. The King says all rumours about his attacking the Protectorate are false. He desires to be friendly. The gold axe means nothing.

So far the message is peaceful in its bearing, but all the envoys give such different accounts to different people, when questioned, that it is difficult (knowing the mendacity of the Ashantis) to ascertain the real truth.

That envoys from a King such as the Monarch of Ashanti is represented to be should state anything they have not previously been told to say, seems incredible. My opinion is that the first embassy, accompanied with the axe, was meant to intimidate. Seeing, however, that the fugitive was not to be given up, and that preparations were being made to resist aggression, more peaceable councils have probably prevailed at Coomassie, the Ashantis not being ready for immediate war.

The different embassies have, for the time being, been dismissed, until His Excellency has made up his mind how to act . . .

[1] *Parl. Papers*, 1881, lxv [C. 3064], p. 7. *Commander J. W. Brackenbury* was Senior Officer, West Coast Division.

3

GOVERNOR SIR SAMUEL ROWE TO THE EARL OF KIMBERLEY: ASHANTI, 30 MAY 1881[1]

[The Ashanti embassy under Prince Buaki[2] has been received at Cape Coast.]

9. THE Prince has deposited about 1,200 ounces of gold, which is a part of the 2,000 ounces which the King himself begged that Her Majesty would accept as a proof of his sincerity.

10. He also offered in the king's name, as a further proof of the sincerity of his wish for peace, the so called Golden Axe.

11. This important emblem of Ashanti power has been sent down by the king by a special messenger. It has been so sent after a somewhat (I am told) prolonged discussion in Council at Coomassie, on the express understanding that it should not remain on the coast but be sent to England, as a direct proof of the wish of the king and people of Ashanti to be on terms of friendship with Her Majesty's Government.

12. I look on the sending of the axe as more important than the embracing of my knees or the payment of the gold. It cannot have been sent away from Ashanti without the knowledge of the people. Indeed, I believe I cannot exaggerate the value of the presence of this axe as a public demonstration on the part of the Ashanti king of his submission to the authority of Her most gracious Majesty.

13. I am assured by Amuaku Attah, the Chief who was sent by Prince Buaki from Mansue to see the king and chiefs of Coomassie on the subject, and to urge them to complete the 2,000 ounces at once, that its presentation to Her Majesty was a matter of discussion before a numerous assembly, and that it was after consideration unanimously decided that it should be sent if the Governor would consider it a proof that the King of Ashanti really wished for peace . . .

4

CAPTAIN R. L. T. LONSDALE: MISSION TO ASHANTI AND SALAGA, 18 MARCH 1882[3]

. . . ON the 23rd November, at my request, I had a private interview with the King [of Ashanti];[4] by private I mean one attended by the

[1] C.O. 96/134. [2] Asafu Buakyi.
[3] *Parl. Papers*, 1882, xlvi [C. 3386]. Encl. in Rowe to Kimberley, 10 May 1882. *Capt. R. L. T. Lonsdale* was on mission, October 1881–February 1882, and was sent again to Kumasi in 1887. [4] Mensa Bonsu (1874–83).

principal Chief of his household, and possibly one to three of the principal Chiefs of Coomassie. I said to the King that among other things, it was part of my duty, if possible, to cause the roads leading from his country towards Salagha and Kratshie to be opened, so that traffic might be resumed along them; but that before attempting to commence such a thing I required certain information, and I believed he was in a position to supply me with it. I required to know which roads were closed, and who were the Kings or Chiefs who closed or caused them to be closed. He said that the King of Salagha and the Fetish Priest of Denty were the two principal persons. I mentioned that I was aware that the roads to Bontuku, Sefwhi, &c. were also closed, but that I had nothing to do with them at present. I brought to his notice the probability, should the roads be opened, of the people who lived in the countries through which they passed demanding equal rights of free passage through his country as he and his people were seeking to obtain through theirs. Here the King's face plainly expressed that such a thing was an extravagance not to be thought of, and would not pursue the subject further. He said he expected me to compel all persons who had formerly paid him tribute, and recognised his authority to return to their allegiance, and resume the payment of tribute. I informed him that I was not going to attempt to do anything of that kind; that I should merely, by peaceful means, and using any fair argument, try and show the people who prevented him travelling over their roads how much it was to their advantage to have free communication throughout the country, and that he would have to open his roads to them if they opened theirs to him. The king said that now there was going to be peace he should commence to rebuild his capital (which is in a very dilapidated condition). He said he had always been of a peaceful disposition, and that now nearly all the turbulent people in his kingdom were dead, and he hoped for a long continuance of peace, during which he could send messages to and receive messages from Her Majesty the Queen. That he had long wanted a good messenger, but had failed in getting one, and that now I had come he hoped I would take a message to Her Majesty from him. I replied that I should be very glad to take any message he liked to intrust me with and submit it to His Excellency the Governor for conveyance to Her Majesty. He tried to lay the blame of sending the golden axe, and the message which accompanied it, on the Adansis, by saying that they had carried untrue tales as to the meaning of the message and axe. I informed him officially of my wish to leave Coomassie on the 3rd December 1881 . . .

5

GOVERNOR SIR SAMUEL ROWE TO CAPTAIN BARROW: MISSION TO ASHANTI, 29 MARCH 1883[1]

[He is to pay particular attention to encouraging the abolition of human sacrificial.]

10. YOU must on no account make any promise of any action in the affairs of Ashanti, either on the part of Her Majesty's Government or on the part of any representative of Her Majesty's Government.

11. Still, should you in conversation find that there is a general disposition on the part of the Ashanti Chiefs and on the part of the King to do away with the barbarous custom of human sacrifices, I would wish you to do all in your power to encourage that disposition.

12. I am told that the practice has become distasteful of late even to those who are in close relationship with the Court, since (as a consequence of there being no successful war and consequent captives) it has become necessary that the persons sacrificed should be taken from the classes to which they belong.

13. You may go farther than this, and try to discover whether the influential Chiefs at Coomassie would be disposed that their King should break through the ordinary rule of his country and cross the Subine and meet me at some distance south of Coomassie.

14. I should only be disposed to make such a journey and devote the time and incur the cost which would be necessary to receive the King at Prahsue, if I were of opinion that the King and his Chiefs are prepared to publicly renounce the custom of human sacrifices.

15. If they are prepared to make such a public renunciation I should be prepared to meet them at a convenient place . . .

16. You are as well aware as myself that a general movement is tending to break up the Ashanti kingdom.

17. The importance of Coomassie has been very much lessened since the surrounding districts were no longer compelled to resort to it as the only place at which they could obtain European merchandise.

18. The custom, as you well know, was formerly that subjects of any State tributary of Ashanti were not allowed to come to the coast excepting with special permission, and that permission was but

---

[1] C.O. 879/20, no. 268. For an abridged version from *Parl. Papers*, 1883 [C. 3687], see Metcalfe, *Great Britain and Ghana*, p. 408. *Capt. Knapp Barrow* was an officer of the Gold Coast Artillery, Assistant Colonial Secretary, 1882-3, and Colonial Secretary (Gold Coast), 1884-7. For selections from his report, 5 July 1883, from *Parl. Papers*, 1884 [C. 4052], see Metcalfe, *Great Britain and Ghana*, pp. 408-12. The original text has 'Obronie Badaie' not 'Obrodie' as the term reported to describe Maclean's early administration as 'white peacemaker': cf. G. E. Metcalfe, *Maclean of the Gold Coast* (Oxford, 1962), p. vi and n.

rarely accorded, and when accorded it was insisted that the journey should be made through Coomassie.

19. The gradual change which is taking place in this country and the consequences of the burning of Coomassie by the force under Sir Garnet Wolseley in 1873 have done away with this.

20. The policy of this Government is to encourage trade with all the districts lying inland of the seaboard of the Colony by those routes which lead most directly to them . . .

21. It will be clear to you therefore that as I have before said, Coomassie cannot look to enjoy any importance as a trading centre until all obstacles to free movement are done away with . . .

6

THE EARL OF DERBY TO GOVERNOR SIR SAMUEL ROWE: ASHANTI, 31 OCTOBER 1883[1]

In my public Despatch No. 337 of this date, I have suggested the holding of a formal meeting for the purpose of installing the duly elected King of Ashanti, and of arranging a treaty of peace and friendship among the various tribes and nations adjacent to the Gold Coast Protectorate.

2. I observe in Captain Barrow's report that the Kings of Bequoi, Dadiassie, Daniassie, and Inquanta all expressed their unwillingness to remain any longer under the King of Ashanti.

3. On the other hand, in the event of such a meeting as I have suggested taking place, endeavours would no doubt be made by the Coomassie people, and the adherents of the King, to induce the revolted Chiefs to resume their allegiance.

4. I am not quite clear whether it would be more to our interests or not, for the security of the Gold Coast, and for the maintenance of peace and circulation of trade, that the Ashanti kingdom should be re-established as a homogeneous whole, or remain split up into a number of small independent States.

5. I have therefore to request you to consider this question carefully, and should you be inclined to think that division is preferable to re-union, you will take care that the Chiefs to whom I have above referred are encouraged to speak their minds freely at the meeting, and that they clearly understand that in summoning them to attend you have no desire or intention to persuade them to place themselves again under the control of the King of Ashanti.

[1] C.O. 96/152; C.O. 879/20, no. 268. This confidential dispatch should be compared with the public version, cited in Metcalfe, *Great Britain and Ghana*, p. 412. Kwaku Dua was enstooled in April and died in June 1884. *Edward H. Stanley*, 15th Earl of Derby, Secretary of State for Colonies, 1882–5.

7

ADMINISTRATOR F. B. P. WHITE TO CAPT. R. L. T. LONSDALE: MISSION TO ASHANTI, 22 JUNE 1887[1]

WITH reference to our former correspondence upon the subject of the state of affairs in Ashantee, I have decided that an effort should be made at once by this Government to effect a cessation of hostilities, and the establishment, by consent of the parties concerned, of a central government in that country.

2. It would seem to be the case that all parties are tired of a state of things which involves continual fighting, with a series of successes and reverses so evenly balanced, and it is probable that they would not only welcome the proffer of advice from this Government, but would be largely influenced by the counsels of an officer sent in the name of the Governor of this Colony; while, on the other hand, it is of paramount importance to the commercial welfare of this Colony that the roads to the interior, especially to Gaman, should be opened up to trade.

3. I select you to conduct the necessary negotiations, and I have every confidence that from your knowledge of the existing state of affairs in Ashantee, and the experience of that country which you possess, you will succeed, if success is possible.

4. I am of opinion that you should commence operations by sending trustworthy messengers to the influential Chiefs on each side, explaining my desire for the restoration of peace, and adding that I have sent you to offer advice and assistance in procuring an understanding between them; but that they must clearly understand that this Government is only actuated by a desire to put an end to the unhappy existing state of affairs, and, while prepared to recognise any form of government upon which they may agree, does not in any way wish to interfere with their right of choice; and until all parties have expressed their willingness to accept your assistance, and have ceased from hostilities, you will be unable to visit them.

5. Your conduct must be influenced by the replies you will receive, but I must impress upon you that you must not enter Ashantee until you have good reason to know that your presence will be acceptable.

6. You will be accompanied by the escort now with you, and I will direct the District Commissioner at Cape Coast and the Inspector General to furnish you with money, &c. as you may require.

[1] C.O. 879/25, no. 333. Encl. in White to Holland, 22 June 1887. White was accompanied by E. A. Barnett, who was present at the preliminary election of Kwaku Dua III (Prempeh). See David Kimble, *A Political History of Ghana, 1850–1928* (Oxford, 1963), p. 278.

7. I fully recognise the advisability of your being accompanied by another officer, but the present very unhealthy season has so diminished the number of officers serving on the coast as to cause me serious embarrassment and difficulty; if possible, however, an officer will be sent to you.

In dealing with the Chiefs you might, as an instance of the desire of this Government to assist them in restoring order, allude to the recent operations in Denkera, and explain what has been done in punishing our Chiefs who have rendered assistance to either party.

8

ASSISTANT INSPECTOR BARNETT TO GOVERNOR SIR W. B. GRIFFITH: PREMPEH'S ELECTION, 29 MARCH 1888[1]

I HAVE the honour to report, for the information of your Excellency—

1. That Prempeh, now known as Quaku Duah, Princess Yah Kiah's son, was elected King and handed over to the linguists, to whom he paid, according to custom, 60 periguins of gold dust.[2]

2. The ceremony took place at midnight on the 26th instant, at which I was present.

3. At 11 a.m. on the 26th instant messengers from Kokofu arrived, and said their King could not come into Kumasi unless every one was forgiven for the following offences: 1. Rebellion; 2. Adultery with Chiefs' wives (this was specially mentioned to save Archiriboanda); 3. Murder and other capital offences (paragraph 3, letter No. 57, Colonial Secretary, 31.2.88). This shows your Excellency more than anything could the enviable position taken up by the King of Kokofu during the late disturbances, viz., guardian and champion of every scoundrel who came to him.

4. I, after a long palaver, negotiated a very successful issue to the request, paragraph 3. Princess Yah Kiah, Bantama Awuah, and Asafu Buaki offered to go personally with me and meet King Eseybi outside Kumasi, and there drink fetish, to wipe out and forget the past conduct of anyone in his camp. On my imparting this to the Kokofu messengers they went away very elated.

Your Excellency can fancy my disgust and regret when messengers from Mampon and Kokofu arrived at 2.30 p.m. on the same day (26th instant), saying their Kings could not be ready and

---

[1] C.O. 879/28, no. 351. Encl. in Griffith to Knutsford, 29 March 1888. *E. A. Barnett* of the Gold Coast Constabulary also left a second report giving more details in Griffith to Knutsford, 30 June 1888. *W. B. Griffith*, Lieut.-Governor and Governor of the Gold Coast, 1880–94.

[2] A periguin was worth about £8; William Tordoff, *Ashanti under the Prempehs 1888–1935* (Oxford, 1965), p. 27.

requesting me to postpone the election to next Big Adai. The representatives of both these Kings, who are with me, were even more astonished than I was at the message.

5. I pointed out to them that it was not my policy to prevent a King being put on the stool, and that they knew as well as I did that an order had come from your Excellency for me to return to the Coast, and that I was no more able to disobey orders from my Chief than they were from theirs.

6. The messengers then admitted that the ceremony could not be postponed, and that their Kings were to blame. The Mampon King's representative also added that they had no objection to Prempeh.

7. The Mampon representative afterwards came to me (he is an old and much respected Prince), and expressed his unqualified regret at the behaviour of his King, saying, He is young, head-strong, and is led away by lying and bad advice sent from the Kokofu camp (which we are led to understand comes from the Coast); the old Chiefs will force him to come to Kumasi or give up the stool; some of them have taken the big oath.

8. Dr. Sullivan, whom I informed your Excellency I had sent to the King of Mampon, returned here on the afternoon of the 26th instant.

9. I attach his report, which corroborates in a way my paragraph 7.

10. I also attach list of Chiefs, representatives,[1] &c., &c., present at the election. Everything went off with great éclat. The speeches, &c. all impressed one with the idea that Ashanti is tired of war.

11. Both the Mampon and Kokofu representatives said that after all they heard I might rest assured there would be no trouble as to their Kings and people settling the long feud which has been carried on since Kofi Kalkali's time.

12. The newly elected King has requested me to allow my messengers to accompany his to witness the drinking of fetish between the different antagonistic Chiefs, in which they bury the past of Ashanti, and all offences are forgiven. This I have complied with.

13. I have thoroughly impressed on the King and his counsellors (that in case of any future disturbances either with his own people or neighbouring tribes) that they must not expect any further help from the British Government.

14. During the orations delivered at the election, and the handing over of the 'royal stool' to the care of Prempeh, it was repeatedly stated, and gratefully acknowledged, that peace was brought about solely by your Excellency's good advice, which they were only too glad they had accepted.

15. To-day, according to what Awuah had stated, all prisoners,

---

[1] This list of 82 titles is included in Griffith to Knutsford, 29 March 1888, C.O. 879/28, no. 351.

political and otherwise, have been released. This was in honour of the new King.

16. Bantamah Awuah has just been to see me, and on my informing him I was writing to your Excellency, requested me to write this: 'I, Awuah, of Bantama, send my good mornings and best wishes to the Governor, and thank my God that he has taken care of Ashanti, and brought peace, otherwise I might have been said to have brought ruin to my country.'

17. I am informed by the King that all Ashanti will send down the nine representatives who have been attached to my mission to thank your Excellency in person. As there will be no time to receive an answer to this letter before I leave for the Coast, would you cause what arrangements your Excellency may see fit to make, to be told me on my arrival at Cape Coast, for their reception.

9

GOVERNOR SIR W. B. GRIFFITH TO LORD KNUTSFORD: EXPEDITION TO TAVIEVI, 7 JULY 1888[1]

IN my Despatch No. 216, of 26th June, it was stated in paragraph four that I thought it would be advisable to instruct Mr. Akers to communicate, through the Adaglus or otherwise, with the Tavieves, and inform them of the terms on which hostilities against them would cease. This was immediately done and in the terms stated in the Despatch. . . .

5. On the 24th of June Mr. Akers telegraphed to the Colonial Secretary from Tavieve as follows: 'Belo Quabla, King of Tavieve, and perpetrator of all outrages, has surrendered himself to me to-day. Have fixed 3rd of July as day for meeting of all Krepi Chiefs.' The telegram was followed by a letter from Mr. Akers dated 23rd June in which he stated that messengers had arrived that day from Tavieve bearing a flag of truce. He enclosed a copy of the proceedings of the interview he had with them, as also of the terms upon which he agreed to allow them to return to their towns; and stated that a portion of the Adaglu people were then in his camp, and that he expected the remainder in the course of the next few days. A copy of this letter and copies of its enclosures are annexed.

6. In the interview referred to, the Tavieve messengers, in reply to Mr. Akers's inquiry, 'how many of your people have been killed in this war?' stated: '167 fighting men that we know of ourselves are

---

[1] C.O. 879/28, no. 351. See W. Walton Claridge, *A History of the Gold Coast and Ashanti* (2 vols., London, 1915), ii, chap. xvi.

killed, exclusive of women and children. A number of women and children were killed in some of the fights, and a great many have died from starvation and exposure. The Tavieve people have had scarcely any food for six days past; soon as ever we tried to congregate in numbers we were scattered and shot,' and they stated that five of their chiefs had been killed.

7. This is terrible retribution, but there was no avoiding the struggle for supremacy. Any hesitation as to taking prompt and energetic action in the circumstances which led to the fighting in Tavieve would have resulted disastrously to the Colony, while in the end severe measures would still have had to be resorted to, and at a far greater cost and probable loss of life on all sides. Much as I deplore the loss of life, and especially the lives of women and children, I have no hesitation in declaring my opinion, which is shared by the members of the Council, that there was but one course for the Government to pursue in the position in which it was placed. That course has been followed, and its result will never be forgotten in Krepi, whilst it will be a warning to other tribes, who previously would have been ready to give trouble at any moment, that their interest lies in loyal and dutiful obedience to the commands of the Government. . . .

10

GOVERNOR SIR W. B. GRIFFITH TO PREMPEH: ASHANTI GOVERNMENT, 16 JULY 1890[1]

. . . 15. I HAVE so far dealt with the word 'districts,' as used by the deputation, in the sense of its meaning only the inhabitants of the places referred to, and not to the countries they inhabited, and looking at the context I think it was so meant by the deputation, because the Government has had nothing to do with countries in Ashanti as districts. Well, they state that you request me to assist you to restore to Ashanti the districts of Juabin, Adansi, Kokofu, and Bekwai, adding that some of the districts named have claimed the protection of the English Government, and some have declared independence. As I have already stated a large party of Kokofus and some Dadiassies have sought refuge in the Protectorate, and I have informed you of the policy adopted with reference to them. As regards any Ashantis who have declared their independence, but whom you do not name, and who cannot be meant as of Juabin in Ashanti or Bekwai, because their representatives are included in the deputation, you must be well aware that this Government has no right to interfere with any line of action any such parties have decided upon, in their own interest. They are not British subjects, and are quite outside of the sphere of influence of this Government. If that of Ashanti cannot induce them to return to their allegiance to its authorities it is clearly no part of the duty of this Government to take such action on behalf of Ashanti. . . .

II

PREMPEH TO GOVERNOR SIR W. B. GRIFFITH: ASHANTI GOVERNMENT, 22 AUGUST 1890[1]

I BEG to acknowledge the receipt of your interesting letter of the 16th July per my messengers, swordbearer, and court crier, as also the enclosed one which you were directed by the Right Honourable the Lord Knutsford, Her Majesty's Principal Secretary of State for the Colonies.

2. I am greatly surprised of the great mistake and wrong conduct of my representative Chief Appia, for I prepared the deputation to meet you at Accra, and upon their earnest request I wrote you on the 7th of April last, soliciting your kind favour to meet them at Elmina, and which you kindly replied, and I believe I informed them of the same when they were still on the road, for which or what reasons of their going down to Elmina, and I pray you will excuse him for this mistake and forgive him for his wrong conduct. It is said that black does not know the value and the preciousness of time; you white people know it, therefore I trust you will excuse him. I have requested him to leave at Elmina at once to meet you at Accra, and I beg you to receive him.

3. I find that it is the policy and firm determination of Her Majesty's Government not to advise any Ashanti subject that sought refuge in the Protectorate on the Gold Coast to return to Ashanti, and as it is not fair and reasonable for me to send for the Ashantees that sought refuge in the Protectorate, without acquainting you of the fact, and if I have said that I wish my good friend the Governor will assist in restoring to me the Juabin, Adansi, Kokofu, Bekwai and the Dadaissie peoples, or any Ashanti, I do not mean that he should force them to come, but simply to call them in the presence of my messengers that they may deliver my message politely to them, that it is my great wish that they should return to me, and that if there is any mis-understanding still existing between us it shall be clearly settled, but should you not feel yourself in any way justified in assuming this

[1] C.O. 879/35, no. 415.

responsibility, then may I ask you to refer to the last clause of the 14th paragraph of your last letter, and if you kindly do so your gratitude will ever remain in my memory, it runs thus:

'I will, however, let the Kokofus and the Didiassies also if any still remain know of your wish that they should return to Ashanti, and that you would receive them kindly and regard them as your subjects, leaving it to them to decide for themselves whether they will or will not return to their countries.'

4. It shall be ungrateful for me to say that Her Majesty's Government does not wish the welfare of Ashanti, for many proofs I find that Her Majesty's Government have the good will and desire to promote the interest and peace of my Ashanti kingdom, and for which cause I am greatly thankful.

5. With regard to the Juabins I know that it is long since they sought refuge and protection in the British territory, and surely they have been treated kindly and have lived happily under you for so many years, yet still as I have their King with me and part of them are elsewhere, and if it is their wish to return, I think it worthy to seek for them for the last four months or more. I am collecting the Juabin captives that the Ashantis carried during the last war with them, and I am happy to say I have collected large numbers and have delivered them to their King, so if those at Konforodua would choose to join their King, it shall give me much pleasure to receive them for their King.

6. The Adansis, I am sorry I have said too much about them, I know they are troublesome set of people, for once I allow them to come and live in my kingdom as before in an independent position, truly troubles will never cease, for they live in the very main road to the coast and traders will be troubled, and there will be no end of troubles for me. If they choose to live under you in the British territory they may remain, but if they choose to come and live on my land as my loyal subjects, surely I shall gladly receive them and treat them kindly, for my motto is 'Peace.'

7. I beg to bring before your Excellency's notice the present state of my Mansu people, that after the defeat of their leader, that rebel chief Kwasi Mensah, by the British Government, have thought better to return to me, but sorry to say that one Kwofi Tinn and friend Quamin Asamoah, of Acquabusu, in Denkera, have strongly stopped them from returning to me. . . .

12

GOVERNOR SIR W. B. GRIFFITH TO
LORD KNUTSFORD: ASHANTI, 19 MAY 1891[1]

... 12. In view, then, of the information both particular and general in my possession relative to Ashanti, it appeared to me to be matter for serious consideration whether the time had not arrived to pursue a firm, decided, and strong policy on the part of the Government with regard to that country, not only in its particular interests, but also in regard to those of this Colony, in its business, and political, and geographical connexion with its neighbour, and for the following reasons *inter alia.*

13. For some time past, since the present King was elected, this Colony has often been put to great and costly inconvenience in dealing with refugees from, and preventing raids on, Ashanti by those who have fled from it for safety in the Protectorate, and in sending missions of inquiry for the benefit of the authorities in Kumasi; but it is clearly not in the interests of this Colony that the procedure stated should be continued indefinitely.

14. So far as I can judge from the information in my possession, the indications are that Ashanti as a whole, besides being gradually broken up, is steadily retrograding, both in its entirety as it now remains and in the portions which have separated themselves from the nominal Government at Kumasi, which is powerless to check the downward tendency mentioned, and has latterly been weakened by coolness between Kumasi and Bekwai, and by a disposition on the part of Yow Sapon, of Juabin, to desert his allegiance if he can obtain admission into the Protectorate, whilst Bekwai, almost the only province of Ashanti which has steadily supported the young King, Kwaku Duah, at Kumasi, would gladly see the British flag planted throughout Ashanti. At present Adansi, owing to the absence of population, is rapidly resuming its forest character. The regular trade road of nearly 80 miles leading from the Prah through Adansi to Bekwai has diminished to a narrow track, along which travellers have to cut away the bush to get a passage. Kokofu and Dadiassi are quite neglected, cultivation has diminished, trade has fallen away, the roads to Gamen and Bontokoo are virtually closed, and Ashanti, as a whole, appears to be gradually falling into decay.

15. Looking to the circumstances that Ashanti, except on the north-west—assuming that Gaman is eventually included in the Protectorate—is surrounded by British territory, and that British interests will suffer if a suitable remedy for the injurious position

[1] C.O. 879/35, no. 415. For another version from *Parl. Papers*, 1896 [C. 7917] with gaps in the argument, see Metcalfe, *Great Britain and Ghana*, pp. 448–9.

into which affairs in Ashanti seem to be steadily drifting is not provided, it appeared to me that it would be a prudent and judicious proceeding on the part of the Government if it exercised its influence for the purpose, not of increasing its territorial possessions, but of preventing Ashanti, situated as it is with regard to these possessions, from receding further in the direction indicated by placing before the authorities at Kumasi for their consideration a proposal to extend British protection to Ashanti, and pointing out to them that the object of this Government in making it was to assist, encourage, develop, and elevate Ashanti by the introduction of European influences calculated to secure willing obedience on the part of the people to law and order, to promote civilization, education, industrial trading, and commercial undertakings in, and steady and progressive improvement throughout the country.

16. At the same time I did not conceal from myself that a closer relationship with Ashanti than that existing between it and the Gold Coast would add to the responsibility and labour of this Government, would also at first entail expense, and later might create inconveniences which it was not possible to foresee nor to appreciate until their existence became apparent.

17. On the other hand, I considered that if Ashanti was taken under British protection it was, in the circumstances of the case, naturally to be expected that a great and beneficial change would very probably be the result. The fact of itself would gradually dispose those who have deserted their particular localities to return and re-inhabit them. Some twelve to fifteen thousand Adansis would be again spread over their country. About twenty thousand Kokofus and Dadiassies would seek their former homes; and, in short, all who had left Ashanti and sought refuge in the Protectorate, or who had gone elsewhere from motives of fear and uncertainty as to the safety of their lives, families, and property would in all probability return and clear the roads, rebuild their towns, and resume their previous avocations as farmers, hunters, miners, and traders, influenced by a feeling of freedom from oppression and molestation, security of person, safety of family relationships and of possession, and a sense of security when travelling, all derived from the belief that these advantages would be enjoyed from the fact of the country being under the protection of Great Britain.

18. Having considered with respectful attention your Lordship's Despatches noted in the margin, and, after careful examination of every important point that suggested itself in relation to the subject, and endeavouring to look mentally as far into the future as it was possible to anticipate, I formed the opinion that, all things considered, the best policy for this Government to pursue would be to propose to the Ashantis, through the authorities at Kumasi, to place their

country under British protection; to take action in the matter while it was still possible to do this before the rainy season commenced in the interior, and, in the event of the Ashantis agreeing to the proposal, to leave it open to Her Majesty's Government to ratify or disapprove of the necessary treaty I contemplated making with the Ashantis in the event of their executing it.

19. In the circumstances stated, I convened a meeting of the Executive Council on the 13th of March, and placed the views I had formed upon the subject before members, to whom I read the draft of a letter I had prepared for transmission to the King of Ashanti. I annex an extract from the Minutes of the Council which describes what took place upon the occasion. On inquiring of members if they agreed generally in the views I had expressed, they replied affirmatively, but advised that Mr. Hull, the officer I intended to send to Kumasi with my communication to the King, should be authorised to extend his stay there beyond the limit of 15 days stated in his instructions. The Council also recommended that he should be supplied with 400 l. to distribute as presents to the King and principal chiefs who were loyal to him in the event of their executing the treaty under which British protection would be extended to them. . . .

13

GOVERNOR SIR W. B. GRIFFITH TO PREMPEH: TERMS OF AGREEMENT, 11 MARCH 1891[1]

... 17. I CONSIDER that it is now my duty to press upon the serious consideration of yourself and of your loyal Kings, Chiefs and advisers the grave change which has taken place in Ashanti since you were placed upon the stool, owing to the defection of some of the Ashanti tribes, the uncertain political relationship to you of others whose loyalty you have possibly hitherto counted upon, and the consequent falling back of Ashanti, the spoiling of those large portions of the country which have been deserted by the inhabitants; the consequent gradual decline in the farming, trading, and other business of the country and concurrently, the diminution of the taxes, tolls, and fees collected, the full supply of which are necessary to the proper maintenance, state, and dignity of yourself and your Kings, Chiefs, and principal men, while the happiness, comfort, and faith of the people are unsettled in consequence of the disordered and uncertain state of the whole country.

18. Ashanti to-day is very much changed from when Mensah became King. Then Koranga, Mampon, Insutu, Kumasi, Juabin,

[1] C.O. 879/35, no. 415.

Becquah, Damassi, Kokofu, Inquanta and Dadiassi, altogether 10 provinces, composed the Ashanti Kingdom. How does Ashanti stand today? I am informed, on what I believe to be reliable authority, that, besides Kumasi Becquah is the most loyal of your supporters. Indeed, the King of that country may be said to be your right hand. Half of the people of Koranga; part of the people of Mampon and those of Ofinsu, Jisu (about 1,000 in each place) are loyal to the stool. There is an unsettled dispute between Insuta and Kumasi. Juabin occupies a strong position—apparently one of independence—but professes to be friendly disposed towards you.

19. On the other hand, a part of Korangam and also a part of Mampon, together with Dadiassi, Kokofu, and Inquanta, all powerful tribes, have crossed from Ashanti and sought refuge in the British Protectorate, and the countries they have left are being rapidly over-run by bush and forest, farming and trade operations having ceased in them whereby much food and profit are lost. Adansi also, inde-pendent until it entered into unwise conflict with Becquah, is without population. The country is fast becoming forest and some ninety miles of what used to be a fair road between the Prah and Becquah has reverted to bush, thus offering a great obstacle to that portion of the trade of Ashanti passing through Adansi.

20. This Government has faithfully kept the engagement it made with you when by its interposition the voice of what was then the major-ity of the people of Ashanti caused you to be placed upon the stool of the Ashanti Kingdom. I give you credit for having done the best you could to restore Ashanti, but it is now quite clear that you have been unsuccessful, it appears from all accounts that matters are going on from bad to worse, and in the circumstances I have to suggest for your serious consideration and that of your loyal Kings, Chiefs, and good advisers whether it will not be wisest in the general interests of Ashanti to adopt a course calculated to secure your position, to satisfy your Kings, Chiefs, and people, to promote peace, tranquillity, and good order in Ashanti, and to restore its trade and the happiness and safety of the people generally by making it to the advantage of the refugees to return, inhabit, and cultivate their respective countries, and thus raise Ashanti to a prosperous, substantial, and steady position as a great farming and trading community such as it has never occupied hitherto.

21. The British Protectorate is very extensive, and Her Majesty's Government does not desire to add largely to the enormous responsi-bilities it already has on the Gold Coast, but considering the position of Ashanti—surrounded as it is on the south-west, south-east, and north-east by the Protectorate, and looking to its business relations and friendly connexion with the Gold Coast, it appears to this Govern-ment that if Ashanti desired to come under British protection, for

the reasons stated in this communication, that it would be the duty of this Government to yield to the wishes of the King, and the Kings, Chiefs, and principal men and people of Ashanti, that they should be allowed to enjoy that protection and freedom which exists wherever the British flag flies, and humbly submit the wishes of Ashanti for the gracious consideration of Her Majesty the Queen-Empress.

22. On behalf, therefore, of this Government, and in the best interest of Ashanti, I would ask you and those on whose support and counsel you depend, to consider seriously the important subject I have now placed before you.

23. Assuming that it should be your decision to acquiesce in the suggestion I have made, it appears to me that the arrangement indicated should take the form of a treaty of friendship and protection between Her Most Gracious Majesty Queen Victoria on the one part, and yourself, your chief Kings, Chiefs, and principal men on the second part.

24. In order to point out distinctly what a treaty such as I have proposed would arrange for, and to facilitate matters, I have entrusted my officer Mr. Henry Mitchell Hull with a form which is complete in itself with the exception of blank spaces for names which would have to be filled in.

25. This treaty consists of nine articles.[1] The preamble or introduction describes the contracting parties, that is to say, Her Most Gracious Majesty the Queen by her representative, and the King, Kings, Chiefs, and principal men of Ashanti for themselves, the people of Ashanti and their common country.

26. By the first article it is declared that the contracting parties of the second part for, and on behalf of themselves, their successors, and the people of Ashanti, place all of the foregoing under the protection of Great Britain, and it contains a declaration that they have not entered into any treaty with any other foreign power.

27. By the second article Her Majesty would take Ashanti under her protection.

28. By article three it is proposed to be agreed that the King, Kings, Chiefs, and principal men, together with the other people of Ashanti, will not enter into any war, or commit any act of aggression on any of the Chiefs bordering on their country by which the trade of the country shall be interrupted, or the safety and property of the subjects of Her Majesty shall be lost, compromised or endangered, and that the authorities of Ashanti herein-before mentioned undertake to refer to the Government of the Gold Coast Colony for friendly arbitration, any trade or other disputes or misunderstandings in

---

[1] For treaty terms, see Metcalfe, *Great Britain and Ghana*, pp. 449–50. The initiative of Griffith was not approved by the C.O.: Meade to Griffith, 3 September 1891; and Hull's mission was a failure: Hull to Griffith, 27 May 1891.

which they may become involved before actually entering into hostilities, in order to avoid the same.

29. By the fourth article it is declared that should any difference or dispute arise between yourself and any of your Kings, Chiefs, and principal men it shall be referred to the Governor or the nearest British authority of the Gold Coast Colony for the time being, whose decision shall be final and binding upon all parties concerned.

30. By article five it is declared that British subjects shall have free access to all parts of Ashanti, and shall have the right to build houses and possess property according to the laws in force in the Gold Coast Colony, and they shall have full liberty to carry on such trade and manufacture as may be approved by the Governor of the Gold Coast Colony or by any officer appointed for the purpose by Her Majesty's Government. Any differences or disputes which may arise between the aforesaid British subjects and the King, Kings, Chiefs, or principal men of Ashanti as to the duties or Customs to be paid to the latter authorities in the towns of Ashanti by British subjects, or as to any other matter, shall be referred to the officer mentioned in Article IV., whose decision in the matter is to be binding and final. The article also provides that the authorities of Ashanti will not extend the rights guaranteed by the article to British subjects, to any other persons, without the knowledge and consent of the officer referred to.

31. Article six declares that in consideration of the protection guaranteed on the part of Great Britain to the authorities of Ashanti they bind themselves and their heirs and successors to keep the main roads in good order, that they will encourage trade and give facilities to traders; and will not cede their territory to, nor accept a Protectorate from, or enter into any agreement or treaty with any other foreign power except through and with the consent of the British Government.

32. Article seven declares that Her Majesty's Government will not prevent the King of Ashanti, of his Kings, Chiefs, and principal men, and their lawful successors from levying customary revenue appertaining to them according to the laws and customs of their country nor in the administration thereof; and Her Majesty's Government will respect the habits and customs of the country, so far as they do not militate against the dictates of humanity, but will not permit human sacrifices.

33. By article eight, it is declared that it shall be competent for Her Majesty's Government to appoint a Commissioner to reside in Ashanti who shall assist you by his advice with a view to examining into and reconciling differences and securing law and order in the country, and who shall promote the trading interests of the country and act in accordance with instructions which may be issued to him

from time to time by the Governor of the Gold Coast Colony. The article also declares that Her Majesty may further direct that Ashanti may be visited by a travelling Commissioner of the Gold Coast Colony when it shall seem fit to the Governor to despatch such an officer for the purposes stated.

34. The ninth article provides that the treaty shall come into operation from the date of its execution, but power is expressly reserved to Her Majesty to refuse to approve and ratify it within a year from its date, a provision which is inserted in all treaties made by Her Majesty's officers in West Africa. . . .

14

PREMPEH TO GOVERNOR SIR W. B. GRIFFITH: TERMS OF AGREEMENT, 7 MAY 1891[1]

. . . 6. WITH regard to the countries in Adansi at its present state, I think it is my duty to see what course I should take to remove all uncomfortableness, being one of the highways of communication between peoples and of commerce should remain in that state in which Adansi is at present, myself, Kings, Chiefs, and principal men are under consideration what course to take to remedy this, so you see it is not my wish that you should send the people of Adansi to come and dwell on my land, a land which is over this side of the River Prah, and this River Prah is from olden times a boundary between Ashanti, and Her Majesty's Protectorate on the coast, a land which you know is my patrimonial trust, and if the inhabitants of that land have thrown away my allegiance with them and have crossed the boundary to come under the British Government on the coast, I do not see it fair to say 'as their country is becoming overgrown with bush and forest, there being no population to keep the roads clear and to carry on farming and trade, it appears to me that this government will have to take some action in the matter,' and further you state that, 'and to remedy this it appears to me a question of consideration whether that country should not be taken under British protection.' I may say for the sake of peace and tranquillity and for the future prosperity and good wishes of Ashanti, leave this matter with me, but if you think that Ashanti kingdom is spoiled and by that, you, whom I consider as a friend and supporter, you, who have promised

[1] C.O. 879/35, no. 415. For the background to this exchange, see Tordoff, *Ashanti under the Prempehs*, pp. 38–43. The authorship of these letters ascribed to Prempeh is not discussed in any of the histories of the period. Possibly they were drawn up by John Owusu-Ansa, teacher, clerk, and son of Prince Ansa, sent to England in 1834. Owusu-Ansa is known to have resided in Kumasi from 1889 and to have become Prempeh's adviser; Tordoff, *Ashanti under the Prempehs*, p. 51.

never to harm me, should take this advantage to force me to compel me to receive in my land people I do not recognise as my subjects, rapacious people, people I know if not under my rule and government will bring trouble and shame on Ashanti; I pray you therefore to leave this matter with me but not to act so towards your good friend.

7. With regard to the Juabins, I think I will not drop of touching on the subject. It is true that my object of making any request for Yow Sapon was of propitiating him and endeavouring to secure his support as stated in your letter, but what must I do? must I leave my Jaubin brothers away, must I be silenced to let my brethren slip away from my hands? No, I must try from day to day to pray to you to assist me to receive back my Jaubin people, as well as Adansi people, Quahoo. I learn from your important communication that they have become British subjects for which or what reason I do not know, now it is extending as far as Attabubu which has recently entered into a treaty with Her Majesty's Government, and I ask is it fair for Her Majesty's Government to deal so with me. I, whom you call as a friend, is it fair to take all my subjects from me; so if you say 'it is therefore useless for you to mention the subject again.' I find that you being my friend, I am at liberty to make any requests to you, so do not be annoyed if I am making these requests. I wanted my Jaubin people, Adansi people, Quahoo, and Attabubu may be returned to me as my subjects before.

8. I have summed your very important and interesting communication to me and have found them under three capital heads; 1st. The replies of the Kokofus and Dadiassis. 2nd. That Ashanti in its present state should come and enjoy the protection of the Queen of Great Britain and Empress of India; and 3rd. The course I should adopt for the future prosperity of Ashanti kingdom.

9. The replies of the Kokofus and Dadiassis to my invitation I thank Her Majesty's Government for its assistance in the matter, those of the Kokofus and Dadiassis who have expressed their willingness of returning to me, I shall be glad and happy to receive them, and upon my word of honour, that I have promised to receive them kindly and regard them as my loyal subjects, as there is a rumour amongst those who have expressed their willingness to accept my invitation to them that a white officer should be sent to bring them to Ashanti, and which it was never the intention of Her Majesty's Government of assuming such responsibility, and to drive all fear and anxiety amongst them, and to remedy this it appears to me and my Kings, Chiefs, and principal men a question for consideration, whether I should not send a Chief to come and drink water with them, to bring my people to me; the Government have done their part worthily, and the remainder is now rest with me.

10. The suggestion that Ashanti in its present state should come

and enjoy the protection of Her Majesty the Queen and Empress of India, I may say this is a matter of a very serious consideration and which I am happy to say we have arrived at this conclusion, that my kingdom of Ashanti will never commit itself to any such policy; Ashanti must remain independent as of old, at the same time to be friendly with all white men. I do not write this with a boastful spirit, but in the clear sense of its meaning. Ashanti is an independent kingdom and is always friendly with the white men for the sake of trade we are bind to each other, so it is our Ashanti proverb, that what the old men eat and left, it is what the children enjoyed. I thank Her Majesty's Government for the good wishes entertained for Ashanti; I appreciate to the fullest extent its kindness, and I wish that my power of language could suitably tell you how much and how deeply I appreciate those kindness of Her Majesty's Government towards me and my kingdom. Believe me, Governor, that I am happy to inform you, that the cause of Ashanti is progressing and that there is no reason for any Ashantiman to feel alarm at the prospects, or to believe for a single instant that our cause has been driving back by the events of the past hostilities.

11. The course I should adopt for the future prosperity of Ashanti kingdom, I may add I am most sanguine of success, and where energy is wedded to enthusiasm in any work failure is not to be thought of; it is certainly true that Ashanti to-day is very much changed from what it was before, say 20 years past, and it is through the uncertain political relationship to the Royal Stool, and I believe it will be wisest in the general interest of my kingdom of Ashanti to adopt a course calculated to bring back Ashanti to its former position, to promote peace and tranquillity and good order in my Ashanti kingdom. Many thanks for the advice, and after a good consideration, a thing that is most horrible to white men, as human sacrifices, whatever precious it may cost us, I am happy to inform you I have abolished such acts totally from my Ashanti kingdom.

12. I shall regard very much if Her Majesty's Government will act as referred in the 39th paragraph of your letter towards me, for you pointed out to me as a friend, the course if I choose to adopt, that is to say, to sign treaty of friendship and protection with Her Majesty's Government, and which course myself, King, Chiefs, and principal men after a serious consideration do not find it proper for us to adopt that course, but will remain friendly with you as of old, and by this if you say as stated in that paragraph it will not do, and I know that Her Majesty's Government gave this advice with the most loyal and friendly feeling towards Ashanti.

13. I feel very much for Prince Archiboranda for his simplicity and assertion, in alluding that were he to return to Ashanti that I would soon cut off his head; may I ask, has he heard any of his brothers and

sisters he left here had suffered from decapitation; he ought to think seriously and come back home.

My Queen Mother, as well as myself, beg to render our thanks for the fine presents you so kindly send us.

My best regards, in which Queen Mother joins.

15

GOVERNOR SIR W. B. GRIFFITH TO G. E. FERGUSON: MISSION TO GOLD COAST INTERIOR, 25 APRIL 1892[1]

SECRET

It has been decided that steps should be taken to secure British influence over the territory in the rear of the Gold Coast Colony beyond the 9th parallel of latitude where such territory is not clearly proved to have been already placed under the protection of a foreign Power. I have selected you for the purpose indicated, and I now instruct you to proceed as promptly as you possibly can to execute the mission entrusted to you. You will endeavour to make treaties with the Native authorities of the following countries, viz:—

Dagomba,
Gondja,
Gourounsi, and
Mossi.

2. I append a copy of a treaty such as it is desirable you should obtain and have formally executed. You will observe that it does not imply the protection of the countries referred to, as that would be simply impossible looking to their distance from the Gold Coast, but that it is a treaty of friendship and freedom of trade, with a binding engagement by the native Chiefs that they will not make any treaty with, or accept the protection of, any other Power without the consent of Her Majesty's Government.

3. You are well aware of the fact that Great Britain cannot, under treaty arrangements, exercise any exclusive right over territory situated within the Neutral Zone of the agreement made at Berlin in 1888. It will be for you, therefore, to consider as to the best course for you to take in proceeding to the countries indicated, whether you

[1] C.O. 879/38, no. 448. For a version with verbal differences and some abridgements, see Metcalfe, *Great Britain and Ghana*, p. 451. *G. E. Ferguson*, clerk and surveyor, had been on mission to Krobo and Akwamu, 1886, Kwahu and Atabubu, 1890, and served on the Anglo-German boundary commission, 1891. He sent back valuable reports on interior trade. From this policy resulted some fifty-four treaties, June 1892–7, made in the Gold Coast interior and collected in African no. 1010, *Collection of Treaties with Native Chiefs &c in West Africa*. They were worded to encourage trade and exclude foreign powers; for an example, see the treaty for Daboya, 8 July 1892, in Metcalfe, *Great Britain and Ghana*, p. 457.

should travel to the westward of that zone, via Attabubu, advance in a north-westerly direction, keeping the longitude of the zone well on your right. It appears to me that if you kept well to the westward of that zone, and then travelled west by north, executing treaties as you proceed, that in this way you might anticipate possible explorers who may be bent upon undertakings similar to that which I am entrusting to your special care, with every confidence that by the exercise of tact, policy, judgment, and your knowledge of native character and languages, you will make it a complete success. I do not wish, however, to trammel you as regards the roads by which, on your nearing the sphere of action, it may appear to you most advisable to take in the interest of your mission.

4. You will, of course, understand that you must not make treaties with Native Chiefs whose territories lie entirely within the Neutral Zone. But you would not be debarred from making treaties with Chiefs having territory lying partially within it, as you would be free to negotiate with them respecting those portions of their territories situated outside of it. Any such treaty must then contain a clause stipulating that territory within the zone is not affected by it.

5. The Neutral Zone, as defined, you are well acquainted with. The lines of longitude having been struck and given, the southern boundary is a line drawn on the latitude of the mouth of the River Daka, and the northern boundary is the tenth parallel.

6. After the conversations we have held upon the subject-matter of this communication, it appears to me unnecessary to do more than again impress upon you first, the absolute necessity of your proceeding to the localities where your operations are to be carried on with the utmost promptitude, as the matter is of much urgency, and should be carried out at once. You will leave no stone unturned in endeavouring to bring to a completely successful issue the mission specially entrusted to your care, in my full reliance that nothing will be wanting on your part to accomplish it satisfactorily. Should this prove to be the case, I have no doubt that it will be gratifying to the Imperial Government.

16

ACTING GOVERNOR F. M. HODGSON TO THE MARQUIS OF RIPON: ASHANTI, 13 NOVEMBER 1893[1]

REFERRING to the Despatches noted in the margin and to my telegram of the 10th instant, reporting the return of Mr. Vroom who had been despatched to Kumasi with an ultimatum to the King of Ashanti

---

[1] C.O. 879/39, no. 458. F. M. Hodgson, Acting Governor for periods, 1891–7; Governor, 1898–1900.

in accordance with the instructions contained in your Lordship's telegram of the 28th September, as well as the arrival of messengers at Accra from Kumasi, I have the honour to state that Mr. Vroom arrived at Elmina on the 31st October, and his report, of which I enclose a copy, reached me on the 7th instant.

2. King Kwaku Dua III showed evident signs of nervousness at the arrival of an officer of this Government at Kumasi, and he and his Court were so anxious to hear the object of Mr. Vroom's mission that they forgot the native etiquette observable in important ceremonials, for which the King personally apologized.

3. The King, Mr. Vroom reports, and as I anticipated, disclaimed any intention of interfering with Attabubu, stating that he recognizes that country as being under the protection of the Queen; but I beg once more your Lordship's reference to paragraph 7 of the letter from the King which accompanied the Governor's Despatch No. 179 of the 3rd June 1891. I beg also to call attention to the opinion expressed by Mr. Vroom in paragraph 19 of his report, in which that officer states:

'To me it is a matter beyond doubt that the army in Nkoranza would have invaded Attabubu.' Mr. Vroom adds, 'They seem, however, wise now,' which, I take it, means that the King realizes, by the action which has been taken, the fact that Attabubu is no longer a vassal state of Ashanti.

4. Mr. Vroom considers that the Ashantis have no wish to come into conflict with the English Government again, and that the feelings of the Ashantis generally are most friendly, as shown by the kind reception he obtained in every village he passed through, and the presents of food he was asked to receive. It is no doubt the case that the people as a body are in every way friendly disposed towards this Government and indeed would gladly welcome the light and easy yoke of the Protectorate bringing peace and safety in their midst in place of the tyranny under which they now have to live. Kumasi, Mr. Vroom says, is in a wretched state, overgrown with grass and with many of the huts in a most dilapidated condition. The markets are neglected, and the people appear poor and oppressed, 'their appeal for freedom is only expressed by their glances.'

5. The King of Ashanti in the written message[1] which he has sent to me by Mr. Vroom explains his action in sending his messengers to Native Kings within the Protectorate without acquainting the Governor, and in conjunction with his Council begs that his offence in that respect may be overlooked. He states also that he desires to encourage trade and wishes for peace and quietness and the maintenance 'of the good will of my good friend and the Great Queen.' King Kwaku Dua III states: 'My army in Koranza has not attacked

[1] Kwaku Dua (Prempeh) to Hodgson, 19 October 1893.

the Attabubu people. I have had no intention to do so at any time. The King of Koranza quarrelled with me, he insulted me; my army went to Koranza to punish the King. I sent messengers to King of Attabubu asking him not to mix up himself with the row I had with Koranza people; my messengers have not returned to me as yet; my army defeated King of Koranza and his people. Attabubu sent men, arms, powder, and lead to the Koranzas to fight me. They, fearing the consequences of their actions, sent to my good friend and falsely accused me of interfering with them. Attabubu people belong to the Queen. I will not interfere with them nor with any other country belonging to the Great Queen. I beg you to let my good friend know this. I look to you to speak good on my behalf. I have already sent messengers to bring back my army in Koranza. My messengers will go with you to my good friend and thank him in my name.'

6. I have no doubt whatever that the despatch of Colonel Sir Francis Scott with a force of Hausas to Attabubu, a matter which would have been promptly reported at Kumasi by spies, as well as the feint of war preparations made at Prahsu, had the result of causing the King to withdraw his army to Kumasi, which had in the meantime been left without protection, and to abandon the attempt of invading Attabubu for the dual purpose of chastising the Nkoranzas, and punishing the King for placing his country under the Queen, and supplying assistance in the shape of arms and ammunition to the Nkoranzas.

7. With regard to this latter matter I am instructing Colonel Sir Francis Scott to make inquiry, and, if necessary, to call the King of Attabubu to account for having mixed himself up with the Nkoranza war.

8. The reported murder of the King of Bekwai and his linguist Attobra is stated to be without foundation. An explanation of the matter is given by Kofi Yami, linguist to the King of Bekwai, and by the King of Bekwai himself in the written message which accompanies Mr. Vroom's report. Their version of the matter may be correct, but I am doubtful of it.

9. With regard to the despatch of messengers by King Kwaku Dua III to Prahsu undoubtedly for the sole purpose of seeing and reporting what was going on there, I enclose a copy of a report from Captain Bayly who was despatched to Prahsu when the detachment of Hausas at that place was reinforced and who has been engaged in making a feint there of warlike preparations.

10. On Thursday the 9th instant I interviewed the messengers from Ashanti for the purpose of hearing their message, and I enclose a copy of the notes taken at the interview.

11. On the 7th instant I received from the Inspector-General of Constabulary the letter (copy enclosed) despatched from Abetifi

(Kwahu) on the 31st October, in which he states that the force under his command was well received throughout the route and most enthusiastically welcomed by the King of Kwahu and his Chiefs. He expresses the opinion that the presence of the force in the north-east portion of the Protectorate has already altered the complexion of political affairs and requests to join the Protectorate are about to be made by many of the towns under the Ashanti rule lying to the west and north-west of Abetifi.

12. Colonel Sir Francis Scott in a subsequent letter of the same date (copy enclosed) reports that messengers had arrived from Yao Sapon, King of the Juabins at Konengo, bringing with them the messages of which I also enclose copies. Yao Sapon evidently fears that his action in sending men and arms to the King of Ashanti to assist him in the war against Nkoranza will be punished, and he begs for mercy. In passing through Korforodua Colonel Sir Francis Scott was interviewed by the Juabins at that place under Princess Amba Sewa, and he addressed the letter, dated the 22nd October, of which I enclose a copy. To that letter I sent the reply copy also enclosed.

13. The Rev. F. Ramseyer, who has been most kind in providing quarters at Abetifi for the officers of the force, and in assisting the Inspector-General with information, has forwarded to me the letter (copy enclosed) referring to the present situation. He naturally is most desirous that this Government should take decisive action with regard to Ashanti. Such action if taken would, I believe, be successful, because the old power of Ashanti no longer exists. The confederation of Kings is broken up, and although King Prempeh (Kwaku Dua III) is doing his utmost to consolidate his empire he cannot succeed as long as Asibi, King of the Kokofus, either refuses to coalesce with him, or is hindered from doing so.

14. The Ashantis have exercised such a baneful influence on the English settlements on the Gold Coast in years past, have caused so large an expenditure of money, and have so constantly interfered with trade, that it should, I consider, be a settled policy of Her Majesty's Government, if I may be allowed to say so, to hasten the annexation of Ashanti with all reasonable and proper means. I should have been glad to do so on the present occasion by demanding an indemnity for the loss of trade, and the expenses incurred in sending a force to defend Attabubu in consequence of the menacing attitude of the Ashanti army. But it is not perfectly clear to me that the Hausa Constabulary at its present strength could, if required to do so, cope single-handed with the Ashanti army, and therefore, as your Lordship stated in the telegram despatched to me on the 8th instant, that reliance must not be placed on the despatch of troops from England, I could not conscientiously suggest the demand for an indemnity, that is to say, for a further instalment of the 50,000 ozs. of gold which

by the treaty signed at Fomana in 1874 the Ashantis undertook to pay, but which, unfortunately for this Colony, they were never called upon to pay in full.

15. It is undoubtedly the case that many of the tribes forming the Ashanti Confederation would welcome annexation; the Juabins would do so; so also would the Bekwais, and I think, too, the Kokofus. These are the most powerful tribes.

16. The request of the King of Juabin that his people may be regarded as British subjects is not now made for the first time. He sent messengers with a similar application to Governor Sir Brandford Griffith in February 1891, and was then informed that if he and his people desired to remove into the Protectorate a place of residence would be procured for them in the same way that places had been found for other Ashanti tribes.

17. Yao Sapon and the Juabins with him are not in their own country, but are at Konengo, a town in that part of Ashanti Akim which is under the King of Ashanti. He is, in fact, just outside the boundary of the Protectorate. His present request is genuine enough, although probably dictated by fear, but as he is not located in his own country, and cannot, I should say, make an authoritative assignment of it under the circumstances, I do not think his request should be listened to. It is clear, also, that he has not entirely severed himself from the King of Ashanti, because he has furnished the King with men and arms to assist him in the war with the Nkoranzas, and that in itself is, I think, a reason why the present time is inopportune for dealing with the request.

18. So far as Ashanti proper is concerned, that is to say, the countries of the confederated Kings, apart from vassal countries like Nkoranza, my own opinion is that it should be dealt with as a whole. I believe the present time is propitious for a forward policy with regard to Ashanti in consequence of the real weakness of the country, and I should like to have been placed in a position to take that policy by means of a demand for an indemnity to cover the expenses to which this Government is now being put. But such a policy is impossible unless this Government can rely with certainty in case of need—which, however, might not arise—of receiving such assistance as that referred to in my paragraph 5 of my Confidential Despatch of the 6th October.

19. So long as Ashanti remains a power by itself, so long will there be a state of unrest in the countries of the Protectorate bordering on it, and especially in those which were formerly dependencies of it; and, besides the loss of trade and life which the constantly recurring wars within Ashanti necessarily give rise to, wars which, on account of the instability of the Government of that country, will never cease, there will always be trouble to this Government, and not unfrequently expense.

20. I am aware that, were Ashanti to be placed within the Protectorate, this Government would have to spend at least 6,000 *l.* a year to rule it, but the gain to trade would be enormous, and I doubt not that this additional burden upon the revenue would be met by the impetus to trade. I have not touched upon the sentimental aspect of the matter, but the rescue of thousands from abject misery and slavery, the stamping out of degrading customs, which are horrible to civilised people, cannot be lightly passed over and should count for something.

21. I enclose an extract from a semi-private note addressed to me by Captain Lang, R.E.,[1] who has accompanied the Expeditionary Force into Attabubu, in which he advocates the absorption of Nkoranza into the Protectorate, but I consider that such a course is out of the question unless this Government is prepared to reckon with Ashanti. I hold the same view as regards application for protection from Chiefs of towns on the east and north-east of Ashanti, as, for example, Agogo, to which reference is made in his letter by Mr. Ramseyer.

22. Should your Lordship, upon a reconsideration of the whole matter, think it desirable to demand an indemnity from the King of Ashanti, I would suggest that the indemnity be fixed at not less than 2,000 ounces of gold, and that I be instructed by telegraph to send a letter to the King at the hands of Mr. Vroom, requesting payment of that amount on account of the loss of trade which has resulted from the action which this Government had to take in stopping the sale of gunpowder and lead, and to cover the expenses incurred in sending a force into Attabubu consequent upon the menacing attitude of his army. . . .

17

THE MARQUIS OF RIPON TO
ACTING GOVERNOR F. M. HODGSON:
ASHANTI, 30 JANUARY 1894[2]

I HAVE under my consideration your despatches noted in the margin and also your telegram of 13th instant, furnishing information with respect to the relations of the Colonial Government with Ashanti, and the condition of affairs in the interior, and urging that the time has arrived when action should be taken with a view of bringing Ashanti under a British Protectorate.

In reply I have to acquaint you that Her Majesty's Government, while fully appreciating the ability and judgment which you have

---

[1] Lang to Hodgson (Private), 1 November 1893.
[2] C.O. 879/39, no. 458. For a version omitting in the public dispatch the rate of stipend, Metcalfe, *Great Britain and Ghana*, pp. 463-4.

displayed, and the clearness with which you have placed your views before them, are not inclined to adopt the policy which you advocate, which they consider would greatly increase the responsibilities of the Gold Coast Government.

Moreover, Her Majesty's Government could not sanction the adoption of any course which might involve the employment of British troops, and as, in your Despatch of 18th November, you have stated that 'such a contingency has to be provided for' and that you 'are not prepared to advocate the despatch of a further ultimatum to Kumasi unless it is,' they find it impossible to authorise you to send such an ultimatum, or to entertain the question of assuming a Protectorate over Ashanti by force.

At the same time they are fully alive to the risk, which, under present conditions, constantly exists, of Attabubu, and other territories which are under the protection of Her Majesty, being invaded by the Ashantis, and they are therefore anxious to ascertain whether some *via media* cannot be found whereby the object of controlling the power of Ashanti may be attained without the use of force.

I have, therefore, to request you to consider and report to me whether, in your opinion it would be possible to get the King of Kumasi, and his principal Chiefs, to accept stipends, which might be fixed at a liberal rate (in the King's case even as high as 1,000 *l.* a year), on condition that they should consent to receive a British Agent at Kumasi, and should agree to refrain from making war upon, or disturbing, any of the tribes beyond a certain frontier which should be laid down by the Governor of the Gold Coast, and which should exclude from Ashanti the Nkoranzas, Bekwais, and other tribes who have asked for British protection.

In case of any dispute between the King of Kumasi and any of these outside tribes the matter should be referred to the agent, who should enquire into it and give his decision, and if he found that the Ashantis were in the right the question should be referred to the Governor of the Gold Coast, who would require the offending tribe to make such reparation as he might deem expedient.

The agent would, of course, have a strong guard of Hausas under one or more white officers, for his own protection, but it would be clearly understood that he must interfere as little as possible with the domestic affairs and policy of the country, but would confine himself to the duties mentioned in the preceding paragraph, of inquiring into disputes between the Ashantees and tribes beyond this border, of preventing the outbreak of war and disturbances, and of using his influence and authority to promote the development and security of trade.

I have to request you to communicate your views on these proposals, if possible by telegraph, and, pending a decision, I have to authorise you to exercise your discretion as to keeping the expeditionary force in Attabubu, or withdrawing it. In the event of its withdrawal, you should send a messenger to the King of Kumasi saying that this step has been taken on the faith of his assurances that he has no intention of invading any portion of the British Protectorate; he must, however, understand that the question as regards his conduct, is not concluded by the withdrawal of the troops for the present, and that the question of what action should be taken in the future has been referred to the Queen, and that her decision, will, to a great extent, depend upon the King's conduct, as he cannot be allowed to continue with impunity to make war upon and destroy his neighbours, and that if he desires in any way to avoid Her Majesty's serious displeasure he must remain quiet and desist from further warlike operations.

18

ACTING GOVERNOR F. M. HODGSON TO DISTRICT COMMISSIONER H. VROOM: MISSION TO ASHANTI, 23 FEBRUARY 1894

... 6. You are at liberty to pledge this Government in the matter of stipends to the extent of 1,500 *l.*, or even, if necessary, 2,000 *l.* a year and I would suggest the following as suitable stipends:

	£	
To the King of Ashanti	600	(50 *l.*, a month.)
,, ,, ,, ,, Mempon . . .	200 ⎤	These are the four principal Kings of the
,, ,, ,, ,, Kokofu	200 ⎱	country and the stipends
,, ,, ,, ,, Bokwai	200 ⎱	in the case of those who
,, ,, ,, ,, Juabin	200 ⎦	are now fugitives from Ashanti would be paid upon their return to it.
,, ,, Queen Mother Yakia . .	80	

7. I desire you to let King Prempeh understand that the agent will be an officer who will assist him in putting his country in order, a matter which cannot but be one he has at heart; that with the arrival of the agent wars will cease and the country will in time again become flourishing and the people happy and contented knowing that their lives, homes and property will be safe.

8. You are at liberty to tell King Prempeh that this Government has made a treaty with the King of Nkoranza and with all the tribes known as the Brong tribes, as well as with the King of Bole. ...

[1] C.O. 879/39, no. 458. Encl. in Hodgson to Ripon, 26 February 1895. *Hendrick Vroom* was District Commissioner of Wassaw.

19

DISTRICT COMMISSIONER H. VROOM TO GOVERNOR SIR W. B. GRIFFITH: MISSION TO KUMASI, 24 APRIL 1894[1]

... 13. THE palaver arranged for the 5th did not [come?] on till the 7th instant. At this meeting the question of stipends to be paid to the Kings of Ashanti was carefully introduced. To the King of Ashanti himself the sum of 600 l. was named and to the Queen Mother 80 *l.* a year. To the other Kings 200 l. each per annum, in the event of their subscribing to the agreement I took with me and which was also read and explained to them.

14. It appears to me that in their assembly on the night of the 5th instant Mr. J. O. Ansah, whose assumed office and supposed influence retire into the shade with a British Agent Resident at Kumasi, and those few councillors whose counsels to King Kwaku Dua III are influenced by self-interest rather than honest devotion to the King or his country set their wits to work to thwart at the last moment the negotiations terminating successfully, in order to gain time further to plot and intrigue.

15. From my confidential man in Kumasi I learnt that these men are counselling an embassy to Christiansborg headed by some of them (and perhaps with Mr. Ansah as the spokesman) to dictate to, and force upon, the Government certain terms which they think will secure to the Kings of Ashanti better advantages than those contained in the present proposals. ...

20

GOVERNOR SIR W. B. GRIFFITH: MEMORANDUM AS TO THE POLICY TO BE ADOPTED TOWARDS ASHANTI, 25 OCTOBER 1894[2]

21. At present, it appears that there is a general feeling in Government, native and commercial circles that Ashanti might be taken without a blow. The question for consideration and decision is, What policy should the Gold Coast Government adopt in the circumstances described?

22. It would appear to be neither humane nor politic to continue the policy of non-intervention. It has had a fair trial and has not

[1] C.O. 879/39, no. 458.
[2] C.O. 96/248; C.O. 879/41, no. 478; and Metcalfe, *Great Britain and Ghana*, pp. 472-3.

succeeded, and further non-intervention will mean constant interference with the trade of the Gold Coast, frequent costly missions
to Ashanti, a never-ending state of disorder in that country, one
district flying at another's throat, or Kumasi and other districts
warring against a recalcitrant state. Bloodshed and disorder has been
our experience of non-intervention, and will continue to be the result
of non-intervention. A further result of non-intervention will be
loss of influence which might be exercised for good.

23. It is needless to consider rebuilding Ashanti so as to make it
independent and self-reliant. That would require a military organisation, which would be used against us and our protected states.
Indeed, we cannot suffer Ashanti to remain independent of us, as it
commands our trade routes; and our previous relations with it
entitle us to take this position, while we cannot with safety to the peace
of the protectorate permit Ashanti to continue to occupy the position
of a country in a state, more or less, of antagonism to the interests of
this Colony, whilst its barbarous and cruel customs are a disgrace to,
and an outrage upon, humanity, and all parties in the Colony are
unanimous in the opinion that we must not aid Ashanti to attain to
any part of its old position of dominance.

24. I am convinced that by far the best solution would be to include
the several tribes forming the Ashanti combination in the protected
territories, and this could be accomplished practically by annexing its
several sections in detail, or by at once asserting our power over the
whole country. And it seems to me that the last will be the most
sagacious and least troublesome course to take.

25. The present state of things cannot be permitted to continue,
and, in default of our determining to take over the whole of Ashanti
at once, I repeat, I am of opinion, that the best course to pursue
would be to accept the offer of any of its tribes to come under our
protection, and I will proceed to show that circumstances and events
justify this course.

26. After the Treaty of Fomana, by which Ashanti lost the
Adansis, the Kwahus threw off the yoke of Kumasi and subsequently
came under British protection. The Juabins followed suit but,
becoming involved in war with Kumasi and being defeated, the
greater part of them came into the protected territories. Then the
Kokofus and Dadiassies, being also defeated by the Kumasis and
Bekwais, came into the protected territories, but before these occur-
rences, Gaman also had thrown off its allegiance to Kumasi. Quite
lately, Nkoranza strove in vain to make itself independent. From our
experience of Ashanti we know that as soon as any Chief thinks himself able to do so he forthwith sets himself up as independent, and
thereupon Ashanti ranges itself into two camps, one in favour of such
Chief, and the other for the authority of Kumasi.

27. Their union in arms was the only bond which formerly held together the various Ashanti tribes. As long as they had a common enemy, viz., the Fantis, or the Denkerahs, or one or other of the tribes now under British protection, they were able to keep together. But now things are changed. All their former foes are under British protection. The bond which formerly bound them together no longer exists, and it is contrary to experience to expect them to hold together. It must be remembered that they have no special language, or dress, or habits, or religion; they are practically the same in language, dress, habits, and religion as the Accras, Fantis, Denkerahs, Assins, and other tribes in the protected territories, except that the Accras speak a language of their own.

28. Ashanti is no longer the more or less compact state that it was. After 20 years earnest endeavour on our part to make it at unity with itself, and self-reliant, it is nothing but a few tribes with difficulty held together by the power and recollection of the former influence of Kumasi, each tribe biding its time to become independent.

29. Probably if any tribe merely declared its independence the Kumasi authorities would take no heed and suffer it to go its way. But as such a declaration is invariably accompanied by insulting messages and murder of messengers war is bound to follow.

30. In these circumstances, I am of opinion that it will be false policy to continue treating Ashanti as a compact state. We should recognise the fact that it is only composed of a bundle of states kept together by no common interest, but which by their internal wars and intrigues, menace the interests and the security of the trade of the protected territories. I would, therefore, submit for consideration the adoption of either of two lines of action with regard to Ashanti; first, the policy of accepting any advances from any of these tribes, and if they ask to be taken under our protection I consider it would then be our duty to extend it to them; and as to the second line of action, where no such offers were made, then we should exercise our power, and compel obedience to it by bringing recalcitrant tribes under our supreme control.

31. Should we decide upon either of the lines of action stated, I think due notice of the change of attitude to the Government ought without delay to be given to the King of Ashanti. For 20 years we have striven loyally and earnestly to prop up Ashanti, but all to no purpose. Ashanti is now practically in a state of disintegration, and to any tribe who seeks it we should grant our protection as a preliminary course of procedure; but I am most strongly of opinion that the wisest, safest, most prudent and inexpensive course of action will be to pursue a resolute policy, and if the sections of Ashanti which are still independent of the Gold Coast decline to accept its rule they should be compelled to do so.

21

GOVERNOR W. E. MAXWELL TO THE
MARQUIS OF RIPON: ASHANTI, 13 JUNE 1895[1]

... 7. IN anticipation of the possibility of being able to enter upon negotiations with a view to a peaceful settlement, it would be useful to me to be favoured with your Lordship's instructions on the subject of slavery as it exists now in Ashanti, and its possible modification when there is a British Residency at which escaped slaves may claim asylum. The subject is governed in the Colony and in the protected territories by Ordinances I and II of 1874, and it is, no doubt, to the immediate application of these Ordinances that objection is entertained by slaveowners in Ashanti.

8. The other subjects for negotiations are:

Acceptance by Kumasi and by all Ashanti tribes of British protection and flag to such extent as your Lordship may direct.

Free trade between Ashanti and the coast and *vice versa*.

Free passage through Ashanti for goods from the interior on their way to the coast.

Protection for missionaries.

Abolition of human sacrifices.

Appointment of a British Resident with an adequate guard.

Guarantee by Kumasi to abstain from warfare with neighbouring tribes, not to close trade roads, and to refer all disputes to the Governor.

Payment by Colonial Government of stipends to certain persons, should these be acceptable.

As to these I believe that I am fully in possession of the views of Her Majesty's Government. There remains the claim of the British Government to the balance of the 50,000 oz. of gold remaining unpaid under the Treaty of Fommanah. Probably this claim can remain in abeyance, if a peaceful settlement can be arranged as regards the other subjects.

9. The return of the messengers from Europe cannot, I suppose, be very long delayed. In any case, I feel that, while their mission continues, no fresh representations at Kumasi, unaccompanied by a display of force, can be of the slightest use. If, after their return, the King of Kumasi fails within a reasonable time to give a satisfactory answer to our letter of February 1894, or if negotiations, whether carried on at Kumasi or at Accra, prove, in spite of all my efforts, that a peaceful settlement is impossible, the time will have come for the

[1] C.O. 879/42, no. 490. The section on slavery is omitted from the public dispatch in Metcalfe, *Great Britain and Ghana*, pp. 478–9. (*Sir*) *W. E. Maxwell*, Governor of the Gold Coast, 1895–6.

despatch of an ultimatum to King Prempeh in accordance with your Lordship's instructions in paragraph 13 of the despatch under reply.[1] The period within which compliance with the request of Her Majesty's Government is demanded should terminate not later than the 31st October, so as to allow the whole of the ensuing dry season for military operations if necessary.

10. I have tried to form a reasonable conjecture as to whether the Ashantis really intend, in the last resort, to oppose us by force of arms or not. It is generally stated that they have been arming for some time for this purpose, and I may refer your Lordship to the statements dated September and October 1894, regarding importation of arms and ammunition which occur on pages 31 and 34 of the printed official correspondence. Mr. Brew, an African trader living in London, in his letter to your Lordship of February 9th, 1885, spoke of the visit of Ashantis to England as an opportunity for an object lesson of the might, power, and vast resources of Great Britain which would have a tendency to avert 'collision and unnecessary bloodshed.' From this it would seem that he regarded a collision and consequent bloodshed as not improbable. On the other hand, Mr. Frank Russell, who is credited with knowing more than anyone in the Colony about Ashanti affairs, believed, in July 1894, that there was a sincere desire to avoid any conflict with the Government, and this I am prepared to accept as the most probable view, for the love of money is one of the most strongly marked characteristics of the African, and the King and Chiefs of Kumasi must know that by fighting they risk all the treasure of the kingdom, irrespective of the cost of the campaign, which they may have to pay and the sum already due under the Treaty of Fommanah. The most recent letters of Mr. Ansah to Sir W. Brandford Griffith contain protestations of the earnest desire of King Prempeh for peace, but these must be taken for what they are worth. Acheriboanda, at a recent interview with me, stated that he has recently received information that the King of Kumasi has been buying a large quantity of arms and gunpowder 'in order to fight against the Government if any expedition is sent to Kumasi to force him to accept a British flag.' The Rev. E. Perregaux, a missionary at Abetifi, wrote to me on the 6th May, mentioning rumours of war and preparations for war in Ashanti. I have attempted, therefore, to test these statements by reference to our trade statistics, and I have caused to be compiled two returns, which I have the honour to transmit to your Lordship. The first is a return for the first three months of 1895 (compiled from the merchants' books at the various ports) of the sales of gunpowder and lead-bars in the whole Colony. This shows the sale for the quarter to be 32 tons 12 cwts. 1 qr. 20 lbs. of gunpowder, and 28 tons 11 cwts. 3 qrs. 20 lbs. of lead-bars. The

[1] Ripon to Maxwell, 15 March 1895.

second return, compiled from the monthly returns of the clerk at Prahsu, shows the quantity of arms and ammunition imported into Ashanti, *via* Prahsu, between August 1894, when a previously existing prohibition was removed, and the end of March 1895 (the month preceding my arrival in the Colony). In these eight months Ashanti obtained from the Colony, *via* Prahsu, 2,034 muskets, 18 tons 4 cwts. 0 qrs. 12 lbs. of gunpowder, and 8 tons 7 cwts. 2 qrs. 5 lbs. of lead. This is independent of supplies imported by other routes than Prahsu. Of course this must not all be regarded as available warlike material, stored in Ashanti and ready to be used against a British force. There is probably a considerable trade in muskets and gunpowder between Ashanti and the interior and a large quantity of gunpowder must be fired away annually on the occasion of native 'customs.'

Sir W. Brandford Griffith was, I presume, aware of the extent of the Ashanti purchases when he telegraphed on the 11th February last, in reply to your Lordship's confidential despatch of the 13th December. He then stated his opinion that, unless immediate operations were to be taken against Ashanti, it would not be advisable to prohibit the sale of arms and ammunition as this would be most injurious to commercial interests in the Colony and would be regarded as an indication of contemplated hostile operations against Ashanti. When I despatched to your Lordship my telegram of the 29th of April, I regarded the mischief as already done, and I do not think it is now worth while to prohibit the export of arms and ammunition to Ashanti, pending the return of the messengers from Europe and the resumption of negotiations.

11. It may, I think, be safely assumed that there will be at Kumasi a fairly strong party who will be unwilling (when it is realised that we are in earnest) to enter upon a struggle in which all that they have of value is risked, and which can only end disastrously for the Ashanti cause. It should also be possible to detach from Kumasi and admit within the Gold Coast Protectorate the majority of the tribes who contributed to form the Ashanti nation when there was one, thereby isolating Kumasi almost completely. Simultaneously with the despatch of an ultimatum to King Prempeh, I should propose to send messengers to the Kings of Bekwai, Sefwhi, Juabin, Kwahu, Nkoranza and Mampong and also to the scattered remnants of the Kokofus, Adansis, Dadiassis, Daniassis, etc., offering formal admission within the Protectorate and warning all persons that the quarrel of the Colonial Government is with Kumasi only, and that tribes which do not actively help us must hold aloof or take the consequences. . . .

22

GOVERNOR W. E. MAXWELL TO PREMPEH:
ULTIMATUM, 23 SEPTEMBER 1895[1]

I WHO write to you am the Governor of the Gold Coast Colony and the representative of Her Majesty the Queen. I send two of my officers, Captain Stewart and Mr. Vroom, to you to deliver and explain to you the following important message to which I beg you to give your most serious attention.

I have been for more than five months at Accra and you have no doubt been expecting to receive a letter from me, for you know well that things are not settled between this Colony and Kumasi. When now at length I write to you, you will, I hope, understand that my words are not light ones, and that I require an explicit answer.

This is what I have to say:

Her Majesty's Government are satisfied, upon evidence submitted to them, that you have violated the treaty of Fommanah by the encouragement and practice of human sacrifices, by placing hindrances in the way of trade and by failing to carry out the guarantee contained in Article 7 of the said treaty with regard to the construction and maintenance of a road from Kumasi to the Prah river.

You and your people have often made attacks upon tribes who are in friendly relations with the British Government and who have sought the protection of Her Majesty the Queen.

By your conduct and the state of war and unrest in which the country has been involved, the development of trade and freedom of communication between this Colony and the interior have been checked and interfered with.

Her Majesty's Government regard this condition of affairs as intolerable and cannot allow it to continue.

They must therefore require you to fulfil your treaty engagements, and to refrain from attacking your neighbours, and, in order that these objects may be effectually secured, it is necessary that you should consent to the establishment of a British Resident at Kumasi who will exercise control over you in these respects, but will not otherwise interfere with the administration or institutions of the country.

I desire to remind you also, though I do not at this moment demand the amount, that the indemnity of 50,000 ounces of gold, the payment of which was stipulated for in the treaty of Fommanah, has not yet been paid.

I now ask for your answer to the demand of Her Majesty's Government that you shall consent to the establishment of a British

[1] C.O. 879/43, no. 490. Encl. in Maxwell to Chamberlain (Secret), 26 September 1895. Based on Chamberlain to Maxwell, 6 September 1895: C.O. 96/258.

Resident at Kumasi who will see that what was promised by treaty
will be performed.

My officers are not instructed to wait for this. They will return as
soon as this letter has been fully explained to you. Your answer can
be sent to me by your own messengers, but I give you notice that there
must be no undue delay and that your reply must reach me at Accra
by the 31st October next.

Before concluding, I have to inform you that Her Majesty has
decided to extend her protection to the King of Nkoranza and to
all other tribes who have asked for it, and I warn you against interfering with any of the tribes to whom that protection is extended.

The messengers whom you sent to England have not been, and
will not be, recognised there in any way and you must clearly understand that Her Majesty's Government can only receive your answer
through me, who am Her Majesty's representative.

The Secretary of State has invited your messengers to return to
Kumasi at once, and if they are wise they will act upon this advice
so that they may be of use to you in your deliberations. It must be
understood, however, that your answer to the demand which I have
communicated to you must not be delayed because they have not
arrived.

23

LORD LANSDOWNE TO COLONEL
SIR FRANCIS C. SCOTT:
ASHANTI, 22 NOVEMBER 1895[1]

I HAVE the honour to inform you that the command of Her Majesty's
land forces on the Gold Coast has been conferred upon you, in
connexion with the difficulties which at present exist with the King of
Kumasi, and I request that you will at once proceed to assume the
command.

The object of the expeditionary force is to reach Kumasi without
any unnecessary delay, and to enforce the acceptance by King
Prempeh and the Ashantis of the terms demanded by the Government.

It had been the intention of Her Majesty's Government, if the
King had accepted the ultimatum, to be satisfied with the establishment of a Resident at Kumasi under certain conditions. As, however,
it has become necessary to take the extreme measure of sending an
expeditionary force, Her Majesty's Government will, in addition to
the terms of the ultimatum, require, as the messengers now in this

[1] C.O. 879/43, no. 490. Encl. in War Office to C.O., 22 November 1895.

country have been informed, that the cost which has been incurred should be repaid by the King, and the Governor will be instructed to make this one of the provisions of any treaty which may be concluded.

The action of the King having rendered the despatch of a military expedition necessary, it has been decided that, whether the King submits or not before the expedition crosses the Prah, a force must proceed to Kumasi to escort the Resident and enforce the terms of peace. In the event of his submission, the extent and the composition of the force to be sent to Kumasi will have to be settled in consultation with the Governor, and reported by telegraph for the approval of this Department.

If the King's submission is not received before the Prah has been crossed, no stoppage *en route* to Kumasi should be permitted for purposes of negotiation. If the Prah be once crossed, the terms of peace must be arranged and concluded in Kumasi.

Further instructions as to the course to be adopted after you reach Kumasi will be communicated to you either direct from me or through the Governor of the Gold Coast.

When you have reached Kumasi, and subdued opposition on the part of the Ashantis, you will fortify the position selected for the Residency and will leave there such a detachment of Houssa constabulary as, in consultation with the Governor, may be considered sufficient to hold Kumasi and protect the Resident. . . .

24

GOVERNOR W. E. MAXWELL: 'NOTES OF A PALAVER', KUMASI, 20 JANUARY 1896[1]

. . . GOVERNOR.—The situation is now changed. The terms which might have been had in October last are no longer open to the King and Chiefs. The other day, a few days before Her Majesty's troops entered Kumasi, a message was conveyed by my orders to King Prempe by an officer in the service of the Gold Coast Government to the effect that it was not the desire of Her Majesty's Government to depose him if he should make submission and if he should pay the full expenses of the Expedition. Subject to the orders of Her Majesty's Government, I will believe no promises—I will make no treaty—unless the cost of the Expedition, or a large sum on account of it, is paid here at once. Twenty-two years ago we believed Ashanti promises, and we made a treaty; none of the articles of that treaty have been observed on the part of the Kings of Kumasi. This time I

---

[1] C.O. 879/44, no. 504. Encl. in Maxwell to Chamberlain, 20 January 1896.

will not believe in words. It is no small matter to bring a large body of Her Majesty's troops from Great Britain to this place, and those by whose fault this Expedition has been necessary must pay the cost, or suffer the consequences of default. I am ready now, on behalf of Her Majesty the Queen, whose representative I am here, to receive the submission of King Prempe in the manner known to the Ashantis. I am also ready to receive the sum which I have demanded—50,000 ounces of gold. These two preliminaries having been settled, I shall be prepared to draw up a treaty, the chief articles in which have already been mentioned to the King's messengers at Cape Coast Castle. That is all I have to say. I am ready to receive a reply.

The King.—I have already stated my willingness to give the submission, and I am prepared to do it now. But I have something else to say. My Chiefs will consider and bring it to the notice of the Governor.

Governor.—I can allow no hesitation. I have made two formal demands. There must be instant compliance.

The King.—I am willing to make the submission. (The King took off his head-dress and sandals, and, accompanied by Yah Kiah, his mother, came and held his Excellency's feet and made the necessary submission.) I now claim the protection of Great Britain. The Governor himself knows that there is not much money in the country. I have got 340 bendas (700 ounces) and this I am prepared to pay, and I beg the Governor to make arrangements with the officer placed here as Resident that I may pay by instalments. I consider myself now as a subject of the Government.

Governor.—It is child's play to talk in this manner. An Expedition of this kind costs a very large sum and I cannot believe that a King who thinks himself sufficiently important to send Ambassadors to Her Majesty Queen Victoria can only find in his kingdom the paltry sum which he offers me.

The King.—I am not playing with the Governor. This is all I can afford to pay. I am now under the British Government.

Governor.—On behalf of Her Majesty, and subject to her commands, I accept the proposal that this country shall be placed under the protection of Great Britain, but it must be remembered that the Kings already in the Protectorate are subject to my orders, and that their independence is limited. Even in the British Protectorate, subject to the commands of the Queen, I claim the right to punish those Kings and Chiefs who misbehave, even to the extent of deposing them from their stools, if necessary. Only one of my two preliminary demands has been complied with.

The King.—I do not refuse to pay the amount demanded, but I beg the Governor to let me pay the sum I have now mentioned and then the rest by instalments.

Governor.—Twenty-two years ago a similar promise was made. They paid 2,000 ounces down, and promised to pay 48,000 ounces afterwards. Have they kept their promise?

The King.—We have never been pressed for the money. We were allowed to pay by instalments as convenient, and since then no demands have been made. That is why we have been hanging on all this time. But this time I only beg the Governor to accept what I have got just now, and to allow me time to pay the balance. I beg to call the Governor's attention to the expense I have incurred in sending messengers to England.

Governor.—There is no kind of security that payment will be made. I cannot go away from this country myself, nor can I permit Her Majesty's troops to leave, unless I have ample security for the future peace of the country, and it is only on payment of the sum which I have mentioned, or a very large portion of it, that I am prepared to accept the assurances of the Kumasi people. Say, therefore, that, my second demand not having been complied with, I must require King Prempe to proceed to the Coast with others whom I shall name.

The King.—I am willing to pay the amount. We beg the Governor to take the first instalment, that is, the money which I have just offered. It is usual for a man before he sits down to a meal to take something to whet the appetite, and so I ask that the Governor may take this as a first instalment before the whole sum is paid.

Governor.—I require that he is to be accompanied by the Queen-mother Yah Kiah. His father and uncles who are here must also go; his brother Baidoo Agyiman, and the two War Chiefs, Amankwatsia and Asafu Buakyi; there are other persons of minor importance whom I may require to go also. Say that I require all the persons whom I have named to go now to a building which will be pointed out. I shall then have quarters assigned to them, and they shall be guarded until an escort can be arranged to conduct them to the coast. The Kings of Mampon, Ejisu, and Ofisu must go also.

The King.—I beg the Governor to accept what I have now. I am going to pay the money. What is ready I will pay now, and in the course of to-day I will arrange to pay the rest. (Here Mr. Albert Ansah produced a telegram from Mr. Tipping at Cape Coast, mentioning readiness to pay an unnamed sum on account of a concession.)

Governor.—Say that my statement is final, but that, in consideration of the King's submission, which I have accepted, I will undertake that he shall be treated with all the respect due to his rank on his way down. Neither he nor those who accompany him shall be harmed, so long as no resistance is attempted, and no attempt made at rescue.

Asafu Buakyi.—I want the Governor to question Ansah. We have never had any communication with England. It was Ansah who told us that the King of Dahomey had sent Ambassadors to England before, and that we must send him as an Ambassador to England. Why should we suffer and he be left alone?

Governor.—Say that the Ansahs will be made prisoners, and will be taken to the coast as criminals to answer to a charge of forgery.[1] The King and the others named will now consider themselves as prisoners in the hands of the Colonel Commanding.

Palaver set. . . .

25

GOVERNOR W. E. MAXWELL TO JOSEPH CHAMBERLAIN: ASHANTI, 28 JANUARY 1896[2]

. . . 10. I PROCEED now to consider the question put in your second telegram of the 22nd instant, namely, 'having regard to submission by the King, what grounds are there for insisting on a British Protectorate, with all its legal consequences rather than the establishment of British protection to the extent defined by the ultimatum?' On general grounds, when British protection is extended to surrounding tribes, such as Bekwai, Mampong, Insuta,[3] Juabin, and Nkoranza, I know of no particular reason for leaving Kumasi with a larger measure of independence than that retained by the Chiefs of the neighbouring places. The submission of the King does not, I submit, alter the position, for the acceptance by these minor Kings or Chiefs of British protection is also in a manner an act of submission. The effect, within what is generally accepted as the Gold Coast Protectorate, of British protection is, I think, supposed to be much greater than it really is. Its chief and most valuable effect is a general understanding that there must be no more killing, and a feeling of security is thus established. But of the machinery of a civilized Government the people see little or nothing. No British officers are stationed in the interior except at Tarkwa and Akuse. The remoter districts like Sefwi, Kwahu and Upper Wassaw, and even nearer ones, such as Denkera and Akim, are seldom visited, unless some dispute or complaint compels the Government to despatch a Travelling Commissioner to investigate it. I have been astonished when travelling through the Protectorate to find how little there is of anything approaching to any system of district administration practised in any of Her Majesty's eastern possessions. No revenue is collected in the interior, no police are maintained or required there, and there are no Government

---

[1] For the trial of the Ansah brothers, see Kimble, *Political History of Ghana*, p. 296.

[2] C.O. 879/43, no. 490. Written while Maxwell was still at Kumasi.

[3] For an example, see the treaty with Nsuta, 30 January 1896, Metcalfe, *Great Britain and Ghana*, pp. 485–6.

establishments, except at the two places which I have mentioned. The people are left to manage their own affairs in their own way, provided that there is no breach of the peace and that no cruelty or inhumanity is practised. The Kings and Chiefs administer justice in their own courts according to native custom. This freedom is, however, modified by the jurisdiction of the Supreme Court, which it is possible to assert and enforce to a somewhat inconvenient extent. Political considerations are not necessarily present to the minds of judicial officers, who, sitting in some court or fort on the coast, sign warrants or orders for execution by bailiffs or police in some remote inland district and these subordinate officials cannot always be trusted to refrain from abusing their powers when beyond the supervision of superior officers. Not long ago, in consequence of the death of a police-constable in Sewfi, I had to address a circular to the District Commissioners on this subject.

11. I admit, therefore, that the full legal consequences of a British protectorate, namely, the unrestrained exercise of the jurisdiction of the Supreme Court of the Colony, have their inconveniences, and, as it may be expected that Kumasi will, before long, be an important centre of native trade, I do not want to place the local Chiefs and their people at the mercy of the sharp traders of Cape Coast, who in cases of trade disputes will always threaten to have them brought down to the coast by a summons from the Supreme Court. I am not, therefore, an advocate of annexation or of any unrestricted scheme for the inclusion of Ashanti within the Gold Coast Protectorate.

12. The proposal in the ultimatum addressed to the King of Kumasi in September last was that the British Resident should exercise control as regards the fulfilment by the King of his treaty engagements, but should not otherwise interfere with the administration or institutions of the country. Under such circumstances, there would not be wanting about the person of the King clever and unscrupulous advisers, inspired by native lawyers in Cape Coast, who would define for him the limits of the Resident's possible interference, and the probability is that the country would continue to be governed with much less security for life and property than is established where British protection is accepted and the British flag hoisted. The position would probably be found very soon to be intolerable, the Resident being constantly appealed to against acts of cruelty and injustice which he would be powerless to remedy.

13. The course which I recommend is a middle one. I believe that among all the Ashanti tribes, as among the Fanti tribes, in the Gold Coast Protectorate, respect for human life can be secured by the declaration of a British protectorate, under which it is universally known no inhumanity or cruelty is allowed to be practised. The establishment of a British Residency at Kumasi will create a centre

where complaints can be heard and redressed by a representative of the paramount Power. But for the present I should be inclined to limit or take away altogether the jurisdiction of the Supreme Court in all places north of the Prah. It might be enacted that actions should be brought or prosecutions instituted, in regard to matters arising in those places, only with the leave of the Governor first obtained. The Resident, for some time to come, can be trusted to administer justice on ordinary principles of equity and common sense. There is no pressing need for the settlement of the question at once, and with the re-establishment of confidence and the resumption of trade it may be expected that the people of Kumasi, like those of the surrounding countries, will themselves desire to see British protection permanently established. In the meantime, I am confident that no Chief will venture to assert absolute independence and the Resident will be able gradually to assert and exercise a very wholesome control, which will be more and more value as the people feel the security engendered by it.

14. I have not yet been able to collect the scattered headmen of Kumasi and the surrounding villages, but as soon as I can do so I will make temporary arrangements for the establishment of some kind of central native authority, working in connexion with the Resident or Acting Resident.

15. Regarding permanent settlement, I am making inquiries as to the persons from whom candidates may be selected according to native custom to fill the vacant stool of Kumasi, should this be decided to be vacant by the removal of Prempeh, whose return I could in no case recommend. It cannot be expected that any of the persons who have been taken to the coast as political prisoners should acquiesce in the arrangement which secures the independence of Bekwai, Mampong, Insuta and other tribes, and the re-establishment of Prempeh would, notwithstanding any assertions or promises made on his behalf to the contrary, be the signal for resumptions of attempts to procure the subjection of adjoining countries. I cannot hope for the settlement of the country, the prevention of atrocities, the security of trade and communications, the successful introduction of civilising influences, the improvement of the people and their institutions, or the permanent removal of the anxieties which have so frequently been caused to the Government of the Gold Coast by the action of Kings and Chiefs of Ashanti, unless those who have been responsible for the intolerable misgovernment and hostile and offensive behaviour of the last few years, culminating in the neglect to comply with the ultimatum of Her Majesty's Government, are deprived of all power to interfere with the gradual establishment of a better state of things by being kept for some years in a place where they can do no mischief. . . .

D. DAHOMEY, NIGERIA

I

T. V. LISTER (FOREIGN OFFICE) TO THE SECRETARY TO THE ADMIRALTY: DAHOMEY BLOCKADE, 11 MAY 1876[1]

[Lord Derby has considered the complaints of Turnbull, agent of F. and A. Swanzy at Whydah.]

. . . I T would appear . . . the Commodore deputed certain officers under his command to seek an interview with the principal authorities at Whydah with the view to obtain redress for Mr. Turnbull, but that the interview proving unsatisfactory he inflicted a fine of 500 puncheons of Palm Oil on the King and published notification to the effect that if the fine were not paid in oil or its value (about £6,000) by the 1st of June next he should institute a blockade of the whole Dahomian coast and enforce it until the fine were paid. Since the receipt of the above intelligence the Commodore has been instructed to postpone the time of payment till July.

I am to state that as it does not appear from the information which has been recvd. on this matter that the life or death of any British Subject was in danger, Commodore Hewett shld. be told that he would have done better to have referred home for instructions before he imposed a fine.

Having, however, imposed this fine and threatened a blockade in case of non-payment, I am to state that the Commodore shld. be authorized to establish such blockade. He shld. at the same time be informed that he shld. be careful not to commit himself to continue the blockade until the payment of the fine and that he must await further instructions from home on this subject. . . . H.M.G. is not prepared to entertain the Commodore's proposals for the organization of an expedition to attack the King by land.

2

KING OCKIYA AND CHIEFS OF BRASS (NEMBE) TO LORD DERBY: NIGER TRADE, 21 FEBRUARY 1877[2]

W E the undersigned Kings and Chiefs of Brass West Coast of Africa beg and pray that you will take our case into consideration.

[1] C.O. 147/32. The fine was paid by the French firms of Régis and Fabre. See C. W. Newbury, *The Western Slave Coast and its Rulers* (Oxford, 1966), pp. 103–4.
[2] F.O. 84/1498. Followed by twenty-eight signatures. For the background to Niger trade at this period, see J. E. Flint, *Sir George Goldie and the Making of Nigeria* (Oxford, 1960), p. 28; and no. 40, below.

Many years ago we used to make our living by selling slaves to Europeans which was stopped by your Government and a Treaty made between you and our country that we discontinue doing so, and that we should enter into a legitimate trade and that if we did so an allowance or Comey as it is called should be paid us by the traders on all produce bought. This we did and our trade gradually increased . . . [missing] We shipped . . . about 4,500 to 5,000 tons of palm oil per annum.

To do all this we had to open up place[s] on the Niger, trading Stations or markets as we call them up as far [as] a place called Onitha [sic] on the Niger. Some years ago the White men began trading on the Niger with the intention of opening up this River, this did us no harm as they went up a long way farther than we could go in their Steamers and also bought a different kind of produce to what we were buying, but lately within the last six years they have begun putting trading Stations at our places and consequences [sic] they have stopped our trade completely as well as of those in the Lower part of the River Niger, our living made out of the brokerage and formerly when we sent nearly 5,000 tons of oil away we do not send 1,500 per annum. This means starvation to my people as well as Natives of the Niger under my rule I have about 8,000 people and there are another 8,000 in the lower part of the Niger suffering with me.

It is very hard this on us; in all the other rivers in the Bight viz Nun, New Calabar, Cameroons, Benin, Bonny, Opobo and Old Calabar the markets are secured to them and why should a difference be made for this my river. We have no land where we can grow plantains or yams and if we cannot trade we must starve, and we earnestly beg and pray that you will take our case into consideration, we do not want anything that is not fair, we only want the markets that we and our money [?] have made to be secured to us and that the white men who have had nothing to do with opening up the Palm Oil trade shall not come and reap all our benefits.

One of the steamers has just been up the Niger and the people over whom I have no rule and who are starving have fought with her and the white men now accuse me and my people of having done it although I assure them I have nothing to do with it. I have asked the consul out here two or three times to write home and lay our case before your Lordship and he has promised to do so but I have never received an answer. I can truly say that I have never myself nor have I ever allowed my people to break the treaty we have with England nor will I allow them to do so again. I beg that you will look into this affair for me and my people. What we want is that the markets we have made between the river and Onitha should be left to ourselves . . .

3

KING GLELE TO COMMODORE SULLIVAN: ANGLO-DAHOMEAN RELATIONS, 28 MAY 1877[1]

I BEG to say that I have heard all that you did in the Treaty Book, but in my part I have no occasion with the English. My law in my country Whydah is, nobody has to kill any English or any Europeans in my country. Just having heard by other people that [the] English are coming to break Whydah, Godomy & Cootenoo which I am astonished of it.

In my father King Gezo's time there came some misunderstanding like this, which first brought by the Englishmen, that we have settle it all these come by false letters [sic]. If you wish us to be friends to them I hope you will not listen to any false letters but hear from me before you can believe.

In my father's time we build a fort for French, English and Portuguese at Whydah which the English merchants have theirs but the others are still with theirs trading & repairing their fort. All these I have consider of it some time ago which I am doubt of it. In my part I like to trade with all Europeans also in my Grand Father King Argarjah's time English is a best friend like a son to us through this King Argarjah send his son to England which I believe you might have seen. In the old books again in King Tabessoo's time English always take one part whenever we are going to fight with any country which some English man named Argargan sold big guns to the King Tabessoo to fought with Zas [?] Peoples.[2]

Having received a letter by Captain Leese[3] when his affairs took place that H.M. the Queen said that I may not go to Abeokuta again, but what they have done to my Father & myself is very hard, but now they become your friend more than I, but it is your place to take my part but not theirs as England and Dahomey are friends from the Beginning as Peace & Tranquillity has many between us now. I am ready to receive any English traders in my country to trade with also they may come to repair their fort & keep Factory in it. My Caboceere Avogah will attend them well at Whydah and they also may obey the laws in my country. Also I beg tell you that in this month of August I wish you to send me one of H.M. Ships so that I may send my own Ambassadors to H.M. the Queen of Great Britain.

P.S. Again say that you may not listen to the false letters as you may believe me & I also may believe you.

[1] C.O. 147/34. A treaty between Sullivan and the *Yevogan* of Whydah had been signed in the interests of friendship and trade, 12 May 1877: encl. in Admiralty to C.O., 5 July 1877.
[2] References to the eighteenth-century kings of Dahomey, Agaja (1708–38) and Tegbessu (1739–74).
[3] Possibly *C. C. Lees*, Acting Administrator of Lagos, 1873–5, and Lieut.-Governor, 1876–8.

4

TREATY WITH ONITSHA, 15 OCTOBER 1877[1]

W E, the Undersigned, King Ha na ezé oun, and Chiefs of the District of Onitsha, being desirous of developing the resources of our country by means of legitimate trade with the subjects of Her Majesty the Queen Victoria of Great Britain, have this day met at the town of Onitsha, in the King's residence, and in the presence of Henry Chaster Tait, Esq., Her Britannic Majesty's Acting Consul for the Bights of Benin, Biafra, the Island of Fernando Po, &c., and the other British subjects who have hereunto subscribed their names, have declared our intention of abiding by the following Articles:

Art. I. We will use all the means in our power to put a stop to human sacrifices, as we know that this custom is displeasing to the Queen and people of Great Britain; and it is now our wish to enter into and maintain for ever friendly relations with the English.

II. We also promise to assist and protect all missionaries of any Christian denomination that are now or may hereafter settle among us, and to make use of the advantages offered to us by sending our children to school.

III. We agree to cede to the owners of the present factories established in Onitsha, and to the Church Missionary Society, all right and title to the land on which the church and mission station stand, and the British trading stations occupy, being to the extent of their present respective enclosures, with this understanding, that should any factory be removed and not occupied for two years, the land will revert to us, and we have then the right to sell it to any British trader; but it is distinctly understood and agreed that no native houses are to be erected there, nor will any native be allowed to enter into or occupy the land.

IV. Should any British subject wish at any time to remove his factory and goods, he will be permitted to do so without let or hindrance.

V. The size of the measures and prices to be paid for produce must be arranged between the agents and the natives themselves.

VI. Should any native steal any goods or any articles from the English people in their employ, it will be the duty of the King and Chiefs to find out the offender and punish him, and also make restitution to the value of the goods or of the articles stolen.

VII. Should any question arise between a native and any British subject, the King will refer the matter to the Chairman of the Court

---

[1] Sir Edward Hertslet (ed.), *A Complete Collection of the Treaties and Conventions, and reciprocal regulations at present subsisting between Great Britain and Foreign Powers* (31 vols., London, 1835–1926) vol. xiv (1880), pp. 49–51.

of Equity, and take no steps until the matter has been thoroughly examined and a decision given by the Court of Equity, it being perfectly understood that no disputes on trade matters, or differences about or concerning prices of cloth, goods, or produce, are to be included in this clause of this Treaty—these matters being subject to the decision of the chief agents themselves, or whomsoever they may appoint to represent or act for their firms.

VIII. In consideration of the faithful observance of all the foregoing articles of this Treaty, each factory will make unto the King a yearly dash, the amount of which hereafter be settled by the principal agents, but it is understood and agreed that the church, mission and schools are exempt from all taxes or dashes.

IX. Should a favourable report be made to Her Majesty's Consul in the commencement of the season of 1878, that this Agreement and Treaty has been faithfully carried out by the King and Chiefs of Onitsha, Her Majesty's Consul may suggest to Her Most Gracious Majesty Queen Victoria the desirability of making suitable presents to the King and his principal Chiefs . . .

X Ha Na Eze Oun, *King of Onitsha.*
X Agedi, *Chief*, Amodi Amrafaro, *Chief*, Menjuru, *King's Messenger.*

Witnesses: Hy. Chaster Tait, *Her Britannic Majesty's Acting Consul,* S. A. Crowther, *Bishop, Niger Territory,* Isaac Thos. George, Jacob P. Romaine, Henry S. Fletcher, H. Johnson, Wm. Romaine, Sol. Perry, Edward Phillips.

5

MOMO LATOSA, *ARE ONA KAKANFO,*
IBADAN, TO ADMINISTRATOR
C. A. MOLONEY: YORUBA WARS,
16 JULY 1878[1]

WE beg to tender our compliments to your Excellency.

2. We need perhaps not refer again to the oft repeated occasion of the unpleasant war with the Egbas; but if we mention it at all, it is to assert our own right that we are not the provoker of the war: and when once aroused to resentment, we mean to carry it on to an issue.

3. We are not so pressed as to lay down arms, as we heard that the report was circulated there, but we determine to open a way to the Coast, by means of which the whole Country will be opened to

---

[1] C.O. 147/37. Encl. in Moloney to Lees, 17 January 1879. (*Sir*) *C. A. Moloney,* Governor of Lagos Colony, 1886–90; he had been Acting Administrator and Deputy Governor for periods, 1878–83.

traders from the interior &c., &c. We wish your Excellency to be
neutral and indifferent until the project is carried out.

4. Our constant communication is to show the respect which we
have for your Government.

6

SIR MICHAEL HICKS BEACH TO
LIEUTENANT-GOVERNOR C. C. LEES:
IJEBU, 28 DECEMBER 1878[1]

. . . I HAVE the honour to ack: the receipt of your despatches[2] . . .
enclosing others from the Acting Administrator of Lagos, on the
subject of the outrages recently committed in the Eastern portion of
the Lagoon.

In reply I have to refer you to my despatch no. 71 of the 6th Inst.,
in which I suggested for your con[sideration] whether it would be
advisable to offer the King of Jebu a subsidy on condition of his keeping
the rivers & roads under his jurisdiction open & safe for traders.

Should his proposal be undesirable or fail of effect, it may then
become a matter for con[sideration] whether, when the new lagoon
steamer, now in course of construction, has reached Lagos, some
action should not be taken to punish the perpetrators of the recent
outrages on British Subjects, and show them that they cannot be
committed with impunity.

7

A. C. WILLOUGHBY TO ACTING
ADMINISTRATOR C. A. MOLONEY:
IJEBU, 20 AUGUST 1879[3]

. . . THE King [of Ijebu] said that the Governor did not wait for a
reply from the messenger before proceeding to visit his waters, that
it was not a friendly act on the part of the Governor. His desire was
that the Governor should not have gone at all although the intention
for the extension of trade was good and that it should not be interrupted. Yet he had rather wished it to be confined to Ejinrin market.[4]
He believed the Governor was urged to make the visit beyond Makun
by the ill-disposed and intruding traders at Lagos who are greed[y]

[1] C.O. 147/36. *Sir Michael E. Hicks Beach*, Conservative politician, and Colonial
Secretary, 1878–80.
[2] Lees to C.O., 15 November 1878; Moloney to Lees, 7 November 1878. This
suggestion was not acted on for the moment; see below, no. 15.
[3] C.O. 147/38. Encl. in Ussher to Hicks Beach, 30 August 1879. *A. C. Willoughby*
was Superintendent of the Lagos Constabulary.
[4] A lagoon market on the trade route to Ibadan.

of gain and endeavour to deprive his people at Makun[1] of their trade with the Ijos. To prevent this the Makuns acted under his orders to detain all traders other than the Ijos, especially the Ibadans, who make his back door their passage to go to Lagos. Let the Lagos traders bring their goods to Ejinrin, the Jebus will buy from them there and sell the same to the Ibadans and other people in the interior.

With regard to the communications between himself and the Governor he is not forgetful and he believes they are on record at Lagos as other communications between him and former governors. Let the Governor take care of those places under his Government and do not visit his waters and towns in his territory.

In the matter of slaves he knows that the English Government does not at all countenance slavery, but he considered it an unfair dealing with his people, who, after having been advised to cease from selling slaves are deprived of those whom they bought to use as servants to carry their produce to Ejinrin market, by the Lagos traders who are inducing them to run away from their masters at the market and using them at Lagos . . .

[A case of three slaves escaping is cited.]

The King then said he would consider the rendition of these slaves as a demonstration of the friendship to be continued between himself and the Lagos Government, that it was his intention to have stopped the Ejinrin market, but through the pleadings of the Balogun and other traders of Epe he refrained doing so.

That the friendship should be binding the Government must accede to these following terms which the King submits:

1st. That his waters be no more visited and his people at Makun disturbed and the Ibadans be encouraged to go by his back road to Lagos, notwithstanding the cannons and ammunition the Governor may have in the steamer on the waters, yet he the King can remain inland and pronounce his curse which will not fail to effect the destructions of both steamer and her contents.

2nd. That a stop be put to the meddling Lagos traders in going to other markets beyond Makun.

3rd. That Lagos traders confine themselves to Ejinrin market for trading purposes.

4th. That his runaway slaves be sent back to him as without them he has no other means of conveying his produce to Ejinrin and other markets. . . .

[1] A market on the route to Ondo and Ilesha; see vol. i of this edition, map 4, p. 368, and Glover's explanation of these trade routes, pp. 367–70.

The steamer *Gertrude* had shown the flag on the eastern sector of Lagos lagoon in July 1879. In the C.O. Hemming was in favour of forcing the Ijebu markets to open trade: Minute, 29 September; Herbert was opposed to 'the old Glover policy' of force, but wanted freedom of navigation: Minute, 10 October. The steamer continued to police the lagoon: Ussher to Hicks Beach, 21 October 1879.

8

P. P. MARTINS TO ACTING
ADMINISTRATOR C. A. MOLONEY:
EGBA, 10 NOVEMBER 1879[1]

. . . I PROCEEDED to Abeokuta [on 27 October] and found that a mediation from this Government is very necessary and the Egbas will gladly come to terms of peace with the Ibadans, if proper men are sent by this Government to treat with them, and also a well-qualified man who knows the Country well and their Customs, to show to the Agents, the principal Chiefs and Headmen of the Country who have the reins of the Egba Government in their hands, as they do not yet recognize King Oyekan as their ruler. Notwithstanding all that, this Government will not be successful at the first interview with the authorities of Abeokuta, but they will have to make two or three trips before they come to a good result for the undermentioned reasons.

1. During the present year especially the last three months, the Egbas believe that they have the upper hand over the Ibadans, and that through the Administration of Onilado, king of a part of the Egba confederation and Prime Minister of the Egba Government and its Chief ruler they have succeeded in raising all the Ilorins, Ijesas, Efons, Ados, and other smaller states around Ibadan against the latter, and that in this dry season (next month) all of them will come out with their forces to join them (the Egbas) and fight with the Ibadans, if this fails them (which is more probable) up to April or May next when the rain begins, then they will take the best way which is, to accept the proposal from Lagos.

2. The Egba Confederation is now divided into two different parties, one in favour of, and the other against King Oyekun; the latter with King Onilado at the head of the Chiefs or Civil people, and War Chief Ogundipe at the head of the Warriors or military board (these being the most influential). The former with King Okpena of Ijehun at the head of the Civil side and Ogundeyi (brother of the late Basorun) at the warriors'. The messengers that came from the interior in the name of the King of Oyo in September last (whose message was not sincere) delivered two different messages, one in public and the other in private, whilst they asked publicly to interfere and mediate negotiations for peace in the name of Alafin King of Oyo, they made the Egbas to understand privately that unless they ask the death of Latosa Field Marshal of Ibadan, because instead of the latter obeying him as his King and master as his predecessors did, he never

---

[1] C.O. 147/39. Encl. in Moloney to Ussher, 19 November 1879. Pedro Martins and John A. Payne (who had also been sent) were two Lagos traders with close relations with the Egba. See Payne to Moloney, 11 November 1879, ibid.

obeys but commands him [sic]. Upon these circumstances King Onilado as Prime Minister of the Egba Confederation received both the public as well as the private message and sent the messengers or Ambassadors away with words that he will not treat for peace until Latosa goes to sleep (kills himself) and the Ibadans scatter all over the Yoruba Country and abandon the place, that the Egbas, Ijebus and the Yoruba Kings and their people to colonise there (Ibadan) and put it under the subjection of the three principal Aku kingdoms viz. Yoruba, Egba and Ijebu [sic].

3. Though this message was sent by the Prime Minister alone yet it pleased the whole nation for their present policy is not to show cowardice in any way whatever, though Onilade and Ogundipe and even their opposite parties do not wish the continuation of the war, but they dare not confess it when they are divided, and he who first shows it out will be considered the coward. Except men who are acquainted with our African Policy none will believe my Report that after showing that the people are pleased with the war in one way, they are too anxious to see it come to a close, for their anxiety for peace surpasses their wishes for war . . .

[Ibadan is important in the wider strategy of containing the Hausa, Fulani, and Fon. The Ijebus are considered as temporary allies of the Egba.]

9

PEACE TREATY BETWEEN THE KING AND CHIEFS OF BONNY AND NEW CALABAR, 19 NOVEMBER [?] 1879[1]

WE, the undersigned Kings and Chiefs of Bonny and New Calabar, considering that our mutual security and the good of our country require that we should be united in friendship, did this day meet on board Her Majesty's ship *Dido* in the Bonny River, and in the presence of Captain Compton E. Domvile, the Senior Naval Officer on the West Coast of Africa, Her Britannic Majesty's Acting Consul, S. F. Easton, and the officers and gentlemen who have hereunto attached their signatures, solemnly agreed that from this day no quarrel, war, or strife shall arise amongst us, and having chosen Her Britannic Majesty's Consul for the time being as Arbitrator for the settlement of the troubles that have so long disturbed the peace of our

[1] Hertslet, *Commercial Treaties*, vol. xiv (1880), pp. 1195–7. And F.O. 84/1541, Easton to F.O., 21 November 1879: reporting treaties and adjudication by Opobo in courts of equity held on H.M.S. *Dido*. For another example see the treaty between New Calabar and Will Braid, 1879, in G. I. Jones, *The Trading States of the Oil Rivers. A Study of Political Development in Eastern Nigeria* (Oxford, 1963), pp. 239–41.

countries and injured our commerce, we further most solemnly bind ourselves to abide by his decisions under the penalties as set forth in this Treaty or Agreement.

Art. I. The King and Chiefs of Bonny will not in any way aid or assist the Okrika men against the New Calabars. They bind themselves under a penalty of 100 puncheons to observe this Article, and the New Calabars also bind themselves in the same penalty not to assist the Okrikas should they go to war with Bonny.

II. The Kings and Chiefs of Bonny for themselves, and the Kings and Chiefs of New Calabar for themselves, agree to let all old palavers to be bygones, and never to bring them up again.

III. The Kings and Chiefs of the countries mentioned in Article II, that in any further misunderstanding between them, they will refer their case to the arbitration of Her Britannic Majesty's Consul for the time being, and that they will be bound by his decision.

IV. The Kings and Chiefs agree to put an end to, at once and for ever, the disgusting and horrible practice of cannibalism.

V. The Okrika men shall have the right to fish in all the creeks and waters in which they have hitherto fished, without molestation, so long as they are on friendly terms with the New Calabars.

VI. Seeing the deadly enmity that has so long existed between the people of Okrika and New Calabar, it is decided for the better and more efficient maintenance of peace, and for the lasting welfare of the country, that they shall not use the same oil markets, and further, that the New Calabar men have, by a long possession of the Obiar-tuboo markets, proved their rights to them, and it is, therefore, decided that they shall retain undisturbed possession of the same.

VII. The Bonny people shall have the exclusive right of trading in the Andelli markets only on and after the 21st January, 1880, and the New Calabars shall have the exclusive right of trading at all the other so-called Brass Markets. A penalty of 500 puncheons of palm oil shall be inflicted upon the New Calabars for any act of aggression upon Bonny people, or *vice versa*.

VIII. The King and Chiefs of New Calabar shall open the creeks leading to Brass and Bonny, and shall not prevent the Abassa men from passing through with their canoes, but shall give them their safe convoy.

IX. The Bonny Chiefs having sworn Ju-Ju with the Okrikas, against New Calabar, are ordered to at once remove their Ju-Ju's.

In the event of any of the Articles of the Agreement being broken, a fine of 100 puncheons of palm oil will be enforced from the aggressors, except in Article VII.

All trade shall be stopped until the fine shall have been paid.

X. That this Treaty and all the stipulations therein contained shall be binding between the two Contracting Powers of Bonny and Calabar perpetually from the date hereof.

XI. That the Billa people are not to be molested by either Contracting Party, but are free to go where they please under a fine of 100 puncheons.

XII. That the usual traders coming to Andelli are to be allowed full liberty to trade without the slightest restriction, under a fine of 100 puncheons of oil.

X King Amachree.	X Manilla Pepple.
X George Amachree.	X Oko Jumbo.
X Horsfall Manuel.	X Adda Allison.

Witnesses:

Compton Domvile, *Captain and*	R. B. Knight.
Senior Officer.	R. D. Boler.
Harry A. Ogle, *Lieutenant.*	F. W. Batty.
John Ashworth, *Lieutenant.*	Thos. Welsh.
S. F. Easton, *Acting Consul.*	W. H. Robinson.
	S. Cardi.

10

REVISED CODE OF COMMERCIAL REGULATIONS: BRASS, 3 DECEMBER 1879[1]

... T H E following articles have been mutually agreed to by the undersigned on the part of themselves and their successors with the Kings of the territories adjacent to the Brass River on the part of themselves and the people of their districts.

Sanctioned by S. F. Easton Esquire H.B.M. Consul for the Bight of Biafra and the Island of Fernando Po.

Article First. That the Kings and Chiefs of the country connected in trade with the Rio Bento duly appreciating the benefit of legitimate traffic do hereby guarantee that from this day forward they shall not engage in or sanction the exportation of slaves from their country.

Article Second. That Comey shall be paid to the two Kings at the rate of one piece satin stripe between them for each puncheon hove—an arrangement may be made with the traders which shall stand good.

Article Third. That the Comey being paid no other tax or payment is to be demanded under any pretence whatever, and that the Kings shall give Beaches for trading purposes, and such beaches shall be considered inviolable British Property, and the occupant for the time being is authorised by the parties hereto subscribing to expel trespassers and to maintain his right of occupancy, and to defend himself and property against any unlawful aggression.

[1] F.O. 84/1541. Encl. in Easton to F.O., 18 December 1879.

Article Fourth. That it shall under no circumstances be compulsory on the traders to give goods out on trust, but when trust is taken it is only to be given out to boys with the consent of their Chiefs, a list of which has been given to the traders, such Chiefs holding themselves responsible for such trust given out to them or their boys. Workbar to be paid to chiefs only, and the traders in the River agree that the Chiefs whose names have been handed in to them, shall be paid the workbar of their boys, and that it shall be incumbent on the Kings and Chiefs and those to whom Comey is paid to see that no losses accrue to British Traders or subjects from defalcating debtors.

Article Fifth. That a limit of time to pay in debt be given to each Trader to be settled by private contract.

Article Sixth. That should any trader or gentleman being indebted to a trader or British Subject in the River fail to pay his debt when it becomes due, a notice of the same is to be given to the Chiefs of the town where such trader resides, who are hereby requested to see justice done to the British Trader or Subject and if necessary are to take possession of the trader's oil or other property and herewith liquidate the debt.

Article Seventh. That any Chief of the Trading Town neglecting to act in conformity herewith be held personally responsible for the debt. The Chiefs receiving Comey are required and engaged to see this article is executed.

Article Eighth. That in the event of any white man's trade being stopped, either directly by the Chiefs or indirectly and secretly by their connivance without just ground for such proceeding the authorities receiving Comey will be held responsible for the said stoppage of trade, and a fine or penalty of one puncheon of oil per day will be levied from them as compensation to the trader so interrupted, during the period of such interruption.

Article Ninth. That upon the death of any trader in the River, no second Comey can be demanded from his successor for oil upon which it has already been paid. That the bar mutually agreed upon by the Natives and Europeans shall alone be paid. No further dashes or gratuities of any description shall be demanded or given to any of the Chiefs or their boys.

Article Tenth. That a copy of this Treaty shall be furnished to each Chief receiving Comey, and the Chiefs to produce it when receiving Comey, and that these articles be held to be the law existing between the British Traders and the Natives for the regulation of trade. Matters to be observed so long as they continue law by those who were not present at their own enactment as by those who were.

Article Eleventh. That considering unpleasantness has frequently arisen between Natives and Europeans by the boys of the former making public property of the beaches, it is decided that henceforth no boys shall be allowed to land except those really required to try the oil and remove Cargo, and that under no circumstances shall any person light a fire on any beach, without having first obtained permission of the trader or his representative to do so.

Article Twelfth. That differences having arisen about fires being made in the Bush behind the Beaches it is understood by this that no Native has a right to come, or make use of any place within a mile—equalling eighteen fathoms of any European Beach.

Article Thirteenth. That a copy of this Treaty be furnished to the Chiefs and Gentlemen of Brass, and they hereby engage to fulfill the conditions of this Treaty, and to become severally and conjointly responsible for the due payment of all fines, to which they or any Brass Subject of subjects may become liable under its provision.

Article Fourteenth. That any dispute arising between Natives and Europeans shall be referred, at the instance of either party to the Court of Equity. Upon being duly summoned by the Court, the attendance of the other party shall be compulsory, and the decision arrived at by the Court shall be final and binding on both parties.

Article Fifteenth. That considering the frequent loss of Ships, it shall not henceforth be compulsory to employ a Native Pilot, but it shall remain in the option of the 'Master' or consignee to do so.

Article Sixteenth. That Tobacco be sold to Chiefs only, but in case it is given to boys, it must be with the sanction of such Chiefs.

Article Seventeenth. That the Chiefs of the Bento hereby pledge themselves that no British Subject shall from the date of this be detained, maltreated, or molested in any way or under any pretence whatever. If any such maltreatment, detention or molestation take place, the Chiefs of the Bento will incur the displeasure of Her Majesty the Queen of England, and be declared enemies of Great Britain.

Sgnd. S. F. Easton H.M. Acting Consul.
King Ockya, Brass.

11

TREATY: KING AND CHIEFS OF
OPOBO, 1 JULY 1884[1]

HER Majesty the Queen of the United Kingdom of Great Britain and Ireland, Empress of India, &c., and the King and Chiefs of Opobo, being desirous of maintaining and strengthening the relations of peace and friendship which have for so long existed between them;

[1] Hertslet, *Commercial Treaties* vol. xvii (1890). For the treaty with New Calabar, 4 July 1884, see Jones, *Trading Estates of the Oil Rivers*, pp. 243–5.

Her Britannic Majesty has named E. H. Hewett, Esq., her Consul for the Bights of Benin and Biafra, to conclude a Treaty for this purpose.

The said E. H. Hewett Esq., and the said King and Chiefs of Opobo have agreed upon and concluded the following Articles:

Art. I. Her Majesty the Queen of Great Britain and Ireland, &c., in compliance with the request of the King, Chiefs, and the people of Opobo, hereby undertakes to extend to them, and to the territory under their authority and jurisdiction, her gracious favour and protection.

II. The King and Chiefs of Opobo agree and promise and refrain from entering into any correspondence, Agreement, or Treaty with any foreign nation or Power, except with the knowledge and sanction of Her Britannic Majesty's Government.

III. This preliminary Treaty shall come into operation from the date of its signature.

Done in duplicate this 1st day of July, 1884, on board Her Britannic Majesty's ship *Flirt*, anchored in Opobo River.

Edward Hyde Hewett.
King Ja Ja.
Cookey.

12

AGREEMENT BETWEEN ONITSHA AND THE NATIONAL AFRICAN COMPANY, 20 AUGUST 1884[1]

WE, the undersigned King and Chiefs of Onitsha, after many years experience, fully recognize the benefit accorded to our country and people by their intercourse with the National African Company (Limited), and in recognition of this we now cede the whole of our territory to the National African Company (Limited) and their administrators for ever.

In consideration of this, the National African Company (Limited) agree:

1. The said Company will not interfere with any of the native laws, and will not encroach on any private property unless the value is agreed upon by the owner and the said Company.

2. The said Company will not interfere with any of the ground now occupied by the natives of the country unless agreed to by both sides.

3. The said Company reserve to themselves the right of excluding foreign settlers other than those now settled in the country.

[1] *F.O. Confidential Print*, 5064 (1884), p. 23.

4. The said Company agree to respect the rights of native land-owners, and the said Company will not take possession of their land without payment for same.

(Signed) D. McIntosh
(*Pro* The National African Company (Limited), and marks-signed on the part of Onitsha by the King, Queen, and sixty-three Chiefs, and forty-three land-owners, whose signatures were duly witnessed.)

13

ONITSHA PROTECTORATE TREATY,
9 OCTOBER 1884[1]

[Made between the King, Queen, and Chiefs of Onitsha and Consul E. H. Hewett.]

...ARTICLE I

HER Majesty the Queen of Great Britain and Ireland, &c, in compliance with the request of the King, Queen, and Chiefs, and people of Onitsha, hereby undertakes to extend to them, and to the territory under their authority and jurisdiction, her gracious favour and protection.

ARTICLE II

The King, Queen, and Chiefs of Onitsha agree and promise to refrain from entering into any correspondence, Agreement, or Treaty with any foreign nation or Power, except with the knowledge and sanction of Her Britannic Majesty's Government.

ARTICLE III

It is agreed that full and exclusive jurisdiction, civil and criminal, over British subjects and their property in the territory of Onitsha is reserved to Her Britannic Majesty, to be exercised by such Consular or other officers as Her Majesty shall appoint for that purpose.

The same jurisdiction is likewise reserved to Her Majesty in the said territory of Onitsha over foreign subjects enjoying British protection, who shall be deemed to be included in the expression 'British subjects' throughout this Treaty.

ARTICLE IV

All disputes between the King, Queen, and Chiefs of Onitsha, or between them and British or foreign traders, or between the aforesaid

[1] *F.O. Confidential Print*, 5064 (1884), pp. 21–3.

King, Queen, and Chiefs and neighbouring tribes, which cannot be settled amicably between the two parties, shall be submitted to the British Consular or other officers appointed by Her Britannic Majesty to exercise jurisdiction in Onitsha territories for arbitration and decision, or for arrangement.

ARTICLE V

The King, Queen, and Chiefs of Onitsha hereby engage to assist the British Consular or other officers in the execution of such duties as may be assigned to them, and, further, to act upon their advice in matters relating to the administration of justice, the development of the resources of the country, the interests of commerce, or in any other matter in relation to peace, order, and good government, and the general progress of civilization.

ARTICLE V [I]

Permission to trade in the country of the King, Queen, and Chiefs shall be regulated according to the terms of the Agreement entered into on the 20th August, 1884, between the said King, Queen, and Chiefs and the National African Company (Limited) copy of which Agreement is hereunto annexed.[1]

ARTICLE VII

All ministers of the Christian religion shall be permitted to reside and exercise their calling within the territories of the aforesaid King, Queen, and Chiefs, who hereby guarantee to them full protection.

All forms of religious worship and religious ordinances may be exercised within the territories of the aforesaid King, Queen, and Chiefs, and no hindrance shall be offered thereto.

ARTICLE VIII

If any vessels should be wrecked within the Onitsha territories, the King, Queen, and Chiefs will give them all the assistance in their power, will secure them from plunder, and also recover and deliver to the owners or agents all the property which can be saved.

If there are no such owners or agents on the spot, then the said property shall be delivered to the British consular or other officer.

The King, Queen, and Chiefs further engage to do all in their power to protect the persons and property of the officers, crew, and others on board such wrecked vessels.

All claims for salvage dues in such cases shall, if disputed, be referred to the British Consular or other officer for arbitration and decision.

[1] See Document 12.

ARTICLE IX

This Treaty shall come into operation, so far as may be practicable, from the date of its signature.

Done in duplicate at Onitsha, this 9th day of October, 1884 . . .

14

SIR HENRY HOLLAND TO GOVERNOR C. A. MOLONEY: EGBA TREATIES, 17 AUGUST 1887[1]

I HAVE the honour to transmit to you a copy of the correspondence which has passed between this department and the Foreign Office on the subject of your semi-official letter of the 19th of June last.[2] A copy of your letter, which has been printed, is also enclosed for convenience of reference.

As you will learn from the enclosed correspondence, you have authority to negotiate treaties of friendship and commerce with the chief authorities of Abeokuta and the other interior tribes, including a provision that they will not cede their territories to any other power, or enter into any agreement with a foreign Government except through Her Majesty's Government, or with their consent.

This authority is, however, subject to the proviso that the conclusion of such treaties will not bring Her Majesty's Government into collision with legitimate French interests; and I have to impress upon you the necessity of exercising extreme care in respect of this point.

Sir Samuel Rowe did not take out any draft treaty with him to the Gambia; he had only general instructions to the same effect as those now given to you.

It is desirable that the Chiefs should agree, if they are willing to do so, to grant protection and facilities to British traders, and to refer any quarrels which may occur among themselves to the arbitration of the Government of Lagos. You may, if you find it necessary, grant moderate stipends to the Chiefs to secure their observance of the treaties; but you will, of course, be careful not to incur any great expenditure without my sanction.

[1] C.O. 879/26, no. 334. See also I.A. 9, p. 11.
[2] F.O. to C.O., 12 August 1887.

15

GOVERNOR C. A. MOLONEY TO SIR HENRY HOLLAND: STIPENDS, 19 SEPTEMBER 1887[1]

. . . 3. THE suggestion put forth [by Administrator F. Evans] not by any means for the first time would be, were it practicable to carry it out, very desirable, but in my opinion it is impracticable in the form it takes for the simple though important fact, among others, that it is opposed to the custom and public opinion of the country known as Yoruba . . .

4. In his despatch No. 157 of the 15th October 1879 to Governor Ussher, Sir Michael Hicks-Beach advocated the promotion by negotiation of the free and unrestricted development of trade and advanced the question of subsidizing annually some of the principal Chiefs, pointing to Gambia and Sierra Leone as examples where such a plan is worked: but under different circumstances and with questionable advantage in my opinion and experience.

5. I remarked then that the light in which stipends were viewed should be of weight in the consideration of the question. Presents to people beyond our jurisdiction would not attract any particular attention, beyond perhaps envy, and would be in accordance with custom prevailing generally among themselves, but to offer any direction of annual subsidizing in view of the suspicious and jealous character of the people towards each other and particularly so towards ourselves would most probably be interpreted as a bid for jurisdiction in such direction, or as indirect acquisition of territory, or the first move towards actual possession . . .

16

THE MARQUIS OF SALISBURY: MINUTE, JA JA, 25 AUGUST 1887[2]

IT is evident we can do nothing until Ja Ja's embassy has been heard. But the papers sent in this box are incomplete. The whole case against Ja Ja is that he has broken faith: because unless he has made some

[1] C.O. 147/60. This view was approved in the C.O.
[2] F.O. 84/1828. On Consul Hewett's memorandum, 27 August 1887, in favour of Ja Ja's deportation—approved by T. V. Lister, Assistant Under-Secretary in the F.O. In Hewett's absence (in London), (Sir) H. H. Johnston was Vice-Consul, from 1886–8. See Sir William Nevill M. Geary, *Nigeria under British Rule* (London, 1927), Appendix I, for an account of this episode, from *Parliamentary Papers*; and Roland Oliver, *Sir Harry Johnston and the Scramble for Africa* (London, 1957), pp. 107–23, for a detailed analysis.

promise to the contrary, we are not entitled to call upon him to admit our traders into parts of his country where they have never been admitted before. Please let me have the papers showing the nature of the promises made by Ja Ja which he is alleged to have broken.

17

ACTING CONSUL H. JOHNSTON TO THE MARQUIS OF SALISBURY: JA JA, 11 SEPTEMBER 1887[1]

[Following a Protectorate treaty with the Obako district, Ja Ja's attitude to penetration of the Opobo river by European traders has become more threatening.]

. . . WHAT I regard as much more serious than Ja Ja's plans for opposing our settlement at the [Obako] markets are the rumours which reach me from various sources as to his intended course of action in case his Envoys return from England with unsatisfactory tidings. If your Lordship declines to forbid British subjects to trade directly with the markets outside Ja Ja's territory, for such prohibition would mean the withdrawal of the bulk of British commerce from the Opobo River, and constitute a complete reversal of our foregoing policy, there is no further reliance to be placed on Ja Ja's good faith or friendship. He may either attempt to sell his country to France (he has now, I am informed, an agent in that country), or he may sack the factories, kill the white men, and retire into the inaccessible interior with his plunder. If there is any truth in the hints and admissions of two or three of Ja Ja's Chiefs, their Ruler is contemplating some very inimical action towards us if his Envoys bring back an unsatisfactory reply. Nothing will be done until his Chiefs and his son, whom he regards as hostages, are safely landed at Opobo, and then it would appear that Ja Ja will throw off all restraint and become a declared enemy of the British Power. I cannot yet say what plan he has in view, but it is one which seems to cause considerable consternation among his Chiefs and those who are in his confidence. One Chief (at the time I am writing) is removing all his people or endeavouring to remove them without exciting Ja Ja's suspicions, to the number of 300, and is also little by little transporting his portable property to Bonny, because he believes that what Ja Ja is about to do will entail some heavy punishment on Opobo town. He promises, as soon as he and his are out of Ja Ja's clutches, to make some surprising revelations. Ja Ja himself, and, indeed, almost every one but the British subjects, is clearing all his valuables out of Opobo; the whole town, in fact, expects a bombardment. No word or hint of mine or of any of the naval authorities can ever have given rise to such apprehensions. Except as regards the stoppage of his trade with British subjects (which has now been enforced for three weeks), I have never uttered or written any threat whatever to Ja Ja or to any one else in the river. I have scrupulously avoided doing so. Besides, I have always recognized this principle, that our dispute lay with Ja Ja personally, and not with the Opobo people. Consequently, I can only conclude that the panic which prevails in Opobo town is in anticipation of some contemplated action on Ja Ja's part unfriendly to the British . . .

Under circumstances like these, prevention is better than cure. As long as Ja Ja remains here I cannot leave this river, nor, in the opinion of the naval authorities and myself, is it safe to withdraw the gun-boat. Your Lordship will appreciate the serious loss of time and inconvenience this situation causes. I am practically obliged to forsake the rest of my district. I can get no satisfaction from Ja Ja. He signs Agreements today and breaks them tomorrow. He is in open contumacy to Mr. Hewett's orders and to my own. He still declines to pay the last fines (very small sums) inflicted on him by Mr. Hewett for disobedience and disrespect. I have never visited his wrong-doing by the punishment of a fine, because I saw the futility of expecting him to pay without a recourse to force. Ja Ja's acts of deliberate disregard of Consular orders and decisions are too numerous to recount at the present time. The situation, in fact, has come to this, that either Ja Ja must be deposed or removed, or Consular authority is a mockery in this district . . .

18

THE MARQUIS OF SALISBURY: MINUTE, JA JA, 25 OCTOBER 1887[1]

SIMPLY approve his conduct. His suggestions must be considered more carefully.

We need not discuss the principles developed in this despatch. They amount to this—that when a merchant differs from a native chief as to their respective rights, the native chief is to be deported. I am not surprised that he does not admire the conduct of our naval officers.

[1] F.O. 84/1828. On Johnston, 24 and 28 September 1888 (motives for the arrest and deportation). Approved in F.O. to Johnston, 25 November 1887. For the preparation of another dispatch ratifying Johnston's conduct, dated 6 April, and published in *Parliamentary Papers*, see Oliver, *Sir Harry Johnston*, p. 123.

19

TREATY WITH IFE, 22 MAY 1888[1]

We, the King, Chiefs, elders, and people of the kingdom of Ife, hereby declare that from henceforth there shall be peace and friendship between the subjects of Her Majesty the Queen of England and those under her protection and the King, authorities, and people of the kingdom of Ife.

2. The kingdom of Ife is perfectly independent and pays tribute to no other power, and territorially is bounded on the north by Ibadan territory (by Oshun River) and on the south by Ondo and Jebu territories, on the east by Ijesha and Ondo territories, and on the west by the Oshun River.

3. We hereby further declare that subjects of Her Majesty the Queen may always trade freely with the people of Ife in every article they may wish to buy or sell within the territory known as Ife, and we pledge ourselves to give no favour or privilege to other countries which we do not give to subjects of the Queen.

4. We further engage to give to British subjects and others under the Queen's protection the first consideration in all trade transactions with the people of the Ife territory; that no toll, duty, fee, impost, or charge shall be charged or levied on the persons or property of any British subject or other person under Her Majesty's protection other than and beyond that or those which are customary and reasonable or may from time to time be agreed upon to be so levied or charged by the Governor of Lagos and the King and authorities of Ife, and that any dispute which may arise will not be allowed to interfere with or stop the markets in the territory of Ife.

5. We further promise that all differences or disputes that may arise other than trade disputes shall be adjusted by the King and authorities of Ife or referred for adjustment and settlement to the decision of an arbitrator to be appointed by the Governor of Lagos, and the decision of such arbitrator shall be final and conclusive.

6. It is hereby further agreed that no cession of territory and no other treaty or agreement shall be made by the King or authorities of Ife than the one they have now made, without the full understanding and consent of the Governor of the Colony of Lagos on behalf of Her Majesty the Queen.

Signed and sealed on behalf of the King, Chiefs, elders, and people of Ife by their authorised representative.

(L.S.) Amodu Adetokunbo,   his X mark
heir to the throne of the
kingdom of Ife.

[1] C.O. 879/28, no. 355, Encl. in Moloney to C.O., 10 October 1888.

Witnesses to mark and seal, made in our presence this 22nd day of May 1888:

       (Signed) Geo. Stallard, Private Secretary,
            A. L. Hethersett, Clerk and Interpreter.
            Thos. M. Williams, 2nd Clerk,
                Governor's Office.

On behalf of Her Majesty the Queen of England:
       (Signed) Alfred Moloney, Governor.

20

DECLARATION: KING AND CHIEFS OF ILARO, 21 JULY 1888[1]

WE, the undersigned, Olugbenle the Oba (King), Taiwo the Elemo, Oshagua the Apena, Bankole the Ashipa, and Odu the Balogun of the Kingdom of Ilaro, declare as follows:

1. Ilaro is an independent kingdom. It does not pay tribute to any other Power. Nor is it under the protection of any other Power.

2. We and the rest of the people of Ilaro earnestly solicit Her Britannic Majesty to accord to ourselves and our country her gracious protection; and we entreat Her said Majesty to take our territory under her gracious protection accordingly, and to include it in the Protectorate of her Colony of Lagos.

3. Our said territory is bounded on the west by Dahomey and Porto Novo, on the north by Ketu, Ineko, Iboro, Shawonpa, and Okele, on the east by Otta and the Egba country, and on the south by Ipokia (Pokra), Addo, and Igbessa.

4. The following are our principal towns, viz., Ilaro, Ajilete, Pahai, Ijalo, Itolu, Gbotodu, Epoto, Ogbogu, Ilugboro, Igbin, Iwoye, Ibeshe, Ijana, Idode, Ilobinuwa, Ikernon, Ilobi, Palaka, Shasha, Mori, Akaba, Erodo, Ologuntaba, Pakoso and Inonkere.

5. To show our sincerity we are ready to forthwith enter into any Agreement into which the Governor of Her Majesty's Colony of Lagos may reasonably require us to enter.

6. We the undersigned fully represent the people of Ilaro to all intents and purposes, and have full power and authority to bind them by executing this or any other document . . .

    X Olugbenle, *King of Ilaro*, Taiwo, *Elemo of Ilaro*, Oshagua, *Apena of Ilaro*, Bankole, *Ashipa of Ilaro*, Odu, *Balogun of Ilaro*.

---

[1] Hertslet, *Commercial Treaties*, vol. xviii (1893), pp. 195–6; C.O. 879/28, no. 355. Lord Knutsford and the C.O. agreed to postpone ratification of these and other treaties with Oyo and Igbessa, until negotiations were completed with France. Hemming, Minute, 20 September 1888: C.O. 147/64. And, below, no. 23.

Signed, sealed and delivered by the above-named Olugbenle, Taiwo, Oshagua, Bankole, and Odu in the presence of: Jacob Emanuel Medium Cole, 96 Broad Street Lagos, *Writing Clerk*, William Augustus, Onanla, Ilaro, *Shoemaker*.

Certified true copy: Alfred Moloney, 3 August 1888.

21

TREATY WITH OYO, 23 JULY 1888[1]

I ADEYEMI, Alafin of Oyo and Head of Yorubaland the four corners of which are and have been from time immemorial known as Egba, Ketu, Jebu, and Oyo embracing within its area that inhabited by all Yoruba-speaking peoples, being desirous of entering into and maintaining for ever friendly relations with the subjects of Her Majesty the Queen of Great Britain and Ireland, and of developing the resources of Yoruba by means of legitimate trade with the subjects of Her Majesty and those under her protection, or who may hereafter come under her protection, and in gratitude for what the Queen has at so much expense and risk to life done from time to time for my country, have this day at the city of Oyo, in the presence of those who have hereunto subscribed their names as witnesses, declared my intention of abiding by the following Articles:

Art. I. From henceforth there shall be peace and friendship between the subjects of Her Majesty the Queen, and those under her protection, and the Alafin of Oyo and the King of Yorubaland and his people, and all other peoples over whom he has authority and influence.

II. The subjects of the Queen may always trade freely with the people of Oyo and the Yoruba-speaking countries in every article they may wish to buy and sell, in all towns, rivers, creeks, waters, markets, and places within territories known as Yoruba; and I, Adeyemi, pledge myself to show no favour and to give no privilege to the traders or people of other countries which I do not give or show to those of the Queen.

III. British subjects and others under the Queen's protection are to have the first consideration in all trade transactions with my peoples.

IV. No tolls, duties, fees, imposts, or charges shall be charged or levied upon the persons or property of any British subject, or other person under Her Majesty's protection, other than and beyond that or those which are customary and reasonable, or may from time to time be agreed upon to be so levied or charged by the Governor of Lagos and myself.

[1] C.O. 879/28, no. 355. Encl. in Moloney to Knutsford, 21 August 1888. Again, the C.O. delayed approval. Hemming thought that Clause III 'may savour too much of exclusive trade privileges for which it is contrary to our policy to negotiate', but let it stand. Minute, 26 September 1888, C.O. 147/65.

V. I will not allow any disputes that may arise between people frequenting or visiting the markets in my territory to interfere with or stop the markets, and all differences or disputes that may arise, other than trade disputes, between my peoples and those of other nations and tribes visiting the markets, shall be adjusted by me or referred for adjustment and settlement to the decision of an Arbitrator appointed by the Governor of Lagos, and the decision and award of such Arbitrator shall be final and conclusive.

VI. I engage, as far as in me lies, to bring about new markets between the Oyos and the other Yoruba-speaking peoples, to promote the enlargement of existing ones, and to keep open all the roads through my kingdom to the Niger and towards the coast.

VII. It is hereby further agreed that no cession of territory and no other Treaty or Agreement shall be made by me, other than the one I have now made, without the full understanding and consent of the Governor for the time being of the said Colony of Lagos.

VIII. In consideration of the faithful observance of all the foregoing Articles of this Agreement, the Government of Lagos will make unto me a yearly dash to the value of 200 bags of cowries, but such dash may, upon breach or neglect of all or any one or more of the provisions of this Agreement, and at the discretion of the Governor of the Colony, be altogether withdrawn or suspended.

IX. Provided always that the terms of this Agreement be subject to the approval of Her Majesty . . .

X Adeyemi, *Alafin of Oyo.*

In the presence of:
Samuel Johnson, *Clerk in Holy Orders.*
William Moseri, *Scripture Reader.*
On behalf of Her Majesty the Queen,
  Alfred Moloney, *Governor and Commander-in-Chief of the Colony of Lagos.*

22

GOVERNOR C. A. MOLONEY TO
MAJOR C. M. MACDONALD: ILORIN,
2 APRIL 1889[1]

YOU were good enough to say at Lagos you would gladly receive a note from me embodying the salient points of a conversation I had

[1] C.O. 879/29, no. 365. (*Sir*) *Claude MacDonald* had been Military Attaché in Cairo, 1882–7, Acting Agent and Consul-General at Zanzibar, 1887–8; in 1889 he was sent by the F.O. to investigate the Niger territories and returned as Commissioner and Consul-General of the Oil Rivers (Niger Coast) Protectorate, 1891–6. The C.O. approved this proposal and allowed £50 for presents. MacDonald reported the early National African Company treaty with Ilorin to be worthless: MacDonald to Salisbury, 18 October 1889: C.O. 879/33, no. 399.

with you on the attitude of Ilorin towards the Yoruba country where peace was substituted by the Lagos Government in 1886 among its tribes for a war which began in 1877.

2. It is unnecessary for me to trouble you with the history of the war. I presume you have in your possession Parliamentary Papers C. 4957 and C. 5144 of 1887, which embody the correspondence respecting it, and the negotiations for peace conducted by the Lagos Government.

3. Those negotiations were confined, or rather intended to be confined, to the Yoruba speaking tribes. Ilorin was considered outside of such. It is peopled chiefly by Fulanis and Gambaris; it is nominally under the Sultan of Gando or of Sokoto. The Emir of Nupe, who resides at Bida, has also influence with Ilorin. With both Gando and Sokoto the Royal Niger Company has treaties; so has the British Government. *Vide* Hertslet's Treaties.

4. At the time of the negotiations there were two camps in the neighbourhood of the town of Ofa, which was situated near Ilorin. In the one camp was the Ilorin army with a contingent of the Yoruba Confederation known as the Ekiti parapo: in the other the Ibadans with an Ofa contingent. The Ofa (Yorubas) at the time were, if not under the Ibadans, at least their active allies. It was agreed in 1886 by the Ibadans and Ekitis to solve *inter se* and with Ilorin, the Ofa question, if the Lagos Government settled the differences in Yoruba proper. The Yoruba differences were settled, *vide* Treaty of 1886, copy herewith, but the aboriginal negotiations in reference to the war between the Ilorins and Ibadans failed: hostile activity continued in that direction. Ofa was abandoned (in 1887, I think) by a large part of its occupants, who took refuge in the border towns of Yoruba, such as Ekirun, Ilobu, Ejigho, &c., where they might best have the protection of the Ibadans. It is said that most of the Ofas who remained and trusted the Ilorins were killed or sold by the latter. The Ilorin camp has since continued at its old site. It is commanded by Kara, a Mohammedan fanatic, who seems to act as he pleases, and independently of the King of Ilorin, who has all along more or less leaned towards peace. Kara is described as having a bee in his bonnet which at times is exceptionally active—so much so that mechanical means of restraint have to be resorted to. If he could be got into Rider Haggard's lion's trap (Maiwa's revenge), and kept there, it would be indeed a very good thing for the country and its general peace.

5. Between the Ibadans, Ekitis, &c., a treaty of peace, friendship, and commerce was made in 1886. I have appended a copy. The Ekitis were the allies of the Ilorins. Their contingent in the Ilorin camp has not, the Ekitis allege, been allowed to return to Ekiti since the establishment of peace. While the Ekitis have held to the Treaty

of 1886 their position has been an awkward one, and, unless the Ilorins are soon curbed, may prove too much for them.

6. It is of considerable moment to Yoruba land and the internal peace that has been there established, and to the commerce of Lagos, to have the difference between the Ilorins and Ibadans settled, and as soon as possible. Such a settlement would, besides, enable the Ibadans to return from Ekirun to Ibadan if they found peace clearly and sufficiently assured.

7. It must be remembered that the Ilorins had of old overrun most of Yoruba, and had in such towns as they had overcome placed representatives. The Ibadans in the past took up the national cause and succeeded in driving out and back the Ilorins. The Ibadans were within their rights; in consequence of their successes they for some years have posed as cocks of the walk, and did not show that deference and obedience to the Alafin of Oyo, the acknowledged head of all Yoruba, and whose subjects they were and are, they should have done; they have since 1886 acted more becomingly and loyally, under the influence of the Government of Lagos.

8. The Ibadans are still at Ekirun, although they agreed in 1886 to return to their town Ibadan. The aggressive attitude of Ilorin they advance as their excuse, also their desire and intention to protect Yoruba from being overrun by Ilorins, as they threaten. The Ekitis, also a party to the 1886 Treaty, view with distrust the continued presence at Ekirun of the Ibadan army, and complain of their non-return to Ibadan. The Ekitis are also reproached by the Ilorins for their part in the peace negotiations of 1886, and for their present passive and friendly attitude towards Ibadans.

9. The treaty of peace, friendship, and commerce of 1886 will be found printed in Command Paper 4957 of 1887. The Ilorins, as will be gathered from my previous remarks, are out of it. A similar document should be concluded between the Ibadan and Ilorin authorities, to which the Alafin of Oyo, the King of Jebu, the Ekiti Kings and Ogudembe with advantage might be parties, and the Bale of Ogbomoso and the King of Iwo witnesses.

10. It might be found that the way would be made easy towards the production of such a treaty by proceeding *pari passu* with one of peace, friendship, and commerce with the Government of Lagos as per form herewith. To help such negotiations it would be well worth the while of the Government of Lagos to guarantee an annual issue in money or presents to the extent of 200 *l*. This is a mere suggestion, and would be naturally subject to the consideration and approval of the Home Government.

11. Although Yoruba land may be viewed generally as heathen, Mahommedanism is visibly growing therein and is making itself felt. In Lagos island itself, while in Sir R. Burton's time—*vide* account

of his visit when Consul for the Bight of Benin and Biafra to Abeokuta 1863–4—he gave the population as eight or nine hundred, it may now be said to have grown to so many thousand, indeed, more.

12. The Ibadans may be properly viewed as the buffers between Islamism and Heathenism. Among Lagos Mahommedans, for whom I entertain the greatest respect, there is found the usual sympathy for their co-religionists, which extends in association with great respect, I may say reverence, to Ilorin, which the former view practically as their local Mecca, with which they have now constant communication, *via* (1) Abeokuta, Iseyin, Oyo, and Ogbomoso, and (2) *via* (Artijere, Odeondo, Ilsa, and Ila, the countries of the Ekitis). Both routes favour, I fear, the slave traffic.

13. Before I left Lagos, it was my duty to convey to the Legislature, when I intimated my intention to leave for Europe, that in Yorubaland peace prevailed to a gratifying and encouraging extent; that there were no inter-tribal differences; that although circumstances beyond them, and which they could not at present control, the Ibadans advanced as keeping them still at Ekirun, whence they expressed themselves as desirous of withdrawing as soon as they could, [*sic*] yet there continued social and commercial intercommunication between them and the Ekitis; that the former were endeavouring to come to some understanding and friendly settlement with Ilorin (which is, it should be remembered, outside Yoruba and within Niger territories) which would justify their early return home.

14. I further communicated that I had availed myself of the opportunity of conversing with you on the subject, and intended, before I reached England, to convey my own views as to the possibility of further action calculated to establish a more lasting and complete peace in Yorubaland by the friendly settlement of the differences between the Ibadans and Ilorins. I also said that it was your hope to visit Ilorin by way of the Niger.[1]

15. I append a copy of a treaty made with the Government of Lagos by the Alafin of Oyo. It has not been ratified by Her Majesty's Government, but it is under their consideration. The Alafin is allowed, however, to have and receive his annual dash. . . .

23

JOHN BRAMSTON (COLONIAL OFFICE) TO FOREIGN OFFICE: YORUBA TREATIES, 21 DECEMBER 1889[2]

I AM directed by Lord Knutsford to request you to inform the Marquis of Salisbury that he has under consideration, in connexion

---

[1] See above, no. 21.
[2] C.O. 879/29, no. 365. See also below, II, no. 37, p. 200.

with the agreement with France of the 10th August, the question of the confirmation of the treaties made by Governor Moloney in 1888 with various native states in the neighbourhood of Lagos.

These treaties have all been communicated to you, and a list of them accompanied the letter from this department of 25th June last. This list, however, did not include the treaty with Ondo, which was enclosed in the letter from this department of the 22nd April last.

In three cases, those of Igbessa, Ilaro, and Ketu, the Chiefs, in addition to concluding a treaty of friendship and commerce, have offered the cession of their territory to Her Majesty, and the people of Ilaro have sent frequent messages to Lagos to know whether the offer would be accepted.

Lord Knutsford is disposed to think that, as the agreement of the 10th August will dispose of any apprehension of the French extending their territory to the back of Lagos, and cutting off the Colony from the interior, it is not necessary to take any cessions of the country, but that the Treaties of Commerce, &c. will suffice.

The only one of the Treaties to the confirmation of which there appears to be any objection is that with Ketu, as it seems probable that the line of demarcation fixed by the agreement will pass through that country.

Lord Knutsford therefore proposes, with Lord Salisbury's concurrence, that when Governor Moloney returns to Lagos, which he will do next month, he should be authorised to convey the confirmation by Her Majesty of the various Treaties he has concluded, except that with Ketu, but to inform the Chiefs and people who have offered the cession of their territories that Her Majesty does not desire to accept it, but wishes only to remain on terms of friendship with them, and to leave them to govern their countries, as heretofore, themselves.

24

A. W. L. HEMMING: MINUTE,
YORUBA INTERIOR, 10 JANUARY 1890[1]

MR. MEADE,

See Sir A. Moloney's Memo:[2] annexed, on this and previous papers. With regard to his proposals we might:

(1) send a telegram to Capt. Denton directing him to send Mr. Millson[3] up to Ibadan Ekirun to hold the Ibadans in hand, & make

[1] C.O. 147/73.   [2] Memorandum, 3 January 1890, ibid.
[3] Knutsford to Denton (telegram), 14 January 1890. For the Alvan Millson expedition, January–February 1890 to report on the Ilorin–Ibadan war, C.O. 879/33, no. 399.

preparations for a general meeting of the representatives of the Ibadans & Ilorins?

(2) Answer 21801 by saying that the matter has been considered in conjunction with Sir A. Moloney & that on his return to the Colony he will take such steps as he may find advisable & practicable with a view to the restoration of peace in the interior, & the reopening of the roads?[1]

(3) With regard to the appt. of a Travelling Commr. Sir A. Moloney should submit his suggestions more definitely. We ought to have before us the terms of the appt. as to salary, allowances, leave &c. and a statement as to the probable cost.

I have no doubt that such an appt. would be useful, & in the result would probably repay the expense, but we can't proceed on such a vague recommendation.

(4) I see no objection to the Govr. being authorized to visit Abeokuta & other places in Yorubaland. As regards the subsidies it might be well to give Sir A. Moloney a caution that, whilst not 'spoiling the ship for a ha'porth of tar' he must bear in mind that the revenue of the Colony at present only just equals the expenditure, and must not be too liberal.

(5) The question of the stoppage of the importation of guns & ammunition may wait for later & further reports from Sir A. Moloney. If the proposals before the Slave Trade Conference take further shape the matter will be dealt with in connection therewith . . .

25

A. W. L. HEMMING: MINUTE,
IJEBU, 27 OCTOBER 1891[2]

. . . I STILL adhere strongly to the views I expressed . . . and I think that some decided action should be taken to exact reparation from the Jebus & to punish them & that the opportunity should be seized to break down 'the middle wall of partition' which they have set up between the trade of the interior and Lagos. Their impudent pretensions to prevent free intercourse and as the Awujale stated 'to allow neither white man nor Yoruba to pass through Jebu in future', cannot, I submit, be allowed, and, weak and insignificant as they are, they must be shown that they will not be permitted thus to stifle trade & hinder the development of the interior countries.

[1] F.O. to C.O., 21 December 1889, ibid.
[2] C.O. 147/83. There had been considerable pressure from Liverpool and Manchester to open the trade routes, 6 April, 31 March 1891. From the Honduras, Moloney also advised strong measures: Moloney to C.O., 9 October 1891: C.O. 879/36, no. 428.

I would therefore write in the sense of what I proposed[1] . . . and leave it to Mr. Carter to settle the exact time and mode in which, if necessary, coercion should be applied.

I do not myself believe that any action on the part of the Egbas need be feared. We should not interfere with their trade, & they would be afraid if they sided with the Jebus of exposing themselves to attack from the Yorubas who would soon discover that our action was taken in their interests & with the view of giving them a free road to Lagos. You will see . . . that all the principal merchants & traders of Lagos are anxious that steps should be taken to break down the Jebu monopoly.

26

GOVERNOR G. T. CARTER TO LORD KNUTSFORD: IJEBU AGREEMENT, 25 JANUARY 1892[2]

. . . 14. I THEN proceeded to the question of the roads, briefly alluding to the past history of the question, and speaking very plainly on the subject of their backwardness as compared with the neighbouring tribes. I particularly adverted to their folly in refusing to receive missionaries in the country; and though I could not coerce them into adopting such a policy, yet I strongly advised them to follow the example of those who had done so. I bade them compare the position of Lagos with that of their own country, and told them that the results which they could see with their own eyes had not been achieved by the policy of isolation which they had adopted, but by liberal and advanced views, by free trade, and by the encouragement of missionaries, who established schools and endeavoured to introduce a higher standard of morality and a purer form of religion than at present existed amongst those natives which were ignorant of the Bible. I added that Her Majesty's Government had determined that in future all roads and water-ways through their country were to be free and open to all, and while I should be glad to hear anything they had to say on the subject, it must be distinctly understood that a decision such as I had intimated was imperative.

15. The spokesman replied that he was authorised to say that there was war in the interior, and that I should see to that being settled first before demanding that the roads should be opened.

16. I said I was perfectly aware of the fact he had mentioned, but

[1] Knutsford to Carter, 5 November 1891. Both Meade and Herbert agreed with the policy of sending an ultimatum.

[2] C.O. 289/36, no. 428. Some twenty-two Ijebu officials had visited Lagos. This was followed by an ultimatum: Carter to the *Awujale* of Ijebu, 16 December 1891, and a mission by Haddon Smith at the end of December.

did not see what that had to do with the question, and told them plainly if they did not open the roads of their own free will I should be compelled to use harsh measures.

17. The spokesman here prevaricated, and said that the roads were already open.

18. I replied by recounting to them their well known habits of restrictive tolls, and their practice of compelling all produce to be sold in their own markets at their own price, and said that was not the English idea of open roads. I impressed upon them that the Queen did not want to take over one inch of their territory, but merely to open it up to free and unrestricted commerce, which they would find to be far more paying to themselves in the long run. I said that we did not wish them to surrender their privileges for nothing, and that I was prepared to consider that question in an agreement I proposed to submit to them.

19. The spokesman then replied that the King was ready to agree that all the roads should be open and free.

20. I then enquired if they were prepared to sign an agreement to this effect?

21. The spokesman said that they were ready to agree to what had been proposed, but they did not understand 'Book.'

22. I endeavoured to remove their objection by saying that, although they did not conduct their business in this fashion, it was the practice in England to keep record of all transactions of this nature, and that I must have something to send to the Queen in proof of what had taken place. I said I would have a proper paper drawn up, and hoped that they would sign it. If they preferred to trust to their memory, I would not compel them to take away a copy of the agreement, because there were numbers of witnesses to what they had promised, and it would be sufficient for me to have the agreement placed on record at Lagos.

23. As the deputation had nothing further to say, the meeting broke up with the understanding that an agreement should be drawn up for signature, embodying the terms to which they had assented, and arranging for compensation to be made to the King in view of his losses consequent upon the abolition of tolls.

24. On the 21st January the Jebus again assembled, when I brought forward an agreement which had been drawn up, under my direction, by the Queen's Advocate. I found that they had an invincible objection to sign the document; and, moreover, to my surprise, again raised the question of the tolls which they still wished to retain. I, however, expressed my mind very freely upon this subject, and told them frankly that unless this concession were made, the Government would take immediate steps to free the roads in its own fashion, in which case the King would get nothing. The Jebus then gave way,

and definitely promised that all the roads and waterways should be open for produce and goods passing both ways, and that all tolls should be abolished.

25. I then read the agreement, which was carefully explained to them, and they unanimously agreed to all its provisions, but every argument failed to induce them to affix their signature. They said they understood nothing about 'Book', and that the promise they had given was quite as binding as if they touched the pen, as I wished them to do. Seeing that it was hopeless to get any further, I called upon Mr. Payne and Mr. Jacob Williams, the two Jebus they had expressly asked to be present, to sign the document on their behalf, as witnessing the solemn promise their compatriots had made. Both these gentlemen then addressed the deputation, and obtained from them a unanimous declaration of agreement to the terms of the compact; and further, at Mr. Payne's request, they took the oath of their country on Kola nuts and water. This was regarded as satisfactory by all parties present, and Mr. Payne and Mr. Williams then affixed their names to the document.

26. There can be no doubt that the agreement, as it now stands, is far more likely to be kept than if it had been made out according to English ideas, and the general impression is that the Jebus will faithfully observe their compact. . . .

27

JOHN BRAMSTON (COLONIAL OFFICE)
TO THE WAR OFFICE: EGBA AND
IJEBU, 23 MARCH 1892[1]

I AM directed by Lord Knutsford to transmit to you, to be laid before Mr. Secretary Stanhope, copies of correspondence with the Governor of Lagos respecting the conduct of the Egbas and Jebus in stopping the trade routes between the Colony and the interior, and of the latter in repudiating an agreement into which they had very recently entered with the Colonial Government.

It appears to Lord Knutsford that it has become necessary to consider whether some action should not be taken under these circumstances, especially as the closing of the roads has completely paralyzed the trade of the Colony, and is causing much anxiety and impatience on the part of the merchants in this country.

[1] C.O. 289/36, no. 428. The War Office agreed to send an officer of the Gold Coast Constabulary empowered to ask for up to 300 men of the West India Regiment at Sierra Leone. W.O. to C.O., 25 March 1892.

Great pressure has been brought to bear upon this Department by the Chambers of Commerce both of Liverpool and Manchester.

To deal at once with both Abeokuta and Jebu Ode is, however, beyond the resources at the disposal of the Colonial Government; and it will be seen that it is therefore proposed, in the first instance, to adopt coercive measures against the Jebus, who are the greater offenders.

It is hoped that when the Egbas learn that possession has been taken of Jebu Ode they will offer to come to terms; but should they not do so, and it should become necessary to use force against them, they can be dealt with during the next dry season.

Jebu Ode is reported to be a walled town of some 35,000 inhabitants, and is situated within 16 miles of the Lagos Lagoon at Ejinrin. Mr. Haddon Smith, of the Lagos Constabulary, who has recently visited the place, is now in this country, and can give full information with respect to it.

The Governor of the Gold Coast Colony, who has been communicated with, has stated that he can send 150 Houssas, with two European officers and a Nordenfeldt gun on tripod, and the Lagos Constabulary can supply a similar number.

The Lagos Government possess three 7-pounder steel guns, two Nordenfeldt guns, and a Gatling.

The Inspector-General of the Lagos Constabulary, Major Stanley, is the only officer now in the Colony, but two others, Captain Tarbet and Mr. Haddon Smith, will be sent out by the steamer of 30th instant.

It is proposed to entrust the command of the expedition to Colonel Scott, C.B., Inspector-General of the Gold Coast Constabulary, who is recommended to Lord Knutsford by the Adjutant-General as a thoroughly competent and efficient officer.

Lord Knutsford proposes to endeavour to secure the co-operation of the Navy, so far at least as to obtain the presence of H.M.S. 'Alecto;' and, if the Lords Commissioners of the Admiralty will consent to allow a small force of seamen and marines to be landed, their assistance would have a most beneficial moral effect both on the houssas and the enemy, the support of any of Her Majesty's forces showing that the matter in hand is not merely one in which the Colonial Government alone is concerned, but is, to use the expression of the natives, a 'Queen's palaver.'

It is further proposed that when the Jebus have made terms of peace, a force of (say) 100 houssas should be left at Jebu Ode for some little time to come, and the possibility of this being done with safety must be considered.

Lord Knutsford would be obliged by an expression of Mr. Stanhope's opinion as to the sufficiency of these proposals, and in what manner, if any, they should be supplemented.

In particular, I am to inquire whether the number of officers referred to as available would seem to be sufficient, or whether Mr. Stanhope would suggest that any additional ones should be sent out on a temporary engagement.

In asking for this expression of opinion, I am to observe that the organization and direction of active military operations is altogether outside and beyond the business or experience of this Department, and doubtless Mr. Stanhope and his military advisers will appreciate the readiness with which the Colonial Government is willing to undertake the task of dealing with the Jebus without calling for the employment of regular troops.

28

GOVERNOR G. T. CARTER TO LORD KNUTSFORD: IJEBU, 5 MAY 1892[1]

IN reference to my telegram of this date . . . it will be necessary that I should explain in detail the reasons which impelled me to urge upon Her Majesty's Government the policy of including Jebu in the British Protectorate of Lagos. First and foremost, the existence of this race, in its present wilful disregard of all attempts at enlightenment, is a blot on the civilization of this Colony; they have persistently refused to allow missionaries to reside in their country, and throw every obstacle in the way of their passing into the interior. The Jebu capital is situated only about 15 miles from the bank of the Lagoon, and yet there is no reasonable doubt that the inhabitants still practise the abominable rite of human sacrifices. I have already reported in my Despatch, No. 129, of the 20th ultimo, that a considerable number of slaves have recently been killed in honour of a deceased king, and this report has been confirmed by several persons who have lately passed through Jebu Ode. It is difficult to obtain absolute proof of the fact from eye witnesses, as the fetish priests carry out these sacrifices with great secrecy, but it is perfectly well known in Lagos that the Jebus have never abandoned this horrible practice.

2. In regard to my statement to the messengers, that we do not want 'one inch of their territory,' this is perfectly true at the present moment, but I submit that circumstances now render it practically necessary that we should incur the responsibility of taking the government of the country out of their hands.

3. The Jebus will never voluntarily open their roads to the interior

[1] C.O. 289/36, no. 428. Military action against Ijebu ending in the capture of the *Awujale* took place on 20 May. Knutsford also agreed to the occupation of Sagamu, Ijebu Ode, Ikorodu (as a temporary measure), 3 June 1892.

tribes, and it is hopeless to expect them to press for a British Protectorate, unless they are absolutely compelled to do so by an invasion of Ibadans. There can be no doubt that the past policy of the Lagos Government has been a wise one, in preventing the Ibadans from exterminating the pusillanimous Jebus, as they could easily do, in view of the fact that it is in one sense better that a people of that character should occupy the country than the warlike Ibadans, who might be very troublesome neighbours in a more objectionable sense, even than the Jebus. Unless the Lagos Government adopt a firm policy, now that so good an opportunity offers, there can be little doubt that the Ibadans will take advantage of the demoralization of the Jebus to overrun the country, and possibly establish themselves there to carry out a similar policy to that pursued by their predecessors. It is idle to shut one's eyes to the fact that, if the positions of the Ibadans and Jebus were reversed, the former would not be one whit more complaisant to the latter than the Jebus are to the Ibadans at the present moment.

4. The key to the situation seems to me to lie at Sagamu, the capital and market town of Jebu Remos. This section of the Jebus are undoubtedly friendly to the Lagos Government, and if they were certain of our support they would throw off the yoke of the Jebu Ode without hesitation.

5. If your Lordship will consult the sketch map of Yoruba, compiled by Mr. Macaulay, under the personal supervision of Sir Alfred Moloney (though it must be admitted that the map is very incorrect), it will be observed that the direct road to Ibadan is through Ikorodu, immediately on the Lagoon, via Sagamu, but the Ibadans are not allowed to use that road, and are compelled to come through Oru and Jebu Ode, where their produce is disposed of. My idea is that Sagamu should be occupied by a strong force, and advance posts established towards Ibadan if necessary. A good road should be constructed right through from Ikorodu to Ibadan, and it might be a question whether the Government should not collect tolls at Sagamu to defray the cost of the maintenance of the road. If this were done, Abeokuta would cease to be of any consequence. Ibadan would become a large centre of commerce, and the whole of the produce of the rich Yoruba country would come down direct to the Lagoon by this road. I would suggest that an engineer should be despatched from England to make a proper survey of this route, and to frame an estimate of the cost of the construction of such a road as I have proposed. I have good reason to believe that the Ibadans would enter heartily into such a scheme, and that a plentiful supply of labour would be forthcoming.

6. The position of Abeokuta with regard to Sagamu in the map is clearly incorrect. These places are about 40 miles apart, while Jebu Ode is approximately half the distance from Sagamu. It will be

observed that the map places Abeokuta within about 15 miles of Sagamu, while the latter place is placed about 25 miles from Jebu Ode. 7. I have considered it my duty to place these matters before your Lordship, though it is hardly necessary for me to say that I shall always be prepared to carry out the wishes of Her Majesty's Government.

29

COMMISSIONER CLAUDE MACDONALD TO THE MARQUIS OF SALISBURY: BENIN, 16 MAY 1892[1]

THIS is the first instance of any Treaty having been made between Her Majesty's Government and the King of Benin, though several attempts have been made by Consular officers; amongst others by the late Sir Richard Burton when Consul at Fernando Po. There is no doubt that the Benin Territory is a very rich and most important one. Minerals, Gum Copal, Gum Arabic, Palm Oil, Kernels &c., are to be found in large quantities. Trade, Commerce and Civilization however are paralized [sic] by the form of Fetish Government which unfortunately prevails throught. the Kingdom; the present Ruler it appears from all the information I can gather would be willing to put an end to the present state of affairs but he is overawed by the priesthood and executions for the most trivial offences or as sacrifices to the Gods, are of daily occurrence. The Crucifixions spoken of by Capt. Gallwey in his Report were made to propitiate the rain gods, the wretched victims were slaves who were crucified and left to die.

I hope before long to be able to put a stop to this state of affairs, and I look upon the Treaty, so ably effected by Capt. Gallwey, as the first step towards carrying out this much to be desired end.

I shall be surprised however if these barbarous practices which have been the Custom of the Country for centuries will be abandoned by the Priesthood without a severe struggle, and a display, and probable use of force on the part of the Government of the Oil Rivers Protectorate which however I should only recommend as a last extremity . . .

[1] F.O. 84/2194. Encl. Treaty of protection, 26 March 1892; and report by Vice-Consul Major H. L. Gallwey, 30 March 1892. See A. F. C. Ryder, *Benin and the Europeans* (London, 1969), pp. 265–72.

30

GOVERNOR G. T. CARTER TO THE
MARQUIS OF RIPON: EGBA,
18 JANUARY 1893[1]

I HAVE the honour to enclose herewith a copy of a Treaty which I
have negotiated with the King and Authorities of Abeokuta on behalf
of the Egba Nation.

2. It has not been without considerable difficulty that I have been
able to induce the Egbas to enter into a Treaty at all, no doubt owing
to the unfortunate incidents connected with the Jebu question; and
there is moreover such an undercurrent of intrigue and misrepresentation in Abeokuta, encouraged by disloyal residents in Lagos,
that it has been no easy task to impress the authorities with the bona
fides of my mission.

3. The first Treaty which I submitted for their consideration was
objected to on several grounds, which I need only briefly indicate
here, as the subject will be fully dealt with in my general report at
the conclusion of the expedition. The most important point, however,
has been secured, viz., a guarantee that the roads shall not be closed
again without the consent and approval of the Governor of Lagos.

4. There was a strong disinclination to any provisions in regard to
the protection of missionaries, the abolition of human sacrifices, the
cession of their country to any other power, detailed provision for
arbitration in case of dispute, and the right of British subjects to build
houses, own property, and carry on manufactures in the country.
They argued that, except in the case of one township, human sacrifices had been long abolished, and they were prepared to take steps
to prevent any recurrence of the practice in the future. In regard to
the other questions, they were prepared to refer disputes to Lagos,
but they desired that they should be settled between the authorities
and the Governor without any reference to arbitrators or a final
appeal to the Governor. No argument was of any avail to turn them
from the opinion which they had formed on this subject. As to missionaries, they had always received protection, and British subjects
had always been able to own property and carry on any manufacture
which they desired; there was no reason, therefore, to provide
specially for these subjects in the Treaty. What they wanted was
a treaty of friendship with the British Government, and they were
quite prepared to give a guarantee that the roads should not be closed
again without the consent of the Governor of Lagos.

5. As it was useless arguing the question further, I said I would

[1] C.O. 289/36, no. 428. *George F. S. Robinson, 1st Marquis of Ripon* was Secretary
of State for Colonies, 1892–5.

endeavour to frame a Treaty which would meet their wishes, and drew up the enclosed, which seems to meet all the exigencies of the case. It will be noticed that I have in clause 6 recited the points which were objected to by reason of their being unnecessary, so that a record should exist of the grounds upon which the insertion of special provisions were opposed, and in regard to the Missionary question I have met the objection by inserting the words 'as heretofore' between the words 'will' and 'afford'.

6. The clause providing for the independence of the country was inserted at the urgent request of the Magaji, but your Lordship will see that I have made it conditional upon the strict observance of the Treaty. I had no hesitation in giving way on this point, as the general policy of Her Majesty's Government has always been in favour of non-interference with Native territories and institutions except in cases of urgent necessity.

7. I have endeavoured to impress upon the authorities the advantages which their country would derive if railway communication could be established between Lagos and Abeokuta, and although I have received no absolute pledge that permission will be accorded, I have good reason to believe that the authorities themselves are favourably disposed towards the project, but they are of opinion that it will take a little time to reconcile the people to such a scheme, who would look with suspicion upon so radical a change in the transport arrangements of their country.

8. I have not been able to induce the authorities at present to accept any stipend from the Lagos Government. The Egbas are by nature so suspicious that such an act would be regarded in the light of a reward for the sale of their country, but I gather that the authorities do not despair of removing these unworthy suspicions.

9. Your Lordship has been advised by telegram that I arrived in Abeokuta on the 7th instant, and that my reception was all that could be desired. I will only add that further experience has only confirmed the pleasant impressions which this reception gave me. It would have been impossible to hope for a more cordial welcome, and with trifling exceptions I have received nothing but the utmost civility and good humour, both from the authorities and from the inhabitants of the town wherever I have shown myself.

10. I believe that the authorities are honestly desirous of securing a permanent alliance and friendship with the Lagos Government; and, although it is rash to prophesy in regard to the fate of West African Treaties, there is good reason to hope that the present one will be strictly observed. If it should ever be flagrantly violated, the same policy should be adopted with the Egbas as that which has been carried out in the case of the Jebus with such conspicuous success.

11. It is a remarkable circumstance that the grievances which the

Egbas professed to have against the Lagos Government have been very lightly touched upon. The Ilaro question has been mentioned it is true, but there has been no suggestion that the country should be given back again, and I think that nothing further will be heard of it. The Magaji desired that the boundary between the Egba country and Ebute Metta might be defined, and I was able to tell him that as soon as Mr. Fowler's survey of the country was finished I should be in a better position to give him specific landmarks; with this answer he was quite satisfied.

12. I have been delayed in Abeokuta longer than I anticipated, but to be successful in West African negotiations too much regard must not be paid to the question of time.

13. I propose to leave Abeokuta on the morning of the 19th instant, and am proceeding to Isehin, and from thence to Oyo; the journey to Isehin will, I calculate, take five or six days, and from thence to Oyo two days.

31

EGBA TREATY, 18 JANUARY 1893[1]

BETWEEN His Excellency Gilbert Thomas Carter, Esquire, Companion of the Most Distinguished Order of Saint Michael and Saint George, Governor and Commander-in-Chief of the Colony of Lagos, for and on behalf of Her Majesty the Queen of Great Britain and Ireland, Empress of India, &c., Her heirs and successors on the one part, and the undersigned King (Alake) and Authorities of Abeokuta representing the Egba kingdom, for and on behalf of their heirs and successors on the other part. We, the undersigned King and Authorities do, in the presence of the elders, headmen, and people assembled at this place, hereby promise:

1st. That there shall be peace and friendship between subjects of the Queen and Egba subjects, and should any difference or dispute accidentally arise between us and the said subjects of the Queen, it shall be referred to the Governor of Lagos for settlement as may be deemed expedient.

2nd. That there shall be complete freedom of trade between the Egba country and Lagos, and in view of the injury to commerce arising from the arbitrary closing of roads, we the said King and Authorities, hereby declare that no roads shall in future be closed without the consent and approval of the Governor of Lagos.

3rd. That we, the said King and Authorities, pledge ourselves to use every means in our power to foster and promote trade with the countries adjoining Egba and with Lagos.

[1] C.O. 289/36, no. 428.

4th. That we the said King and Authorities will as heretofore, afford complete protection, and every assistance and encouragement to all Ministers of the Christian religion.

5th. It is further agreed and stipulated by the said Gilbert Thomas Carter on behalf of Her Majesty the Queen of England, that so long as the provisions of this Treaty are strictly kept, no annexation of any part of the Egba country shall be made by Her Majesty's Government without consent of the lawful Authorities of the country, no aggressive action shall be taken against the said country, and its independence shall be fully recognised.

6th. The said King and Authorities having promised that the practice of offering human sacrifices shall be abolished in the one township where it at present exists, and having explained that British subjects have already freedom to occupy land, build houses, and carry on trade and manufacture in any part of the Egba country, and likewise that there is no possibility of a cession of any portion of the Egba country to a foreign Power without the consent of Her Majesty's Government, it is desired that no special provision be made in regard to these subjects in this Treaty.

Done at Abeokuta this Eighteenth day of January, 1893.

		his		
(Signed)	OSOKALU	x	King Alake	
		mark		
		his		
„	OSUNDARE, Onlado	x		
		mark		
		his	Representatives	
„	SORUNKE, Jaguna	x	of King Alake and	
		mark	Egba United Kingdom.	
		his		
„	OGUNDEYI	x		
		mark		

(Signed) G. T. CARTER,
 Governor and Commander-in-Chief
  Colony of Lagos.

Witnessed at Abeokuta this Eighteenth day of January, 1893.

(Signed) G. B. HADDON-SMITH, Political Officer.
 „ R. L. BOWER, Captain, Assistant Inspector, Lagos Constabulary.
 „ J. B. WOOD, Missionary of the Church Missionary Society.
 „ A. L. HETHERSETT, Clerk and Interpreter, Governor's Office.
 „ E. R. BICKERSTETH, Trader.
 „ W. F. TINNEY SOMOYE, Clerk to the Egba Authorities.

I, the undersigned, do swear that I have truly and honestly interpreted the terms of the foregoing Treaty to the contracting parties, in the Yoruba language.

Witness to signature (Signed) A. L. HETHERSETT
(Signed) E. R. BICKERSTETH, Trader.

32

OYO TREATY, 3 FEBRUARY 1893[1]

TREATY made at Oyo, in the Yoruba Country, this third day of February, in the year 1893, between His Excellency Gilbert Thomas Carter, Esquire, Companion of the Most Distinguished Order of Saint Michael and Saint George, Governor and Commander-in-Chief of Lagos, for and on behalf of Her Majesty the Queen of Great Britain and Ireland, Empress of India, &c., Her Heirs and Successors, on the one part, and the undersigned King Alafin of Oyo and Head of Yoruba land for and on behalf of His Heirs and Successors on the other part.

I the undersigned Alafin of Oyo do hereby promise:

1st. That there shall be peace between the subjects of the Queen of England and Yoruba subjects, and should any difference or dispute accidentally arise between us and the said subjects of the Queen, it shall be referred to the Governor of Lagos for the time being whose decision shall be final and binding upon us all.

2nd. That British subjects shall have free access to all parts of Yoruba land and shall have the right to build houses and possess property according to the laws in force in this country. They shall further have full liberty to carry on such trade and manufacture as may be approved by the Governor of Lagos.

3rd. That I the said Alafin of Oyo agree to allow a right of way to Lagos to all persons wishing to go there.

4th. That I the said Alafin of Oyo pledge myself to use every means in my power to foster and promote trade with countries adjoining Yoruba land and with Lagos.

5th. That I the said Alafin of Oyo will afford complete protection and every assistance and encouragement to all ministers of the Christian Religion.

6th. That I the said Alafin of Oyo solemnly promise to abolish the practice of offering human sacrifices and to prohibit it throughout the country under my control.

7th. That I the said Alafin of Oyo will not enter into any war or commit any act of aggression on any of the Chiefs bordering on Lagos

[1] C.O. 289/36, no. 428. Encl. in Carter to Ripon, 8 February 1893.

by which the trade of the country with Lagos shall be interrupted or the safety of the persons and property of the subjects of the Queen of England shall be lost, compromised or endangered.

8th. That I the said Alafin of Oyo will at no time whatever cede any of my territory to any other power, or to enter into any agreement, treaty, or arrangement with any Foreign Government, except through and with the consent of the Government of Her Majesty the Queen of England, &c.

9th. It is hereby agreed that all disputes that may arise between the parties to this Treaty shall be enquired into and adjusted by two arbitrators, the one appointed by the Governor of Lagos, the other by the Alafin of Oyo, and in any case when the arbitrators so appointed shall not agree the matter in dispute shall be referred to the Governor of Lagos, whose decision shall be final.

10th. In consideration of the faithful observance of all the foregoing articles of this Treaty the Governor of Lagos will make from 1st January next ensuing unto the King of Oyo a yearly present of one hundred pounds but such present may upon breach of all or any one or more of the provisions of this Agreement, and at the discretion of the Governor of Lagos for the time being, be altogether withdrawn or suspended.

11th. I likewise pledge myself to obtain the consent and co-operation of all the sub-ordinate Kings and Authorities of representative Towns in Yoruba land to the provisions of this Treaty.

his
ADEYEMI   x   Alafin of Oyo and Head of
mark   Yoruba land.

(Signed) G. T. CARTER,
Governor and Commander-in-Chief,
Colony of Lagos.

33

GOVERNOR G. T. CARTER TO
THE MARQUIS OF RIPON: IBADAN
AND ILORIN, 14 MARCH 1893[1]

...41. AFTER the usual compliments had passed, I briefly recounted to them the events which had led up to the present meeting, and said that the King of Ilorin had agreed with me as to the only means of bringing their unhappy differences to an end, and had instructed the authorities at Ofa to accept me as a mediator between themselves and

---

[1] Ibid. Encl. Declaration of the Emir of Ilorin (peace with Ibadan), 25 February 1893. Written from Carter's 'camp between Ikirun and Offa'.

the Ibadans, and to act upon my decision, whatever it might be. I said that they must be conscious of my disinterestedness, and that I had nothing to gain personally from one side or the other, and that therefore they could rely upon my impartiality. I pointed out that I had made myself thoroughly acquainted with the past history of their differences, and plainly saw that as each side distrusted the other, there was only one way of coming to a settlement, which was for both parties to break up their camps simultaneously, and for me to see that each side strictly adhered to the compact. Addressing the Ilorins I told them that the Ibadans had unanimously agreed to do what I told them; their interests were bound up in Lagos, and it was impossible that they could act contrary to my wishes. Both parties had now agreed to accept me as arbitrator, and it only remained for me to fix a day for their common departure, and it was my decision that they should each break up their camps on the fifth day from the date of this assembly, viz., on Monday the 13th instant.

42. There was not the smallest disposition on either side to question this ruling. The Ilorins repeated that it was their King's wish that they should accept my decision, and that settled the question. The Ibadans, of course, agreed to my terms, and then both sides split kola nuts together, and ratified the compact amongst themselves. The only thing they asked was that I would allow them to count the five days from Wednesday, instead of Tuesday, as this was an unlucky day to them. As this did not appear to me to be a very important matter, I readily conceded the point, and it was finally arranged that the camps should be evacuated on Tuesday the 14th March.

43. Before the meeting broke up I asked if there were any other details they desired my assistance to settle, more especially as to any question of boundaries, because, if so, I would gladly render them any assistance in my power. . . .

34

GOVERNOR G. T. CARTER: MINUTE,
IBADAN, 23 JUNE 1893[1]

I would venture to suggest that the S[ecretary] of State should communicate with Captain Denton and inform him that His Lordship had under his consideration the proposal contained in my Desp: of the 6th April[2] and that it had been decided to carry out the policy therein recommended to station a force of Houssas at Ibadan in

---

[1] C.O. 147/93. On Carter to Meade (London), 30 May 1893. Carter wrote his own Minute to his own dispatch which was used as a draft for Ripon to Denton, 4 July 1893.
[2] Carter to Ripon, 6 April 1893: C.O. 289/36, no. 428.

charge of a European officer, the details of which would be arranged upon my return to the Colony.

In the meantime, Captain Denton should be instructed to communicate with the Ibadan authorities and inform them that this policy had been decided upon, not with a view to any serious interference with the Native Government, but to act as a protection to the poorer people and to assist the Authorities in keeping the roads open and in the suppression of slave raids.

The duty of the European officer would be to act as an Intermediary between the Ibadan Authorities and the Lagos Government, to visit the neighbouring towns, and to endeavour by diplomatic means to preserve the peace which has been established between the Ibadans and Ilorins.

The Authorities should also be informed that, although the practice is viewed with disfavour, it is not the intention of the Government to interfere [D with domestic slavery] with local customs and observances, so long as they do not conflict with the ordinary principles of humanity, the sole object of the Government being to preserve peace, to secure open roads, and reasonable freedom of action to the inhabitants generally.

It would I think be desirable that Captain Denton himself, or at any rate an officer whose discretion could be relied upon should visit Ibadan and convey this decision to the Authorities. They should also be informed that Her Majesty had learned with some surprise their refusal to carry out the wishes of the Governor during his visit to Ibadan in March last, which they must have been aware could only have been dictated with a view to their interests. They should be reminded that the Jebu Expedition was undertaken principally to enable them to have free access to the Lagoon, and to dispose of their produce to the best advantage, and that the visit of the Governor to the interior had resulted in putting an end to a war which for many years had inflicted great hardship on their Countrymen.

In view of these circumstances H.M.'s Government hoped that they would now atone for their ingratitude by rendering every assistance to the Lagos Government in carrying out the policy which had been determined upon and which would so obviously tend to their advantage in securing peace and good order in the Yoruba country.

It would also be desirable to communicate with the King of Oyo by letter and inform him that it had been decided to station a white officer & some Houssas at Ibadan. He will I am sure approve of this policy. He is nominally King of all Yorubaland, and the Ibadans accord to him a sentimental recognition, but for all practical purposes the Ibadans rule themselves.

35

VICE CONSUL W. CAIRNS ARMSTRONG TO COMMISSIONER CLAUDE MACDONALD: OPOBO, 10 JULY 1893[1]

[He has toured the creeks to Opobo.]

... THE market question was the next subject they touched on. The retirement [of Europeans] from the markets had taken place during my absence on leave. I was therefore very much interested in what they had to say. They expressed their satisfaction in once more having the markets to themselves, they informed me that they worked in conjunction with the Bonny chiefs and had bought out the African Association and Messrs Miller Brothers, that now perfect harmony existed between the European traders and themselves which used not to be the case whilst the white man was at their markets ...

[Trade has increased, compared with the quarter ending 30 June, 1892.][2]

... This improvement no doubt is due to a great extent to the White Trader having left the market as undoubtedly the great advantages of working these markets at a profit lies with [sic] the middlemen whose experience of years and cheap slave labour make competition for the white man with his necessary launches, establishment up country and European employees almost impossible ...

36

AGREEMENT, IBADAN, 15 AUGUST 1893[3]

... WE the undersigned Bale and Authorities of Ibadan on behalf of ourselves and of the people of Ibadan do hereby agree and declare as follows:

1. That the general administration of the internal affairs of the following Yoruba towns viz: Iwo, Ede, Osogbo, Ikirun, Ogbomoso, Ejigbo, and Isein and in all countries in the so called Ekun Otun Ekun Osi is vested in the general Government of Ibadan and the local Authorities of the said towns act in harmony with and are subject to Ibadan notwithstanding that the Alafin is recognised as the King and Head of Yoruba Land.

[1] F.O. 2/51.
[2] Imports: £71,859; exports: £85,929; customs duty: £15,196.
[3] C.O. 146/90. Encl. in Denton to C.O., 28 August 1893. Signatories were: Acting Governor G. C. Denton; Fijabi, the Bale; Suntoki, the Otun Bale; Fajinmi, the Osi Bale; Akintola, the Balogun; Oyeniye (representative of Akintola); Babalola, the Otun Balogun; Kongi, the Osi Balogun; Sumanu Apanpa, the Asipa; Ogundipo, the Seriki; and witnesses.

2. That we fully recognise all the provisions of the Treaty dated the 3rd. February, 1893, made at Oyo . . .

3. That we fully agree to carry out within the territory of Ibadan all the provisions of the said Treaty.

4. That we further agree in amplification of the said Treaty on our own behalf to the following terms and conditions:

First. That we will use every effort to secure the free passage of all persons coming through Ibadan either from the interior to Lagos or from Lagos to the interior and we promise to afford protection to all persons and property so passing.

Second. That for the purpose of better securing the performance of the said Treaty of the 3rd. February, 1893, and of this Agreement we do hereby agree to receive at Ibadan such European Officers and such a force of the Lagos Constabulary as the Governor shall from time to time deem necessary for the said purpose and for securing to us the benefits of the said Treaty and Agreement, and we also agree to provide land for the occupation of such Officers and Force.

Third. We further agree, upon the request of the Government of Lagos, to provide land for the construction and maintenance of a Railway through our Territory, should the construction of such a Railway be determined upon, and to accept for such land such compensation, if any, as shall be agreed upon between the parties hereto or between the Authorities of Ibadan and the persons undertaking the construction of such Railway.

5. And we do finally agree that all disputes which may arise under or in reference to this Agreement shall be enquired into and adjusted by two Arbitrators, the one to be appointed by the Governor of Lagos for the time being, the other by the Bale and Authorities of Ibadan, and in any case where the Arbitrators so appointed shall not agree the matter in dispute shall be referred to the Governor of Lagos whose decision shall be final . . .

37

[SIR GILBERT CARTER] TO THE SECRETARY OF STATE FOR THE COLONIES: IJEBU REMO, 6 AUGUST 1894[1]

. . . 10. As I informed your Lordship in my telegram of the 31st July, I regard this question as one of considerable urgency to the future of Lagos, and am still of opinion that the absolute cession should be

[1] C.O. 879/41, no. 475. Sagamu was occupied in February 1894. This dispatch was signed for Carter by Smalman Smith, and approved by the C.O. in Ripon to Carter (telegram), 26 September 1894. Ikorodu was formally annexed on 9 November 1894 and Ijebu Remo attached to the Lagos Protectorate.

accepted. The position of Ikorodu is a most important one, forming as it does the terminus of one of the main arteries of the Yoruba country. A large market is held there, and there are not wanting agitators of the semi-civilized type in Lagos who are impressing upon the Acarigbo the value of this port to his country, and the practicability of using it as a source of revenue by imposing duties on English goods and spirits landed there. I need hardly point out how undesirable such a proceeding would be, and, as all other salient points on the Lagoon have been secured to the Colony, it seems to me a most unwise policy to neglect the opportunity of acquiring it now that it is within our grasp. I venture, therefore, to urge once more the desirability of making this place an integral portion of the colony. The authorities have been advised of the precise position they will occupy in the event of cession, and they are prepared for the result. The slave question has now practically settled itself, and all those who were dissatisfied with their position have deserted their masters.

11. The ruling spirit of Ikorodu is undoubtedly Jasimi, the Balogun, and I have provided a stipend of 100 l. a year for him. It is only recently that he has recognized the authority of the Acarigbo, a result which was due to my intervention, but, if he chose to assert his independence, there is no power in Jebu Remo to coerce him.

12. I have ascertained that the Olojo had no authority to offer the cession of Ikorodu upon his own initiative; he was appointed by the Acarigbo upon the recommendation of the Ikorodu representative personages, and was placed in the position he occupies mainly because he was poor and obscure and could be ruled by the elders. I gather that he was advised to assert himself, at the instigation of certain missionaries who assured him of support from Lagos. It is clear, however, that he has incurred the hostility of the Acarigbo and of the ruling section in Ikorodu, and he has been refused recognition on all sides. Unquestionably, but for the Lagos Government, he would be put to 'sleep'.

13. I am proceeding at once to Jebu Ode where I propose to obtain a modification of the strip of the Jebu country formerly ceded to Lagos, so as to include Majada, and complete the junction, I trust, with Ikorodu, and extending the strip of Colony from the river Ogun on the west to the river Oshun on the east. From thence, as I have already advised your Lordship, I propose to visit Ibadan, dealing as I might judge expedient with Ogedemgi's case, and then proceeding via the eastern towns of Ijesa, and returning to Lagos through Ondo.

38

COMMISSIONER CLAUDE MACDONALD TO THE FOREIGN OFFICE: BENIN, 13 DECEMBER 1894[1]

I HAVE the honour in accordance with Section 5 Paragraph 102 of the 'African Order in Council 1893' to report for the information of Lord Kimberley that I have passed sentence of deportation for life on Nana Allama late chief of the Benin District.

'The grounds thereof and the proceedings thereunder' are enclosed herewith. I would respectfully beg to state that first count in the indictment is drawn up in accordance with the provisions laid down in Section 16 of the African Order above mentioned, which lays down that 'the provisions of any Treaty with Her Majesty or Her successors for the time being in force with respect to any place within the limits of any local Jurisdiction, shall have effect as part of the law to be enforced under this Order in relation to such, and in case of inconsistency between such provisions and the law in force in England, or anything contained in this Order, effect shall be given to such provisions.'

Nana has been deported to the Upper Cross River, one wife and his eldest son accompany him, a house has been provided for him and he receives subsistence at the rate of £10 a month.

39

NOTES.—PALAVER HELD AT IKIRUN.— IBADAN AND ILORIN BOUNDARY QUESTION, 21 DECEMBER 1894[2]

PRESENT:—Captains Bower, Lugard and Tucker.

On behalf of Ibadans.—Messenger of Bale of Ibadan and Ibadan Authorities,—Bale of Onisha and Akermu of Ikirun, Bales of Oyon Ijabi and Igbayi.

[1] F.O. 2/64. Minutes in the Foreign Office raised points of disagreement with this interpretation of the Order of 1893, but agreed 'to let things slide and to take no official notice of the despatch': Minutes 18 and 19 June by Kimberley. For the background to Nana's deportation, see J. C. Anene, *Southern Nigeria in Transition 1885–1906* (Cambridge, 1966), pp. 160–1.

[2] C.O. 879/41, no. 475. Encl. in Carter to Ripon, 29 December 1894. For Lugard's account of the negotiations and the demarcation of the boundary from Awere to Nupe (without orders), see Margery Perham and Mary Bull (eds.), *The Diaries of Lord Lugard* (4 vols., London, 1963), vol. iv, pp. 254–6. *Capt. R. L. Bower* was Resident of Ibadan, 1893–7; *Capt. W. R. Reeve Tucker* had been Assistant Inspector, Gold Coast Constabulary and the Lagos Constabulary; he became Lagos Commissioner of Police and a Travelling Commissioner. *F. J. D. Lugard*, after his expedition from Mombasa to Uganda, had entered the service of the Royal Niger

On behalf of Ilorins.—Messenger of Emir Balogun Ali and Magagi Ingeri. Messenger of Emir of Ilorin, asked to state what were the grounds for refusal to accept Captain Bower's decision, states:—

'The Ilorins wish Consuls to be left in those towns in which they existed before Captain Bower came to settle the boundary.'

Captain Bower states:—

'His Excellency the Governor has already given his decision with regard to those towns. Ikirun must remain an Ibadan town,' and proceeds to explain what took place when his Excellency the Governor put an end to the Ibadan and Ilorin war, that Ikirun and towns behind it *must* remain Ibadan, and Offa and towns behind that town be Ilorin territory, that a boundary should be drawn over the ground intervening between Ikirun and Offa, but that the Ilorins and Ibadans then stated that no boundary was necessary as they were brothers. Captain Bower then proceeds to state that he received instructions last year to arrange boundary with Emir of Ilorin, who had previously told his Excellency the Governor that he was prepared to abide by his decision. His Excellency the Governor forwards agreement proposing Awere as boundary, but Emir does not agree, claiming Ikirun and Ilesha, and states Awere runs through Ilorin farms, and ultimately refuses to sign any agreement. Captain Bower, who had taken agreement to Ilorin for signature, then left Ilorin: messenger of Emir in reply states—'The Emir is a friend of both Captains Bower and Lugard, and appeals to Captain Lugard to settle the matter.'

Captain Lugard recalls state of affairs when the respective fathers of the Emir and Bale of Ibadan ruled, that the cause of war then was practically the same question as was now before the Palaver, that his Excellency the Governor had stopped the war and sent the respective armies home, the question then being in dispute only where the boundary should be. His Excellency decided[1] Offa to be Ilorin, but that any people who had left that town during the war and gone to Ibadan towns could remain there. Ilorins are aware that a treaty exists between Ilorin and the Niger Company, and that the Niger Company agreed to his Excellency's proposals. All that remained was that a line should be fixed between Offa and Ikirun, which Captain Bower was deputed to do, settling the Awere as the boundary, as no Ilorin farms existed on the Ibadan side of that river.

Messenger of Emir states:—

'We will agree to Captain Lugard's decision.'

Ilorin messengers asked what Ilorin farms exist on Ibadan side of Awere, reply that farms exist at Okuku belonging to Erin.

Company in 1894 and commanded the expedition to Borgu (Nikki). For his later career, see Margery Perham, *Lugard the Years of Adventure 1858–1898* (London, 1956), and *Lugard the Years of Authority 1898–1945* (London, 1960).
[1] i.e. Sir Gilbert Carter.

Bale of Okuku states:—

'We gave the people of Erin lands to make farms before the war. Erin then being an Ibadan town. These are the only Ilorin farms. An Ilorin Consul was only placed at Erin in December last.'

Captain Lugard suggests to the Ibadans, as a solution to the difficulty, that the *Awere River* be the boundary having reference to Ilorin, and a swamp, called the *Awo Wotun*, be the boundary having reference to Ibadan, and that the intervening ground be *neutral*.

Captain Lugard states that this is his decision and that if the Emir does not agree he does not obey the wishes of either the Governor of Lagos or the Niger Company.

Captain Bower explains that his Excellency the Governor agreed that if Ilorin farms existed on the Ibadan side of the Awere, the boundary could be withdrawn to the Otin River, but that he, Captain Bower, has explained to his Excellency the falsity of the statements made by Ilorin messengers to Lagos that Ilorin farms existed on the Ibadan side of the Awere River. Captain Lugard states that the Emir writes him that the Olofa of Offa should remain in Offa under Ilorin, and with regard to that explains that his Excellency the Governor decided that the Offa people who remained in Offa at the end of the war should remain Ilorin subjects, but that those who resided in Ibadan territory should be Ibadan subjects if they so desired; that now Offa is an Ilorin town, Captain Lugard points out the Emir is at liberty to place whom he chooses at the head of affairs there, or do anything else he chooses with regard to the government of the place.

The messenger of the Emir states that he is only a slave and cannot decide for the Emir, but that the decision of Captain Lugard would be communicated and a reply returned.

W. R. Reeve Tucker,
R. L. Bower, Captain.
Resident.

40

MEMORANDUM: CASE OF THE BRASS CHIEFS, 8 JUNE 1895[1]

[The slave trade has been abolished; Article VI of the Treaty signed with Consul Hewett in 1886 guaranteed free trade.]

... THE Company which is now known as the Niger Company, has done us many injuries, which were made known to Consul Hewitt [*sic*] in writing; for some time after the Charter was granted they drove us away from our markets in which we and our forefathers had traded

---

[1] *F.O. Confidential Print*, 1468 (1895), F.O. 83/1382. Encl. in Kirk to Salisbury, 25 August 1895. For the Akassa rising and its consequences, see Flint, *Sir George Goldie*, chap. 9.

for generations, and did not allow us to get in our trust, or trade debts, some of which remain unpaid to this day. Neither will they permit the Ejoh or market people to come down and pay us.

In 1889, Major Macdonald, now our big Consul, came to us, and we told him of all these things, and he promised that he would lay our complaints before the Queen's Government; Consul Hewitt was still in the Rivers.

In 1891, he, Major MacDonald, came again and explained to us that it was the intention of the Queen's Government to send Consuls to these rivers and that we should then have a Consul of our own who would specially look after our interests. He pointed out to us that this could not be done without money, and explained how the money could be raised by means of duty, and asked whether we consented to pay these duties. At first we refused, because we could get no satisfactory answer about our markets; but eventually we signed, but begged the Major that he would do what he could to get some of our markets back for us. He then appointed a Vice-Consul, Captain MacDonald to the River.

Since then we have seen the Major many times, and he has always told us to be patient, but latterly things have gone from bad to worse, and the markets that we have are quite insufficient to maintain us.

We thoroughly understand that all markets are free, and open to everybody, black and white man alike; and we are quite willing to trade side by side with the white man at those markets. We do not now ask for any exclusive privileges whatever, but only that we may be allowed to trade without molestation at the places we and our fathers have traded in days gone by.

We are willing to pay fair duties: but we cannot understand, however, if all markets are free and open to black and white man alike, why there are many villages or markets in the Niger where neither are allowed to go and trade.

We submit that, if we have to go to Akassa, a distance of nearly 40 miles, to pay our duties, and are only allowed to trade at certain places selected by the Niger Company called 'ports of entry,' and have to take out trade and spirit licences, and pay a very heavy duty going into the territories and a heavy duty coming out, it is the same thing as if we were forbidden to trade at all.

The Niger Company say, 'We (the Company) have to do these things, why not you?'

We can only say that, with our resources, to carry out these Regulations and pay these duties means ruin to us.

The Niger Company are cleverer than we are. We humbly submit that we have a right, confirmed by our Treaty, to go and trade freely in the places we have traded at for all these generations. We are ready to pay to do so, but let us pay a fair duty, and conform to fair Regulations.

The duties and Regulations of the Company mean to us ruin; of this there is no doubt.

We do not deny that we have smuggled, but under the circumstances can this be wondered at?

We have suffered many hardships from the Company's Regulations. Our people have been fired upon by the Company's launches, they have been fired upon from the Company's hulks, our canoes have been seized and goods taken, sometimes when engaged in what white men call smuggling, and sometimes when not.

The 'chop' canoes coming from the Ejohs have also been stopped.

Within the last few weeks the Niger Company has sent messengers to the Ejohs and other tribes with whom we have always traded and said that any of them who traded with us at all, or who paid us their debts, would be severely punished, and their villages burnt.

We have evidence to prove all this, which we would like to lay before the big man who has been sent by the Queen.

All these unjust things that have been done to us, the many times we have been told to be patient and have been so, and the wrongs which we consider we have suffered are now worse than ever, all these drove us to take the law into our own hands and attack the Company's factories at Akassa.

We know now we have done wrong, and for this wrong we have been severely punished; but we submit that the many unjust oppressions we have borne have been very great, and it is only in self-defence, and with a view to have our wrongs inquired into, that we have done this thing. We have frequently asked the Consuls that have been put over us, from Consul Hewitt to the present time, to tell us in what way we have offended the Queen to cause her to send this trouble on us.

Traders we are, have been, and always will be.

The soil of our country is too poor to cultivate sufficient food for all our people, and so if we do not trade and get food from other tribes we shall suffer great want and misery.

We fervently hope and pray that some arrangements may be arrived at which will enable us to pursue our trade in peace and quietness.

Warri, his x mark.

Karemma ditto.

Thomas Okea, ditto.

Nathaniel Hardstone, ditto

Witnesses:

    H. L. Gallwey,

      Deputy Commissioner and Vice-Consul,

      Benin District.

    Cuthbert E. Harrison,

      Acting Vice-Consul, Brass District.

41

CAPTAIN R. L. BOWER TO THE ACTING COLONIAL SECRETARY, LAGOS: OYO, 12 NOVEMBER 1895[1]

I HAVE the honour to state that the Alafin and his chiefs, not having agreed to the conditions imposed on him by me, I early this morning started to bombard the town and advanced towards the big square.

On arriving there I was received with a heavy fire from the houses each side of the square, and from several hundred men posted at the top of the square. I halted to return the fire, and sent round flanking parties, whereupon they dispersed in all directions.

I then set fire to the Alafin's palace and the houses round it, and returned to the mission.

One of the head Chiefs, Onasokun by name, has given his submission to me, and I have informed him that all people desirous of peace can return to their houses and will not be molested.

The Alafin, I am informed, has escaped to Ogbomosho.

42

HENRY MORLEY (ROYAL NIGER COMPANY) TO COLONIAL OFFICE: ILORIN, 20 NOVEMBER 1895[2]

I AM directed to acknowledge the receipt by the Governor and Council of your letter of yesterday's date—marked 'Confidential'—inclosing copy of a letter from the Colonial Office, on the subject of the Emir of Ilorin: and they at once telegraphed imperative instructions to the Niger Territories to urge on the Emir that he should maintain friendly relations with the Government of Lagos. They are not, however, confident that very effective action can be taken at the moment, beyond withholding the Ilorin subsidy. Diplomacy is of very little use during a revolution such as is now going on in Ilorin. The late Emir has quite recently been murdered, together with five of his sons, and a number of his principal followers, and the new Emir's position is unstable.

The proper course would be for the Company to occupy Ilorin with an armed force; but this step cannot be taken until some settlement is arrived at which will put an end to the critical state of affairs on the

[1] C.O. 879/45, no. 509. Encl. in Denton to Chamberlain, 20 November 1895. This action was approved in Chamberlain to Carter, 13 January 1896.
[2] C.O. 879/41, no. 475.

frontiers of the Niger Coast Protectorate, which fully occupies all the force that the Company is able to spare from the regions of the Benue, where the slave raiders are giving very serious trouble.

43

JOSEPH CHAMBERLAIN TO ACTING GOVERNOR F. ROHRWEGER: ILORIN, 4 NOVEMBER 1896[1]

NOVEMBER 4.—Secret and Confidential. Referring to your telegrams of 2nd October and 9th October, I am afraid that for us to raise blockade, or take initiative in overtures, Ilorin, might be regarded as a sign of weakness. I am informed confidentially that Company are about to undertake military operations right bank of Niger, and at request of Goldie I have decided not to authorise hostile operations against Ilorins at present. In the meantime Denton should endeavour to get into friendly communications with Ilorin if this can be done without any appearance of weakness.

44

J. R. PHILLIPS TO THE MARQUIS OF SALISBURY: BENIN, 16 NOVEMBER 1896[2]

... 13. To sum up, the situation is this:—the King of Benin whose country is within a British Protectorate and whose City lies within fifty miles of a Protectorate Customs Station and who has signed a treaty with Her Majesty's representative, has deliberately stopped all trade and effectually blocked the way to all progress in that part of the Protectorate. The Jakri traders, a most important and most loyal tribe whose prosperity depends to a very great extent upon the produce they can get from the Benin Country, have appealed to this Government to give them such assistance as will enable them to pursue their lawful trade. The whole of the English merchants represented on the River have petitioned the Government for aid to enable them to keep their Factories open, and last but not perhaps least the Revenues of this Protectorate are suffering.

[1] C.O. 879/45, no. 509.
[2] F.O. 2/102. The Foreign Office agreed and arranged the expedition with the War Office: W.O. to C.O., 24 December 1896. For the ambush and death of Phillips, see *Parl. Papers*, 1897 [C. 8440]; Anene, *Southern Nigeria*, pp. 188–96. *J. R. Phillips* was Deputy Commissioner of the Niger Coast Protectorate, 1896–7.

14. I am certain that there is only one remedy, that is to depose the King of Benin from his Stool. I am convinced from information, which leaves no room for doubt, as well as from experience of native character, that pacific measures are now quite useless, and that the time has now come to remove the obstruction.

15. I therefore ask his Lordship's permission to visit Benin City in February next, to depose and remove the King of Benin, and to establish a Native Council in his place and take such further steps for the opening up of the Country as the occasion may require.

45

SIR GEORGE GOLDIE TO ACTING GOVERNOR G. C. DENTON: ILORIN, 18 FEBRUARY 1897[1]

IN view of the interest felt by your Government in the Ilorin question, I venture to trouble you with the following brief report, and I shall be obliged if you will forward a copy to the Secretary of State for the Colonies. I am, of course, preparing a full report for the Secretary of State for Foreign Affairs, who will doubtless communicate it to the Colonial Office, but this fuller report cannot be completed at once, and I shall take it home with me, as I am returning at once to London, having fully succeeded, and to an extent beyond my expectations, in the three expeditions which I came out to direct.

Believing that Ilorin would accede peacefully to my suggestions after the fall of Bida, and having received the written submission of the Emir Suliman, I only brought from Jebba one half of the troops, and less than half of the guns, with which the battle of Bida had been won. I knew, however, that I could not find an opposing force more than one-fourth that of Bida; and, moreover, that our troops, flushed with success, were fit to combat much larger numbers.

On the 14th instant, at the River Araibi, ten miles from the City of Ilorin, I learnt from my spies that the four Baloguns, or War Chiefs, had compelled the Emir to agree to fight, and that the whole Ilorin forces were drawn up near the River Oyon, three or four miles from Ilorin, and were advancing to meet us.

The battle commenced about 8 a.m. on the 15th inst. and lasted till the afternoon of the 16th. We were compelled to inflict very heavy losses on the enemy. The Balogun Alanamu, the most warlike

---

[1] C.O. 879/45, no. 509. *Sir George Goldie* formed the United (National) African Company, 1879, and became Deputy-Governor and Governor of the Chartered Royal Niger Company; he personally directed the Niger–Sudan campaign in 1897, after working out the details in a confidential circular, 1 January 1897: Royal Niger Company Papers, vol. iv, Rhodes House Library, Oxford.

of the four War Chiefs, has just told me that we killed over 200 horsemen; and as the foot soldiers were in the proportion of about six to
one, it may be assumed that their total loss exceeded a thousand. We
then bombarded the town (which unfortunately caught fire) and took
possession of it, the Emir, four Baloguns and all other Chiefs flying
dispersed to distant villages.

While the troops were occupied in stopping the conflagration,
I took active steps to enter in communication with the Emir, who
has always been most faithful to his treaty with the Company. To-
day, at noon, the Emir and four Baloguns with other Chiefs surrendered to us and came here to negotiate a new treaty, which was
signed in the presence of all the troops and many spectators in the
great square. The Emir recognises the entire power of the Company
over all the Ilorin territory, and that he will govern in accordance
with the directions given him from time to time; that he must not
make war without consent of the Company; that he must accept such
frontier between Ilorin and Lagos as may be directed.

I told the Emir and Baloguns that, pending Her Majesty's decision,
the frontier must be that fixed by Captain Bower some time ago on
behalf of Sir Gilbert Carter. I carefully abstained from holding out
any hopes that this frontier line would be rectified, but I think it
right to inform you that I reserve to myself the liberty to reopen this
question with Her Majesty's Government.

The Emir and Baloguns were greatly concerned with the difficulty
they would have, after their crushing defeat, in organising any
government in the Ilorin territory. I told them, however, that the
Company felt that any government is better than anarchy, that they
were at liberty to take the steps taken by all governments to enforce
order in the regions left under their authority; but that they must
wait for one month before taking such steps in the southern portion
lying to the north of the Lagos frontier and Odo Otin, so as to give
me time to inform you of what had taken place and to give you time
to issue instructions to your officials and troops, so that the approach
of Ilorin horsemen to the neighbourhood of the Lagos frontier should
not be mistaken for a renewal of hostilities.

There is no fear of such renewal for a generation to come. The
Ilorin power is completely broken. The four Baloguns, Alanamu,
Salu, Ajikobi, and Suberu, were far more humble and broken than
the peaceful Emir Suliman, whom they had forced into war, and who
behaved today with great dignity, although with a keen sense of the
entirely new position created by our conquest of Ilorin.

I have arranged that some of our troops shall move frequently
along the Ilorin side of the *temporary* Lagos frontier, so as to ensure
order and the roads being kept open. No garrison will be left
permanently in Ilorin City, but troops will visit it occasionally.

We leave here to-morrow to receive the submission of another Sokoto province, Lafiagi, so that letters to me should be addressed via Buruthu, Forcados, that being far more rapid than via Akassa . . . I find to my regret, that the greater part of the City of Ilorin has been burnt.

46

GOVERNOR SIR H. E. McCALLUM TO JOSEPH CHAMBERLAIN: EGBA, 4 SEPTEMBER 1897[1]

[Captain Denton has been sent to Abeokuta to discuss tolls and the railway.]

. . . IN para: 5 of his report Captain Denton refers to [the Alake] as an imbecile drunkard incapable of taking any active interest in public affairs. Competent or incompetent however, he is the titular head of the Government and in view of clause 5 of the Treaty of January 18th 1893, it is important that this Government should take no step which might be characterized as aggressive action but that we should do what we can to lead and not to drive the Egbas.

5. I have therefore approved of the arrangement made by Captain Denton (para: 4 of his report) by which the Alake will continue to be recognized by the Lagos Government as the principal authority of Abeokuta assisted by the Balogun and the Seriki. I have accordingly addressed him a letter . . . in which I take the opportunity of informing him that Abeokuta must not be allowed to stand still but that we must look to material progress being made.

6. I must confess that I cannot regard the present arrangement as a stable one. It is right however to give it a trial though it will probably end before very long in the Alake being invited 'to go to sleep' and my being obliged to visit Abeokuta to see how best the Government of that town can be conducted.

7. From Sir Gilbert Carter's despatch . . . it appears that in 1893 he invited the Egba authorities to accept a Resident to assist them in the Government but they would not listen to this proposal. Since 1893 the situation has undergone important changes. A railway constructed at the expense of this Government will before long be at the gates of Abeokuta and complicated questions may at any time arise through our having at present no locus standi in the country except that it is included in our sphere of influence.

[1] C.O. 147/117. Denton's report, 27 August 1897 (valuable for its discussion of labour recruitment) enclosed. *Lieut.-Col. Sir H. E. McCallum* had served as a surveyor and colonial engineer in the Straits Settlements; Governor of Lagos, 1897–9. For his policy, see Newbury, *Western Slave Coast*, pp. 188–9.

8. The French, moreover since 1893, have adopted an aggressive attitude in the direction of territories under our influence lying to the north and west of the Egba boundaries and threaten trade routes . . . unless we adopt suitable counter-measures which will involve closer relations with the territories in question.

9. Abeokuta itself under the present régime is not progressing; there is also much oppression of the people . . . From all the information which I can gather the people themselves would much like closer connection with the British Government but dare not oppose their Chiefs who through self interests are inimical to the idea, a feeling in which they are supported by a certain section of the Lagos community.

10. Captain Denton discussed privately with the Chiefs the idea originally submitted to them by Sir Gilbert Carter with the result that he is persuaded that they will never dare to ask for a Resident of their own accord . . .

11. The situation therefore is that whilst willing to give the present régime a fair trial, the political and material condition of the Egba country is such that unless this régime be more successful than in the past we may find it extremely difficult if not impossible to avoid concluding with the Alake and his Chiefs a new Treaty giving the British Government greater control than we have at present whilst preserving to the nation its independence as secured to them by the treaty of 1893. . . .

47

SIR GEORGE GOLDIE TO THE FOREIGN OFFICE: SOKOTO AND GWANDU, 15 NOVEMBER 1897[1]

. . . Turning to the more important point of the letter, I am inclined to believe that the relations of French officers to the west of the Niger with the Sultan of Gandu are at present excellent. So long as they remain to the west of the Niger, they will not be felt by him as a menace to his capital; and if they have committed the folly of supplying him, as Lieutenant Mizon supplied the Emirs of Muri and Adamawa, with rifles and ammunition, he will doubtless display a degree of friendship calculated to produce further gifts.

It must not be forgotten that the Sultan of Gandu has felt some soreness towards the Company since the commencement of this year, when two provinces of his section of the Sokoto Empire were wrested from him, and practically the only sources of his slave supply were dried up.

---

[1] C.O. 879/50, no. 538. Encl. in F.O. to C.O., 22 September 1897.

There is reason to believe that Gandu's Suzerain, the Sultan of Sokoto, has also been tampered with by messages and presents from the French. Until quite recently the Sultan of Sokoto had shown unexpected moderation in the delicate questions of Nupe and Ilorin, and had exercised restraint over the declarations of the Sultan of Gandu. Two or three months ago the Company became aware that emissaries from the French were penetrating the Sokoto Empire, and distinctly menacing news has now been received from that quarter. This is a matter of indifference to the Company, which, in its present positions, is perfectly able to take care of itself. I have not any expectation that, after the experiences of Bida and Ilorin, any Fulah force will be found ready to advance against the Company. Nor is there any ground for fear that the Emirs of provinces near the waterways, such as Yola (Adamawa), Muri, Bautshi, and so forth will depart from their present prudent and friendly attitude. I should, perhaps, state here that Yola and Muri have just signed new treaties with the Company, giving it the fullest powers of jurisdiction.

The menacing tone of Sokoto is no doubt adopted in the hope of inducing the Company to restore the late Emir of Nupe, Abu Bokari, and I do not wish to be understood as saying that this may not be ultimately the best course, under sufficient guarantees. Abu Bokari has expressed his intention to follow the wishes of the Company if he is replaced on the throne. The present Emir of Nupe, Mamadu or Mohammed, is an excellent man and peaceably inclined, but he has not the strength of character of Abu Bokari, and a strong man is needed in Bida.

I have not the slightest doubt that when an arrangement is arrived at with France, the Sultan of Sokoto will immediately revert to the peaceful attitude adopted by him between the fall of Bida and the commencement of September 1897. Apart from French intrigues, there is no reason why friendly relations with Sokoto need be disturbed for generations to come, if ever. The gradual extinction of the immense slave-raiding operations to the south of the River Benue, between 1889 and 1894, was finally accepted by him in the latter year. The same but more summary process in Nupe and Ilorin was, until recently, passing off without serious complaint. All the benefits of developing the Sokoto Empire can be attained without the cost and bloodshed of conquest. I do not believe that the Foulah Empire could be fully conquered, even by the Company for less than £750,000.

It is undoubtedly inconvenient to have French officers on our frontiers intriguing with the rulers of a portion of our territories which was, in the Anglo-French Agreement of August 1890, expressly excluded by name from the French sphere of influence and left to the Royal Niger Company. The inconvenience is only temporary, but the system is unfair and one-sided, as the Company could not carry on similar intrigues in French territory, believing that disasters to one European nationality in Equatorial Africa rebound on all other such nationalities.

48

CHIEF JUSTICE H. C. GOLLAN TO HIGH COMMISSIONER SIR F. D. LUGARD: NORTHERN NIGERIAN TREATIES, 19 SEPTEMBER 1902[1]

[The Sultan of Sokoto retained his full rights of sovereignty by the Treaty of 1 June 1885, and he might have been entitled to abrogate it.]

. . . IT is, of course, clear that the rules of international law do not apply to dealings between civilised and uncivilised states, but I cannot see by what principle it could be said that the Sultan would not have been entitled to abrogate the Treaty of 1st June 1885, for failure to pay the subsidy . . .

The Treaty of the 16th April 1890, merely confers jurisdiction upon the Company over non-natives, but no more affects the independent sovereignty of the Sultan than the capitulations do that of the Sultan of Turkey.

The Treaty of the 26th June 1894, contains, in this connection, two most vital clauses, 6 and 8. By the former clause the Sultan agrees not to recognise any other white nation 'because the Company are my help', and by Clause 8 the Company undertake 'not to interfere with the customs of the Mussulmans, but to maintain friendly relations' . . .

The Sultan no longer speaks as an independent Sovereign conferring rights and franchises as his predecessor did in the two former Treaties, but expressly acknowledges his dependence upon the Company, and expressly stipulates for by the 'helping' or 'protecting' power for non-interference with the rights of Mussulmans. It appears to me that this Treaty constitutes a surrender of the status of the Sultan of Sokoto as an independent ruler, and relegates him to the position of the Ruler of a protected Native African State . . .

[The transfer of the administration from the Royal Niger Company to the Government of the Protectorate has resulted in the lapse of subsidies.]

The payment of the subsidy promised was in no way made a condition for the surrender of independence—it was an independent term of the Treaties, and I am, therefore, of opinion that mere failure

[1] C.O. 879/80, no. 718. For the details of the conquest of Northern Nigeria, see D. J. M. Muffett, *Concerning Brave Captains* (London, 1964), Parts I and II; Perham and Bull, *Lugard*, vol. ii, pp. 87–136.

or even refusal to pay it—which would have entitled an independent Sovereign to denounce them—does not affect the validity of the Treaties made with Sokoto . . .

[The position of the ruler of Gwandu is similar, by the treaties of 13 June 1885, 7 April 1890, and 4 July 1894.]

49

HIGH COMMISSIONER SIR F. D. LUGARD TO THE EARL OF ONSLOW: KANO, 12 DECEMBER 1902[1]

. . . REFERRING to your telegram . . . information received that Kano preparations completed for provoking war, demonstration in favour of murderer of Moloney. Safety of the garrison of Zaria, prestige of British Government, possibility of delimitation of frontier depend on energetic action. Paramount chiefs in this country await result and if action deferred they would attribute to fear of them, possibility of deplorable result. Probable number of troops 1,000. Despatch sent.

50

THE EARL OF ONSLOW TO HIGH COMMISSIONER SIR F. D. LUGARD: SOKOTO, 28 JANUARY 1903[2]

[Relations with Sokoto have deteriorated, especially since Lugard's Proclamation of 1900.]

. . . 6. YOU are aware that the policy of His Majesty's Government has always been to avoid, if possible, any rupture with Sokoto, although they have not concealed from themselves that the measures which they authorized you to take to suppress slave-raiding would probably bring us into conflict sooner or later with the Sultan. It is necessary in the interests both of humanity and of trade, that slave-raiding by organized bands, causing widespread misery and blood-shed and depopulating the country, should be met by force and suppressed so far as this can be done with the troops at your disposal; but there is no desire on the part of His Majesty's Government to destroy the existing forms of administration or to govern the country otherwise than through its own rulers . . .

[A march on Kano has become necessary; but it has not been planned to attack Sokoto.]

[1] C.O. 879/79, no. 713.   [2] C.O. 879/80, no. 718.

51

HIGH COMMISSIONER SIR F. D. LUGARD
TO JOSEPH CHAMBERLAIN:
SOKOTO, 15 JANUARY 1903[1]

... 7. REFERRING to the strong feeling which you inform me exists in England that military operations should, if possible, be avoided, and the desirability of conciliatory measures, the following is the translation of a letter I received from the late Emir of Sokoto last May, and which has not been withdrawn by his successor:—
'I do not consent that anyone from you should ever dwell with us. I will never agree with you; I will have nothing ever to do with you. Between us and you there are no dealings except as between Mussulmin and unbelievers (Karifi)—war, as God Almighty has enjoined on us. There is no power or strength save in God on High'.

To send a messenger to Kano [sic] would probably be tantamount to condemning him to death and courting insult myself. When the time comes that the Administration of Northern Nigeria is content to allow the murder of an unarmed Resident to pass unavenged, and witness his reception with honour by a State within the Protectorate itself without effective protest, the advocates of a conciliatory policy may look with some confidence to such a widespread contempt for the British as would lead to constant uprising and bloodshed ...

[Conciliation is impossible; military force has suppressed the slave trade at Bida, Kontagora, Yola, Bautshi, Ilorin, Zaria.]

52

HIGH COMMISSIONER SIR F. D. LUGARD
TO JOSEPH CHAMBERLAIN:
SOKOTO, 27 MARCH 1903[2]

SOKOTO March 19. Sokoto occupied 15th March: feeble resistance: Sultan (and) chiefs fled. I arrived this morning: hope to effect full settlement early: Wazeri and Sultan's brother returned home today: many native followers. I am breaking up expeditionary force: Kemball leaves for Zungeru day after tomorrow: Lagos (and) Southern Nigeria reserve men returning home. All well. Boundary Commissioners are here.

---

[1] Ibid. For a discussion of this translation of the Emir's letter, see Muffett, *Brave Captains*, pp. 40–51, and for a full text, pp. 83–5.
[2] C.O. 879 80, no. 718.

53

ACTING HIGH COMMISSIONER W. WALLACE TO JOSEPH CHAMBERLAIN: BURMI, 18 SEPTEMBER 1903[1]

I HAVE the honour to transmit herewith, for your information, copies of reports received from Major Barlow and Major Plummer relating to the capture of Burmi and final overthrow of the ex-Sultan of Sokoto's forces which resulted in his death along with many of his principal chiefs who had taken part in the defence.

Without a doubt the later phases of this rising have been watched with the keenest interest by all the Mohammedan States, Captain Sword's repulse at Burmi, which check to our arms was greatly exaggerated throughout Hausaland, having raised hopes among the ruling race that there might still be a chance of their regaining their old status; however, after the crushing defeat inflicted, their last hope must have fallen to the ground, as practically the whole of the irreconcilable chiefs who dared to put it to the touch to win or lose, have perished along with their leader, and with, from first to last, over 1,000 of their fanatical followers, who, as a rule, bravely faced our rifle fire, but always refused or failed to charge right home, wherein lay their only chance of success against our troops. Of course, one must take into consideration the great stopping power of our bullets, Mark IV., which was one of the principal factors leading to our success. Without this ammunition, I am of opinion that our success would have been very doubtful. The ex-Sultan fought bravely, leaving the shelter of the mosque when he heard that the troops had effected an entrance into the town; he was killed . . . and round his body were piled the corpses of 90 of his followers . . .

[The whole country has been 'sitting on the fence'; casualties were one European killed and eight wounded, sixteen Africans killed and 148 wounded.]

[1] C.O. 879/80, no. 718. (Sir) William Wallace, former Agent-General of the Royal Niger Company; Resident-General and Deputy High Commissioner, Northern Nigeria, 1900–10.

II

EXPANSION AND INTERNATIONAL PARTITION

Introductory Note

THE need for territorial expansion was a late development in British West African policy. Primarily, the establishment of interior protectorates was a reaction to French and German expansion, plus a traditional interest in preserving and pre-empting existing and potential markets. The timing of advances and the compromises reached in European diplomatic negotiations derived from complex local factors in Africa and international considerations beyond Africa. But, in the main, the motivation for British decisions to expand stemmed from a need for increased customs revenues in the 1870s and a fear that French protectionist policies might be applied in vast areas of the West African interior in the 1880s.

Between 1875 and 1880 attempts were made to offset the rising cost of the West African posts by expanding customs jurisdiction and taking strategic river and coastal ports under British protection. These efforts in the Scarcies river basin, at Katanu in Southern Dahomey, and in the Volta markets east of the Gold Coast were the consequence of the breakdown of another of the many Gambia exchange schemes, 1875–6, and the refusal of the Sierra Leone administration to agree to tariff equalization with French posts south of Senegal. By 1880, these minor imperial advances had been checked by Lord Salisbury's decision that Cabinet approval was required for further territorial acquisitions in West Africa.

Nevertheless, in conditions of trade recession on the coast, both the Colonial Office and the Foreign Office remained anxious about French activities in Southern Dahomey and on the Lower Niger. The unratified Anglo-French Convention of 1882 left open many questions about Sierra Leone and Guinea boundaries. This check to the rationalization of European rivalries on the coast led to an excessive reliance on paper treaties among colonial administrations, as a method of keeping open their hinterland for trade. The same concern for 'free trade' underlay the British position during the Berlin Conference which allowed Great Britain to consolidate her position on the Lower Niger and in the Oil Rivers Protectorate. The entry of Germany into West African partition added a new and unexpected dimension to international agreements about boundaries and spheres of influence, 1887–90.

These agreements which extended British jurisdiction, often in advance of administrative occupation, roughed out the main lines of future advances from bases in the Gambia, Gold Coast, Sierra Leone, and Nigerian enclaves. By 1890 the long official reluctance to make such advances was largely dispelled.

The second phase of West African partition to settle the details of the Anglo-French Declaration of 1890 and the provisions of the Anglo-German Heligoland Agreement, threw into relief the weakness of reliance on treaties to counter French or German advances. British diplomacy on West Africa aimed, in the main, at salvaging the British conception of 'free trade' in negotiations with France over Gyaman in 1893 (II. 41) and in the Sierra Leone–Guinea demarcation with its separate clauses on tariffs in 1895 (II. 46). More important, the rapid French advance into Borgu after 1894 and the numerous, but defective, Niger Company treaties gave rise to the long series of negotiations in Paris over the Niger–Chad boundary. The French challenge led Chamberlain to authorize the use of force in September 1897 in the manœuvres for posts in the Nigerian and Gold Coast interiors. In June 1898 the West African difficulties with France were smoothed out in an extensive agreement which offered access to the navigable Niger, in return for a conventional tariff zone from the Ivory Coast to Lake Chad. The following year the principles governing the partition of the neutral zone were laid down by agreement with Germany. The rest was left to boundary commissions on the ground.

I

LORD CARNARVON TO THE OFFICER ADMINISTERING SIERRA LEONE: MATAKONG, 25 FEBRUARY 1875[1]

I HAVE to acknowledge the receipt of Mr. French's[2] despatch of the 13th ultimo, furnishing information respecting the Island of Matacong and the adjoining territories.

In the 13th paragraph of his despatch Mr. French states that the courts of Sierra Leone exercise jurisdiction in the territories ceded to Her Majesty by the two Treaties of 29th November, 1847, but that not a single civil officer in the service of the Settlement is stationed in those territories.

With reference to the statements which have from time to time been made to this Department as to the evasion of the payment of Customs duties at Sierra Leone by landing goods on the neighbouring coasts and conveying them thence into the interior, I should wish to be informed whether much illicit trade of this kind is carried on in the territories above-mentioned, and whether any gain to the Colonial revenue would be likely to accrue from collecting duties there.

[1] *Parl. Papers*, 1876, lii [C. 1409], p. 24. *The Earl of Carnarvon* (Henry H. M. Herbert), Under-Secretary, 1858–9; Secretary of State for Colonies, 1866–7, 1874–8.
[2] Chief Justice G. French, Acting Governor, to Carnarvon, 13 June 1875, ibid.

If upon inquiry you should be of opinion that payment of duties may, with advantage and profit to the Settlement, be enforced in these territories, I have to instruct you to take the necessary steps for stationing Customs officers at the different trading posts.

2

MEMORANDUM RESPECTING PROPOSALS FOR AN EXCHANGE OF BRITISH AND FRENCH TERRITORIES ON THE WEST COAST OF AFRICA [JUNE 1875][1]

HER Majesty's Government propose to transfer absolutely to the Government of France, in exchange for the territories hereinafter named, all the territory constituting the British Colony of the Gambia, with its territorial and Sovereign rights; and Her Majesty's Government further undertake not to acquire any Possessions, or to exercise any political influence or protection over any tribes or territories, on the West Coast of Africa lying between the northern branch of the River Pongas and the northern limit of the existing French Possessions.

The French Government, in return for the foregoing concessions, undertake to transfer to the British Government the French Settlements of Dabou, Grand Bassam, Assiné, and the Establishment in the Mellicourie river, together with all the Sovereign or territorial rights which they may possess over the adjacent territories; and the French Government further agree not to retain or acquire any Possessions, or to exercise any political influence or protection over any of the territories or tribes, on the West Coast of Africa lying between the northern branch of the River Pongas, on the north, and the French Settlement of the Gaboon, on the south.

The foregoing arrangements will not prevent either the English or French Governments from enforcing redress from natives for any wrongs which British or French subjects may have suffered at their hands in the territories within which either Government has agreed not to acquire Possessions nor to exercise any political influence or protection.

A Joint Commission shall be appointed to examine on the spot and to define the limits of the territories to be surrendered on either side, or in which either party undertake not to retain or acquire Sovereign rights or jurisdiction, and to report the value of the public buildings and stores which on either side may have to be taken over in consequence of the interchange of territories; and the difference in value of the said public buildings and stores will be made good in money to the Government in whose favour the excess of value may be found to exist.

It is further agreed that British subjects in the territories of the Gambia about to be exchanged with France shall enjoy the same facilities, and be placed in the same position in regard to trade, as French subjects; and, on the other hand, French subjects shall, in the territories about to be transferred by France to the British Government, enjoy the same facilities and privileges for trading as British subjects.

3

R. H. MEADE TO T. V. LISTER: NEGOTIATIONS WITH FRANCE, 15 MARCH 1876[1]

. . . 2. FROM the *note verbale* sent to Lord Lyons by the Duc Decazes . . . Lord Carnarvon understands that the French Government object to the acquisition by Her Majesty's Government of jurisdiction over the coast line between the present boundaries of the Gold Coast and those of Lagos, more particularly from the apprehension that such jurisdiction might result in the establishment of tariffs prohibitory of the importation of those French products which are stated to be indispensable for purposes of exchange in countries now independent.

3. Lord Carnarvon would suggest to the Earl of Derby that, in reply to this note, the French Government should be clearly informed that the object of Her Majesty's Government was undoubtedly to acquire the entire control over the trade along the whole length of coast on which it has been proposed that French should cease to exercise any influence, Her Majesty's Government reserving to themselves the right to consider at what particular points English officials should be stationed, and that nothing short of the acquisition of power to control and regulate all tariffs, and, in case of need, even to prohibit absolutely the importation of arms and ammunition, without being obliged to seek the concurrence of any other Power purporting to have a political interest in any part of this line of coast, would justify the cession in exchange of so important a post as the Settlement on the Gambia.

4. As therefore there is a material divergence between the views of Her Majesty's Government and those of the French Government with regard to a very important part of the subject-matter of the negotiations, and as Lord Carnarvon would not feel himself at liberty to propose to Parliament any less favourable exchange than that

[1] C.O. 879/9, no. 92; C.O. 87/109, F.O. to C.O., 1 and 10 March 1876 (for French refusals). The above was based on a minute by Herbert, 10 March 1876, and was summed up in F.O. to Lord Lyons, 18 March 1876 (draft).

which he has already indicated, he would suggest that the French Government should be informed that, for the above reasons, the present negotiations for an exchange of territory must be considered as closed . . .

4

LORD CARNARVON TO GOVERNOR C. H. KORTRIGHT: SCARCIES CUSTOMS POSTS, 16 JUNE 1876[1]

. . . 4. As, however, the position of affairs is now entirely altered by the failure of the negotiations with France, I am prepared to authorise you to open communications with the Chiefs of the Great and Little Scarcies in order to acquire from them the right of placing Customs officers in those rivers, and collecting duties there upon terms similar to those sanctioned in the case of the territories to the south of Sierra Leone. I need hardly inform you that Her Majesty's Government do not in this case desire any extension of local sovereignty, and that the jurisdiction to be acquired should be fiscal and not political.

5. I have recently authorised you to retain Dr. Rowe for a short time in order to enable him to inquire into and report upon the civil establishment of the Settlement, and if you desire to make use of his experience in conducting these negotiations you are at liberty to do so, and to defer his departure to the Gambia accordingly.

6. In my Despatch above quoted I pointed out that before commencing any negotiations for acquiring the right of collecting Customs duties, it would be necessary for you to assure yourself that the revenue likely to be obtained would warrant the expense of placing a Customs establishment to collect it, and you will be guided by the same instructions in the case of Matacong and the Scarcies districts.

7. Before taking any action in the matter you will clearly satisfy yourself that no other European power has any claims over the Scarcies districts, and you will make no final and definitive agreement with the Chiefs without a previous reference to me.

8. With respect to the Island of Matacong the case appears somewhat different. It appears that that island was ceded to this country by clause 6 of a Treaty dated 18th April 1826, but as I understand no steps have yet been taken to exercise British jurisdiction there. As, however, it is represented that the establishment of a Customs station on that island is necessary in order to control the importation of goods through the rivers of the adjacent mainland, this arrangement may be made on securing a final report from you after you or Dr. Rowe have personally visited the island . . .

[1] C.O. 879/11, no. 139.

5

LAW OFFICERS TO COLONIAL OFFICE: SCARCIES CUSTOMS POSTS, 29 MAY 1877[1]

. . . WE have the honour to report—

That, although there would be no objection in principle to enforcing the duties if they were granted to Her Majesty as lessee from the Native Chiefs, yet inasmuch as the act of enforcing them would in that case depend for its validity upon the title of the lessors, we think it would be extremely difficult to prove that title in the event of being questioned, especially as we understand that the area over which the duties are intended to be levied is not an area held in common by all the Chiefs, but an area made up of several territories, each of which is claimed by a separate Chief.

Under these circumstances, we submit for your Lordship's consideration whether it would not be safer and at all events free from the difficulties we have pointed out, if a slip of territory along the beach and the banks of the rivers were ceded to Her Majesty. In that event Her Majesty could enforce as one of the ordinary rights of sovereignty the duties from all vessels frequenting the coast line in question.

6

REPORT OF THE DEPARTMENTAL COMMITTEE ON SIERRA LEONE: EXPANSION FOR REVENUE, 20 JULY 1877[2]

[Revenues which depend on customs have declined since 1871. Agreements have been made with chiefs to the south and north of Sierra Leone for cession of customs, and in the past portions of coast have been acquired for fiscal purposes.]

23. HAVING regard, then, to all the circumstances of the case, we recommend that,—

(1.) Her Majesty should be advised to confirm the Treaty made by Lieutenant-Governor Rowe with the Chiefs of the Great and Little Scarcies Rivers, and to accept the offer of a cession of coast line made therein, the amount to be taken to be limited to so much as will give the command over the mouths of the rivers, and confer the right to

---

[1] C.O. 879/11, no. 139. Signed by John Holker, Hardinge S. Gifford. Also Law Officers to C.O., 19 June 1877 (a customs protectorate could not be enforced against foreign vessels).
[2] Ibid. The members of the committee were: Sir Julian Pauncefote, Assistant Under-Secretary for Colonies, 1874–6, Assistant Under-Secretary, Foreign Office, 1876–82; R. H. Meade, C.O.; and an official from the Treasury.

prohibit the importation of goods which have not previously paid duty at Freetown, or other port of entry of the Colony, reserving to Her Majesty the right to extend the limits along the banks, if at any time it may be found necessary or desirable to do so.

(2.) That the Governor of Sierra Leone should be authorised to negotiate with the Chiefs of the Ribbee, Bompeh, and Cockboro' Rivers Treaties in substitution of those made in December 1875, by which they shall cede to Her Majesty (in terms similar to those of the Scarcies agreement) so much of the coast line as she may require for the purpose of the collection of revenue.

24. In addition to the territories with which we have dealt in the foregoing remarks, there are other districts to the north of the Scarcies Rivers, over the coast line of which it would be desirable that the Government of Sierra Leone should have power to exercise similar control.

25. These are (1) the Samoo Bullom country, between the Scarcies and Mellicourie Rivers, with the Chiefs of which the Administrator of the West African Settlements, Chief Justice Huggins, has recently concluded a Treaty by which sovereign rights are ceded to Her Majesty; and (2) the country between the Mellicourie and Mahniah Rivers, of which the sea coast and the sovereignty over all the waters was ceded to Great Britain by a Treaty of 18th April 1826. This last-mentioned Treaty was not acted upon for many years, but the Government of Sierra Leone, acting under instructions from the Secretary of State, has recently issued a notice that the island of Matacong, which was ceded by another article of the same Treaty, is British territory.

26. It appears, however, that the French have a post at Benty, on the Mellicourie River, and therefore all action on the Treaty made by Mr. Huggins has, for the present, been deferred. They also claim the sovereignty, by virtue of Treaties made in 1865 and 1866, of a large portion of the country referred to in the Treaty of 1826.

27. A lengthened correspondence took place in 1868–69, respecting the encroachments of the French in this neighbourhood, in which it was held both by the Foreign Office and the Colonial Office that the occupation of these countries was an infraction of 'the British rights acquired under Treaties of long standing.'

The correspondence gradually developed into the negotiations with the French Government for an exchange of territories on the West Coast of Africa. These, however, were suspended in 1870 in consequence of the outbreak of the Franco-German war, and having been renewed by Her Majesty's Government in 1875, they were finally abandoned last year on account of the declaration of the French Government that they could not consent to the acquisition by Great Britain of exclusive rights over the seaboard between the Gold Coast and Lagos, and consequently the question of the right of the French to establish themselves in the territory ceded to Great Britain in 1826 has not yet been disposed of.

28. Under these circumstances we think that, before any steps are taken to exercise the rights conferred by the Treaty of 1826, and Mr. Huggins' Treaty with the Samoo Bullom Chiefs, it will be desirable that the French Government should be asked to explain their position in regard to these territories, and to establish their claims, pointing out to them that the rights of Her Majesty are of very old standing, and that it has now become a matter of great importance to the Colony of Sierra Leone that they should be enforced.

29. We have not failed fully to consider the question whether it might not be possible to come to some arrangement with the French, by which they should agree to levy in the Mellicourie River duties similar to those in force at Sierra Leone, but we have come to the conclusion that it would be useless, for many reasons, to make any such proposal. So far as we can ascertain, the French have never yet attempted to levy any duties at Benty, and it appears probable that they have not done so mainly on account of their knowledge of the very insecure basis on which their so-called rights at this point rest. The policy of the French Government on the West Coast of Africa is, moreover, as is well known, very considerably influenced by the firm of Régis Aîné & Co., and M. Régis has openly expressed his dislike of all duties, as well as of all Government interference with or protection of the merchants.

30. But in addition to these reasons, the experience gained on the Gold Coast furnishes very strong arguments against the likelihood of any satisfactory agreement being arrived at. In that case, which was much stronger than the present one, the Dutch Settlements being interwoven with the English, three several attempts, [sic] in 1849, 1856, and 1859, were made to induce the Netherlands Government to impose an equal tariff, but the local opposition prevented them from acquiescing, and an exchange of territory was at last found to be the only solution of the difficulty.

31. In reporting in favour of the proposed acquisition of the coast line of the neighbouring territories for fiscal purposes, we entertain a hope that the result will be so to increase the revenue of Sierra Leone, that within a few years it will considerably exceed the expenditure, and when this point has been attained, we think that the opportunity should at once be taken to lower the Customs duties and charges on shipping, and gradually to make the Colony a free port. Freetown possesses unusual advantages as the only safe harbour along many hundred miles of coast, and as affording the greatest facilities for communication with Europe by steam and telegraph, *via* Madeira. If its commerce could be relieved of the burdens at

present imposed upon it, the trade now carried on in the adjacent rivers, to the detriment of the Colonial Customs, might be attracted once more to the Colony, and result in the establishment of a large commercial community, and in such an increase in the revenue arising from Crown rents and other sources, independent of Customs duties, as would suffice to defray its expenses.

32. It is no doubt to be regretted that, owing to the great and unavoidable expense of maintaining a Colony such as Sierra Leone, its commerce inland cannot be allowed at once to compete with that of the French and other nations on the basis of free trade; but the conditions of the Colony, and its urgent necessities, are such that, in the absence of an annual grant from Parliament, there would appear to us to be no alternative but to revert to the scheme inaugurated in 1847, of protecting the Customs revenue of the Colony by securing as much of the adjacent coast line as may be necessary for the purpose.

33. Therefore, to recapitulate, the Committee recommend:—

1. That the Treaty made by Lieutenant-Governor Rowe with the Scarcies Chiefs in June 1876 be confirmed, and the proffered cession of coast line be accepted as regards so much thereof as may be desirable.

2. That the Governor be authorised to negotiate similar treaties with the Chiefs of the Ribbee, Bompeh, and Cockboro' Rivers, in substitution of those made with them in December 1875.

3. That before any action is taken with respect to the treaty made by Mr. Huggins with the Samoo Bullom Chiefs, and the territory ceded by the Treaty of 1826, an endeavour should be made to arrive at an understanding with the French as to the extent and validity of their alleged rights in these countries.

7

DR. S. ROWE, MINUTE: EXPANSION NEAR SIERRA LEONE, 13 AUGUST 1877[1]

. . . I T is of great importance to the peace of the outlying districts of Sa. Leone that the aborigines should have no ground for doubting the intention of HMG. to enforce her treaty rights.

I respectfully but earnestly entreat Lord Carnarvon not to countenance the cession of any part of the rights granted to H. Majesty by the Treaty of 1826.

The French are pushing their authority in the Mellicourie river only to obtain if possible a cession of the Gambia on their terms.

[1] C.O. 267/331. On H. J. Huggins, Acting Governor, to C.O., 26 July 1877 (reporting the French occupation of Samu Bulom).

8

SIR MICHAEL HICKS BEACH TO
GOVERNOR SIR SAMUEL ROWE:
EXPANSION NEAR SIERRA LEONE,
24 JANUARY 1879[1]

2. I APPROVE of your proposal to station a Customs officer on the
island of Kikonkeh, at the mouth of the Scarcies River, to see that
ships do not go there or attempt to land goods without a permit, on
the understanding that before doing so you will communicate to the
Scarcies Chiefs, who signed the Agreement of 10th June 1876,[2] Her
Majesty's ratification of the treaty and Her acceptance of the cession
which they have offered; and that you will issue a proclamation notifying
the same, and stating, in accordance with your suggestion, that all
merchandize entering the districts referred to will from and after a
certain date (to be fixed with reference to the following instructions)
be subject to the same Customs dues as are levied at Freetown.

3. Referring to your recommendation that the duties should be
enforced at once, I am of opinion that it would be desirable, even at
the risk of incurring some loss of the revenue, which may be expected
immediately to accrue from the extension of fiscal jurisdiction, not to
provoke hostility and reclamations from the mercantile community
by suddenly imposing upon them payments from which they have
hitherto been exempt, and I think therefore that, unless you have
good reason to anticipate grave evils from such a course, it will be
best to allow a short interval (the duration of which your local
knowledge will enable you to decide) to elapse before the exaction of
duties, within which they may dispose of stocks already despatched,
and make arrangements for carrying on their business under the new
regulations.

4. I observe that in paragraphs 9 and 14 of your despatch you speak
of the island of Matacong as being a depôt from which goods are at
present taken into the Scarcies and Ribbee Rivers without payment
of duties.

5. As you are aware, much correspondence took place last year
with respect to Matacong, in which it was distinctly laid down by my
predecessor that the sovereignty of the island is vested in Her Majesty,
and he only consented, in reply to the representations of Messrs.
Randall and Fisher, that the levying of duties in respect to goods
landed there should be suspended until a further report had been
received from you. This report was called for by Lord Carnarvon's
despatch of 20th July 1877, to which I do not find that any reply has

---

[1] C.O. 879/14, no. 159.   [2] See above, I no. 3, p. 18.

yet been returned. I have therefore to call your attention to it, and to request to be informed what steps have been taken in pursuance of the instructions contained in it.

6. In the 16th and following paragraphs of your despatch you point out that by the Charter of 1799 the Camaranka or Bompeh River was defined as the southern boundary of the Settlement of Sierra Leone, and that Major General Sir Charles Turner in 1825 obtained a cession of the territory from the Camaranka southwards to the Gallinas River. You argue from this that it would appear to be unnecessary to make treaties with the Chiefs of the Ribbee, Bompeh, and Cockboro' districts for the cession of the coast line, all that is required being the issue of a proclamation stating that Her Majesty has determined to exercise and put in force certain rights which for various reasons have been allowed to remain in abeyance.

7. It appears, however, upon examination of the records of this Department that the King's Government declined to advise His Majesty to ratify the treaties made by Sir C. Turner, and their disavowal was conveyed to that officer in two despatches from Earl Bathurst, dated 18th and 19th December 1825, copies of which are enclosed herewith for your information.[1]

8. It is clear therefore that Her Majesty has no territorial rights over the Bompey and Cockboro' districts, and I am of opinion that the evidence of any acquisition, under the Charter of 1799, of the territory lying between the Bompey and Ribbee Rivers is too vague and uncertain to be acted upon.

9. It will therefore be necessary that you should proceed, in accordance with the instructions already conveyed to you, to negotiate with the Chiefs of the rivers above mentioned, treaties for the cession of the coast line of their territories, similar to the one concluded with the Scarcies Chiefs.

10. When these treaties have been arranged you will act as regards the levying of Customs duties in the manner already prescribed in relation to the Scarcies River; but I need hardly point out that you will of course be very careful, in considering the propriety of placing a Customs officer on the coast of Yawry Bay, to be assured that this can be done with perfect safety as regards the Natives in the neighbourhood, who may not be as peaceably disposed as those of the coast to the north of Sierra Leone . . .

---

[1] See Vol. I: Bathurst to Turner, 22 April 1826, p. 418.

9

WILLIAM WYLDE: MINUTE, ANGLO-
FRENCH WEST AFRICAN QUESTIONS,
14 APRIL 1879[1]

THE French Govt. having now made known to us the extent of the
acquisitions recently made by them at Kotonou,[2] admittedly with the
object of counteracting the Financial Policy pursued by our Colonial
Authorities on the Afn. Coast, it remains for us to decide whether we
will accept the position in which we are now placed by the action of
the French Govt., or whether we will adopt countervailing measures
which it is perfectly in our power to do, and by accepting the Protectorate of the two districts of Appa and Katanu turn the flanks of
the French and make ourselves masters of the position. We should
be perfectly justified in doing this considering the action of the
French at Matacong[3] and in the neighbourhood of Lagos. But is it
advisable to do so? We must enter into communication with the
French Govt. on the subject of their recent action at Matacong, and
would it not be better to deal with the whole of the African Coast
question at once rather than to raise separate questions, each of which
only becomes an additional source of irritation likely to lead to
entanglements. There are four other letters of the same date as this
from the Colonial Office, all of them mixed up with French questions,
and I would submit whether it would not be expedient to deal with
them as a whole rather than to continue a correspondence in which it is
difficult if not impossible to take a line without compromising ourselves pending a decision as to the Policy to be pursued on the African
Coast.

10

GOVERNOR H. T. USSHER TO
SIR MICHAEL HICKS BEACH:
KATANU, 29 SEPTEMBER 1879[4]

IN continuation of my despatch of this date upon the subject of my
proceedings in Porto Novo, I have the honour to inform you that
while I was at Badagry, en route to the former place, a deputation
consisting of the King and Chiefs of Ajido, who are also the King and

---

[1] F.O. 84/1552. On Meade to F.O., 12 April 1879 (requesting new negotiations
on the Gambia exchange scheme). William Wylde (see vol. I, p. 121 n.)
[2] Cotonou in Southern Dahomey.
[3] Occupied in March 1879; see John D. Hargreaves, Prelude to the Partition of
West Africa (London, 1963), pp. 222–31.
[4] C.O. 147/38.

Chiefs of Katanu, waited upon me to request a reply to their former petition addressed, in 1876, to the Administrator of Lagos, M. Dumaresq,[1] in which they earnestly begged that the town and territory of Katanu should be taken under the protection of Her Majesty's Government. They added that, up to the present moment, beyond threats, nothing had been done by either the French or the King of Porto Novo to annoy them or annex their country; but that King Tofa was daily becoming more and more threatening, and had, moreover, killed several members of the family of Prince Konu, of Katanu, merely because he piloted the 'Eko' up the Whemi River at M. Dumaresq's request; that Tofa had burnt down their toll-house on the Katanu (or Toh-ché) Creek, and that they were deprived thus of their tolls in an arbitrary manner; and that they begged me to take the territory—at all events, provisionally—under British protection, adding their complete willingness to abide by the decision of the Queen.

2. I informed them that, on my return from Porto Novo, I would again see them on this subject; and I added that I should require a letter from them, setting forth all the circumstances, as well as the prayers of their petition, before I could act in any way.

3. After long consideration of the matter, and having consulted the Acting Administrator, and Mr. Thomas Tickel,[2] of Badagry, the most experienced European in this Settlement in native affairs, who was good enough, although far from well, to act throughout as my interpreter and informant on native law and matters generally, I arrived at the following conclusions:—

(1.) That the King of Katanu was an independent Prince, and that no attempt had been made by either Tofa or the French to impose a King or a flag upon them.

(2.) That, taking into consideration the activity recently exhibited by the French in these waters, as well as the continued threats of the King of Porto Novo, any delay in obtaining possession of the key to the road between Cootenoo and Porto Novo would be injudicious, and might result in its immediate annexation by the French.

(3.) That the Katanu Creek also commanded the road to Whemi, and would infallibly keep open the lagoons for the future.

(4.) That the King of Dahomey had never at any time laid claim to Katanu, nor had the Katanus ever paid him, or any one, tribute; thus rendering improbable a complication with the Dahomian Monarch.

(5.) That, in case of necessity, the possession of Katanu would enable this Government to abolish the drawback now refunded on goods destined for Porto Novo, and also to regulate such duties as to it should for the future seem fit.

[1] *John d'A. Dumaresque*, Acting Administrator of Lagos Colony.
[2] Vice-Consul and Political Officer, Western District.

4. I therefore determined to take on board the King and Chiefs, and to proceed to Katanu, there installing them under the British flag. Having received the petition hereto appended, I drew out the inclosed Provisional Agreement; and, having landed at Katanu on the morning of the 24th September, I formally hoisted the British flag, in the presence of the Administrator and Colonial Secretary and under a guard of Houssas, to the inexpressible delight of the wretched people of this poor place, who appear to have been in constant fear of tyranny and oppression. I also made King Seto and his Chiefs a present of 10 *l.* to rebuild their toll-house, and I distributed sundry small presents as well.

5. On the same day I returned to Badagry, and, having anchored there all night, arrived in Lagos the next day, Thursday, the 25th instant, having been absent from the morning of the 19th.

6. I beg to transmit an official notice in regard to the annexation of Katanu, which I have caused to be published throughout the Colony under my command. I have heard that the measure gives general satisfaction, with perhaps the exception of the firm Regis Ainé.

7. I am of opinion that, in case you should advise Her Majesty to confirm the arrangement, the position of this Government is unassailable as a matter of right and title. The importance of Katanu has been hitherto overlooked by both the French Agents and the King of Porto Novo. Probably it has been taken for granted as belonging to the latter State in consequence of its proximity thereto; nothing can pass from Cootenoo to Porto Novo except through this creek, which is about 50 yards wide.

8. I am informed that the beach of Cootenoo is unworkable, as the canoe-men have all absconded in terror of the numerous sharks which infest the beach. Moreover, the King of Dahomey has placed an embargo upon goods being sent from Cootenoo to Porto Novo until the French houses shall have landed more, which they are not in a position to do. The occupation of Katanu Creek should prove a final blow to their proceedings in this direction, and they would gain nothing now by annexing Porto Novo. As to the latter place, I am of opinion that, by skilful and timely negotiation, a voluntary offer might be made to us by King Tofa to cede his country to Great Britain. He is said to be prepared at any moment for an English occupation.

9. In case you advise Her Majesty to confirm my action in this matter—and I admit that I have taken upon myself a great responsibility—I consider it necessary that a travelling Agent for Native Affairs alone should be at once appointed; and that the only person at all suitable for this purpose is Mr. Thomas Tickel, whose claims I propose to discuss in a subsequent despatch.

11

SIR MICHAEL HICKS BEACH TO GOVERNOR SIR SAMUEL ROWE: EXPANSION NEAR SIERRA LEONE, 30 SEPTEMBER 1879[1]

... I HAVE the honour to acknowledge receipt of your despatches ... on the subject of the necessity of exercising jurisdiction over the sea beach of Turner's Peninsula, with the view of checking the importation of contraband goods into British Sherbro' and the adjoining districts.

2. This matter has for some time past engaged my serious attention, and I am fully alive to the danger which threatens the financial position of the Colony of Sierra Leone and the importance of taking steps to avert it. I have accordingly consulted the Law Officers of the Crown as to whether the treaty made by Sir C. Turner in 1825, under which the territory known as Turner's Peninsula was ceded to the British Crown, could still be held to have any force, and they have informed me in reply that in their opinion the treaty ought to be regarded as valid, and now in force.

3. As it follows from this opinion that the rights acquired by the treaty in question are still vested in Her Majesty, you will in future be justified in asserting them, if occasion should arise, over the whole of Turner's Peninsula. It is, however, another question as to how far they should at present be enforced, and the information now before me does not enable me to come to a satisfactory decided conclusion upon this point.

4. As you are well aware, Her Majesty's Government are extremely reluctant to sanction any extension of jurisdiction in West Africa beyond what may be absolutely necessary, whilst at the same time it is most inconvenient that such questions should from time to time be re-opened.

5. Recent events to the northward of Sierra Leone show that the Chiefs are not able in all cases to carry their people with them, more especially when influenced by the intrigues of those who have a direct interest in opposing the measures it is desired to introduce. I wish you, therefore, in the first place to consider whether without the actual exercise of any jurisdiction, which for many reasons it is desirable, if possible, to avoid, a general announcement of the rights of this country such as I have already suggested, would not suffice to check the danger which you apprehend ...

6. It will, however, in any case be desirable that you should state

[1] C.O. 869/17, no. 206. A new agreement with the chiefs of Bulom and Shebar was made, 18 November 1882.

clearly and distinctly, and, if possible, define accurately upon a map
the precise amount and position of the territory over which it will be
requisite to exercise jurisdiction should it unfortunately be found
impossible otherwise to protect the revenue of British Sherbro' . . .

12

A. W. L. HEMMING: MINUTE,
KATANU, 10 NOVEMBER 1879[1]

MR. USSHER has taken a very important step—and one to which the
F.O. had refused to assent until it had been discussed & decided by
the Cabinet. It is unfortunate that he should have gone down to
Lagos before he could have received the desp. of 23 Augt. (Gold
Coast), the 5th para. of which distinctly told him that he was to do
nothing in the matter of Katanu.

However he had not that desp. and undoubtedly the circes. which
he reports were such as might well induce him to think that the matter
was one of urgent importance, & would justify him in incurring the
responsibility of acting without instructions. At the same time he has
without doubt placed the Sec. of State in an awkward position.
Though I should very much doubt if any difficulty would arise with
Dahomey from this action, still knowing as we do the plots & intrigues
of the French officials & traders, we cannot be certain that such will
not be the case. The French Govt. can have no ground of complaint
as they have distinctly defined . . . the extent of the territory they have
acquired at Cootenoo, & it does not even reach the mouth of the creek
on which Katanu is situated. Moreover as no Comm[unication] had
yet been made to them as to the proposal to include Cootenoo in the
negotiations arising out of the Matacong affair, they cannot say that
we are acting unhandsomely or forestalling them—but our possession
of Katanu would probably go some way to induce them to give us
Cootenoo—of which the value wld. be much diminished.

To withdraw now the protection given by Govr. Ussher would
undoubtedly tarnish our prestige in that part of Africa—already as
we know from many sources impaired by our weakness of our treatment of Dahomey in the matter of the fines—such withdrawal would
of course be attributed to fear of Dahomey or France—or both—&
this feeling would be cherished & encouraged by the French agents.
Again it must not be forgotten that if we withdraw we leave these poor
people to the tender mercies of Porto Novo—possibly of Dahomey
who will naturally be additionally incensed with them for having
invoked the protection of the Lagos Govt. And finally, now that
attention has been drawn to Katanu its value will be at once perceived,

[1] C.O. 147/38. On no. 10, p. 168. Hicks Beach agreed: Minute, 11 November 1879.

and as soon as we step out there can be little doubt that the French will step in—and if this occurs there will not be much chance of their agreeing to surrender Cootenoo and they will make their presence an additional lever with which to work to obtain the transfer of the Gambia—the object which they will use every means to attain.

On the whole I would submit that, altho' disapproval should be expressed of Govr. Ussher having taken such an important step without first obtaining sanction from H.M.'s Govt., yet that his action should not be reversed, & that the Protectorate of Katanu should be accepted.

13

R. G. W. HERBERT TO THE FOREIGN OFFICE: EXPANSION EAST OF THE GOLD COAST, 17 JANUARY 1880[1]

. . . WITH reference to the letter from this Department of 9th. Instant, I am directed by the Secretary of State for the Colonies to transmit to you, to be laid before the Marquis of Salisbury copies of two further despatches from the Governor of the Gold Coast, reporting the peaceable cession by the Agbosomé and Afflowhoo Chiefs of the Coast line of their territory.

2. As the action taken by Governor Ussher in this matter is in accordance with the instructions he has received, which have been communicated to you, Sir Michael Hicks Beach proposes, unless Lord Salisbury is aware of any objection, to express his approval of what has been done, and to confirm the arrangements made with the Native Chiefs.

3. I am to observe that from the information in this Department, it would appear that the whole extent of the Coast line now acquired does not exceed 8 or 9 miles in length . . .

14

THE MARQUIS OF SALISBURY: MINUTE, EXPANSION EAST OF THE GOLD COAST, 29 JANUARY 1880[2]

DRAFT that Instructions under which Governor Ussher has acted were not sent to us before being sent to him. That if they had been, we should have expressed even stronger disapproval of any further annexions in W. African territory & that I must decline except under specific instructions in each case from the Cabinet to assent on the part of this Department to any further annexions in West Africa.

[1] F.O. 84/1581.   [2] Ibid.

15

A. W. L. HEMMING: MINUTE, LIBERIAN BOUNDARY, 25 OCTOBER 1880[1]

[A common frontier with Liberia is required to end disputes about the area from Shebar to Cape Mount.]

. . . THE most satisfactory course therefore appears to be that an arrangement should be come to with Liberia by which we should be at liberty to acquire by cession from the Native Chiefs so much of the coast line beyond our present boundary as may be deemed necessary for the due security of our commercial & revenual interests, and that we should then recognize her right to acquire such portions as should remain between our new boundary & her present limit at Cape Mount. It would of course be necessary that she should relinquish a portion of her claims, for enquiry into which the recent Boundary Commission sat. Judging from what took place before the Commission those claims are not of much value & it would be difficult for Liberia, even if the Commission were renewed, to substantiate them.

But such a proposal as I have made would have to be carried out, not by a Commission, but by negotiation with the Liberian Govt., and we have, I think, the means ready to our hands for opening such negotiations with every prospect of success.

As you are aware, certain British subjects (natives of Sierra Leone) have considerable claims against the Govt. of Liberia on account of property &c. destroyed in the disputed territories in 1871—and I understand that Mr. Harris has also a claim against them on a similar account. H.M.'s Govt. can hardly allow these claims, which it was originally proposed to refer to the Boundary Comm[issioners] to remain unsatisfied, but it is well known that Liberia is poverty stricken, & would find it difficult, if not impossible, to discharge them. We might therefore offer to the Liberian Govt. that, in consideration of the relinquishment of their pretentions to the territory which H.M.'s Govt. might consider it necessary to acquire, the Govt. of Sierra Leone should take over & satisfy the pecuniary claims of British subjects against the Republic. It might be pressed upon them that these claims have been long outstanding & cannot be indefinitely postponed, & that if the offer made be declined, H.M.'s Govt. must reserve the right of considering what steps should be taken to enforce payment. If British jurisdiction over the proposed coastline were

---

[1] C.O. 267/343. On Rowe to Kimberley, 21 October 1880. Liberia resisted this pressure till 1884, when the Government agreed to Mano as the frontier with Sierra Leone, by treaty, 11 November 1885. See Fyfe, *History of Sierra Leone*, pp. 384–5, 431.

assured the revenue of B. Sherbro' would probably increase so much & so rapidly that there would be no difficulty in paying off the debts taken over from Liberia . . .

16

ANGLO-FRENCH CONVENTION, 28 JUNE 1882[1]

Article I

THE line of demarcation between the territories occupied or claimed by Great Britain and France respectively to the north of Sierra Leone, on the West Coast of Africa, shall be drawn between the basins of the Rivers Scarcies and Mellicourie.

The exact position of the said line of demarcation shall be determined by inquiry on the spot, by Commissioners to be appointed for that purpose in the manner provided in Article VII of the present Convention.

The said line of demarcation shall, however, be drawn in such a manner as to insure to Great Britain the complete control of the Scarcies Rivers and to France the complete control of the Mellicourie River.

The Point and Factory of Mahela and the adjacent water communication shall belong to the nation to which, by the aforesaid inquiry, their possession may be found necessary for the control of the Scarcies Rivers, or of the Mellicourie River, as the case may be. If the water communication at Mahela should be found to open into the Mellicourie River as well as into the Scarcies River, the said line of demarcation shall start on the coast from the centre of the stream which joins the sea at Mahela, and shall be continued in such manner as to assign to Great Britain the communication with the Scarcies River, and to France the communication with the Mellicourie River.

Article II

The Island of Yelboyah, and all islands claimed or possessed by Great Britain on the West Coast of Africa lying to the south of the said line of demarcation as far as the southern limit of the British Colony of Sierra Leone, shall be recognised by France as belonging to Great Britain, and the Island of Matacong, and all islands claimed or possessed by France on the West Coast of Africa to the north of the said line of demarcation as far as the Rio Nunez, shall be recognised by Great Britain as belonging to France; with the exception of the

[1] C.O. 879/18, no. 233. Although not ratified by the French Chamber, the 1882 Convention was accepted in both countries as a working definition of spheres of interest.

Isles de Los, which last-mentioned islands shall continue to belong to Great Britain.

ARTICLE III

Her Majesty the Queen of the United Kingdom of Great Britain and Ireland engages to abstain from holding any territory, and from exercising or countenancing the exercise of British political influence in the country lying between the line of demarcation which is to be fixed in accordance with Article I and the Rio Nunez.

It is understood that nothing contained in this Article shall affect any rights which may be possessed by France, on the stream of the Rio Nunez, or to the north of that river.

ARTICLE IV

The President of the French Republic engages to abstain from holding any territory and from exercising or countenancing the exercise of French political influence in the country lying between the line of demarcation which is to be fixed in accordance with Article I and the northern limit of the Republic of Liberia.

ARTICLE V

British subjects in the French possessions on the West Coast of Africa, and French citizens in the British possessions on the West Coast of Africa, shall receive equality of treatment with the citizens or subjects of France and Great Britain respectively as regards the protection of life and property.

ARTICLE VI

The right to hold real property within the British possessions on the West Coast of Africa shall be accorded to French citizens in the same manner as this right is or may be granted by law to aliens in the United Kingdom of Great Britain and Ireland.

The right to hold real property within the French possessions on the West Coast of Africa shall be accorded to British subjects in the same manner as this right is or may be granted by law to aliens in France.

ARTICLE VII

The Commissioners for determining on the spot the exact position of the line of demarcation provided for in Article I of the present Convention shall be appointed in the following manner, that is to say:—

Her Majesty the Queen of the United Kingdom of Great Britain and Ireland shall appoint two Commissioners, and the President of the French Republic shall appoint two Commissioners. The said Commissioners shall meet at Sierra Leone for the purpose of commencing their labours within six months after the ratifications of the present Convention shall have been exchanged, or sooner if possible. In the event of any question arising upon which the aforesaid Commissioners are not able themselves to come to an agreement, the matter shall be referred for decision to the governments of the two high contracting parties.

ARTICLE VIII

The present Convention shall be ratified, and the ratifications shall be exchanged at Paris as soon as possible.

In witness whereof, the respective Plenipotentiaries have signed the same in duplicate, and have affixed thereto the seal of their arms.

Done at Paris, the 28th of June 1882.

(L.S.) LYONS.

(L.S.) C. DE FREYCINET.

17

T. V. LISTER TO SIR ROBERT HERBERT: FRANCE AND THE LOWER NIGER, 22 MAY 1883[1]

[Lord Granville agrees that French occupation of the Oil Rivers would damage British West African commerce; negotiations for a demarcation of spheres of interest will probably fail.]

... IF the idea of negotiation with France is set aside as impracticable, it will have to be considered whether any active steps should be taken. The tendency of events seems at present to point to the gradual absorption of the west coast by various European nations. If this tendency should be unchecked, it is probable that public feeling in this country would be strongly averse to the incorporation of the Oil River coast into the possessions of any foreign country; but at the present moment annexation by this country would be distasteful, and the idea of it could not be entertained. The question then arises whether effective steps could be taken, without annexation, to keep other nations from

[1] C.O. 879/20, 265. See, too, C.O. African no. 259 for British reactions to Brazza's Congo treaty and its ratification in Paris, November 1882. Aberdare to Granville, 28 February 1883, encl. in F.O. to C.O., 12 March 1883. The C.O. decided the French threat was a Cabinet matter: Meade, Minute, 28 March 1883; Derby, Minute, 6 April 1883. For French consular and naval activity on the Lower Niger which gave rise to this alarm, see C. W. Newbury and A. S. Kanya-Forstner, 'French Policy and the Origins of the Scramble for West Africa', *Journal of African History*, x, 2 (1969), p. 269. The Colonial Office demanded a 'remonstrance' for this and news of the French occupation of Porto Novo: Meade to F.O., 4 June 1883.

interfering with this territory, and it is clear that, if any such steps are practicable, they should be taken at once; for if the Chiefs, or any of them, should be induced to place themselves under the Protectorate of any Power, whatever that Power might be, any other Power would be debarred from dealing with them. Should the French, for instance, induce Native Chiefs to accept Treaties of the character of that recently concluded with the King of Loango, they would become virtually masters of their territories.

Lord Derby is doubtless aware that treaties are in existence with Chiefs on the Niger under an Article of which it is stipulated that no cession of territory and no Treaty or Agreement shall be made without the full understanding or consent of Her Majesty's Government. Copies of these Treaties, which were made in 1863, are inclosed for reference.

It may well be considered whether, if these Treaties should be now renewed and confirmed, and similar Treaties should be made with other Chiefs on the coast, a check might not be put upon the advance of the French. It is possible that such treaties might have the effect, but it is necessary in a matter of such importance to look the question fully in the face, and it is to be feared that it is not impossible that they might fail altogether. The French might look on them as a challenge; they might disregard them. If the Chiefs made engagements or concessions in spite of them, we should unquestionably have grounds for complaint against those Chiefs, but it might be doubtful whether we should be able to call on a foreign Power to cancel its engagements. Should this prove to be the case, the object we should have in making the Treaties would be altogether defeated. An adventurer of the character of M. de Brazza, or a naval officer of the type of the Commander of the 'Saggittaire' might make engagements with the Chiefs similar to the Loango Treaty (which is probably a model of those likely to be offered), the French Government might express its inability to cancel them, and this country might find itself merely in possession of Treaties valueless in face of a hostile Protectorate, and powerless to save its trade from destruction.

Lord Granville thinks that these considerations should be well weighed, but that, as is above stated, a decision should not be delayed; and his Lordship would therefore be glad to learn as soon as possible Lord Derby's views upon the existing situation.

18

H. P. ANDERSON: MEMORANDUM, FRENCH OCCUPATION OF PORTO NOVO, 11 JUNE 1883[1]

[Because of French annexation of Cotonou and renewal of the Porto Novo Protectorate there is a serious clash of interests along the Dahomey–Lagos seaboard; the Colonial Office urges that a strong protest be sent to the French Government.]

... WHATEVER the decision may be as to the remonstrance, I cannot avoid pointing out that there are questions involved the solution of which is forced on us. As regards the remonstrance, I believe we may discount the answer. We cannot be sanguine enough to believe that the French will retire; they will probably reply as before that, knowing the liberality of their African commercial policy, we should welcome them as neighbours. The position will then be practically the same as if we had not remonstrated, though it will be so far improved, in the opinion of the Colonial Office, if I rightly understand their view, that it will be impossible for the British public to misunderstand the object of the French advance. The question then will have to be decided what is to be done. I think we should be prepared beforehand with the decision. If we remain passive, we shall see our trade stifled, we shall find our traders furious, and we shall hardly escape grave complications with the French as successive Protectorates produce fresh irritation till, when the field is finally closed against us, we shall have to deal with chronic grievances and complaints. If it is thought that the field will not be closed, my reply is that Consul Hewett assures me (and I have questioned him closely on the point) that, though we have now the vantage-ground with the Oil River Chiefs, *these Chiefs, if we do not within a given time accept the Protectorate for which they are prepared, will unquestionably put themselves in the hands of the French.*

How can we doubt that the French will take them? If there is one thing clearer than another, it seems to be that the French have a settled policy in Africa, both on the East and West Coast, and that the policy is antagonistic to us. The progress of this policy is sometimes sluggish, sometimes feverish, but it never ceases. Admiral Wilson, who has had some forty years' experience of African waters, called my attention some months since to the sagacity which the French had shown in occupying the unobtrusive position of Mayotte, an island in which there was good anchorage for their ships, so protected by

---

[1] *F.O. Confidential Print*, 4819 (1883). (*Sir*) *H. Percy Anderson*, Senior Clerk in the Foreign Office, 1883, and Assistant Under-Secretary, 1894-6.

nature that it could be held by a handful of men against a fleet, and giving easy access to Zanzibar, the Comoros, and, with Nossi Bé as an outpost, to Madagascar. Its utility is now being proved. On the West Coast the policy is more marked. Railways are being pushed in Senegal from St. Louis to the Upper Niger. Connection is being established with the Soudan, and a push is being made towards Timbuctoo. New stations have recently been established at Grand Bassam and Assinie. M. de Brazza is on the Congo; a vessel sent direct from France has brought Punta Negra and Loango under her sovereignty, and the gap between this district and Gaboon will probably be closed, while the question of the Congo mouth is kept an open one with Portugal; from Porto Novo the trade of Lagos is attacked; a French official agent is at work above the delta of the Niger, while the Captain of the 'Voltigeur' is trying to induce the natives of the mouths of that river to accept his Treaties. If he succeeds in this, the final step will have been taken, and British trade will have no chance of existence except at the mercy of French officials.

Action seems to be forced on us, and if this is so, we are fairly forced into a corner as to the direction of it. Only one course seems possible; that is to take on ourselves the Protectorate of the native States at the mouth of the Oil Rivers, and on the adjoining coast. Reasons were given in the letter to the Colonial Office of the 22nd May, the force of which was admitted in their reply, why any step short of Protectorate would be worse than useless; the step beyond it—Annexation—is inadmissible. Partial Protectorates would result in an unseemly and dangerous race with the French; Porto Novo, for instance, is now said to be a reply to Whydah; Mr. Hutton,[1] of Manchester, tells me that it is openly spoken of thus by the French merchants. Protectorates are unwelcome burdens, but in this case it is, if my view is correct, a question between British Protectorates, which would be unwelcome, and French Protectorates, which would be fatal. Protectorates of one sort or another, are the inevitable outcome of the situation. In our case, if Consul Hewett and Captain Moloney are to be trusted (and they do not speak impulsively), they could be imposed almost without an effort on the majority of the Chiefs; they would not be difficult of management, for one gun-boat in the Bights would suffice, under ordinary circumstances, to keep the protégés in order, and they would not be burdensome to the Treasury, for expenses could be managed by manipulating the traders.

There remains to be considered the effect on our relations with France. That there would be irritation in France cannot be doubted; but would this be a more important factor than the irritation in this

---

[1] *James F. Hutton*, President of the Manchester Chamber of Commerce, 1884–5, and M.P., 1885–6.

country if the Protectorates go to France? Ground for minor grievances, of the character already referred to, would disappear, for the
battle-ground would be closed. There would be no more opportunity
for surprises and countersurprises, intrigues, and underhand work.
Working above ground we should come to open negotiation, and it
can only be by negotiation that the African question between the two
countries can be ultimately settled.

At present the French have nothing particular to gain by negotiation,
for they are playing the game their own way, and we are making no
serious attempt to interfere with them, but the position would be
reversed if we had the Oil Rivers in our hands. Then negotiation
would be the only escape from the situation. Hesitation on the part
of the French to treat would probably be overcome if they were to
understand that the question of the Gambia would enter into the
discussions. The remarks made by Admiral Sir F. Richards in his
comments annexed to the Admiralty letter of the 31st May are
pertinent to this point. 'My belief,' he says, 'is that the real Naboth's
vineyard of the French in Africa is the Gambias.' This view apparently
represents correctly the opinion on the Coast.

On the other hand, the consensus of opinion seems to be unanimous
among the best instructed that British interests on the Oil Rivers are
incomparably superior to those on the Gambia. This being so, if we
should be in the position of having in our hands what we chiefly
want, and of being able to offer to the French what they chiefly want,
a settlement should not be impossible, and public opinion in both
countries, when duly enlightened, might fairly be expected not to be
opposed to it. If we could surrender the Gambias, and obtain in
exchange the Gaboon, the acknowledgement of our already existing
Protectorate over the Lower Niger, and the retirement of the French
from the Gold Coast, leaving the question of M. de Brazza, which it
would not be safe to touch, to solve itself, the African commercial
policy of the two countries would, with this exception, have separate
fields, ample for both, in which there need be no collision and no petty
rivalries. Relations would thus be placed on an amicable footing, with
every prospect of permanency.

To sum up: I venture to suggest that a remonstrance against the
Porto Novo Protectorate should be addressed, as the Colonial Office
suggest, to the French Government; that we should be prepared for
an unsatisfactory answer; that, on receiving it, we should take steps
for assuming the Protectorate of the Oil River Coast; and that, when
established there, we should endeavour, by negotiation on the basis
of our retirement from the Senegambias, and the French retirement
from the Gaboon, the Lower Niger, and the Gold Coast, to define
the respective fields of the future commercial enterprise of the two
countries.

19

CONSUL E. H. HEWETT TO LORD GRANVILLE: CAMEROON AND DELTA ANNEXATIONS, 11 JUNE 1883[1]

IN my despatch No. 4, Africa of the 7th June, I addressed your Lordship on the annexation of the territory in the Cameroon district. I have now the honour to inclose a Petition to the same purport from the King and Chiefs of Akassa (Nun entrance of the Niger).

Their Petition is strongly supported by the representative of the National African Company, who is well acquainted with the character and condition of the various tribes and races of the Delta of the Niger, and of the countries bordering on the River. This Gentleman in his letter to me, covering the Petition, expresses a strong opinion that the measure proposed would be highly advantageous to British interests, and would tend to the peace of the country by placing some check on the increasing encroachments of the French, who are seeking by every means to extend their influence in that part of Africa, and would also be of great benefit to the natives.

Of the different tribes between Cameroons and Akassa, I may mention that Old Calabar is expecting that the country will be taken over by England. Indeed, Prince James Eyamba, the head of the powerful House of Eyamba has already applied to your Lordship seeking British protection for himself and his people, and King Eyo of Creek Town, on one occasion asked me confidentially when the Queen was going to take the country. This shows that he expects, as I believe does also King Duke of Duke Town, that Her Majesty's Government will take that step.

The Qua Eboes, when they were attacked by Ja Ja, wrote to me for protection, and renewed their request when I went to their River.

At Opobo the Chiefs have no voice in the Government; they are entirely under subjection to Ja Ja, who would demur to his country being surrendered to us, but he, of all the Kings, is the one whom it would be most desirable to remove.

At Bonny there is a strong party, particularly among the young Chiefs, who would be very glad to see the present system of government superseded by British rule.

At New Calabar there is a powerful faction opposed to the King. Neither is sufficiently strong to attain undivided sway, and there will probably be a conflict between the two. Our intervention would be welcomed as affording them an excuse for retiring from the position they have respectively taken up.

[1] *F.O. Confidential Print*, 4825 (1883). *E. H. Hewett*, Consul in Loanda, 1861–70, Consul, Bight of Benin, 1880–1.

With respect to Brass, no one has been elected to succeed the late King who governed that part of the River where the factories are situated. There is but one Chief who I believe would accept the office of King, and he is not fit for it. It is very necessary that some authority should be established there for the protection of traders.

There is another King of Brass 16 miles up the River at Nembé, who might object to his country being surrendered to a foreign Power, but it would probably be unnecessary to interfere with him, as his district is not on the branch of the River generally frequented by European traders.

Between Akassa and Benin is the river Forcados, one of the most easily entered on the coast, which leads to Warri,—a good field for trade. Some years ago two English houses established factories there, but the Chiefs of Benin finding that opening of Warri interfered with their trade, compelled them to withdraw.

I heard shortly before I left the coast that Alumé, who had been appointed head Chief at Benin by Mr. Easton, the late Acting Consul was dead. He and another Chief there were constantly at variance, and how matters will be settled I am unable to say, but here, as in other places, it is very evident that a strong hand to rule both parties is necessary.

Unless some steps are taken in the direction that I have indicated, I feel confident that no advancement will be made in the development of the country and the civilization of the inhabitants, or in the prevention of the gross injustice and cruelty which now obtain.

20

CABINET MINUTE: EXPANSION IN WEST AFRICA, 22 NOVEMBER 1883[1]

THE Cabinet also agreed with the report of its Committee recommending the acceptance of certain ports offered to the British Power in Western Africa, with a view to the maintenance of an unfettered trade, which unhappily is not favoured by the arrangements of the French in those latitudes.

[1] Cabinet Papers 41/17. See no. 21.

21

JOHN BRAMSTON (COLONIAL OFFICE) TO FOREIGN OFFICE: APPA PROTECTORATE, 23 NOVEMBER 1883[1]

WITH reference to previous correspondence, and in particular to the letter from this Department of 31st July last, I am directed by the Earl of Derby to transmit to you, to be laid before Earl Granville, copies of further Despatches from the Governor of the Gold Coast Colony, on the subject of the proceedings of the French at Porto Novo, and the prayer of the King and Chiefs of Appah that their country may be admitted within the British Protectorate.

Lord Granville will remember that the question of Appa was brought before the Committee of the Cabinet which met recently to discuss various points relating to the position of affairs on the West Coast of Africa, and that it was then decided that it is expedient to grant the prayer of the King and Chiefs as conveyed in their memorial of 18th April last.

Lord Derby proposes, therefore, with Lord Granville's concurrence, to authorise Sir S. Rowe to intimate to the King and Chiefs of Appa that Her Majesty accedes to their prayer, and to instruct him to take the necessary steps for placing the district under British protection, and under the care and superintendence of the Government at Lagos.

22

T. V. LISTER TO CONSUL E. H. HEWETT: CAMEROONS PROTECTORATE, 16 MAY 1884[2]

[Consular expenditure is to be increased to protect British trade and administer the treaty ports.]

... IT is arranged that on your arrival you shall be met by a man-of-war at Bonny, and you should lose no time in visiting in her the various native Chiefs, with many of whom you are already acquainted. You should explain to them that you have special instructions to express to them the desire of Her Majesty to maintain and strengthen

[1] C.O. 879/20, no. 265. The Lagos boundary was extended to Appa in March 1884. Similar moves on the Gold Coast by Governor W. A. G. Young were delayed, and Southern Togo was annexed by the Germans. Young to Derby, 29 April 1884: C.O. 879/22, no. 283.

[2] Parl. Papers, 1885 [C. 4279], pp. 16–17. Hewett arrived in July 1884 at Amboises Bay and found the German flag over Bell and Akwa Towns, but went on to treat with chiefs of Old Calabar and Victoria.

the relations of peace and friendship which have for a long time existed; you should state that she is willing, if requested to extend to them her favour and protection, on condition that they give such guarantees as shall be considered satisfactory for the lives and property of British subjects, and for the freedom of commercial intercourse and religious worship. You will further make it clear to them that it is not Her Majesty's desire to obtain any exclusive privileges for British subjects, but that, in order to prevent such exclusive privileges being granted to the subjects of other Powers, you are instructed to require of them that they should refrain from entering into agreements with other Powers without the knowledge or sanction of Her Majesty. Should you succeed in obtaining assent to these terms, you will be authorized to conclude engagements binding the Chiefs to observe them. The Chiefs will understand that the British Consular officers to be stationed on the coast will watch to see that the conditions are faithfully executed, and will be ready to assist at all times with friendly advice. The Chiefs will, as hitherto, manage their own affairs, but will have always at hand counsellors and arbitrators in matters of difficulty or dispute.

A somewhat exceptional treatment will be required as regards the Chiefs of the Cameroons, who have expressed an urgent wish to cede their territory to Her Majesty. In their case it is not proposed to accept the cession at present, as by so doing the necessity would be entailed of establishing in that particular spot a British Colony or Settlement, with the requisite machinery for government; but the Chiefs will be asked to undertake that they will, if required, cede such portions of their territory as it may be thought desirable to acquire.

Special treatment will also have to be accorded to the Settlement at Ambas Bay, which is the property of the Baptist Missionary Society. You should take an early opportunity of visiting the Settlement, and of informing the residents that Her Majesty's Government have acceded to the request made by them and by the parent Society that it should be taken under the protection and control of the British Crown . . .

23

H. P. ANDERSON: MEMORANDUM 1,
WEST AFRICA CONFERENCE,
14 OCTOBER 1884

. . . I T seems incontrovertible that, though as regards the Congo, we can appear at the Conference as one of many Powers interested, as

<hr/>

[1] F.O. Confidential Print, 5023 (1884), p. 15. For the background to the Conference, see S. E. Crowe, *The Berlin West Africa Conference, 1884–1885* (London, 1942).

regards the Niger we should take our seat as *the Niger Power*, the one Power at present concerned in the trade of the Lower Niger and Oil Rivers.

Appearing in this character, we should have to refer in Conference to our Treaties. The first question to be decided (and which seems to me to call for decision at once) is what interpretation we put on those Treaties. They contain, besides their stipulations for freedom of trade, provisions for placing the territory under British protection, forbidding Treaties with other Powers without our assent, and conferring on our Consular officers a position similar to that of Resident. They do not, like the French Treaties, mention the word 'suzeraineté', but they are believed to be much on the same lines as the German Treaties. The Germans, as we know, interpret these as conferring an exclusive German Protectorate; what view should we say that we take of ours?

Having in Conference referred to the existence of our Treaties, and explained our interpretation of them, we should next have to consider whether we should maintain them or cancel them to make way for an international arrangement.

If we maintained them, I presume that it may be taken for granted that we should not do so under such conditions as to preserve our Protectorates under the control of a Commission, as by so doing we should be undertaking the responsibilities of police for the benefit of Europe; but that we should maintain them in their entirety, retaining the coast under our protection, giving guarantees to the Powers for freedom of navigation, and compelling respect for the Treaties and the guarantees, as we could without much difficulty, through our Consular Corps and our squadron; if this were our idea, and it were accepted, it might be worked out eventually through Lord Aberdare's scheme of conferring a Charter on the African Company.

If we did not maintain our Treaties altogether, we might do so partially, adhering to them as regards the smaller rivers and assenting to the internationalization of the stream of the Niger itself; but this course might place us hereafter in an embarrassing position.

If we prefer to cancel our Treaties, have we not the right to insist upon them—*i.e.*, to preserve our position as the Niger Power—until we are satisfied as to the conditions on which we could consent to withdraw them? I mean that instead of appearing in the Conference to listen to what France and Germany have to say, should we not appear for them to listen, in the first instance, to what we have to say? And should we not explain that, as regards the Niger, we must shape our decision after hearing what is proposed; that we are alone on the spot, and alone have the trade; that we are protecting it with our Consular Corps and our ships; that we have Treaties with the Chiefs; that we understand the markets; and that, though our sole wish is to open the trade to the world, we require to be convinced that the proposals will have that effect? The above are the points which appear to me to press for considera- tion, and if there is any force in my observations, I would further suggest that it should be considered whether it should be intimated, before the Conference, that we hold an exceptional position as regards the Niger.

24

EARL GRANVILLE TO SIR E. MALET (DRAFT): WEST AFRICA CONFERENCE, OCTOBER 1884[1]

... THE second basis for discussion deals with the question of the application to the Congo and the Niger of the principles adopted by the Congress of Vienna with regard to liberty of navigation.

Her Majesty's Government would wish that those principles might be applied not only to the Congo and the Niger, but also to the other rivers of Africa.

Count Münster, in his note of the 22nd instant, expressed the concurrence of the German Government in this wish. You are, therefore, authorized to join in discussion, or even to raise it, on this broader basis, with reference not only to the other rivers of Western Africa, but also to the Zambesi.

The question for practical consideration will be, as far as Her Majesty's Government are concerned, not the acceptance of the general principles, to which they cordially assent, but the mode of their application. Count Münster, in his note of the 22nd instant, referred to the Regulations for the Elbe and the Danube; in the cases of those rivers, as in those of other European rivers to which the principles of the Congress have been applied, no great difficulty has been experienced in the adaptation of the principles to the varying conditions, as each river runs through the territories of well-defined States, and the geographical position and peculiarities of navigation have been well known or easily ascertained; in the African rivers the difficulties will be undoubtedly greater, though probably not insuperable.

The Congo in its lower course is a navigable river with one mouth comparatively easy of access; on its banks factories of many nations are established, and Her Majesty's Government have already con- vinced themselves that the navigation might be regulated by an International Commission, the creation of which they have repeatedly urged; if, therefore, it is proposed to establish such a Commission on

[1] *F.O. Confidential Print*, 5023 (1884).

that river, you will be authorized to give their assent, subject to the examination and approval of its constitution. The position of the Niger is altogether different; on that river the establishment of a Commission is believed to be impracticable. The river itself, in a great part of its course, is very imperfectly explored, consequently there is no connection between its sources and its lower stream; the latter, when it approaches the sea, is split into a network of creeks little known, and in many instances unsurveyed; the trade of the interior passes through the medium of coast tribes, who act as middlemen, and who, being keenly alive to their interests, are difficult to manage and control; the commerce owes its development almost exclusively to British enterprise: the trade is [almost, if not][1] altogether, in British hands, and the most important tribes, who have for years been accustomed to look on the agents of this country as their protectors and counsellors, have now, in consequence of their urgent and repeated appeals, been placed formally under British Protectorate. On this river, therefore, a difference of application of the principles of the Congress of Vienna would seem to be imperative; the coastline and lower course of the river are sufficiently under British control for Her Majesty's Government to be able to regulate the navigation, and they are prepared to give in Conference the most formal assurances as to the freedom of the navigation. The manner in which these assurances should be recorded will form a proper subject for deliberation; it is only, therefore, as a suggestion that I observe that they might possibly be conceived in the sense of the provisions of the XVth Article of the Treaty of Paris.

If the Conference shall decide to extend the principles of the Congress of Vienna to other rivers, the question of the mode of application will, as in the case of the Congo and Niger, have to be considered separately after study of the individual conditions of each of these rivers as they may successively be discussed.

The third basis related to the definition of the formalities to be observed in order to render future occupations on the coasts of Africa effective; this has been explained by Count Münster to mean that assurances shall be given that in future the principles unanimously laid down by the jurist and Judges of all lands, including England, shall be practically applied.

Her Majesty's Government have no hesitation in accepting the discussion of this basis . . .

---

[1] Note by Anderson: 'We hope that, before instructions go, the African Company will enable us to cut out the words in brackets. H.P.A.'

25

THE EARL OF DERBY TO GOVERNOR W. A. G. YOUNG: EXTENSION OF LAGOS PROTECTORATE, 10 NOVEMBER 1884[1]

I HAVE the honour to acquaint you that I have this day telegraphed to you that Her Majesty's Government proposed to give instructions to the Consul for the Bights of Benin and Biafra to conclude treaties of protection with the natives on the seaboard between the Benin River and the eastern boundary of the Lagos Protectorate, but that Consul Hewett was at present in the Niger River, and instructions could not reach him.

I instructed you, therefore, to take immediate steps for making provisional agreements with the natives for a British Protectorate, and where no responsible authority existed with which a treaty might be made, to hoist the British flag and proclaim a Protectorate.

26

SIR EDWARD MALET TO EARL GRANVILLE: WEST AFRICA CONFERENCE, 1 DECEMBER 1884[2]

WITH reference to my despatch No. 154, Africa, of the 29th ultimo, I have the honour to report that the draft of the Act of Navigation for the Congo and Niger, inclosed therein, will be discussed at once in the Conference. I shall urge that the question of the Congo and of the Niger be taken separately, similar treatment for both rivers being impossible.

In all probability I shall be asked in the Conference how Her Majesty's Government propose to deal with the Niger, and I should consequently be glad to receive from your Lordship instructions giving me a certain amount of latitude in dealing with the point.

The following is the substance of the Declaration suggested by my advisers founded on the precedents established in the Argentine Treaty of 1853, the Oregon Treaty of 1846, and in the Treaty of Paris.

I should add that the text of the Declaration has been revised by Sir Travers Twiss,[3] who tells me he sees no objection to it.

---

[1] C.O. 879/21, no. 278.

[2] F.O. Confidential Print, 5033 (1884). Sir E. B. Malet, diplomat and British envoy to Brussels, 1883, and Berlin, 1884–95.

[3] Former Professor of International Law, London, and Civil Law, Oxford, Admiralty Advocate-General, and legal adviser to the Foreign Office.

'Her Majesty's Government engage that the navigation of the River Niger and of its affluents so far as they are, or shall be, under the sovereignty or Protectorate of Her Majesty the Queen, shall be free, the merchant-ships of all nations being put absolutely on the same footing as British ships in those waters, and not subjected to any differential treatment whatever.

'Her Majesty's Government engage to levy no toll nor any duty on goods which may be on board of merchant-ships, founded solely on the fact of the navigation of the River Niger and its affluents.

'The Regulations to be established by Her Majesty's Government for the security and control of the Niger navigation shall be framed so as to facilitate as much as possible the passage of merchant-ships of all nations.

'It is understood that nothing in the above engagement shall be construed as preventing, or as intended to prevent, the Queen's Government from making any rules or regulations respecting the navigation of the Niger, not inconsistent with the engagement above referred to.'

27

LORD SELBORNE TO EARL GRANVILLE: WEST AFRICA CONFERENCE, 20 JANUARY 1885[1]

I ENCLOSE a draft which I have prepared, as promised, of the form in which we might enter into an engagement as to protected territories in Africa, so as to give effect to the view taken by Gladstone, which is the same (in principle) with my own.

Perhaps it would not be necessary to ask questions if this is accepted. But, if the other Powers press for more, I would suggest that some practical explanation should be given of the sense attached to the supposed obligation: as, *e.g.*, whether Germany would hold herself bound to create and maintain judicial establishments capable of securing the objects in view, throughout the extent of the 300 miles coast-line of which she has assumed the Protectorate at Angra Pequena, &c., and hold *us* bound to do the same throughout every district protected by us on the banks and near the mouths of the Niger; or, in the alternative, to admit a direct and absolute responsibility, under all circumstances, for all wrong-doings towards foreigners, of the natives of the protected territories?

[1] *F.O. Confidential Print*, 5033 (1884). *1st Earl of Selbourne*, Lord Chancellor, 1880–5.

Enclosure
Draft as to Protected Territories in Africa.

The Signatory Powers also undertake, so far as relates to any territories on the coasts of Africa placed under their Protectorate, to use, in favour of foreigners of every nation, as effectual means of insuring the maintenance of peace, and obtaining justice or due reparation in respect of privately acquired rights, and securing liberty of commerce and of transit in the conditions in which they may have been established, as they are enabled to use in favour of their own rights, or of the rights of their own subjects.

28

NIGER DISTRICTS PROTECTORATE:
NOTIFICATION, 5 JUNE 1885[1]

I T is hereby notified for public information, that under and by virtue of certain treaties concealed between the month of July last and the present date, and by other lawful means, the territories on the West Coast of Africa, hereinafter referred to as the Niger Districts, were placed under the Protectorate of Her Majesty the Queen from the date of the said Treaties respectively.

The British Protectorate of the Niger Districts comprises the territories on the line of coast between the British Protectorate of Lagos and the right or western river-bank of the mouth of the Rio del Rey. It further comprises the territories on both banks of the Niger, from its confluence with the River Benué at Lokoja, to the sea, as well as the territories on both banks of the River Benué from the confluence, up to and including Ibi.

The measures in course of preparation for the administration of justice and the maintenance of peace and good order in the Niger Districts will be duly notified and published.

29

TREATY: CESSION OF MAHIN BEACH,
24 OCTOBER 1885[2]

[King Amapetu of Mahin has ceded sovereignty rights to G. L. Gaiser, 29 January 1885, and has signed a protectorate treaty with Dr. N. G. Nachtigal, 11 March 1885, which has not been ratified.]

. . . N o w, therefore, be it known to all whom it may concern, that King Amapetu, King of Mahin, by this Treaty . . . doth hereby for

---

[1] Hertslet, *Commercial Treaties*, vol. xvii (1890), pp. 108–9; C.O. 879/22, no. 296.
[2] Hertslet, *Commercial Treaties*, vol. xviii (1893), pp. 178–9. Based on agreement with Germany regarding spheres of influence in Derby to Young, 6 April 1885.

himself and his lawful successors cede unto Her Most Gracious
Majesty Queen Victoria, her heirs and successors, all that part of the
Mahin country which is known as the Mahin Beach, wheresoever the
Mahin country is bounded by the sea, the whole of such coast line
being hereby ceded to Her Majesty, such cession being without
prejudice to the rights of the said Gottlieb Leonhard Gaiser, as set
forth in the deed of sale to him of the 29th January, 1885, hereinbefore
referred to, the grant to him of such land rights extending on the sea
beach in the Gulf of Benin from Abejanure on the west, to Abetobo on
the east, and being bounded inland by the next lagoon . . .

[This cession is accepted in its entirety.]

30

EDWARD STANHOPE TO GOVERNOR W. BRANDFORD GRIFFITH: GOLD COAST EXPANSION, 19 NOVEMBER 1885[1]

I HAVE under my consideration your Despatch No. 345 of 14th
September, on the subject of the desire of the people of Sefwhi to be
taken under the protection of Great Britain.

You are aware of the reluctance of Her Majesty's Government to
increase, without very strong and sufficient reason, the existing
responsibilities of this country on the West Coast of Africa, and they
feel it, therefore, their duty to examine most carefully any proposals
which may be submitted to them for extending the area of British
authority and jurisdiction in that part of the world.

In the present instance the advantages likely to be derived from the
further opening up of intercourse with the interior tribes, and from
the increased development and security of trade which may be looked
for, appear largely to outweigh the possible inconveniences arising
from the extension of the Protectorate, and render compliance with
the prayer of the Sefwhi people both desirable and expedient.

I have therefore to inform you that Her Majesty's Government are
prepared to sanction the inclusion of Sefwhi within the Gold Coast
Protectorate, on the understanding that this does not involve the
responsibility of defending the country against any native aggressions,
or of supporting the King and Chiefs in any demands which may seem
unreasonable or undesirable.

You should therefore communicate this decision to the King and
Chiefs, and, if they are willing to accept Her Majesty's protection

[1] C.O. 879/25, no. 333. And for control of the Volta by treaty with Akwamu
(based on the treaty of 1874) by declaration, 9 May 1887, see Metcalfe, *Great
Britain and Ghana*, no. 354. A treaty with Sefwi was made by Lonsdale, 8 February
1887.

on these terms, a treaty should be drawn up and signed and transmitted to me for Her Majesty's approval and ratification.

31

SIR SAMUEL ROWE TO SIR HENRY HOLLAND: EXPANSION ON THE GAMBIA, 14 JUNE 1887[1]

... 10. THERE would thus seem to be five principal questions which demand consideration. Taken in the order of their importance, they are as follows:—

First. On the north bank a clear knowledge of the position in which this Government stands towards the French as a consequence of recent events in Baddiboo; without this knowledge it is difficult and it seems almost impossible to respond to the invitations from the heads of the trading villages to visit them or to attempt to assist in restoring peace and order in the land.

Secondly. On the south, the removal of Brima NJie from the scene of his plundering and an attempt to restore the district to some approach to a peaceful and orderly state.

Thirdly. Also on the south bank and probably quite as important as the second of these points to the trade of Bathurst, some interference by which a stop may be put to the fighting between Musa Molloh and Fodey Cabba; it may be by causing or persuading Fodey Cabba to remove to some other district or by causing Fodey Cabba to desist from his plundering and slave catching; this I imagine would be difficult if he be allowed to remain in the district to which he has temporarily attached himself.

Fourthly. On the north bank, and of considerable importance though perhaps less so than the foregoing because the trading district which will be influenced by it is at a greater distance from Bathurst, the removal of Momodu Lamin from Toobacoota; so that there may remain no excuse for the French to direct an attack on the Nyani district nor for the Nyani and Wooli district to fall out.

Fifthly. To obtain information as to conditions of the treaty according to which Musa Molloh is stated to have placed the kingdom of Ferdhoo and certain neighbouring districts under the protectorate of France—Among other districts mentioned as so placed under the protectorate is the kingdom of Wooli. Wooli is on the north bank of the river; so far as I can learn it has not been subordinate to Ferdhoo, it was overrun by Bondou, but has been allowed to recover more or

---

[1] C.O. 876/26, no. 341. There was no intention of handing over Gambia territory to the French by this date: C.O. to British and African Steam Navigation Company, 9 September 1887.

H

less its independence and pays only a nominal tribute to Bondou. Yarbutenda, the riverside wharf to which trade is supposed to come from the Bondou country and for keeping the trade highways free to traders and some other privileges we pay to the King of Bondou under Treaty No. 22. November 12, 1869, 50 *l.* a year, is situated in the Wooli country which lies between the river bank and the kingdom of Bondou.

11. I have no doubt that much may be done towards effecting what can be done locally by personal influence; the tribes in this district are not insensible to it so far as I have seen, but to effect this time is needed and personal intercourse with those whom we wish to persuade.

12. I see no other way to produce these results. They seem to me to be necessary not only to the peace of the banks of the river so far as concerns the dwellers there, but to prevent them being overrun and probably annexed as a consequence by the Government of the neighbouring Colony of Senegal, and to prevent this last it would be necessary that a line of separation should be agreed on between the English and French which line should form a boundary beyond which English influence or interference should not be exercised, on the north towards the Senegal, on the south towards the Casamance, and beyond which line the French should equally admit that they are restrained from passing. . . .

32

H. BRACKENBURY: NOTE,
RELATIONS WITH FRANCE, 27 JUNE 1887[1]

The differences between France and this country as to territory in the neighbourhood of Porto Novo have doubtless become a source of constant irritation between the French and British local authorities, and a collision has actually taken place between the French and British native troops.

But the interests here concerned are purely local and not of a high order. The settlement of the dispute in favour of the French would not in any way affect the general strength of the Empire, nor would it in any way interfere with Imperial interests so far as Imperial defence is concerned in case of war with a great maritime power.

The one spot in West Africa where Imperial interests of a high order are concerned is Sierra Leone, which has been selected as the intermediate coaling station between Gibraltar and the Cape; and it

[1] C.O. 879/26, no. 334. *General (Sir) H. Brackenbury*, Deputy Quartermaster-General, had served with Wolseley in the Ashanti campaign and was head of the War Office Intelligence branch, 1886–91. Salisbury, as a result of this note, asked the C.O. to agree to an extension of the area of negotiations with France: F.O. to C.O., 12 August 1887; C.O. to F.O., 29 August 1887 (agreed).

is of the utmost importance to us to prevent the extension of French influence to the neighbourhood of that settlement. Of this the French are well aware. They have recently made a treaty with Samadu, a powerful native whose rule extends over territories directly in contact with the tribes under British influence, by which, according to the published versions, they have gained a Protectorate over his country. And it is my opinion that the French are keeping this Porto-Novo sore in a state of irritation in order to give to this question a fictitious importance in our eyes, that it may be used as a lever to obtain concessions from us in the neighbourhood of Sierra Leone, whenever the question of the Gambia again comes to the front. It appears to me therefore that it should be our object to use it in exactly the opposite way, attaching no value in our own minds to the disputed territory, but making the French yield other points to us in exchange for a settlement of the Porto Novo question in their favour.

33

RECOMMENDATIONS OF THE BRITISH AND GERMAN COMMISSIONERS: GOLD COAST COLONY AND THE GERMAN TOGO PROTECTORATE, SEPTEMBER 1887[1]

1. THAT the boundary line laid down in the Agreement signed by the German and British Commissioners on the 14th July, 1886, should be continued in such a manner as to include within the German Protectorate the territories of Towe, Kowe and Agotime, and to leave within the British Protectorate the countries of Aquamoo and Creppe (or Peki). The exact definition of this boundary to be hereafter determined, if necessary, by a joint commission on the spot.

2. That between the northern limit of the territory of Creppe and the mouth of the River Daka, the river Volta shall form the line of demarcation between the spheres of influence of the two countries, Great Britain undertaking not to acquire any protectorates to the east of that river, and Germany entering into a similar agreement with regard to the territories to the west.

3. That a conventional line be drawn on the latitude of the mouth of the River Daka, and that the two Governments shall mutually agree to regard the territories lying to the north of this line, within the limits marked on the accompanying map . . .

[The 'neutral ground' on the map was fixed at 10° north, with its eastern limit at 0° 33′ east and the western limit at 1° 27′ west.]

<hr>

[1] C.O. 879/27, no. 33. The recommendations of commissioners Krauel and Scott were accepted by an exchange of notes, 12 and 14 March: C.O. 879/28, no. 356.

. . . and to abstain from seeking to acquire within them protectorates or exclusive influence.

4. If the second of these recommendations is adopted, the Commissioners are of opinion that an agreement might properly be concluded that, in the event of Germany extending her protectorate up to the River Volta, within the limits mentioned, the Imperial Government will engage not to levy duties upon goods in transit, nor to place any other impediment in the way of trade between the British Protectorate and the interior; the British Government undertaking on their part, in the event of the extension of the German Protectorate above-mentioned, not to levy transit duties within their Protectorate east of the River Volta upon goods passing from the German Protectorate into other districts east of the Volta, not being British, or from the same into the German Protectorate.

34

PROVISIONAL CONVENTION: LAGOS, 2 JANUARY 1888[1]

PROVISIONAL convention regulating the relations between the British Colony and Protectorate of Lagos and the French Protectorate of the kingdom of Porto Novo.

Between his Excellency Cornelius Alfred Moloney, Companion of the Most Distinguished Order of Saint Michael and Saint George, Governor for Her Britannic Majesty, and Commander-in-Chief of the Colony and Protectorate of Lagos,

On the one part.

And Administrator Victor Ballot, Chevalier of the Order of the Legion of Honor, Director of the Political Affairs of the Colony of the Senegal, entrusted with the command of the French establishments of the Gulf of Benin and of the Protectorate of the kingdom of Porto Novo,

On the other part.

Who, provided with the powers and instructions of their respective Governments, which have been found in good and due form, have provisionally adopted what follows until the conclusion of the definite convention regulating the differences concerning the territory of the French Protectorate of Porto Novo and the English Colony of Lagos, in order to put an end to the regrettable situation actually existing, and to establish with common accord the *modus vivendi*, which ought in the future to exist between the two Protectorates.

[1] C.O. 879/27, no. 345. Encl. in Moloney to Holland, 2 January 1888.

Article 1. The French flags and military posts of Afotonu and of Zunu will be withdrawn.

Article 2. The English flags and military posts of Zumi north, Zumi south, Agege Kanji, and Wheetah will be withdrawn.

Article 3. The Channel of Zumi will be absolutely free.

Article 4. The Channel of Toché will be open to traders and to French officers not in uniform.

Article 5. No new occupation will take place. The two parties engage mutually not to hoist in future the national flag upon any point where it had not been already.

Article 6. The stipulations of the present Convention shall be executed within eight days from the signing thereof.

Article 7. The duration of the said Act is subject to the decisions of the Cabinets of Paris and of St. James.

Done, at Lagos, in quadruplicate, the 2nd January 1888.

Alfred Moloney,
Governor.

In this convention Zumi, Zunu, and Kanji Agege are synonymous, and Wheetah synonymous with Ouetah.

35

A. W. L. HEMMING: MEMORANDUM: WEST AFRICAN QUESTIONS, 5 MARCH 1889[1]

I. *Without any proposal for the cession of the Gambia.*

IN our letter to the Foreign Office of 5th December 1887, we proposed the following scheme, which, it was stated, appeared 'to present a reasonable basis for negotiation.'

'1. That Her Majesty's Government should agree to relinquish their Protectorate over Katanu and Appa and withdraw from these districts, stipulating that such of the Chiefs and inhabitants as desire to do so should be permitted to come into the Lagos Protectorate.

'2. That the boundary between the Protectorate of Lagos and that of Porto Novo should be drawn at a point somewhat west of the Addo River, as shown upon the sketch map C enclosed in the letter from this Department of 16th November 1887.

'3. That in return for the very important concession made to the French Government by the proposed abandonment of Katanu and Appa they should be asked to yield to the representations of Her Majesty's Government respecting their proceedings at the Gambia, and to relinquish all claims to exercise authority or influence in the countries bordering upon that river; to settle the Assinee boundary

[1] C.O. 879/29, no. 365. Encl. in C.O. to F.O., 7 March 1889.

question in accordance with the recommendations of the English Commissioners and accept the boundary proposed by them; and to agree to a demarcation of British and French spheres of influence in the interior of Africa behind Sierra Leone.

'4. In the event of the French Government agreeing to the proposal which has been made to them to refer the Assinee boundary dispute to arbitration, this question should, of course, be omitted, and it will be possible to press all the more strongly for the acceptance of the other demands of Her Majesty's Government.'

I do not think that any different or better scheme than the above could be devised, assuming the cession of the Gambia to be left out of the question. We have nothing but Katanu and Appa which we could offer to the French in return for the concessions we desire to obtain from them.

The arrangement would certainly not be a satisfactory one—but it is probably the best that could be effected.

II. *If the cession of the Gambia is to be entertained.*

In this case we should of course be in a much stronger position and be entitled to ask for very much larger and more important concessions in exchange for what we should be prepared to surrender.

In a letter of 10th October last Mr. Hutton stated as follows what he understood the French Government would be prepared to agree to in exchange for the Gambia:—

'One of my French correspondents, who is consulted by his Government on matters connected with their administration on the West Coast of Africa, informs me that at the Colonial Office in Paris there is now a disposition to come to an agreement with Great Britain relative to the delimitation of respective interests in West Africa, and that he believes there would not be an insuperable difficulty relative to France withdrawing from Porto Novo and the whole coast westward of Gaboon provided that Gambia is given in exchange, and that the right bank of the river Scarcies is accepted as their eastern boundary; also that in the interior a line be drawn from the sources of the Grand Scarcies to the Upper Djolibah (or Niger sources) about Farannah and thence north-east until the 10th degree North lat.—Samadoo's country north of about 10° North, and the whole of the territories on the right bank of the Upper Niger within a line drawn, say, from Burrum (about 18° North lat. and 0° long.) to a point at about 10° North lat. and 4° West long., all to be accepted as under French influence.'

In writing to the Foreign Office we said that these proposals, if they represented the views of the French Government, appeared to present a prospect of a satisfactory settlement.

But I think that, in the first instance, we ought certainly to ask for considerably more than we should get under Mr. Hutton's proposals. I would suggest that we should revert to the scheme which formed the basis of the negotiations commenced in 1875, viz.: that the French should withdraw from the whole of the coast line between the right bank of the Rio Pongas and the Gaboon, or, it would now be sufficient to say, between the Rio Pongas and Lagos, as the whole of the Oil Rivers and Camaroons territory is now occupied by us and the Germans. We should also of course stipulate for a line of demarcation in the interior in order to prevent the French from occupying the countries in the rear of Sierra Leone and of the Gold Coast.

I think the French would probably very strongly demur to giving up the rivers north of Sierra Leone between the Rio Pongas and the Scarcies, and we might in such case agree to a compromise by allowing them to come as far north as (say) the Mahniah river, but if we do not in the first place ask for something more than we are finally prepared to accept, the negotiations will break down by our being required to take less than we can possibly agree to.

There is no doubt that in the Gambia we have a valuable property (for the French) to offer, and we must ask a high price for it.

If we agree to the line being brought south of the Rio Pongas, we should demand, in return, an undertaking that there should be no differential treatment of British trade at the Gambia or in other parts of the sphere reserved to French influence.

I think that, in the last resort, we might, rather than make no settlement at all, accept an arrangement somewhat on the lines of that suggested in Mr. Hutton's letter; but a strenuous effort should be made to obtain better terms, and it is somewhat difficult to fix a *minimum* until we have some idea of what the French are likely to offer.

36

WAR OFFICE TO FOREIGN OFFICE: RELATIONS WITH FRANCE, 21 MAY 1889[1]

. . . IF, in the development of the government of the Rivières du Sud, the French hold out advantages to Samory, they will in course of time strengthen their hold over his southern provinces; and it is precisely in these provinces, those immediately surrounding Sierra Leone, that Major Festing found his power to be strongest, and himself personally held in the highest esteem and respect. The Director of Military Intelligence cannot but look upon this as a constant source of anxiety. If, on the other hand, the French were to abandon all

---

[1] C.O. 879/31, no. 377. C.O. to F.O., 28 May 1889 (agreement with this argument), and see above, I, pp. 35-7.

influence south of the 10th parallel of latitude, the mere knowledge of this would have a powerful effect upon Samory's mind, would strengthen our position greatly in his eyes, and would enable us to enter into treaties of friendship and alliance with him, which would be of great value in case of war with France. Even an agreement that the existing boundary-line between the Rivers Scarcies and Mellacoree should be prolonged inland so as to strike the 10th parallel of latitude would effect this end.

In short, the Director of Military Intelligence would urge that any minor sacrifice should be made at Lagos and Assinie for the sake of securing the proposed line of demarcation at Sierra Leone; but is not prepared to recommend the surrender of the Gambia for that purpose unless it were accompanied by the surrender by the French of their Gold and Slave Coast possessions.

As regards the question put by Mr. Egerton, 'Will the French keep up the efforts they have lately been making, and of which the Intelligence Division observes diminution?' the Director of Military Intelligence is of opinion that they will keep up efforts to consolidate their power and influence between the River Senegal and the southern limits of their possessions in the Rivières du Sud; that they will endeavour to draw trade from the English to the French ports; and that they will continue to send commercial and geographical missions into these territories; but that they will not endeavour at present to push further up the Niger, or to establish communications between their Niger possessions and their Protectorates in rear of the Gold Coast. . . .

37

E. H. EGERTON TO THE MARQUIS OF SALISBURY: ANGLO-FRENCH AGREEMENT, 2 JULY 1889[1]

YESTERDAY Mr. Hemming and I attended at the Ministry for Foreign Affairs, in order to arrive at a more detailed settlement of the West African questions, respecting which we had come to a rough general understanding, as reported in my No. 88 of the 27th ultimo.

MM. Nisard and Bayol were present, and having naturally had opportunity of becoming acquainted with each other's views on various points connected with the settlement, we were enabled to proceed somewhat rapidly.

[1] C.O. 879/29, no. 365. Encl. in F.O. to C.O., 10 July 1889. (Sir) E. H. Egerton, Secretary to the Paris Embassy, 1885–92. Full text of the Arrangement, 10 August 1889 in Hertslet, The Map of Africa by Treaty, 2nd edn. (London, 1896), vol. ii, pp. 558–63.

Without wearying your Lordship with the discussions, I will merely state the agreements come to, subject to approval by our Governments. They are as follows:—

1. *Gambia.*—The Jinnak Creek on the coast will be the starting-point of the northern frontier-line of the British Gambia Protectorate, which will follow eastwards the parallel of latitude of that creek, viz., about 13° 37' north. This line will cut Baddiboo in two, leaving the northern portion, or Rip, to France, the southern to Great Britain, and will stop at a point 10 kilom. distant from the Gambia; thence it will leave the parallel and follow the course of the river eastwards at a distance of 10 kilom. (6 miles 376 yards), as far as Yarbutenda.

The southern frontier of British Gambia will start at the mouth of the San Pedro River, and ascend that river as far as 13° 10', from whence it will follow that parallel of latitude eastwards to a point at the head of the Vintang Creek, near Sanding, leaving the whole of the Vintang district in British hands; the line will then turn northwards until it reaches a point 10 kilom. distant from the Gambia River, which it will follow eastwards at that distance until opposite Yarbutenda, where it will stop.

This arrangement leaves the navigable channel of the Gambia and the Vintang Creek free from all foreign interference, and though the sphere of influence into the interior is circumscribed, there is not, apparently, unmixed evil in this—it is improbable that the trade, such as it is, of the surrounding country will be diverted from the Gambia, whilst our position will be clearly defined, and our responsibilities will be diminished by the limitation of our sphere of political influence to districts which we can easily control from the water. The islands, it is true, on the coast north of the entrance to the River Gambia, and now in dispute, will not be considered as forming part of the Gambia Protectorate. The French Delegates did not appear inclined to give way to our contention that they should be so, and as this point is inferior in importance to the possession of the Vintang country, we did not press it.

It must be remembered in connection with the present proposed arrangement that the French have of late displayed much activity and have made great sacrifices and efforts in developing their Senegambian Colony, and that they have made Treaties with the Chiefs on the Gambia and surrounding districts; consequently they are to some extent at an advantage in discussions with us on the affairs of the populations neighbouring that river, our Gambia attitude having been a passive one.

2. *As regards Porto Novo.*—It was agreed that the meridian of the Agera River, which divides Pokra from Porto Novo, shall be followed as a line of demarcation, both to the sea through Appah, and also to the interior northwards up to the 9th degree of north latitude,

where it will stop. The French negotiators were willing, and indeed anxious, that the line should continue far into the interior, but we did not think it necessary or desirable that it should approach nearer the Niger than the 9th, or at most the 10th, degree.

It is clearly understood that each party has entire political liberty of action on its side of this line of demarcation, and be free from any interference by the other.

I may mention that M. Bayol informs me confidentially that there is every probability of the French Tariffs being assimilated to those of the neighbouring English Colonies. Also, that one reason of the anxiety of the French to draw the line of demarcation well into the interior is that they wish to be undisturbed in their operations against Dahomey; but of course they thus entirely renounce any action to the east of the meridian in question. He promises that the Katanu Chiefs shall be protected from any vengeance of King Tofa.

3. In the direction of Assinee we proposed that the line of frontier should start slightly from the west of New Town on the shore and be continued across the neck of land to the Tendo Lagoon. There was some little question as to the exact point near New Town where the line should be drawn, the French holding that there are two New Towns; this matter is not conclusively settled, but we recommended them to take the line as suggested by the French Commissioners in 1883.

The Gold Coast line of frontier will then follow the shore of the Tendo Lagoon to the entrance of the Tendo River, and be continued to a point south of Nougoua and north of Ellubo, from whence it will be directed west towards the line, or continuation of the line, of demarcation between the Kinjabo and Brissam Kingdoms.

We explained that Great Britain held Protectorates over Brissam (Aowin) and Sefwhe, and had assumed the Gaman or Bontouku Protectorate; the French on their side held claim, by M. Reich La Plène's Treaty, to that Protectorate, and desired that the Gaman question should be considered outside the present settlement.

The navigation of the Tendo and Ehy Lagoons, and of the Tendo River, are to be free to the craft and subjects of both countries, and it is decided that should we establish customs at the mouth of the River Tendo, we shall have the right of insisting on certificates of the destination of the goods entering the river, and that they shall have paid in full, without rebate, the French duties.

The acquiescence of the British Government in this arrangement is further to depend on a scale of duties being established in Assinee in which the duties on tobacco and spirits will not be less than those mentioned in the proposed Tariff which I submitted to your Lordship in my No. 79 of the 6th ultimo.

With reference to those duties M. Bayol informed me that he was confident of the proposed Tariff being accepted, and further that the duty on cotton goods would be diminished from 30 per cent. to 10 per cent. *ad valorem.*

4. As regards the Sierra Leone frontier, the arrangement as laid down in the French Memorandum which I had the honour to enclose in my No. 88 of the 27th ultimo is maintained, with the exception that there will be no mention of a line of demarcation following the meridian 13 of French longitude, at which the line of demarcation from the coast will stop.[1]

I shall hope shortly to submit to your Lordship a rough draft of the text of the proposed General Agreement, for your examination and approval, which draft is now being drawn up at the Ministry for Foreign Affairs, founded on our conversations and written notes.

There will be no mention, except as regards Assinee, of the change of the French Tariff, the assimilation of which generally to that of the English neighbouring Colonies will, if brought about, be of undoubted value in keeping harmony in the relations of the French and English establishments on the West Coast.

38

BRITISH AND GERMAN AFRICA AND HELIGOLAND AGREEMENT, 1 JULY 1890[2]

[Art. I: East African spheres of influence; Art II: withdrawal of the German Protectorate over Witu; Art. III: South West Africa.]

Line of Boundary between the British Gold Coast Colony and the German Protectorate of Togo. Volta Districts.

Art. IV. In West Africa—

1. The boundary between the German Protectorate of Togo and the British Gold Coast Colony commences on the coast at the marks set up after the negotiations between the Commissioners of the two countries of the 14th and 28th of July, 1886; and proceeds direct northwards to the 6° 10′ parallel of north latitude; thence it runs along that parallel westward till it reaches the left bank of the River Aka; ascends the mid-channel of that river to the 6° 20′ parallel of north latitude; runs along that parallel westwards to the right bank of the River Dchawe or Shavoe; follows that bank of the river till it reaches the parallel corresponding with the point of confluence of the River Deine with the Volta; it runs along that parallel westward till it reaches the Volta; from that point it ascends the left bank of the

---

[1] i.e. the line to the north of Sierra Leone would run according to the provisions of the 1882 Convention.

[2] Hertslet, *Map of Africa*, vol. ii, pp. 646–8.

Volta till it arrives at the neutral zone established by the Agreement of 1888, which commences at the confluence of the River Dakka with the Volta.

Each Power engages to withdraw immediately after the conclusion of this Agreement all its officials and employés from territory which is assigned to the other Power by the above delimitation.

Gulf of Guinea. Rio del Rey Creek.

2. It having been proved to the satisfaction of the two Powers that no river exists on the Gulf of Guinea corresponding with that marked on maps as the Rio del Rey, to which reference was made in the Agreement of 1885, a provisional line of demarcation is adopted between the German sphere in the Cameroons and the adjoining British sphere, which, starting from the head of the Rio del Rey Creek, goes direct to the point, about 9° 8' of east longitude, marked 'Rapids' in the British Admiralty chart.

Freedom of Goods from Transit Dues between River Benué and Lake Chad.

Art. V. It is agreed that no Treaty or Agreement, made by or on behalf of either Power to the north of the River Benué, shall interfere with the free passage of goods of the other Power, without payment of transit dues, to and from the shores of Lake Chad.

Treaties in Territories between the Benué and Lake Chad.

All Treaties made in territories intervening between the Benué and Lake Chad shall be notified by one Power to the other.

Lines of Demarcation subject to Modification.

Art. VI. All the lines of demarcation traced in Articles I to IV shall be subject to rectification by agreement between the two Powers, in accordance with local requirements . . .

[Non-interference in spheres of influence; application of the Berlin Act and freedom of trade; cessions to be made by the Sultan of Zanzibar; recognition of the British Zanzibar Protectorate; cession of Heligoland.]

Signed: Edward B. Maslet; H. Percy Anderson; V. Caprivi; K. Krauel.

39

DECLARATION BETWEEN GREAT BRITAIN AND FRANCE RESPECTING TERRITORIES IN AFRICA, 5 AUGUST 1890[1]

[The French Government agrees to recognize the British Protectorate over Zanzibar and Pemba.]

... 2 THE Undersigned, duly authorized by Her Britannic Majesty's Government, declares as follows:—

1. The Government of Her Britannic Majesty recognizes the Protectorate of France over the Island of Madagascar, with its consequences, especially as regards the exequaturs of the British Consuls and Agents, which must be applied for through the intermediary of the French Resident General.

In Madagascar the missionaries of both countries shall enjoy complete protection. Religious toleration, and liberty for all forms of worship and religious teaching, shall be guaranteed.

It is understood that the establishment of this Protectorate will not affect any rights of immunities enjoyed by British subjects in that island.

2. The Government of Her Britannic Majesty recognizes the sphere of influence of France to the south of her Mediterranean possessions, up to a line from Say on the Niger, to Barruwa on Lake Chad, drawn in such a manner as to comprise in the sphere of action of the Niger Company all that fairly belongs to the Kingdom of Sokoto; the line to be determined by the Commissioners to be appointed.

The Government of Her Britannic Majesty engages to appoint immediately two Commissioners to meet at Paris with two Commissioners appointed by the Government of the French Republic, in order to settle the details of the above-mentioned line. But it is expressly understood that even in the case the labours of these Commissioners should not result in a complete agreement upon all details of the line, the Agreement between the two Governments as to the general delimitation above set forth shall nevertheless remain binding.

The Commissioners will also be intrusted with the task of determining the respective spheres of influence of the two countries in the region which extends to the west and to the south of the Middle and Upper Niger.

Salisbury, London, August 5, 1890.

[1] Hertslet, *Commercial Treaties*, vol. xviii (1893), pp. 437–9.

40

A. W. L. HEMMING: MINUTE,
WEST AFRICAN EXPANSION,
10 NOVEMBER 1890[1]

... THE old dread of increasing our responsibilities by taking over more territory has, I venture to think, been proved by experience to be somewhat of a bugbear.

When, in the old days, we confined ourselves on the Gold Coast to the Coast line we emboldened the Ashantees to invade the country, & as a consequence were involved in war. Since our jurisdiction & control have been extended no serious difficulties have occurred & the development of the country is steadily advancing. So at S. Leone the extension of authority and protection of the Sherbro district has been followed by a state of peace and order hitherto unknown there, and an immense increase of trade. The fact is, as it seems to me, that in W. Africa it is very difficult to stand still. If we don't go forward we practically recede for the natives regard a refusal to take them under protection as a lack of power to protect, & are therefore always disposed to turn their eyes in search of more potent friends & allies.

I would suggest, therefore, that Sir A. Moloney should be authorized to extend British protection to Ilaro ...

41

FOREIGN OFFICE TO LORD DUFFERIN:
ANGLO-FRENCH AGREEMENT (DRAFT),
MARCH 1893[2]

WITH reference to my Despatch ... of the 6th ultimo, I transmit herewith copies of the correspondence which has passed with the Colonial Office on the suggestions submitted in Mr. Phipps's[3] despatch to your Excellency of the 29th December last for the settlement of the Anglo-French boundary to the west of the Gold Coast Colony.

[1] C.O. 147/76. On Moloney to C.O., 13 September 1890. For acceptance of the Yoruba protectorates, see I.D.

[2] C.O. 879/37, no. 435. Despite instructions from Salisbury to Phipps, 6 July 1892 (Metcalfe, *Great Britain and Ghana*, no. 379), local demarcation failed. Lord Ripon was against the expense of a new local boundary commission and urged a compromise between Binger and Lang's boundary lines for the Assini–Gyaman frontier. The Foreign Office accepted this view which provided the basis for the Anglo-French Gold Coast–Ivory Coast boundary agreement, 12 July 1893. See Metcalfe, *Great Britain and Ghana*, no. 385.

[3] *E. C. H. Phipps*, First Secretary, 1890, Minister Plenipotentiary in Paris, 1893.

The decision of the Marquess of Ripon, in which I concur, has been come to after a very careful study of Mr. Phipps's despatch, in consultation with the British officials best acquainted with the subject, and after full consideration of the arguments advanced by Captain Binger and the French experts. The line which it indicates is, in our opinion, in conformity with the Agreement of June 26th, 1891, though on points of that Agreement respecting which doubts have been raised, it involves a considerable concession on the part of Her Majesty's Government. It appears to them to be an acceptable compromise of the conflicting views of the Commissioners, and they trust that it will be viewed in that light by the French Government.

It will be seen that Captain Binger's line has been traced with as much accuracy as possible on Captain Lang's map; this map has been drawn carefully, and is based on local surveys more recent than those on which Captain Binger's map was founded. Her Majesty's Government hope that it will be accepted as the map on which the new line should be traced.

The object which both Governments have in view is to avoid a fresh delimitation on the spot, and to settle the frontier by a clearly marked line on a trustworthy map.

Her Majesty's Government would, in order to secure a settlement, be disposed to abandon their claim to the town of Nougoua. They would accept the River Tanoe as the boundary for, say, five miles above that town, which would thus be comprised in the French sphere. At the five-mile point the line would leave the river, and strike northward to the centre of the Ferra Ferrako Hill, whence it would run either in the direction marked by Captain Lang, or directly north-west to a point between Souacron and Akuakru, leaving the former to France and the latter to England. Thence it would follow the line indicated in the 13th, 14th, and 15th paragraphs of the Colonial Office letter.

It is unnecessary at the present stage to define the line with greater precision. Mr. Phipps is thoroughly conversant with the points at issue. I trust that, adhering to the indications above given, he will be able to arrive at some agreement with Monsieur Hanotaux which is likely to be acceptable to both Governments. In that case he should draw the line as clearly as possible on Captain Lang's map, if that is admitted as correct by the French Government, and submit it for final consideration and approval.

42

SIR GEORGE GOLDIE TO THE
FOREIGN OFFICE: YOLA–CHAD
BOUNDARY, 7 AUGUST 1893[1]

... THE points on which German Colonial opinion is really anxious are (1) the shore of Lake Chad, and (2) the possession of the valuable River Chari; and on these points I think we should now yield, provided—but not otherwise—they recognize that the mouth of the Faro shall be taken as the point (to the east of and near Yola) referred to in the 1886 Agreement.

The German Government has strangely misunderstood that Agreement. They now propose to start from 'the point where the boundary-line determined in the 1886 Agreement traverses the Benue'. But that point has not yet been determined, and one object of the last British despatch to Berlin was to determine it at the junction of the Faro with the Benue, some 20 miles above Yola, and, therefore, within the vicinity of that town ... It would not be tolerable to have the 1886 line passing within cannon range of Yola, nor was this contemplated.

In the proposed new demarcation line, all the concessions are being made by England to Germany, which has no Treaties there—in hopes of her support against others—and none by Germany to England, which has Treaties with all the regions to the west of the new line, except Bornu, where Germany cannot reach, and even with some regions to the east of the line, which England would then have to give up. It would therefore be far better to make no new arrangement unless Germany agrees to the proposed settlement of the point left vague in the 1886 Agreement.

But Germany is certain to agree to this if put before her as an absolute condition of our conceding what she most cares for, the shore of Lake Chad and the Chari River.

43

EDWARD FAIRFIELD TO THE FOREIGN
OFFICE: LAGOS–DAHOMEY
BOUNDARY, 27 FEBRUARY 1894[2]

I AM directed by the Marquess of Ripon to acknowledge the receipt of your letter of 20th instant, forwarding a note from the French

---

[1] *F.O. Confidential Print*, 6471 (1893). The Yola–Chad boundary agreement with Germany, 15 November 1893, was approved by the Royal Niger Company in October.
[2] C.O. 879/37, no. 446. News of French expeditions into Borgu did not reach the Colonial Office till April. Denton to C.O., 6 April 1894 (telegram). *Edward Fairfield*, Assistant Under-Secretary for Colonies, 1892–7.

Ambassador, in which he proposes that the delimitation of the boundary line between the British and French Protectorates in the neighbourhood of Lagos should be continued up to the 9th parallel of North Latitude.

As this delimitation is in accordance with the Anglo-French Agreement of 10th August 1889, Lord Ripon sees no ground for objecting to it, and I am to request you to inform the Earl of Rosebery that a copy of your letter and its enclosure will be sent to the Governor of Lagos, with instructions to place himself in communication with the Governor of Porto Novo, and arrange with him as to the details of the work.

I am, however, to suggest that it would seem desirable to warn the Royal Niger Company of what is about to take place.

On reference to the correspondence respecting the negotiations of 1889, Lord Ripon finds that the French Government at first proposed that the boundary line should be continued as far north as the 10th parallel, and it was so inserted in the first draft of the agreement.

It will be seen, however, that, in the memorandum enclosed in the letter from this Department of 27th July 1889, the Intelligence Department suggested that it would be better not to go beyond the 9th parallel, as the Niger Company had treaties with Borgu, and the effect of extending the boundary further north would be to cut off a portion of that State from British influence.

The Secretary of State for the Colonies concurred in this objection, but suggested that the Niger Company should be consulted before any alteration was made.

It appears from Lord Salisbury's despatch to Lord Lytton of 31st July 1889 (enclosed in your letter of the same date) that it was decided, after personal communication between Mr. Egerton and Sir G. Taubman Goldie, that the line of demarcation should stop at the 9th parallel, and Mr. Egerton subsequently secured the consent of the French Government to this arrangement.

The Royal Niger Company was therefore apparently satisfied in 1889 that their interests had been sufficiently safeguarded in the Agreement.

Lord Rosebery will probably consider whether the French Government should not be informed that the territory north of the 9th parallel is already under British influence, and that it is therefore not open to them to make any advance in that direction. . . .

44

SIR CLEMENT HILL: MEMORANDUM, ROYAL NIGER COMPANY TREATIES, 6 APRIL 1894[1]

THE thirty-seven Treaties of the Charter were, of course, approved by its issue on the 10th July, 1886.

On the 21st March, 1887, the Company sent in a list of 237 Treaties with native tribes on the Benué and Lower Niger and with the States of Gandu and Sokoto.

On the 2nd August, 1887, these Treaties were approved. But in approving them, the Secretary of State reserved the right to withdraw this approval if necessary or expedient. The Company pointed out that this provisional approval might, if published, give a handle to their opponents to work for the overthrow of the Treaties, and it was agreed not to lay it before Parliament.

On the 5th September, 1888, thirty-five additional Treaties were communicated to us. A conditional assent was given on the 27th October, and on the 1st November we were assured that the Company accepted and would observe the conditions.

Some of the Treaties, however, referred to the Forcados River, as to which there was a question of the rights and jurisdiction of Nana, Chief of Benin, and these were reserved till the matter could be reported on by Sir C. MacDonald . . .

[MacDonald reported the Headmen of Goolah and Buentu had a right to make these treaties.]

Treaties between the National African Company . . . and Ilorin (18th April 1885) and Borgu or Boussa (12th November, 1885) were communicated by the Niger Company on the 19th June, 1889, but nothing seems to have been said by us in regard to them.

Treaties with Sokoto and Gandu were sent on the 20th July, 1891, and on the 29th of the same month forty others were communicated. They were acknowledged on the 22nd August, 1891, without comment.

Sir G. Goldie visited Nupe in 1891 and 1892 with a letter from the Queen, when the Emir declared that he considered the Treaty of 1884 (?1885) to be binding on him and his successors, so it was not thought necessary to make a fresh one.

A further Treaty with Ilorin of the 9th August, 1890, was

---

[1] *F.O. Confidential Print*, 6572 (1894), pp. 69–70. *Sir Clement Hill* Assistant Clerk, 1886, and deputy to Sir Percy Anderson, Senior Clerk, 1894. All 306 of the Company treaties were confirmed in Kimberley to Royal Niger Company, 23 April 1894, ibid.

communicated on the 26th April, 1892, which does not appear to have been approved.

On the 14th August, 1893, the Treaty of the 7th May, 1893, with Yola was received, and it was acknowledged on the 21st of the same month, but not formally approved.

We have got a printed list of all the Treaties, which shows on what form they are respectively drawn.

It will be seen that there are ten different forms, and some variously worded.

Form 1 . . . is a Treaty of Cession with no objectionable clause. It covers the Treaties.

Form 2 covers six Treaties and cedes the Territory.

Under clause 3 the Company reserve to themselves the right of excluding foreign settlers other than those settled in the country at the time of signature . . . We could not now approve that clause.

Form 3 covers . . . seven Treaties, all of 1884. It cedes the territory, but contains a clause as to foreigners similar to that in Form 2.

Form 4 . . . embraces fifty Treaties, of which forty-seven are dated in 1885 and three in 1886. The cession clause exists, but it also gives the Company the right of excluding foreigners. It is perhaps not so objectionable, as the right is given to the Company, and is not reserved by them, but still we could hardly approve it.

Form 5 . . . is used for 174 Treaties, dating from 1885 to 1888. It cedes the territory, and does not contain the objectionable clause.

Form 6 . . . covers nineteen Treaties, all dated 1885. It cedes territory, but contains the two following clauses:—

'No one shall have a right to mine in our country (either foreigner or native) without the sanction of the National African Company, their heirs, or assigns. We also give to the National African Company, their heirs or assigns, the power to exclude all or any foreigners from our country'.

The latter clause like its fellow in the other forms, should not stand, even if the former is not considered as conferring a monopoly.

Form no. 7 . . . is used for the Muri Treaty of 1885 only. It is not a cession of territory, though it binds the Sultan not to enter into treaties with strangers or foreigners without the Company's consent. It grants certain monopolies of trade.

Form 8 . . . is used for fourteen Treaties of 1885. It cedes the territory, and grants sole powers to mine, farm, and build, and the power to exclude all foreigners.

Form 9 . . . embraces thirteen Treaties, of which twelve are dated 1889, and one is dated 1890. It cedes territory, and gives sole mining rights.

Form 10 . . . covers thirty Treaties, ranging from 1890 to 1893. It contains the cession clause and sole mining rights, but expressly bars 'any monopoly of trade, direct or indirect, by the Company, or others', and 'any restriction of private or commercial intercourse'. The remaining twenty-two Treaties . . . are on various Forms. They date from 1884 to 1890 . . . Most of them cede the territories, or place the signatory Chiefs under the protection of the Company; some grant sole rights in certain industries; some have the exclusion of foreigners' clause; in some, on the other hand, the Company specially agree not to exclude foreigners. The most important are those with Bautshi . . . Borgu . . . Gandu . . . Ilorin . . . Nupe . . . and Sokoto. Bautschi cedes territory, and contains no objectionable clauses. Borgu grants full jurisdiction over foreigners, and agrees not to cede territories or make Treaties or arrangements with any foreign Government, except with the consent of the Company, or of Her Majesty's Government. It further engages to place the territory under British protection whenever required. The Company agrees to admit all foreigners. Gandu ceded territory on the banks of the Benué and Kworra, and grants the sole right among foreigners to trade, with full jurisdiction over and power of taxing foreigners. Ilorin is similar to that with Borgu. Nupe gives entire charge of trading interests, sole rights of mining, and power over foreigners. Sokoto grants jurisdiction over foreigners, the entire rights of the Sultan to the country on both sides of the Benuéa and rivers flowing into it, for such a distance from the banks as the Company desires, and the sole right among foreigners to trade.

The Treaty of the 7th May, 1893, with Yola is on form 10, that is, cession of territory, jurisdiction, and sole right to mine, but reservation of freedom of trade with any person or nation.

45

SIR GEORGE GOLDIE: MEMORANDUM, THE UPPER NIGER, 10 JULY 1894[1]

THE question for England in Northern Africa is how to satisfy France without sacrificing any material British interests. Apart from Imperial aims in other parts of Africa, the Niger Company itself would benefit by such a policy, as colonial hostility in France means aggression, under the disguise of private enterprise, in regions already secured to England by International Agreements. The Niger [Company] Council are not, therefore, sacrificing unduly the interests of their shareholders in agreeing to the proposal I now put forward.

Fortunately, the outcry in France during the last ten years has not been to secure the most accessible parts of Africa, within moderate

[1] *F.O. Confidential Print*, 6572 (1894). This was forwarded to Phipps by the F.O., 24 July 1894.

distance of navigable waterways, but to unite across the continent her Mediterranean colonies—Senegambia, the Ivory Coast, Dahomey, and the French Congo.

With one exception, this idea has been completed, on paper, by the Anglo-French Agreement of 1890, the Franco-German Agreement of 1894, and M. Binger's Treaties with the native Rulers between Upper Niger and the Ivory Coast. The French possessions in Dahomey are, however, cut off from the rest of her North African Empire by the Niger Company's territory of Borgu (otherwise known as Barba), and a French Ministry which could show that it had completed the connection of the African Colonies would probably be able to justify to public opinion a recognition of British rights in the Basin of the Upper Nile.

There is another reason for France desiring to limit the advance of the Niger Company westward from the Middle Niger. She has acquired Treaty rights on the lines of routes followed by MM. Monteil and Binger, but these do not cover great breadths of country, so that the greater part of the vast regions between the Upper and the Middle Niger—known as the 'boucle du Niger'—is still open to acquisition by England through the Niger Company. The latter has, in fact, a well equipped expedition now starting to make treaties with every important tribe not already secured by France.

I have drawn on the accompanying map the line . . . which the Niger Company would, if necessary, be prepared to accept, provided that this concession formed part of an Agreement by which all pending Anglo-French disputes in Northern Africa were settled.

The sacrifices of the Niger Company would be as follows:—

1. All the country (north of the latitude of the Say-Barua line and to the west of the Middle Niger which falls within the Empire of Gandu. Mr. Joseph Thomson asserts that this Empire, with which the Niger Company has Treaties, extends nearly to Timbuctoo. The Anglo-French Agreement of 1890 does not prevent the Niger Company from retaining this region, as that Agreement deals only with districts to the direct north and south of the Say-Barua line, and not with districts east and west of the meridians of longitude bounding that line. France has already acted on that principle.

2. A considerable portion of Gandu, and also of Borgu (or Barba), south of the latitude of the Say-Barua line, but lying to the west of the new frontier which I propose. Borgu (or Barba) extends certainly as far west as the 1st degree east of Greenwich, and probably much further.

3. The right to extend westward into regions unsecured by France.

The proposed arrangement would not interfere with any rights of Germany.

Two very important considerations must be mentioned:—

1. The proposed line gives the absolute maximum of concession consistent with the security, for revenue purposes, of the British position on the Middle Niger, and, therefore, owing to the free navigation up to the really unnavigable cataracts, of her position on the Lower Niger.

2. The Niger Company trusts that no such concession will be made as a set-off for French recognition that Bornu, as far as that country lies to the south of the latitude of the Say-Barua line, lies within the British sphere. The 1890 Agreement which settled that question is sufficiently clear. It did not draw the line so as to exclude from the British sphere all that did not belong to the Sokoto Empire, but so as to include all that *did* belong to that Empire. France is, therefore, distinctly precluded from interference in Bornu, as Lord Salisbury carefully pointed out in his speech in the House of Lords, immediately after the Agreement was concluded, without calling forth any contradiction either from the French Government or the French press, which, indeed, generally complained of France having sacrificed the possibility of acquiring Bornu at some later date.

46

THE MARQUIS OF DUFFERIN TO GABRIEL HANOTAUX: SIERRA LEONE– GUINEA AGREEMENT, 22 JANUARY 1895[1]

I HAVE the honour to acknowledge the receipt of your Excellency's note of the 22nd instant, in which you observe that during the course of the recent discussions relative to the delimitation of the British and French possessions to the north and east of Sierra Leone, the Commissioners of the two countries had arrived at an understanding as to the principle of the arrangements intended to regulate the commercial relations between the British Colony of Sierra Leone and the neighbouring French possessions. Your Excellency points out that it was at the same time understood that the conditions of this understanding should form the subject of an exchange of notes immediately after the signature of the Agreement.

In consequence, your Excellency does me the honour of intimating to me that the Government of the Republic is disposed to give its assent to the following stipulations:—

[1] C.O. 879/42, no. 481. The boundary agreement for the area from the coast to Tembi-Kunda was signed 21 January 1895. *1st Marquis of Dufferin and Ava*, diplomatist and administrator in Egypt and India, British Ambassador to Paris, 1891–6. *A. A. G. Hanotaux*, Minister for Foreign Affairs in France, 1894–5, 1895–8. For tariff negotiations, see no. 22, p. 456, below.

1. In the territories dependent on the Colony of Sierra Leone, on the one hand, and in those dependent upon the Colonies of the French Guinea (including Fouta Djallon) and of the French Soudan, on the other hand, the traders and travellers belonging to the two countries shall be treated upon a footing of perfect equality in so far as the use of roads and other means of land communication are concerned.

2. The roads crossing the frontier indicated by the agreement of the 21st January 1895, between the British Colony of Sierra Leone and the neighbouring French Colonies shall on both sides be open to commerce on payment of such duties and taxes as may be established.

3. The two Governments reciprocally engage not to establish on the land frontier defined by the Agreement of the 21st January 1895, between their respective Colonies any duties, either import or export, higher than those which shall be levied on the maritime frontier either of the Colony of Sierra Leone or of the Colony of French Guinea.

The duties on exports shall not in any case exceed 7 per cent. *ad valorem*, calculated according to the official tables of valuation of each Colony.

4. Posts at which the duties or taxes on imports and exports shall be paid shall be established at certain fixed points on the frontier, in order that caravans may not be diverted from the roads which they might desire to follow in order to pass from the Colony of Sierra Leone into the neighbouring French Colonies, or *vice versa*.

I am instructed by Her Majesty's Government to express their acceptance of the arrangement above recorded, which they have no doubt will prove beneficial to the trading and commercial interests of the two countries.

47

HENRY MORLEY (ROYAL NIGER COMPANY) TO FOREIGN OFFICE: BORGU, 31 DECEMBER 1895[1]

I AM directed to acknowledge the receipt by the Governor and Council of your letter of the 27th instant inclosing copy of the French 'Bulletin Officiel' transmitted in Lord Dufferin's Despatch No. 326, and I am to make the following remarks on the list of Treaties, therein enumerated, in the hinterland of Dahomey, for the information of the Marquess of Salisbury.

The system followed by the French explorers appears to have been that of describing as independent countries many territories

[1] C.O. 879/45, no. 506. Encl. in F.O. to C.O., 15 January 1896.

which are really dependent on other States. Taking the Treaties
in turn, it is not possible to accept on the *ex parte* statement of
Commandant Decoeur that Ouari, Ouavo, and Kafiri are independent
of Borgu (Nikki), with which the Company has a Treaty, made on
the 10th November 1894, by Captain Lugard. The same remark
applies to the implication that Gourma, Boti, and Tchampango, are
independent of Gandu, with which the Company has several Treaties
and ratifications of Treaties. Bikini is plainly within the jurisdiction
of Gandu, and Ilo within the jurisdiction of Boussa, which even the
French press admits to be within the Company's sphere. But these
last two places, Bikini and Ilo, are also specially secured by falling
to the east of the meridian of Say.

Passing to the two Treaties of Lieutenant Baud, I am to point out
that, Say being the starting-point of the Say–Barua line, it is not
competent for one of the Contracting Parties to obtain rights to
exclude the other Contracting Party. The possession of Say and
Barua ought, my Council submit, to be settled by mutual arrangement,
or be neutralized. The postion of Malla is not marked on the French,
German, and English maps in the possession of the Company.

To M. Alby's Treaty with Sansanné-Mangou the Company has
no objection to raise.

M. Deville's Treaty with Bouay and Kaudi may be questioned
on the ground of both of these places falling within the jurisdiction
of Borgu (Nikki), while the greater part of Bouay is to the east of the
meridian of Say.

While the Governor and Council are quite prepared to accept
as a compromise the prolongation of the Dahomey–Lagos demarcation line up to its reaching the Middle Niger below Say, they earnestly
hope that until this compromise is effected everything to the east of
the meridian of Say and north of the 9th parallel of latitude will be
held to be British. The Council submit that the Say–Barua line must
either have been an ordinary demarcation line which protects from
aggression the territories lying within the lines passing through its
extremities at right angles to it, or must have been intended to divide
the Niger River between France and England, in which case both
banks of the Niger above Say, would fall within the French sphere,
and both banks of the Niger below Say would fall within the British
sphere. There seems no escape from this dilemma; because, if only
one bank of the Niger (the left) is secured to Great Britain by the
1890 Agreement, then—on the principle of it being a division of the
river—only the same bank was secured to France, so that that Agreement would have left open to British enterprise all the right bank of
the Upper Niger from its source down to Timbuctoo and on to Say,
an interpretation which would have been indignantly repelled in
France.

The final words of the Anglo-French Agreement of the 5th August 1890, referred plainly, not to the banks of the river, but to the vast territories inclosed in what is known as the 'boucle du Niger'.

48

THE MARQUIS OF SALISBURY TO THE MARQUIS OF DUFFERIN: NIGER BOUNDARY COMMISSION, 12 MAY 1896[1]

I HAVE received your Excellency's Despatch, No. 75, Africa, of the 8th instant, forwarding a report from the Niger Commissioners[2] of the meeting held on that day, at which their French colleagues, acting under instructions from M. Hanotaux, put forward the following counter-proposal, namely, that a line starting from the eastern frontier of Dahomey at its intersection with the 8th degree of north latitude should follow that parallel eastward to the Niger, and thence ascend that river to Say, the right bank falling to France and the left to Great Britain.

In dealing with this proposal, it is necessary to consider the origin of the Niger Commission and the questions which it was appointed to examine.

The arrangement between Great Britain and France of the 10th August 1889, concerning the delimitation of their respective possessions on the West Coast of Africa, settled, by Article 4, a line of demarcation between the British and French spheres of influence on the Slave Coast. The direction of the frontier was definitively laid down by that article as far as the point where it meets the 9th degree of north latitude, where the demarcation ceased.

From the date of the signature of that agreement, the territory west of this line up to the 9th parallel has been comprised in the French sphere, that to the east of it up to the same parallel in the British sphere.

By Article 2 of the Declaration of the 5th August 1890, Her Majesty's Government engaged to appoint two Commissioners to meet at Paris two Commissioners appointed by the Government of the Republic, in order to determine the respective spheres of influence of the two countries in the region which extends to the west and to the south of the Middle and Upper Niger. The agreement referred only to the portion of the spheres as yet undetermined. The Commission was duly appointed, and has at various times examined

---

[1] C.O. 879/45, no. 506.
[2] A. W. L. Hemming, C.O., and H. Howard, F.O., Envoy Extraordinary and Minister Plenipotentiary, 1896, Paris.

the matter so referred to it. The Commissioners originally appointed, in 1892 were—for Great Britain Mr. Phipps and Sir J. Crowe, and for France, M. Hanotaux and M. Haussmann.

These Commissioners were disposed to agree in principle that the boundary between the spheres west of the Niger should run from Say to the north-west angle of the neutral zone and thence to the French town of Bonduku. No definite agreement was, however, made. In 1894 another effort was made to arrive at a settlement. A line was discussed by Mr. Phipps and M. Hanotaux which would have been drawn from the termination on the 9th parallel of the eastern frontier of Dahomey to the intersection of the Niger by the 12th parallel of north latitude. There was, however, a divergence of opinion respecting the possession of Nikki, and no definitive settlement was reached.

The conclusion at the beginning of the present year of an arrangement with France on certain matters respecting Siam and Tunis appeared to offer a favourable opportunity for proposing that the Niger Commission should resume its meetings.

This view was adopted by France; fresh Commissioners were appointed to act under the original stipulations already referred to, contained in the Declaration of the 5th August 1890, and they have held several meetings at which the titles on which the claims of the two countries rest have been exhaustively examined. At the meeting of the 28th April, the British Commissioners proposed to draw a boundary line eastward from the intersection of the 9th parallel of latitude with the meridian forming the eastern frontier of Dahomey along the 9th parallel as far as 1° east of Paris (3° 20' east of Greenwich), and thence northward along this meridian up to its intersection with a line drawn direct from Say to Barrawa. This proposal was prompted by a spirit of conciliation, for it involved a large sacrifice of territory secured to Great Britain by treaties the absolute validity of which has been proved by the British Commissioners.

Her Majesty's Government has learnt with surprise the nature of the counter-proposal now made by the French Commissioners, which would deprive Great Britain of the whole of her sphere of influence to the west of the Niger north of the 9th parallel of latitude. The basis of the agreements of 1890 and 1894 was the existence of two spheres requiring delimitation by a commission, and this has also been the basis of the subsequent negotiations to which I have referred.

The present proposal is an entirely new departure. It renders the past work of the Commissioners inoperative, and leaves no ground open for future discussion by them. It substitutes absolute surrender by one party for an amicable arrangement between the two Powers. The plan proposed by the British Commissioners had the latter object in view, but the counter-proposal is wholly unacceptable.

Her Majesty's Government deeply regret the present position of the negotiations.

The counter-proposal goes further in proposing the abandonment by Great Britain of the portion of her existing sphere lying between the 8th and 9th parallels, now administered by the authorities of Lagos. Such a proposition could, if it were seriously made, only be discussed between the two Governments. It is outside the sphere of the task assigned to the Commissioners appointed under the Agreement of 1890, and Her Majesty's Government could not authorise their Commissioners to discuss it.

I have to request your Excellency to instruct the Commissioners in the sense of this Despatch.

49

COLONEL W. EVERETT TO SIR CLEMENT HILL: UPPER NIGER, 31 DECEMBER 1896[1]

PRIVATE.

My Dear Hill,

Whilst thinking, last night, of the somewhat uncompromising character of the proposed Despatch to Monson,[2] and of the great unlikelihood of its leading to the resumption of the negotiations—seeing how bent the French are on getting to the Niger below the rapids—I discovered what I think might constitute a very satisfactory *quid pro quo* for, at least, the triangle of territory which lies south of the 9th parallel in Hanotaux's second proposal.

Briefly, it consists in such a rectification of the western frontier of the Gold Coast agreed to in July 1893 (see map in Hertslet to face p. 589) as would give to the Colony all that is wanted in Gaman. Though I have no knowledge of how such an exchange would be viewed by the Colonial Office, I should think they would gladly sacrifice this bit of Lagos for the Gaman country, and I believe the French would agree without even a formal protest. I need not now go into the details, but, if we got this, together with Bona, Lobi, and a frontier to the north, leaving Dafina and Yatenga to France, and giving us Mossi, and if, in addition, we obtained, as we ought fairly to obtain in any case, the 14th parallel of latitude from the Niger to Lake Chad, the French might have Borgu and the right bank of the

---

[1] C.O. 879/48, no. 529. *Colonel William Everett*, Director of Military Intelligence, War Office. And see his memorandum, 7 September 1896, in Metcalfe, *Great Britain and Ghana*, no. 409, recommending occupation of territory north of the Neutral Zone. This suggestion of Everett's on access to the navigable Niger was reserved by the C.O. 'for consideration' and seriously examined in 1898.

[2] *Sir E. Monson*, British Ambassador in Paris, 1896–1904.

Niger down to Liaba and welcome. So far as we know, it is a worthless tract of country which would never be of much use to us or to anyone else. There would remain the question of the port. You know Goldie's views as well as I do. He has said to me more than once, 'If ever the French get a port on the Niger I will sell up the whole business and clear out.' As long, then, as the Niger Company are there, I do not see quite how that port is to be managed; but if Her Majesty's Government took over the administration and were prepared to spend a little money—which Goldie cannot afford to do—neither I nor Howard can see any solid objection to the arrangement. Only we ought not to let them have a port opposite Jebba or Rabba, or any other place just in the bend of the river, if we can help it. I have had several talks with a fellow (lately in the employ of the Niger Company) who knows every inch of that part of the country, and he told me that all the trade from the Hausa States—even from Gando and Sokoto—comes through those places, owing to the insecurity of the northern routes lying east and west through Gomba and Boussa.

To escape from this difficulty I should propose to modify Hanotaux's line from the intersection of 9° latitude with 4° east longitude, by producing it to the Niger, instead of turning it eastward along 9° latitude. I believe it would cut the Niger somewhere in the vicinity of Arenberg, but, in any case, I should be inclined to let the French have that place so that their *amour propre* might be satisfied. They would then have a port on the navigable portion of the Niger, and we could establish ourselves firmly at Jebba, or Rabba, and turn all the trade from the east down the river.

If these proposals were agreed to by you and Colonial Office, your Despatch to Monson might perhaps be modified to suit them; and, if we were to get all I have noted, it would be worth while resuming negotiations, for I believe we could do good business and probably finish the whole thing off in a month, or six weeks at the outside.

On the other hand, if matters are delayed much longer, you may take my word for it that the French will be found in occupation all through Borgu, and also in country further west north of the Gold Coast, for they are active, whilst we are, at least immediately west of the Niger, doing nothing. In that case all our present 'concessions' will have vanished, and then our position will be even worse than it is now.

50

JOSEPH CHAMBERLAIN TO GOVERNOR SIR W. E. MAXWELL: GOLD COAST INTERIOR, 4 JUNE 1897[1]

YOU are aware that the French have recently occupied not only Mossi but also Boussa and other places with which treaties had previously been concluded by agents of the Gold Coast Government and the Royal Niger Company, binding the kings and chiefs not to accept the protection of, or to make any treaty with, another Power without the consent of Her Majesty's Government.

2. When the terms of these treaties were settled, it was considered that they would be sufficient to bar the conclusion of subsequent treaties by agents of a foreign Government; but, although the French Government have not expressly repudiated this view, they have not as yet made any reply to the remonstrances which have been addressed to them by Her Majesty's Government with reference to the occupation of Mossi and Boussa, and in the French newspapers it is openly stated that no treaty with native authorities will be respected unless it has been followed up by effective occupation.

3. It has been a source of weakness to Her Majesty's Government in all the negotiations which have taken place with regard to West Africa that the French have usually been in occupation of the principal places in dispute, and it was therefore decided, when the negotiations in Paris last year were suspended, that British officers should be despatched by the Gold Coast Government to occupy Gambaga, Wa, Bona, and, if possible, Wagadugu. Captain Stewart succeeded in occupying Gambaga, but the French had seized Wagadugu before he could get there, and Mr. Henderson has been prevented by the Sofas from remaining in occupation of Wa and Bona.

4. The situation is, therefore, a difficult one, as we have to deal with the Sofas as well as the French, and it has been made still more complicated by the action of the Germans, who are intriguing against us in the Neutral Zone, and supplying the Sofas with arms and ammunition.

5. I have learnt with much satisfaction from your telegram of the 31st of May that Mr. Henderson has been released, and is now on his way to the coast with a letter from Samory. It appears to Her Majesty's Government that, while the tribes with which we have made treaties of friendship or protection must be protected against

[1] C.O. 879/48, no. 529, and Metcalfe, *Great Britain and Ghana*, no. 417 (with abridgements and slight verbal differences). *Joseph Chamberlain*, Secretary of State for the Colonies, 1895–1903.

Sofa raids, it would not be advisable to commence military operations against Samory without the strongest cause and without a very clear perception of the results to which they might lead. An expedition against him would be a very serious undertaking, and it is to be feared that the French would derive more advantage than we should from the sacrifices which such an expedition would entail upon us. You have suggested that the French Government might be invited to join with us in breaking Samory's power, and I am awaiting the remarks which, as stated in your telegram of the 23rd of May, you are sending me by post with regard to making representations to them on the subject. I think, however, that joint action would be attended with great difficulties, and in particular that it would tie our hands in asserting our claims to Mossi and other countries which the French are endeavouring to secure for themselves. It would certainly lessen our prestige with the natives and our own subjects, who would suppose we were unable, without assistance, to assert our authority. If, therefore, it should ever unfortunately become necessary for us to break the power of Samory, I am of opinion that we shall have to carry out this operation with our own resources. But upon this point I will not express a final opinion until I am in possession of your views.

6. If, however, as I hope, a satisfactory arrangement can be made with Samory, the most urgent question for you to consider will be the arrangements to be made in view of the recent aggressions of the French and Germans. As regards the latter I shall address you in a separate Despatch, but in respect to the former I am disposed to think that you should, if your forces are sufficient, immediately occupy all the important places in the Gold Coast hinterland, which can be claimed as properly belonging to Great Britain, and which are not already in the occupation of the French. It remains to consider what measures can be taken to procure the evacuation of those places which have been occupied by them in violation of the rights which we have acquired by treaties.

7. They have no doubt been encouraged in their action by the belief, based on their experience of the facility with which we have yielded to their demands and abandoned our rights on other similar occasions, that we were not in earnest in urging our claims, and that we should not be willing to incur any expense to make them good by effective occupation; and the best evidence of our determination to adopt a different course in the present instance will be the presence of a force superior to theirs.

8. The French are believed by the Intelligence Division of the War Office to be in no great strength in the region behind the Gold Coast; but it is thought that they could, if so disposed, concentrate from 500 to 1,000 men at Wagadugu in three months' time by drawing

on their reserves in Senegal and the Soudan; and in this connexion it is important to note that Bandiagara is in telegraphic communication with Senegal, and that a field telegraph is being laid from Bandiagara to Wagadugu. Two small flying columns are believed to be in Mossi—the one under Captain Voulet and another under Lieutenant Baud. The latter is said to consist of about 50 regular soldiers, and to be accompanied by a small native levy. A more important force, under Captain Destenave, was reported to be at Wagadugu on the 23rd of March last en route to Say.

9. It is possible that on finding themselves confronted by a superior force, and being made aware that we are determined and prepared to substantiate our claims, the French might withdraw from places which we claim under treaties with native authorities, as the Germans, according to a report published in the Revue Geographique for May, have recently done at Bafilo and Kirikri when confronted by the French themselves. But in case they should not do so, I wish you to consider whether there are any places which it would be practicable for us to seize and hold as a material guarantee for dealing with the French seizures of Mossi and Boussa when negotiations are resumed with the French Government.

10. You will, of course, understand that French rights in any place, like Bontuku, which has formed the subject of an arrangement between the two countries, must be scrupulously respected, but to the north of the 9th parallel there is nothing to prevent our seizing any place outside the Anglo-German Neutral Zone which would answer our purpose, with the exception of such places as are included in the agreement which Captain Stewart made with Lieutenant Voulet at Tenkrugu. As I have mentioned Bontuku, I should add that you are not debarred from occupying it if it should be necessary to do so in the course of operations against the Sofas; but in that case you should explain to the Governor of the Ivory Coast that it has been done under the pressure of necessity, owing to the hostile action of men living in the territories assigned to France and placed under French protection by the agreement of the 12th of July 1893. The case is different with regard to places which have not been the subject of an Anglo-French agreement, although considered by the French to be within their sphere of influence. It is open to you, without offering any explanations, to occupy any places north of the 9th parallel to the west, as well as to the east, of the Komoe river, or in the Gurunsi country, or (if you should be strong enough to do so) in Gurma. The chief point to consider is whether the importance of the places to the French is such that they would be induced by our occupying them to relinquish their hold on those which we claim.

11. You will also, of course, understand that you are not to take the offensive against French troops. The discretionary permission

accorded to you in this Despatch to advance to, and occupy places claimed by the French as theirs, does not apply to any town or village garrisoned by French regular troops or in which a French officer is stationed.

12. To carry out this policy it will be necessary that a strong force should be raised, and I hope that it may be possible to get recruits through the Royal Niger Company in addition to those whom you may be able to obtain on the spot. The chief difficulty will, I am afraid, be to get the men. I am prepared to apply to the War Office for more officers as soon as I learn from you that they are required. The question of expense must not be allowed to stand in the way of dealing effectively with the present emergency. It is proposed that the force, although raised in the first instance by the Gold Coast Government, should eventually be employed in occupying the territories claimed as British, not only behind the Gold Coast, but on the Niger, and in that case Lagos and the Niger Coast Protectorate and the Royal Niger Company would be called upon to contribute towards the cost of what would be in effect a small West African army.

51

JOSEPH CHAMBERLAIN TO
GOVERNOR H. E. McCALLUM:
LAGOS INTERIOR, 23 JULY 1897[1]

I HAVE the honour to inform you that the representations which have been addressed to the French Government having failed to induce them to withdraw their forces from Boussa and other places which are claimed under treaties concluded with the native authorities as falling within the British sphere of interest in West Africa, Her Majesty's Government have been compelled to consider what steps should be taken to procure the evacuation of those places and to prevent further aggressions by the French.

2. I transmit to you a copy of a Despatch addressed to the Governor of the Gold Coast on the 4th of June,[2] in which I suggested that, if the forces at his disposal were sufficient, he should immediately occupy all the important places adjacent to the Gold Coast which could properly be claimed as British and were not already in the occupation of the French, and that he should consider whether there were any other places which it would be practicable to seize and hold as a material

---

[1] C.O. 879/48, no. 529.
[2] No. 50. An inter-department conference was summoned at the end of August and in September which planned use of Niger Company troops in order to make Bussa 'untenable'. Sir C. Hill, Memorandum, 2 September 1897: C.O. 879/50, no. 538.

guarantee for dealing with the French seizures of Mossi, &c. when negotiations are resumed at Paris.

3. Her Majesty's Government think it desirable that the same policy should be pursued with regard to the territories on the Niger, and it was proposed, as you will see, that the additional force to be raised by the Gold Coast Government should eventually be employed in the Niger territories, and that Lagos and the Niger Coast Protectorate, as well as the Royal Niger Company, should be called upon to contribute towards the cost of what would be in effect a small West African army.

4. Since then it has become clear that action must be taken on the Niger without delay and independently of what is being done on the Gold Coast, and, as neither the Company nor Lagos and the Niger Coast Protectorate can provide the necessary funds, it has been decided that the cost of the force required shall be defrayed from the Imperial Exchequer.

5. The force will not, however, be an Imperial one; but it is proposed that it should be raised by increasing the strength of the Lagos Constabulary, and the expenses incurred beyond what is at present provided in the Colonial Estimates will be repaid to Lagos from the Exchequer.

6. The rights of Great Britain over the territories immediately behind Lagos as far as the 9th parallel of north latitude have, as you are aware, been recognised by France in the arrangement of the 10th of August 1889, and the boundary has been delimited by British and French Commissioners on the ground. There is, however, reason to think that this arrangement is not being respected by the French, and you should endeavour to ascertain whether this is so or not. On the east of the Niger the French Government have, by the arrangement of the 5th of August 1890, as understood by Her Majesty's Government, engaged not to interfere in the territories to the south of a line from Say on the Niger to Barruwa on Lake Tchad, drawn in such manner as to comprise in the sphere of the Niger Company all that fairly belongs to the Kingdom of Sokoto, but this interpretation of the agreement is disputed by the French Government. The extent of the territories claimed as British on the west of the river is shown in the treaties concluded by the Royal Niger Company, which you will find printed at pages 32 to 39 of the accompanying volume (African No. 506), [C.O. 879/45] as enclosures to a Despatch which the Marquess of Salisbury addressed to Her Majesty's Ambassador at Paris on the 7th of February 1896, containing the instructions to be given to the British representatives on the Niger Commission.

7. Since the sittings of the Commission in Paris were suspended last year, the French have occupied all that portion of Gandu which is situated on the right bank of the Niger, as well as the whole of

Borgu to the river bank, while in the country behind the Gold Coast they have occupied Wagadugu, and are endeavouring to establish themselves in Gurunsi and the adjoining countries, and it seems not improbable that, if Her Majesty's Government continue to do nothing but make protests and appeal to treaties, the French will proceed, as already advocated in the press, to cross the Niger and occupy territory on the left bank.

8. The occupation of places in the Empire of Sokoto would, however, be a serious undertaking, and for the present it is only necessary to consider what should be done on the right bank.

9. The first thing to do is to establish posts in any important places such as Saki, which are within the British sphere as defined by the arrangement of 1889. The next step is to establish posts in Kiama, and any important places between Nikki and Boussa which are not already in the occupation of the French, and also, if possible, in places which are in the 'hinterland' of Dahomey, but north of the 9th parallel. It is hoped that by the establishment of British posts in the immediate vicinity of the French posts, the position of the French might be rendered untenable, and they might thus be induced to retire. The most convenient base of operations for the force employed on this service would probably be some place like Liaba on the Niger, and the assistance of the Royal Niger Company would be required to convey the force to its base on the river. It is possible that Her Majesty's Government may send gunboats to the Niger in order to patrol the river, but on this point I shall communicate with you again.

10. As to the strength of the force required to carry out this policy, it is difficult to form any estimate in this country. Her Majesty's Government are prepared to assist in defraying the cost of a force of 2,000 men, and it is suggested that two or three white officers, including a doctor, and 100 to 150 Hausas, would be required for each of the more important posts. The force at each post should be distinctly stronger than the French force in the neighbouring posts.

11. The chief obstacle in the way of carrying out this policy will, I fear, be the want of men. Sir George Goldie has undertaken to obtain some recruits from the Niger for the Gold Coast Government, but none have yet arrived, and it seems doubtful whether even the needs of the Gold Coast can be supplied from that source. Lagos will have, therefore, to depend upon the recruits to be obtained within the Lagos sphere of influence.

12. There will be no difficulty in obtaining officers from the regular army, and they will be sent out as they are required.

13. I have to request that you will consider and report to me whether you would be able to carry out the policy which I have indicated in this Despatch. You should in the first instance state your

views briefly by telegraphy, and you should also write to me explaining more fully what you would propose to do. I have already asked you by a telegram of this date how many men you could raise in Lagos and in what time.

52

JOSEPH CHAMBERLAIN TO GOVERNOR H. E. McCALLUM: UPPER NIGER, 28 SEPTEMBER 1897[1]

ON the receipt of your telegram of the 11th instant, Her Majesty's Government addressed a complaint with regard to the proceedings of Lieutenant Brot to the French Government, and M. Hanotaux states that the Minister of the Colonies has been requested to repeat instructions by telegraph to the authorities of Dahomey to prevent such an incident from recurring.

You have authority to prevent violation of British territory by resort to force if it should be absolutely necessary. You must, however, use great caution, and you should be clear that the case is a perfectly clear one and that the force which you have is distinctly superior.

53

COLONEL WILLIAM EVERETT: MEMORANDUM, UPPER NIGER, 30 OCTOBER 1897[2]

... BRIEFLY, it would appear that—

1. But for wording and subsequent application of the second part of clause 2 of the Declaration of the 5th August, 1890, the whole of the territory now in dispute, falling eastward of a meridian passing through the town of Say, should belong to Great Britain under the first part of that Article.

2. The claim of the Niger Company to the Provinces of Bussa, Kiama, Kishi, and Ilesha can be fully established.

3. The claim of the Niger Company to the whole of Borgu, under the 1890 Treaty with the King of Bussa, appears to rest on so slender a foundation as to make it doubtful whether an Arbitrator would give a decision in their favour.

4. The claim of the Niger Company to Nikki and its dependencies, with the exception of Kiama and Ilesha, under Captain Lugard's Treaty of the 10th November, 1894, cannot at present be established.

5. The claim of the Niger Company to the country now known as

[1] C.O. 879/50, no. 538.   [2] C.O. 879/50, no. 539.

Gurma and contained within the boundaries marked on Intelligence Division Map No. 1150, cannot be established.

6. The claim of the Niger Company to the territory lying to the south of Say, between Gurma and the Niger cannot be established.

7. The claim of the Niger Company to the provinces of Libtako, Yagha, Torode, and Say with the Sultan of Sokoto, can be established under the 1890 Treaty with the Sultan of Sokoto, but not under the 1894 Treaty with the King of Gando.

8. The claim of the Niger Company to the province of Aïr, or Ashen, appears to rest on a very slender foundation. In the absence of further evidence as to the suzerainty of the Sultan of Sokoto over this district it is very doubtful whether an Arbitrator would admit the claim.

54

JOSEPH CHAMBERLAIN TO GOVERNOR H. E. McCALLUM: UPPER NIGER, 5 FEBRUARY 1898[1]

NEW situation has developed since my despatch of 12th November. General idea is now that advance from Lagos into Borgu and occupation of posts should be continued by Lagos Constabulary and 2nd Battalion West India Regiment. Accordingly three companies have been sent to Lagos to be placed at your disposal. At the same time Lugard will make parallel advance from a base of operations on the bank of Niger with Company's troops and with the new force. The two movements of troops must be in co-operation with and support each other. Before finally deciding on instructions to be given, anxious to know what is your opinion of best means to secure joint action and undivided responsibility. All troops must be under the command of Lugard when possible for him to exercise it.

55

JOSEPH CHAMBERLAIN: CABINET MEMORANDUM: NIGER NEGOTIATIONS, 24 JANUARY 1898[2]

[The British Commissioners in Paris have been too lenient in their presentation of the British case.]

. . . WHAT are the alternatives?

I suggest that, in the first place, our Ambassador should be directed to tell M. Hanotaux formally that the policy of this country is directed,

---

[1] C.O. 879/52, no. 550. For the expedition, see Perham and Bull, *Lugard*, vol. iv, part ii.　　[2] Cabinet Papers 37/46. Dated 25 January on the cover.

not so much to the acquisition of new territory as to the maintenance of free markets, open on equal terms to all the world; and, as this fact may have an important bearing on the present controversy, to ask him, before proceeding further with negotiations, whether the French Government would be willing to enter into a reciprocal arrangement that all our respective territories in West Africa, including Senegal, Gambia, Sierra Leone, Ivory Coast, Gold Coast, Dahomey, Lagos and Nigeria, should be open to the nationals of each country on the same terms as regards customs and conditions of trade as to its own subjects.

I have no doubt M. Hanotaux will refuse. If so, the offer will place our policy clearly before the world, and will be satisfactory to all our people. If, on the other hand, he should accept, his agreement would materially alter the position, both as regards troops and as regards a great part of the disputed territory behind Lagos.

Assuming his refusal, however, I would then instruct the Commissioners to say categorically that Great Britain will not consent to give territorial rights to the French in any part of the Hinterland which we claim as ours.

But if they are serious in saying that they have chiefly humanitarian objects in view, and the maintenance of their rights under the Berlin Act, we will endeavour to meet them.

This we can do—

1. By amending the Regulations for the navigation of the Niger, so as to remove any restriction to the disadvantage of their trade.

2. By an Agreement (similar to that which they have made with the Germans in Togoland) to allow their invalids, accompanied by an escort, to pass freely through our territories to the Niger. This Agreement to be for a short term, seven years (seven or ten), as in the German case.

3. To allow them a lease (say, for fourteen or twenty-one years) of a small piece of land at a convenient spot on the Niger, where they may make a wharf, and erect such warehouses or other purely commercial buildings as may be necessary, with the direct understanding that such lands and buildings are subject to our jurisdiction and to our Customs Regulations . . .

56

FOREIGN OFFICE TO SIR EDWARD MONSON: NIGER CONVENTION (DRAFT INSTRUCTIONS), 15 FEBRUARY 1898[1]

HER Majesty's Government have given their most careful attention to the criticial position of the negotiations between the Niger Commissioners, as shown in your Excellency's recent despatches.

[1] F.O. 27/3408. Signed by F. Bertie, in the absence of Salisbury, and sent privately to Monson in Paris, before the officially signed dispatch, 25 February 1898.

It is still their earnest desire to arrive at a solution compatible with the interest and dignity of both countries, and they are, therefore, ready to consider the statement made by the French Commissioners, at the eighteenth meeting, to the effect that the project already put forward has broken down, as affording an opportunity for laying before the French Government a scheme of a comprehensive and definite character for the settlement of all the questions coming within the scope of the Commission.

In so doing, they put aside the questions of international comity arising out of those movements of French troops, of which it has been your Excellency's duty so frequently to complain. They make large territorial concessions in regions where they have Treaty rights which, in their opinion, have stood the test of the minute inquiry to which they have been subjected by the Commissioners, and which were obtained before France attempted to extend her influence over the Chiefs with whom the British Treaties were concluded. The value of the territories in question is incontestable, and the measure of the sacrifice which their renunciation entails upon Great Britain may be gauged by the keenness of the rivalry which their possession has excited.

In addition to these territorial concessions, the proposals of Her Majesty's Government embrace the remodelling of any provisions of the Regulations for the navigation of the Niger which may be proved to tell disadvantageously on French commerce, although the highest legal authorities of the Crown have advised that there is nothing in the present rules which is inconsistent with the letter or spirit of the General Act of Berlin, by which the navigation is regulated.

If Her Majesty's Government are unable to grant territorial access to the Niger, it is from no feeling of unfriendliness to the Government of the Republic, and from no desire to hamper the great work which France is accomplishing in West Africa. It is their sincere conviction that such a concession, besides being incompatible with the position secured to Great Britain at the Berlin Conference, would defeat the objects which the two Governments have at heart of securing an arrangement in West Africa which will admit of their working side by side in their own spheres of action without friction and to their mutual advantage.

Whilst dealing in this spirit with the concessions which they themselves are willing to make, Her Majesty's Government ask nothing from that of the Republic but (1) the recognition of the rights of Great Britain over territories which were placed under British protection years ago with the full official knowledge of the French Government, and which, in spite of that knowledge, and in face of repeated protests from Her Majesty's Embassy, have since been occupied by French forces; (2) an adjustment of territory in rear of the Gold Coast Colony, under which the larger share goes to France; and (3) an extension of that identity of fiscal policy which has already been applied in parts of West Africa. Any territorial arrangement which gave to France the whole of the territories under discussion to the west of the Niger would clearly defeat the purpose of the Commission, which was to divide them between the two countries. The following is the scheme which the British Commissioners are authorized to lay before their French colleagues.

Behind the Gold Coast Her Majesty's Government would recognize Mossi and the northern part of Gurunsi as falling within the French sphere, whilst Bona, Lobi, Southern Gurunsi, Mamprusi, and all territory lying between any of these districts and the 9th parallel of latitude would be recognized as falling within the British sphere.

No alteration would take place in the frontiers as already settled south of the 9th parallel. North of that parallel they would be delimited on the spot by a Joint Commission.

Her Majesty's Government hope, however, that, if this arrangement is come to, the King of Mossi, with whom Great Britain has a Treaty, and who has appealed to Her Majesty's Government for protection, will be allowed to resume his former position, or, if this is impossible, that adequate compensation will be given him.

Behind Lagos the line proposed by the British Commissioners on the 28th April, 1896, from the 9th parallel of latitude as far as its intersection with the Niger would be recognized as the frontier. In order, however, to avoid the objections inseparable from a frontier defined solely by a meridian, and in order to assure to the populations of Bere, Okuta, and adjacent places now occupied by the British the protection so recently confirmed to them, the line of 1896 would be deflected in the southern portion, so as to include within the British sphere these districts, together with the towns of Ashigéré and Bété. In the northern portion the line would be deflected from a point north of Ilo, so as to leave within the British sphere all territory belonging to the Province of Boussa. This line would be delimited on the spot by a Joint Commission.

The territories west of that line after being deflected as mentioned in the preceding paragraph would be recognized as French. This would give to France a connected territory, comprising Northern Gurunsi, Mossi, Gurma, Libtako, Yagha, Torode, so much of Say as lies west of the Niger, and a considerable portion of Borgu, including Nikki west of the 1896 line.

As to access to the Niger, Her Majesty's Government would endeavour to meet the wishes of the French Government—

(a.) By amending the Regulations for the Navigation of the Niger, so as to remove any restrictions which may be found to exist to the disadvantage of French trade, and by making an arrangement under which, subject to proper Regulations for the protection of the Customs, the transit of merchandize (other than arms and ammunition and trade spirits) across British territory to and from Nikki and a point on the river between the Moshi River and Leaba would be exempt from the payment of import or export duties.

(*b*.) By an Agreement similar to that contained in the recent Agreement between France and Germany in regard to Togoland, to allow French invalids, accompanied by an escort, to pass freely through British territories to the Niger. This Agreement to be for a short term, as in the German case.

(*c*.) By granting to the French Government a lease of a small piece of land at a convenient spot on the Niger, where they may make a wharf and erect warehouses, or other purely commercial buildings, as may be necessary, it being understood that such land and buildings are and remain subject to British jurisdiction and to British Customs Regulations.

The fiscal arrangement proposed by Her Majesty's Government is that the Tariffs of the British and French territories respectively should apply to all merchandize alike, irrespective of origin, and that no charges should be imposed on British merchants in a French Colony, or on French merchants in a British Colony, beyond those payable by the nationals of either Colony. The same duties would thus be levied on goods of British and of French origin in British and French territories respectively, but the rates in the two territories would not necessarily be identical. The arrangement would apply to all the British and all the French possessions from the western frontier of the Ivory Coast to the eastern frontier of the Niger Coast Protectorate, to possessions on the coast as well as to those in the interior. It would embody the special commercial arrangements between the two countries already existing in West Africa, and would be drawn up by Commissioners selected by the respective Governments.

Before concluding this despatch, it is necessary that I should allude to the communications which have passed relating to the territories east of the Niger. The position of Her Majesty's Government in these regions has been defined by Agreement with France, and the withdrawal by the French Commissioners of the conditional assurance in regard to that Agreement, which was recorded in your Excellency's despatch No. 394, Africa, of the 27th November last, and accepted in my despatch No. 406 of the 9th December, makes it incumbent upon me to remove all doubt as regards that position.

Your Excellency has already pointed out to M. Hanotaux on more than one occasion that the Say–Barruwa line laid down in the Agreement was entered into by Her Majesty's Government to define the spheres of influence of Great Britain and France to the south and north of it respectively. You should now remind his Excellency of these communications, and state that Her Majesty's Government decline to admit that their rights are in any doubt.

Any incursion of a French force into the territories lying between the Niger and Lake Chad and south of the Say–Barruwa line would be a distinct breach of that Agreement, and be regarded by Her Majesty's Government as the invasion of a territory to which their rights have been recognized by a Convention between Great Britain and France.

Her Majesty's Government cannot doubt that, on reconsideration, the Government of the Republic will recognize the justice of the British view, and will give assurances which will remove the anxiety now caused by the existence of so serious a difference between the two countries.

57

GOVERNOR H. E. McCALLUM TO JOSEPH CHAMBERLAIN: BORGU TREATIES, 1 MARCH 1898[1]

I HAVE the honour to inform you that I have this day sent you a cypher telegram, of which the following is a paraphrase:—

'Important information has been given me by the Chief Minister of the new King of Borgu in respect to the Treaties made by Captain Lugard with Nikki and Kyama . . . As regards the Nikki Treaty, it was actually made with Siré Toru, who is the son of Waru Kura, and nephew of Pe Lafia, a predecessor, who possessed much power and had reigned well for a period of 30 years, during which time he had restored the town of Nikki. The name of Absalamu was a false one, and is one which is unknown amongst the Baribas. Siré Toru, who became blind about nine years ago, and was an old man, was a cruel king, and was afraid of Lugard; he, therefore, gave his name as Pe Lafia, who had been a good king. The French gave him valuable presents, and to them he gave his right name. As regards the Kyama Treaty,[2] the name of the King is Kemura, as stated by the French. Musa Pobida, or properly Foruda, was the confidential secretary of the King, and possessed no authority. As a matter of fact, Kyama has really no King, but only a Balé under the King of Nikki. Borgu is not divided into independent kingdoms, but all the divisions, including Boussa, are subject to the King of Nikki'.

2. This information was given to me by the Lemamu of Bodé, who was sent to Saki with full powers by the King of Bodé-Béré—

---

[1] C.O. 879/52, no. 550. For Lugard's account of the Nikki treaty, 10 November 1894, and a copy from F.O. 2/167, see Perham and Bull, *Lugard*, vol. iv, pp. 179–88.
[2] It is not clear from *Lugard*, p. 154, when the Kaiama treaty was signed.

Woru Yaru—as his representative to welcome me in the name of the Bariba nation and of himself, he—according to Mr. Rohrweger—having been acknowledged spontaneously and universally as being the proper successor of Siré Toru. The Lemamu is a man of between 60 and 70 years of age, and has an intimate knowledge of everything that has taken place in Borgu for a long time past.

3. Pe Lafia rebuilt Nikki, which has been deserted in consequence of intestine wars, and was regarded with much affection by the Baribas, over whom he ruled very well. He died 34 years ago, and was succeeded by the following kings, who reigned before Siré Toru came to the throne, namely: Siré Kura and Siré Tasu.

4. Siré Toru, when he heard that Captain Lugard was coming to Nikki, was very much afraid that he would be arrested on account of his misdeeds, kept out of the way, and gave his name as Lafia. He is said to have had no such fear of Commandant Decoeur, who was profuse in his presents, and who obtained a Treaty signed in the King's right name. The Lemamu informed me that, at the time, Siré Toru knew no difference between the French and the English, and that he thought the two missions belonged to the same white nation, but that he did not fear Commandant Decoeur as he had done Captain Lugard.

5. Why Siré Toru gave a letter to Captain Lugard signed Absalamu I cannot make out, for the Lemamu tells me that it is a name which he has never heard of amongst the Baribas.

6. For some time I could not ascertain from the Lemamu who Musa Pobida, who signed the Kyama Treaty, really was. It was the Lemamu's brother who eventually said that it must be intended for Musa Foruda, who was King Kemura's clerk and confidential secretary, and a man of no importance whatever. However, Kyama appears to be a division of the Borgu Kingdom, which is directly under Nikki, and as the so-called King is not of royal blood he is regarded by the Baribas as the Chief or Balé of the town, and not as a king in any sense of the word . . .

[The King of Bodé-Béré is a son of Pe Lafia and nephew of Sire Toru by a Yoruba mother. The French candidate for Nikki—Sabi Erima—has no claim. The King of Bussa does not ratify the Nikki election and is subject to Nikki.]

58

DIRECTOR OF MILITARY INTELLIGENCE TO COLONIAL OFFICE: GOLD COAST INTERIOR, 2 MAY 1898[1]

SECRET.

. . . But, even on the assumption that the Kiepert boundary is correct, it would appear that Governor Hodgson has overlooked the fact that both Daboya and Yaboum on Kiepert's map, and also on the later and more accurate maps, lie within the Neutral Zone, and should therefore be excluded from any project of route to Gambaga intended to lie outside that Zone.

Sir John Ardagh[2] is, however, strongly of the opinion that both for administrative and military reasons the partition of the Neutral Zone between the two Imperial Governments should be arranged as soon as circumstances permit. If the present moment be inopportune for again approaching Germany with a view to the definite settlement of the main question, it is suggested that, having regard to the inconvenience experienced by both nations in being debarred from using the routes running through any portion of the Zone as lines of military supply, some temporary compromise may be arrived at which would tend to eventually facilitate a fair partition.

In the note of Baron von Bülow, addressed to our Ambassador at Berlin on the 13th October last and printed in Colonial Office Proof 4672, it is implied that the main line of German communications with Sansanne Mango has hitherto run through Yendi, and that with a view to the mutual evacuation of the Neutral Zone the Germans are endeavouring to open up some other route to the Hinterland.

The four proposals contained in Colonel Everett's memorandum[3] above quoted all agree in surrendering Yendi to Germany, and it may therefore be assumed that by an offer to permit the Germans to continue to exercise a right of way through Yendi on condition that similar concessions were granted to us in the western portion of the Zone, we should not be giving up any portion of the Zone which is likely to fall ultimately within our territory. Germany might perhaps be asked in the first place to agree to our using the route Salaga–Zong–Sogne–Patenga–Gambaga (*vide* Colonel Northcott's telegram of 13th March, in Colonial Office Proof 9214). If that route should be refused, then the Pigu–Savelugu and Yegi route might be pressed (*vide* Colonel Northcott's telegram of 1st March, in Colonial Office Proof, 6393); or, in default of this, that suggested in Governor Hodgson's telegram of the 28th April might be asked for.

---

[1] C.O. 879/54, no. 549.   [2] Director of Military Intelligence, 1896–8.
[3] Sent to the F.O. in April 1897: C.O. 879/48, no. 529.

It will be remembered that in the recent Franco-German Agreement the necessities of lines of military communication have been very fully recognised by allowing the French a right of way through the north of Togoland.

59

CONVENTION BETWEEN GREAT BRITAIN AND FRANCE, 14 JUNE 1898[1]

Article I

. . . THE frontier separating the British Colony of the Gold Coast from the French Colonies of the Ivory Coast and Sudan shall start from the northern terminal point of the frontier laid down in the Anglo-French Agreement of the 12th July, 1893, viz., the intersection of the thalweg of the Black Volta with the 9th degree of north latitude, and shall follow the thalweg of this river northward up to its intersection with the 11th degree of north latitude. From this point it shall follow this parallel of latitude eastward as far as the river shown on Map No. 1, annexed to the present Protocol, as passing immediately to the east of the villages of Zwaga (Souaga) and Zebilla (Sebilla), and it shall then follow the thalweg of the western branch of this river up stream to its intersection with the parallel of latitude passing through the village of Sapeliga. From this point the frontier shall follow the northern limits of the lands belonging to Sapeliga, as far as the River Nuhau (Nouhau), and shall then follow the thalweg of this river up or down stream, as the case may be, to a point situated 2 miles (3,219 metres) eastward of the road which leads from Gambaga to Tenkrugu (Tingourkou), via Bawku (Baukou). Thence it shall rejoin by a straight line the 11th degree of north latitude at the intersection of this parallel with the road which is shown on Map No. 1, as leading from Sansanne Mango to Pama vïa Jebigu (Djebiga).

Article II

The frontier between the British Colony of Lagos and the French Colony of Dahomey, which was delimited on the ground by the Anglo-French Boundary Commission of 1895, and which is described in the Report signed by the Commissioners of the two nations on the 12th October, 1896, shall henceforward be recognised as the frontier separating the British and French possessions from the sea to the 9th degree of north latitude.

From the point of intersection of the River Ocpara with the 9th degree of north latitude, as determined by the said Commissioners,

[1] Encl. in Monson to Salisbury, 15 June 1898: *Parl. Papers*, 1898 [C. 8854].

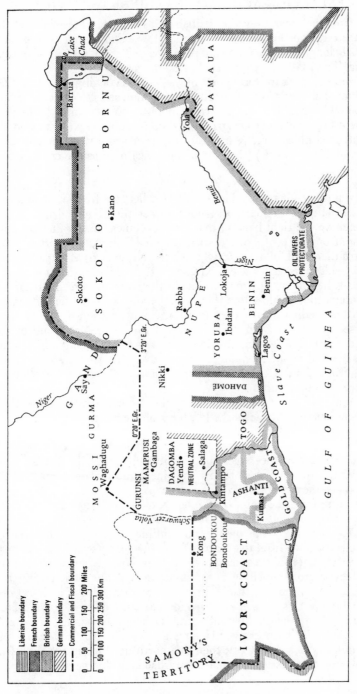

Map 1. Anglo-French Partition, 1898.

the frontier separating the British and French possessions shall proceed in a northerly direction, and follow a line passing west of the lands belonging to the following places, viz., Tabira, Okuta (Okouta), Boria, Tere, Gbani, Ashigere, (Yassikéra), and Dekala.

From the most westerly point of the lands belonging to Dekala the frontier shall be drawn in a northerly direction so as to coincide as far as possible with the line indicated on Map No. 1 annexed to the present Protocol, and shall strike the right bank of the Niger at a point situated 10 miles (16,093 metres) up-stream from the centre of the town of Gere (Guiris) (the port of Ilo), measured as the crow flies.

Article III

From the point specified in Article II, where the frontier separating the British and French possessions strikes the Niger, viz., a point situated on the right bank of that river, 10 miles (16,093 metres) up-stream from the centre of the town of Gere (Guiris), (the port of Ilo), the frontier shall follow a straight line therefrom at right angles to the right bank as far as its intersection with the median line of the river. It shall then follow the median line of the river, up-stream, as far as its intersection with a line drawn perpendicularly to the left bank from the median line of the mouth of the depression or dry water-course, which, on Map No. 2 annexed to the present Protocol, is called the Dallul Mauri, and is shown thereon as being situated at a distance of about 17 miles (27,359 metres), measured as the crow flies, from a point on the left bank opposite the above-mentioned village of Gere (Guiris).

From this point of intersection the frontier shall follow this perpendicular till it meets the left bank of the river.

Article IV

To the east of the Niger the frontier separating the British and French possessions shall follow the line indicated on Map No. 2, which is annexed to the present Protocol.

Starting from the point on the left bank of the Niger indicated in the previous Article, viz., the median line of the Dallul Mauri, the frontier shall follow this median line until it meets the circumference of a circle drawn from the centre of the town of Sokoto with a radius of 100 miles (160,932 metres). From this point it shall follow the northern arc of this circle as far as its second intersection with the 14th parallel of north latitude. From this second point of intersection it shall follow this parallel eastward for a distance of 70 miles (112,652 metres); then proceed due south until it reaches the parallel of 13° 20' north latitude, then eastward along this parallel for a distance of 250 miles (402,230 metres); then due north until it regains the 14th parallel of north latitude; then eastwards along this parallel as far as its intersection with the meridian passing 35' east of the centre of the town of Kuka, and thence this meridian southward until its intersection with the southern shore of Lake Chad.

The Government of the French Republic recognizes, as falling within the British sphere, the territory to the east of the Niger, comprised within the above-mentioned line, the Anglo-German frontier, and the sea.

The Government of Her Britannic Majesty recognizes, as falling within the French sphere, the northern, eastern, and southern shores of Lake Chad, which are comprised between the point of intersection of the 14th degree of north latitude, with the western shore of the lake and the point of incidence on the shore of the lake of the frontier determined by the Franco-German Convention of the 15th March, 1894.

Article V

The frontiers set forth in the present Protocol are indicated on the annexed Maps, which are marked 1 and 2 respectively.

The two Governments undertake to appoint within a year as regards the frontiers west of the Niger, and within two years as regards the frontier east of that river . . . Commissioners who will be charged with delimiting on the spot the lines of demarcation, between the British and French possessions . . .

Article VI

The two Contracting Powers engage reciprocally to treat with consideration ('bienveillance') the native Chiefs who, having had Treaties with one of them, shall, in virtue of the present Protocol, come under the sovereignty of the other.

Article VII

Each of the two Contracting Powers undertakes not to exercise any political action in the spheres of the other as defined by Articles I, II, III, and IV of the present Protocol.

It is understood by this that each Power will not, in the spheres of the other, make territorial acquisitions, conclude Treaties, accept sovereign rights or Protectorates, nor hinder nor dispute the influence of the other.

Article VIII

Her Britannic Majesty's Government will grant on lease to the Government of the French Republic, for the objects, and on the conditions, specified in the Form of Lease[1] annexed to the present Protocol, two pieces of ground . . . one of which will be situated in a suitable spot on the right bank of the Niger between Leaba and the

[1] *Parl. Papers*, 1898 [C. 8854] pp. 8–10.

junction of the River Moussa (Mochi) with the former river, and the other on one of the mouths of the Niger . . .

[Area of the leased plots of land; conditions of transit are to be discussed after signature of the Protocol.]

Article IX

Within the limits defined on Map No. 2, which is annexed to the present Protocol, British subjects and British protected persons and French citizens and French protected persons, as far as regards their persons and goods, and the merchandize the produce or the manufacture of Great Britain and France, their respective Colonies, Possessions, and Protectorates, shall enjoy for thirty years from the date of the exchange of the ratifications of the Convention mentioned in Article V the same treatment in all matters of river navigation, of commerce, and of Tariff and fiscal treatment and taxes of all kinds.

Subject to this condition, each of the two Contracting Powers shall be free to fix, in its own territory, and as may appear to it most convenient, the Tariff and fiscal treatment and taxes of all kinds.

In case neither of the two Contracting Powers shall have notified twelve months before the expiration of the above-mentioned term of thirty years its intention to put an end to the effects of the present Article, it shall remain in force until the expiration of one year from the day on which either of the Contracting Powers shall have denounced it.

In witness whereof, the undersigned Delegates have drawn up and signed the present Protocol.

Done at Paris, in duplicate, the 14th day of June, in the year of our Lord, 1898.

Signed Martin Gosselin; William Everett; René Lecomte; G. Binger.

60

CONVENTION BETWEEN GREAT BRITAIN AND GERMANY, 14 NOVEMBER 1899[1]

[Articles I, II, III, IV: Great Britain renounces rights in Samoa; Germany renounces rights in Tonga and the Solomons; the territories of the Neutral Zone, West Africa, as established in 1888, are partitioned as defined in Article V; Germany remains free to engage labourers in the Solomon Islands.]

Article V

IN the Neutral Zone the frontier between the German and English territories shall be formed by the River Daka as far as the point of its

[1] C.O. 879/64, no. 631.

intersection with the 9th degree of north latitude, thence the frontier shall continue to the north, leaving Morozugu to Great Britain, and shall be fixed on the spot by a Mixed Commission of the two Powers, in such a manner that Gambaga[1] and all the territories of Mamprusi shall fall to Great Britain, and that Yendi and all the territories of Chakosi shall fall to Germany.

Article VI

Germany is prepared to take into consideration, as much and as far as possible, the wishes which the Government of Great Britain may express with regard to the development of the reciprocal Tariffs in the territories of Togo and of the Gold Coast.

[Article VII: Germany renounces her extra-territoriality rights in Zanzibar.]

---

[1] *Sic*, Mamprusi: 'Gambaga' was not a separate territory. Supplemented by the treaty of 25 June 1904, for the boundary north of the 9th parallel, this arrangement led to lengthy surveys on the ground, 1900–5.

III

JURISDICTION AND ADMINISTRATION

Introductory Note

THE period of financial stringency and expanding administration, after 1875, saw the formal separation of the British West African colonies, when Lagos, the Gambia, and Sierra Leone received new Charters of Government in 1886 and 1888. These Charters followed the pattern of Crown Colony government elsewhere, instituting (as in the Gold Coast Letters Patent of 1886) the office of Governor with Executive and Legislative Councils, though only the Gold Coast and Lagos Legislatures had power to pass ordinances for protected territories (Orders in Council of 1874 and 1887). At the same time, the sphere of English law on the Gold Coast and Lagos had been widened by the Supreme Court Ordinance of 1876. Supreme Courts for all four colonies were reconstituted in 1888 and 1889. The period of administrative and judicial separation saw, too, a slight expansion of unofficial representation in the legislatures and the beginnings of municipal government at Accra and Freetown in 1889 and 1893. District administration in the Gold Coast towns was carried out by District Commissioners from 1875. In the areas near Freetown and Lagos experiments were made, after 1887, with travelling commissioners and frontier police (A. 12, 21). Plans for a regular West African Civil Service were prepared for the Gold Coast in 1901 and extended to other colonies and protectorates in 1904 (A. 58, 63).

The main problem of government in the period of rapid expansion in the 1890s was to settle the relationship between the interior and the colonial capitals. In the Niger Delta and along the Lower Niger—traditionally a Foreign Office responsibility—consular jurisdiction and administration by a chartered company produced very different styles of local government. The consuls inevitably exceeded the powers allowed them under the Order in Council of 1872; and a special commission was required to settle the Onitsha murder case of 1882 (A. 7). Jurisdiction was extended by the African Orders in Council of 1885 and 1889, and colonial ordinances were applied in the new Niger Coast Protectorate after 1893. The hinterland of the Lower Niger gradually opened to consular courts and native councils (A. 27); but in the area of Royal Niger Company rule, 1886–9, administration was left to a few district agents with regulated political and judicial powers, backed by an armed force which extended Company control as far as Nupe.

It is to be noted that after 1874 the separate land forces of the colonies and the Company decreased dependence on regiments from the West Indies and the Royal Navy. The crisis of 1897–8 on the Upper Niger and the need for a military unit which could be employed in any of the four

colonies and their hinterlands led to the formation of the West African
Frontier Force of some two to three thousand men (C. 3-9). This policy
was confirmed by the Selborne Committee of 1898 which completed the
amalgamation of the West African forces, against the objections of the
Governor of the Gold Coast.

As the partition and military conquest of the West African interior proceeded, the Protectorates of the Gambia and Sierra Leone were organized
by the Orders and Ordinances of 1893-7 (A. 22, 25, 28, 29, 32), partly on a
Gold Coast and Zululand model, under the Foreign Jurisdiction Act of
1890. Despite the opposition of Temne and Mende chiefs, the Sierra
Leone Protectorate administration survived the Hut Tax rebellion, 1897-8.
In Ashanti, after *ad hoc* administration by a resident at Kumasi, Prempeh
was deposed, and a decision was made (A. 50) to annex the conquered
territory to the 'Colony'. By the Administration Ordinance no. 1 of 1902
the familiar Commissioners' Courts and Native Tribunals were set up in
Ashanti and later in the Northern Territories. By contrast, the Lagos
hinterland, 1893-1903, was left under a variety of jurisdictions and treaties
which partially preserved Egba independence, installed a resident at
Ibadan, applied the Native Council experiment of 1901 to Ijebu, and kept
the old Lagos Protectorate under Commissioners and the Lagos Legislative
Council. In 1904 Lagos Supreme Court Jurisdiction was, in theory,
extended throughout Yorubaland.

By the end of the century, the geographical and administrative separation
of the extended colonies and protectorates, except in matters of defence,
was balanced by a need to co-ordinate and amalgamate the different
administrations that had grown up in Nigeria. As the Company Charter
was revoked and its territory partitioned, 1899-1900, the Niger Coast
Protectorate was placed under the Southern Nigeria High Commission,
while Northern Nigeria fell to a separate High Commission with power to
legislate by proclamation. In 1906 the Colony and Protectorate of Lagos
were merged with Southern Nigeria; the old Lagos Protectorate became
the new Western Province, governed by former laws. In both Northern and
Southern Protectorates, Commissioners' Courts and Provincial Courts
were introduced; but those in the south were controlled by the Supreme
Court, while the northern courts were under the High Commissioner. The
former native courts of the Niger Coast Protectorate were re-established as
Native Councils in the Central and Eastern Provinces, presided over by
district commissioners. In the north, the Native Courts Proclamation of
1900 recognized officially approved indigenous legal institutions; and in
1906 this system of retaining Muslim and pagan courts was refined, giving
the Residents increased powers of appointment and dismissal. The final
step towards the amalgamation of Northern and Southern Nigeria was
exhaustively planned by Lugard in 1913. This amalgamation ended all
that remained of Yoruba autonomy, combined administrative departments,
set limits to Supreme Court jurisdiction, and aimed at re-structuring
southern administration on the northern model (A. 66-70).

The 1870s and 1880s saw little relaxation of the Treasury control of
West African finances. It was also a period of demonetization of the dollar
after 1880 and the large-scale importation of British silver coin by local

administrations, the African Banking Corporation and the Bank of British West Africa (B. 3, 5). But there was little management of the new coinage before 1912, when the West African Currency Board was set up (B. 24). In general, customs increased in incidence; direct taxation was avoided, with the exception of the Sierra Leone Hut Tax, until the establishment of Native Treasuries in Northern Nigeria. The principle of 'self-sufficiency' on which the Colonial Office still prided itself as late as 1897 (B. 13) did not long survive the cost of rapid expansion into the interior and military operations in the Northern Territories and on the Upper Niger (B. 14).

The rapid growth of trade after 1890 encouraged other forms of public investment. Although there was little public debt in the West African colonies before 1895, some loans were made under the Stock Act of 1877, before Chamberlain helped initiate the programme of public works finance under the Colonial Loans Act of 1899 and the Colonial Stock Act of 1900.

A. COLONIES AND PROTECTORATES

I

LAW OFFICERS TO LORD CARNARVON: WEST AFRICAN SUPREME COURTS, 1 SEPTEMBER 1877[1]

WE are honoured with your Lordship's commands signified in Mr. Meade's letter of the 20th August ultimo stating that he was directed by your Lordship to transmit to us copies of the following documents:—

An Order in Council dated the 26th day of February 1867, establishing the 'West Africa Courts of Appeal'

The Administration of Justice Ordinance 1876 of the Legislature of Sierra Leone.

Letters Patent constituting the Gold Coast Colony.

The Supreme Court Ordinance of 1876 of the Legislature of the Gold Coast Colony.

Three draft Orders in Council

(1) Revoking the Order in Council of 26th February 1867
(2) Providing for appeals from the decision of the Supreme Court of the Gold Coast Colony
(3) Establishing an Appeal Court for Her Majesty's Settlements on the Gambia.

[1] C.O. 267/332. Signed, John Holker, Hardinge S. Giffard. For the institution of appellate jurisdiction, see W. C. Ekow Daniels, *The Common Law in West Africa* (London, 1964), pp. 38–9; and for the Gold Coast Supreme Court Ordinance of 1876, Kimble, *Political History of Ghana*, p. 304.

That the changes which had been effected by the enclosed Ordinances in the constitution of the Supreme Court of Sierra Leone, and the creation of the Gold Coast Colony with a separate Supreme Court, appeared to render necessary those or similar Orders in Council and Mr. Meade was to state that your Lordship would feel obliged if we would consider the enclosed drafts . . .

We have the honour to report that in our opinion the Draft Orders in Council enclosed are proper and sufficient for the purposes for which they are respectively intended.

2

LAW OFFICERS TO LORD DERBY: CONSULAR JURISDICTION, 27 MARCH 1878[1]

WE were honoured with Y L's commands signified in Sir Julian Pauncefote's letter of the 15th Instant stating that he was directed . . . to transmit to us the Papers . . . in relation to a question which had arisen as to the power of H.M's Consul at Fernando Po to send a British Subject for trial to Lagos on a charge of slave dealing. That the judicial powers of H.M's Consul were regulated by H.M's Order in Council of the 21st of February 1872[2] a copy of which accompanied the papers. That by that Order in Council the Consul had power to deal with the offences against the Slave Trade Acts mentioned in § 16, but he had no authority to send offenders for Trial to a British Colony under the provisions in that behalf contained in the Foreign Jurisdiction Act. That we would observe however that the Colonial Office considered that power might be exercised by him under the terms of the concluding paragraph of § 26 of the Slave Trade Act of 1873 (36 and 37 Vict. cap 88) and they inquired whether Y. L. concurred in the Instructions to that effect which they proposed to send out to the Governor of the Gold Coast Colony . . .

We have the honour to Report

That in our opinion the Consular Office has not by 36 and 37 Vict. cap. 88 Sectn. 26 the power to send a person charged with an offence under that Act for trial to a British Colony for we think such Consular Officer is not a judge having jurisdiction to try within the meaning of that Section.

---

[1] C.O. 147/36. Signed, Hardinge S. Giffard, W. Deane. The C.O. referred the case to Governor Freeling (who made no comment), but not to the Foreign Office, whose consul had begun proceedings against the African British Subject, A. Williams.

[2] Vol. I, pp. 579–80.

3

ACTING CONSUL S. F. EASTON TO THE SECRETARY OF STATE FOR FOREIGN AFFAIRS: TRIAL FOR SLAVE DEALING, 3 NOVEMBER 1879[1]

I HAVE the honour to inform Your Lordship that whilst at Onitsha I arrested three British Subjects viz Nathaniel Adolphus Palmer, native of Sierra Leone, John Nathaniel Ogoo, native of Sierra Leone, John Obadiah Astrope, native of Lagos.

They were arrested on 25th October. They were brought before me on the 1st November, charged with extensive slave-dealing. I proceeded to try them on that count and the evidence adduced was so overwhelming and conclusive that I sentenced Ogoo and Astrope to penal service for fourteen years and Palmer to penal servitude for seven years.

The evidence taken before me forms Enclosure No. 1. I have forwarded them to Lagos along with a request to the Lieut-Governor (Enclosure No 2.)[2] of that Colony that he will detain them pending Instructions from Your Lordship as to their final disposition.

These men have been the scourge of Onitsha for the past two years, and the merchants were so desirous to see them removed that they have offered to defray the expense of their interim incarceration . . .

4

GOVERNOR SIR SAMUEL ROWE TO SIR MICHAEL HICKS BEACH: SIERRA LEONE NATIVE AFFAIRS, 6 NOVEMBER 1879[3]

IN reference to the proposed addition which I have placed on the Estimates for the year 1880 of £800 for the salaries of two Assistants in the Secretariat Department, I have the honor to report as follows;

2. In deference to the wishes of Council, I have put one of these officers under the head of Aborigines, but it appears to me necessary that it should be understood that they should both be available for any duties which it may be necessary for them to discharge . . .

---

[1] F.O. 84/1541. Encl. 'Evidence in Support', November 1879. The F.O. noted these proceedings were illegal: Pauncefote, Minute, 3 January 1880. Easton also arrested Edward Bickersteth at Akassa on a charge of slave-dealing, tried and sentenced him to ten years imprisonment at Lagos. Easton to F.O., 3 November 1879.

[2] Easton to Moloney, 2 November 1879, ibid.

[3] C.O. 267/338 (Sierra Leone).

3. There are at present 9 Executive Officers entitled to European leave on the fixed Establishment of the Settlement, exclusive of the Judicial, the Ecclesiastical and the Medical Establishments, and exclusive also of the Auditor, Gaoler, and the Sanitary Inspector.

4. Without considering these 9 officers as interchangeable, it is necessary when any of these goes on leave, that his duties should be taken up by some one of those who are remaining here.

5. By the Colonial Regulations Officers whose parents are not Natives of West Africa are entitled to an absence of 8 months in every twenty four; this is exactly one third of their time, and if the reliefs were carried out regularly it would reduce the number of officers present at any time in these 9 different offices to 6.

6. If you should see fit to be pleased to approve this increase to the General Staff, it is my intention that one of these officers should more particularly devote himself to duties in connection with the Aborigines Branch, and that he should indeed be a Secretary for Native Affairs.

7. The duties of this office have hitherto been distributed. The Records relating to stipends are kept in the Colonial Secretary's Department, that officer is also responsible for the correctness of the accounts of the Board and Lodging of Native Chiefs and their followers.

8. Much of the political work also in connection with this branch was in former years carried on through the Colonial Secretary, which is not, I would respectfully submit, the most desirable arrangement in these political matters. Indeed, it is not possible for the Colonial Secretary to properly carry on his local duties and give to Aboriginal matters, the time necessary for this full supervision.

9. Since I have had the honor to assume this Government much progress has been made in organising this Department and in collecting information in reference to it, in which I have been most ably assisted by Mr. Lawson[1] the Government Interpreter who indeed has practically been the Secretary for Native Affairs so far as it regarded the relation of this Government with tribes to the northward.

10. Mr. Lawson is now over 64 years of age, and the Settlement cannot hope to retain the advantage of his services for more than a few years longer.

11. I have done as much as has been possible in committing to paper some of the valuable local knowledge which he has accumulated during a long lifetime, and am very wishful to obtain the assistance of an officer who will so classify and arrange the Records belonging to it as to make them available in the interest of the Settlement for the use of any fairly educated person. It is absolutely necessary also that there should be at the disposal of the Governor an officer who

---

[1] *Thomas George Lawson*, government interpreter, 1852–88. He was succeeded by the Creole, J. C. E. Parkes.

should be detached on journeys to such Native Chiefs within or without the Settlement as it may be necessary from time to time to visit . . .

5

GOVERNOR H. T. USSHER TO LORD KIMBERLEY: ASSESSORS AND JURIES, 26 JULY 1880[1]

[Astrope, Bickersteth, Palmer, and Agoo have been tried for slave-dealing at Onitsha; all except Astrope have been convicted and sentenced to fourteen years' penal servitude at Elmina.]

. . . 2. IN the course of this prosecution, undertaken by the desire of the Secretary of State for Foreign Affairs, at the great inconvenience and expense of the Gold Coast Colony, it has become more and more evident that it is impossible to rely upon an impartial decision from either a jury or assessors, in cases where the accused—as in this instance—can command local influence.

3. Had it not been for the determination of the Queen's Advocate whose exertions have been beyond all praise, and the decisive conduct of the Judge, Mr. Hector Macleod, in overruling the preconcerted opinion of the native assessors, these great criminals would have escaped, and have returned to the Niger, to renew their nefarious traffic, in defiance of the authorities. I am informed that in every case the assessors stolidly and consistently declined to convict, in the face of the clearest evidence. There is no doubt in my own mind that the whole of the proceedings too nearly touched the whole African semi-educated community, to permit them to condemn men whose proceedings were possibly no worse than their own . . .

[The prisoners have been transported from Lagos to Elmina.]

5. A still greater commotion has been raised by the application of the Queen's Advocate to remove a person of great local influence, Mr. J. P. L. Davies, to be tried at Accra under the powers given by the Supreme Court Ordinance of 1876. It has become a matter of certainty that no Lagos jury will give an impartial verdict in the case of this person whose local influence is immense; and in the interests of his creditors, and of the ends of justice, Mr. Woodcock, seconded by Mr. Moss, the agent of the principal English creditors, applied to change the venue.

I still think it possible that a demonstration may be made for which I am quite prepared . . . The state of society here in these matters

[1] C.O. 147/41. Proceedings of the trial held at Lagos, encl. in Griffith to Ussher 8 May and 19 July 1880.

gives great cause for alarm; and it will become a question how far and in what manner it will be necessary to modify the present system of trial by jury. Intimidation of a flagrant kind is resorted to here, and latterly, I regret to observe, on the Gold Coast, and it will shortly become impossible to obtain a conviction . . .

6

PROVISIONS FOR EXTENDING THE GOLD COAST NATIVE JURISDICTION ORDINANCE, [MAY 1882][1]

1. A SUITABLE district must be found.

2. This must be a district presided over by a head chief known as Ohen Ohene, Manche, or Amagh.

This district may be subdivided under the Ordinance, but I should advise a trial of a single tribunal in a single district at first.

3. The head chief sitting with his captains, headmen, and councillors, constitute a native tribunal under the Ordinance.

4. The tribunal will have jurisdiction over such an area as is at present under the supervision of the head chief.

5. The head chief, his captains, headmen and councillors, should be called together and the intentions of the Government to constitute them a native tribunal should be explained to them.

6. All the powers rights, duties, obligations and jurisdiction imposed by the Ordinance should be carefully explained to them by some competent person, especially mentioning the fact that the native tribunals would be done away with upon the new one proposed.

7. When this has been done, the head chief should be asked if he desired to come under the terms of the Ordinance.

8. If he replied in the affirmative, it should be ascertained from the head chief what he considers are the limits and boundaries of his present supervision.

9. The names of the villages therein should be ascertained, and the boundaries of the proposed native jurisdiction carefully ascertained, and marked out by name.

10. It would be advisable before constituting the district a division to ascertain if any other chief or chiefs laid claim to exercise jurisdiction over any part of it.

11. This may be done by notices to the neighbouring chiefs of the intention of forming such a native jurisdiction, naming the villages

---

[1] C.O. 879/19, no. 249. Ordinance no. 8 of 1878 (Native Jurisdiction) had never been applied. It was repealed and re-enacted in Ordinance no. 5 of 1883, constituting chiefs and councillors into tribunals.

and boundaries over which it was to have jurisdiction, and request to
know if they claimed any villages or jurisdiction over such country.
Such notices should be published in the proposed division.

7

COLONIAL OFFICE TO FOREIGN
OFFICE: ONITSHA MURDER TRIAL,
23 OCTOBER 1882[1]

I AM directed by the Earl of Kimberley to transmit to you to be laid
before Earl Granville . . . a copy of a Despatch from the Governor of
Sierra Leone,[2] forwarding a letter from the Commissioners appointed
for the trial of certain persons[3] for murder at Onitsha on the river
Niger, reporting that the accused had been found guilty of manslaughter, and that two of them were sentenced to 20 years imprisonment, one to 18 years and six months, and the fourth to two years.

With regard to the Commissioners' remarks as to the necessity for
providing a better machinery by which trials of this kind may be
conducted, I am to observe that the proposed new Order in Council
for regulating Consular Jurisdiction on the West Coast of Africa
will if passed, be more effective than the proposals of the
Commissioners . . .

8

EARL OF KIMBERLEY TO
ADMINISTRATOR C. A. MOLONEY:
TARQUAH GOLD MINING DISTRICT,
7 NOVEMBER 1882[4]

2. I HAVE perused Commander Rumsey's report with much interest,
and I appreciate the very satisfactory manner in which he carried out
the duty intrusted to him.

3. With regard to the remarks contained in the report, and in your
Despatch, respecting the formation of a District, you will perceive
from the correspondence relating to the Native Jurisdiction Ordinance
which has recently been sent to you, that it is not proposed to declare
the interior portions of the 'protected territories' to be districts of

[1] *Parl. Papers*, 1882 [C. 3430]; *F.O. Confidential Print*, 3932 (1878).
[2] Havelock to Kimberley, 21 September 1882, encl. Commissioners Francis
Pinkett (Chief Justice), T. Risely Griffith (Colonial Secretary), Francis Smith
(Chief Magistrate), W. M. Huggins, to Havelock, 19 September 1882. The Commission, appointed under the Great Seal to hear the case, suggested an Act of Parliament to extend the jurisdiction of Gold Goast courts to the Niger districts.
[3] W. F. John and John Williams and his wife were the principal accused.
[4] C.O. 879/19, no. 249.

the Supreme Court and place them under resident Commissioners. The best mode of providing for the maintenance of peace and order at the Gold Mines, and directing affairs in the neighbourhood, will of course be considered by Sir Samuel Rowe in connexion with his scheme for putting in force the Native Jurisdiction Ordinance . . .

9

ORDER IN COUNCIL: BRITISH JURISDICTION IN WEST AFRICA, 26 MARCH 1885[1]

[Under the Foreign Jurisdiction Acts, 1843-78, power and jurisdiction are conferred on consular courts and consuls appointed as judicial officers.]

. . . 4. THE jurisdiction hereby conferred shall extend to the persons and matters following, in so far as by Treaty, capitulation, grant, usage, sufference or other lawful means Her Majesty has jurisdiction in relation to such persons and matters, that is to say:—

(1) All persons within the limits of this Order who are British subjects by birth or naturalization, or are otherwise for the time being subject to British law.

(2) All persons properly enjoying Her Majesty's protection within the said limits.

(3) The property and all personal or proprietary rights and liabilities within the said limits of any such persons as before mentioned, or situate for the time being within the said limits, and belonging to British subjects or protected persons, although such subjects or persons may not be within the said limits.

(4) All other persons, whether natives of Africa or not, and whether subjects of any non-African Power or not, who submit themselves to the jurisdiction, and who give such security as the Consular Court requires for obedience to the Order of the Court.

(5) British ships, with their boats, and the persons and property on board thereof, or belonging thereto, being on the coasts or in the harbours or waters of any country or place within the limits of this Order.

(6) Natives of Africa, being subjects of any native King or Chief who, by Treaty or otherwise, consents to their being subject to the jurisdiction . . .

[Civil and criminal law administered under the Order shall be that in force in England at the date of commencement of the Order, or such laws and ordinances of the West African settlements, as directed by a Secretary of State. Rules of procedure; registration of British subjects.]

[1] Hertslet, *Commercial Treaties*, vol. xvii (1890), pp. 83-99.

10

LETTERS PATENT CONSTITUTING
THE COLONY OF LAGOS, 13 JANUARY 1886[1]

... WHEREAS by our Letters Patent under the Great Seal of our United Kingdom of Great Britain and Ireland, bearing date at Westminster, the 22nd day of January, 1883, we did constitute the office of Governor and Commander-in-Chief of the Gold Coast Colony, then comprising our Settlements on the Gold Coast and of Lagos, and did provide for the Government of our said Colony: and whereas we are minded to make separate provision for the Government of our Settlement of Lagos hitherto comprised within our Gold Coast Colony: Now know ye that we have by Letters Patent of even date herewith, revoked and determined our said Letters Patent of the 22nd day of January, 1883, but without prejudice to anything lawfully done thereunder: And further know ye that we do hereby erect our said Settlement of Lagos into a separate Colony, to be called the Colony of Lagos . . .

2. Our Colony of Lagos (hereinafter called the Colony), shall, until we otherwise provide, comprise all places, settlements, and territories belonging to us in Western Africa, between the second degree of east longitude and the sixth degree of east longitude.

[The Governor is empowered to carry out his instructions.]

5. In the first instance the Government of the Colony shall be vested in an Administrator, and every such Administrator, and every Lieutenant-Governor, if we shall think fit to vest the Government in such an officer, and every person appointed to fill the office of Governor shall, with all due solemnity . . . [He shall take an oath of allegience   Sections 6–21 are the same as those for the Gold Coast Letters Patent, 13 January 1886.]

11

CHARTER OF THE NATIONAL AFRICAN
(ROYAL NIGER) COMPANY LIMITED,
10 JULY 1886[2]

[The Company, incorporated in 1882 and with a capital of £1,000,000, has declared its objects as trading and banking, carrying and acquiring factories, applying for concessions and privileges in mining, forests,

---

[1] Hertslet, *Commercial Treaties*, vol. xvii (1890), p. 109. For Gold Coast Letters Patent of the same date, see Metcalfe, *Great Britain and Ghana*, no. 350.

[2] Ibid., pp. 118–25. For the opening text of the petition of the Company, see Flint, *Sir George Goldie*, Appendix II.

fisheries; territories have been ceded to the Company which should be developed under Royal Charter.]

Authorization to Company.

1. THE said National African Company Limited . . . is hereby authorized and empowered to hold and retain the full benefit of the several cessions aforesaid, or any of them, and all rights, interests, authorities, and powers for the purposes of government, preservation of public order, protection of the said territories, or otherwise of what nature or kind soever, under or by virtue thereof, or resulting therefrom, and ceded to or vested in the Company in, over, or affecting the territories, lands and property comprised in those several cessions, or in, over, or affecting any territories, lands, or property in the neighbourhood of the same, and to hold, use, enjoy, and exercise the same territories, lands, property, rights, interests, authorities, and powers respectively for the purposes of the Company, and on the terms of this our Charter.

Fulfilment by Company of Promises given.

2. The Company shall be bound by and shall fulfil all and singular the stipulations on their part contained in the Acts of Cession aforesaid, subsequent to any consequent agreement affecting those stipulations approved by one of our Principal Secretaries of State . . .

British Character of the Company.

3. The Company shall always be and remain British in character and domicile, and shall have its principal office in England; and its principle representative in the territories aforesaid and all the Directors shall always be natural-born British subjects, or persons who have been naturalized as British subjects by or under an Act of the Parliament of our United Kingdom.

Restriction of Transfer by Company.

4. The Company shall not have power to transfer, wholly or in part, the benefit of the cessions aforesaid, or any of them except with the consent of our Secretary of State.

Foreign Powers.

5. If at any time our Secretary of State thinks fit to dissent from or object to any of the dealings of the Company with any foreign Power, and to make to the Company any suggestion founded on that dissent or objection, the Company shall act in accordance therewith.

Slavery.

6. The Company shall, to the best of its power, discourage and, as far as may be practicable, abolish by degrees any system of domestic servitude existing among the native inhabitants; and no foreigner, whether European or other,[1] shall be allowed to own slaves of any kind in the Company's territories.

Religions of Inhabitants.

7. The Company as such, or its officers as such, shall not in any way interfere with the religion of any class or tribe of the people of its territories, or of any of the inhabitants thereof, except so far as may be necessary in the interests of humanity, and all forms of religious worship and religious ordinances may be exercised within the said territories, and no hindrance shall be offered thereto, except as aforesaid.

Administration of Justice to Inhabitants.

8. In the administration of justice by the Company to the peoples of its territories, or to any of the inhabitants thereof, careful regard shall always be had to the customs and laws of the class, or tribe, or nation to which the parties respectively belong, especially with respect to the holding possession, transfer, and disposition of lands and goods, and testate or intestate succession thereto, and marriage, divorce, and legitimacy, and other rights of property and personal rights.

Treatment of Inhabitants generally.

9. If at any time our Secretary of State thinks fit to dissent from, or object to, any part of the proceedings or system of the Company relative to the people of its territories, or to any of the inhabitants thereof, in respect of slavery or religion, or the administration of justice, or other matter, and to make to the Company any suggestion founded on that dissent or objection, the Company shall act in accordance therewith.

[The Company shall provide facilities for British ships and may fly a distinctive flag.]

General Powers of the Company.

12. The Company is hereby further authorized and empowered, subject to the approval of our Secretary of State, to acquire and take by purchase, cession, or other lawful means, other rights, interests, authorities, or powers of any kind or nature whatever in, over, or affecting the territories, lands, or property comprised in the several Treaties aforesaid,[2] or any rights, interests, authorities or

---

[1] The text in Flint, *Sir George Goldie*, p. 333. has 'or not'.
[2] Ibid., p. 334, has 'in the region aforesaid' for this phrase and omits part of the subsequent sentence.

powers of any kind or nature whatever, in, over, or affecting the territories, lands, or property in the region aforesaid, and to hold, use, enjoy and exercise the same for the purposes of the Company and on the terms of this our Charter.

Question of Title.

13. If at any time our Secretary of State thinks fit to object to the exercise by the Company of any authority or power within any part of the territories comprised in the several cessions aforesaid, or otherwise acquired by the Company on the ground of there being an adverse claim to that part, the Company shall defer to that objection.

Prohibition of Monopoly.

14. Nothing in this our Charter shall be deemed to authorize the Company to set up or grant any monopoly of trade; and subject only to Customs duties and charges as hereby authorized, and to restrictions on importation similar in character to those applicable in our United Kingdom trade with the Company's territories under our protection shall be free, and there shall be no differential treatment of the subjects of any Power as to settlement or access to markets, but foreigners alike with British subjects will be subject to administrative dispositions in the interests of commerce and of order.

The customs duties and charges hereby authorized shall be levied and applied solely for the purpose of defraying the necessary expenses of government, including the administration of justice, the maintenance of order, and the performance of Treaty obligations, as herein mentioned, and including provision to such extent and in such manner as our Secretary of State may from time to time allow for repayment of expenses already incurred for the like purposes or otherwise, in relation to the acquisition, maintenance, and execution of Treaty rights.

The Company from time to time, either periodically or otherwise, as may be directed by our Secretary of State, shall furnish accounts and particulars in such form, and verified in such manner as he requires, of the rates, incidence, collection, proceeds, and application of such duties, and shall give effect to any direction by him as to any modification of the description, rate, incidence, collection, or application of any such duties.

Conformity to Treaties.

15. The Company shall be subject to and shall perform, observe, and undertake all the obligations and stipulations relating to the River Niger, its affluents, branches, and outlets, or the territories neighbouring thereto, or situate in Africa, contained in and undertaken by ourselves under the General Act of the Conference of the Great

Powers at Berlin, dated the 26 February, 1885, or in any other Treaty, Agreement, or Arrangement between ourselves and any other State or Power, whether already made or hereafter to be made.

Foreign Jurisdiction.

16. In all matters relating to the observance of the last preceding Article or to the exercise within the Company's territories for the time being of any jurisdiction exercisable by us under the Foreign Jurisdiction Acts, or the said General Act of the 26th February, 1885, the Company shall conform to and observe and carry out all such directions as may from time to time be given in that behalf by our Secretary of State, and the Company shall, at their own expense, appoint all such officers to perform such duties and provide such Courts and other requisites for the administration of justice as he directs.

General Provisions.

And we do further will, ordain and declare that this our Charter shall be acknowledged by our Governors, and our naval and military officers, and our Consuls, and our other officers, in our Colonies and Possessions, and on the high seas and elsewhere, and they shall severally give full force and effect to this our Charter, and shall recognize and be in all lawful things aiding to the Company and its officers.

And we do further will, ordain and declare that this our Charter shall be taken, construed, and adjudged in the most favourable and beneficial sense for and to the best advantage of the Company, as well in our Courts in our United Kingdom, and in our Courts in our Colonies or Possessions, and in our Courts in foreign countries, or elsewhere, notwithstanding that there may appear to be in this our Charter any non-recital, mis-recital, uncertainty, or imperfection.

And we do further will, ordain, and declare that this our Charter shall subsist and continue valid, notwithstanding any lawful change in the name of the Company or in the Articles of Association thereof, such change being made with the previous approval of our Secretary of State signified under his hand.

And we do lastly will, ordain and declare, that in case at any time it is made to appear to us in our Council expedient that this our Charter should be revoked, it shall be lawful for us, our heirs and successors, and we do hereby expressly reserve and take to ourselves, our heirs and successors, the right and power, by writing, under the Great Seal of our United Kingdom, to revoke this our Charter, without prejudice to any power to repeal the same by law, belonging to us or them, or to any of our Courts, Ministers or officers, independently of this present declaration and reservation . . .

[Schedule of treaties, January–November 1884.]

12

R. G. W. HERBERT TO SIR SAMUEL ROWE: TRAVELLING COMMISSIONERS, 8 MARCH 1887[1]

I AM directed by Secretary Sir H. Holland to acquaint you that he has had under his consideration the question of the policy to be pursued in future by the Government of Sierra Leone with regard to the tribes inhabiting the adjacent interior districts of which the produce forms the bulk of the exports of the Colony.

The disastrous effect on the prosperity of the Colony which has resulted from the succession of disturbances in these districts during the last few years has abundantly proved that so long as the inhabitants of that area are permitted to wage their constant inter-tribal warfare uncontrolled it is impossible to carry on the Government of Sierra Leone without financial assistance from the Imperial Government. The Settlement is already in receipt of an annual grant in aid of 5,500 *l.*, and a balance of 8,000 *l.* of the loan made to it from the Imperial Exchequer in 1877 is still outstanding, so that it appears to Sir H. Holland that its claims on Her Majesty's Government have been amply recognised and that no expectation of further assistance should be entertained.

The removal of the artificial obstacles to the trade of the Colony created by the present tariff has been dealt with in the letter from this Department of this day's date, but Sir H. Holland is satisfied that that alone will not be sufficient to ensure financial stability, and that arrangements must, if possible, be made for permanently securing the observance of peace in the producing areas.

Three schemes have been put forward.

In the memorial from the inhabitants of Sierra Leone, which was enclosed in your despatch No. 23 of 14th January 1886,[2] the desire was expressed that measures should be adopted 'for the enlargement of the boundaries of the Settlement by a policy of peaceful annexation,' and that as the finances of the Colony were unable to bear the cost of such annexation the Imperial Government should grant a loan to the Settlement for the purpose. It is hardly necessary for Sir H. Holland to observe that for many reasons it would be wholly impossible for Her Majesty's Government to entertain this proposal.

In the next place, it has been suggested that, as in the case of the Gold Coast Colony, a protectorate should be declared over the adjacent interior districts which are still independent, leaving the jurisdiction in the hands of the native Chiefs as at present.

[1] C.O. 879/24, no. 323. Based on a minute by J. Anderson, 4 September 1886; and Rowe to C.O., Memorandum, 21 December 1886: C.O. 267/365.
[2] C.O. 267/362.

This arrangement has unquestionably worked well hitherto on the Gold Coast, not a single disturbance having occurred among the tribes in the protectorate with which the ordinary police force of the Colony has been unable to deal. Tribal disputes have been settled amicably by a visit from an officer with a few police, or by summoning the Chiefs who are disposed to quarrel to head-quarters, with a view to an arrangement. Sir H. Holland is not, however, satisfied that the analogy between the circumstances of the Gold Coast and of Sierra Leone is so complete as to justify the assumption of the responsibility involved in this proposal, and, in view of the general reluctance of Parliament to regard with favour any extension of British authority over the inland districts of West Africa, he does not feel able to press it upon Her Majesty's Government as a desirable solution of the difficulty.

The third scheme is that submitted in your despatch No. 134 of the 24th April last,[1] viz., the appointment of Commissioners who should be constantly travelling through the districts in question, advising the Chiefs, and endeavouring to arrange inter-tribal disputes.

Such an arrangement is no doubt open to the objection that it depends for its success very much on the character of the men selected to carry it out, and any rashness or mistake on the part of a Commissioner might lead to serious complications.

Sir H. Holland does not, however, think that, if due care be taken in the appointment of the Commissioners, this objection is one to which much importance need be attached, or that it can be held to outweigh the other manifest advantages of the scheme. He approves, therefore, of the policy sketched in paragraph 16 of your memorandum of the 18th December last, and authorises you, on your return to Sierra Leone, to carry out the scheme embodied in your despatch of 24th April last, on the lines laid down in paragraph 18 of your memorandum above mentioned.

Sir H. Holland would propose that only two out of the three Commissioners suggested by you should be appointed in the first instance, leaving the third appointment to be filled up later, in the event of the plan being found to work satisfactorily.

Sir H. Holland is, moreover, disposed to think that it would be desirable to arrange for the insertion in the agreements which have been or may be made by the Government of Sierra Leone with all the Chiefs in the districts of a clause binding them to impose no restrictions on trade, and to refer all their disputes with their neighbours to the Government of Sierra Leone, whose decision shall be final.

It should at the same time be pointed out to them, that these engagements with the Queen's representative are not to be lightly entered into, and that any violation of them would be regarded as a grave offence.

[1] C.O. 267/362.

This proposal involves no responsibility for the defence of the tribes in the districts concerned against attack from tribes outside, and avoids all interference with the internal economy and institutions of the people. Sir H. Holland entertains a strong hope that the occasions upon which the police would have to be actively employed beyond the borders of the Settlement, in order to punish any breach of the agreements with the Chiefs, would be extremely rare, and he is glad to find that this hope is shared by you, whose experience of West Africa has been so varied and extensive. In the event, however, of your finding it necessary to take such action, you should of course in each and every case report by telegraph what you propose, and obtain the sanction of the Secretary of State. And it is hardly necessary to observe that when making your recommendation you should entirely satisfy yourself that you are in a position, with the force at your disposal, to carry out your action successfully.

It will probably be necessary, in order to carry out this policy, that the police force should be increased by the addition of a hundred men and an officer, so as to enable it to deal with any disturbances that may arise without the assistance of Her Majesty's Imperial forces, which it is of course undesirable to employ, except in case of absolute necessity.

It is essential to the working of this or any other arrangement for the pacification of the country that the means of communication should be improved and the proposal submitted by you for the construction of a road joining the points where the navigation of the rivers terminates, and leading to Freetown via Songo town, is one which should be carried out without delay, and the Commissioners should arrange with all the Chiefs through whose territory it will pass for assistance in its construction and for its maintenance. The frequent patrolling of this road by small parties of police will have a good effect in securing the peace of the country and the safe transit of produce to the various markets. . . .

13

A. W. L. HEMMING: MINUTE, LAGOS JURISDICTION, 4 NOVEMBER 1887[1]

. . . In all our West African Colonies the exact limits of jurisdiction & the amount it is desirable to exercise are, & must be somewhat undefined. This, especially to the judicial mind, is a dreadful thing— & the tendency is always towards exact definition & direct adminis- tration. But unless we are prepared to see the establishments costing a

[1] C.O. 147/60. On Moloney to Holland, 17 August 1887, reporting the views of Smalman-Smith, Chief Justice, on Lagos jurisdiction under the Supreme Court and the District Commissioners.

vast deal more than they do now, this cannot be allowed, & certain things must be winked at which are perhaps outside the law.

In the present case I would only notice the action taken by Capt. Moloney in authorizing the establishment of a post on Igbagun Island & granting of stipends to the Chiefs of Isseh & Ode. His proceedings may be approved, & he might receive authority to give, if he thinks it desirable, the stipend of £100 per ann. to the Epes . . .

14

ORDER IN COUNCIL: JURISDICTION IN TERRITORIES ADJACENT TO THE GOLD COAST COLONY, 29 DECEMBER 1887[1]

[Recital of the Foreign Jurisdiction Act, 1843, the Letters Patent (Gold Coast), 24 July 1874, the Letters Patent (Lagos and Gold Coast), 13 January 1886.]

. . . Now, therefore, Her Majesty is pleased by and with the advice of her Privy Council, to order as follows:

1. It shall be lawful for the Legislative Council for the time being of the Gold Coast Colony, by Ordinance or Ordinances, to exercise and provide for giving effect to all such powers and jurisdiction as Her Majesty may, at any time before or after the passing of this Order in Council, have acquired in the said territories adjacent to the Gold Coast Colony . . .

[The Governor may refuse such ordinances which may be disallowed.]

15

LORD KNUTSFORD TO SIR W. B. GRIFFITH: GOLD COAST MUNICIPAL BOARDS, 8 JANUARY 1889[2]

. . . The formation of a municipal board for Cape Coast should also be pressed forward with as little delay as possible. I am aware that the local promoters of this measure do not contemplate the levy of any local taxation, but the creation of a representative municipal authority will at once relieve the Colonial Government from the necessity of devoting its funds to minor local improvements and other charges. In the course of time it will no doubt be possible to induce the

---

[1] Hertslet, *Commercial Treaties*, vol. xviii (1893), pp. 127–8.

[2] C.O. 879/31, no. 379. The proposal arose from the deteriorating financial condition of the Gold Coast and the failure of earlier attempts at direct taxation; also C.O. 267/376, Hay to Knutsford, 13 February 1889; Wingfield, Minute, 9 March 1889. A Municipal Ordinance was enacted in 1889 and revived in the Town Councils Bill, 1894. A council was elected for Accra in 1895. See Kimble, *Political History of Ghana*, p. 421.

municipal board to undertake whatever local services are really required by the people, and I look for much useful experience to be gained by this body, provided that the European and leading inhabitants of the town will consent to take part in it. It is therefore desirable that the necessary Ordinance should be promptly enacted and the subsequent steps taken without delay.

I should, indeed, wish you to consider whether many of the difficulties connected with the collection of a poll tax could not be overcome by the creation of nominated sanitary boards in the leading coast towns, presided over, perhaps, by the District Commissioner, and having power to levy a graduated house tax, fixed perhaps at a very low figure as a commencement, the proceeds of which would, at first, at any rate, be wholly devoted to local purposes. In the 13th paragraph of your confidential Despatch of the 24th of November, you have yourself indicated this as a possible measure, and it appears to be deserving of consideration.

By far the largest part of the public works and improvements to be executed will principally benefit Cape Coast Castle and the other coast towns, and if local revenues could be raised at these places the Colonial Government might gradually be relieved of a large part of its duties in this respect.

There would, however, always remain works of general colonial utility, or exceeding the capacity of local resources, to be executed out of the general revenues of the Colony, and the formation of local bodies is suggested only as likely to afford minor relief, and as tending to free the Public Works Department from the harassing supervision of small local improvements.

Whilst therefore suggesting the desirability of the formation of these urban authorities, I shall be prepared to consider your further proposals of increased taxation in the light of the additional information which you will doubtless send to me.

16

ORDER IN COUNCIL: JURISDICTION IN CERTAIN PARTS OF AFRICA AND MADAGASCAR, 15 OCTOBER 1889[1]

[The territories of Morocco, Tunis, Liberia, Zanzibar, the South African Republic, and the Orange Free State, and possessions of European powers.]

7. FOR preventing doubts, it is declared that the power of constituting, altering, or abolishing local jurisdictions for the purposes of this Order, may be exercised with reference to the whole or any parts of any of the districts or territories for the time being included in Her

[1] Hertslet, *Commercial Treaties*, vol. xviii (1893), p. 3.

Majesty's Protectorate of the Niger districts, or in any other existing or future Protectorate, or any part or parts of the territories for the time being under the Government of the International Association of the Congo, or under the Government of the Free States under its administration, subject to, and in accordance with, the provisions of the Convention between Her Majesty and the said International Association, signed at Berlin, the 16th December, 1884.

17

T. V. LISTER TO MAJOR C. M. MACDONALD: OIL RIVERS PROTECTORATE, 18 APRIL 1891[1]

I AM directed by the Marquis of Salisbury to communicate to you the following general instructions for your guidance in your duties as Commissioner and Consul-General in the Oil Rivers Protectorate and the adjoining districts, in the performance of which you will be assisted by an adequate staff of Deputy Commissioners and Vice-Consuls. You will understand that Consular Commissions are given in order to enable the Commissioner and his subordinates legally to perform acts as to which powers are conferred on Consular officers by Acts of Parliament.

The district over which you will have jurisdiction is comprised, on the coast, between the Colony of Lagos on the north and the German Protectorate of the Cameroons on the south. In the interior it includes the whole of the territory placed within the British sphere by the Anglo-German Agreement of 1885, and the Supplementary Agreement of 1886, with the exception of the territories administered by the Royal Niger Company under its Charter. The boundaries between those territories and your district, as well as those to the westward separating your district from Lagos and the territories connected with and dependent on it, will be defined in subsequent instructions. The present frontier on the side of the Cameroons is laid down in the IVth Article of the Anglo-German Agreement of the 1st July, 1890, which supplements and corrects the Agreement of 1885. It is open to rectification by agreement between the two Powers; and it will be your duty to endeavour to settle, whenever an opportunity may offer, by friendly negotiation with the German authorities, the basis of such a rectification for submission to the two Governments . . .

[He is to study the treaties made with African chiefs and supplement them if necessary.]

---

[1] *F.O. Confidential Print*, 6351 (1893). MacDonald had recommended a consular administration in his report of 12 June 1889. See Anene, *Southern Nigeria*, pp. 115–31.

Copies of the Acts of Berlin and Brussels are annexed.

I am to direct your special attention to the Articles of the former concerning the navigation of branches and outlets of the Niger, by which the Act is applied to portions of your district, and to the provisions of the latter respecting the control over the importation of spirits and of munitions of war. I am also to impress upon you the importance of careful observance of the stipulations of the arrangement with Germany excluding differential treatment and restricting the levying of duties to the amount necessary for the purposes of administration.

You should, however, remember that the fiscal portion of that arrangement is subordinate to the rules of the Act of Brussels of which the two Powers are signatories, which fixes a maximum duty on certain articles.

[Friendly relations are to be maintained with the German Cameroons.]

As regards the internal affairs of your district, I am to observe that your object should be, by developing legitimate trade, by promoting civilization, by inducing the natives to relinquish inhuman and barbarous customs, and by gradually abolishing slavery, to pave the way for placing the territories over which Her Majesty's protection is and may be extended directly under British rule. It is not advisable that you should interfere unduly with tribal government; the Chiefs should continue to rule their own subjects and to administer justice to them; but you should keep a constant watch so as to prevent injustice and check abuses, making the Chiefs understand that their powers will be forfeited by misgovernment. If you should, in special cases, find it essential, for the benefit of the natives, you will be authorized to insist on the delegation to you of a Chief's judicial and administrative powers, which you will then exercise in their interests. In such cases you should not fail to apply without delay for the sanction of the Secretary of State. You should be careful, however, not to arouse discontent by attempting too abrupt reform.

You will take under your immediate control the intertribal and foreign relations of the native Chiefs.

The question of raising revenue to cover the expenses of administration requires your immediate attention. The system hitherto in force under which the coast Chiefs have exacted 'comey' from traders must be finally abolished. Duties must be raised on a regular system, and applied for purposes of government. You will make the Chiefs understand this, explaining to them that they must surrender to the protecting Power their claims to levy imposts of any description on trade, and to regulate commercial intercourse. You will arrange that, in return for the abandonment of the 'comey', compensation shall be given to them by annual payments out of the revenue.

[A scale of duties is to be fixed and expenditure allowed for salaries, buildings, police, steamers, scientific departments and stipends; justice will be administered under the African Order in Council of 1889; he will keep in touch with the Royal Niger Company and Lagos; smuggling from German territory is to be prevented; naval forces are not to be called on except in urgent circumstances.]

18

A. W. L. HEMMING: MINUTE,
SIERRA LEONE MUNICIPAL COUNCIL,
17 APRIL 1893[1]

[Municipal Council Ordinance no. 6 of 1893 has been drafted by Governor Fleming and is approved.]

THE policy of the Ordinance is in accordance with the views of this Dept. as expressed in Lord Knutsford's desp. of 17th Oct./88 . . . We have urged the establishment of Municipal Councils also at the G. Coast & Lagos.

I see nothing to object to in the Constitution of the Council. The qualification for electors very properly cuts out all those who do not contribute to the Municipal funds . . . I am not quite sure whether in the present state of society in Freetown it is altogether wise to prohibit Govt. Officers from being elected as Councillors. They probably comprise a very large section of the educated portion of the community. But of course, on the other hand, there are very strong & obvious reasons against their election.

As regards the mode of raising municipal revenue it would of course have been much better to adopt the usual system of rates—but it is clear from the Govr's. desp. . . . that the prejudices of the people on the subject are too strong (owing to the unwise abolition of direct taxation by Sir Pope Hennessy in 1872) & that it would have been impossible to carry into effect at present any proposition for the imposition of a rate. Under these circes. the method adopted of raising a revenue by means of Licences appears to me the best that could have been found.

Provision is made for the levying of a rate, if the funds otherwise raised prove insufficient. Lord Knutsford agreed . . . to the revenue derived by the Govt. from Boat and Canoe Licences being handed over to the Municipality.

---

[1] C.O. 267/401. The Ordinance was approved in Ripon to Fleming, 12 May 1893. Twelve councillors were elected and three appointed in 1895.

19

HIGH COMMISSIONER SIR CLAUDE MACDONALD TO THE FOREIGN OFFICE: OIL RIVERS COURTS, 20 APRIL 1893[1]

... I HAVE the honour to append a detailed statement of the said Fees and Fines of Court collected in 1892.

1892	Old Calabar	£57	9	0
	Warri	33	19	0
	Opobo	88	17	0
	Bonny	74	14	6
	Benin	5	9	6
		£260	9	0

I would respectfully draw the attention of Her Majesty's Government to the fact that the fees in this case represent the sums paid into Court for summonses by Natives, British Protected Subjects, who are very prone to litigation, the cases were heard by the various Vice Consuls, none of whom are in the pay of the Imperial Government, and who receive no extra salary for sitting in Court, the fines are those imposed upon native Chiefs for various offences.

For the information of the Lords Commissioners of Her Majesty's Treasury I beg again to state that the entire expense of the upkeep of the six Vice Consular Courts falls upon the Revenue of the Protectorate.

20

GOVERNOR SIR W. BRANDFORD GRIFFITH TO THE MARQUIS OF RIPON: GOLD COAST LEGISLATIVE COUNCIL, 12 JUNE 1893[2]

... 95. IN paragraph 17 of their paper the 'complainants' state:

'We would, therefore, respectfully invite your Lordship's attention to the urgent necessity of securing an adequate representation of the general public on the Legislative Council. At the present time there is only one unofficial member, who has practically no influence whatever on the Council from the fact that even on matters of mere detail,

---

[1] F.O. 2/51. See, too, *Report on Administration of Niger Coast Protectorate,* 1891–4 [C. 7596]; and the F.O. Annual Series: 1834, *Niger Coast Protectorate* [C. 8277].

[2] C.O. 879/39, no. 453. Encl. merchants and traders to Ripon, 31 October 1892. signed by W. Waters, chief agent for F. & A. Swanzy, and 517 others.

apart from all questions of Government policy, the official members are bound to vote as instructed, and he is, therefore, in hopeless minority when opposed to measures that chiefly affect the classes whom he is supposed to represent, and of whose requirements he has special knowledge, and whose interest he has at heart.' . . .

96. The Gold Coast Colony is, as regards the question of education of the negroes, not so well off as the Island of Dominica was in 1865, although, undoubtedly, a great deal has been done here in the way of improvement in that direction in the last few years. But whilst in the West Indies the English language is that of the vast majority of the inhabitants, and, with the exception of immigrants from the East, there are no different tribes and few conflicting interests, on the Gold Coast, on the contrary, very few of the people—and these almost altogether in the towns on the littoral—speak English, whilst among themselves they use various languages and dialects, as the Accra, Adangme, Ashanti, Appolonia, Cherepong, Ewe, Hausa, and Tchi.

97. Again, the various nations, peoples, and tribes have strong hereditary antipathies and dislikes to each other. Some of the tribes east of the Volta, such as the Krepis and Akwamus, are unfavourable to those on the right bank. The Akwapims and Eastern Akims hate the Krobos, who in turn would like to destroy these neighbours. Eastern Akim is opposed to Western Akim, the Accras hate and detest the Fantis to the full extent to which the latter reciprocate those feelings, and the Elminas entertain similar sentiments to those of the Accras towards the Fantis, who do not dislike Elminas less. I could add to this enumeration, but enough has been stated to show your Lordship how diametrically opposed the people of the Gold Coast are to each other. This feeling is not lessened in any sensible degree by education, and therein lies one of the great difficulties of this Government with regard to the selection of Natives for seats in the Legislative Council, for an Accra man will no more be trusted by the Fantis than one of these would be relied upon by the Accras.

98. So strong is the antipathy which many of the tribes feel for each other, that oldstanding feuds are handed down from father to son for generations, and no sooner does a favourable opportunity present itself than old questions are reopened, and not infrequently the Government is compelled to take prompt action in order to prevent a sanguinary encounter between the contending parties. In fact, some Kings and Chiefs have told me, when referring to neighbouring nations, that if they were not afraid of the Government they would 'sweep these neighbours off the face of the earth'.

99. The policy of this Government has always been to refuse to recognise, and to endeavour to allay, these existing inter-tribal jealousies, but the passive resistance with which its efforts are unhappily met renders the promotion of more harmonious relations very

difficult. Such a feud may sink below the surface, but it is always there.

100. In support of this statement, I may mention the difficulty which exists in obtaining the conviction of an Accra or a Fanti man in the Courts by a jury selected from their respective races, no matter how strong are the proofs which may be brought against him; whilst on the other hand, it is lamentable to observe the eagerness with which they are only too ready to bring in a verdict against each other, and which has, I fear, frequently nearly succeeded in bringing about a scandalous miscarriage of justice. In support of this grave statement I would respectfully ask reference to Despatches which I had the honour to address to your Lordship's predecessor on the 8th of December 1888, the 9th of May 1889, as well as to the Minutes of the Executive Council of the 6th and 9th of May 1891.

101. Besides the initial difficulties indicated there are others, originating in them, with regard to securing the representation of the general public on the Legislative Council. Natives to be eligible for such representation should speak English, possess some culture, with a substantial and respected position in the Colony, and should be free from connexion with any circumstances calculated to affect their integrity and independence of character. Now it is difficult to find Native candidates possessing generally the qualifications described, whilst as regards European British subjects, in a country which they resort to to make money in, and to escape from as soon as their object is accomplished, it is difficult to get mercantile agents to leave their business to attend to the discharge of functions, which do not touch their interests so keenly as to make it a matter to which they should devote time that could otherwise be more profitably employed for their own personal interests. Again, ill-health often compels men to leave their occupations and seek for recovery in a temperate climate. This breaks in upon the discharge of all duties, and when they return their time is so absorbed by looking into what has taken place in their absence and in bringing up arrears, that they have little to spare for the performance of outside obligations. As corroborative of this statement, a European agent at Cape Coast, who not long ago had taken a fortnight's holiday to recruit his health, informed me that on returning he found such an accumulation of correspondence and other work awaiting him that he should not again be inclined to leave his business except to go to England, when his responsibility would cease during his absence. Men so situated at outstations would not be much disposed to give up a fortnight to attend to legislative duties. Sir Samuel Rowe, in a letter dated 16th August 1884, addressed to the Secretary of State, remarked upon the subject under notice (in paragraph 22):—'The reason why no un-official members have been asked to attend the Council at Accra has

been rather that there were no British subjects resident there, who were not officials, who it was thought would be considered representative by the whole Colony, than that there was any disinclination to seek the opinion of gentlemen who were not connected with the Government service.' Moreover, the usefulness of an unofficial member is greatly detracted from by his necessary lack of acquaintance with official matters, of which the bulk of legislative work is composed. It is only in the course of debate that he begins to comprehend the question under discussion, and any opinion of it that he may then form is of small value, though doubtless the best according to his lights. The view I take of the matter is that the unofficial member gains the little knowledge he possesses of how an administration is carried on from the few meetings of Council which he attends. Even in questions of trade and commerce, when hitherto the opinion of a person—whose profession it is to engage in such matters—is sought with the object of guiding the Government, or is expressed on independent grounds, the view taken by unofficial members often appears to be so short sighted and restricted by motives of present self interest as to deprive any expression of it of any real legislative value. Granting, however, that it was practicable to find several persons eligible for the position of a Legislative Councillor, in view of the Imperial policy as explained in the Duke of Buckingham's Despatch, it appears to me that in a Colony situated as the Gold Coast is, it is out of the question that there should be in the Legislative Council a majority of unofficial members, by whose combined votes the Government could be overruled with regard to its policy and measures. But the question is set at rest in principle by the views entertained by Her Majesty's Government, which were distinctly announced in the Despatch already quoted from. I think, therefore, my Lord, that the reasons I have stated, together with the authoritative announcement referred to, completely dispose of the point put forward in paragraph 17 of the 'Complaint'. . . .

21

J. C. ERNEST PARKES TO THE COLONIAL SECRETARY: SIERRA LEONE FRONTIER POLICE, 28 JULY 1893[1]

1. RECENT reports from the Chiefs and people of certain places, as to the conduct of members of the Frontier Police stationed therein, compel me with reluctance to submit for His Excellency's consideration the important question whether the interests of the Government are being studied or its influence increased by the presence in many

[1] *Parl. Papers*, 1899, lx [C. 9391], ii, pp. 561–2.

stations of indiscreet and semi-civilised members of the native community, far away from Headquarters amongst an ignorant people, without the careful and constant supervision of proper officers.

2. My reason for bringing forward this question at the present time is that during the past few months no less than four serious charges have been brought against sub-officers of important stations of insulting the Chiefs, in one case handcuffing one, and keeping him in custody for a considerable period, flogging their people, and in other ways taking advantage of them . . .

[The papers concerning these and other examples are enclosed.][1]

3. The main cause of this much-to-be-regretted state of things is, I am inclined to think, the absence of Officers on the spot or near at hand capable of maintaining that strict discipline and supervision to make the force useful and respected, and to whom immediate complaints could be made and redress obtained, and if this difficulty could be overcome the force might some time in the near future arrive at that state of perfection which Sir James Hay expected of it at its establishment. Up to the present time, however, unfortunately, the greater number of the European officers who have been sent out have not been able to keep their healths and have had to return home, I believe, invalided. I venture, therefore, most respectfully to submit the following scheme for His Excellency's consideration, as a tentative measure to mitigate the evil referred to.

4. Having already . . . suggested the establishment of a Protectorate, the appointment of Political Agents, and the reduction of the Frontier Police, I would venture now to suggest that instead of keeping a large number of Police scattered as at present near and far without adequate supervision, that detachments of 30 or 50 men be stationed at certain centres under responsible officers, who should use them for patrolling in the district under his charge, and such other duties as the officer administering the Government might be pleased from time to time to direct. I would further suggest that as a large body of disciplined troops are stationed here, and they have, in the only engagement which the Frontier Force has undertaken, been obliged to go to their assistance, that the services of these (if there is no military objections thereto) should be used for patrolling the Hinterland during the dry season, so that they would be able to obtain information as to the country around in which they may at any time have to take action, and permit the natives to see some of the disciplined troops of the Sovereign to whom they owe allegiance.

5. I need hardly point out that as British jurisdiction extends so the duties of the Frontier Police will necessarily be lessened, as there will be more civil than quasi-military duties to perform, and in case of any

[1] Ibid., pp. 562–6.

punitive expeditions it is to be presumed that after the experience of Tambi it would be a military one, which, as matters were arranged for Tambi, I believe has proved less expensive as regard to transport than that of the Frontier Police. Of course if it were deemed necessary by the officer commanding the troops, some of the force might accompany such an expedition to gain experience in action . . .

22

THE MARQUIS OF RIPON TO ADMINISTRATOR R. B. LLEWELYN: GAMBIA PROTECTORATE, 10 OCTOBER 1893[1]

I HAVE read with much interest the valuable reports of the travelling Commissioners, Messrs Oxanne and Sitwell, which were transmitted in your despatch No. 49, of 1st July last,[2] and I have had the advantage of gaining from yourself personally, during your recent visit to England, much useful and interesting information respecting the territories lying between the Anglo-French boundary and the River Gambia, and the measures which you would wish to see adopted for extending and consolidating British jurisdiction over these territories.

2. By the agreement of August 10, 1889, between England and France, followed in 1891 by the delimitation effected by boundary commissioners appointed by the two countries, a strip of territory on each side of the river running back 10 kilometres (and something more near the mouth) has been assigned to England. The river itself, with its islands and some small portions of this territory, have long formed part of the Queen's dominions, but the remainder has never been formally annexed to the British Crown, though it is now under the protection of Her Majesty.

3. It is necessary to keep this distinction in view, for the Colony of the Gambia, as defined in the Letters Patent of 28th November 1888, constituting the office of Governor, consists only of such places within the specified limits as are British territory, and the power of the Legislative Council to make laws is confined to the Colony as thus defined. The power of making laws applicable to the Protectorate must be sought elsewhere, and I cannot consequently authorise you to submit to the Council for enactment the Ordinances which you proposed to introduce for establishing courts of summary jurisdiction in the territories outside the island of St. Mary, and for preserving peace in the villages of the same territories.

4. It is hardly necessary to add that the jurisdiction of the Courts of the Colony is limited to matters occurring within the boundaries

[1] C.O. 87/44.   [2] C.O. 87/143.

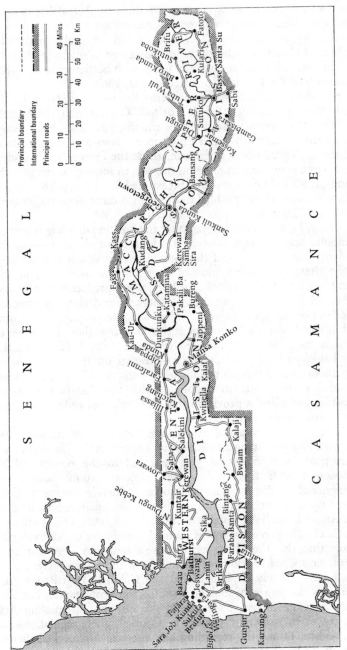

Map 2. Gambia, 1912

of the Colony, except so far as it is extended by Act of Parliament, as has been done in the case of crimes committed within 20 miles of the boundary, by the Act 34 Vict. c. 8, and in Admiralty matters by the Colonial Courts of Admiralty Act, 1890, and as might be done by Order in Council under section 4 of the British Settlements Act, 1887 or section 9 of the Foreign Jurisdiction Act, 1890.

5. St. Mary's Island, which contains the town of Bathurst, the Ceded Mile, including Albreda, British Combo, the river itself, with Macarthy's Island and its other islands, have long been recognised as British territory and subject to the laws and the Courts of the Gambia. These places in fact constitute the Colony, but I understand that an erroneous impression prevails in some quarters that the landing-places and towns at which Sir Samuel Rowe hoisted the British flag in 1887 were thereby added to the British dominions and became part of the Colony and subject to its law.

6. I may, however, remind you that the hoisting of a flag is merely a symbolic act, the significance of which must depend upon the attendant circumstances and the intention with which it was done. In 1887 there was no intention of annexing the country. You will remember that on the 14th of April 1887, my predecessor informed Sir Samuel Rowe, who was then in England and about to proceed to the Gambia on special duty, that he was 'not prepared to recommend to Her Majesty's Government that any steps should be taken to assume or exercise a protectorate over these districts (Barra on the north bank, and Foreign Combo and Fogni on the south), or to annex them in any way to the Gambia settlement.' But he was instructed 'to endeavour to negotiate with the Chiefs treaties of friendship, including a provision that they will not cede their territories to any foreign Power.'

7. Treaties of friendship, as you are aware, were subsequently made with Fogni Vintang and Kiang, and approved by Her Majesty's Government, but no answer was returned to the request which accompanied each treaty—that Her Majesty would accept the sovereignty of the district. The situation as defined by the instructions of April 14th, 1887 remained in fact practically unaltered at the date of the Anglo-French Agreement of August 10th, 1889, and it must be taken that the flags hoisted by Sir Samuel Rowe were meant to signify no more than that the Chiefs with whose assent they were displayed were under special relations of friendship with Her Majesty. . . .

13. I have already explained that the Colonial Legislature does not possess the power of making laws for the Protectorate, but Her Majesty in Council has, by virtue of the Foreign Jurisdiction Act, 1890, power to make, by Orders in Council, such regulations (or laws), as she thinks fit, regarding the exercise of her jurisdiction within its limits. This jurisdiction applies to all British subjects, and

to the subjects of the signatory Powers of the General Act of the Brussels Conference; that is, of virtually all the Powers of Europe and the United States of America, and some few other extra-European Powers, as well as to the subjects of any native Chief or Government which, by treaty or otherwise, has agreed or consented to the exercise of power or authority by Her Majesty.

14. The Gambia Protectorate is within the limits of the Africa Order in Council of the 15th of October 1889, of which a copy is enclosed. There is, however, no Consul within the Protectorate, and in other respects this Order seems not altogether suited to the present circumstances. I propose therefore to advise Her Majesty to issue a new Order in Council dealing only with the Gambia Protectorate.[1]

15. It will obviously not be convenient that every regulation or law affecting the Protectorate should be made by Order in Council; the want of local knowledge would render such a course impracticable, while the delay might be productive of inconvenience. It will therefore be desirable that the power of legislation should be exercised locally. In the Bechuanaland Protectorate south of the Zambesi this power is vested in the High Commissioner for South Africa, and I had thought at first of advising Her Majesty to place it in the hands of the Administrator of the Gambia, but on further consideration it seems to me preferable that the necessary laws should be made by Ordinance of the Legislative Council.

16. A similar power in regard to the Gold Coast Protectorate was conferred upon the Legislative Council of the Gold Coast by an Order in Council of the 6th of August 1874, which will be found in the accompanying Parliamentary papers relating to the Queen's juris-diction on the Gold Coast and the abolition of slavery within the Protectorate. The whole of this paper merits your careful perusal, and will, I have no doubt, be of assistance to you in the duties you are about to undertake. The Government of the Gambia has hitherto exercised to some extent influence and authority similar, though in a far less degree, to that exercised on the Gold Coast before 1874, but Her Majesty's Government are not in possession of that detailed information as to the relations between master and slave which enabled the Earl of Carnarvon to address to Governor Strahan the important despatch of the 21st of August 1874.[2]

17. The points to which, as it seems to me, you should first direct your attention are—the sale of human beings as slaves, the transfer of slaves upon death of the owner, either by bequest or inheritance, and the removal or exportation of slaves from the limits of the Protectorate; and if it be possible to check these transactions, and, further, to stop the introduction of slaves, a death blow to slavery will

[1] Order in Council, 23 November 1893; and no. 25.
[2] Vol. I, p. 582 for Draft Proclamation of the Order in Council, 6 August 1874.

have been struck. But the task is a difficult one, and it is obvious that no measures taken with this object are likely to succeed unless they receive the general assent of the people; it should therefore be the duty of the travelling Commissioners, who at present are the only representatives of British authority in the country, to endeavour, during the coming season, to familiarise the natives with the idea of these first conditions of personal liberty, and to obtain their adherence to the principle of them. In anticipation of such assent, I should wish you to furnish me with the drafts of such laws as you consider likely to be accepted by the people, and suitable to the objects in view.

18. Simultaneously with, or perhaps before, the adoption of these measures some simple method of administering justice should be devised and introduced. For this purpose it would be desirable, at any rate at first, to execute justice through the native authorities, the magistrate being rather the assessor of the Alcaide than the judge of an independent court. The more serious case might be remitted to the Court at Bathurst, and I propose that the necessary jurisdiction should be conferred by the Order in Council, which can be done under the provision of section 9 of the Foreign Jurisdiction Act, 1890.

19. As any increase of security to life and property in the Protectorate will tend to prosperity and development of the country, and to the increase of the trade and consequently of the revenue of the Colony, it is reasonable that the latter should contribute to the expense of bringing about so desirable a result. The financial resources of the Colony are, however, limited, and you should consider whether any revenue can be obtained from the Protectorate itself. You have already devised a system of trading licenses, which, if carried out, will, you believe, yield a considerable sum, of which a portion is to be paid in stipends to the native authorities; and you think that money may be obtained from farm rents—a question upon which I shall doubtless hear further—the scheme being, as I understand it, to substitute reasonable and fixed rents for the capricious and arbitrary exactions which were taken under the Chief system, and for the British Government to receive a portion of these rents, paid in kind, in return for the security afforded by its protection, the remainder being paid to the native authorities.

20. This scheme deserves a trial, though I fear the collection and disposal of the Government share of the produce may prove a practical difficulty. And there seems also to be a risk of possible trouble in the future if the Alcaide draw considerable revenues from their people without giving to the latter any benefits in return. The income derived by the Government from the Protectorate should naturally be spent within it, and you have doubtless already considered the propriety of keeping separate accounts of these receipts and expenditure.

21. It will be wise not to extend the administration too far at first, but gradually to work your way up the river, making good the authority of the Government in one district before extending it to the next, and with this object it will probably be found advisable to declare in each law when made that it is only to apply to such places as the Administrator may direct by proclamation. . . .

23

A. W. L. HEMMING: MINUTE, SIERRA LEONE FRONTIER POLICE, 9 FEBRUARY 1894[1]

. . . WE must have a strong Frontier Police force at S. Leone, as we shall have to keep in order the whole Territory which will become our Protectorate when we have settled the boundary question with France—and altho' we may hope to have fewer formidable expeditions there will no doubt often be small disturbances to be put down.

I agree with Mr. Hamilton that the Forces (Frontier & Civil) should be separate. Sir F. Fleming agreed to this recommendation of the Governors[2] & he shews no good reason for altering it.

A Civil Inspector should therefore be appointed— . . .

As to Govt. Agents I don't like the idea. They must be Natives & it would be extremely difficult, if not impossible, to get satisfactory men for the posts. We could not depend upon them, & they would be likely to get us into all sorts of difficulties. I should much prefer a couple of good European Travelling Commrs., who should go about thro' the country & hear complaints & settle differences, taking with them an escort of Police. I feel sure this would work on the whole more satisfactorily . . .

24

ACTING GOVERNOR F. CARDEW TO THE MARQUIS OF RIPON: SIERRA LEONE INTERIOR, 9 JUNE 1894[3]

. . . 12. As to the process by which the slave trade could be stopped, I have reason to believe that its total suppression could be effected

---

[1] C.O. 267/407. On Fleming to Ripon, 2 January 1894 (recommending a force of police and government agents).
[2] The West African governors had agreed to keep civil and frontier police distinct.
[3] C.O. 879/39, no. 460. *Colonel (Sir) Frederic Cardew*, Governor of Sierra Leone, 1894–1900. Meade favoured declaring a protectorate by an ordinance under the Foreign Jurisdiction Act (as for the Gambia): Minute 28 July 1894: C.O. 267/409. Cardew increased the Frontier Police from 300 to 500 men in five companies. This was approved in Ripon to Cardew, 25 July 1894: C.O. 267/409.

without any rupture of our friendly relations with the Chiefs within our sphere of influence provided we have sufficient force at hand to insist upon the orders of the Government being carried out, and this can only be done by a substantial augmentation of the Frontier Police. Such an augmentation would probably mean an additional annual outlay of, say, about 7,000 *l.* a year, but I am not certain of these figures as, owing to the absence of the Inspector-General of Frontier Police at Port Lokko, I have not yet been able to consider in detail a scheme for an augmentation, nor how the extra expenditure should be provided for. I propose, shortly, to submit a scheme for your Lordship's consideration, but I may here say that I think the extra outlay would be more than compensated by the increased trade that would result from the entire suppression of the slave traffic, and that it need only be incurred for a few years, that is to say, until our power in the interior is consolidated, when a gradual reduction of the Frontier Police might take place, especially as by that time a scheme for the regular administration of the country would probably have been carried out.

13. I have said above that I have reason to believe that the total suppression of the slave traffic could be effected without any rupture of our friendly relations with the Chiefs within our sphere of influence, and I am led to form the opinion by the manner in which all the Chiefs I have seen have received the orders which the police have had given to them for the prevention of the traffic, and with which I have made them personally acquainted. They have all appeared to acquiesce in them, and some have voluntarily expressed their readiness to assist in carrying them out.

14. But, next to the augmentation of the police force, the first essential is the settlement [of] the boundary question so that we may know how far our limits extend with a view to bringing about peace along our borders. At present, as I have already stated above, there is the war between Chief Kai Lunou on the one side, and his Sub-Chief Kafara, assisted by the Sofas, on the other, and which, from reports received, may by this have extended into the Waima district; and there are the recent raids in Samu district. Now, the several theatres of these disturbances are in debatable territory, and the Government, therefore, cannot actively interfere with a view of bringing about a peace between the combatants until the settlement of the boundary question.

15. A second essential is a complete prohibition of the importation into British territory of trade guns and powder. It seems to me most inconsistent, as well as unjust to the natives, that while, on the one hand, we are using either moral suasion or armed force to suppress these disturbances we are, on the other, furnishing the combatants with an unlimited supply of arms and ammunition, that is to say,

with the very means which keep alive these disturbances. I have, with the concurrence of the Executive Council, recently issued a notice prohibiting the sale of trade guns and powder in the Sanda Lokko districts and surrounding regions which have been so long disturbed by war, and I would further propose to extend the prohibition throughout the whole of British territory were it not for the fact that it would place at a disadvantage Kai Lundu and his people, who are fighting the Sofas, and whom we cannot adequately protect until the settlement of the boundary question. In this connection may I suggest that the governments of France and Liberia be approached with a view to their acting in concert with Great Britain for the entire prohibition of trade guns and powder at least within those of their territories which adjoin the British sphere of influence connected with the Colony of Sierra Leone? I am informed by the Collector of Customs that, under the present amount of trade done, there would be a loss to the Revenue of not more than 500 *l.* a year if the importation of trade guns and powder were entirely abolished, the sum which would be forfeited by the revenue sinks into insignificance compared with the incalculable mischief done by such a trade, and it is needless to say that it would be recouped again and again by the increase of trade that would result from the establishment of peace.

16. A third, and last, essential is a declaration of a Protectorate over the British sphere of influence, after which, and as soon as our power is thoroughly consolidated by the entire suppression of the slave traffic the means of an efficient and augmented Frontier Police Force, the country might be gradually brought under a settled scheme of administration. I am of opinion that in any such scheme the leading principle involved in it should be the administration of the country, as far as possible by native law and through the Chiefs, I say *as far as possible*, for it is well known that there are some native crimes, such as cannibalism, withcraft, and cognate offences, and some native laws the penalties of which are altogether repugnant to our ideas of humanity and civilisation; these, with all capital offences, might be tried by a Court of Chiefs presided over by a District Commissioner, of which there would be one in each of the districts into which the interior might be divided, the proceedings of such courts should be subject to the review of the Governor of Sierra Leone, and the sentences awarded to his confirmation or otherwise. Offences relating to the contravention of orders with regard to the slave traffic, and hereafter all slave customs, such as domestic slavery, I think should be dealt with by the District Commissioner alone. . . .

19. With regard to the administration of the interior, I think it should be entirely separate from that of the Colony of Sierra Leone, the only connexion between them being the Governor of the Colony, who would act as paramount Chief of the interior, but who could,

however, take the advice of his Executive Council in matters which would mutually concern the Colony and the interior.

20. At present there is imported into the Colony some of the vilest compounds known as trade rum and gin, &c.; these liquors are a great medium for trade with the natives of the interior, as far as my experience goes it seems at present to have only penetrated into the fringe of the country, but the question arises whether an effort should not be made on the part of the Government as soon as practicable after a Protectorate is declared to save those people from the ill-effects of this traffic which in the end must lead to their further degradation and ruin.

21. In giving expression to my views as to the best scheme for the future administration of the Interior, I have only dwelt briefly on a few of the most salient points as they occur to me in writing this Despatch, in fact, only some general principles have been touched on, the details would have to be worked out if at any time it was thought advisable to adopt such a scheme as I have attempted to foreshadow. It may be asked how a revenue could be obtained for the expense of such a scheme of administration, which would involve the payment of the Frontier Police, the salaries of a certain number of District Commissioners, with their respective staffs, and of a road surveyor and overseers. The revenue of the Colony would be quite inadequate for the purpose, but I think the interior itself would in course of a short time furnish a sufficient revenue. Apart from her share of the Customs' dues of the Colony to which she would be entitled, a revenue could be derived from the following sources:

(a.) Hawkers and store licenses.

(b.) Licenses for the purchase by individuals of arms, and powder, and caps, in small quantities.

(c.) A house tax.

22. With regard to a house-tax, this would be the most prolific source of revenue, and, as far as I am advised, its imposition hereafter would not meet with opposition on the part of the Chiefs, the houses might be classified according to their size and taxed accordingly. During my recent tour I caused, without revealing my object, the houses to be counted in each of the towns we put up at, and the dimensions of the houses we occupied to be taken; these statistics might furnish a basis of calculation hereafter . . .

25

GAMBIA PROTECTORATE ORDINANCE, 28 DECEMBER 1894[1]

... 3. THE Administrator, with the advice of the Executive Council, may, from time to time, by Proclamation, declare any portion of the Protected Territories to be a District for the purpose of this Ordinance, and may appoint a Head Chief to exercise authority over a District. The Administrator may, in like manner, alter the boundaries of any District, and may dismiss any Head Chief and appoint a successor.

4. The Administrator may, if he thinks fit, from time to time, subdivide any District into convenient groups of villages, and may appoint a Headman, subordinate to the Head Chief, to have supervision of any such group. The Administrator may dismiss any Headman and appoint a successor, and may at any time re-arrange the grouping of the villages.

5. Except in so far as they are expressly altered, all native subdivisions of territory and grouping of villages for purposes of jurisdiction existing at the commencement of this Ordinance shall continue.

6. A Head Chief is responsible to the Administrator for the good order of his District, and may at any time apply to the Administrator or to a Commissioner for advice or assistance.

7. The Headman of a group of villages is responsible to the Head Chief for the good order of the group, and if he neglects to keep order may be punished by the Native Court.

8. The Administrator, with the advice of the Executive Council, may make, alter or revoke Regulations for promoting the peace, good order and welfare of the Protected Territories in respect to the following matters:

Constructing, repairing, clearing, regulating and protecting roads, wells, springs, watercourses, watering and bathing places;
Taking care of unoccupied land, and conserving forests;
Making and preserving land marks and fences;
Regulating public fisheries;
Preventing accidents in hunting by gunshot or otherwise;
Preventing and abating nuisances;
Cleaning weeds and brushwood from the outskirts of towns and villages;
Providing grounds for the burial of the dead and regulating burials.

... All Regulations shall be published in the Government Gazette and thereupon shall have the force of law ...

[1] No. 11 of 1894 in Llewelyn to C.O., 28 December 1894: C.O. 87/147.

[Provisions for Native Courts and appeals to the Administrator or Commissioner. Chiefs and Headmen shall have powers to end disturbances, carry out laws and orders, apprehend offenders.]

26

GOVERNOR F. CARDEW TO THE MARQUIS OF RIPON: LEGISLATIVE COUNCIL MEMBERSHIP, 23 MAY 1895[1]

In reply to your Lordship's despatch no. 61 of the 28 March on the subject of the appointment of Unofficial Members, I have the honour to report that I laid the matter before the Executive Council on the 17th Instant the majority of members of which concurred in your Lordship's views and it was accordingly decided as follows:

(a) That the term of five years should commence from the present time.

(b) That in order to avoid changing all the Unofficial Members at the same time there should be an interval of one year between each change.

(c) That it be in the power of the Governor to decide the rotation in which the Unofficial Members should be called upon to retire.

2. As of the three Unofficial Members the Honourable T. S. Buckley only holds his position in virtue of his appointment as President of the Sierra Leone Chamber of Commerce the election for which office is held annually and the occupant of which is therefore subject to change and as the same remark would apply to the Mayor of Freetown when the time arrives for him to be elected and to become an *ex officio* Member of the Legislative Council, the above decisions really affect the Honourable Samuel Lewis C.M.G. and the Honourable T. C. Bishop and as the former is the senior member I am of the opinion he should be called upon to retire last and I have therefore arranged that the decisions of the Executive Council should first come into operation with the Honourable T. C. Bishop whom I have caused to be informed that subject to your Lordship's approval and confirmation he will be expected to resign his appointment on the 17th May 1900. At one year from the 17th Instant a similar notification will have to be sent to the Honourable Samuel Lewis C.M.G. The interval of one year was decided on as it was considered that that period was necessary for the new member to become conversant with the procedure of the Legislative Council before the next member retired.

3. Before adopting the decisions set forth above there was some discussion as to the desirability of placing any limt to the term of the

[1] C.O. 267/417.

appointment of Unofficial Members, the Honourable Samuel Lewis being of contrary opinion, though he did not oppose the decision by his vote. Mr. Lewis was of opinion, as I understand him, that such a measure would tend to sacrifice the independence of Unofficial Members, as in their desire to remain on the Council they would be inclined especially when their term of office was expiring, to vote contrary to their convictions rather than oppose the Government on whom their future re-appointment depended . . .

27

HIGH COMMISSIONER SIR CLAUDE MACDONALD TO THE MARQUIS OF SALISBURY: OIL RIVERS COURTS, 12 JULY 1895[1]

. . . THE so called High Court of the Native Council of Old Calabar and the Minor Native Courts which latter have been established as the country was opened up, have done most excellent work. The Native Court at Calabar was instituted by Mr. Vice-Consul Johnstone, now Commissioner and Consul-General, Central Africa. It was declared by the late Consul Hewitt [sic], was re-instituted by Consul Annesly, but gradually fell into disuse. I append copy of the present Regulations of the Court as well as of the Minor Councils established in various parts of the Cross River District. It will be seen that the Calabar Court consists of a President, Vice-President, and is at present constituted of thirty-seven members. The President is ex-officio the senior Consular Authority; the members consist of all important Chiefs of the Efik speaking (Calabar) people. When the present Administration was first instituted (1891) this Court had not sat for nearly a year, and had practically ceased to exist. It was soon seen that there were elements of great good and usefulness in this system of legislation, and the Court was again constituted. It is held every Thursday in the Court House at the Consulate General, and there is now nearly always an average attendance of three fourths of the members, some of whom come from considerable distances. It will be seen that so far as the Calabar Court is concerned, the cases heard are mostly civil out of a total of 395 cases adjudicated on, 369 were civil cases; the more serious criminal cases which come under the knowledge of the Native Chiefs being referred to the Consular Court.

In addition to this Native Court, Minor Councils of perhaps even greater importance, in discovering and dealing with the many

[1] F.O. 2/84.

barbarous practices which prevail throughout the country, have been instituted at the following places. In the Akpayafe District in the neighbourhood of the German frontier, at Tom Shot's District on the right shores of the Calabar estuary, called in the Efik language the Abaka District, at Ekpa lying to the north of this and bordering on the Ibibio tribe, at Uwet within sight of the rapids of the Calabar River, in the Okoyon District which stretches from the Calabar to the Cross River, peopled by a tribe notorious for its turbulent disposition and much given to human sacrifice and similar atrocities, at Adiabo where the Efik people and the Okoyons meet, and at Itu on the Cross River where a large market exists and which is the commencement of an important trade route to the interior; in this Court there are representative members from the Efik, Ibibio, Enyong, Umon and Akuna tribes.

Cases which a few years ago would inevitably have led to bloodshed and the kidnapping of women and children, are now settled in these Courts or 'Palaver Houses'. Each plaintiff knows that his case will be judged by an assembly consisting of influential members of his own and other tribes and that he always has the power of appeal to 'the Consul', also, and this the most important of all, . . . he knows that the decisions of the Court will be enforced if necessary by the supreme authority of the Consul, as representing the Great Queen of the White men.

The Regulations of these Minor Councils have been made as simple as possible, they are practically embodied in the 14th Paragraph which has to be read and explained to the people at every sitting of the Court for the first six months after its establishment, and which is summed up in the last sentence: 'Anyone guilty of taking the life of any innocent person whether man or woman or child shall suffer death or such other punishment as the Commissioner and Consul General may direct' . . .

The High Court of the Native Councils of Old Calabar. The High Court of the Native Councils is constituted as follows:

President.

Her Britannic Majesty's Commissioner & Consul General.

Vice-President.

[elected by the Court for three months.]

Members.

1. Prince Eyo Honesty IV
2. Prince Ekpenyon Eyo II
3. Prince Eyo Eyo Ita (Political Agent for Ikpa Market District).
4. Chief Ibitam Ibitam.

5. Chief Eyo Efiom Eyo.   6. Chief Okon Ekpenyon Oku.
7. Chief Okon Efiom Nsa.   8. Chief Okpo Itam.
9. Chief Esien Andiyo.

Duke Town.

1. King Duke Ephriam Enyamba   2. Prince James Enyamba V
   IX.   (Political Agent for Ikpa
                                   District).
3. Prince John Eyamba V   4. Prince Archibong Eyo
   (Political Agent for Adiabo   Archibong II.
   District).
5. Prince Archibong Edam   6. Chief Adam Ephraim Adam.
   Archibong III.
7. Chief James Ephraim Adam.   8. Chief Coco Otu Bassey
                                    Offing (Political Agent for
                                    the Cross River District).

Cobham Town.

1. Chief Bassey Ibitam Antikha. 2. Chief Antikha Bassey
                                    Cobham.
3. Chief Etim Henny Cobham.   4. Chief James Egbo Bassey
                                    (Political Agent of Ibaka
                                    District).
5. Chief Henny Egbo Bassey.   6. Chief Egbo Bassey.

Henshaw Town.

1. Chief John James Henshaw.   2. Chief Henshaw James
                                    Henshaw.
3. Chief Hogan Henshaw.   4. Chief Henshaw Bassey
                                    Henshaw.
5. Magnus James Brown.   6. Asuquo Ukpon.

Edim Ebani or his representative for Aqua Obio Abakpa.

Abasi Ja-Ja or his representative for Akim.

Okon Etim Asuja or his representative for Old Town.

Efiom Otu Okon (Political Agent for the Uwet District).

Bassey Ukot Ebi; Eyo Offiong Eniang Representative of Ikoneto;
Offiong Inyan Etok for Mbia Obo Edera; Eyo Etim Ntok for Ikot
Offiong.

Clerk of the High Court of the Native Councils Magnus Adam Duke.

Assistant Clerk James Joseph Henshaw.

28

GOVERNOR F. CARDEW TO COLONIAL OFFICE: PROTECTORATE JURISDICTION IN SIERRA LEONE, 22 JULY 1895[1]

PURSUANT to a conversation I recently had with Mr. Bramston on the subject of the proclamation of a Protectorate over the British sphere of influence behind the Colony of Sierra Leone, I beg to offer the following suggestions for its government.

2. I think the principles which should govern any legislation consequent on the Proclamation are, that the jurisdiction of the Protectorate should be continued as far as possible through the Chiefs, and its administration kept, as far as practicable, distinct from that of the Colony.

3. The rules and regulations for the government of the Protectorate might be on similar lines, *mutatis mutandis*, to those issued by Proclamation No. II, 1887, for Zululand, and I would suggest a scheme of government somewhat as follows:

Courts of Law, Procedure, Jurisdiction.

4. A District Commissioner, with a clerk and interpreter, and, say, 12 court messengers, to be appointed to each of the five districts into which the Protectorate is at present divided for Frontier Police purposes.

5. Native Chiefs to have jurisdiction according to Native laws in all criminal cases other than murder, culpable homicide, cannibalism, pretended witchcraft, slave raiding and slave dealing, leopard or alligator killing, and cognate offences, provided always that such Chiefs shall in no case be permitted to inflict any punishment involving death, mutilation, or grievous bodily harm.

6. Native Chiefs to have jurisdiction according to Native laws in all civil cases.

7. It might be necessary for the District Commissioner alone to have jurisdiction in civil and criminal cases between Natives of different tribes, but this is not desirable if the prevailing custom of dealing with such cases between Chiefs is found to be workable.

8. The crimes of murder, &c., set forth above, but with the exception of slave raiding and slave dealing, to be tried by a court consisting of the District Commissioner, as President, and two or more Chiefs as members, the proceedings of the court to be, *mutatis mutandis*, and as far as the circumstances of the country will admit,

---

[1] C.O. 879/43, no. 497. Approved in C.O. to Cardew (in London), 16 October 1895. This was carried out in Protectorate Ordinance, 31 August 1896; see, too, Daniels, *Common Law in West Africa*, pp. 63–4.

the same as those of the Supreme Court of Sierra Leone. The finding and sentence to be subject to the confirmation or otherwise of the Governor.

9. With regard to offences relating to slave raiding and slave dealing, the District Commissioner to alone have jurisdiction.

10. As it appears to me desirable to interfere as little as possible with the jurisdiction of the Native Chiefs, I should not be inclined to allow any right of appeal against their decision in the civil and criminal cases in which they are allowed to exercise sole jurisdiction; at any rate such right of appeal might for the present be withheld, until it can be hereafter ascertained whether, in the interests of justice, it is actually required.

11. The above suggestions apply to the Aborigines, as distinct from the Natives of the Colony, but in the case of the latter, of whom there are a large number resident in the interior for trading and other purposes, and in the case of Europeans, all criminal and civil cases between themselves, or between them and the Aborigines, should be decided by the District Commissioner of the district in which the cases occur, and conducted, *mutatis mutandis*, as regards procedure and right of appeal, in the same manner as in the courts of the District Commissioners of the Colony of Sierra Leone, but a District Commissioner in the Protectorate should have greater powers, both in criminal and civil cases, than those conferred on District Commissioners within the Colony.

12. As an appeal to the Supreme Court of the Colony from the decision of a District Commissioner, owing to distance, would be a long and expensive process, and often tend to defeat justice, to prevent frivolous and vexatious appeals the deposit to be made on making an appeal should be proportionately high.

Lands.

13. As far as I am aware, all lands are the property of the tribe or community which possess them, and cannot be alienated by the Native Chiefs or people either by sale or transfer; but I think it should be made lawful for the Governor to deal with such lands for the following purposes:

(a) Assigning locations for Native Chiefs and tribes.
(b) Authorising the occupation of waste and uninhabited lands for colonisation by Natives from Sierra Leone or other British Colonies elsewhere.
(c) Authorising the occupation of land by Europeans and Natives (not Aborigines) by leasehold (but not freehold) from the Chiefs.
(d) Dealing with all mineral rights, and conferring such powers as may be necessary for the working of mines.

(e) Acquisition of land for all Government purposes, such as roads, railways, buildings, customs, and police stations, &c. &c.

Administration.

14. Last year the Frontier Police were largely augmented, and the total annual cost of the force is now about 19,000 *l*. The finances of the Colony cannot bear the strain of such a large expenditure, except at the sacrifice of many useful works and reforms in other directions which are pressing for action, and to relieve the strain and at the same time obtain a revenue for the administration of the Protectorate it will be necessary to impose taxation on its inhabitants, and this taxation should be introduced as soon as practicable after the District Commissioners have been appointed and are in exercise of their full functions. The taxation should, I think, be imposed gradually, that is to say, in the first instance it should be limited to districts nearer Freetown which have been longest under our control, and afterwards extended to those farther off, as soon as it is found that these latter, which have in the past, suffered so much from Sofa and other raids, and large areas in which are still uninhabited, have become more settled.

15. The taxation might, as a commencement, be confined to a house tax and trading license . . .

29

SIERRA LEONE PROTECTORATE ORDER IN COUNCIL, 24 AUGUST 1895[1]

WHEREAS by the Foreign Jurisdiction Act, 1890, it was amongst other things enacted that it should be lawful for Her Majesty to hold, exercise, and enjoy any jurisdiction which Her Majesty then had, or might at any time thereafter have, within a foreign country, in the same and as ample a manner as if Her Majesty had acquired that jurisdiction by the cession or conquest of territory:

And whereas by certain Letters Patent under the Great Seal of the United Kingdom of Great Britain and Ireland, bearing date at Westminster the 28th day of November 1888, Her Majesty's Settlement of Sierra Leone was erected into a separate Colony, to be called the Colony of Sierra Leone, and by the said Letters Patent provision was made for establishing a legislative council for the said Colony of Sierra Leone, with certain powers and authority to legislate for the said Colony as by the said Letter Patent will more fully appear:

And whereas Her Majesty hath acquired jurisdiction within

[1] C.O. 879/43, no. 497.

divers foreign countries on the West Coast of Africa, near or adjacent to Her Majesty's said Colony of Sierra Leone, and it is expedient to determine the mode of exercising such jurisdiction:

Now, therefore, Her Majesty is pleased, by and with the advice of Her Privy Council, to order as follows:

1. It shall be lawful for the Legislative Council for the time being of the Colony of Sierra Leone by Ordinance or Ordinances to exercise and provide for giving effect to all such jurisdiction as Her Majesty may, at any time before or after the passing of this Order in Council, have acquired in the said territories adjacent to the Colony of Sierra Leone.

2. The Governor for the time being of the Colony of Sierra Leone shall have negative voice in the passing of all such Ordinances as aforesaid. And the right is hereby reserved to Her Majesty, Her heirs and successors, to disallow any such Ordinances as aforesaid, in whole or in part, such disallowance, being signified to the said Governor through one of Her Majesty's Principal Secretaries of State, and also to make and establish from time to time, with the advice and consent of Parliament or with the advice of Her or their Privy Council, all such Laws or Ordinances as may to Her or them appear necessary for the exercise of such jurisdiction as aforesaid as fully as if this Order in Council had not been made.

3. In making and establishing all such Ordinances, the said Legislative Council shall conform to and observe all such rules and regulations as may from time to time be appointed by any Instruction or Instructions issued by Her Majesty under Her Sign Manual and Signet, and until further directed, the Instructions in force for the time being as to Ordinances passed by the said Legislative Council for the peace, order, and good government of the said Colony of Sierra Leone shall, so far as they may be applicable, be taken and deemed to be in force in respect of Ordinances passed by the said Council by virtue of this Order in Council.

4. The Courts of the Colony of Sierra Leone shall have in respect of matters occurring within the said territories adjacent to the said Colony, so far as such matters are within the jurisdiction of Her Majesty, the same jurisdiction, civil and criminal, original and appellate, as they respectively possess from time to time in respect of matters occurring within the said Colony, and the judgements, decrees, orders, and sentences of any such court made or given in the exercise of the jurisdiction hereby conferred may be enforced and executed, and appeals therefrom may be had and prosecuted in the same way as if the judgement, decree, order, or sentence had been made or given under the ordinary jurisdiction of the court.

5. In the construction of this Order in Council the term 'Governor'

shall include the Officer for the time being administering the Government of the Colony of Sierra Leone.

And the Right Honourable Joseph Chamberlain, one of Her Majesty's Principal Secretaries of State, is to give the necessary directions herein accordingly.

C. L. Peel.

30

SIR JOHN KIRK TO THE MARQUIS OF SALISBURY: REPORT ON THE AKASSA RISING, 25 AUGUST 1895[1]

. . . 1. THE Chiefs of Brass allege that the Royal Niger Company's officials have been in the constant habit of firing upon their canoes, without cause, whenever seen on the Niger, of shooting their people, and seizing both canoes and cargo . . .

[The Company admits the charge for canoes violating Company regulations or the provisions of the Brussels Act.]

. . . Under conditions such as these, the Company's Regulations being what they are, and having been issued with the full sanction and previous approval of Her Majesty's Government, to whom they had in the first place been submitted, it is difficult to see how the law could be carried out without recourse in the end to force. These laws may be harsh, or even not in keeping, as the Brassmen allege, with Treaties, but those engaged in setting them aside ought to have been fully prepared for the consequences and to run the risk of accidents to the agents they employed in carrying on this contraband trade, and the occasional loss of these vessels and goods when captured.

[2. He does not find that canoes carrying food have been prohibited by the Company; nor have the Brass people suffered from starvation or privation.]

3. With reference to the complaint that the Brass people have been excluded by the Regulations of the Royal Niger Company from their old trade markets on the Niger, and that they have no others open to them, it is first necessary to bear in mind that the Rules they complain of were approved by Her Majesty's Government five years before what is now known as the 'Niger Coast Protectorate' was established, or the present boundary-line defined which cuts them off.

---

[1] F.O. 83/1382. Flint, *Sir George Goldie*, p. 212, indicates that Goldie may have helped with this report and its ideas. He certainly approved in his memoranda: 'The Public Revenues of the Niger Company', 9 December 1895, and 'A Niger Customs Union', 11 December 1895: Royal Niger Company Papers, *Meetings*, vol. i, Rhodes House Library. See, too, Anene, *Southern Nigeria*, pp. 172–3; and for MacDonald's plans for reform of administration, p. 175.

The Agent-General of the Company stated, in the presence of the Chiefs of Brass, in answer to questions put by me, that, in order to be able to trade legally on the Niger, any native of Brass, being technically regarded under the Company's laws as a foreigner in the Company's territory, would be required to comply with the same Rules as affect the largest trading Corporation. He would thus, I was told, be required to pay yearly a sum of 50 *l.* for licence to trade, with a further sum of 10 *l.*, also yearly, for every station he traded at, and he would then only be allowed to trade at such stations as had been declared open for that purpose and nowhere else. He would next be required to pay 100 *l.* annually if he intended to trade in spirits, without which, I may remark, trade in the delta is at present impossible.

Having thus acquired the right to commence trade in the Niger Territory, he would on first entering have to report his arrival and obtain a clearance either at Akassa or higher up at the mouth of the Ekole Creek, and pay the Company's duties of 2s. per gallon on spirits, the same spirits having already paid at the rate of 1s. to the Protectorate at Brass, and so on with other articles, the duty on which is in some cases still greater than on spirits. After his barter was over, he would, before leaving the Territory, be called on to pay 20 per cent. export duty on the value of all produce . . .

It will thus be seen that the Rules in force are practically prohibitory to native trade, and the Brassmen are right in saying that this is so . . .

[4. Ethnic composition of the Brass population; domestic slavery; population; language.]

5. The charge brought by the Royal Niger Company against the people of Brass of smuggling, is by them openly admitted. I have shown how impossible it would be for the Brass people to pay taxes and duties to both Administrations, and carry on trade at a profit. Under existing conditions they are and must be smugglers, if they are to trade at all, for from the New Calabar markets they are excluded by apparently a stronger people . . .

[Revenue lost through smuggling is estimated at £30,000 a year.

6. Premeditated nature of the attack on Akassa; difficulties of estimating the value of material losses.

7. Details of the attack.

8. Arms traffic and evasion of the Brussels Act. Inclusion of Brass within the Company frontier would be opposed.]

. . . The first or partial scheme which I would submit is as follows:

1. To divide the Company's territories into two parts, the maritime and the inland, the first to include the whole of the Niger Delta from

the sea between Forcados and Akassa and inland for about 90 to 100 miles as far as the head of the delta, where the river is limited to one channel, and before any of the branches that take its waters to the sea have left the main stream.

Under this scheme all the river valley and inland territory above the delta would be left as at present, with the Customs and Licence Rules and Regulations as they now are. The inland customs frontier now established at Lukoja, where secondary duties are collected, would, however, require to be brought down to the head of the delta where the second system of duties, now levied higher up, would then be applied, and where customs duties on exports from the upper river would be levied.

2. The maritime region of the Niger Territory thus separated for revenue purposes, while remaining under the administrative jurisdiction of the Company, would be united in a Customs Union under identical tariffs and Arms Regulations with the Niger Coast Protectorate . . .

[Licences would be abolished and the common tariff raised; Company trade might suffer by diversion of traffic.]

. . . The second plan which I would venture to submit for removing the present difficulties, and at the same time developing the whole Niger territory by means of a common system of taxation to be applied to both branches of the Administration, would be as follows:

1. A Customs Union and a common tariff and system of taxation to be established between the Company and the Coast Protectorate, to extend to both the interior and the coast. The Tariff to be fixed by Her Majesty's Government so as to meet the charges necessary.

2. To treat the two divisions of the British Protectorate in the Niger Region financially as one, by means of a common fund to be established into which all the revenues of the two provinces shall be paid, to be divided as Her Majesty's Secretary of State may direct for meeting the administrative charges and obligations of the two Governments.

3. The Company, at an early date to be fixed (if possible on the first January 1896), to cease to carry on trade on its own account, and to devote itself only to the work of administering and developing its Territory as a Government. But in view of the stock of trade goods which will remain on hand, to realize such goods as rapidly as it can to advantage, but on account of the administrative fund.

4. The Company to be entitled to divide amongst its shareholders the profits earned up to the date when this agreement begins to operate, including any reserve fund, so as to leave its capital intact. All accounts connected with this to be subject to approval by accountants selected by Her Majesty's Secretary of State.

5. The Company to relinquish, on behalf of the Administration, all its private rights over lands, minerals, and forests, but as a Government, to retain such rights as the Secretary of State may consider desirable for purposes of development and administration, or in the public interest, but not otherwise unless as may be agreed to.

6. The Company to derive no profit whatever from its Territory, save as provided in the foregoing section, and the fixed interest on its capital, as provided for in section 9.

7. The Company to reduce its capital from that at present nominally subscribed and partly paid up, of 1,027,080 *l.* to 400,000 *l.*, which is understood to be the amount of its present working capital, and to employ this capital for purposes of development and administration as a Government only . . .

[8. Capital of the Company to be used for steamers, stations, expeditions, judiciary and police, plantations, payment of interest.

9. Shareholders are to be paid 6 per cent. for use of capital.]

10. No one personally engaged in trade in either of the two divisions of the Niger Protectorate to be qualified to be a member of the Board of the Company.

11. Her Majesty's Government, while retaining the right reserved in the Charter to withdraw the same in the event of the Company failing in its duties, to have the additional power hereafter of at any time taking the government either into its own hands, or of otherwise providing for the same, and, in such case, the Company to have no other claim, than that of receiving their capital paid up, or of continuing to receive interest on the same, as is here mentioned, viz., 6 per cent. per annum, as Her Majesty's Government may elect . . .

[Eventually the interior will pass under Crown rule; as a transition, the Company's capital can be paid off or carried over as part of the Protectorate debt.]

31

A. W. L. HEMMING: MINUTE,
SIERRA LEONE JURIES, 30 AUGUST 1895[1]

[By Jury Ordinance No. 8 of 1895 public officials charged with criminal offences are to be tried by a judge and assessors; juries remained optional for other criminal cases.]

. . . THERE can be no doubt that such an Odce. as this is required. It is almost impossible for the Govt. at S. Leone to get a conviction in the case of defalcations or Embezzlement by public officers.

[1] C.O. 267/418.

The juries are scandalously corrupt & Col. Cardew is convinced & the judge's report in 15285 confirms this, that the jurors in Spaine's case who held out against a conviction had been bribed. The question of abolishing trial by jury altogether at S. Leone has more than once been mooted. It was done away with in civil cases in 1866. Col. Cardew suggests, if the Odce. be sanctioned, that the C. Justice should no longer be on the Exec. Council. This (the fact of his being on the Council) is one of the objections urged in Mr. Spaine's memorial in 15273.

32

JOHN BRAMSTON TO COLONEL CARDEW: SIERRA LEONE PROTECTORATE, 16 OCTOBER 1895[1]

I AM directed by Mr. Secretary Chamberlain to inform you that he has given very careful consideration to your letter of the 22nd of July,[2] submitting your views upon the future administration of the territories adjacent to Sierra Leone, and under the protection of Her Majesty, and I am to acquaint you that Mr. Chamberlain agrees in substance to your recommendations.

2. It may be of assistance to you to explain that the principle which governs these cases is, that the existence of a Protectorate in an uncivilised country carries with it a right on the part of the protecting Power to exercise within that country such authority and jurisdiction —in short, such of the attributes of sovereignty—as are required for the due discharge of the duties of a Protector, for the purpose not only of protecting the Natives from the subjects of civilised Powers, and such subjects from the Natives and from each other, but also for protecting the Natives from the grosser forms of ill-treatment and oppression by their rulers, and from the raids of slave dealers and marauders. It then becomes a question of fact, what are the powers which in any particular case it is proper for the Protector to assert? In the present case, the circumstances of the territories adjacent to Sierra Leone render it necessary to assert the authority which your letter specifies.

3. The machinery for giving effect to these powers is supplied by the Foreign Jurisdiction Act, 1890, which provides that Her Majesty may have, hold, exercise, and enjoy, any jurisdiction which she now has or may at any time hereafter have within a foreign country in the same and as ample a manner as if Her Majesty had acquired that jurisdiction by the conquest or cession of territory. The meaning of these words is, that in territory acquired by cession

[1] C.O. 879/43,, no. 497.   [2] No. 8, above.

or conquest Her Majesty may make laws by Order in Council, and, therefore, when she possesses jurisdiction in a foreign country she will in like manner proceed by Order in Council to give effect to it. The words are used in distinction to territory acquired by settlement, in which laws are made by Parliament alone or by persons acting under powers conferred by Act of Parliament. The Legislative Council of Sierra Leone will in future furnish an instance of both methods.

4. So far as regards the Settlement (or, as it is now called, the Colony) of Sierra Leone, the Legislative Council makes, and will continue to make, laws under the powers delegated to it by Letters Patent which Her Majesty was authorised by Parliament to issue for that purpose. The authority was originally contained in the Act 6 & 7 Vict. c. 13, enlarged by the Act 23 & 24 Vict. c. 121, both of which Acts have since been replaced by the British Settlements Act, 1887, 50 & 51 Vict. c. 54, under which Act the existing Letters Patent of the 28th of November 1888 were issued.

5. As regards the territories adjacent to the Colony, it would be practically impossible for Her Majesty in Council to regulate by Order in Council the various matters for which legislative sanction will be required. The want of local knowledge would render such a course impracticable, while the delay might be productive of inconvenience. Her Majesty has therefore been pleased by Order in Council, dated the 24th August last, to empower the Legislative Council by Ordinance to exercise and provide for giving effect to all such jurisdiction as Her Majesty may at any time before or after the passing of this Order have acquired in the said territories adjacent to the Colony of Sierra Leone. The Order will be transmitted to the Colony, and I am to enclose a copy for your information. Similar powers are already possessed by the Legislative Councils of the Gold Coast, Lagos, and the Gambia; and you will probably defer the publication of this Order until you issue the Proclamation hereafter referred to.

6. I am to call your attention to the 4th article of the Order by which jurisdiction is conferred upon the courts of the Colony in respect of matters occurring within the Protectorate. The administration of justice is one of the subjects referred to in your letter, and the establishment of the necessary courts will, no doubt, be dealt with in due course by Ordinance, but, in order that there might be means at once for punishing crime should any serious cases arise in respect to which Her Majesty's jurisdiction is exercisable it was thought right that Her Majesty should, under the powers conferred on Her by the 9th section of the Act, expressly empower the Colonial courts to deal with such cases. It is possible that these courts may not be required to act, and in that case this special power would remain in abeyance; it is also possible that their services may be frequently wanted, and then the value of this power would be apparent; and

if any rules of procedure or supplementary machinery were found necessary, these could be supplied by Ordinance.

7. Mr. Chamberlain consents to your issuing a Proclamation formally declaring that the territories on the British side of the boundary line fixed by the agreement with France, dated January 21st, 1895, are under the protection of Her Majesty.

You will make this Proclamation at such time as you may think convenient, and you should consider whether it is desirable to defer it until you are ready to give effect to the scheme of administration to which I am now to refer more in detail.

8. Mr. Chamberlain has referred to the Zululand Proclamation No. II, 1887, to which you call attention, and he infers that you mention it as indicating the source from which you have drawn the principles of the scheme embodied in your proposals. I am to inform you that the system of law, procedure, and jurisdiction embodied in paras. 4–12, of your letter appears to him to be well considered and likely to answer the desired purpose. You will therefore be at liberty on your return to the Colony to take measures for bringing it into force as soon as the necessary preparations are complete. You should, however, instruct the District Commissioners to watch carefully, and report to you from time to time upon, the manner in which the Native courts discharge their functions, for, if it should be found that they commit injustice or do not in other respects answer the purposes for which they are designed, it may be necessary to restrict or even to abolish their powers, and to increase the jurisdiction of the Commissioners' courts.

9. The question of the land is very important, perhaps the most important of all the subjects with which you will have to deal. The objects which you specify in par. 13 are those at which it is proper to aim, and Mr. Chamberlain observes with satisfaction that you recognise that, as the land is owned by Natives, it will be necessary that titles should emanate from them. You will recognise the necessity of proceeding cautiously in these matters, and of carrying the Natives with you in the steps which you take. If the land regulations meet with the general assent of the Natives, all will go well; but if you have the misfortune to introduce measures to which they are opposed, serious difficulty may arise. He thinks it also right to invite your serious consideration of the question whether an Ordinance should not be passed declaring that no concessions to Europeans will be valid unless approved by the Governor. Such a measure seems desirable in the interests of the Natives themselves, and to protect them from making improvident concessions to speculators.

10. It is clear that the Protectorate should as far as possible provide for its own administration, and, on the other hand, that any revenue obtained from it should be spent there. Mr. Chamberlain agrees to

the proposals contained in paras. 14–22 of your letter, and, subject to any modifications which on further consideration you may think advisable, he authorises you to give effect to them. He desires me, however, to request you to consider whether the reasons for exempting the aborigines from the obligation to take out trading licenses are sufficiently strong to over-ride the sound principle of treating alike all persons who are engaged in the same kind of business.

11. Mr. Chamberlain agrees that it will be prudent not to attempt at present any measure for abolishing summarily the institution of domestic slavery; but the courts should not recognise any claims on behalf of the masters. It will also be proper to extend to the Protectorate the laws of the Colony against slave raiding and dealing in slaves; and it might be well if, before your departure, you were to examine in the library of this office the law recently passed in the Gambia upon this subject, of which a copy can be furnished to you if desired.

12. It would seem judicious not to complicate the present scheme of administration by introducing questions relating to the supply of arms. I am, therefore, only to observe that the question of an international agreement is before Her Majesty's Government, and that Mr. Chamberlain would be glad to receive any report which you may be able to furnish at any time, and which may help to a solution of the question.

13. As regards the provision of funds for the initial expenses of the Protectorate, Mr. Chamberlain does not feel able to give you any definite instructions, and he feels that he may safely leave this to your discretion; but it seems inevitable that the money should in the first instance be provided from the funds of the Colony.

14. A copy of this correspondence will be forwarded to the Officer Administering the Government, so as to be on record when you arrive, but he will be instructed to take no action until your return.

33

GOVERNOR W. E. MAXWELL TO
CAPTAIN D. STEWART, RESIDENT OF
KUMASI: ASHANTI ADMINISTRATION,
10 FEBRUARY 1896[1]

1. You will consider yourself as the agent of the Governor resident in Ashanti and responsible for the conduct of business with all the Ashanti and other tribes between the Prah and the ninth parallel of latitude.

[1] C.O. 879/44, no. 500. Encl. in Maxwell to Chamberlain, 22 February 1896. Approved in C.O. to Maxwell, 15 April 1896.

2. A list of the tribes with whom Treaties of protection have already been concluded will be furnished to you.

3. You should interfere as little as possible in the ordinary administration carried on by the King and Chiefs of a tribe. They should be encouraged to manage their own affairs, and they are entitled to hold their own courts of justice. Your interference will only be necessary in case of gross injustice or cruelty or any case involving loss of, or danger to, human life.

4. The Kings and Chiefs of a tribe are not authorised to inflict the death penalty. Every case of murder should be investigated by you or by some competent officer detailed by you for that purpose, sitting in conjunction with the King and Chiefs of the tribe. In case of conviction the death sentence may be carried out under the orders of the King in the manner prescribed by native custom, provided that no cruelty or barbarity is permitted.

5. You can exercise all ordinary civil and criminal jurisdiction, being guided by the general principles of English law and of equity and good conscience. No sentence of imprisonment exceeding one year should be imposed without reference to the Governor. The probability is that for some time, at all events, the only cases that will come before you will be petty offences committed in the town and its vicinity by members of the foreign population. With regard to these you should be guided by the laws of the Gold Coast Colony, a copy of which will be furnished to you, though you are not to infer that these are in force in Ashanti.

6. A suitable building should be erected as soon as possible to serve as a gaol. It should be construed to accommodate about 20 prisoners, and you will report at some future time what arrangements are made as to guarding and rationing persons under sentence of imprisonment.

7. You should give close attention to the laying out of the town according to a plan which will be furnished to you by the Officer Commanding the Royal Engineers. Government reserves must be laid out. All building must be prevented upon reserved spaces. A quarter will be assigned to the foreign trading community, and within this merchants and traders may acquire building allotments, provided that substantial buildings are erected thereon within one year. You will be furnished with forms of licences for issue to persons who obtain allotments. Persons who build new houses must be required to adhere to the proper alignment and to provide such drainage as may be required.

8. Public latrines must be erected and their use insisted on. Cases of nuisance should be summarily punished.

9. Sites for mission schools and other mission premises can be allotted on the outskirts of the town away from the trading quarter.

Building licences may be issued to missionaries in the manner above described.

10. No concession of land in any part of Ashanti, whether dated before or after the 20th of January 1896, is to be recognised in any way by you. Every such concession to be valid must be sanctioned by the Governor.

11. The encouragement of trade will be one of your most important duties. You should inform yourself of the conditions under which trade is carried on both with the coast and with the interior, and you must require the Kings and Chiefs of tribes to keep all roads clean. No road should be permitted to be closed or to be regarded as unsafe by reason of any difference or hostility between tribes. You will doubtless take an opportunity of making yourself acquainted with all the more important roads leading to Kumasi.

12. It is very desirable that the road to the north should be cleared as soon as possible, so as to afford free access to the open country beyond the forest. As soon as you can do so, you should yourself visit the upper country, going, if necessary, as far as Kintampo, where it may be advisable, at some future time, to establish a station for the encouragement and security of traders. It is probable that this would serve as a centre of trade to which Mohammedans from the various states in the bend of the Niger would be attracted for the purchase of kola-nuts, salt, &c. If a trading centre is established there or in some other favourable situation in that direction, it may be expected that a brisk trade would rapidly spring up between that place and Kumasi, and if the road is kept reasonably clean there seems to be no reason why horses, which abound in the upper region, should not be used.

A flying column is being sent to the districts lying northwards of Kumasi, and the officer in charge will be instructed to conclude treaties of protection with Ahafu, Wam, Berekum, Poliano, Banda, and other places. You will have authority to make similar treaties on behalf of the Governor. The necessary forms will be furnished to you . . .

34

SIR ROBERT MEADE: MINUTE,
POLITICAL PRISONERS, 18 JULY 1896[1]

[Sierra Leone Ordinance No. 12 of 1896 for detention of prisoners from the interior has been received and approved.]

. . . In the present state of the country behind S. Leone order can only be kept by the strong hand, & it is impossible to allow Sir S. Lewis

C.O. 267/425. On Cardew to Chamberlain, 10 June 1896.

[by use of writs of *habeus corpus*] to pose as a greater power than the Governor, if peace is to be preserved at all. The short facts are that in a land dispute outside British territory three or more investigations by Govt. officials have all resulted in favour of one side, & the other side intrudes on the land & defies the Govt. by force, & the ring leaders have been brought down to Freetown & will be detained under this Ordinance until legal machinery is introduced into the back country by laws now in the process of incubation.

35

TEMNE CHIEFS TO ACTING GOVERNOR J. E. CAULFIELD: THE PROTECTORATE ORDINANCE, 28 JUNE 1897[1]

[The petition is to be forwarded to Queen Victoria; since the Yonni expedition British administration and laws have been spreading.]

. . . THE substance of the laws in question is as follows:

1. That the country is no more your petitioners', it is the Queen's; and that your petitioners have no more power over their lands and property; and that their Chiefs cannot do even so much as to settle matters respecting their common farms. All gold and silver found in the country to be the property of the Government.

2. Your petitioners are to pay for their houses from 5s. to 10s. a year.

3. Your petitioners are not to carry on any trade unless they pay to the Queen £2 a year.

4. No rum is to be sold in any part of the country unless your petitioners pay the £2 a year.

5. Native Chiefs may be deposed and deported at the Governor's pleasure.

6. The country is to be in charge of the District Commissioners, whose decision in all cases, and that by the English laws, is final, against which there is no appeal except by paying a large amount of money.

7. That there are three courts in the country:—1. Native Court; 2. District Commissioners' and Native Courts; 3. District Commissioners' Court. In the two latter your petitioners are to be judged by English laws, both in civil and criminal cases: that any Chief

---

[1] *Parl. Papers*, 1899, lx [C. 9391], ii,pp. 575–8. Signatories were: Nemgbana (Kwaia), Dick Wola for Bey Compay (Kwaia), Almamy Bundu (Kwaia), Bey Suba (Magbele), Alkali Kozar Bubu (Gambia), Kombor for Bey Sarma (Loko Masama), the Alkali of Port Loko, Bey Kobolo (Marampa), Almamy Sater Lahai, Almamy Anamodu, Bey Farama.

hearing any case not belonging to his Court will be punished by fine, imprisonment, and flogging.

8. No slave-dealing of any kind to take place in the country.

9. All case of witchcraft to be tried by the Government.

These and many others were the laws interpreted to us by Mr. Renner,[1] and others, but those which have thrown your petitioners into the greatest consternation are the following:

(a) That your petitioners are to have no more power over their country. They are not to hear any cases relating to their lands, farms, and the boundaries of their country; this your petitioners take to mean nothing short of total dispossession of their country; and knowing the humanity of the English people, your petitioners feel sure that this is a misrepresentation of the mind of the English Government on the subject particularly as your petitioners are not aware that they have done anything to merit such great calamity from their friends and benefactors.

(b) That your petitioners are to pay for their houses and huts. The nature of their houses, built of mud and sticks, and thatched with grass and leaves, your Excellency, will show the true condition of your petitioners. The numberless deserted villages to be met with in the country tell of the present unsettled state of the country; your petitioners fear that taxing houses will certainly hinder the return of the poor people to their homes. Again, as big as some of our towns are, the houses in them are, in most cases, owned by not more than half a dozen Chiefs and Headmen; having not to pay for their building materials, the Chiefs can afford to put up most of these huts for the accommodation of strangers and the poorer members of their families. Chiefs own the villages, and the huts therein are built for them by their retainers, the majority of whom can scarcely save enough to provide a suit of clothes for themselves, their children, and wives for the whole year; the burden of paying the tax must necessarily fall upon the Chiefs, and, failing to pay, the villages must fall to the ground; the moral consequence of a forced accommodation will be better imagined than described. Again, the name of the tax recalls to the minds of your petitioners the dreadful days of Kwaia; when, for house tax, men and women were ruthlessly dragged from place to place, plundered, and some flogged almost to death by the tax-collectors. The dreadful disclosure of which moved Her Most Gracious Queen and Her Government to set up that lasting monument of English pity and benignity. They not only abolished the tax, but returned the country to its former owners. This has endeared your petitioners to England, stamped their confidence in the Government, and established their loyalty to their great friend and benefactor the Queen for ever. The thought of the revival of those dreadful days is

[1] Dr. William Renner, Assistant Colonial Surgeon.

what has plunged your petitioners in the greatest alarm. They have not the means to pay these taxes, and therefore fall at your Excellency's feet and pray to be saved from so much dreaded misfortune. Your petitioners are not unmindful of the great expense the Government must have undergone, and is undergoing, to bring about and maintain the peace and order they are now enjoying in their country; and your petitioners will not grudge any contributions in their power to lighten the burden of the Government in any way. As part of these contributions towards the maintenance of this peace for which the Government is now expending thousands of pounds, your petitioners will guarantee for the present at least, with the aid of one European or other Government resident and a dozen policemen, to keep the peace in their country.

Your petitioners beg to assure your Excellency they have now seen and felt the power of the Government, there is not one amonst them who has now the most distant ideas for war-making. Your petitioners repeat that one officer with a few police are sufficient to carry out the wishes of the Government in their country.

(c) That any Chief having any case not in his jurisdiction shall be punished by fine, imprisonment and flogging. Your petitioners regard this as a terrible punishment for a right they had enjoyed from their forefathers, and not for any wrong done to the Government or the community at large. The Government are possibly not aware that by our country laws and fashion, every Chief, Headmen of a town or family, is responsible for the conduct of his children and people under him; and as your petitioners feel confident that it is not the desire of the Government to abolish their cherished institutions, and fearing that in the midst of it they might fall into the bad grace of the Government, your petitioners respectfully beg your Excellency to save them from the serious disgrace and pending scourge of a fine, imprisonment, and flogging, by being allowed to continue their ancient privileges of settling all their cases, subject to an appeal to the District Commissioner. Your petitioners, moreover, pray that in their country they be judged by their native laws so long as they do not affect their loyalty to the Queen or Her Government.

(d) That your petitioners have to pay for some of the attempts of their children to follow the example of the English people in doing what is called lawful trading, that is, to buy and sell their merchandise instead of human beings, is something to them quite unexplainable. When the White people stopped the slave-trade in their country, to give your petitioners no cause of complaint for want of business, they introduced the timber trade. When that traffic failed, the growth and exportation of ground-nuts was encouraged; as soon as that crop began to show signs of decay, palm oil and kernels were introduced into the market. All these have fallen so low as to make scarcely worth any one's while to devote any serious attention to the trade; and since the Government has been doing so much for peace and order, the parents of commerce, your petitioners have been expecting to hear of some new lines of industry and commerce from the Government; instead of this, your petitioners have been surprised by a direct order not to do any more in merchandise trading; and there are some of the traders in their midst who would be pleased to clear at the end of this year's trade as much as 30s., one head of money in our country. Not all men are made for farming—some farmers and some traders. Your petitioners respectfully request that the freedom of trade accorded to the people trading in the Colony be granted to them as loyal friends and subjects of the Queen.

The Government may possibly have overlooked the fact that the greater part of the duty on dry goods and spirits indirectly falls upon your petitioners.

(e) What your petitioners complain of in the question of the spirit traffic is, the very bad and cheap sort that is brought into the country; thus any one owning a shilling takes to drink. In former years, the best of spirits in casks and earthenware jugs was imported into their country, and as such only very little of it could be drunk at a time. Your petitioners desire then that the Government act the father for them, and see that no spurious stuff be brought into the country; this will be the only way of bringing about the object desired by the Government. To stop drinking is a sheer impossibility, but to check its spread in the country is a very desirable object. In your petitioners' humble opinion, this can only be obtained by raising the quality of the spirits imported, which will consequently raise the price and confine it to the very few who would be able to afford it, and so keep it out of the reach of the many.

(f) As regards the question of Slavery, your petitioners beg to assure your Excellency that from so many years' experience they now know something of the mind of the English Government on the subject. To buy and sell slaves is now out of the question, and it would be useless to trouble the Government about it. All your petitioners desire is, that the few domestics left to them by their people, and who have become part and parcel of their family, should not be encouraged to leave them and come to Freetown. Your petitioners have not the means of keeping money in banks as the White people; a few of them, it is admitted, run away from ill-treatment, but the greater part of the runaways are those who are lazy and who refuse to work. Hundreds of them have found their way to Freetown: these your petitioners are aware have become subjects of the Queen . . .

[This drain of labour through the loss of domestic slaves should be stopped.]

(g) That it shall be left to the discretion of the District Commissioner to advise the deportation and banishment of persons from their homes without any charge or judgment, and the persons so named to be left without any place of appeal for redress or protection. Where human nature is so varied in its form, the liberty of every individual in the country is, under this arrangement, left to hang on a very slender thread. This is certainly a misrepresentation to your petitioners of English fashion . . .

36

GOVERNOR SIR H. E. McCALLUM TO JOSEPH CHAMBERLAIN: IJEBU ADMINISTRATION, 7 DECEMBER 1897[1]

. . . I HAD a discussion with the Awujale at Jebu Ode and the decisions come to thereon are as follows:

(a) That considering this Government has incurred the expense of making roads in the Jebu territory from Jebu Ode to Epe, Ejirin and Mamu, the Awujale is held responsible that the said roads are kept clean and in repair according to African customs.

(b) That I declined to re-open the question of the Jebu Ode–Ibadan boundary but adhered to the decision arrived at some two years ago. The Jebu Chiefs however are to be given control over Jebu forests on their side of the boundary line and to introduce measures for their protection.

(c) That I agreed to an arrangement by which one third of all fines imposed in any Jebu Towns are to go to the Awujale, one third to the Chiefs, and one third for the maintenance of prisons and general improvement of the country . . .

37

SIR GEORGE GOLDIE TO FOREIGN OFFICE: ROYAL NIGER COMPANY, 14 SEPTEMBER 1897[2]

. . . 3. HER Majesty's Government desire that almost the whole of the Company's force shall be employed in this work for an indefinite period, and, therefore, that the greater part of the Company's river fleet shall be diverted to this purpose, as also the most energetic, experienced, and able of its white and coloured officials. Under any other conditions, military action would end in disaster.

[1] C.O. 147/121.   [2] C.O. 879/50, no. 538.

4. The military force has been gradually created during ten years, and especially during the last five years of exceptional effort, with the sole object of carrying out the Company's obligations under the Charter or establishing and maintaining order amongst the native States and tribes in its sphere, to the utmost extent and with the utmost rapidity permitted by its scanty revenue. It has, therefore, been maintained at the lowest point consistent with the above obligations, and at the highest point consistent with revenue considerations; but no margin has ever been provided for the unforeseen contingency of having to do the work of the Imperial Government in preventing European Powers from invading a British Protectorate.

5. It has always been held that a Charter is a contract by which the Imperial Government undertakes protection from external and civilized Powers while the Chartered Company undertakes all internal and native wars. It is obvious that the Niger Company could not contend with the French Republic.

[The actions against Nupe and Ilorin have been undertaken in the shadow of impending dissolution of the Company which has been taxed with the question of Brass and fiscal frontiers with the Niger Territories.]

8. Since that time the grounds have been largely increased for supposing that Her Majesty's Government are considering or are open to consider the question of making some vital changes in the system of administration. I need not refer to the main grounds for this belief. I would however like to note that the very dispatch to which I am now replying terminates with the words, 'if the administration of the Niger Territories should be withdrawn from the Company'. This is, I believe, the first time that such a trenchant solution of the question has been referred to in official correspondence. Moreover, I yesterday learnt, incidentally and again for the first time, that two Government vessels were being built, and were nearly completed, for patrolling the Niger. As this patrolling work has been done by the Company's large and specially-constructed fleet ever since the issue of the Charter, and as its fleet has never been found insufficient—at the time of the French dispatch-boat, the 'Ardent', it was diplomatic action and not naval action that the Company requested and obtained, with due success—I was naturally struck with such a far-reaching measure having been taken without any communication with the Niger Company.

9. In these circumstances, I would point out that it would be a real breach of trust on the part of our Council, unless the future position of the Company were first clearly ascertained, to risk the whole existence of the Company, and to divert its entire energies from their normal channels for an undetermined period, certainly to incur heavy indirect losses, which could not be accurately measured or recovered,

in order to perform a duty which really rests on the Imperial Government, namely, that of protection against external and civilized Powers.

[The risk of failure is high, even with 700 men, in the circumstances of restraint imposed by the Government.]

11. The Company is, however, willing to risk its future, and I am willing, personally, to risk my reputation—to say nothing of the lives of all engaged—in this hazardous venture, provided some definite decision is arrived at as to future fiscal and other arrangements, for the Company cannot administer without revenue.

12. If, on the other hand, Her Majesty's Government desire to take over the Company altogether, with its troops, ships, stations, &c.—an operation which could be arranged in a few hours' discussion—I shall be glad to offer my services, of course without pay, for directing (with competent military assistance) the proposed operations, so as to avoid any break in continuity of direction at a period of difficulty.

38

EDWARD WINGFIELD TO FOREIGN OFFICE: ROYAL NIGER COMPANY, 30 OCTOBER 1897[1]

... Sir George Goldie proposes that the Company should place at the disposal of Her Majesty's Government a special force of 300 trained men, who would be under the command of an officer appointed by the Government; but that the posts at Leaba, Fort Goldie, Jebba, and (if one should be established there) Boussa, should remain at the charge and at the orders of the Company. He also states that the Company could arrange to send out all the officers (other than the commanding officer) required for the special force; that it could also supply horses, carriers, and various stores, as required, and that it would gladly organise and maintain the entire expedition if the Government wish it to do so.

3. Mr. Chamberlain is of opinion that this offer to arrange for the supplies for the entire expedition should be accepted, the funds required being, of course, provided from the Imperial Exchequer. In the case of an expedition having a Colony as its base, the organisation of the Colonial Government is available for this purpose. But in the present case the base will be a point on the Niger, and it will only be possible to carry out the proposed operations successfully by making use of the Company's organisation and Sir G. Goldie's ability and experience.

4. It appears to Mr. Chamberlain, however, that the proposal that the posts at Leaba and the other places mentioned should remain

[1] C.O. 879/50, no. 538.

under the orders of the Company, would involve dual control, which, as Sir Geo. Goldie observes, must always result in failure; and it was with the object of avoiding this difficulty that, in the letter from this Department of the 14th of August, it was proposed that the sphere of operations of the Commissioners and Commandant (for which appointment Major Lugard has been selected), should be the territories on the right bank of the Niger, from the 9th parallel northwards, that he should be independent of the Company, and that he should correspond direct with the Colonial Office.

5. I am to submit, for the consideration of the Marquess of Salisbury, that, unless Her Majesty's Government are prepared to take over immediately the whole of the Company's administrative rights (which would for some reasons be the best solution of the difficulty), these proposals should be adopted; and, on learning that his Lordship approves of this course, Mr. Chamberlain will at once enter into direct communication with the Company, and will endeavour to come to an agreement as to the terms on which the Company would, subject to the control of this Department, undertake the duty of keeping the force under Her Majesty's Commissioner supplied with ammunition, provisions, and all other necessary stores.

6. In the meantime, the arrangements for raising the new force are being pushed on as rapidly as possible. Recruits are being enrolled in Lagos, and Sir G. Goldie has undertaken to have men enrolled in the Company's territories; arms, ammunition, and uniform for 1,500 men, as a first instalment, have been ordered, and a large proportion has been already shipped; and most of the officers and non-commissioned officers who will be required have been selected, and are being held in readiness to embark at short notice.

39

SIR FREDERIC CARDEW: MINUTE,
ENFORCEMENT OF THE HUT TAX,
15 JANUARY 1898[1]

[The Acting District Commissioner in Ronietta (Temne) reports refusal to pay the tax.]

1. I THINK it is necessary on this report, to increase the number of officers and Frontier Police in the Ronietta district.

2. Captain Moore will proceed on Tuesday next in the Colonial steamer *Countess of Derby*, *via* Waterloo, with such a reinforcement as the Inspector General can supply, to Kwalu, and being the senior officer, on arrival there he will take over the duties of District

[1] *Parl. Papers*, 1899, lx [C. 9391], ii, p. 594.

Commissioner from Dr. Hood. He will take all necessary steps for enforcing law and order in the district and the due payment of the house tax, giving reasonable time when he observes a disposition to pay, but he should make a severe example of those who incite or intimidate others not to pay . . . the offenders should be severely punished; it may be expedient, at first, to sentence such to periods of imprisonment not exceeding three months, so as to prevent the delay that would be occasioned should the offender desire to appeal, but I leave this to Captain Moore's discretion. Such examples should be made of the most influential Chiefs should they offend, and I think it is desirable in all these cases for the prisoners to be sent to Freetown gaol for imprisonment.

3. With reference to para. 3, no time should be lost to bring the offenders to justice, and the Frontier Police must be protected.

4. In cases where the Paramount Chiefs are unable to make their authority felt, the house tax must be exacted from the Sub-Chiefs and Headmen of towns and villages.

5. With reference to my Minute of to-day's date on the subject of the prohibition of the carriage of arms by natives, I consider, owing to the state of unrest in the Ronietta district, that the prohibition should be extended to all natives in that district. Captain Moore will therefore issue instructions to the police to disarm any native that may be met with arms, and confiscate his weapons . . .

40

GOVERNOR SIR H. E. McCALLUM TO JOSEPH CHAMBERLAIN: EGBA GOVERNMENT, 2 FEBRUARY 1898[1]

. . . 17. The general plan of Government which I laid before the Alake and his Chiefs was to form a State Council of the following eight persons:

Egba Osili   King of the Osili section of the Egbas
   ,,   Olowo   ,,   Olowo   ,,   ,,
   ,,   Agura   ,,   Agura   ,,   ,,
The Seriki
Sule representative of the Mohammedans
Josiah Olumide   ,,   ,,   Christians
Sarunhin—President Native Board of Trade
Apena Iporo—Representative of the Alake Section.

[1] C.O. 147/30. And McCallum to Chamberlain, 5 March 1898. See S. O. Biobaku, 'The Egba Council, 1899–1918', *Odu Journal of Yoruba and Related Studies* (1955), pp. 14–20. The *Seriki* and *Apena* were omitted from the Egba National Council as it met in practice.

18. To each of these eight persons I proposed, in addition to their advisory duties, to entrust a department of State, and I explained the broad principles of those different departments and their relation to state and individual interests.

19. Turning then to Egba affairs I enumerated different points which required immediate attention in the cause of good order, trade and prosperity and I made it quite clear that if these points were not attended to by the Council and an honest effort made to properly govern themselves the British Government would be obliged to actively interfere for we could not allow the continuance of the retrogression which had for a long time past been going on in Abeokuta.

20. I then agreed to hold a meeting of the New Council on 31st Ultimo in the compound of my house, explain to them the different duties and the general plan of Government and to bring them myself to the Alake who would receive them in state. This was the more necessary for the four kings are by native customs supposed not to come in the presence of each other much less see each others' faces. I looked upon the presence of these four kings together in Council as of paramount importance. The present Alake is a miserable specimen who must however be supported and up to the present his particular section of the Egbas have alone taken any part in the Government of the Country.

21. I sent messages to the other kings that customs and tradition must give way before the good and prosperity of their kingdom and so successful was my appeal that not only did I eventually bring all four kings together before an immense assembly but got them all to discard the bead curtains which usually hang in front of their faces and then photographed the whole group. I may here state that this step was regarded as being impossible by those Egbas who were in the best position to know, and that the utmost enthusiasm prevailed throughout the town at the four kings having been brought together and at all sections of the Egbas being now interested and concerned in the Government of the Country.

22. The Departments to which I have appointed the different Ministers at a very satisfactory and crowded meeting held in my compound are as follows:

Egba Osili	Justice
The Sereki	Justice
Egba Oluwo	Finance
Egba Agura	Roads and Works
Sule	Public Order
Sarunhin	Trade and Agriculture
Olumide	Sanitation
Apena Iporo	Secretary to the Government.

41

LIEUT.-COLONEL H. P. NORTHCOTT
TO THE COLONIAL SECRETARY: NORTHERN
TERRITORIES, 31 JULY 1898[1]

5. THE proximity of the rainy season militates against movements that are not of urgent necessity, and it is objectionable to post Europeans during this season at places where no provision has been made for their accommodation. As soon, however, as travelling becomes possible, and normally healthy conditions return, I propose that every corner of the administrative area shall be visited by an officer, and that it shall be divided into sub-districts capable, from their size, of being effectively regulated by a European. His duties will be to explain to all the chiefs in his sub-district the fact of their subordination to British rule, and the obligations imposed upon them by it; to strictly enforce law and order within the limits of his juris-diction; to discover the natural lines of communication between his own and the neighbouring sub-districts, to improve them into perma-nent highways, and to arrange that they are safe for unarmed parties; to ascertain the wants of the people and the resources with which they can increase their purchasing power; and to encourage an extension of farming and stock-keeping. He will be required to send in a monthly report on the condition of his sub-district, and will be encouraged to make suggestions on any subject appertaining to his duties.

6. These sub-districts will be grouped into districts, each of which will be administered by an officer directly responsible to the Com-missioner and Commandant. The duties of the District Officers will be analogous to those of the Sub-District Officers, but they will be invested with wider powers and they will be required to endorse the reports of their subordinates, with an expression of their own views. Except in cases of urgent and pressing necessity, where the safety of the sub-district establishment is endangered, no punitive expedition will be undertaken without previous submission of the facts to the District Officer, and his permission being obtained. Immediate reports of any such action will be made to headquarters, but in ordinary cases District Officers will have the issue left in their hands. Decentralisation is absolutely necessary in a large country with officers widely spaced, and it is imperative that a sense of responsibility should be encouraged within reasonable limits.

7. I have adverted to the fact that taxation is for the moment unadvisable, but I am disposed to call upon the native chiefs to assist

---

[1] C.O. 879/54, no. 564. *H. P. Northcott* was first Commissioner and Commandant, Gold Coast Northern Territories. Encl. in Hodgson to Chamberlain, 21 September 1898.

in public works to the best of their ability by supplying free labour. One of the first requisites for opening up the country and facilitating commercial intercourse is the construction of good roads, and, in the commencement that has been made in this service, the principle of the corvée has been applied with the full acquiescence of the native dignitaries. I intend to employ it throughout the Northern Territories in the construction and maintenance of roads, in the building of huts for public purposes, and in work of a similar nature, special care being taken to adjust the calls upon the population as not to interfere with the work of agriculture.

8. The whole scheme of administration, foundation, and superstructure, is dependent for its success on the ubiquity of the white man. An officer must be quartered in each sub-district, and he must be supported by an armed detachment of sufficient strength to insure his personal safety in any probable contingency, to support the dignity of his position, and to enable him to quell any minor disturbance with exemplary promptitude . . .

42

REPORT OF THE NIGER COMMITTEE, 4 AUGUST 1898[1]

[The Committee is to examine the future administration of the territories of Lagos, Niger Coast Protectorate, and the Niger Company, defence, revenue, and railways.]

(1) On the question of the future administration of the three territories, Lagos Niger Coast Protectorate, and Niger Company's Territories—whether they should be united under one head—we are of opinion that the object to be aimed at is the eventual establishment of a Governor General for the whole of the territories, resident in the territories.

But we feel that the appointment of a Governor General is inadvisable at present (a) For climatic reasons: it would be impossible under present circumstances, to get any but a young man to do efficient work in West Africa—and even a young man would require to be away to recruit his health one-third or more of the time, so that continuity of policy would be lost.

Sir G. Goldie said that this difficulty would be removed in time by the establishment of a 'Simla' in the Bautshi Highlands.

(b) Because of the absence of telegraphs and roads, which render it really more difficult to communicate with all parts of the territory from any possible point within it than from Downing Street.

[1] C.O. 879/52, no. 550. Members were Lord Selborne, Goldie, Sir Clement Hill, Sir Ralph Moor, Sir Reginald Antrobus, and McCallum.

This difficulty will, of course, also be removed in time.

For the present we are of the opinion that the administration of these territories must be conducted through the medium of provincial Governors under the direct superintendence of the Colonial Office.

The limits and number of the subordinate administrations— We are of opinion that the Niger cannot form the dividing line; both banks of the Niger must be under one jurisdiction on opposite banks, the administration of the criminal and civil law will be more difficult.

The division, we think, should be into a Maritime Province and a Soudan Province, between the Soudan regions governed by Mahommedans and the Pagan regions of the Niger Delta, including, however, with the latter, the Mahommedan Yorubas.

The actual line we suggest as the Southern Boundary of the Soudan Province would leave the Dahomey boundary at the 9th parallel, run east and then south-east, including all the Bariba and excluding all the Yoruba country, and including Ilorin (following Bower's line with necessary rectifications), and on to (but excluding) Idda on the Niger, then east from Idda to Ashaku on the German boundary, leaving Takum in the Soudan Province. The seat of Government of the Soudan Province we think should, for the present, be Lokoja.

The question then arises whether the Maritime Provinces should be further divided.

If it is divided, we are agreed that the division should be into a western province, with its capital at Lagos, and with an area similar to that of the existing Colony of Lagos, and an eastern province, with its capital at Asaba, including the rest of the Niger Delta.

The provinces, whether two or three in number, will have to be divided into divisions and districts.

Sir H. McCallum recommends that the native Chiefs, subsidised as hereinafter suggested by him, should in all cases be organised as village and district councils . . .

[There should be one military force, as part of a West African force, a customs union with the Lagos tariff; no more than £400,000 in revenue can be expected; military and civil expenditure will amount to at least £699,000; there will be no direct taxation at present.]

II. In respect of Sokoto, and as to Bornu and Rabah, the Committee have naturally felt themselves bound to be guided by the advice of Sir George Goldie, who almost alone has knowledge on the subject.

He is of the opinion that the Sultan of Sokoto would not voluntarily receive a Resident accompanied by a sufficient guard. It would, therefore, he thinks, be useless to send one until the Fulah power is crushed.

No attempt should be made to do this by a general *coup de main*. It should be done gradually, each Emir being taken in turn. The necessity for a forward policy is not so urgent now that Her Majesty's Government have come to an agreement with the French Government, and Her Majesty's Government may well wait until the new Governor of the Soudan province can advise them as to the time for making an advance.

Sir George Goldie does not think that the Sultan of Sokoto, if pressed, would refuse to accept a Resident with a small escort, but he would deprecate in the strongest possible manner a Resident being sent to Sokoto under such conditions. He thinks that the fate of Major Cavagnari would probably await him.

With reference to railway construction, the Committee are unanimously of opinion that the great trunk line must be one from Kano, down the valley of the Kaduna, to its junction with the Niger. Thence goods would at first have to be conveyed by water to meet the ocean-going steamers on the coast, but in future the line should be continued to some port where ocean-going steamers can come alongside.

Such a port might either be Lagos or Warri, or Sapele on the Benin river, or some spot on the Niger itself, such as Asaba.

At present the port of Lagos can only accommodate steamers of not more than nine feet draught. Merchandise has therefore to be shipped from the railway into branch steamers and carried to Forcados, and there transhipped into ocean-going steamers. An estimate has been prepared by Messrs. Shelford and Co. for making the harbour of Lagos practicable for ocean-going steamers by the removal of the bar, at a cost of £800,000.

Sir H. McCallum is of opinion that the line now being constructed from Lagos to Abeokuta should be continued to the Niger to meet the line from Kano, as he is of opinion that Lagos harbour when improved at the estimated cost will in every respect form the most suitable port.[1]

Sir Ralph Moor and Sir George Goldie, on the contrary, think that the natural point to which the line from Kano should be eventually extended is either Warri or Sapele on the Benin river, both of which are, they assert already available as ports for ocean-going steamers of the largest size. I understand that Sir H. McCallum does not admit this last assertion . . .

[There is need for consideration of the Lagos railway line and for survey work on the Niger before a decision can be made.]

[1] For railways, see IV. C.

43

SIR DAVID CHALMERS: REPORT, SIERRA LEONE INSURRECTION, 21 JANUARY 1899[1]

... 16. *Summary.*

169. The Hut Tax, together with the measures used for its enforcement, were the moving causes of the insurrection. The tax was obnoxious to the customs and feelings of the people. A peremptory and regularly recurring impost is unknown in their own practices and traditions. The English Government has not yet conferred any such benefits as to lead to a burden of a strange and portentous species being accepted willingly. There was a widespread belief that it was a means of taking away their rights in their country and in their property. That the tax was considered as an oppressive and unjust impost is proved by the unanimous and earnest petitions and representations against its enforcement in the earlier stages, by the general unwillingness to pay reported by District Commissioners in the beginning of 1898, and manifested everywhere by the agreements and oaths of the Chiefs binding themselves not to pay, and their resistance to payment, and by the opinions of Chiefs and others who know their countrymen and their modes of thinking.

170. The amount of the tax is higher than the people, taken generally, can pay, and the arrangement by which liability is primarily placed on the Chiefs to make good definite amounts on demand is unworkable.

171. The mode of enforcing payment provided by the law would probably prove abortive, whether used to meet inability or unwillingness to pay.

172. Repugnance to the tax was much aggravated by the sudden, uncompromising, and harsh methods by which it was endeavoured to be brought into operation, not merely by the acts of native policemen, but in the whole scheme adopted by the Colonial authorities. Before payment of this tax had begun to be demanded, alienation and anger had been produced by the vexatious acts and interferences with the Chiefs and people by the Frontier Police, and this anger and alienation were greatly intensified when these same Police were used subsequently to compel payment of the tax by illegal and overmastering force. The inherent repugnance to the Hut Tax would by itself most probably have led to passive resistance in whatever modes

[1] *Parl. Papers*, 1899, lx [C. 9388], pp. 73-5, 79-81. *Sir Daniel Chalmers*, former Queen's Advocate, Sierra Leone, 1873-4, was sent out as special commissioner to investigate the Hut Tax rising. For an account of the insurrection and its results, see Fyfe, *History of Sierra Leone*, pp. 567-99.

that form of opposition might have been capable of assuming. The sense of personal wrong and injustice from the illegal and degrading severities made use of in enforcing the Tax, coupled with the aversion to the Tax in itself produced in the Timinis a resistance enforced by arms, and led the Medis to venture on an exterminating and plundering raid.

173. The Timinis were hurried rapidly into their hostile attitude through the circumstance that an act for the enforcement of the Hut Tax was directed against a war Chief, Bai Bureh, who in his resistance had a considerable fighting force, both of his own people and those of other Chiefs in sympathy with him, ready at his disposal. The hostility of the Timinis produced no other results than resistance against the attempts of the Government forces to make this chief a prisoner, and afterwards resistance, or attempted resistance, against their operations in laying waste the country.

174. In the Mendi country opposition to the Hut Tax showed itself at a very early period. Owing to the fact that in that country there were a few powerful Chiefs shrewd enough to perceive at the beginning that the English Government was too strong to be opposed, and owing to coercive measures taken against other Chiefs, and owing to the forces for resistance being very much less organised than in the Timini country, the tax was paid to a considerable extent, but unwillingly, and the Mendis undertook their raid at what they deemed a favourable opportunity after their injuries had been piled up and brooded over. The hostility of the Mendis found its outlet mainly in killing people who had no means of defence, and in plunder, and little in resistance to armed force, although they made one or two somewhat resolute stands.

175. The different character of the rising in the Mendi and Timini countries is due in part to the different character of the people, in part to the traditions of predatory raids among the Mendis, in part to the different circumstances which preceded the rising in the two regions. The Mendis are more relentless and revengeful than the Timinis; believing that some of their countrymen had been killed, they would seek to kill in return. There was not that long series of severities amongst the Timinis by which, week after week before the outbreak, fuel was being added to the fire against the Mendis. It was also a material circumstance that the Timini people were under a strong leader, who held them well in hand, and made them subordinate to his own plan, which has clearly appeared, as I have stated, to be merely one of resistance to the police and military forces. The Mendis do not appear to have had any strong leader, and each one, or each little group, appear to have been raiding for their own hand.

176. The Mendi raid being for revenge against the English-speaking people for their share in imposing the Hut Tax, and for plunder,

abundantly accounts for its spreading into such parts of the Colony as Sherbro, where many of the inhabitants were Sierra Leone people, and there were wealthy trading factories.

177. The insurrection was not in any degree caused by writings in the Sierra Leone press. Neither antecedently nor subsequently to the beginning of the insurrection were there incitements to resist the law. After the insurrection had gained a footing in the Timini country there were criticisms, and in some instances the language may not have been enough guarded. The circulation of newspapers in the Protectorate is so small, and so little do they come in contact with the native intellect, that even if the writings had been inflammatory, their influence with reference to these risings may be put as a negligible quantity.

178. I have formed a similar opinion as to the influence of Sierra Leone traders and other natives of Sierra Leone. Instances of Sierra Leone people speaking unwisely may have occurred, but there is very little evidence of such, and none of any general current of incitements to rebellion.

179. Concurrent with the Hut Tax and the mode of enforcing it, there were other causes of discontent felt by the Chiefs and people, amongst which may be reckoned the oppressive behaviour of members of the Frontier Police (apart from the Hut Tax troubles), and the diminution of the Chiefs' jurisdiction, the lowering of their status by the arbitrary appointment by the Government of men as Chiefs having no right, according to native law or usage, to the position, the clauses of the first Protectorate Ordinance for the appropriating and giving away of lands, the repeal of which was never sufficiently explained. There is no reason to think that these, or any other concurrent grievances, would have brought about the insurrection, apart from the overmastering grievance of the Hut Tax with its implied meaning and the incidents connected with it.

180. In the course of this Report it has been my duty to point out many grave errors—errors which, by their joint operation, have been the cause of this deplorable insurrection. I have done so with much regret. If I could have found that the insurrection was the result of an inevitable conflict between ancient barbarism and an advancing civilisation, I would willingly have taken this view, but to have done this would not have been consistent with the faithful discharge of the Commission with which I have been entrusted . . .

. . . 18. *Administration Through Chiefs.*

189. If the scheme of the administration of the Hinterland by Magistrates be discarded, as I think it must be, I come to that which appears to me to be the only practicable alternative—a regulated administration through the Chiefs, coming back thus to the schemes

which was originally proposed and sanctioned. The native organisation is one to which the people are accustomed, and are prepared to pay respect, which is suited to them, and capable, with some guidance and control, of keeping the peace and doing substantial justice. It must be admitted that such a scheme is handicapped in respect that matters are not entire: it would be necessary to go back and undo some things as well as to endeavour to guide others into the situation they would have occupied if the measures I advocate had been taken some years ago. But I do not think that the task is an impossible one if undertaken by some one having organising ability, willing to take trouble in building up peacefully, and not biassed by prepossessions drawn from the recent past. The measures to be adopted can now, of course, only be stated in brief outline, and subject to elaboration and amendment. The leading principle must be to bring back and strengthen the confidence of the Chiefs in the English government, and their sense of loyalty and dependence upon it.

190. With this view, in the first place, I would endeavour to remove the causes of irritation connected with the police. At once I would do away with the small police posts or stations, weeding out from the force all but the very best of the non-commissioned officers and men employed at these posts by offering them their discharge and giving them all practicable facilities for employment in the Congo State, or elsewhere, away from Sierra Leone. Thus some reduction on the numbers and cost of the Frontier Police would be effected. The only reservation would be of such police posts, if any, as it might be necessary to retain, to prevent smuggling on the frontiers. The men on such posts should be frequently changed and absolutely prohibited from interfering with questions between natives . . .

[The Force might be further reduced by absorbing part of it in the West African Regiment, leaving only detachments of fifty to eighty men at the station of each District Commissioner.]

But as it became practicable, as with proper management I believe that in a short time it would be, to use the authority of the Chiefs themselves, if necessary, against a recalcitrant brother, it would be very soon advisable to withdraw these detachments from all places within moderately ready access from Freetown, or other centre, where there would always be a reserve of perfectly mobile troops in the highest state of discipline and efficiency . . .

191. The principle of the scheme I suggest, so far as concerns the Frontier Police, is that they should cease altogether from taking part in the ordinary administration of the Protectorate, and that they should be stationed at such places, and kept in such state of preparation and discipline, that a force could be detailed and sent rapidly to any point where their services were required. Perhaps it might be advisable for

a time to place garrisons near the Liberian frontier or other parts where there may be a risk either of internal disturbance or attack from outside. Since the defence of Freetown, as an Imperial coaling station, concerns the Empire, as does also that of the whole of Sierra Leone, the Imperial Government might arrange that the West African Regiment (or its Houssa or other substitute) might furnish the requisite detachments, and thus the need for the Colony keeping up a large Frontier Police would be still further diminished. The Civil Police work of the Protectorate would be done by the Chiefs, with the help perhaps of a very small number of messengers attached to the establishment of the District Commissioners. These messengers should be picked men for intelligence, honesty, and discretion, and act under carefully drawn up rules.

44

SIR FREDERIC CARDEW: OBSERVATIONS
ON THE CHALMERS' REPORT,
SIERRA LEONE INSURRECTION, 1 MAY 1899[1]

. . . 17. *Administration through the Chiefs.*

172. The Royal Commissioner advises: (1) A regulated administration through the Chiefs; (2) The entire withdrawal of the Frontier Force, and the merging of that force in the West African Regiment; and (3) The civil police work to be done by the chiefs, with the help, perhaps, of a very small number of messengers attached to the establishment of the District Commissioners.

173. From the time of the inception of a Protectorate it has always been the idea of the Government to rule through the Chiefs; the Ordinance was framed on this basis, and the principle has been put in practice, but with the necessary supervision by the District Commissioners and Frontier Police, for if this were not done and the chiefs left to carry out their own administration without interference, the Police being entirely withdrawn, I think it may be safely predicted that there would be a return of intertribal squabbles which, however much they might be kept from resulting in acts of war on any large scale by the military force proposed by the Royal Commissioner at the headquarters of each District Commissioner, would be constantly occurring, and occasionally leading to the raiding of some towns or village by one party or other of the combatants,

[1] *Parl. Papers*, 1899, lx [C. 9388], pp, 123-4. Chamberlain decided to continue with a reduced hut tax: Chamberlain to the Officer Administering Sierra Leone, 7 July 1899.

besides slave dealing would certainly become more rife, even extending it may be to slave raiding, and the extortion of the chiefs through the woman palavers would increase.

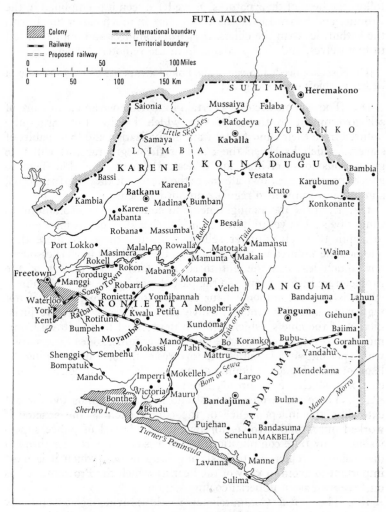

Map 3. Sierra Leone, 1912

174. I think it would be a very retrograde step to relegate the administration of the Protectorate to the chiefs without supplying proper supervision over them, which I do not think the scheme of the Royal Commissioner sufficiently provides. The history of West Africa under the administration of its chiefs has been all along one of slavery,

oppression and wrong. In saying this I do not wish to be hard or unjust towards the chiefs of the Protectorate, of whom I know nearly all, and of whom I have many kindly recollections, but they will follow the bent of their natures, as we have seen it exemplified in the Frontier and Sierra Leone trader, who are in much closer touch with the authorities than the chiefs, they *will* domineer and oppress if left to themselves, and that particularly in the remoter districts . . .

[Outposts are needed to watch the boundaries; civil police work cannot be left to chiefs or messengers.]

183. The scheme accords a certain independence and a measure of self-government to the chiefs for which I think they are quite unfitted from their almost total want of civilization and their habits of slavery, which has been the curse of the negro race. It will take generations to so civilize and educate them as to enable them to govern properly their own affairs, in the meantime they need a paternal and just government to regulate and order them.

184. Even the most enlightened and educated negro communities cannot be said as yet to have reached such a state of advancement as to acquit themselves under self-government—there are more than one notable failures in this respect in the world as object lessons—how much less can the untutored and uncivilized natives of the Protectorate be fitted for even the partial measure of self-government which is now recommended for them, a measure too, which if not regulated—and that would involve an interference with the jurisdiction of the chiefs, which is much deprecated by the Royal Commissioner—would reinstate the barbarous criminal code of the natives which permits such cruelties and tortures as the ordeal of dipping the hand of the offender in boiling oil and the drinking of poisoned concoctions, which I have already referred to.

185. There are strong political and military grounds too for not extending the independence of the chiefs, such as the scheme if worked out would involve, for by the withdrawal of police supervision at any time complications might arise on the frontier through dissensions of chiefs or their slaving propensities, which it is most important to avoid in view of the bearing which the Protectorate has on Freetown as an imperial coaling station.

186. The Royal Commissioner would provide against this by stationing troops at the headquarters of the various districts, but without outposts or patrols. I may mention that the areas of these districts are wide, the distances long and communications slow owing to the different nature of the country, and that if timely information were not brought of actions tending to disturbance, which could best be done by detached posts and patrols from the police or the troops, the disturbance itself might break forth and spread

dangerously before the troops could be pushed up to the scene of action for its suppression.

187. In concluding my observations under this heading, I would submit that if the Royal Commissioner's scheme were adopted any hope of collecting revenue direct from the chiefs or natives, such as hut tax, or tribute, or voluntary contributions, would, in my opinion, be utterly futile, for the withdrawal of the police would be immediately construed by the chiefs as a surrender, and I doubt whether all the coaxing in the world would get anything out of them, and then it would become a problem as to what is to be done for a revenue to meet the growing expenditure of the Colony, a problem which the Royal Commissioner has, I think, by no means solved in his report.

45

EDWARD WINGFIELD TO THE TREASURY: TRANSFER OF NIGER COMPANY TERRITORY, 6 JUNE 1899[1]

[Royal Niger Company territories will be divided between the Niger Coast Protectorate and Northern Nigeria.]

Customs Union.

5. THE Customs Tariffs of Lagos and Southern Nigeria will be assimilated, and goods on which duty has been paid in either division will be free to pass into the other or into Northern Nigeria, except that the importation of trade spirits into Northern Nigeria will be absolutely prohibited. It is already prohibited there by the Royal Niger Company, in accordance with the provisions of the General Act of the Brussels Conference (1889–90) by which the Powers agreed to prohibit the importation of spirits into parts of Africa where, either on account of religious belief or from other motives, the use of distilled liquors did not exist or had not been developed. The preventive service in Northern Nigeria will be carried out by the military forces. As it will not be possible to determine precisely what proportion of the Customs revenue is derived from the duties on goods for consumption in Northern Nigeria, it is proposed that the Customs receipts should be allotted to the three divisions in such proportions as the Secretary of State may from time to time direct, having regard to the requirements both of the divisions on the coast and of the inland division.

[1] C.O. 879/58, no. 591.

Compensation to the Company.

6. With regard to the compensation to be paid to the Company on the revocation of their Charter, Mr. Chamberlain understands that the arrangement which has been made by their Lordships with the Company is as follows:

(a) The Company will assign to the Government the benefits of all its treaties, and all its land and mining rights. It will retain all its plant, trading assets, stations, buildings, wharves, workshops, sites, except as hereafter provided.

(b) The Government will assume the Niger debt of £250,000, and will pay within one month of the revocation of the Charter £450,000 for settlement of all accounts to date, and will impose a royalty on minerals exported from ports in what are now the Company's territories, of which the Company shall for 99 years receive one half (but not less than 2½ per cent., unless the Secretary of State shall consider that a less rate is requisite for the development of the mining industry).

(c) The Government will take over so much of the Company's war materials and administrative buildings as may be fit for the public service, according to a schedule to be approved by the Government not later than two months before the revocation of the Charter; and the Government will be entitled to take over so much of the Company's plant, including steamers, buildings and land at stations, wharves, slips, workshops, &c., as the Government may select.

7. It is understood that the Company also claim that the Government should either compensate or find other employment for those members of the Company's staff in London, five in number, who have been employed on the administrative as distinguished from the trading business and are not willing to take service in West Africa.

8. The estimates which have been prepared by Sir Ralph Moor and Colonel Lugard for the purpose of the Company's war materials and administrative buildings and plant (including steamers, buildings and land at stations, wharves, slips, workshops, &c.) have already been sent to you in the letter from this Department of the 9th May. The value of the buildings &c., to be purchased for Southern Nigeria is estimated at £78,645, and that of those to be purchased for Northern Nigeria at £42,113, making £120,758 in all . . .

[The actual revenue for Lagos, Niger Coast Protectorate, and Royal Niger Company territories for 1897 was £424,648; the estimated revenue for 1899 is £432,365.]

46

W. BRANDFORD GRIFFITH: MEMORANDUM, JURISDICTION IN ASHANTI, 9 AUGUST 1899[1]

9. I WILL now deal with my second contention. I admit that to any one not intimately acquainted with the conditions on the Gold Coast to apply to new territories the entire legal system of the Colony must seem unsatisfactory. But there is a most important fact to be borne in mind. Alongside our Courts are native courts with indefinite, but unlimited, jurisdiction—except in the case of the few courts which have been brought under the Native Jurisdiction Ordinance. In Accra, Cape Coast, Axim, and all the coast towns, as well as inland, native tribunals sit and deal with cases; to many tribunals are attached authorised prisons (see p. 1136 of Revised Ordinances). On the coast their powers are on the wane, but inland they deal with the majority of cases only the more important matters being brought before English Courts. Further inland only cases of murder and the most important land cases are brought to the English Courts, the native courts dealing with all other cases. Although Kwahu is part of a district under the Supreme Court Ordinance, there has not been for the last six months a single case brought from there either to the District Commissioner's Court or to the Divisional Court; there having been no Resident District Commissioner, the native courts have dealt with all the cases that have arisen. In Sefwhi there has been of late a District Commissioner, but his work has been of the smallest dimension, the great majority of the cases being taken to the native courts. Of course when a District Commissioner is permanently established at these places, the court work will rapidly drift from the native to the English Court, and the District Commissioner can then be given larger jurisdiction (as at Wassaw) so as to avoid the necessity for any but important cases being brought to the Divisional Court. For years Kwahu and Sefwhi, and other outlying posts have been under our entire legal system, but have experienced no ill effects, as they have been also under their original native legal system, which has done practically all the work.

I quite admit that it is unsatisfactory to have two legal systems in force, but the answer to that argument is that the whole uncivilized state of things on the Gold Coast is unsatisfactory, and that it is only by very gradual advance that we can hope to civilize. The native courts were formerly the only courts to which the natives had access, and they were better than no courts; now any native can, if he chooses,

[1] C.O. 96/342.

have the benefit of the English Courts, but as these latter are often at a great distance, the native has recourse in minor matters to his original native Court. And, too, these native Courts exist and are made use of in the coast towns.

What applies to Sefwhi applies *a fortiori* to Ashanti, which is nearer; it applies also to posts more inland; the native Courts in such inland post would go on with their jurisdiction until such time as we could introduce English Courts in their midst, then they might be regulated or might be allowed to die out.

47

ORDER IN COUNCIL: BOUNDARIES
AND ADMINISTRATION IN NORTHERN
NIGERIA, 27 DECEMBER 1899[1]

[Recital of the powers and responsibilities of the Royal Niger Company.]

Now, therefore, Her Majesty, by virtue and in exercise of the powers by 'The Foreign Jurisdiction Act, 1890,' or otherwise in Her Majesty vested, is pleased, by and with the advice of Her Privy Council, to order, and it is hereby ordered, as follows:—

1. This Order may be cited as the 'Northern Nigeria Order in Council, 1899.'

2. The limits of this Order are the territories of Africa bounded by the following line, namely, a line commencing at the point of intersection of the River Okpara with the 9th degree of north latitude, and then proceeding in a northerly direction along a line passing west of the lands belonging to the following places, viz., Tabira, Okuta (Okouta), Boria, Tere, Gbani, Ashigere (Yassikéra), and Dekala. From the most westerly point of the lands belonging to Dekala the line runs in a northerly direction, coinciding as far as possible with the line indicated on the map marked No. 1, which is attached to the Convention with France of the 14th of June, 1898, and striked the right bank of the Niger at a point situated 10 miles (16,093 metres) up stream from the centre of the town of Gere (Guiris) (the port of Ilo), measured as the crow flies. From this point the line runs at right angles to the right bank of the Niger as far as its intersection with the median line of the river. It then follows the median line of the river, up-stream, as far as its intersection with a line drawn perpendicularly to the left bank from the median line of the mouth of the depression or dry watercourse, called Dallul Mauri, situated at a distance of about 17 miles (27,359 metres), measured as the crow flies, from a point on the left bank opposite the above-mentioned village of Gere

[1] Hertslet, *Commercial Treaties*, vol. xviii (1893), pp. 250–7.

(Guiris). From this point of intersection the line follows this per-pendicular till it meets the left bank of the river, and then follows the median line of the Dallul Mauri until it meets the circumference of a circle drawn from the centre of the town of Sokoto with a radius of 100 miles (160,932 metres). From this point it follows the northern arc of this circle as far as its second interesection with the 14th parallel of north latitude. From this second point of intersection it follows this parallel eastward for a distance of 70 miles (112,652 metres); then proceeds due south until it reaches the parallel of 13° 20' north latitude, then eastward along this parallel for a distance of 250 miles (402,230 metres); then due north until it regains the 14th parallel of north latitude; then eastwards along this parallel as far as its intersection with the meridian passing 35' east of the centre of the town of Kuka, and thence this meridian southward until its inter-section with the southern shore of Lake Chad. From this point the line goes direct to the point of intersection of the 13th degree of longitude east of Greenwich and the 10th degree of north latitude, and thence in a south-easterly direction to a point on the left or southern bank of the River Benue, which it crosses 5 kilometres below the centre of the main mouth of the Faro River. Thence the line follows south of the Benue, the circumference of a circle, the centre of which is the centre of the town of Yola as it existed in 1893, and the radius of which is the distance between the centre of the town of Yola and the point on the left bank of the Benue 5 kilometres below the centre of the main mouth of the Faro River, until the circum-ference meets a straight line drawn from the point on the right bank of the Old Calabar or Cross River, marked 'Rapids' in the English Admiralty Chart, direct towards the centre of the town of Yola. It then follows that line in a south-westerly direction to a point near Ashaku, whence it runs west to Idda on the Niger, leaving Takum to the north. From Idda which it leaves to the south, the line runs west to Owo, leaving to the south the Benin territories, and then northward to the frontier of the Kabba district, whence it passes westward through Aiedi, Awton, and Illa, leaving to the north the towns subject to Ilorin and to the south the towns subject to Ibadan or Oyo. Thence it runs in a north-westerly direction along the frontier of Ilorin, past Odo Otin and Ikirun, both of which it leaves to the south, until the frontier of Ilorin meets the 9th parallel of north latitude. It then runs west, leaving all Borgu towns to the north and all Yoruba towns to the south, as far as the point of intersection of the Okpara River with the 9th parallel of north latitude.

The territories so bounded shall be known as Northern Nigeria . . .

4. Her Majesty may appoint a High Commissioner for Northern Nigeria, and such High Commissioner may, on Her Majesty's behalf, exercise all powers and jurisdiction which Her Majesty, at

any time before or after the date of this Order, had, or may have, within Northern Nigeria, and to that end may take, or cause to be taken, all such measures, and may do, or cause to be done, all such matters and things therein as are lawful, and as in the interest of Her Majesty's service he may think expedient, subject to such instructions as he may from time to time receive from Her Majesty, or through a Secretary of State.

5. Subject to the approval of a Secretary of State, the High Commissioner may appoint so many fit persons as, in the interest of Her Majesty's service, he may think necessary to be Deputy Commissioners, Residents, Assistant Residents, Judges, Magistrates, or other officers, and may define from time to time the districts within which such officers shall respectively discharge their functions . . .

[The High Commissioner shall issue Proclamations for administration, respecting native law and custom, subject to approval; he shall exercise a grant of pardon; the provisions of the Africa Order in Council, 1889, cease to apply to Northern Nigeria.]

48

GOVERNOR F. M. HODGSON: PUBLIC PALAVER AT KUMASI, 28 MARCH 1900[1]

THE Kings and Chiefs having been presented by the Resident to the Governor, who spoke to each separately, the Governor addressed the meeting as follows:— . . .

The paramount authority of Ashanti is now the great Queen of England, whose representative I am at this moment. In order that the powers of the King paramount may be exercised properly, inasmuch as the seat of the Government is far away at the Coast, it is necessary to place here a white officer, who bears the title of 'Resident.' Under the Governor the Resident at Kumasi exercises the powers of King paramount. You know perfectly well what those powers are, but for a moment I should like to refer to them. You know perfectly well that with the entry of the British Government into Ashanti the power of making human sacrifices ceased; that your lives are now safe. You have only to advise the white officer who is resident in Kumassi when there is any danger, and you have the strong arm of the British Government to defend you. There is one other matter that came to an end at the same time, that was the buying and selling of human beings as if they were cattle or bales of goods. In all countries of the Queen everybody is free. Now what are the powers which were formerly

[1] C.O. 879/62, no. 623. Encl. in Hodgson to Chamberlain, 7 April 1900. For the Ashanti uprising, see Kimble, *Political History of Ghana*, pp. 317–19.

exercised by the King paramount which the Government now exercises. You will recollect that whenever there was any fighting to be done the King paramount had the power of calling out the young men to come and assist him. The Queen is not likely to solicit your assistance in that way. But the Queen reserves to herself the right of calling out the men of the tribes for peaceful purposes, for example, to serve as carriers, to make roads, and to build houses. Then, again, the King paramount had the power when there was any great enterprise on hand to call his Council together, and say that he wanted to carry out such and such an enterprise, and the cost of it had to be provided for in such proportions as are well known to you all by the heads of the tribes. Now the British Government has been in charge here for four years, and it has not as yet disturbed you with any request for money. Why is that? If your country had been conquered by a stronger tribe than all of you put together, you know what would have happened to you—you would have been required to pay a heavy tribute, such as your wealth would enable you to pay. Why, then, has the great Queen not disturbed you, and asked you for money? Because she knew that many of the tribes had been driven out of their country, and wished all of you to have time to return to your country and rebuild your villages, and to get accustomed to the kind of life which you are able to lead under British rule. You know by this time what the state of things is under the British Government. You have had four years of it, and I venture to say that if you were to speak out what is in your hearts you would say that you do not want to return to the old dissensions among yourselves, and that, in fact, you do not want to return to the old state of things.

Now you will recollect that after the war was conducted on our side by Sir Garnet Wolseley there was a treaty signed at Fomena. In that treaty was a clause in which you Ashanti Chiefs undertook to pay to the British Government a sum of 50,000 ounces of gold—25,000 pereguins. To that sum has to be added the expenses incurred in connection with the last expedition, which amounted also to upwards of 25,000 pereguins. I daresay you are wondering amongst yourselves what I am going to say next. Some of you are saying amongst yourselves, Is the Governor going to ask us to pay the money down at one time? To this I say, No, but what I am going to say to you is this, that there must be paid annually to the Resident a sum which will be called interest on this expenditure by the British Government. You must understand this also, that in order to provide you with the protection which the British Government can give you, namely, security to your lives and peace among yourselves, there is a large annual expenditure of money by the British Government. The sum to be paid as interest is 2,000 pereguins . . .

49

JOSEPH CHAMBERLAIN TO GOVERNOR
MAJOR NATHAN: ASHANTI JURISDICTION,
5 FEBRUARY 1901[1]

I HAVE the honour to call your attention to the confidential despatch
which I addressed to Sir Frederic Hodgson on the 19th of February,
1900,[2] with regard to the question of the exercise of jurisdiction in
Ashanti and other territories near or adjacent to the Colony of the
Gold Coast.

2. Owing, no doubt, to the events which occurred shortly afterwards in Ashanti, I have received no reply to that despatch. In the
meantime, however, the question of jurisdiction in Ashanti has been
raised at the trial of the European manager and two native assistants
of the Ashanti Goldfields Corporation, on a charge of torturing persons
in order to obtain evidence in connection with a robbery which had
been committed at the Obassi mines, when the Supreme Court
decided that it had jurisdiction in Ashanti and heard the cases; but
on the 12th of March, 1900, Sir F. Hodgson issued an Order of the
Governor in Council, under section 20 (a) of the Supreme Court
Ordinance, excluding Ashanti from the jurisdiction of the Court. The
Northern Territories had previously been excluded from the jurisdiction of the Court by a similar Order, made on the 23rd of February,
1900.

3. The present state of the case, therefore, is that the Supreme
Court has no jurisdiction in Ashanti or the Northern Territories; but
I understand that it is regarded in the Colony as having jurisdiction
in Sefwhi and Kwahu, which have been formally, but (as it now
appears) without due authority, included in the Protected Territories,
as they existed when the Order of the Queen in Council, of the 29th
of December, 1887, was made, to which the name of 'Colony' was
given by the Statute Law Revision Ordinance, 1895. I should mention, in passing, that this Ordinance has been repealed, but that the
definition of 'Colony', which it enacted, has been inserted in section 8
of the Interpretation Ordinance, 1876, as printed in the edition of the
Gold Coast Laws which was published in 1898.

4. I now transmit to you a copy of a memorandum which the
Chief Justice (Sir W. Brandford Griffith) submitted to me when he
was on leave of absence in this country last year.[3] You will see that
Sir B. Griffith argues strongly against the proposal that this definition
of 'Colony' should be repealed; and, in view of the difficulty if not
impossibility, of determining precisely the limits of the territories

[1] C.O. 879/67, no. 649.
[2] Metcalfe, *Great Britain and Ghana*, no. 428.   [3] Above, no. 46.

which have already been annexed to the dominions of the Crown, and of the practical difficulties which, as he points out, would arise if the territories which have been treated as forming part of the Colony were now to be declared to be a protectorate, I have come to the conclusion that the necessary steps should be taken to effect the formal annexation of the Protected Territories, as they existed on the 29th of December, 1887, to His Majesty's dominions. The result will be that the natives of these territories will become British subjects, and therefore subject to the provisions of the Acts of the Imperial Parliament relating to slavery and slave dealing, but I understand that under the operation of the Ordinances which were passed in 1874, slavery and dealing in slaves have practically been abolished in these territories, and that no difficulty is likely to arise on that account. Moreover, I am assured by Sir F. Hodgson that the natives are ready for annexation, and that no trouble need be anticipated if the state of affairs which they regard as already existing *de facto* is now established *de jure*.

5. Sir F. Hodgson is, however, of opinion that it would be advisable, at present, to include Sefwhi and Kwahu in the Colony, and it would certainly not be advisable to include the Northern Territories; but with regard to Ashanti it is not clear to me what course would be best. You will observe that in the 14th paragraph of my despatch of the 19th of February, 1900, I stated that I had come to the conclusion that it would not be advisable to extend to Ashanti the system in force in the Protected Territories, and I suggested that the Resident should be entrusted with judicial as well as executive powers, but that it should be provided that certain cases or clauses of cases, and cases relating to concessions certainly, might, with the concurrence of the Governor, be referred by the Resident to the Supreme Court for trial. Since then the war has taken place, and Ashanti has been conquered. The effect will be, no doubt, to make the people ready to acquiesce in whatever form of Government may be decided upon, and, having regard to the large gold-mining operations which are now in progress, and which will increase when the railway is completed to Coomassie, I am inclined to think that Ashanti should be annexed to the Colony, provided that this could be done without injustice to the chiefs and peoples who remained loyal during the war, and without risk of difficulties in connexion with the abolition of slavery. The matter is, however, one requiring very full and careful consideration, and I shall come to no conclusion until I have your views before me after you have visited the country and consulted with the Resident. It is also a question, upon which I desire to have your opinion, whether it would not be convenient that Kwahu, Sefwhi, and British Gaman, should be included for administrative purposes in Ashanti.

6. Meanwhile, I have had drafts prepared of the following instruments:

(A.) An Order in Council annexing to His Majesty's dominions the 'Protected Territories.'

(B.) An Order in Council providing for the government of Sefwhi and British Gaman.

(C.) An Order in Council providing for the government of Kwahu.

(D.) An Order in Council providing for the government of Ashanti.

(E.) Instructions to the Governor of the Gold Coast with reference to the administration of Ashanti.

(F.) An Order in Council providing for the administration of the Northern Territories.

(G.) Instructions to the Governor of the Gold Coast with reference to the administration of the Northern Territories.

(H.) An Order in Council revoking the Order of the Queen in Council of the 29th of December, 1887, but providing that acts done under its provisions shall be valid. Copies of these drafts are enclosed, but as the arrangements contemplated when they were prepared may have to be modified, I do not propose to proceed further with them until I have learnt your views.

7. I am anxious, however, to have the descriptions of the boundaries revised with as little delay as possible. The descriptions which have been inserted provisionally in the drafts are based upon the Order of the Governor in Council, dated the 9th of March, 1900, a copy of which was enclosed in Sir F. Hodgson's despatch, No. 280, of the 3rd of August last; but it is obvious that they require revision, and it is especially important in view of the questions likely to be raised in connexion with concessions, that the limits of Ashanti should be clearly defined.

50

GOVERNOR MAJOR NATHAN TO JOSEPH CHAMBERLAIN: ASHANTI JURISDICTION, 6 FEBRUARY 1901[1]

. . . 3. THE only divergence of opinion between the Chief Justice and myself was that he considered that it should be laid down in the draft for Ashanti that the Native Courts of that country should administer justice in criminal matters in accordance with the Criminal Code of the Colony, so that we should not have two sets of laws

[1] C.O. 879/67, no. 649. (*Sir*) *Matthew Nathan*, Acting Governor of Sierra Leone, 1899, Governor of the Gold Coast, 1900–3.

working alongside each other in the same country. It appeared to me that were this laid down it could not be practically enforced, and that it would be better that the jurisdiction heretofore exercised by native tribunals, and the manner in which such jurisdiction has been heretofore exercised by them, in accordance with native laws and customs, should be recognized and regulated, than that a Code should be forced on the Chiefs and people which they would, at any rate, at first, but imperfectly understand, and which would not be adhered to without constant interference with the native tribunals by the Resident. The restrictions imposed in the draft on the parties, and offences with which the native Courts are competent to deal (Clause 17 (1) and (2), and the facts that appeal lies from them to the Resident's Courts (Clause 18), and that the Resident can remove any case he thinks fit from the Native Tribunals (Clause 19) should be sufficient to prevent any gross abuse of their powers. In time it is probable that the natives will sufficiently appreciate the Criminal Code, as it will be administered in the Resident's Courts, for them to bring all their criminal cases to those Courts. When this happens we shall have to face the difficulties brought about by the native chiefs ceasing to have power, and, therefore, ceasing to be of use in the administration of the country.

4. Clause 17 (3) of the Proclamation for Ashanti, which takes away from certain tribunals their jurisdiction in land matters, and specially limits their jurisdiction in other civil matters, has been drafted with a view to the punishment of those chiefs, towns, or districts that recently made war against us, and of any that may seriously misbehave in the future. The Schedule referred to in the Clause will be made out after consultation with the Resident.

5. Clause 56 of the draft for Ashanti, originally submitted by the Attorney-General, which it has not appeared necessary to send to you, but which is referred to in the Chief Justice's Minute of 19th January, 1901, deals with the case of disaffected chiefs, as follows:

'Any chief who shall be ordered by the Governor either directly or by a deputy or messenger to do or refrain from doing any public act or acts, and shall either defy or neglect promptly to obey such order, shall be guilty of an offence, and on conviction shall be liable to a fine not exceeding ten pounds, or imprisonment with or without hard labour for a term not exceeding three months.'

The definition of the offence and the nature of the punishment, as embodied in this Clause, did not appear suitable, and I am disposed to concur in the view of the Chief Justice that the power of restricting a chief's jurisdiction (Clauses 17 (3, and 20)) is sufficient power of punishment to insert in the original Ashanti Proclamation. It must be borne in mind in connection with this matter of punishing disaffected chiefs, and also in connection with their deposition and banishment

referred to by the Chief Justice in his Minute that the power of the
Governor to legislate directly by Proclamation would enable him to
deal quickly with any case that might arise with regard to which
existing Proclamations gave him imperfect powers . . .

51

GOVERNOR MAJOR NATHAN TO
JOSEPH CHAMBERLAIN: ASHANTI
ADMINISTRATION, 6 MARCH 1901[1]

. . . 2. ASHANTI should be divided into four districts, to be called
the Central, Southern, North-Eastern, and North-Western districts.
The Central district should include the towns, villages, and lands
directly under Kumasi, and those under Ejisu (spelt Atwiso, on
I.D.W.O., map No. 1097), Juabin, Bompata, Obogu, Agogo,
Kumawu, Manpon, Insuta, Aguna, Ofinso (spelt Ofesu on the map)
and Atchima. The district as now proposed contains the Central
and Eastern districts as recommended by Sir Frederic Hodgson, and
also Aguna, Insuta, and Mampon, from his Northern district. It
embraces the politically most important part of the country. The
inclusion in it of Sir Frederic Hodgson's Eastern district will not
add much to the work of administering it as this part is easily accessible
from Kumassi, and is not one giving much trouble.

The Southern district should include Dengiasi, Bekwai, Kokofu,
Adadum, and Adansi. This is the Southern district, as recommended
by Sir Frederic Hodgson, and in addition Dengiasi from his Western
district. It embraces the part of the country where the gold mining is
at present most developed.

The North-Western district should include British Gaman,
Wanki, Tekiman, Berekum, Wam, and Ahafu. It embraces the
British Gaman, the Northern half of the Western, and the Western
part of the Northern districts proposed by Sir Frederic Hodgson as
well as the Wam and Ahafu countries, which he included in Sefwhi.
It has some trade importance, and abuts on the French Boundary.

The North-Eastern district should include Nkoranza, Attabubu,
and Abiassi. It only embraces part of Sir Frederic Hodgson's
Northern district, but its area is, nevertheless, as extensive as that of
the other districts now proposed. It will be of considerable trade
importance, and abuts on the German Boundary.

The above divisions are shown, as far as our present knowledge of
the ownership of villages, and the doubtful accuracy of the Intelligence
Department map allow, on the copy of that map forwarded herewith;
the northern boundaries of the North-Western and North-Eastern

[1] C.O. 879/67, no. 649.

districts being the 8th parallel of latitude, where they abut on the Northern Territories, and the boundary between the two districts being the main road north to Kintampo.

3. Kumassi would, of course, be the headquarters of the Central district.

I propose that the headquarters of the Southern district should be at the post in the Moinsi Hills, which Colonel Sir James Willcocks recommended to command the Adansi country. It is at a considerable elevation (1,300 feet) on the main line of communication, between Cape Coast and Kumassi, dividing nearly equally the distance between the latter place and Prahsu, and it is centrally situated with regard to the mining properties in the district. The telegraph office at Kwisa would be removed to within the post. The labour for the construction of the works and buildings should be provided free by the Adansis, as part of the punishment for their treacherous conduct of last year.

The position of the headquarters of the North-Western district will have to be selected by the Resident when he is able to visit that district. It would probably be somewhere in the neighbourhood of Wanki, where there is high ground and good water. Telegraphic communication will eventually have to be extended to whatever place is selected. The labour for the necessary buildings and defensive works of the station should be provided without payment by the people who fought against us last year in those parts, as a punishment.

Attabubu, where a medical officer, supported by 10 Hausas, has, for some time past, been exercising administrative functions under the title of the Resident at Attabubu, would probably be the best headquarters for the proposed North-Eastern district, in which it is centrally situated at the crossing of the road from Abetifi, in Kwahu, to Kintampo, in the Northern Territories, with the trade route from Nkoranza to Salaga. The telegraph to Salaga and Gambage will eventually pass along the latter road.

4. The administration of the Central district should, as proposed by Sir Frederic Hodgson, be in the hands of the Resident. He should be assisted as now, by a Cantonment Magistrate for Kumassi, but that officer should be regularly appointed, and paid at the same rate as a District Commissioner, and should not be an officer of Constabulary withdrawn from his proper duties.

The Southern district should be administered by a specially appointed district Commissioner.

The North-Western and North-Eastern districts should, for the present, be in charge of the Officers Commanding the companies of Constabulary, which will be stationed in them, or of the Medical Officers in them, in cases where these Officers may have special administrative qualifications. They would receive a duty allowance . . .

7. I have already proposed to you that 7 out of the 9 companies, and 1 out of the 2 batteries of the Gold Coast Battalion of the Gold Coast Regiment of the West African Frontier Force should be stationed North of the Prah. Four of these companies, and two-thirds of the battery should be at Kumassi, in the Central district, available to garrison that place, and furnish when required a column of 3 companies, with 2 2.95 in. and 3 .303 in. Maxim guns (about 500 men). One company with one maxim gun should be stationed in each of the other districts. That in the Southern district should, with the remainder of the artillery battery, garrison the Moinsi Hill post, and it should furnish a detachment for the protection of the mines, and of the railway survey and construction in Ashanti as long as this may be necessary. That in the North-Western district would furnish detachments at Sikassiko and Sefwi. That in the North-Eastern district would be available to furnish immediate reinforcements to the Northern Territories, in the event of emergency. With the proposed establishment of 4 officers to a company, there should never be less than 3 doing duty in each of the outlying districts, and it should be possible to avoid detachments of natives being posted anywhere without a European officer in charge.

8. The provision made by Sir Frederic Hodgson for Civil Police in his despatch above referred to is sufficient. I concur in there being a central prison at Kumassi, which already exists, but consider that there should also be prisons at the headquarters of the Southern, North-Eastern, and North-Western districts for men sentenced to imprisonment for 6 months or less. There would be a military guard over each prison, and only trifling expenditure would be involved, while the labour of the prisoners would be available for roads and other works at the station. A Foreman of Works should be available for Ashanti, and also a Telegraph Foreman.

9. The expenditure involved by the system of administration proposed above will be approximately the same as that required by the arrangements recommended by Sir Frederic Hodgson, and detailed in enclosure 2 to his despatch, except, of course, that the personal emoluments for the Constabulary will be much greater. The cost of 7 companies and 1 battery will be over £36,024, against £14,370, the cost of 3 companies, and the total cost for the administration of Ashanti, including expenditure on departmental services as well as on general administration will thus amount to about £60,000 per annum . . .

52

W. LOW TO JOSEPH CHAMBERLAIN: ASHANTI, 8 MARCH 1901[1]

(Telegram.)

FOLLOWING telegram received from Governor of Gold Coast, Kumasi:

Telegram begins: Propose, after consultation with Resident in Coomassie, who has gone carefully into each case, deportation of 17, and detention of 27, leaders of rising; and to issue proclamation (of) amnesty to cover all offenders, with exception (of) those persons in custody, which include murderers of Branscombe and others, and, except a few chiefs not yet arrested, who will be mentioned by name. Propose that tribute referred to in my predecessor's despatch of 7th April, should be paid. All the chiefs here, including most in country, have acquiesced in this to Resident in Coomassie. I do not propose additional tribute for last year's war, but that rebel tribes should be punished for this by not being allowed to carry guns, and by being forced to provide free labour for additional barracks and military posts, rendered necessary in their districts by their conduct. Propose to fill all vacant stools with men duly elected and recommended to me by Resident in Coomassie, as these essential for administration of country, and do not propose any alteration in ownership of lands. Most important points should be decided before departure of myself (from) Kumasi. Please telegraph if approved as soon as possible.

NATHAN.

53

GOVERNOR SIR WILLIAM MacGREGOR TO JOSEPH CHAMBERLAIN: LAGOS BOUNDARY, 9 APRIL 1901[2]

I HAVE the honour to enclose herewith a rough sketch map prepared by Mr. L. Cecil Woodman, representing the High Commissioner of Southern Nigeria, and by Mr. Gerald Ambrose, Travelling Commissioner of this Colony, on which is shown the boundary recommended by these two officers between Lagos and Southern Nigeria.

2. It will be seen that the boundary proposed begins at Ogbo on the coast, and proceeds thence in a straight line in a north-easterly

---

[1] C.O. 879/67, no. 649. *William Low,* Gold Coast Colonial Secretary. Some forty-six Ashanti leaders were sent down to the coast and fifteen to join Prempeh in exile in the Seychelles.

[2] C.O. 879/58, no. 580. *Sir William MacGregor,* Governor of Lagos, 1899–1904.

direction till it reaches the junction of Lagos Creek with the Addabrussa Creek; thence it follows the 'Unnamed Creek' to Siluko, thence ascends the Ofusa-Owena to the junction of the Owena with the Ofusa, then follows the Ofusa till it cuts the boundary line that proceeds nearly due east from Akure to Owo.

3. I have had an opportunity of considering this boundary with Sir Ralph Moor; and I concur with him in recommending the boundary as described above for your sanction.

54

HIGH COMMISSIONER SIR F. D. LUGARD TO COLONIAL OFFICE: NORTHERN NIGERIA, 1 MAY 1901[1]

... NATIVE courts, under the supervision of residents are gradually being formed. Mr. Hewby, in the Upper Benue province, has been especially successful, and has set up a native court in most of the larger towns of his province. He receives regular reports of the cases tried, and informs me that very fair justice is done. The Assistant Resident in Illorin assures me that the public slave market there is now a thing of the past, and that great improvement is visible in the methods of trial, and the sentences inflicted by the new native court. There was much unrest in this province during the absence of the troops, but I hope that substantial progress is being made. Borgu has improved greatly during our occupation. The able chief, Kiama, is making roads in every direction, which he frequently superintends himself. The small patch of country on the east of the Niger, in the neighbourhood of the Dalul Mauri, has recently been occupied by troops, a course rendered necessary by French aggression, and the raids of the Fulani from Raha. I have instructed the Officer Commanding to punish the latter. There is no resident in the Bassa province, which, I am informed, is a very important one from a trade point of view, and the people have expressed great eagerness for a white man to live among them and settle their differences without recourse to intertribal warfare. The deficiency of staff has, however, prevented my taking this district in hand and assuring the safety of the roads for traders. The Gwari district belongs rather to the coming than to the past year. It contains many large pagan towns, from which I hope to obtain a cheap labour supply for work on the new cantonments, and I am using every effort to avoid the introduction into this new centre of the preposterous labour rates which have obtained on the Niger, and which hamper all development and progress.

[1] C.O. 879/58, no. 580.

Vide infra.) In the Lower Benue Major Burdon[1] and (later) Dr. Cargill have made some progress in cultivating the friendship of the Munshi tribe, and also with the Fulani sub-emirate of Nassarawa and Keffi. Slave-raiding by the Mohammedan chiefs still continues, and produces continual unrest among the neighbouring pagan tribes, with the usual reprisals and closing of trade routes. I anticipate that this will cease without any recourse to drastic measures, as soon as I can place a small garrison at Nassarawa and establish the Resident there, but the telegraph line must first be made. The trade routes to the Lower Benue will then be free from danger. During the past year we can hardly be said to have had any relations with Sokoto, Gando, Kano, and Katsena. A copy, in vernacular, of the proclamation announcing the transfer was sent to Sokoto, and my messenger was treated with indignity. The annual subsidy payable to these chiefs under the treaties of the Royal Niger Company would, I presume, fall due on January 1st, 1901—a year after His Majesty's Government had taken over their obligation. It has not yet been paid, and, in view of the unfriendly attitude of these Emirs, I have had some hesitation as to whether it should be continued. I understand Sir G. Goldie to say that, had the Company continued to administer, the subsidy would have been discontinued. If, however, the Crown rights to minerals are dependent upon the payment of this sum, it would, of course, be advisable to send it, and for this reason no repudiation of the obligation, which would vitiate the contract, has been made. It is merely three months over-due. I have, however, strongly expressed my view that all minerals throughout the Protectorate should be declared by proclamation to be the property of the Crown. A prophecy of the founder of the Fulani dynasty predicted the fall of the empire during this year, and I believe that the fatalism of these Mohammedans has prepared them to accept their destiny. So far as I can learn the vast bulk of the population—Pagans, Hausas and Mohammedan slaves—who hate the Fulani oppression, would welcome the advent of Europeans. Dr. Cargill (who speaks Hausa) even writes, 'that it is impossible to exaggerate the eagerness with which they await our coming.' The Fulani themselves, I am told, hate us rather as the Power which is destined to accomplish their fall, and to put an end to their slave-raiding and extortion, than on any religious or racial grounds. That Sokoto no longer exerts its former strength is evident from the fact that the French expeditions which have crossed British territory from Dosso to Zinder, via Konni and Maradi, have probably passed within 14 miles of Wurno, the residence of the Sultan of Sokoto, and yet the Fulani army has remained

---

[1] (*Sir*) *John Burdon*, former Commandant, Royal Niger Constabulary; Resident, Northern Nigeria, 1900; Resident, Kano and Sokoto, 1903–1910. *Dr. Cargill*, for a period Resident of Kano.

inactive. The ill-advised mission, under Bishop Tugwell,[1] served only to demonstrate the hostility of the King of Kano, but the members of the mission maintain that the ill-feeling was confined to the chief and his immediate clique. Pending the establishment of the new headquarters, I have not attempted to open up any relations with these distant Fulani emirates in the north. They still remain great centres of the slave-trade, as do also Yola and Bautshi, in the east. There is, probably, no part of the 'Dark Continent' in which the worst forms of slave raiding still exist to so terrible an extent, and are prosecuted on so large and systematic a scale as in the British possession of Northern Nigeria. Nor are they even provident of their hunting grounds, for those who are useless as slaves are killed in large numbers, the villages burnt, and the fugitives left to starve in the bush. The first great step to check this evil was taken by the Royal Niger Company in 1897, when, after the defeat of Bida, they severed from the rule of that emir all the territories south of the Niger (Kabba province). The relief came almost too late, for the country is depopulated, and hundreds of ruins attest the former existence of a population and prosperity which has gone. Deprived of their hunting grounds, and anticipating the advent of European control, with its prohibition of slave-raiding, the Fulani and Nupes began early in the year to ravage the districts nearer home, and, with Kontagora the 'Gwamachi' (destroyer), who bears the title 'King of the Sudan,' laid waste the country from the Niger banks, on the west and south, to the eastern highlands, and to the north as far as the borders of Sokoto and Zaria. At the beginning of July, information reached me that they had planned a combined attack on our small garrison at Wushishi, and I hurried thither myself with reinforcements, under Major O'Neill, Royal Artillery. The headmen of Wushishi itself were secretly murdered, and outrages on our soldiers within a few yards of camp followed. Meanwhile, the two armies raided for slaves almost to the very banks of the Niger, and close to Jebba, while messages were sent to pursuade Illorin to join in a rising, and to expel the white men, whose troops (it was said) had been exterminated in Ashanti. The people began to desert Wushishi, and the absolute necessity for obtaining supplies for our troops, and of protecting the villages which had shown us friendship, compelled me to instruct Major O'Neill to place small forts in neighbouring villages, and to patrol the country. This task he performed most ably and with great dash, defeating the horsemen of Kontagora and Bida in a series of skirmishes, and occupying the country for some 20 miles south and east of Wushishi. Great loss was inflicted on the slave raiders, and

[1] In 1900 Bishop Tugwell of the C.M.S. Niger Mission and five missionaries had prospected the North and encountered Lugard at Jebba: Perham and Bull, *Lugard*, vol. ii, p. 498.

thousands of refugees crowded the protected villages for safety, while his handful of men had hardly any casualties. Mr. Dwyer, meanwhile, managed with much tact and pluck to keep things fairly quiet in Illorin, where he had succeeded Mr. Carnegie, an officer of exceptional promise, whose sad death was a very great loss to the Protectorate. In November, I directed Major O'Neill to endeavour to clear the waterway of the Kaduna. With a small force, ably assisted by Lieutenant Porter, he defeated a band of Kontagora's levies, at Daba, and, crossing the river, he met and dispersed the gatherings of the Bida horsemen, and on December 19th pursued them to the walls of the town. With great gallantry he entered the city with only 30 men, and endeavoured to arrest the emir with his own hand. This action was, however, opposed to the definite orders he had received from me not to approach Bida. He exposed his small party to a most imminent risk of extermination, and only escaped, himself badly wounded, by the greatest good fortune. This was at a moment when such a disaster might have involved most serious consequences to the Protectorate, and when such a risk was the more unnecessary, since our troops were already arriving from Ashanti. They returned at the end of December, and I immediately gave orders for an expedition to be organised against Kontagora. Colonel Kemball, Acting Commandant, himself took command, and in the middle of January marched north, with a strong force to Ngaski, along the Niger bank. There he met Lieutenant Keyes, with a detachment from the Illo garrison. The combined force marched on Kontagora, keeping to the north of the town to prevent the escape of the chief towards Sokoto. The town was captured, and the enemy defeated, with the loss of one man on our side, while the Fulani horsemen suffered very heavily. Colonel Kemball despatched two strong parties in pursuit of the flying chief, and these compelled him to abandon all his slaves and retinue, and he only escaped with a handful of followers. The town was saved from constant attempts at incendiarism, by great efforts, during the night. A company was left as garrison, and the force marched to the Kaduna, meeting with demonstrations from the villagers, who were overjoyed at the fall of the 'Gwamachi' (destroyer). On their upward march the troops had passed through an absolutely depopulated country. On February 9th, at Egbaji, I met Mr. Wallace (who had just arrived from England) and Mr. Watts[1] of the Niger Company, who for years has been an intimate friend of the Bida chiefs, and who speaks Nupe. I had sent messengers to the Emir and all the principal chiefs of Bida to meet me there, but only the Markun's party arrived. This man was appointed emir, by the Company, after the defeat of Bida in 1897, but the ex-emir, Abu Bakri had returned and

[1] *Walter Watts* had been a Company agent, Political Agent, 1895, and Agent-General, Niger Company, 1900.

ousted the Markun, and had since been recognised as emir by the Company. I sent further messages to tell Abu Bakri to meet me on the Kaduna, whither I was proceeding, and assuring him that, no matter what the result of the interview, his return, in safety, would be guaranteed. Again, only the Markun's party met me. Colonel Kemball and his troops joined me here, and we marched on Bida prepared, if necessary, to fight. I had, however, assured the chiefs that not a shot would be fired unless I was attacked, but that all who attempted flight would be treated as enemies. Abu Bakri I could no longer recognise as emir, but if he would yet meet me at Bida, I would arrange to provide for his future in comfort. He, however, elected to fly, and was pursued for a great distance by troops sent to watch the rear of the town, towards Lapai. He barely escaped, with six followers only, while several important chiefs were wounded and captured. They were liberated later, after their wounds had been treated. The troops marched through the town in a long procession, and formed a hollow square in front of the Markun's 'palace', where I proclaimed him emir before the assembled people. Following the custom in British India I gave him 'a letter of appointment,' containing the conditions on which he held the emirate. These, briefly, were, that he should rule justly and in accordance with the laws of the Protectorate, that he should obey the High Commissioner, and be guided by the advice of the Resident; that minerals and waste lands should be the property of the Crown. In the case of Kontagora, I wrote to the emir of Sokoto, asking him to nominate a successor, and explaining the reason why I had deposed the chief. He will receive a similar letter of appointment. The broad principles achieved may be thus summarised. Two of the most powerful Fulani emirs have been smashed, because, after repeated warnings, they would not desist from laying waste the whole country and carrying off the people as slaves. Both the fine cities, which were the Fulani capitals, have been preserved from destruction. The loss of life has been confined almost entirely to the Fulani horsemen, viz., to the slave-raiders themselves, and they have suffered heavily, while the peasantry and slaves have suffered little. The emirs themselves have been pursued with such energy that they abandoned everything, and reached Zaria, or elsewhere, in so miserable a plight that the effect will be very far-reaching indeed, and will not admit of the usual misrepresentation. The Fulani rule has been maintained as an experiment, for I am anxious to prove to these people that we have no hostility to them, and only insist on good government and justice, and I am anxious to utilize, if possible, their wonderful intelligence, for they are born rulers, and incomparably above the negroid tribes in ability. It was with this object that I invited Sokoto to nominate a new emir for Kontagora, and I have hopes that the effect of such a message may lead to a better understanding between us and the Mohammedan rulers. The defeat of these chiefs has—again almost too late—checked the great organised slave raids towards the Niger. There still remain the great slave raiders in the east—Yola and Bautshi—and these I propose to coerce this year, and to open up the trade routes in that direction. Meanwhile, the new provinces thus acquired urgently need political officers. Already, with the removal of the fear of the Fulani, each petty village is claiming its ancient lands, or raiding those of its weaker neighbour, and interminable feuds are the result. I greatly desire to properly survey the country, and make a rough land settlement, which it will be the duty of the new emirs, under the supervision of the Resident, to enforce, and so to put a stop to this unrest.

55

HIGH COMMISSIONER SIR F. D. LUGARD: NORTHERN NIGERIAN COURTS, 1 MAY 1901[1]

SEVENTEEN legislative proclamations have been enacted during the year 1900, and seven during the first quarter of 1901, while ten or twelve are still awaiting His Majesty's approval. Of those enacted the more important are:

(1.) *The Courts Proclamation*,[2] setting up a Supreme and Provincial Court. The appointment of a Chief Justice in September last has necessitated a revision of this Proclamation, and a draft of a new Supreme Court Ordinance has already been submitted. Generally speaking the system I have inaugurated is as follows. The Supreme Court will have original and appellate jurisdiction over all non-natives and in all cantonments. Judges of inferior Courts are Commissioners of the Supreme Court within its jurisdiction. In the provinces, which are separated by such vast distances that the Supreme Court could not act effectively, the residents have a jurisdiction (co-existant with the Native Courts) over natives, limited only by the necessity for confirmation by the High Commissioner of all serious sentences. Their cause lists operate as appeals, and the High Commissioner, advised by his legal advisers, can refer any case to the Supreme Court. In practice, where it is possible to set up a Native Court, that tribunal would deal with most cases of ordinary crime by natives, and with native civil actions, but crimes against specific laws of the Protectorate, such as those triable under the 'Slavery,'

---

[1] *Colonial Reports: Northern Nigeria*, 1902 [Cd. 788], pp. 16–17.
[2] No. 5 of 1900. For details of the working of the Native Councils and Minor Courts in Southern Nigeria, see E. A. Kay and S. S. Richardson, *The Native and Customary Courts of Nigeria* (London, 1966), pp. 13–14; and for the review of the northern system in 1906, ibid., pp. 25–6.

'Liquor,' 'Firearms,' and 'Personation' Proclamations, being foreign to native law and custom, would usually be dwelt with by the Provincial Courts. The Supreme Court administers strict law; Provincial Courts administer English law, modified by native law and custom. The administration of justice by Residents is frequently intimately associated with their political and executive functions, and their cause lists, therefore, are submitted to the Head of the Executive, the High Commissioner, advised by his legal adviser. In practice I am convinced that this system produces better results than would be obtained by making the Provincial Courts more directly subordinate to the Supreme Court, while it enables the High Commissioner to keep in closer touch with the work of the district officers. The Provincial Courts have, on the whole, worked well, and uniformity of sentences is gradually being arrived at.

(2.) *The Native Courts Proclamation.*—The system of Native Courts which I established has worked fairly well in the districts in which it has been possible to establish such Courts, but the greater part of the Protectorate with which we are in touch is occupied by pagan tribes, without cohesion, and in a primitive state of development, in which regular Native Courts are not possible, since there are no chiefs and councillors of which to constitute them. I am considering certain modifications to the Native Courts Proclamation, which shall meet the requirements and conditions of these tribes . . .

56

SIR RALPH MOOR TO JOSEPH CHAMBERLAIN: SLAVERY IN SOUTHERN NIGERIA, 7 JULY 1901[1]

. . . I have held meetings with the representative chiefs at the following places—Old Calabar, Opobo, Okrika, Bonny, Degema, Brass, Warri, Sapele, Benin River, Benin City, and subsequently a large meeting was held at Bonny . . . which lasted several days. The question of slavery was very fully gone into in all its aspects, and, though the chiefs on many grounds are averse to the changes contemplated, they recognize that such changes must come, and that in some respects they will be immediately beneficial to the country, though the matter will require most careful and judicious handling to avoid immediate and serious difficulties which might give rise to entire dislocation in the affairs of Government, Trade and Tribal control . . .

[1] C.O. 520/12. *Sir Ralph Moor*, High Commissioner Niger Coast Protectorate, 1894–9, Protectorate Southern Nigeria, 1900–2.

2. The existing sources from which slaves are at present originally obtained in the Territories are:

(a) Natives seized by organized slave raiding and sold in slave markets.

(b) Natives accused of witchcraft or crime forced by local public opinion to proceed and consult the oracles of the Aro Ju Ju hierarchy, many of whom are seized and sold by Ju Ju priests as slaves.

(c) Natives seized in inter-tribal and other wars between towns and rival parties of the same tribe.

(d) Natives, mostly children sold by their parents, guardians, or the Chiefs of a Tribe, in trade transactions to liquidate debts or obtain trade goods.

(e) Native children born in a state of slavery. These children are generally regarded as free in the tribe or house in which they are born, but are liable to be sold or pawned.

3. The slaves referred to at paragraph 2 (a) are obtained on the East of the Niger principally from the Aro tribe, portions of which are engaged more or less in continuous slave raiding, while one branch of the tribe—the Inokuns—are the business people engaged principally in the slave dealing and doing but little in the manipulation of produce. The raiding sections of the tribe are the Abams, Ehoffias, and Baribas. The four sections may regard themselves as separate tribes forming a portion of the Ibo Nation, but they are undoubtedly closely connected and work together in all transactions, fighting, slaving, trading, &c. The Inokun section is divided into fourteen families, each having its own business route and any interference by one family with the business route of another leads promptly to internal dissension. The points at which these Inokuns come in contact for business purposes with the middlemen carriers of trade goods and produce are:

(1) Various points on the Cross River

(2) To the North of Opobo around Agumini, Akwete, and upper Kro [?] River.

(3) To the North of New Calabar.

(4) Around Oguta Lake, and,

(5) Some little distance inland to east of Niger . . .

[There are slave markets at Itu and Enyong; few are made slaves through wars; children are obtained mainly west of the Niger. The main purchasers are middlemen traders who use them as canoe boys and carriers. Slave-owning has declined among the coast people.]

. . . 12. After careful consideration and enquiry I am satisfied that it would be impracticable to bring the [Slave Dealing Proclamation] into force in portions of the Protectorate only but that it must take effect throughout the entire territories at the same time. An opportunity for this course will arise when the Aro expedition is carried out and slave raiding with the slave markets put a stop to. The greater part of the slave supply will then cease and the same movement should be taken advantage of to put a stop to the demand. This course will give rise to a further difficulty however which must be met before such action is actually taken. For some years past there has been talk and some slight agitation among the slaves of the Coast Tribes with regard to their freedom—or as the Chiefs themselves describe it 'The Boys have become more arrogant', and it has only been by the improvement in their condition of life generally and with a view to individual advancement effected by the advice of the Government that serious difficulty has been avoided. Before, therefore, the Proclamation is actually enforced, and the position of slavery practically abolished for the future, something further must be done to improve the condition of these slaves by removing them in some way from the state of slavery or there will be a danger of a general uprising which would mean anarchy, crime, and a general stoppage of trade. I propose, therefore, to bring into force a Proclamation . . . by which all such slaves and any that may be born in slavery in future . . . will become actual members of the Houses to which they now belong or in which they are born with all the rights and privileges of that position and subject to all the obligations imposed by Native Law and Custom . . .

57

HIGH COMMISSIONER SIR RALPH MOOR TO JOSEPH CHAMBERLAIN: 'ARO' EXPEDITION, 24 NOVEMBER 1901[1]

Memorandum of Instructions, 12 November 1901

THE Objects of the Expedition are as follows:

(a) To put a stop to slave-raiding and the slave trade generally with a view to the Slave Dealing Proclamation No. 5 of 1901 being enforced throughout the entire territories as from the 1st of January next.

(b) To abolish the Ju Ju hierarchy of the Aro tribe which by superstition and fraud causes much injustice among the coast tribes generally and is opposed to the establishment of Government. The power of priesthood is also employed in obtaining natives for sale as slaves and it is essential to finally break it.

(c) To open up the country of the entire Aro Tribe to civilization.

(d) To induce the natives to engage in legitimate trade.

[1] C.O. 520/10. Anene, *Southern Nigeria*, pp. 222–32.

(e) To introduce a currency in lieu of slaves, brass rods, and other forms of native currency and to facilitate trade transactions.

(f) To eventually establish a labour market as a substitute for the present system of slavery . . .

[Plan of military operations; list of Political Officers.]

10. *Loot.* Questions with regard to loot taken on expeditions of this nature continually arise, and it is well therefore to lay down a definite ruling at the commencement. While there is no objection to the officers and men taking a reasonable trophy as a momento of the operations I will not sanction promiscuous loot on the part of either officers or men for the purpose of disposing of same . . .

58

GOVERNOR MAJOR NATHAN TO JOSEPH CHAMBERLAIN: GOLD COAST CIVIL SERVICE, 25 NOVEMBER 1901[1]

8. WHEN all the changes suggested above have been carried out, and when the strength, as well as the rates of pay to staff have been increased in accordance with the various proposals that I have placed and shall continue to place before you, the expenditure on European officials in the Colony will be much greater than it is at present. It seems, however, that when the revenue of the Colony exceeds, as it will this year, by more than £100,000 the expenditure, while the staff is obviously insufficient, and in many cases unsatisfactory, it is time to take up its improvement on a generous scale, and on some definite plan, such as is here submitted.

9. It now remains to explain the red lines on the diagram. They represent possible courses of promotion. It will be seen that to the Assistant District Commissioner, who, it is hoped, in future will have entered the service as a cadet, but who should as a rule have legal qualifications, all the senior appointments, except those requiring special professional qualifications (law, engineering, medical, or military), will be open. To those that enter the service as accountants or in the Treasury, Audit, Customs, Transport, Postal, Public Works, Forestry, Medical, Educational, Ecclesiastical, Military, Police, and Prisons Departments, advancement will be as a rule confined to their own departments, except that from certain grades in the Preventive, Medical, and Military services, and in exceptional cases from others, it will be possible to obtain Travelling Commissionerships, which will lead to the administrative services in Ashanti and the Northern Territories. This scheme would practically be the formation of a

[1] C.O. 879/72, no. 679.

Gold Coast Civil Service on the lines of the Covenanted Civil Service of India, to fill the Secretariat and higher administrative posts in the Colony, leaving those posts in Ashanti and the Northern Territories to be filled as in the non-regulation provinces of India by military and other officers, who have proved themselves to have special qualifications for dealing with natives. The departmental services would correspond to the uncovenanted services (Public Works Department, Police, Customs, &c.) in India.

10. To carry out such a scheme it will be necessary to have an entrance examination for Civil Service Cadetships, to extend the scheme to cover all the West African Colonies, and probably to offer still higher inducements in the way of pay than here proposed, as well as good pensions, made up partly by deductions from salary. There are many difficulties in the way (particularly those due to climate), which I am aware have already been considered. I propose when I am in England to go more fully into the matter than it is possible for me to do here, where information with regard to previous proposals for a Covenanted West African Civil Service is not available . . .

59

HIGH COMMISSIONER SIR F. D. LUGARD
TO THE SULTAN OF SOKOTO: NORTHERN
NIGERIA, 21 MARCH 1903[1]

'. . . ALL these things which I have said the Fulani by conquest took the right to do now pass to the British. Every Sultan and Emir and the principal officers of State will be appointed by the High Commissioner throughout all this country. The High Commissioner will be guided by the usual laws of succession and the wishes of the people and chiefs, but will set them aside if he desires for good cause to do so. The Emirs and Chiefs who are appointed will rule over the people as of old time and take such taxes as are approved by the High Commissioner, but they will obey the laws of the Governor and will act in accordance with the advice of the Resident. Buying and selling slaves and enslaving people are forbidden. It is forbidden to import firearms (except flint-locks), and there are other minor matters which the Resident will explain. The Alkalis and the Emirs will hold the law courts as of old, but bribes are forbidden, and mutilation and confinement of men in inhuman prisons are not lawful. The powers of each Court will be contained in a warrant appointing it. Sentences of death will not be carried out without the consent of the Resident.

[1] *Colonial Reports: Northern Nigeria*, 1903 [Cd. 1768].

'The Government will, in future, hold the rights in land which the Fulani took by conquest from the people, and if Government requires land it will take it for any purpose. The Government hold the right of taxation, and will tell the Emirs and Chiefs what taxes they may levy, and what part of them must be paid to Government. The Government will have the right to all minerals, but the people may dig for iron and work in it subject to the approval of the High Commissioner, and may take salt and other minerals subject to any excise imposed by law. Traders will not be taxed by Chiefs, but only by Government. The coinage of the British will be accepted as legal tender, and a rate of exchange for cowries fixed, in consultation with Chiefs, and they will enforce it.

'When an Emirate, or an office of state, becomes vacant, it will only be filled with the consent of the High Commissioner, and the person chosen by the council of Chiefs and approved by the High Commissioner will hold his place only on condition that he obeys the laws of the Protectorate and the conditions of his appointment. Government will in no way interfere with the Mohammedan religion . . .'

60

CHIEF JUSTICE W. NICOLL TO GOVERNOR SIR WILLIAM MacGREGOR: EGBA JURISDICTION, 14 DECEMBER 1903[1]

. . . THE treaty proposed [of 13 January 1904] . . . between His Majesty and the rulers of Egba land grants to His Majesty for a period of twenty years criminal and civil jurisdiction over all persons in Egba land who are not natives of that country.

It grants an *original* jurisdiction in the following cases:

(1) Criminal jurisdiction in indictable cases over all persons who are not natives of Egba land;

(2) Civil jurisdiction over matters in difference where one or more of the parties to the suit is not a native of Egba land and the amount involved is £50 or upwards.

(3) Civil jurisdiction for the administration and control of the property and persons of all persons who are not natives of Egba land.

It grants an *appelate* jurisdiction in the following cases:

(1) an appelate criminal jurisdiction in non-indictable cases over all persons who are not natives of Egba land;

(2) an appelate civil jurisdiction over matters in difference where

---

[1] C.O. 147/167. Encl. in MacGregor to Lyttelton, 15 December 1903 (and draft treaty).

one or more of the parties to the suit is not a native of Egba land, and the amount involved is over £5 in amount.

The Treaty provides for the formation of a Mixed Court with jurisdiction in non-indictable cases over persons not being natives of Egba land, and over matters in difference where one or more of the parties to the suit is not a native of Egba land and the amount in dispute is under £50. The President of the Court will be appointed by His Majesty and this will in practice be almost equivalent to granting His Majesty an original jurisdiction in these matters.

The Treaty further grants to His Majesty for a period of twenty years jurisdiction over all persons whatsoever in Egba land for the repression and punishment of the crimes of murder and manslaughter.

The Treaty does not interfere with the jurisdiction of the Native Courts over matters between and affecting natives of Egba land *only* except in cases of murder and manslaughter.

Under sections 3 & 12 of Ordinance No. 4 of 1876 the Supreme Court of Lagos can exercise the jurisdictions ceded by the Treaty . . .

61

MR. EZECHIEL; MINUTE, YORUBA JURISDICTION, 16 JANUARY 1904[1]

. . . (2) WE have also to consider what to say with regard to Ibadan, Oyo, and the other places mentioned in par. 7 of the present despatch.

In the first place I should mention that the point is one of immediate importance because Europeans have already settled in Ibadan, & the question of jurisdiction in offences against the tolls regulations there has been directly raised . . .

Sir W. MacGregor says in par. 7 of this despatch that in the territories in question no jurisdiction has ever been ceded, or been practically exercised, & that up to the present time it has been held that Lagos Courts possess no jurisdiction there. This opinion practically bears the inference that Ibadan is in the same position in regard to jurisdiction as Abeokuta; & it will never do to admit that Ibadan has any jurisdiction over Europeans to 'cede' to the King. The fact that the formal independence of Ibadan & the other places has never been recognized, as that of Abeokuta has unfortunately been, does constitute a real difference in the position; and as regards Ibadan & Oyo in particular, our position is strengthened by the first clause of the Treaty with Oyo (of Feb. 3 1893) which was confirmed by an Agreement with Ibadan . . .

[1] C.O. 147/167. On no. 60.

62

ACTING GOVERNOR C. H. H. MOSELEY TO ALFRED LYTTELTON: IJEBU ADMINISTRATION, 3 MAY 1904[1]

IN continuation of my despatch, Lagos, No. 154, of the 14th April, I have the honour to report that I have again visited Jebu Ode, and returned to Lagos on the 26th of April.

2. Some of the Mohamedan [sic] Members of the Native Council whose resignations were tendered to me on my previous visit complained to me that they were being ostracised by their co-religionists, and I accordingly sent for the Lemomu and Naibi, their Chief Priests, and questioned them thereon. The Lemomu and Naibi denied that there was any feeling in the matter, but as it was plain that the Mohamedans were divided into two camps, I pointed out to them the harm they would cause to peace and good order and to trade unless they were on friendly terms, and I was at last able to effect a reconciliation between them.

3. The Christian Members of Council who tendered me their resignations on my previous visit also complained that they were being subjected to much insult and persecution on account, as they said, of the progressive and enlightened manner in which they had carried out their duties as Members of the Council.

4. On Saturday morning, the 23rd instant, I received the Awujale and all his principal chiefs resident in Jebu Ode. The Awujale gave a general denial to the allegations of the Mohamedan and Christian Members of Council, and late in the day informed me that in very many cases, these members had extorted money from persons applying in the bush for permits to cut timber under the provisions of the Forestry Ordinance.

5. I would briefly mention here the system under which Major Reeve-Tucker has, with the Native Authorities, been hitherto putting into operation the provisions of the Ordinance. Certain members of the Native Council were appointed at monthly salaries to supervise the applications for permits to cut trees, the cutting of the trees, and the collection of a royalty of 10s. per tree authorised to be cut. These members were assisted by a staff of clerks and Forest Guards. The Forestry Ordinance was passed on the 23rd day of May, 1902, but was adopted by the Jebu Ode native authorities only in the latter part of 1903, and it had been made to operate retrospectively, i.e., as from the date of its passing instead of on the date on which it was

[1] C.O. 879/72, no. 684. *Alfred Lyttelton*, M.P., Secretary of State for Colonies, 1903–5.

adopted in Jebu Ode. The permits or licenses to cut timber were in all cases granted by Major Reeve-Tucker himself, and he undertook the custody of such moneys as were collected and paid to him by the Members of Council or the Forest Clerks. I may add that I have expressed my inability to approve of Members of Council acting as paid servants of the Council, and also of the Ordinance being given a retrospective operation.

6. Resuming the subject matter of paragraph 5 of this despatch, the Awujale and chiefs were so decided in their desire not to act again with those members who expressed a wish to resign, that I accepted the resignations, and provisionally approved of the nomination of 16 other persons, all Pagan chiefs, to sit in their places. The Council as now constituted consists entirely of Pagan chiefs, as both Mahommedans and Christians decline to sit on it. This is in accordance with native custom, which forbids a man of chiefly rank to accept a post on terms of equality with an inferior in rank, and none of the resigned members was a person of rank.

7. I impressed upon the new Council that quarrelling and persecutions must at once cease, and I forcibly explained to them that if there was any recurrence of the disturbance I would interfere in the administration of the district in such a way as to effectively and severely punish those responsible.

8. I was assured by the Awujale and the chiefs that they would do their utmost to see that my injunction was loyally and literally obeyed, but they again renewed their complaints mentioned in paragraph 5 above, and asked that the resigned Members of Council might be expelled from the district. This I at once declined to accede to in the absence of satisfactory proof that such a course ought to be taken in the interests of the country.

9. During the period between my two visits, only one such complaint had been preferred to the Travelling Commissioner, Major Reeve-Tucker, and upon inquiry it entirely fell to the ground. I am informed by Mr. Hornby-Porter, who was present at the inquiry, that he concurs in the opinion of Major Reeve-Tucker that this particular complaint was not substantiated. Other complaints are being made by the Awujale, however, and I think it best, in view of all the circumstances, to appoint a Commission to thoroughly investigate the whole matter; although, so far as I can at present see, the immediate cause of the trouble has been removed by the above resignations from the Council, there must inevitably remain a certain amount of friction and ill-feeling until all complaints as to the administration of the Forestry Ordinance have been dealt with.

10. I transmit, enclosed, a report received after my return to headquarters from Major Reeve-Tucker, which shows a satisfactory state of affairs.

11. I have arranged for Captain Blair, who is thoroughly acquainted with the district, to be temporarily stationed in Jebu Ode during the absence of Major Reeve-Tucker on a visit to the surrounding villages; and, in view of Major Reeve-Tucker's report, have issued instructions for the withdrawal of the troops, as I think I can safely say that as far as one can judge, there are not the slightest signs of further trouble; at any rate for some time to come.

63

COLONIAL OFFICE MEMORANDUM: WEST AFRICAN CIVIL SERVICE, 2 NOVEMBER 1904[1]

A GREAT improvement has taken place in our West African Services during the last few years, but much remains to be done and I think that we should consider whether any further reforms can be made at the present time.

The following appear to be some of the points which might be considered.

(A.) Unification of the Civil Services of the Colonies and Protectorate in the matter of Salary.

We have already amalgamated our West African Military Forces, with great advantages in every direction. The formation of the West African Medical Staff has been equally successful and we have recently laid down a uniform scale of pay for the Native Medical Officers (who are not eligible for the West African Medical Staff and were in receipt of different rates of pay in different Colonies). We should now consider to what extent the salaries of the appointments in the other branches of our West African Services can be unified.

In 1901 Sir M. Nathan[2] submitted a scheme in which the salaries of the officials of the Gold Coast Service were arranged in accordance with the Table in Appendix I.[3] Increments were not proposed in the case of salaries of £400 per annum and over, as it was not clear that any special advantage is derived from the system of increments, except in the case of officers whose pay is so small that a small increase to it is a matter of importance. Promotion in West Africa is generally rapid, and an officer of standing has more incentive to work in the prospect of promoting to a higher appointment than in that of an increment to his salary in the grade in which he is serving.

In accordance with this scheme, appointments of £400 a year and over, with one exception, carry with them a duty allowance of

---

[1] C.O. 879/88, no. 787. The authorship within the Department is not clear.
[2] No. 51.   [3] Not printed.

20 per cent., to be drawn by the holder of the office when discharging its duties, and by the officer acting for him when he is absent or temporarily transferred to other work. In the case of the Puisne Judges this allowance did not seem necessary, if they received a uniform salary of £1,000 per annum, as special provision could be made in the unusual case of an officer appointed to act as Puisne Judge.

The Governor pointed out that the system of duty allowances had the double advantage of remunerating officers for undertaking work and responsibilities in addition to or above those of their substantive appointments, and of ensuring higher remuneration to officers when in the Colony, where their necessary expenses, especially in the case of married officers, are greater than when they are on leave.

Sir M. Nathan stated that, after careful consideration of various cases, he had come to the conclusion that it would not be convenient or advantageous for junior officers drawing salaries of less than £400 per annum to have duty allowances attached to their offices, and he proposed that they should continue to draw incremental salaries.

Some progress has been made with the introduction of this scheme into the Gold Coast, and we have recently made a beginning in the same direction at the Gambia and in Sierra Leone.

I think that we should now consider the question of introducing the scheme universally throughout our West African Colonies and Protectorates, especially as the approaching amalgamation of Lagos and Southern Nigeria affords a favourable opportunity for re-arranging the salaries of those possessions.

Certain advantages connected with the scheme are mentioned above, and it appears to be well suited to West Africa. The arrangement for the payment of duty allowances is particularly suitable for countries where the officials are so frequently coming on leave or being invalided; there will be greater order and simplicity in the classification of appointments, and as the salaries of the appointments are arranged in a nicely graduated series, the trouble of re-arranging salaries when the appointments increase or diminish in importance is minimised. Also this unification of the salaries of the services will be a preliminary step to a still more complete unification in other respects, to which reference will be made later.

Some appointments must, of course, be excepted from the scheme. The question of the salaries of the Puisne Judges on the Gold Coast is referred to above. Then there are the Travelling Commissioners in the Gambia, who come away during the rainy season and are not replaced by other officers, and there are no doubt a few other appointments which must be excluded from the scheme.

The majority, however, of our West African appointments (apart, of course, from those of the West African Frontier Force and the West African Medical Staff, which stand on a special footing) can be brought within the scheme, and I think that we should now, in consultation with the Governors and High Commissioners, classify all these appointments in accordance with the system proposed by Sir M. Nathan and introduce the new salaries, as opportunity offers, i.e., when vacancies occur, or in cases where the new salary is practically the same as the old salary. Meanwhile no new appointments should be made without first considering whether the new scale of salary should be adopted . . .

. . . I think, therefore, that we should go carefully through our West African appointments and consider which of them, in addition to those which are already so filled, could be filled by officers seconded from the Home or Indian Services. As showing what might be done in this direction, I would call attention to our recent action with regard to the appointment of Director of Public Works on the Gold Coast. Hitherto the appointments of Director of Public Works in our West African Colonies have generally been regarded as permanent appointments and they have not always been filled by men who were best qualified to hold them. When, however, the appointment of Director of Public Works on the Gold Coast recently fell vacant, a new departure was made and a Royal Engineer Officer was seconded and appointed to the post for a limited period. The post of Director of Public Works in Northern Nigeria has also been filled by an officer seconded from the Indian Public Works Department and the arrangement is working well. I think that a similar course might be followed with advantage in the other West African Colonies. In a developing country like West Africa, conditions are constantly changing and different Directors of Public Works with different qualifications may be required at different periods, according as this or that scheme of Public Works comes into prominence. New men bring new ideas, and are more likely to have the necessary initiative and energy to carry them out. It was not until Sir W. Maxwell had been transferred from an Eastern Colony to the Governorship of the Gold Coast that official quarters, suitable for the tropics, were constructed on Eastern lines in the latter Colony . . .

64

HIGH COMMISSIONER W. EGERTON TO
ALFRED LYTTELTON: SOUTHERN
NIGERIA AMALGAMATION, 29 JANUARY 1905[1]

I HAVE the honour to forward herewith my scheme for the amalgamation of the two Administrations of Lagos and Southern Nigeria,

[1] C.O. 879/72, no. 684. (*Sir*) *W. Egerton*, from Straits Settlements; High Commissioner, Southern Nigeria (Protectorate), Governor of Lagos Colony, 1904, and

which I recommend for the future should be called Southern Nigeria, with its capital at Lagos.

2. Southern Nigeria is as good a name for the entire territory as can be found both geographically and ethnologically, and the territory of the present Southern Nigeria Administration is larger and far more important, commercially and otherwise, than that of Lagos, although the trade of the former is as yet undeveloped, and a large portion of the Protectorate is still unexplored and unsettled.

3. It was only after long considerations that I decided to recommend that Lagos should be the capital. Even after the care that sanitation has had, for several years, at Lagos, Lagos is not, and I fear never can be, so healthy a place of residence for Europeans as Calabar. Moreover, while Calabar has an excellent harbour for ocean steamers, Lagos suffers from a dangerous bar, over which steamers of greater draught than 11 ft. 6 ins. cannot pass. But Calabar is still undeveloped, and shares with eight other ports the trade of Southern Nigeria, while Lagos is a large town in which is concentrated the whole trade of the Colony and its hinterland; which has been, and is being, developed under the stimulus of free competition, a condition sadly lacking at present in its eastern neighbour. Lagos has also large vested interests and possesses much better communication with Europe. A railway has been built from it into the interior and is being extended and, after two millions of money have been sunk in that railway, it cannot be long before steps are taken to remove the bar and thus make Lagos a safe and commodious port for the largest steamers trading to West Africa. I feel, therefore, that I cannot but recommend that Lagos should be the headquarters of the Administration, but it may be possible, and even advisable, some 10 or 20 years hence, to move the centre of the Administration to Calabar, or even to Onitsha or Lokoja, on the Niger, if Northern Nigeria is joined to the Southern Administration, the interior opened up by roads and railways and communication between the coast and the hinterland made easy.

4. I believe it has been already decided to add Northern Nigeria to this Administration in the near future. Such an amalgamation would be easy, and should show a much greater economy than the present one.

Such an amalgamation would be much simpler than that between Lagos and Southern Nigeria, for the different systems of Government, of laws and methods adopted in the latter two Administrations forbids a complete union for some time to come.

Southern Nigeria, 1906–12. Amalgamation had been decided in 1904: Lyttelton to Egerton, 12 August 1904, though an earlier scheme had been submitted by Sir Ralph Moor, 14 January 1901. See A. O. Anjorin, 'The Background to the Amalgamation of Nigeria in 1914', *Odu University of Ife Journal of African Studies*, vol. 3, no. 3 (1967), pp. 72–86. The new Colony and Protectorate was constituted 1 May 1906.

There could, and should, be a complete fusion between Northern and Southern Nigeria, and one system of law could be adopted for both. Further, the Heads of Departments proposed for the present Lagos–Southern Nigeria amalgamation should be capable of directing the larger departments if Northern Nigeria were added to the Administration. The chief alteration that would then be required would be that the Governor's deputy would have to reside in Lagos, and that the Governor would have to be freed from all petty details of administration. Many causes of friction would then be removed, and the objection to large sums being taken from Lagos and Southern Nigeria revenues to meet expenditure in Northern Nigeria would cease, as in the spending of those sums the general welfare of the whole country would be considered—this is not and cannot be the case under the present system of independent administration. The enforcement of a 'caravan' tax on traders travelling between Lagos and the Niger by land while transport via Southern Nigeria and the Niger is free is a good instance of this. Moreover, the present unscientific boundary by which some chiefs find their territories placed under two independent administrations could be rectified.

5. The scheme I now submit is not one of complete amalgamation, but is devised to effect a rather more complete amalgamation than that which at present exists between the Colony of the Straits Settlements and the Federated States of the Malay Peninsula. If the future of this dual Administration proves as successful as that of its eastern counterpart, my scheme will be fully justified.

6. I propose:

(a) That the revenues of the Southern Nigeria Protectorate and those of Lagos should still be kept separate, though each should lend such monies as one may require and the other has to lend, and that the combined revenues should be available as security for any loans raised. This should enable money for development purposes to be raised more cheaply with the ample security given by an Administration commanding a revenue already approaching a million sterling.

(b) That legislation should continue to be separate. I do not see how it can be otherwise; the two places have, unfortunately, been ruled and legislated for so very differently, and the Lagos Council can hardly be given control over the revenues of, or law-making powers over, Southern Nigeria, about which they know nothing, and in which they have no interests. Except on these two points the amalgamation is to be complete.

7. The whole territory will be under one Administrator, who should (as in the Straits) continue to be Governor of Lagos and High Commissioner for the Southern Nigeria Protectorate; each department

is to have one head who will control the staff throughout the whole Administration. The only exception to this is in the Secretariat. I propose that there shall still be a Colonial Secretary for Lagos, who will deal direct with the Governor on everything relating to the present Lagos territory, and a High Commissioner's Office, to assist the Governor, as High Commissioner, with correspondence relating to the Administration of the present Southern Nigeria Protectorate.

8. I have only divided the combined territory into three provinces. There are several reasons for doing this:

First.—That it is possible in this way to provide higher salaries for the administrative officers in charge (who should, as a rule, be men trained in a Colony with a Civil Service selected by examination), and this has a further advantage that they can be given fuller administrative powers, and when the Governor is away there will always be an officer of experience to take his place.

Second.—Geographical reasons. Lagos town is in easy communication with all parts of the Lagos coast and hinterland. Southern Nigeria divides naturally into two: the western half or Niger valley, the future Central Province, receives all its mail and trade through the port of Forcados. All parts of the future Eastern Province (including the present Eastern, Calabar and Cross River Divisions) are in fairly easy communication with Calabar. The Eastern Division having an overland mail service with Calabar to supplement the present inconvenient fortnightly mail . . .

65

GOVERNOR E. P. C. GIROUARD: NORTHERN
NIGERIA, 15 OCTOBER 1908[1]

. . . V.—ADMINISTRATION.

(25). Central Administration.

ON my arrival in the country I found the central administration undergoing changes. Previous to the departure of my predecessor all political work was directly dealt with by the High Commissioner through a personal Political Secretariat, as apart from the Administrative Secretariat. The Political Secretariat dealt with provincial matters in detail, and all questions affecting the administration of the

---

[1] *Colonial Reports: Northern Nigeria*, 1909 [Cd. 4448], pp. 27–8. (*Sir*) *Percy Girouard*, engineer and administrator in the Sudan and South Africa; High Commissioner and Governor of Northern Nigeria, 1907–9.

provinces other than matters of departmental routine were referred direct to the High Commissioner. Prior to my arrival, the office of Political Secretary was abolished, the High Commissioner retaining the remainder of the old political staff. As a new-comer to the country, I preferred to carry the change to its logical conclusion, viz., the creation, by amalgamation, of the usual Colonial Secretariat.

(26). Provincial Administration.

Prior to 1907, the Protectorate was divided into 14 provinces, all reporting direct to headquarters. These provinces were of immense size, ranging from the smallest, Bassa, with about the area of Wales, to Kano, Zaria, Sokoto, Bauchi, and Bornu, all having areas approximating to that of Scotland. The administration of the provinces varied as to policy. In the great Mohammedan Emirates where we found old established systems of native administration, the Residents were directed to guide and improve the native rule. In the pagan communities, however, where numerous tribes speaking different dialects are found contiguous, more direct general rule became necessary, tribal native law and custom where not repugnant being retained.

To administer and control the provinces, form their provincial courts, and collect the revenues, there were available about 100 political officers, or an average of under six per province, allowing for one-third on leave, but this proportion has frequently been exceeded owing to invaliding, and at the most four officers were available in the smaller provinces, five to seven in the larger. My predecessor had the intention of amalgamating the provinces into larger units. This policy has been pursued, but is advisedly making slow progress. By the end of the next financial year it is hoped, however, to have reduced the number to nine provinces, and they will be reduced eventually to eight. All the old provinces are retained as divisions of the united provinces, thus ensuring continuity of administration, but relieving headquarters of details more readily dealt with by the central authority of the united provinces. Continuity of administration is one of the most necessary factors for the good government of African races; continual change of Residents or other officers only too often entailing a change in provincial administrative methods unsettling to the native mind. For the present it is sought to retain officers in the same provinces, if not in the same divisions of these provinces, for as long a period as possible.

One of the further factors necessary for successful provincial administration is the knowledge of native languages. Reliance upon interpreters is, I am glad to say, rapidly becoming unnecessary except for new arrivals and in dealings with the many pagan tribes. Residents are fully aware of the necessity of acquiring languages and of the fact that other things being equal promotion in the service will be largely dependent upon linguistic attainments. A very real knowledge of the Hausa tongue is possessed by many, and every endeavour is being made to acquire and vocabularise other languages less widely diffused.

Provincial administration, as a whole, is progressing very satisfactorily. My predecessor in a valuable series of memoranda gave Residents that guiding help which makes for the adoption of similar methods of administration without binding too rigidly the action of the man on the spot. The general policy thus laid down has been carried on with those alterations necessary for changing circumstances. One of the main guiding principles in provincial administration has been that of ruling through the native authorities. In the Mohammedan communities, before our arrival, the emirates had been divided into districts, but these districts were in no sense coadunate, i.e., they consisted of villages or towns dotted all over the emirate. The heads of the districts were only too often mere figureheads residing in the capital, and their rulers too jealous of power and fearful of intrigue to permit of their residence in the districts. Our endeavour since the occupation has been to break down this system, which led to much maladministration, illegality, and extortion. It has been sought to create coadunate districts by a re-allocation of villages, and, further, to insist upon the permanent residence of district heads within the areas told off to them. A very great measure of success has been attained, and Emirs themselves are gradually recognising that, far from reducing their influence, the system will lead to an increase of prestige, just as it will, a matter it is feared at present of less importance to them, lead to far greater efficiency in native government.

66

GOVERNOR SIR F. D. LUGARD: MINUTE,
NIGERIA SUPREME COURT,
24 SEPTEMBER 1912[1]

. . . 8. THE Supreme Court jurisdiction will be limited territorially to the larger centres in which there are several Europeans and many educated natives (such as Calabar, Opobo, Bonny, Onitsha, Warri, &c.). It will include the whole of the Colony and also all places where,

[1] C.O. 879/113, no. 1005. See Perham and Bull, *Lugard*, vol. ii, p. 411. The important amalgamation report of May 1913 contains a supporting memorandum on the organization of the Supreme Court by Sir E. Speed, Chief Justice, Northern Nigeria, dated 10 January 1913. It is included in the valuable edition of A. H. M. Kirk-Greene, *Lugard and the Amalgamation of Nigeria: A Documentary Record* (London, 1968), as Appendix IV, pp. 259–61. Both the confidential report and the

by treaty with native rulers, Supreme Court jurisdiction has been established in independent or semi-independent territories, such as Abeokuta, Oyo, and Ibadan, &c. In Northern Nigeria it has concurrent jurisdiction, in certain easily accessible districts, with the Provincial Courts; but this, I think, is inadvisable and leads to divided control and depreciates the Provincial Court in the eyes of the natives. The power is rarely exercised, and Chief Justice Speed states that he has never known a case of conflict of jurisdiction. It has also an original jurisdiction over non-natives and persons in Government employ, and although a non-native has no right of appeal to the Supreme Court in criminal cases, an application for transfer would probably be granted as a matter of course. It may, however, possibly be advisable to grant a right of appeal in cases subject to confirmation, provided the appeal is lodged before the case is sent for confirmation. The jurisdiction of a Provincial Court can at any time be suspended in any place where the Supreme Court has an original jurisdiction by a general order of transfer, which makes the transition easy when occasion may arise. The Governor may at any time order (or the Provincial Court may, with consent, transfer) any case at any stage of hearing to the Supreme Court. In civil matters there is an appeal to the Supreme Court in cases over a certain value.

9. The Provincial Court has complete and original jurisdiction throughout a 'Province', subject to the conditions already stated. The Resident in charge alone has full powers *ex officio*. All officers subordinate to him are Commissioners of the Provincial Court, with powers varying according to their experience and ability. These powers may from time to time be increased by the Governor. The Resident, or any Commissioner, exercising full powers has power to transfer any case from a Native Court at any stage—but this refers primarily to criminal cases. No sentence which exceeds a fixed limit (which may be varied by the Governor in different Courts) is valid until confirmed by the Governor, and the sentence or award is not complete till confirmed. The Cause Lists are submitted to the Governor and operate as appeals. The power of confirmation and appeal may be delegated by the Governor to the Chief Justice, but to no one else. Here, again, it may be advisable to allow of delegation to a Provincial Commissioner (1st Class Resident), if advised by a legal officer, up to a certain limit. The remainder can be dealt with by the Governor, advised by his Legal Adviser in his executive capacity, but the prerogative may be separately exercised by the Governor in his capacity as representative of the King.

later compilation on amalgamation, 1912–19, repay careful study. See, too, the Introduction, pp. 1–44. Only documents not included in this edition have been reproduced here.

Litigants may not be represented by counsel in Provincial Courts. No error of venue to invalidate a trial.

10. Native Courts, established by warrants defining their powers in each case, are of two classes—Alkali's Courts (mainly limited to Mohammedan districts) and Judicial Councils (mainly in pagan districts). They are classified according to their powers, and some may award a capital sentence subject to confirmation by the Governor. These Courts are composed entirely of natives and exercise no jurisdiction over non-natives. The Ordinance constituting them and the warrants setting up each Court are very simple and translated into the vernacular. An appeal lies to the Native Court at the headquarters of the Native Court at the headquarters of the Province, which may also, on application, order a re-trial in the Provincial Court. No errors of venue matter.

11. From this brief summary it will be seen that the principles which I had in view in setting up this system were:

(a) A territorial limitation of Supreme Court jurisdiction, partly because of the physical impossibility for the Supreme Court to deal with so vast an area, together with a limitation chiefly to non-natives because the country was not ripe for Supreme Court jurisdiction over natives, for whom a much less costly, more rapid, and simpler form of justice was preferable.

(b) The concurrent training, on the one hand, of Residents and District Officers to dispense justice—an education greatly assisted by the legal adviser's comments on his monthly cause list; and, on the other hand, of the best and most intelligent of the natives to deal more especially with their own civil matters themselves under the close supervision and instruction of British officers.

12. It may be objected that under this system executive and judicial functions are vested in the same officers, a procedure condemned by the concensus of opinion in civilised countries. I regard it deliberately, nevertheless, as the best possible system in the very early development of a new country, where the staff is limited, and where the policy is to rule through the chiefs themselves. But as the country develops it will be possible to separate these functions while still maintaining the leading features of the present system—simplicity, cheapness, and rapidity . . .

67

GOVERNOR SIR F. D. LUGARD TO THE SECRETARY OF STATE: NIGERIAN COURTS ORDINANCES, 21 MAY 1913[1]

... I HAVE the honour to submit three draft Ordinances:
(a) Setting up Provincial Courts on the model of Northern Nigeria;
(b) Setting up Native Courts;
(c) Amending the Supreme Court Ordinance so as to bring it into line with these . . .

[He has conferred with the Chief Justice of Northern Nigeria, Sir E. Speed, the Chief Justice of Southern Nigeria, Mr. Willoughby Osborne, and the Acting Attorney-General, R. J. B. Ross.]

4. I also consulted Mr. Boyle (Colonial Secretary), who, as Officer Administering the Government, had been responsible for the draft Ordinance formerly submitted to you, and from which the present drafts differ *toto coelo*. He concurred in the new drafts when I had explained to him the working of the system. The Acting Attorney-General also declared himself satisfied with them, after some consultation with Sir E. Speed, more especially on the point whether the wording of the drafts was entirely adequate to exclude legal representatives from appearing as counsel in Provincial and Native Courts . . .

5. These Ordinances cannot come into force until the area and extent of the new 'provinces' have been decided upon and notified. I have dealt with this re-division in my report on the amalgamation . . .

[The draft on the Supreme Court is incomplete and requires definition on points of detail; general principles are explained in his original minute.]

8. Referring to Mr. Willoughby Osborne's memorandum,[2] in paragraph 6 he says he is of opinion that legal representatives should not be allowed to appear in appeal cases from the Provincial to the Supreme Court. In this I concur with His Honour, and differ from Sir E. Speed.[3] The Chief Justice, like Mr. Ross (Acting Attorney-General) and every officer to whom I have spoken, emphasised strongly the great evil which has been allowed to grow up in Southern Nigeria by the extension of the Supreme Court Jurisdiction into the interior, and the consequential influx of a swarm of native legal practitioners, who emply touts to prompt ignorant people to litigation,

[1] C.O. 879/113, no. 1005.
[2] Memorandum, 12 December 1912, reproduced later in *Lugard and the Amalgamation of Nigeria* (ed. Kirk-Greene), pp. 176–9.
[3] Memorandum, 3 February 1913, ibid., pp. 179–80.

especially regarding the boundaries and ownership of land. The abolition of this practice is one of the main objects I have in view in restricting the jurisdiction of the Supreme Court 'Local Limits' to only such areas as contain a large number of aliens.

9. In paragraphs 9 and 16, Mr. Osborne proposes that Provincial Courts should only have jurisdiction where the Supreme Court does not possess complete jurisdiction. Sir E. Speed considers that, if the Supreme Court exercises jurisdiction over large areas, the Provincial Courts must (as now in Northern Nigeria) have concurrent jurisdiction, and, therefore, that the Chief Justice should exercise the power to transfer any case to the Supreme Court, or to issue a writ of prohibition to a Provincial Court to prevent a conflict of jurisdiction. If, however, the Supreme Court's jurisdiction is restricted to small areas (as I propose it shall be in Southern Nigeria), it will, he considers, be better to oust the jurisdiction of the Provincial Courts entirely from the area of Supreme Court jurisdiction. I see no objection to this latter course, provided that there is a Commissioner of the Supreme Court available to deal with petty cases.

10. As regards the question whether the power of transfer . . . should be exercised by the Governor or by the Chief Justice in cases in which aliens are concerned throughout the Protectorate, Sir E. Speed writes, 'I do not attach much importance to it, provided that Provincial Court Officers are instructed to report such cases for the Governor's orders.'

Mr. Osborne considers that the power of transfer should be vested solely in the Governor. I concur in this view, and have so amended the draft. If it should not be found convenient to restrict the local limits of the Supreme Court to areas which can be fully dealt with by the Supreme Court Judges and Police Magistrates (as Commissioners of the Supreme Court) the difficulty may perhaps be solved by making Political Officers Commissioners of the Supreme Court within the local limits, in addition to their functions as Commissioners of the Provincial Court outside of these limits . . .

11. Sir E. Speed and Mr. Boyle support my view—from which Mr. Osborne dissents—that the Supreme Court procedure is inapplicable to Provincial and Native Courts.

12. Mr. Willoughby Osborne . . . assumes that the Native Courts would be entrusted with powers of life and death. They certainly would not be. Their powers at first would be extremely limited, as they were at first in Northern Nigeria, and only very gradually increased as any particular Court showed itself fit to administer larger powers. At first their jurisdiction would be chiefly limited to civil causes (marriage, divorce, petty land disputes, &c.), in which they administer native law and custom, together with extremely limited criminal powers (for petty theft, &c.).

13. Mr. Osborne considers that 'the worst evil attendant on the Native Court system is not touched by the Bill', viz., the dishonesty of Native Court clerks. In this I sincerely trust that he will be found to be wrong. The transfer of all but trivial criminal cases to the Provincial Court may possibly render it unnecessary to employ alien clerks and interpreters at all in the Native Courts, and in any case their opportunities for dishonesty would be so greatly reduced as to be almost nil. In so far as the Provincial Court is dependent on them, it suffers under an identical disability with the Supreme Court itself, and, as officers pass in the native languages, this disability will be much less than in the Supreme Court. I cordially agree with His Honour that this feature of the existing system is the worst evil of all, and the main object of the proposed legislation is the endeavour to abolish it . . .

[The terms of drafts are forwarded with detailed amendments; there is need for a definition of 'non-native'.]

68

GOVERNOR SIR F. D. LUGARD TO THE SECRETARY OF STATE: NIGERIA, 30 JUNE 1913[1]

SECRET.

. . . *Control of natives.*—But actual facts (cited in the enclosures) show that the right of interference and control went very much further, and was exercised over the natives themselves. For indeed the inevitable corollary of the action prescribed by the Brussels Act—of disarming the natives and preventing their acquisition of arms for self-defence against their neighbours or for internal control—was the assumption by the suzerain Power of the responsibility and obligation of defending them against external aggression, and of maintaining peace and order within their boundaries, with the consequential right of legislating for these objects.

10. *Actual assertion of Suzerain Rights.*—The local Government in July, 1900, somewhat prematurely no doubt, divided the whole interior country into Supreme Court 'districts'. In the following year His Majesty by Order in Council declared the whole to be a British Protectorate, and the Secretary of State (Mr. Chamberlain) instructed the Governor (*vide* Attorney-General's memorandum, Enclosure 1) that he had power to legislate for the area, except such part as was excluded by treaty. Then followed the Native Councils Ordinance, 1901, which vested administrative powers in such Councils, and

[1] C.O. 879/113, no. 1005. Lugard had returned to England in April 1913 and went back to Nigeria in October.

imposed upon them the duties of preserving peace and good order, and administering justice. The members of these Councils were nominated by the Governor in a series of Gazette notices, and the British Resident was in this way appointed *ex officio* President of the Ibadan Council, which was perhaps the most important of them. (Sir W. Macgregor, No. 44 of 11th November, 1901. Mr. Chamberlain, Confidential, 11th March, 1902.) The Ordinance was enforced throughout the Protectorate, and was acquiesced in by the people. There followed other Ordinances establishing the jurisdiction of the Supreme Court (*cf.* the Egba, Yoruba, and Ife Jurisdiction Ordinances of 1904), and in despatch 549 of 12th July, 1909, the Secretary of State directed that each application of the laws of the Colony to these States must be effected by Ordinance. It is not claimed that these Ordinances conferred jurisdiction on His Majesty, but that His Majesty had already asserted it in the Order in Council of July, 1901, and the Ordinances were consequential on that assumption. In various Orders in Council, as for instance in the Coinage Order of 7th May, 1913, which applies to all Nigeria, it is recited that 'Whereas by treaty grant usage sufferance and other lawful means *His Majesty has power and jurisdiction over the Protectorates of Northern Nigeria and Southern Nigeria*'—words which would appear to indicate that His Majesty has asserted the claim to jurisdiction throughout the Protectorates, unqualified by any reservation. If this jurisdiction is called in question as regards practically the whole of the Lagos Protectorate, the validity of the Order in Council would, I assume, be questionable.

11. The Order in Council of July, 1901, and Mr. Chamberlain's relative despatch were, however (as I have said), limited to countries in which no treaty existed restricting the jurisdiction of the Crown, but the Chief Justice sums up his careful examination of the position by the statement that in his judgement the Crown has acquired complete jurisdiction throughout the Protectorate—except perhaps in Egbaland—and can legislate for natives, as well as for non-natives. The Attorney-General holds that the Agreements of 1904 were only recitals of jurisdiction already acquired, being necessary in regard to aliens who were not amenable to local Councils . . .

16. *Past Policy and Position to-day.* I come now to the policy which has been hitherto followed towards these native States, and the results as I found them. Mr. James (Enclosure 3) complains that there has been no consistent policy in the past, and the result is chaos. The District Commissioners in charge at Abeokuta and Ibadan and elsewhere frankly informed me that they had failed to obtain any indication of the policy of Government, and hence had followed their own. The Ibadan Resident stated that Sir William Macgregor's intention was to create a number of completely independent States,

each, I believe, with its own fiscal frontiers and customs; and he had endeavoured to give effect to that policy. The Egba Resident also stated that he had understood the aim of Government was 'to build up a strong and financially independent State'. The legal officers were unable to say what powers of legislation and control the Governor can exercise. It has been assumed that the consent of each petty State must be obtained before any Ordinance passed by the Legislative Council is operative in its territories. The Governor, therefore, is powerless to enforce laws for the preservation of peace and good order. The Conservator of Forests informs me that within the past three or four years fights have occurred regarding forest boundaries, in which people have been killed. Riots, involving loss of life, between so-called Christian factions and pagans have taken place more than once, and I have had a recent instance. Except by consent, such a law as the Forestry Ordinance cannot be applied, though it is designed to prevent the destruction of the forests and consequent decrease in the rainfall, to the detriment of agriculture. Mr. Thompson urges, in this connection, that it is essential that Government should control the forests, and have the right to acquire reserves, and that the present system, under which some States have accepted the forest laws, while others have done so in part, and others have made forest laws of their own, is most unsatisfactory. In regard to the control of the alienation of land the position is equally unsatisfactory. The District Commissioner reports that 'large areas of land in Ibadan are occupied by aliens, who buy and sell it unbeknown very often to the grantors, and new plots are being almost daily secured unbeknown to the authorities'. (25th November, 1912.) Again, it is reported to me that the natives in Ibadan are taking to tapping the palm trees for liquor, owing to the high surtax on spirits. It is needless to point out the disastrous effects of such a state of things, if allowed to go unchecked and to spread to neighbouring districts, (a) as to its effect on the people, (b) on the palm trees, from which the wealth of the country is at present produced, and (c) on the revenues of the Colony, if locally-made liquor replaces the imported article on which the receipts from Customs so largely depend. Of course, no system of taxation can be introduced, should it appear advisable to institute it. Even the jurisdiction exercised by the Supreme Court under special treaties is unsatisfactory, as will be seen by the letter from the Chief Justice which forms Enclosure 5. Christian marriages performed in these States are, I am told, invalid. The Colonial Government has spent millions in the building of a railway, and the prosperity and wealth of these native States has advanced phenomenally in consequence. Yet the Colonial Government pays rent for the land on which the railway runs, and leases land for the residences of its officials, by whose guidance and control alone these States have avoided disruption and chaos. I recently reported to you that in the insignificant little district of Illesha a threat had been made in the Native Council that if rangers were sent to carry out the Forestry Ordinance (to which Illesha had verbally agreed in 1909) they would be murdered, and a similar threat was inferred to the Resident himself. Yet Illesha was saved from a rebellion of its component villages by the intervention of the Colonial Government in 1908, when troops were sent and force used to support the Owa. In Ibadan a permanent detachment of troops is maintained at the cost of the Colonial Government, while, within a week of my arrival at Lagos, a mutiny of the Egba Police compelled me to send troops in haste to maintain the authority of the Alake. Nor was this the first time that the necessity had arisen; indeed, so critical had the position become in 1906 that the Alake threatened to hand over the country to the British. The so-called independence of these petty States appears, therefore, to consist in the assumed right to decline to be bound by the laws which apply to the Colony and the rest of the Protectorate, while they are dependent on the Colonial Government for the force by which their authority is maintained, and for the guidance which alone has prevented their disruption. In this and succeeding paragraphs I have shown how unsatisfactory is the result in regard to restrictions on trade, the administration of justice, the preservation of good order, the conservation of natural resources, and the promotion of education on sound lines; and I have also endeavoured to show how this state of things may in the future develop into a danger to Nigeria.

17. Whatever may be the merits of a policy of creating independent States and allowing them to set up fiscal barriers, to collect customs dues, and to tax trade, it is obviously of primary importance to ascertain whether there are the elements of permanency in such creations. To this enquiry I have received but one answer. Even Mr. Young, who has with great ability guided the Egba Government towards the attainment of this ideal for the past five years, admitted that there was none. If his hand and that of Mr. Edun—now a very elderly man—were removed from the helm, chaos would ensue. Nor is the material available with which to build up a native State. Officers of long standing assert that it is questionable whether there is any native, even in the Government service, who could be placed in a position of absolute trust. Still less are they to be found in these States, where patriotism is a synonym for sedition, and peculation and bribery are, I am told, chronic. The defalcations of the Egba Native Treasurer compelled me to ask your sanction to the appointment of a European, since the Colonial Government has advanced £30,000 to the Egba Government.

18. The Colonial Government cannot but be influenced in framing its native policy by the fact that these semi-independent

States have shown that they are not animated by a spirit of loyalty and form foci for the seditious elements of Lagos. The documents impounded by the Supreme Court in the case of Prince Ademola revealed an extensive intrigue, in which Mr. Edun, the present Government Secretary (and practically the ruler of Egba-land), was concerned, with certain disaffected persons in Lagos. The correspondence spoke of the Governor (Sir W. Egerton) in contemptuous and insulting language, and it was boasted that the Egba Government had spies in every important office—the Governor's, the Chief Justice's, and the Secretariat—and could obtain copies of any document . . .

21. Again, one is compelled to consider whether the policy of setting up independent States astride the railway which forms the main artery of Nigeria is a wise one. So long as these States are in financial difficulties the risk is less. But if valuable minerals were found (already I have applications from two sources to exploit the minerals, and especially the prospects of coal in Egba-land) the situation would be very different; and incidentally there arises the problem as to how a European mining community could be dealt with in an 'independent State.' Already questions have been asked in Parliament, and the decision as to how minerals are to be dealt with in these States cannot be much longer deferred. The case of the Transvaal is much in point. Doubtless the Colonial Government would be forced to intervene if advisers of any nationality other than British were introduced, but there is nothing to prevent the attempt. It might be hardly less inconvenient if these States introduced British advisers of their own choosing, without reference to the Colonial Government—already the Egba Government has appointed its own Agent in London—and if minerals were discovered such a situation might easily arise. It appears to me wiser to formulate a policy now—late as it is—than to wait until intervention is forced upon us under more difficult circumstances.

There would seem to be three logical courses open:

(a) to withdraw the Resident and refuse the use of troops, and so to allow the artificial creation to fall to pieces;

(b) to treat the country as a foreign State, and retaliate for its customs dues by levying import dues on goods entering British territory;

(c) to modify the existing situation in such a way that these States are incorporated as integral parts of British territory under proper safeguards, and sharing in the general development and progress of Nigeria.

As the first two of these alternatives are impossible and unthinkable, I will, as briefly as possible, lay my suggestions before you in regard to the third.

22. *Policy in Northern Nigeria.*—In framing the policy which should guide the development of Northern Nigeria, these considerations were, of course, present in my mind. In that Protectorate the ideal aimed at is that the central Government exercises complete financial control, while working through and with the native administrations in the collection of taxes, leaving to them sufficient executive powers and financial latitude to interest them in the administration of their territories, and to maintain their prestige. The Ordinances of the Protectorate are operative everywhere, and the orders of the Governor are recognised and obeyed by every native authority and every Court. The policy of the Government is to vest increasing powers in the hands of the rulers who prove themselves capable of using them rightly, and to decrease them where there is maladministration.

23. It would be a task of extreme difficulty to superimpose this policy on the States of the Western Province of Southern Nigeria, and it may prove beyond our abilities; but I submit that it has at least the merit of a definite aim and object. I have already taken some short steps towards its inauguration. But it is obvious that nothing effective can be done until the power to legislate is conceded. The present moment, when amalgamation is effected, appears to me a fitting opportunity to carry out this initial reform. New Letters Patent and Orders in Council will be required on amalgamation, and I would suggest that they should assert in unequivocal terms the right of the Crown to legislate for the whole of Nigeria, and to exercise executive powers, while the Courts should be vested with full jurisdiction . . .

69

L. HARCOURT TO GOVERNOR
SIR F. D. LUGARD: AMALGAMATION
PROPOSALS, 2 SEPTEMBER 1913[1]

. . . I HAVE the honour to acknowledge the receipt of your Confidential despatch of the 9th of May, submitting proposals for the amalgamation of the Government of Northern and Southern Nigeria.

2. In brief outline, you propose that the Colony and Protectorate of Nigeria shall, for administrative purposes, be divided into three parts. The Colony will be known as Lagos, and will be governed by an Administrator, while the two sections of the Protectorate will be administered separately by Lieutenant-Governors. They should, I consider, be known as at present, as Southern Nigeria and Northern Nigeria. The Lieutenant-Governors and the Administrator will all

[1] C.O. 879/113, no. 1005. *L. Harcourt*, Secretary of State for Colonies, 1910-15.

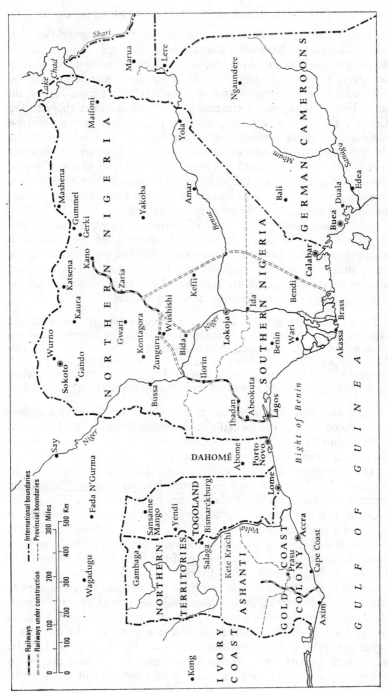

Map 4. Gold Coast and Nigeria, 1912

be subject to the control and authority of the Governor-General, who will have an Executive Council to advise him. Subject to His Majesty's power of disallowance, and to such instructions as he may be given by His Majesty from time to time, legislation will be effected by the Governor-General, or in his absence from Nigeria on duty, by a Deputy, and in the case of Ordinances which apply to the Colony, the advice and consent of a Legislative Council will be obtained. Matters primarily affecting Nigeria as a whole will be dealt with by the Governor-General, who will have advisers for the whole territory in connection with certain branches of the administration. Words will be included in the Letters Patent making it possible for the Governor-General to exercise such functions as may be deemed desirable while on duty in England.

3. All these arrangements will, of course, be purely tentative, and it will probably be advisable to modify them when the process of amalgamation has advanced a further stage. The great advantage of your proposals is that they involve little change from the pre-amalgamation arrangements, and that they can be modified or developed at any time as circumstances may require . . .

[The plan for an absentee Governor-General is without precedent and contains serious risks; some communications with the Nigerian Government will have to be made directly to the Secretary of State; the Lieutenant-Governor in charge will have to be an Acting Governor-General with 'powers a little restricted'; the ill-health of the Governor-General, while he is abroad, could lead to a breakdown in communications.]

10. I may add that, while the title of Governor-General is appropriate to yourself in the special circumstances in which you have been called upon to take up the appointment, I do not propose that it should be continued to your successors.

11. You point out that, while certain Departments will remain separate for Northern and Southern Nigeria, though individual officers will be interchangeable at the discretion of the Governor-General, it will be necessary that certain other Departments should be combined in order to ensure co-ordination. The Railway, Marine, and Customs Departments have already been combined, and, as regards Public Works, the existence of the Director of Railways and Works ensures co-ordination in matters of importance. The remaining Departments which you have proposed to combine are the Medical, the Posts and Telegraphs, the Judicial, and, to some extent, the Legal, Departments. I have addressed you separately with regard to the Medical Department. As regards the Posts and Telegraphs, I agree generally to the proposals made. . . . As regards the Judicial and Legal Departments, I also agree generally to your proposals, except that, in order to ensure the proper working of the system,

I think there should be one judge in addition to the establishment you propose . . .

[Leave conditions for senior personnel are agreed to; the Governor-General or his Deputy may assent to Ordinances and enact them, with Legislative Council advice, when they apply to the Colony of Lagos.]

15. Turning now to the subject of the annual Estimates of revenue and expenditure, I agree with you that the Estimates of Southern Nigeria, Northern Nigeria, and the Combined Departments should be printed separately as in the case of the Estimates for 1913. I am not clear as to what items of expenditure will be regarded as coming within the purview of the Legislative Council, or what source of revenue will be regarded as at its disposal. I shall be glad to receive further information on this point, and also to learn whether you consider it desirable that the Lagos Municipal Board of Health should continue to exist. It would appear that the functions of the Legislative Council and the Board might be efficiently exercised by one body. The proposed composition of the Council appears to be open to criticism, but I will defer consideration of this subject until I have received your views on the larger question.

16. I agree generally to the proposals made in the thirteenth paragraph of your despatch with regard to the Executive Council. As to the composition of the Council, however, I think it desirable that there should be a body of regular members all of whom would have the right of being present, if available, at any meeting. The Governor-General would have power to summon extraordinary members to assist in the discussion of special subjects. I doubt whether seven regular members (the number which you suggest) would be sufficient in the conditions of Nigeria without throwing an undue burden of work upon them. I observe, moreover, that no Financial Officer is included in your list of members.

17. I approve the proposed division of Southern Nigeria into nine provinces, and the reorganisation of the system of administration on the general lines of that obtaining in Northern Nigeria, as explained in paragraphs 42–5 of your report . . .

[Railways and harbours, new capitals, the W.A.F.F., and the Medical Staff will form the subjects of other correspondence.]

70

L. HARCOURT TO GOVERNOR SIR F. D. LUGARD: SOUTHERN NIGERIA, JURISDICTION AND ADMINISTRATION, 14 OCTOBER 1913[1]

SECRET.

. . . I have for some time had under my consideration your Secret despatch of the 30th of June,[2] with regard to the jurisdiction acquired by the Crown in the Protectorate of Southern Nigeria, more especially in the Western Province, and the policy to be followed in future in that Province.

2. On the general question of the jurisdiction acquired by the Crown, your proposal amounts to this: that whereas in the past the onus of establishing any jurisdiction claimed for the Crown has been upon the Government, and for that purpose, when usage or sufferance could not be relied upon, agreements have been made with various native chiefs or communities, in future—apart from Egbaland which occupies a special position—the onus of proof should be thrown on any person or native community denying His Majesty's jurisdiction. After careful consideration, I am prepared to agree to the adoption of this policy. If His Majesty's jurisdiction is challenged in one of the native States, the point will, I presume, come before the local Provincial Court, and if it involves difficult questions of the construction of treaties or agreements the Court will be able to refer the question for the ruling of the Secretary of State under Section 4 of the Foreign Jurisdiction Act, 1890.

3. As regards your suggestion in paragraph 23 that in the Order in Council providing for the Government of the Protectorate on the amalgamation of Northern and Southern Nigeria the right of the Crown to legislate for, and to exercise executive powers over, the whole of Nigeria should be asserted in unequivocal terms, you will see that in the draft Order already sent to you the existing provision of the Southern Nigeria Order in Council of 1911, whereby the legislative authority of the Governor is made subject to all treaties and agreements with natives at present in force, is preserved. I do not think that this saving clause can properly be omitted, and any general assertion in the Order in Council of the right of the Crown to legislate for the whole of Nigeria without such a saving clause would probably excite suspicion and lead the natives to treat as

---

[1] C.O. 879/113, no. 1005.
[2] No. 68. The Egba treaty was abrogated, 16 September 1914: see Kirk-Greene, *Lugard and the Amalgamation of Nigeria*, pp. 174–5.

encroachments on their rights acts on the part of the Protectorate Government to which they would otherwise not object.

4. So far as foreign Powers are concerned, it must, I think, be recognised that these native States are not in any sense independent sovereign States, but are in all their external relations under the protection of His Majesty, who will take such measures as he sees fit to make them carry out any treaty or other obligation towards foreign Powers that His Majesty may have assumed. This does not mean, however, that such States have necessarily lost all internal autonomy. As regards the right of jurisdiction over non-natives residing permanently or temporarily in a native State, it is clear, as pointed out in my Confidential despatch of 20th October, 1911, that the Crown has jurisdiction over such persons.

5. As you justly remark in paragraph 24 of your despatch, Egbaland must necessarily be treated differently from the remainder of the Protectorate. I have already dealt, in my secret despatch of October 7th, with the question of the Egbaland tolls or customs dues, and I have pointed out that it is impossible to regard these tolls as infringing the provisions of the Treaty of 1893 respecting freedom of trade. His Majesty's Government are bound, so long as the provisions of that Treaty are observed by the Egbas, to refrain from interfering with their internal self-Government except with the consent of the Egba authorities; and this obligation must be accepted as binding on the Government of Nigeria. I do not see any objection to the policy sketched in paragraph 24 of your despatch, so far as civil and criminal jurisdiction are concerned, but I do not understand what exactly is meant by 'Leases should be in perpetuity' in this connection, and I presume that in saying that the Egba Government should bind itself to conduct its courts in accordance with English law you probably mean that the courts which deal with matters other than those between Egbas should be governed by Southern Nigeria—not English—law. The 'New Policy' outlined in paragraph 8 of the sixth enclosure to your despatch goes, however, beyond what is stated in your despatch, and does not appear to me compatible with the Treaty of 1893, or subsequent agreements.

6. I entirely approve of your intention to adopt in Southern Nigeria, as far as is possible, the policy, which has been found so successful in Northern Nigeria, of vesting increasing power in rulers who prove themselves capable of using it rightly.

B. FINANCE AND PUBLIC INVESTMENT

I

R. G. W. HERBERT TO THE
SECRETARY TO THE TREASURY:
SIERRA LEONE AND GAMBIA DEBTS,
21 DECEMBER 1876[1]

I AM directed by the Earl of Carnarvon to request you call the attention of the Lords Commissioners of the Treasury to the letters from this Department, of 27th July last, in which his Lordship proposed that Parliament should be asked for grants in aid of the revenues of Sierra Leone, Gambia, and St. Helena. In reply to those letters their Lordships, by your letter of 3rd August, stated that as the supplementary estimates had already been presented to Parliament it was out of their power then to take the question under consideration.

Since that date Lord Carnarvon has intimated to their Lordships on more than one occasion that it would be necessary for him to renew the application for financial assistance to the Colonies already named, and I am now directed to request that you will submit to their Lordships the proposals which it has become his duty to bring before them.

1. With regard to the Colony of Sierra Leone, Lord Carnarvon regrets to be unable to make any more favourable representation of the state of affairs than was presented in July last. It is true that the floating debt, which at that time was stated to be about 26,000 l., has not materially increased, but remains at about the same figure. On the other hand the receipts from Customs dues, which form the chief part of the revenue of the Colony, continue to decline, for whilst during the quarter ended 30th June last the amount received was 12,718 l., the following quarter to 30th September realized only 11,536 l. As was pointed out in my letter of 27th July, much of this diminution of the revenue is owing to the loss sustained by the evasion of the Customs duties through the importation of goods into the adjacent rivers, whence they find their way into the Settlement.

With respect to the desire of their Lordships to be furnished with full information as to the present and prospective financial condition of the Colonies for which aid is asked, I am to state that if anything is required beyond what is contained in this and the previous letters, and their Lordships will be good enough to specify the nature of the information they desire, Lord Carnarvon will endeavour to supply it. His Lordship, however, desires me to observe that owing to a variety

[1] *Parl. Papers,* 1877, lx [C. 1685], pp. 6–9.

of circumstances, not the least important of which has been the constant changes in the official staff through sickness and death, caused by the fatal influences of the climate, the accounts of the West Africa Settlements have not hitherto been kept and rendered with the care and regularity which could be desired, and the necessity of which Lord Carnarvon has not failed to frequently impress upon the Colonial authorities.

In consequence of this defective condition of the accounts, which Lord Carnarvon regards with much dissatisfaction and regret, it is a matter of the utmost difficulty to extract from them any data as to the financial condition of the Settlements which can be considered as really accurate and trustworthy. Isolated facts may no doubt be obtained on which rough guesses may be framed, but for the purposes of instituting a comparison or drawing a correct inference, the accounts are practically useless.

A better system has now been introduced, and Lord Carnarvon believes that in the future there will not be the same difficulty in obtaining from the financial statements the information which he readily admits should be in the possession of this Department.

Whilst, therefore, for the reasons above stated, Lord Carnarvon fears that he cannot lay before their Lordships any further information as to the present financial condition of Sierra Leone, which would be of real use, it is impossible for him to forecast more distinctly the prospects of the Colony.

Like all West African possessions, Sierra Leone is, and must perforce be, dependent upon Customs duties as the main staple of her revenue.

Direct taxation has been tried, but the difficulties of assessment and collection, and the poverty of the greater portion of the inhabitants, render any tax of the kind oppressive in its operation and meagre in its results.

The financial condition of the Settlement is therefore to a great extent at the mercy of circumstances, the course of which it is impossible to foresee, and of influences against which no perfect safeguard can be devised. The condition of a trade which is constantly fluctuating, the existence of war or peace among the tribes of the interior over whom the Government can exercise little or no control, or the possible outbreak of an epidemic, are all elements in the calculation, the value of which cannot be estimated.

Whilst measures for the improvement of the revenue have been considered, the necessity of keeping down expenditure and exercising the strictest economy has not been lost sight of. Reduction and amalgamation of the establishments to the utmost practicable extent has already been effected, and will of course be extended as opportunities offer, but Lord Carnarvon would in his opinion only be misleading the Lords Commissioners of the Treasury if he were to hold out the hopes of the possibility of any considerable reduction of local expenses. The new Governor, Dr. Rowe, C.M.G., an officer of considerable financial knowledge and administrative ability, has already done very much during his tenure of office as Lieutenant Governor to simplify the accounts, and introduce a better and more intelligible system of rendering them, and he is fully aware of the necessity for a vigilant scrutiny of all expenditure of public money.

Lord Carnarvon feels that he can confidently affirm that before coming to their Lordships for aid for Sierra Leone, every legitimate means of increasing the revenue and diminishing the expenditure have been fully considered, and when practicable adopted.

Under these circumstances Lord Carnarvon cannot ask their Lordships to propose to Parliament, for the purpose of meeting existing liabilities and completing the construction of the harbour works, a vote of smaller amount than that asked for on the 27th July, viz., 31,000 *l.*

[In addition, £6,000 will be needed for a colonial steamer and a launch; and £3,000 to redeem the Gambia debt. Since there is to be no exchange of the Gambia for French posts, Parliament must meet the cost of the West Africa Settlements.]

The circumstances, therefore, of the case allow of no option. Due notice has been given of the course which it is now proposed to adopt, and Lord Carnarvon feels both as regards himself and Her Majesty's Government that there ought to be no difficulty in justifying the submission to Parliament of the votes now asked for.

In my letter of 27th July their Lordships were informed that Lord Carnarvon proposed to return to them a portion (20,000 *l.*) of the grant of 35,000 *l.*, made to the Gold Coast in 1874.[1] Since that date, as pointed out in the letter from this Department of 2nd ultimo, the circumstances of the Colony have somewhat changed, and his Lordship does not think that it would be prudent to relinquish so large a sum as he had at first hoped. He believes, however, that 15,000 *l.* can be spared, and he proposes accordingly to instruct the Crown Agents to transfer that amount to the Paymaster General to the credit of Imperial funds.

I am further to remind their Lordships that the advance of 20,000 *l.*, which, on the recommendation of Lord Carnarvon's predecessor, they were good enough to make to the Settlement of Lagos in 1873, has been fully and punctually repaid . . .

---

[1] Vol. I, Herbert to Law, 22 May 1874, p. 645.

2

THE SECRETARY TO THE TREASURY TO THE COLONIAL OFFICE: SUPPLEMENTARY ESTIMATES, 6 MARCH 1877[1]

[Supplementary Grants of £60,700 have been requested for Sierra Leone, the Gambia, and St. Helena.]

... My Lords regret that it should not be in the power of the Department to supply more information in regard to the financial condition of the two Settlements of Sierra Leone and the Gambia ... but under all the circumstances of the case, they are prepared to consent to supplementary Estimates of £4,200 for the Gambia and £5,500 for St. Helena being presented to Parliament in the ensuing session.

My Lords also assent to a Supplementary Estimate in the case of Sierra Leone for such amount as may prove to be necessary; but they trust that Lord Carnarvon may be able to see his way to reducing the very large grant asked for for this Colony by (at the least) the amount (£10,000) proposed to be taken by way of compensation to Mr. Heddle whose claim does not appear to have been ascertained and admitted by any judicial tribunal ...

3

C. PIKE TO ACTING ADMINISTRATOR C. A. MOLONEY: LAGOS CURRENCY, 26 AUGUST 1879[2]

... I have the honour to state as follows:

1. That the coins in question consist chiefly of Mexican, Peruvian, Chilian, and Brazilian dollars the first of these being three times as many as the others. The cause of so great an importation of these from England is the depreciation of silver in the European markets, which has enabled merchants to purchase them at prices sufficiently low to yield a profit in the Colony after paying expenses. The weight of a silver dollar is 17½ dwts., which at 4s. 1d. per ounce, the average price quoted in London between January and June of the present year, makes the cost of each dollar only 3s. 7d., while the local value is

[1] C.O. 267/333.
[2] C.O. 879/18, no. 239. For the timing of demonetization, see no. 5, and A. G. Hopkins, 'The Currency Revolution in South-West Nigeria in the late Nineteenth Century', *Journal of the Historical Society of Nigeria*, vol. iii, no. 3 (1966), pp. 471–83.

4s. 2d., a difference of 7d. or 14 per cent, and as the whole expense of importation is covered by 4 per cent, there is left to the importer a clear profit of 10 per cent. While the above accounts for the large preponderance of foreign silver in the Treasury, it does not explain why the surplus revenue is so much greater than usual. This is to be attributed to the recent refusal of canoemen to work at Whydah and other Windward ports, causing the diversion of transport through Lagos by inland waters to those ports, all merchandise, but particularly spirits, so passing contributing greatly to the augmentation of the revenue.

2. So long as a profit on the importation of dollars is possible merchants will not of course issue bills of exchange, which must be met in Europe by gold payments and bankers' expenses. It is evident, therefore, that the price alone of silver must determine the duration of the importance of dollars.

3. As to whether it is desirable or not to remit these dollars, the following facts should be considered, namely, that the difference in value against them in England is 14 per cent, which added to 4 per cent, the expense for remitting, would make a loss on each dollar of 9d. or 18 per cent, equivalent to six years' interest at three per cent, so that if we could find means of expending them within that time it would be profitable to retain them.

4. I respectfully submit that, should the acceptance at Treasury of this class of money be made optional, or should it be made compulsory, that all payments should consist in part of English money, the importation of them would be checked, and it would be a means of bringing more English money into the Colony, of which there is usually an inconveniently small quantity in circulation . . .

4

GOVERNOR H. T. USSHER TO
SIR MICHAEL HICKS BEACH:
GOLD COAST TAXATION,
21 JANUARY 1880[1]

. . . 5. IN the memorandum attention is called to the altered state of things on the Gold Coast, especially as regards the existence of increased power and more direct authority over Chiefs in the interior. The occasional capture and punishment of a rebellious or troublesome native Chief does not, however, appear to deter the other from deliberately and habitually breaking the law. It is true that the Governor has at his sole disposal an efficient and capable force of constabulary,

[1] C.O. 879/31, no. 379.

and that he is no longer at the mercy of the officer commanding the troops, when he requires to support his moral authority with a display of physical strength. But even this effective weapon is frequently paralysed by the incompetency or paucity of its officers.

If, in conclusion, the mistake were again committed of assembling the Chiefs and consulting them as to the propriety of imposing the poll tax, their reply, instead of confirming Colonel Ord's conviction, embodied in the concluding paragraph of the memorandum, would be simply to the effect that they are too heavily taxed already; and instead of consenting to a poll tax, they would in all probability petition for a reduction of duties, and the return to them of their right to sell and hold slaves and pawns. When the poll tax was imposed there was a want of revenue in the Settlement, and means were sought to increase it by what in those days would have been a respectable sum; for the present, at least, there is no such immediate want, as the Colony has a surplus of nearly 60,000 *l.*; and I doubt whether the net proceeds of a poll tax, with the only mode of collection now possible, would be worth the risk and trouble of collecting it under present conditions.

6. I have now stated my reasons for disagreeing with the conclusions arrived at in the memorandum,[1] the contents of which I have been broadly analysing; and I do not think, *à fortiori*, that I need inquire into the feasibility of applying the far more complicated system of direct taxation in the Senegal, disclosed by the papers you were good enough to transmit with the above-mentioned memorandum in your Despatch No. 354 above alluded to.

7. With regard to the stipends of the Chiefs, you only consider them as a part of a scheme of direct taxation, and therefore on that and many other grounds I would recommend its abandonment for the present; and until very different arrangements are made as to the government of the interior, I am completely of your opinion. . . .

5

R. G. W. HERBERT TO THE TREASURY: WEST AFRICAN CURRENCY, 26 NOVEMBER 1880[2]

I AM directed by the Earl of Kimberley to request that you will inform the Lords of the Treasury that his Lordship has had under his consideration your letter of the 19th of May last relative of the currency of the Colonies on the West Coast of Africa.

2. In that letter, while no conclusive opinion is expressed by their

[1] A. W. L. Hemming, Memorandum, 27 December 1878: C.O. 96/125.
[2] C.O. 879/18, no. 239.

Lordships, it is suggested that the system of sterling currency is best adapted for use in the Gold Coast, but that in the West Africa Settlements silver had established itself as the metal on which a single standard currency should be based, though you added that without further information their Lordships were unable to judge whether it was too late to arrest the steps which has been taken for demonetising the silver dollar in accordance with your letter of the 14th of February, or whether the experiment of a currency, based upon gold should be tried.

3. As regards this last point I am to observe that the Ordinance demonetising the dollar at Sierra Leone came into operation from the date of its proclamation on the 2nd of April; that dollars to the nominal value of 26,000 *l.* (out of 29,000 *l.* estimated to be in the Colony) had already been received at the Treasury by the 10th of the same month, and that 20,000 *l.* worth were shipped home by the same mail as brought the news of the enactment of the Ordinance, leaving 6,000 *l.* to be packed and sent by the steamer of the following week. In these circumstances it had not occurred to Lord Kimberley that their Lordships would desire to reconsider the general question, and prior to the receipt of your letter now under reply he had already directed the Agents to ship 15,000 *l.* in English gold and silver to the Colony as requested by the Local Government.

4. The 'experiment' being thus already in operation Lord Kimberley did not feel that any further immediate decision was required, and he has since had the opportunity of discussing the matter with Governor Sir S. Rowe in this country, and of considering the whole subject in connexion with the demonetisation of the dollars in the other Colonies on the West Coast.

5. The Governor has no doubt whatever that there will be no difficulty in retaining the English currency as the standard at Sierra Leone; and it is in favour of this view that from Sierra Leone itself no further representations in favour of the silver dollar have reached this Department, and so far as his Lordship can learn the new law is now working satisfactorily, and the change has been accepted by the community.

6. As regards their Lordships' disposition to prefer a silver standard in the West Africa Settlements on the ground that the trade is chiefly with silver using countries, I am to enclose for their Lordships' information copies of the abstracts of the trade returns of Sierra Leone and the Gambia for the last three years, from which it will be perceived that although of the exports a large proportion (say, $\frac{1}{3}$ to $\frac{1}{2}$ from Sierra Leone and $\frac{4}{5}$ from Gambia) goes to France, and a small proportion of the trade of Leone is with the United States of America, countries where there exists a double standard, by far the greater portion of the imports to both Settlements comes from the United

Kingdom and the Windward Coast, and in these circumstances there seems hardly any ground for comparing their case with that of Mauritius, or the other Eastern Colonies whose trade is mainly with India and China where there is no gold currency.

7. With respect to their Lordships' remarks on the fact that dollars to the value of 29,000 *l.* were in Sierra Leone at the time of the passing of the Ordinance, Lord Kimberley is informed by Sir S. Rowe that it is only within a very recent period that the dollar has usurped in the circulation the place which for many years was held by English coins; and it would appear from the return of moneys in the Treasury chest at that station that the dollar formed no appreciable part of the balances until September 1879, and that the silver 5-franc piece from 1876 to 1879 seldom constituted 10 per cent of the whole balance.

8. On these grounds Lord Kimberley is not disposed to doubt the probability of being able to retain the English standard in Sierra Leone, and though he regrets that steps were not taken beforehand for supplying the local Treasury with sufficient English money, and that more explicit instructions were not given as to the redemption of the Dollar at its full nominal value, the absence of which occasioned the agitation in the local community; he cannot impute any blame to the Governor for declining to defer the execution of the definitive instructions which was sent him from this Department on receipt of your letter of the 14th of February last.

9. As regards Sierra Leone, therefore, Lord Kimberley has only to recommend that the Ordinance No. 2 should receive Her Majesty's confirmation, and that the Governor should be instructed to consider and report on the advisability of demonetising and redeeming during a limited period the 5-franc pieces now that English money is again in circulation, and of putting a legal limit to the tender of English silver so as to establish the English system in its entirety.

10. As regards the Gambia I am to enclose copies of two Despatches from Mr. Gouldsbury, from which it may be perceived that the dollar was demonetised there without difficulty and at little cost to the community; but that the silver 5-franc piece there occupies a place in the circulation different to that in the other West African Colonies, which makes it extremely difficult to put the currency system on any sound basis. And I am to state that Lord Kimberley would recommend that the Gambia Ordinance No. 2 should also receive Her Majesty's confirmation, but that no steps should be taken to demonetise the French 5-franc piece so long as the French Minister limits the coinage of that piece. The Governor might further be told that it would be a desirable reform if the mercantile community can be induced to conform to the law and the practice of the Government and rate that coin at 3s. 10½d. instead of 4s.

11. With respect to the Gold Coast it was remarked in your letter

under reply that the demonetisation of the dollar had been effected without inconvenience. This statement was made in anticipation of the event, as the proclamation of the Ordinance demonetizing the dollar was not issued until the 30th of April, and the news of its passing and the effect of the measure was not received in this Department until the month of June. But from the enclosed Despatches from Governor Ussher their Lordships will perceive that their remarks proved true as regards the Gold Coast itself, although an inconvenience and an agitation was momentarily occasioned at Lagos of even a more serious nature than that at Sierra Leone. But in this case as in that of Sierra Leone the mischief appears to Lord Kimberley to have been due rather to the fact that the demonetisation was undertaken without a sufficient supply of English coin in the Treasury, and without any promise as to the redemption of the demonetised coins at their nominal value than to any cause which is likely to render it impossible to maintain the English currency system in the future.

12. At Lagos, as at Sierra Leone, early steps were taken to remedy the inconvenience by sending down 5,000 *l.* from the Gold Coast and 10,000 *l.* from England in English gold and silver, and by the shipment of the dollars to England; and Lord Kimberley much regrets that the demonetised coins were not received and exchanged at the Treasury for some limited period, which would probably soon have allayed the excitement.

13. When the dollar was demonetised in the West Indies it was not questioned that the Government should bear the cost, and that of British Guiana was put to heavy expenses in the matter; but Sir Michael Hicks Beach's Despatches to the West African Colonies contained no explicit instruction on this point, and Governor Ussher like Governor Rowe interpreted them to mean that the holders were to bear the loss, the only difference being that the former has adhered at present to his first decision, while the Governor at Sierra Leone yielded to the public outcry.

14. Mr. Ussher's description of the complainants and their grievances, though somewhat contradictory, do not point to any grave injustice having been done; and it is obvious that if instructions are now sent out to redeem the coins at their old nominal value, those who have in the meantime parted with them at a loss cannot be compensated, and the profit will probably be to a greater extent reaped again by the same speculators who imported them. Moreover, holders at the Gold Coast who have not yet complained will have to be treated similarly to holders at Lagos, but Lord Kimberley is disposed to overrule Mr. Ussher's objections on these points, and to instruct him, if their Lordships concur, to receive in exchange for English money at the Treasury for a period of 10 days all dollars still

in the Colony, and to impose such taxation to meet the cost as is contemplated in the 7th paragraph of his Despatch or the 19th of July if his Council consider it necessary.

15. Governor Ussher states that English merchants are already importing English money, and Lord Kimberley has therefore little doubt that, as soon as the redemption question is settled, the new currency system will be established without difficulty, and he recommends that the Ordinance No. 2 should be confirmed.

16. As regards Governor Ussher's apprehensions as to the importation of debased gold coins, Lord Kimberley would suggest that some inquiry should be made as to the probability of such shipments as are mentioned in his Despatch of 31st May, and if necessary an amending Ordinance passed defining the weight and fineness of the gold doubloon.

17. Lord Kimberley wishes their Lordships' attention to be called to Governor Ussher's statement in his Despatch of the 19th of July that spurious silver dollars were manufactured in Birmingham for exportation to the West Coast, though he does not know what importance to attach to it.

6

LORD GRANVILLE TO GOVERNOR SIR SAMUEL ROWE: GAMBIA MAIL SUBSIDY, 12 FEBRUARY 1886[1]

I HAVE the honour to acquaint you that I have had before me your Despatch of the 11th of December, forwarding a Despatch from the Administrator of the Gambia covering the estimates of the revenue and expenditure of the Settlement for the current year.

The estimates appear to have been framed with a due regard to the necessity for strict economy required by the large falling off which has taken place in the Revenue during the last two years, and I have no observations to offer on them.

I take the opportunity, however, of calling your attention to the heavy subsidy paid to the British and African Steam Ship Company, for the mail service with this country. In addition to the direct payment of 1,200 l. a year, remission of tonnage dues is granted to the Company averaging according to the estimate in Captain Moloney's Despatch enclosed in yours of the 9th of Sept. last, 3,000 l. per annum. Looking to the fact that the great bulk of the trade of the Settlement is with France, and that there now exists a regular monthly communication with that country, by which also mails are sent to England, it appears to me undesirable to maintain the direct communication

[1] Parl. Papers, 1887 [C 4978], pp. 10–11.

with this country at so disproportionate a cost. In the Despatch referred to, Mr. Moloney suggests the abolition of the subsidy to the British and African Company, and that arrangements should be made for establishing a second monthly service between Gambia and Dakar, in connexion with the service of the Messageries Maritimes to the latter place, and now that the cable will shortly connect Bathurst both with Sierra Leone and England, it appears to me that Mr. Moloney's proposal would adequately provide for the postal requirements of the Settlement, even if the British and African Company should cease to call, which is not, however, probable. The question should be brought before the Legislative Council with as little delay as possible, in order that, if they agree, the necessary notice may be given to the Company.

The sum which would be liberated by the abolition of the mail subsidy could not, I think, be better employed than in reducing the tonnage dues. The rate of 1s. per ton at which these duties are at present levied, gives a practical monopoly to the Mail Company, and places the trade of the Settlement at a great disadvantage by preventing any competition for freight. It appears from the Blue Book for 1884 that the total amount received from this source in 1884 was about 1,800 l., and, deducting the amount of the present mail subsidy from this, only 600 l. would have to be provided to enable the dues to be entirely removed. This sum might, as it appears to me, be most conveniently raised by adding 1d. a pound to the duty on unmanufactured tobacco, which, judging from the amount received in 1884 from the present duty, should bring in over 700 l. a year. I have little doubt that opening the port in this way would give a considerable stimulus to the trade of the Settlement, and in the end largely benefit the revenue.

You will instruct the Administrator to bring these questions also before the Council, and should they concur in the proposals I have made, the legislation necessary to give effect to them should be forthwith proceeded with.

The abolition of the tonnage dues would of course only take effect from the actual termination of the subsidy, and as the Company are intitled to only three months' notice of the termination of the agreement, it will be desirable, in the event of the Council concurring, to pass the Ordinances at once, leaving the date at which the alterations in the tariff will come into force to be fixed hereafter by Proclamation.

7

J. ANDERSON: MINUTE, SIERRA LEONE TARIFFS AND FINANCE, 4 OCTOBER 1886[1]

... THE policy we have hitherto pursued at Sierra Leone of taking the coast line and levying customs dues, and taking no concern in the country behind—the policy which Mr Fairfield calls the 'robber baron' policy—has been a signal failure as regards the object aimed at of increasing our revenue without increasing our responsibilities. Instead of increasing the revenue, our last stroke of business in the way of erecting fiscal toll-bars made the revenue of Sherbro drop 10,000 *l.* a year, and it has not yet recovered. Every chief through whose territory trade passes levies a toll on it. We place customs duties, and the coast chiefs and those behind them immediately fall to quarrelling because their receipts are diminished. No man trusts another; the interior chiefs naturally accuse those in front of them of taking more than their share, and of having sacrificed the general interest for the sake of the annual present of rum and gin that we make them. War ensues, the women and children who collect the produce are carried off into slavery, the produce rots on the fields, and what little is gathered finds its way to the markets only by success-fully foiling the plunderers who lie in wait for it at every stage. Exhaustion brings the peace of desolation, but the producers are gone, or move about in fear. The evils of war do not die with it, and years must elapse before we can look for the same prosperity as before. I cannot help thinking that this policy of levying duties on trade while we do not in return do anything for it is not one which, if the British public rightly understood it, we should be allowed to continue. We are supposed to maintain our settlements for the benefit of trade, the suppression of slavery, and the spread of civilization. Instead of this we half strangle trade by our customs, we fill the slave markets by causing these wars in the interior, and for civilization we spend a few hundreds a year for schools not amongst the people upon whose produce we levy the duties, but amongst the population of the peninsula who share in the spoils. In these circumstances the wisest thing would be to withdraw from the whole coast, and govern the peninsula in some simple manner such as its revenue could afford. At present this is impossible; the moment we withdrew some other power would step in, and there would be a storm of indignation against any Minister who would thus sacrifice 'British interests.' We have levied taxation on people and not even kept peace among them;

[1] C.O. 879/24, no. 323. Based partly on a memorandum by Rowe, 29 April 1886, recommending increased customs duties after heavy deficits: Rowe to Stanley, 13 January 1886. (*Sir*) *John Anderson*, later Permanent Under-Secretary, 1911–16.

we cannot withdraw, and our only course is to take up the burden we have shirked of keeping peace in the area which produces the revenue. That this will in the result involve no greater responsibility than the present system, and will abolish the financial risk, the example of our other settlements on the West Coast is, I think, sufficient evidence. On the Gold Coast we keep the peace within an area much larger than the producing area behind Sierra Leone, among tribes quite as fond of fighting among themselves as the Timmanis and Mendis, and yet our constabulary force is only 500 men, while at Sierra Leone we have 300 for the small area of the peninsula and the coast stations. At Lagos we do not keep the peace over any but a small part of the producing area, but we police the waterway, and the French do it over the rest, and the result is, as at the Gold Coast, a steadily expanding trade and revenue. In these settlements it is true we have no export duties, but though these duties prevent the expansion of trade, and render it unable to bear competition, they are not responsible for the tremendous fall in our exports from Sherbro since 1881, nor for the fall in our trade from Sierra Leone in the present year. These cannot in any way be traced to the export dues. They are sharp sudden falls, and are coincident with the harrying of the producing districts by the war bands. The only way of preventing this is by doing as we do at the Gold Coast, assuming a protectorate over the producing area, leaving the chiefs their present jurisdiction, but supervising them and preventing them from making war on each other. Tribal wars would then be treated as matters of police, and put down without trouble or bloodshed, instead of spreading all over the country and causing universal desolation.[1] For this purpose it will be necessary to maintain our police at 400 men instead of 300 as at present, and we shall require an additional officer, entailing an extra expenditure in all of 3,000 *l*. This, however, is only apparent, as at present, in missions, presents, and entertainments to native chiefs we spent last year a good deal more than this; in carrying out the policy of 'moral suasion', and after all that expenditure, we know that they are only waiting for the 'dries' to be at it again. Even what success we had in this matter was due to the personal influence of Sir S. Rowe, and we cannot have him always here.

We can save at least 1,000 *l*. a year under this head by establishing a protectorate, and the extra cost will therefore be reduced to 2,000 *l*. This will reduce the saving on the estimates from 4,900 *l*. to 2,900 *l*. We must now consider what revenue we require, and how we can best provide it. The estimates for the current year show an expenditure of 68,700 *l*. against a revenue of 64,600 *l*. The expenditure can, as I have attempted to show, be reduced practically to 65,600 *l*., so

---

[1] Rowe agreed with this protectorate policy: Memorandum, 21 December 1886 (see III. A, no. 12).

that the addition to the estimated revenue of the year must be 1,000 *l.*
With peace in the country the estimate of revenue would be amply
realized, and we may therefore safely take it as a basis for our calcula-
tions. The export and tonnage dues figure in the estimate at 14,500 *l.*,
so that to abolish them and make up the deficit we shall want
15,500 *l.* of additional revenue to make ends meet. We have to make
up a considerable deficit too, so that it will not be safe to estimate our
requirements from fresh taxation at less than 11,000 *l.* . . .

8

M. F. OMMANNEY (CROWN AGENTS) TO THE AFRICAN BANKING CORPORATION: LAGOS CURRENCY, 28 JANUARY 1892[1]

. . . I HAVE to state that the arrangement as to the future importation
of new coin into Lagos, which was agreed to at the interview you had
with Mr. Meade and myself at the Colonial Office, was that so long
as your Bank at Lagos remains bankers to the Colonial Government
and so long as the further importation of coin is not prohibited by the
Governor, we shall cease to grant orders on the Mint for coin for
shipment to the Colony to private firms or individuals and will furnish
you with such orders of this nature as you may require. If, however,
the Governor of the Colony is satisfied that your Bank is making
unreasonable terms, charges or conditions in connection with this
importation of coin, the Governor will, after seven days notice to your
Lagos Manager in writing by the hand of the Colonial Secretary,
resume the practice of granting such orders on the Mint as he may
think fit, to private individuals or firms . . .

9

COLONIAL OFFICE TO ALFRED L. JONES: BANK OF BRITISH WEST AFRICA, 14 MARCH 1894[2]

. . . I AM directed by the Marquess of Ripon to acquaint you that the
Memorandum of Articles of Association of the Bank of British West

---

[1] C.O. 147/87. (*Sir*) *Montagu Ommanney*, Crown Agent, 1877; Permanent
Under-Secretary for Colonies, 1900–7. The African Banking Corporation was
established by G. W. Neville, Lagos agent for the African Steamship Company.
[2] C.O. 147/96. The Crown Agents agreed to the Articles of Association of the
Bank, 7 March 1894. The Agreement lasted till 1911. *Sir Alfred L. Jones*, (1845–
1909) partner of Messrs. Elder, Dempster's Liverpool shipping firm, dominated
the African Trade Section of the Liverpool Chamber of Commerce. He founded
the Bank of British West Africa and the Liverpool School of Tropical Medicine.

Africa, Limited, have been carefully examined, and His Lordship desires me to convey to you the following remarks with respect to them.

Although the Memo: and articles of association do not satisfy the very desirable condition of prohibiting the proposed Bank from engaging in any but bona fide banking business, Lord Ripon is advised that there are practical difficulties in introducing, in specific terms, a limitation of this kind, regard being had to the conditions usually embodied in such articles. This being so you must understand that, in order to protect the Colonial Govt., against such inconveniences as have arisen in the past, any Agreement made with the Bank for the transaction of the business of the Govt. of Lagos will contain a provision for termination at the sole option of the Governor, at three months' notice.

As regards the terms of such an agreement and the question of entrusting to the Bank the control of the importation of silver, Lord Ripon is prepared to approve the Conclusion of an Agreement similar to that made with the African Banking Corporation, and the insertion of a clause by which the Govt. would undertake not to give facilities to Traders to import silver, while reserving to itself full power to do so.

Lord Ripon would also require the insertion of a clause, limiting the charge to be made by the Bank to persons requiring silver to a premium not exceeding 1%.

Lord Ripon feels bound to safeguard the interests of the public by this requirement, and I am to point out that as the silver can be obtained by the Bank from the Royal Mint free of cost, the charge in question could be almost entirely clear of profit.

If you are prepared to accept the conditions above stated you should communicate with the Crown Agents who will be authorized to enter into an agreement with you.

10

M. F. OMMANNEY TO THE COLONIAL OFFICE: LAGOS RAILWAY FINANCE, 11 DECEMBER 1895[1]

I HAVE the honour to inquire whether any decision has been arrived at as to the manner in which funds are to be provided for the Lagos bridges and of the first section of the railway. The estimate for these works is as follows:

[1] C.O. 879/40, no. 464.

£

Railway, Iddo Island to Otta .   .   .   173,694
Bridges   75,000
   „   Engineering supervision in England   3,000
                                               _____
                                               251,694

Say 252,000 *l.*
   If this money is to be raised by loan, the sum of about 3,000 *l.*
must be added to this amount for the expenses of issue, and the
commutation for stamp duty, making a total of 255,000 *l.*
   2. To enable this money to be borrowed as inscribed stock under
the Colonial Stock Act of 1877, ordinances and documents similar to
those recently sent to Sierra Leone will be necessary.[1] I enclose drafts
of these instruments and, if Mr. Secretary Chamberlain should
decide that funds are to be provided in this manner, it will be
necessary to explain, in sending the drafts out to the Governor, that
they must be strictly adhered to.
   3. I also enclose a statistical document which should be verified,
brought up to date, and returned with the other documents.
   4. In the meantime we shall require a considerable command of
funds, and it is desirable to authorise us to realise, if necessary, the
surplus funds of the Colony, amounting in nominal value to about
50,000 *l.*, subject to adjustment when the loan is issued, if the re-
imbursement of the surplus funds is considered desirable.

11

EDWARD WINGFIELD: MINUTE,
SIERRA LEONE RAILWAY FINANCE,
12 MAY 1896[2]

. . . The Governor proposed to pay for the interest on the Railway
Loan by imposing a duty of 6d. on sword blades of which he said
50,000 were annually imported: we were naturally rather shocked at
this large number of murderous instruments and suggested a larger
import duty. It now appears that 50,000 was a flight of fancy and that
there are no means of finding out what the proper number is, as
sword blades are imported under the head of cutlery. The interest on
the loan is now to be provided for by increasing the ad valorem
duties from 7½ to 10 per cent.

   [1] See below, Section IV, for the Sierra Leone railway.
   [2] C.O. 267/425. On Cardew to Chamberlain, 22 April 1896. (*Sir*) *Edward
Wingfield*, Permanent Under-Secretary, 1897–1900.

12

GOVERNOR F. CARDEW TO JOSEPH CHAMBERLAIN: SIERRA LEONE HOUSE TAX, 14 DECEMBER 1896[1]

. . . 6. I HAVE endeavoured to show above my reasons for thinking that the difficulty of collecting the house-tax, in view of the character of the Protectorate and its great extent, will not be so great as anticipated, nor do I think the physical difficulty of doing so in kind will be insuperable. In the first place, I believe the natives will prefer to pay in coin, and, in the second, that it will very soon be, if it is not so already, within their ability to do so. My experience in Zululand, where I used to collect hut-tax and where, after the first year it was paid in cash, leads me to this conclusion, and, from an address recently given by Mr. Alfred Sharpe before the Geographical Society, I gather that a similar experience obtains in British Central Africa, where the conditions as to the habits and customs of the people appear very similar to those which prevail in the Protectorate, but where, I may say, the soil is not so fertile or productive as in this country. . . .

9. Turning to an examination of the estimate, it will be observed that, in order to be on the safe side, I credit the officers with spending in the Protectorate only 80 l. each out of their salaries. I also allow, as not being available for expenditure there, 787 l. of the pay of the non-commissioned officers and privates as family remittances, and on the same account make considerable deductions from the salaries of the subordinate officials of the Administrative Department.

With regard to stipends to Native Chiefs, hitherto these have been paid in Freetown and Bonthe, at which places the cash was converted into goods. Now the Chiefs will receive them from the District Commissioners in the Protectorate, and will probably retain them to pay their taxes.

The estimate shows that the cash in circulation will amount to 17,961 l., but this sum will not nearly represent the gross amount of coin in the country. Many of the Chiefs have considerable sums hoarded, and in the Protectorate there is a large population of Sierra Leoneans, who are familiar with the use of coin, and with respect to the three districts adjoining the Colony, many of the Chiefs levy their tolls on canoes, wharfage dues, and license to cut timber, in coin, and often raise contributions from their people in cash, which facts show there is a certain amount of coin already in circulation.

10. But another important medium for the dissemination of coin

[1] C.O. 267/427

is the railway works, on which will shortly be employed from 2,000 to 3,000 labourers, most of whom will be from the Protectorate, and who may be expected to return there with a certain proportion of their wages in coin, and finally there are the traders from the neighbouring French Colonies, who of late have taken to disposing of their produce on the frontier for cash, with which they purchase goods in Freetown, but no doubt a certain amount of this money is paid away in the Protectorate.

11. I have endeavoured to show above that there is a reasonable expectation of the taxes being paid in coin, and this expectation amounts to almost a certainty, that in the course of a year or two this will be the case in the three districts bordering the Colony. In the two remoter ones, however, coin is certainly scarcer than in the others, but even in these it should not be so very difficult to dispose of the produce that may be offered in lieu of coin for taxes. The principal produce is rice, and a certain portion of the amount paid in for taxes can be disposed of to the police and the officials of the Administrative and Medical Staff, who, together with their followers, will probably number, all told, 1,000, and as the Sierra Leone traders advance further inland, which they will undoubtedly do as soon as they know the law will protect them, they will also become purchasers . . .

13

R. ANTROBUS: MINUTE, SIERRA LEONE FINANCE, 22 JANUARY 1897[1]

I THINK that we must let Col. Cardew have the money proposed . . . but in doing so we should call attention to his remarks as to the sources from which the money would be found, which are unsound. He seems to think that the Colony has a right to appropriate all the customs duties, but as they are raised to large extent on goods consumed in the Protectorate, it is only fair to add that the expenses of the Protectorate should in part be defrayed from them (the late Sir S. Rowe was fond of pointing out that the liberated slaves of Freetown and their descendants were relieved of taxation at the expense of the slaves of the interior.) Col. Cardew also hints at Imperial assistance; but the policy of the Treasury, in which the C.O. has entirely concurred, has always been to make the W. African Colonies self-supporting, and we have prided ourselves on having within the last few years succeeded at length in making S. Leone independent of help from Imperial funds. We do not want to begin asking for assistance again if it can be avoided . . .

[1] C.O. 267/427. (*Sir*) *R. L. Antrobus*, Assistant Under-Secretary, 1898–1909; Senior Crown Agent for the Colonies, 1909–18.

14

H. BERTRAM COX (COLONIAL OFFICE) TO THE TREASURY: COST OF GOLD COAST EXPANSION, 8 JANUARY 1898[1]

WITH reference to the last paragraph but one of the letter from this Department of the 25th October last, on the subject of the Force which it had been decided to raise at the cost of Imperial Funds for service in West Africa, in which it was stated that it was feared that it might also be necessary to ask for some assistance for the Gold Coast and Lagos in order to meet the expenditure which had been forced upon those Colonies by the incursions of French parties into their territories, I am directed by Mr. Secretary Chamberlain to transmit to you, to be laid before the Lords Commissioners of the Treasury, copies of a telegraphic correspondence between the Gold Coast and this Department on the subject of the special expenditure incurred in connection with the territories in the 'Hinterland' of the Gold Coast to the north of Ashanti which have recently been constituted a separate district with the title of the 'Northern Territories,' and placed in charge of a Commissioner specially selected for that purpose.

From the Estimates of the Gold Coast Colony for the year 1898, which have just been sent home, and which are now forwarded for their Lordship's inspection, together with the Acting Governor's covering despatch, it will be seen that it is estimated that there may be a deficit at the close of 1898 of £79,650, which would be reduced to £19,650 by postponing repayment to the War Department of the instalment of £20,000 which it had been arranged to pay on account of advances in connection with the Ashanti Expedition of 1895–6, and by taking a Grant in Aid of the Colony for £40,000 to meet expenditure in connection with the operations in the Northern Territories. From the subsequent telegrams it will be seen that this latter expenditure may amount to £45,000.

In consideration of these figures, and of the fact that the expenditure in connection with the Northern Territories has been brought about by the action taken by a Foreign Power, Mr. Chamberlain considers that while the Colony may at present be left to make its own arrangements as regards the *ordinary* revenue and expenditure of the Colony, the expenses of the Northern Territories must be met from Imperial Funds. So far as can be judged from the information at present before this Department, it would appear that the annual expenditure on this service is approximately £25,000; and as there is at present no

[1] C.O. 879/52, no. 549.

probability of revenue being raised in these territories to meet such additional expenditure, he would propose, for their Lordships' consideration, that a grant for that amount only should be provided in the Colonial Services Estimate for 1898–9, £20,000 being taken as a Supplementary Estimate for the current year, if further information should show that that amount will probably have been expended before 31st March next . . .

15

H. BERTRAM COX (COLONIAL OFFICE) TO FOREIGN OFFICE: NIGER CURRENCIES, 13 JANUARY 1898[1]

I AM directed by Mr. Secretary Chamberlain to acknowledge the receipt of your letter of the 31st of December, enclosing an extract from a despatch from Her Majesty's Commissioner and Consul-General for the Niger Coast Protectorate, containing a proposal to enact that trade shall be conducted on a cash basis, and that the importation of articles to serve instead of coins shall be prohibited.

2. I am to state, for the information of the Marquess of Salisbury, that it would be unnecessary, even if it were practicable, to compel the natives to abandon the measures of value to which they are accustomed. Such articles as brass rods or cowries are not legal tender, but they are in practice current at recognized values in certain districts, and it would seem impossible to force the natives in all parts of the Protectorate to procure and deal in silver in all their trade transactions with one another. As British trade advances into the Interior, the use of silver will no doubt increase, as has been the case in other parts of West Africa; but the process must be gradual, and must take place *pari passu* with the advance of British trade.

3. Mr. Chamberlain would also observe that these brass rods are in fact a medium of exchange, although an inconvenient one, and that therefore trade in the Protectorate can hardly be said to be in a state of barter.

16

NOTES ON THE MEETING OF GOLD COAST TRADERS, COLONIAL OFFICE, 28 MARCH 1899[2]

PRIVATE.

Mr. Chamberlain said:

'Hitherto the concessions which have been obtained have been on a very large scale. In certain districts this is necessary, but in other

---

[1] C.O. 879/59, no. 592.   [2] C.O. 879/57, no. 578.

cases very small concessions of a few square yards have in other countries nevertheless been productive of enormous profits.

If our hopes are fulfilled, these large concessions will be of enormous importance. I do not grudge any profits made by those who have been first in promoting this industry, and I do not want to curtail them, but I want to have my share of them for the interests with which I am concerned, that is to say, I want to come to an understanding with those who are concerned as to the way in which they will be taxed. They have got to be taxed: this must be admitted. Take the £125,000 paid-up capital of the Ashanti Gold Fields Corporation. The shares are at £18 per share. The shareholders have made a paper profit of at least £2,000,000 sterling. They have made this profit entirely because of the expenditure of treasure by the Imperial Government and the Gold Coast Colony. I shall appeal to the patriotism of the Ashanti Gold Fields Corporation to enable me to share in any profit they may be going to make.

In the first place, I would propose that, in giving a title to any concession which may have been obtained from the native chief or owner, besides seeing to the interests of the native, the Government should be entitled to a sum down which should be in some way proportionate to the amount of the concession. A moderate sum, in return for the title which we have made possible, would be recognised, I think, as a fair demand.

The second point is that we ought to have a fair share of the profits made. It was originally suggested that we might have a 5 per cent. royalty on all the gold won. If the profits are what we expect them to be, I think it may be said that this would be too small. This would be nothing compared with what is done in the Transvaal and Rhodesia. If I were to average the share-charge over the whole product, a 5 per cent. royalty on the whole output would not be excessive.

But there are mines and mines, and there may be mines that will be much more difficult to work, and in the case of such mines a 5 per cent. tax might be prohibitive. We do not want to hamper the industry, and if there is a real reason to fear that there are mines which will not sustain a tax levied upon the output, we must find some other means. The only other means that I can find would be to tax profits, and if it should be your feeling that a tax should be levied not upon output, which would suit the Colony best, but upon realised profit, I think that that might be done. That involves something of the nature of the Income Tax. As regards large companies, such a tax might not be so difficult to collect, because you might take the returns to their shareholders. There would have to be some sort of examination, so as to show that if reserves are made they are not unfairly made. As regards small companies, we should have to examine their books.

I do not mean to oppress or in any way to hamper this industry, but I do not mean all the profits to go the private individual.

Another point is the proposed new Ordinance for dealing with concessions. One great object of this Ordinance is to protect the natives, and we shall also have to see that the title is good enough. We have circulated to the Chambers of Commerce a brief abstract of this Ordinance, and I should be glad to know if you see anything further which should be inserted, or which you take objection to.

We must see that the native gets a share, by means of a sum down or a sum payable, if necessary, by instalments.' . . .

Mr. Moorcroft (Tarquah and Abosso Gold Mining Company): We were the first to begin mining on the Coast. We have spent the best part of a million of money, have expended all our capital and all the gold we have produced, which was worth £150,000 to £200,000. This has gone on for the last 22 years, and we think we deserve every consideration at the hands of Her Majesty's Government.

With regard to the question of taxation, we think you should be very lenient. We have paid a considerable amount in taxes in the Colony. The reason we have been unable to pay our way is because we have to deal with low grade ore, and besides, the expense of transport would have killed almost any undertaking. If we have the railway, for which we are grateful, do not let us pay any tax until we are reaping the benefit of the railway. We reconstituted our company, and our capital is £300,000. As to our concessions, on some of them we have paid rents, on others not, because in some cases, by the terms of the concession, we were not bound to pay until working commenced.

Mr. Chamberlain: I should meet your views by means of the income tax.

Mr. Moorcroft: I think that would be the fairest method.

Mr. Hunt: As to the business expert, I think there should be two assessors in case of need. I am not so interested in the mode of taxation, but it would be some convenience to make it an *ad valorem* tax—an income tax.

Mr. Gordon: I represent the Ashanti Gold Fields Company. I rather regret that the shares have gone up to the high price they have. We set to work the moment we got the concession. As regards the mode of taxation the simplest form is on the output, but I think the fairest would be upon profits; but this necessitates a rather complicated method, especially as a considerable amount has to be expended on development.

Mr. Chamberlain: I should not object to anything in the shape of development coming out of profits. If the Company makes profits and spends part of them on development which would hereafter become profitable, I should not object.

Mr. Gordon: Whatever the taxation may be, I think it should be in such a form as not to create discontent among the native labourers. The difficulty of labour has been very small with us in Ashanti. I should be sorry if there was any direct taxation of the native labourers.

Mr. Chamberlain: If you will give me enough, I promise you I will not tax them at all.

Mr. Tarbutt (British Gold Coast Syndicate): The tax on profits in the Transvaal has caused a great deal of difficulty, and I think a tax on profits is objectionable. The most convenient form is to exact so much per cent. on the output of gold. There is a good rule in the Transvaal, that a man who has a large farm has to select within a certain time what he will keep, and the rest is then thrown open. I think this might be followed on the Gold Coast.

Mr. Chamberlain: It would be convenient, as two proposals have been made and two opinions have been expressed, that there should be a show of hands.

This was taken, and those in favour of taxing product were 9.

Those in favour of taxing profits were 17.

Mr. Chamberlain expressed his thanks to the meeting, and Mr. Jones, on behalf of the deputation, expressed their thanks to the Secretary of State.

17

M. F. OMMANNEY TO THE
COLONIAL OFFICE: WEST AFRICAN
LOANS, 16 AUGUST 1899[1]

[The merits of the Colonial Loans Act terms of borrowing are compared with the financial market.]

. . . IT thus appears that, solely from the actuarial point of view, the issue of such a loan as Inscribed Stock would be materially more favourable to the Colony than a loan under the Colonial Loans Act, as it is proposed by the Treasury to apply that Act. There are other disadvantages of a more general character which appear to us to arise from the latter mode of borrowing. The Colony will be called upon to bear the heaviest charges during the earliest years of the undertaking for which the money is borrowed, during which the earning capacity of that undertaking is still in process of development. It does not appear to us that such a system is convenient or consistent

[1] C.O. 147/146. The Treasury, at this time, would not lend money at less than 3¼ per cent for a period of fifty years.

with the assumption on which such works have hitherto been sanctioned, that the debt charges to be provided for out of their net earnings will be equally distributed over the currency of the loan and that that currency will be of sufficient duration to keep those charges within the limits of the probable net earnings. All recent issues of Colonial Inscribed Stock are subject to redemption on notice after a comparatively short currency, in most cases of 25 years. This enables the Colony to take advantage of either accrued surplus funds or improved credit and the system contemplated by the Treasury, under the Colonial Loans Act, appears to involve the sacrifice of this material advantage . . .

18

CROWN AGENTS TO THE COLONIAL OFFICE: LAGOS LOANS, 18 JULY 1900[1]

[The Treasury have given permission for a loan of £792,500 under the Colonial Loans Act; stock will be issued under unfavourable market conditions.]

. . . 2. THE borrowing powers of the Government of Lagos are contained in the following Ordinances:

No. 2 of 1896   £255,000
No. 15 of 1897   £525,000
No. 4 of 1900   £126,000
making a sum of £906,200
and the sum of £792,500 has been borrowed from the Treasury under Ordinance No. 2 of 1900 and the Colonial Loans Act of 1899, leaving a balance of £113,700 to be raised under Ordinance No. 4 of 1900 . . .

[£102,700 in Stock will be issued by the Crown Agents.]

4. In order to meet the requirements of the Colony, and to set our accounts in order, it is desirable that the loan should be offered to the public at the earliest possible moment, but as we cannot hope to be able to place three per cent Lagos stock, ranking after the Treasury loan, at price above 93 per cent the price at which the recent Queensland 3 per cent loan has been left on the Underwriters' hands, it will

[1] C.O. 147/152.

not be safe for the Government of Lagos to rely on receiving more than £95,500 for its loan of £102,700 from which also will have to be deducted £1,200 for the expense of issue, leaving a net sum of about £94,300 available for the purposes of the Colony . . .

19

JOSEPH CHAMBERLAIN TO HIGH COMMISSIONER SIR RALPH MOOR: NIGERIAN FINANCES, 22 MAY 1902[1]

. . . 17. CONTRIBUTION to Northern Nigeria.—With reference to your suggestion that the amount of this contribution should present the amount of duty collected on behalf of Northern Nigeria, less the amount of expenditure incurred for Customs and Postal work done in Southern Nigeria for that Protectorate, I am to observe that, when the question of the contribution was originally under consideration in 1899, it was arranged, with the concurrence of the Lords Commissioners of the Treasury that, as it would be impossible to determine precisely what proportion of the Customs Revenue derived from duties on goods imported for consumption in Northern Nigeria, the Customs receipts should be allotted to the three divisions (Lagos and Northern and Southern Nigeria) in such proportions as the Secretary of State might from time to time direct, having regard to the requirements both of the divisions on the coast and of the inland division. I have accordingly decided that the contribution for the year 1902–3 shall remain at the same amount, £34,000, as in the preceding year, but I hope that it will be possible to provide £40,000 in the next year's estimates, and (probably) £50,000 in 1904–5 . . .

20

CROWN AGENTS TO THE COLONIAL OFFICE: LAGOS RAILWAY FINANCE, 14 JULY 1902[2]

IN the concluding paragraphs of our letter of the 26th April, on the subject of railway construction in Nigeria, we wrote as follows with respect to the financial position of Lagos:

'I regret, however, to say that the financial position of Lagos renders it out of the question that any further railway extension can be proceeded with at present. The sum of £792,500 has been borrowed

---

[1] C.O. 879/72, no. 677.   [2] C.O. 879/76, no. 695.

from the Treasury, under the provisions of the Colonial Loans Act, 1899, and we have still to borrow the further sum of £457,500 to pay for the completion of the railway and its equipment. The Treasury loan carries, moreover, a first charge on the revenues and assets of the Colony so that any subsequent borrowing must rank as a second charge.

'In these circumstances we have not attempted to provide for the requirements of Lagos by raising any further loan, as in the recent and present state of the money market a loan ranking only as a second charge could only be raised on such onerous terms as to be out of the question. We have, therefore, provided for the requirements of the Colony by temporary advances, and we propose to continue to do so as long as possible. As soon, however, as peace is restored and the money market resumes its normal condition, borrowing on reasonable terms may be expected to become practicable, and we are contemplating asking the Secretary of State to approach the Treasury and obtain permission for the paying off of the loan of £792,500, so as to enable us to offer to the market a loan representing the total requirements of Lagos, viz., £1,250,000, unencumbered by any prior charge.

'When this operation has been effected it may become practicable to borrow further on account of the Colony, but until the first charge held by the Treasury is removed, any borrowing operations which we might attempt would be almost certain to result in failure.'

2. I now beg to submit, for the consideration of the Secretary of State, that the Lords Commissioners of the Treasury should be moved to agree to an anticipation of the period of five years laid down by Section 9 of the Lagos Imperial Loan Ordinance (No. 2) of 1900, as the earliest date on which notice can be given for the repayment of the loan, and that they should be asked to agree to accept earlier repayment on receiving six months' previous notice.

3. Such earlier repayment is absolutely necessary unless the Treasury should be prepared to make further advances to the Colony on the same terms as the existing loan, and to an extent sufficient to enable the Colonial Government to carry out the undertakings to which it is pledged.

4. In our letter of the 7th February, the estimated cost of the railway works which have been approved are given at £1,250,000, and these figures remain substantially correct, but if the Treasury should agree to their loan being paid off provision would, of course, have to be made for the expense of raising the necessary loan and for issuing it at a discount, as, in the present condition of the money market, we could not expect to obtain any great advance in the price of issue of a 3 per cent. loan for Lagos over that which we obtained for the Gold Coast 3 per cent. loan, viz., £91 per cent.

5. It would, therefore, be necessary to raise 3 per cent. stock to the nominal amount of £1,374,145, say, £1,374,000 to provide necessary funds, the figures being as follows:

Required for repayment to Treasury	£792,500	0	0
Less amount already paid off . . .	32,851	9	8
	£759,648	10	4
Further estimated expenditure on account of the railway	457,500	0	0
	£1,217,148	10	4
Stock at £91 per cent. required to produce the above sum	£1,374,144	10	7

6. A 3 per cent. loan of £1,374,000 would involve a charge of £41,220 a year for fifty years by way of interest to which would have to be added an additional charge of £13,740 a year for sinking fund three years after the issue of the loan, making together an annual charge for 47 years on the Colony of £54,960 a year. On the other hand, the present Treasury loan is carrying a charge of £41,731 a year, which runs for thirty years from June, 1900, and this charge would be increased by £24,102 a year if the further sum of £457,500 now required to be raised were borrowed from the Treasury on the same terms as the existing loan, viz., at 3¼ per cent. for thirty years. The total charge on the Colony would therefore be at the rate of £65,833 a year, but the currency of the charges would, of course, be much shorter than in the case of a loan borrowed from the public.

7. I beg to add that it would simplify the issue of any loan by us if the Secretary of State should see fit to instruct the Government of Lagos to pass fresh legislation, repealing the five separate ordinances under which the sum of £1,248,500 has been authorised, and providing in one ordinance for the issue of a loan of £1,374,000 for the purpose of repaying a sum of £759,648 10s. 4d. due to His Majesty's Treasury, and for providing the necessary funds for the completion of the railway and to defray the expenses of the issue of the loan.

21

HIGH COMMISSIONER F. D. LUGARD:
TAXATION, NORTHERN NIGERIA,
2 SEPTEMBER 1903[1]

. . . 82. As the period of initial construction of an administration feeling its way cautiously among a great population and gradually

[1] *Colonial Reports: Northern Nigeria*, 1903 [Ed.1768], pp. 53–5.

acquiring a knowledge of the peoples with whom it has to deal gives place to a scheme of rule based on a settled policy, the cost of the machinery necessarily increases, notably on account of the need of more administrative officers and of additional police, and the necessity for raising a local revenue to meet that cost consequently becomes imperative. Beyond doubt the best method of taxation in Africa is the 'indirect,' viz., by customs; but assuming that the revenue from this source, collected on the coast by Southern Nigeria and Lagos, has reached its maximum, the next best in the condition of the country appears to me to be by *class* taxation. I have, therefore, with the concurrence of the Secretary of State, introduced tolls on caravans and licences on canoes and on the sale and manufacture of native liquors. Of these I will speak later. These alone are, however, insufficient, nor do I think that the principle of direct taxation, though it should be cautiously applied, and its incidence should at first be very light, should be wholly set aside in laying down the lines of policy which are to guide the future development of this country. I, therefore, have proposed to levy from all chiefs who collect tribute and whose ability to do so now depends solely on the Government, a certain proportion (limited under present conditions to one quarter) of the tribute so collected; while in the new assessment all those who pay to no chief, having on many cases abandoned their allegiance, through the instrumentality, more or less direct, of the white man, shall pay for the present their tribute direct to Government.

83. To make this system effective and to prevent fraudulent and excessive exactions by agents will need an efficient staff. I should be amply satisfied if at present the product of the tax did no more than pay for the staff, since the machinery thus introduced would effect much more than the sole collection of the tax, and since by the introduction of this system without injustice and friction the basis would be laid of a revenue which would continually grow from year to year and form eventually a substantial contribution to the task of rendering the country self-supporting. If a fully adequate supervision is not supplied *ab initio* the result will be extortion and consequent discontent. It is unfortunately one of those cases in which capital outlay must be incurred with a prospect of deferred returns; but however costly the machinery, the expense should not, in my view, be grudged, for whereas it is now not difficult to find acceptance of such a system, its introduction at a future period would infallibly produce discontent. It is for these reasons that the Secretary of State has approved in the present year (1903–1904) of a small additional department (the Revenue Department) whose duties will consist in the assessment and collection of this revenue and otherwise in work identical with that of the Assistant Residents.

84. The taxation I have proposed is upon the revenue of chiefs or communities. I am opposed to direct taxation by Government upon individuals (as I said in my report for 1900) because (1) I think it premature until individual property in land has become recognised, and (2) until the system of serfdom has given place to one of independent agricultural labour, and (3) until a currency has obtained a footing so as to obviate too frequent a payment in kind. In writing this I do not reverse what I wrote on this subject in my report for 1901. I then said that I deprecated direct taxation in the earlier stages of the development of an African Protectorate 'while maintaining the absolute right of Government to levy such a tax for benefits conferred.' Progress has been somewhat more rapid than I anticipated, while the necessity of finding a revenue has grown even more imperative, and I consider that it is now possible to introduce the *principle* though its application should at first be tentative and gradual. Moreover, I think that it is better to translate assistance rendered in public works, &c., into liquidation of a recognised payment to the revenue than to allow it to drift into something perilously akin to a system of forced labour.

85. The tax is concerned with the ownership of land and its produce, and my remarks, therefore, both as regards the recognition of individual property and as regards independent labour do not refer to the urban or to the trading communities, in both of which these principles are already largely recognised. Property in a city, whether real or personal, descends to the legitimate heir, and in Fulani cities is subject to death duties. Labour employed by traders is largely independent and carriers are often engaged and paid for their services. But the farm slaves or serfs—*adscripti glebae*—'paying yearly little dues of wheat, and wine, and oil,' as their forefathers paid, do not own their holdings or understand individual land tenure, and their contribution to the revenue should, in my view, be deducted from those dues,—fairly assessed,—and not take the form of a poll or hut tax. The land in theory belongs to the Suzerain, hitherto the Fulani Emir and now the British Government, and with that transfer of suzerainty begins the right of Government to a share to an additional impost upon the tenant. In similar fashion the communities not under Fulani rule pay their dues to Government as the immemorial mark of their recognition of suzerainty, and in return they receive immunity from the raids of the Fulani or other slavers and raiders.

86. The other taxes to which I have alluded above are (1) the caravan tolls, (2) canoe licences, and (3) the local liquor tax. The caravan tolls consist of a levy on goods of 5 per cent. in each Province traversed by a caravan up to a maximum of 15 per cent. on its down journey, and a similar levy on its up journey. This is in return for the safety of the roads and their improvement, and is in lieu of the

exorbitant imposts which used to be levied by Emirs, without any such compensating advantages, and which are now abolished. The Royal Niger Company levied, from 1897 onwards, a tax on the staple of trade of 15 per cent., which, since the transfer to Government, has lapsed. The French, I believe, enforce no taxes on caravans but compel them all to pass through Zinder (and Gaya on the west) and take out registration papers.

(2.) A licence on canoes, according to their earning capacity varying from 5s. to £3 per annum. Large transport and ferry canoes in the season can earn £2 and upwards per month. The tax, therefore, is not excessive. Both these taxes are levied on the classes best able to pay in the country, and who have benefited most from the British administration. The canoe owners especially have earned enormous sums by carrying for Government.

(3.) The remaining tax is on the manufacture and sale of locally made intoxicating liquors. The duty formerly imposed by the Royal Niger Company of £1 per ton on salt imported into Northern Nigeria from Southern Nigeria has also been revived . . .

22

E. E. BLAKE (CROWN AGENTS) TO THE COLONIAL OFFICE: LAGOS LOANS, 3 AUGUST 1904[1]

I HAVE the honour to acknowledge the receipt of your letter of the 20th of July, No. 10864/1904, inquiring as to the conditions on which the necessary funds for extending the Lagos Railway to Oshogbo could be raised.

2. In reply, I beg to say that the whole question of the future borrowings on account of the Government of Lagos has continued to engage our attention since we wrote to you on the 2nd of February, 1903, and our reason for not replying to your letter of the 26th of November last, No. 41191/1903, has been that there has been so much uncertainty as to the condition on which money could be borrowed for the West African Colonies that we did not feel that we were in a position to put any definite proposals before the Secretary of State.

3. I now beg to say that the result of the recent Sierra Leone Loan has undoubtedly shown that money for the West African Colonies can be obtained on the basis of short-dated debentures carrying 4 per cent. interest and convertible into longer currency Inscribed

[1] C.O. 879/76, no. 695.

Stock carrying 3½ per cent. interest, and, in our opinion, further issues on this basis will be practicable and probably on better terms than were obtainable in the case of the Sierra Leone Loan, provided that we are not forced to place the loans upon the market at an unfavourable moment.

4. There is no question that the great depression which has lasted so long in the Stock Market is slowly passing away, and although there has recently been a set back, this set back is probably merely temporary, and a better state of things may fairly be looked for next year.

5. If, therefore, the Secretary of State is prepared to entertain the idea of Lagos borrowing on the same terms as Sierra Leone, we think that it should be practicable to raise such a loan some time during the first half of next year, and on receiving the Secretary of State's approval, we would prepare the draft of the necessary legislation and submit an estimate of the amount of money which it would be necessary to raise.

6. I beg to add that we still remain of the opinion expressed in our letters of the 14th of July, 1902, and 2nd of February, 1903, that the getting rid of the first charge upon the revenues and assets of Lagos, which the Treasury possesses in virtue of its loan to the Colony under the Colonial Loans Act, is an indispensable condition to the successful floating of a public loan for the Colony. It will therefore be necessary that the outstanding balance—£725,000—of the Treasury Loan should be added to any other monies which may require to be raised for the Colony.

23

GOVERNOR H. BELL TO LEWIS HARCOURT: NATIVE TREASURIES, NORTHERN NIGERIA, 17 NOVEMBER 1911[1]

. . . 4. THE most important step taken in that direction during the year was the establishment in each native State of a Treasury, locally known as a 'Beit-el-Mal.' This institution regulates the expenditure of that portion of the local revenue which is annually assigned to the native administration of each Emirate for its support and maintenance. The establishment of a *Beit-el-Mal* consolidates the rank and authority of the Emirs and Chiefs in each province. It strengthens the position of the native judiciary and diminishes extortion and corruption. The grant of a definite rank and office in their

---

[1] *Colonial Reports: Northern Nigeria*, 1912 [Cd. 6007]. (*Sir*) *Henry Hesketh Bell*, Governor of Northern Nigeria, 1909–12.

own administrations will rally to the cause of peace and good government a number of influential natives whose attitude might otherwise
become a matter of anxiety. They will be given a permanent stake in
the stability of the Government and in the event of trouble will
probably be found on the side of law and order.

5. To each Emir has been assigned a fixed civil list proportionate
to the population and importance of the country. The native judges
and magistrates will, in future, receive definite salaries, punctually
paid, instead of being dependent on the spasmodic generosity of the
Emirs or on less reputable sources of profit. A fixed percentage of the
taxes will be paid, as commission, to the district administrations, and
every native holding a recognised office will receive remuneration
commensurate with his services. To Mr. Temple and Mr. Palmer
is largely due the credit of initiating this system.

6. Though the *Beit-el-Mal* organisation is still in its earliest infancy,
its merits are already being keenly appreciated by most of the members
of the native administrations. It is, perhaps, too much to expect the
Beit-el-Mal to be a very popular institution with the Emirs. Under the
old régime, and provided he managed to satisfy the demands of his
Suzerain at Sokoto, the Emir of a feudatory state practically had the
unfettered disposal of all the imposts levied on his people. He thus
possessed the means of rewarding personal service with a lavish
hand, and the degree of his power and popularity depended greatly
on the munificence of his largesse. Though the establishment of a
Beit-el-Mal now places a check upon their personal extravagance,
limits their patronage, and requires them to account for the expenditure of public funds, most of the Emirs have acquiesced, if not enthusiastically at all events with a good grace, in the proper regulation of
their finances. They are not slow to appreciate the advantages of
receiving a good income, regularly paid, and of being free from the
constant demands of clamourous parasites who, in many cases, left
their rulers very little for their own personal expenditure . . .

24

DEPARTMENTAL COMMITTEE ON WEST
AFRICAN CURRENCY: REPORT, 5 JUNE 1912[1]

Summary of Conclusions and Recommendations.
Silver Currency

1. THE continuance of existing monetary conditions in British West
Africa is fraught with dangers to the communities there and at home.

---

[1] *Parl. Papers.* [Cd. 6426]: 1912 *Departmental Committee appointed to Enquire into
Matters affecting the Currency of the British West African Colonies and Protectorates*,
p. 17.

2. The introduction of a distinctive local currency based upon a reserve of gold and securities is the only remedy practicable in present circumstances.

3. This measure should not only place the currency on a sound basis, but should be a source of considerable ultimate profit to the Colonial Governments concerned.

4. There is little reason to doubt that coins of the proposed new currency would be well received by the native population, if certain precautions were taken.

5. The supply of coin and the management of the reserve should be entrusted to a Currency Board.

6. The reserve should be held in London in gold and securities. The whole of the profits of coinage should at first be paid to the reserve.

7. The Currency Board should at the outset be placed in funds by means of advances from the Governments concerned.

8. Coin should be issued at appointed places in British West Africa against prepayment made in sterling either at the place of issue or in London. In the former case the issue should be at par. In the latter case a premium should be charged which should ultimately be raised to the equivalent of the cost of sending specie from London, but should at first be at the lower rate of $\frac{3}{4}$ per cent.

9. Holders of coin of the new currency and of silver coins of the United Kingdom should have the legal right to tender them in British West Africa for concessions at a fixed rate of exchange into sterling money to be issued in London. Certain other facilities for exchange should be granted.

Note Issue.

10. An issue of notes might with advantage be made by the Currency Board in Nigeria and the Gold Coast and possibly also in Sierra Leone.

11. The notes should at first be encashable as of right at the office of issue alone, but additional facilities should be granted from the outset as a matter of courtesy, so far as practicable. At a later stage it may be possible to make all notes encashable as of right in any note-issuing Colony in British West Africa.

12. The notes should not at first be legal tender except to the Government of the Colony of issue. The full status of legal tender should be granted to them later.

13. The coin portion of the note reserve should at first amount to

not less than three-fourths of the note issue; but the proportion might be reduced as notes become generally used.

14. The terms of issue for notes should be the same as for coin, except that notes should be issued against silver coin of the local currency as well as against sterling.

15. Holders of notes should have the right of tendering them in West Africa for conversion into sterling to be issued in London on the same terms as holders of coin.

General

16. The Currency Board should have its head-quarters in London with official representatives at appointed centres in British West Africa.

17. The resources and credit of the Governments of British West Africa should be the final security for the discharge by the Currency Board of its obligations . . .

C. DEFENCE: WEST AFRICAN FRONTIER FORCE

I

GOVERNOR H. McCALLUM TO JOSEPH CHAMBERLAIN: RECRUITMENT, 4 AUGUST 1897[1]

. . . 7. I_F_, therefore, the new force is to be employed outside the confines of Yoruba I venture to submit that we should not depend on the Hausas entirely, but make up one battalion of Yorubas, who have a remarkable fine, smart appearance, and learn their drill rapidly. If you wire me authority to engage Yorubas to the number, say, of 700 to 1000, I believe I could recruit them almost entirely from the Ibadan Warboys, who do not like an agricultural life after being so long engaged in warlike operations against the Ilorins. A number of officers would, of course, have to be sent out without delay to assist in the organization, disciplining, and training of the newly enlisted recruits.

[1] C.O. 879/51, no. 545.

2

J. BRAMSTON (COLONIAL OFFICE) TO FOREIGN OFFICE: FRONTIER FORCE, 14 AUGUST 1897[1]

I AM directed by Mr. Secretary Chamberlain to request that you will lay before the Marquess of Salisbury the following proposals with regard to the steps to be taken to secure against French aggression the territories claimed by Her Majesty's Government as falling within the British sphere of influence in West Africa.

2. It has been decided to raise a West African force of 2,000 or 3,000 men, at the cost of the Imperial Exchequer, to operate on the Niger. The commanding officer is to have the title of 'Commissioner and Commandant' with the local rank of Lieut.-Colonel, and a salary at the rate of 1,500 *l.* a year. The Admiralty have also undertaken to provide three gun-boats specially designed to assist in carrying out the proposed operations.

3. The new force will not in the first instance be available for service on the Gold Coast, where the Colonial Government must continue, for the present, to defend the 'hinterland' against the French as far as it can with its own resources—supplemented by the assistance which it now has of 300 Hausas lent by the Lagos Government, and two companies of the West India Regiment from Freetown.

4. The Lagos Government should, in Mr. Chamberlain's opinion, be called upon to maintain all the posts required in the 'hinterland' of that Colony south of the 9th parallel of north latitude, except Ilorin, which might continue to be held by the Royal Niger Company. It is, however, doubtful whether the Colony will be able to maintain all the posts that should be held while so many men are away on the Gold Coast.

5. It is suggested that the territories on the left bank of the Niger might, for the present, remain under the control of the Royal Niger Company, and that, if it should be decided to establish any posts on that side of the river, the Company should be held responsible for making the necessary arrangements with the Sultan of Sokoto.

6. The sphere of operations of the Commissioner and Commandant would then be the right bank from the 9th parallel northwards, and would comprise, not only the countries with which we have treaties, but all territory to the north of the 9th parallel and west of the river in which he could operate to advantage.

---

[1] C.O. 879/48, no. 529. For a summary of the early operations of the Force, see Colonel A. Haywood and Brigadier F. A. S. Clarke, *The History of the Royal West African Frontier Force* (Aldershot, 1964), pp. 31–80. The 'Royal' title was granted in 1928.

7. The Commissioner would be independent of the Company, and would correspond direct with the Colonial Office, sending his Despatches under flying seal through the Governor of Lagos, who would thus be kept informed of what is going on in the Hinterland of that Colony and would be able to communicate by telegraph with the Secretary of State if occasion should arise. The form of his commission, and the authority required for raising and controlling the force under his command, are legal points which will have to be considered.

8. The duty of the Commissioner would be, by establishing posts in the sphere assigned to him, to stop the advance of the French, and to put such pressure on them as he could without fighting to compel them to withdraw from the posts which they have occupied in territory claimed under treaties as being in the British sphere. It is suggested that the operations should be begun from a point on the river, such as Fort Goldie, and that detachments should be pushed forward gradually until all the important positions on the west of the river have been occupied from the 9th parallel up to Say or beyond, if the French do not retire.

9. There is force in Sir G. Goldie's remark in his letter to the Colonial Office of the 19th of July, that 'the most serious objection to adopting the policy of scattering small detachments of troops over regions secured to Great Britain by native treaties' is that it might be taken as an admission of the new French theory with regard to effective occupation: and it appears to Mr. Chamberlain that while pushing on as we propose to do we should be careful not to admit that occupation is necessary and should insist upon the validity of our treaties.

10. It is possible, as Mr. Chamberlain has already suggested in the Despatch which he sent to the Gold Coast on the 4th of June, that the French, on finding themselves confronted by a superior force and being made aware that we are determined and prepared to substantiate our claims, may withdraw from the posts established in our sphere, as the Germans, according to a statement published in the 'Revue de Géographie' for May last, have recently done at Bafilo and Kirikri when confronted by the French themselves. If not, the Commissioner must endeavour to cut off their communications and starve them out. He should on no account attack a town or village garrisoned by French regular troops or in which a French (European) officer is stationed, and it is very unlikely that he will be attacked by the French. The aggressive action of the French appears to be due to the belief that we shall always give way as we have hitherto done, and Mr. Chamberlain trusts that, by making a stand and retaliating on them in the region selected for the operations of the Commissioner, we shall convince them that we are in earnest, and so induce them to

agree to an early settlement of all the outstanding questions in West Africa on the basis of the treaties obtained by either country.

11. If the operations on the west of the Niger should not be sufficient to bring about this result, and the French should advance into the country south of the Say-Barruwa line, the plan now proposed would have to be enlarged. It might then be advisable to make the Commissioner and Commandant responsible for the operations to be undertaken on the east as well as the west of the river, but this would involve relieving the Company of all their administrative functions, and it does not seem necessary or desirable to go so far at present.

12. The question of expenditure must be further considered. If the Company safeguard the territories on the left bank and pay the cost of this, it might be fair that the rest of the cost should be borne by Imperial funds. But, if the whole business is carried out by the Commissioner and Commandant, the Company ought to make a contribution towards the cost.

13. If Lord Salisbury approves of the scheme suggested in this letter, his Lordship will no doubt communicate at once with the Company, as it is necessary to come to an arrangement with them before any further steps can be taken, and, in the meantime, in order to avoid delay, Mr. Chamberlain will consult the Director of Military Intelligence confidentially as to the manner in which the scheme should be carried out.

14. I am to add that, as it will be some time before the new force can be raised and progress made with this policy, Mr. Chamberlain would suggest that a further remonstrance, in the strongest diplomatic language, should be addressed to the French Government protesting against the proceedings of their officers in ignoring our treaties and occupying territory claimed by us, and possibly hinting at retaliation. It might be pointed out that the larger portion of the French sphere in Africa is not effectively occupied and that we cannot recognise their claim unless there is complete reciprocity; and complaint might be made especially of French aggression in Boussa, Kishi, Wa, and Wagadugu, and of the arrangement with Germany by which Gurma appears to have been recognised as French without regard to our claims.

3

GOVERNOR H. McCALLUM TO
JOSEPH CHAMBERLAIN: DISPOSITION OF
FORCES, 25 OCTOBER 1897[1]

REFERRING to Your telegram of 22nd October, Governor Gold Coast informs me carrying out reliefs 100 Lagos Constabulary who

[1] C.O. 879/49, no. 538.

sending home. When forward movement decided on, if one Company of 2nd Battalion West India Regiment replace Constabulary [at] Lagos, Shagamu, Jebu Ode: one company Ibadan, Ogbomosho, Odo Otin: one company garrison frontier towns: I shall be able to lend early in the year about 550 Constabulary inclusive of recruits now in course of preparation. If military operations later, more men available. Under existing circumstances personal influence of Governor all important. Would you be good enough to reply as soon as possible authorizing flying visit to Ibadan; also with respect to reply [to] Ballot. Taking into consideration negotiations Paris consider it desirable to receive instructions. Two companies leave for Saki Tuesday.

4

LORD SELBORNE: MEMORANDUM,
MILITARY FORCES IN
WEST AFRICA, 20 JUNE 1898[1]

IT is proposed to constitute a small West African Army for service in any of the British Colonies and Protectorates of West Africa.

2. There are at present in existence four Military Forces under the Colonial Office, viz.: the Sierra Leone Frontier Police, the Gold Coast and Lagos Constabularies, and the West African Frontier Force. There are also the Military Constabularies of the Royal Niger Company and the Niger Coast Protectorate.

3. It would scarcely be advisable, or feasible if advisable, to maintain the Force recently raised as a distinct one from the older Forces. The following suggestions are made on the basis that these Forces and the new Force should not be distinct from each other. At present the Constabulary of the Royal Niger Company could not be available for any amalgamation with the Colonial Constabularies, and the fact that that of the Niger Coast Protectorate is under the Foreign Office, not the Colonial Office, complicates matters; but the following suggestions are made on the supposition that the administrations of the Niger Territories and the Niger Coast Protectorate cannot long remain so separated as they are now from those of the West African Colonies. In any case the suggestions could apply to the Forces under the Colonial Office alone in the first instance.

4. It is suggested:
(1.) That the separate Military Forces on the West Coast of Africa should be abolished and amalgamated as the West African Frontier Force.
(2.) That there should be four divisions of this Force located

in Sierra Leone, the Gold Coast, Lagos, and the Niger Territories, respectively.

(3.) That each division should have its own head-quarters, and its own depot, and its own Commanding Officer, as at present.

(4.) That all the division should be inspected annually by the same General Officer sent out from England for the purpose.

(5.) That all the officers should bear military titles and have military rank. Any officers of the Regular Army remaining more than seven years to join the Force permanently.

(6.) That there should be general uniformity between all the divisions, of uniform, armament, pay, and conditions of service, both of officers and men.

[There may be difficulty in carrying out this last suggestion immediately in the case of Sierra Leone, where the rates of pay and other conditions differ from those in the other Colonies. This difficulty will have to be overcome hereafter. In the meantime, the scheme can first be adopted for, and developed in, Lagos and the Gold Coast and the Niger Territories, Sierra Leone, if necessary, standing aside for the present.]

5. For any special expeditions in a Colony, or in the British Protectorate adjacent to a Colony, the Force would, if possible, have to be found from the division belonging to that Colony. If, however, help were needed, the other divisions should be called upon to supply contingents of men and officers.

6. The West African Frontier Force, as at present constituted, is a special Force formed for the special work rendered necessary by the political complications on the Niger. It is intended that in course of time it shall form one of the divisions of the new Force. Considering, however, the special circumstances of the Niger Territories, this division will probably for a long time to come have to be maintained at a higher establishment and in a more fully equipped condition than the other divisions.

7. At present the West African Frontier Force, which is under the command of a specially selected officer with a second in command and an aide-de-camp, has an establishment of 2 Battalions, each Battalion consisting of 8 Companies of 150 men under a Lieutenant-Colonel, with the usual Battalion Staff officers, and each Company having 3 white officers and 5 white non-commissioned officers; 2 Companies of Field Artillery, each containing 50 men, with 3 white officers and 6 white non-commissioned officers; one Company of Reserve Artillery with 50 men, one white officer, and 6 white non-commissioned officers; one Engineer Company, containing 2 white officers, 5 white non-commissioned officers, and 46 natives; a Medical Department, consisting of 2 Field Hospitals and one Base Hospital,

with 8 European doctors and 3 European nurses; a Pay and Accounts Department; and a Transport Department.

8. The scale of pay for the native non-commissioned officers and men is the same as that now in use for the Gold Coast and Lagos Constabularies. The pay of the officers is based on that of the Constabulary officers; but the allowances are different, and will have to be reconsidered when the proposed amalgamation takes place. The scale of pay for the white non-commissioned officers is based on those in force for British Warrant and non-commissioned officers serving in the Egyptian Army.

9. This scheme is submitted as an outline of the general form the organisation should take.

5

GOVERNOR SIR F. CARDEW TO
JOSEPH CHAMBERLAIN: SIERRA LEONE
FORCES, 17 SEPTEMBER 1898[1]

3. WITH respect to (1) I have no experience of the other West African Colonies or Protectorates. I will therefore confine myself to the conditions which prevail here. Setting aside the West India Regiment and the Garrison Artillery, which may be regarded as for the special defence of the Coaling Station, we have the West African Regiment, of which one battalion has been raised, and the Frontier Police.

4. The men of these Corps are recruited from the same tribes, have the same rates of pay, and are armed, clothed, and equipped in a similar manner, with some minor variations as regards uniform for purposes of distinction between the two Corps, and I see no reason, as far as administration and interior economy is concerned, why the two Corps should not be amalgamated; but there is the very important fact to be considered that the Frontier Police are trained to carry out police as well as military duties; they act as detectives, effect arrests, serve writs and summonses, and are conversant generally with the affairs concerning the Chiefs and natives of the district in which they are stationed. As the Protectorate is brought under closer administration—and I think it is probable that one result of the recent disturbances will be to bring this about—so must the Frontier Police be required more and more for police duties, and therefore the more necessary it will be that they should be a special corps.

5. The West African Regiment could no doubt be trained to perform the same duties, but unless it was under the immediate

[1] C.O. 879/54, no. 565.

orders of the Executive there would inevitably be friction between it and the Officer Commanding Troops. In my view, and considering the circumstances under which the Protectorate is administered, the Frontier Police should bear somewhat the same relation to the West African Regiment as the Royal Irish Constabulary and the Military Police Force in parts of India and Burmah do to the Troops, or say, as the Miliciens do to the Tirailleurs in French Colonies, though I believe the Frontier Police to be a far superior force to the Miliciens. In other words, the Frontier Police should continue to be a specially trained corps to enforce the administration of the Protectorate, with the West African Regiment in support, to quell riots and disturbances within and protect British territory against foes from without.

6. The principle on which I consider the West African Regiment should be employed for the purposes of this Colony and Protectorate as apart from the question of its co-operation for general service with the corps in the other West African Colonies and Protectorates is somewhat as under, and in this I have the concurrence of the Officer Commanding the Troops.

6

GOVERNOR F. M. HODGSON TO
JOSEPH CHAMBERLAIN: GOLD COAST
FORCES, 17 OCTOBER 1898[1]

. . . BUT an amalgamation on those lines and to that extent would, I have reason to think, by no means satisfy Colonel Lugard and those who think with him. What I understand is wanted by them is a military body worked entirely on military lines, and to be used only, or at any rate primarily, for military purposes; each division, as it may be called, to be exclusively under the command of the officer in supreme authority over the force, and to be moveable even as regards its component parts only after consultation with him. Such an arrangement, I submit, could not possibly work in the Gold Coast. In the Gold Coast, with its recent addition of the Northern Territories, the several companies of which the Hausa Constabulary is composed are scattered up and down the country, and I consider that it would be most undesirable to withdraw from the hands of the Governor the power of moving any part of the force to a particular locality at a moment's notice as circumstances may render necessary. I maintain in fact that it would be most unwise to curtail in any way

[1] C.O. 879/54, no. 565. In reply to the scheme of amalgamation put forward by the Selborne Committee, no. 4.

the power of the Governor over the Constabulary or his position towards them. He alone can know whether a force is required in a particular district or whether the garrison at one of the stations should be strengthened, and if he had, before acting, to consult an officer placed in supreme command—an officer possibly at a place not in direct telegraphic communication—the delay would at times frustrate the object for taking action. I dwell on this point in the first instance because it was one of the points to which, as it seemed to me, Colonel Lugard attached some importance, and because he did not appear to me to appreciate the fact that, excepting when employed on a punitive expedition or an expedition of a military character, the Constabulary forces are at the present time engaged on constabulary duties, and are constantly employed to do work which in more advanced communities with full exchequers can be, and is, undertaken by a body of Civil Police.

5. I consider in fact that, until the Gold Coast can afford to maintain a separate force to be employed entirely on military service and under military conditions, and to be regulated and guided by an authority almost entirely independent of local control, no change should be made in the conditions under which the Gold Coast Constabulary is employed and administered within the colony, but that, when any portion of the force is detailed for duty in connection with military operations of any kind, then and not until then the portion so detailed should come at once under the command of the officer charged with the conduct of the operations and placed under military law and military regulations. I cite the Jebu Expedition and the recent operations in the Northern Territories as cases in which military conditions of service have come into force, and have been applied without difficulty.

6. I am not, I may say, convinced of the necessity, in the event of an amalgamation of the several West African Constabulary and other forces, of having an officer in supreme command; because, if the officer in command of each local division is a military officer of capacity he should be the officer—the proper officer on account of his knowledge of the country and its tribes—to take command of any military operations which it may be necessary to undertake in the colony by the Government of which he is employed.

7

E. A. ALTHAM: MEMORANDUM, THE MILITARY RESPONSIBILITIES OF THE WEST AFRICAN COLONIES, 1 MARCH 1899[1]

Conclusions.

WITHOUT discussing details, the following is therefore proposed, as a rough estimate of the force which should be maintained in the various Colonies, exclusive of the Imperial troops in Sierra Leone:

Sierra Leone	1 battalion.
Gold Coast Colony	1½ battalions.
Lagos.	½ battalion.
Niger Sudan	{ 3 battalions. 3 batteries of Artillery.
Niger Maritime Province	½ battalion.

The establishment of battalions might slightly vary with local requirements, but may be taken generally at 1,000 native combatants, the batteries at 50. This would give a total establishment of 6,750 natives for the whole frontier force, as against 6,161 at present aggregate of the existing establishment of the local forces involved. If this increase be inadmissible, it would be best to reduce the establishment of Infantry for the Niger Sudan by half a battalion.

Each battalion of the Sudan Force should have a mounted company.

The organisation and maintenance of a reserve should be considered in each Colony, both with a view to economy in peace and increased strength in time of war.

The establishments should be annually revised. The increase proposed for Sierra Leone, for instance, is probably only necessary temporarily; on the other hand, the Sudan might next year require an augmentation.

The Lagos half battalion in time could be converted into an 'armed civil police', and perhaps a half battalion in the Gold Coast Colony could be similarly treated in a year or so, as its military duties diminish and its civil duties increase.

[1] C.O. 879/58, no. 588.

9

HIGH COMMISSIONER F. D. LUGARD TO JOSEPH CHAMBERLAIN: DISCIPLINE, 18 MAY 1900[1]

3. I WOULD, however, submit for your consideration the advisability of including the West African Frontier Force with India in the Army Act (by means, if necessary, of a short Act of Parliament for the purpose) as a force to which that act does not apply, so that either a special Military Code as proposed or the Indian Articles of War could be made applicable to it.

4. The Army Act was drafted primarily for European troops. To maintain discipline even among the comparatively civilized and law-abiding troops of India it was found necessary to have a different code giving larger powers to the officers commanding a battalion, and legalising the infliction of corporal punishment by a summary court martial.

5. Such powers are far more necessary with the savage tribes of Africa which compose our frontier troops. Corporal punishment is (unlike India) a custom of the country, and is inflicted by the chiefs upon their subjects and by the people upon each other. It is regarded as a dignity pertaining to the senior native non-commissioned officer that he should be the inflictor of any flogging. It is not looked upon as degrading as it would be by the people of India, upon whom it is legal to inflict it. Offences of looting, rape, and violence to natives of the country, when troops are on the march, cannot be met by imprisonment, and if flogging is illegal the only legal alternative is death.

6. The African is, above all things, excitable and impulsive, and acts of insubordination must be promptly and severely checked if discipline is to be preserved and the troops are not to become a terror to peaceable villagers and a danger to the Protectorate. Though I advocate most strongly that the Power of inflicting corporal punishment should be legal for African troops, I would surround it by restrictions and safeguards.

7. I abhor the punishment myself, mainly because I think it has a brutalising effect upon the Europeans who have to order and to witness it, not upon the man who gets it. It is over 12 years since I first had to organise and control African soldiers. My detestation of flogging is as great now as it was when I first embarked on African work, but I am bound to inform you that in my opinion a grave danger will be incurred if the 'silly sentimentality,' as Lord Salisbury lately described it, which pervades England on this subject is allowed

[1] C.O. 879/61, no. 610.

to overrule the plain dictates of necessity and the opinion of men of experience in this country on this matter. I may add that I would extend the power under Proclamations to certain offences in certain circumstances to civil criminals.

10

JOSEPH CHAMBERLAIN TO HIGH COMMISSIONER F. D. LUGARD: DISCIPLINE, 2 AUGUST 1900[1]

I HAVE the honour to acknowledge the receipt of your despatch, W.A.F.F., No. 70, of the 18th of May last, relating to the legal status of the West African Frontier Force.

2. I do not think that the passing of an Act of Parliament such as you propose in the third paragraph of your despatch is practicable, and I am advised that the best solution of the difficulties as to the status of the West African Frontier Force is to be found in the passing of identical laws for the new (amalgamated) West African Frontier Force in all the Colonies and Protectorates concerned, as to which I have already addressed you in my despatch, Nor. Nig./ Separate of the 26th of June last.

3. In that despatch I have referred to the question of adopting the Indian Articles of War as a model for the new law, and the question of flogging, to which you have called attention, can be dealt with in the same enactment.

4. Pending the re-enlistment of the men in Northern Nigeria under the new law, the Force must, I am advised, continue on active service.

11

R. L. ANTROBUS TO WAR OFFICE: WEST AFRICAN FRONTIER FORCE, 14 JUNE 1901[1]

I AM directed by Mr. Secretary Chamberlain to state, for the information of Mr. Secretary Brodrick, that he has had under his consideration the legislative measures necessary for carrying into effect the amalgamation of the Colonial Military Forces in West Africa, and for applying military law to all portions of the amalgamated force.

[1] C.O. 879/61, no. 610.

2. Of the two methods suggested by the Inter-Departmental Committee on the amalgamation of the forces, on page 15 of their Report (copies of which are enclosed for reference), it appeared to Mr. Chamberlain that the better method would be to have an identical law enacted in each of the Colonies and Protectorates concerned.

3. An Ordinance, copies of which are enclosed, has accordingly been drafted, with special reference to the Gold Coast unit of the force, based partly on the existing Ordinances relating to the Gold Coast Constabulary, and partly on the Army Act of 1881.

4. Copies of the Ordinance have been sent out to each of the Colonies and Protectorates in which a portion of the new West African Frontier Force is to be maintained, with instructions that it should be enacted with such alterations of wording in each case as are necessitated by local circumstances.

5. The instructions for enactment have, however, been given subject to Mr. Brodrick's concurrence on the following points.

6. It is proposed that the Gold Coast, and any other unit of the Force consisting of more than one battalion, or of one or more infantry battalions and a separate artillery corps, should be called a 'regiment' of the West African Frontier Force. This term has been provisionally adopted because it is often used to denote two or more battalions permanently associated by a territorial connection, and because it appeared more suitable than 'brigade', 'division,' or 'corps,' each of which words has a special significance rendering it unsuitable for the purpose. I am to enquire whether, in Mr. Brodrick's opinion, the word 'regiment' can properly be used in this way. In the case of those units of the Force which consist of one battalion of infantry only, without a separate artillery corps, it is proposed to use the word 'battalion.'

7. If Mr. Brodrick has no objection to offer to these proposals, the names of the various units of the West African Frontier Force will be:

Northern Nigeria Regiment (the old 1st and 2nd Niger Battalions).
Southern Nigeria Battalion (the old 3rd Niger Battalion).
Gold Coast Regiment (the old Gold Coast Constabulary).
Lagos Battalion (the old Lagos Constabulary or Hausa Force).
Sierra Leone Battalion (the old Sierra Leone Frontier Police).

If, however, a proposal recently made to organise the artillery in Southern Nigeria as a separate arm is adopted, the name of the Southern Nigeria Battalion will be changed to the Southern Nigeria Regiment.

8. I am also to ask for Mr. Brodrick's concurrence in the proposal that each of the Governors and High Commissioners concerned should hold a warrant for convening and confirming General Courts-Martial under the Army Act, in the same way as if he were a General Officer Commanding a District, in order that he may be in a position to carry out the provisions of the Ordinance with regard to Court-Martial.

IV

ECONOMIC DEVELOPMENT

Introductory Note

THE protection and expansion of British commercial investment in West Africa remained the dominant theme in British policy for the partition period. Both local administrations and the Colonial Office were sensitive to the need for indirect taxes on trade to help pay for this protection; and increasing note was taken of changes in French tariffs in West Africa and the danger to the British conception of 'free trade' (A. 6, 8, 9).

Consequently, military action, territorial acquisition, and the adjustment of fiscal barriers along the coast were the main aspects of official trade promotion in the 1870s and 1880s. The general connection between trade and tariffs was summed up by Governor Rowe in 1886; and his analysis was representative of official thinking about the need for revenue from the development of West African commerce (A. 10). The appeal to force to keep open trade routes was subjected to restraints on the Gambia, but not on the Niger (A. 2, 3, 4).

Finally, commercial information on interior conditions of trade accumulated rapidly in the intelligence reports of the many missions sent to survey, explore, and partition in the period (A. 5, 7, 12, 26, 32).

The details of tariff negotiations involved all the colonial enclaves. The most difficult zones for fixing duties that would avoid excessive smuggling and secure sufficient revenue were along the Gold Coast frontiers with the Ivory Coast and Togo and on the Lagos–Porto-Novo frontier. Special and temporary compromises were reached in these areas; but the general range of duties at British ports of entry increased from under 5 per cent to over 10 per cent *ad valorem*, with higher duties for spirits, arms, and powder. On the Niger, the Royal Niger Company monopoly of ports of entry was challenged by French and German expeditions and by opposition from Lagos traders and officials. Niger duties roughly doubled between 1890 and 1897. The import of spirits was prohibited in the northern area of Company control, but was widespread south of Asaba. The British Government was doubtful of the efficacy of establishing zones of prohibition, but accepted the recommendations of the Bruxelles Conference of 1899 on this and other points concerning European trade.

In the colonies and protectorates transport policy remained fairly elementary and contributed little to economic development in the 1870s. Sierra Leone re-enacted compulsory road repairs in 1879; and regular road clearing surveys were begun in Lagos Colony in 1888. But no extensive road systems were planned, although the possibilities of motor roads were foreseen as early as 1899 (B. 1, 2, 17).

Railways, on the other hand, were looked on as the key to economic development, as surveys and construction plans were initiated by Knutsford and Ripon, and authorized by Chamberlain. Requests for private concessions were rejected, for the reasons given by the Crown Agent in 1891 (B. 5), though there was considerable official co-operation with the Ashanti Goldfields Corporation. But, on the whole, railways, it was decided early, were to be constructed by the State and departmentally financed by public loans, in British West Africa. Most of the first surveys were completed by 1894, and tracks were begun by 1896. Both Gold Coast and Lagos lines depended on the development of deep-water harbours which were unsuccessful at Takoradi and increasingly expensive at Lagos. The long official argument about the Niger crossing was resolved when the railway reached Jebba in 1909; but the eastern railway line, planned as early as 1902, was not completed till after 1914.

These communications were supplemented in each colony by the construction of the interior telegraph. Shipping communications with overseas markets remained a monopoly of the West African 'Conference', investigated in 1907 (B. 26).

The aim of trade protection and communications was to increase the export of West African agricultural produce. The period of administrative expansion saw, too, the first serious attempts at conservation and the rational exploitation of West African natural resources. On the whole, the political aspects of the introduction of legal controls over land and mineral rights are better known than the technological history of West African agriculture and mining. Though limited in its immediate economic effects, British policy aimed at scientific investigation of forests, livestock, and products and laid the foundations for later specialized agricultural services. The Gold Coast administration, however, was slow to improve the quality of cocoa exports; and the potential value of groundnuts for Northern Nigeria does not seem to have been estimated, even as late as 1907 (C. 36).

In all four colonies there is evidence of the rapid transfer of urban lands, confusion of land records, rising values, and lack of provision for accurate survey before the 1880s. The main focus of land legislation lay, however, in the protectorates and the interior. In Sierra Leone, the principle that chiefs could make transfers in the name of local communities was admitted (C. 3). But on the Gold Coast, between 1891 and 1897, the principles of Crown intercession in the transfer of land and mineral rights was asserted in three Bills which were vigorously opposed and allowed to drop (C. 4, 6, 8, 11, 12, 13). Instead, emphasis was laid on the administrative formalities required by the Notification Ordinance of 1895, before transfer of rights to Europeans could be officially recognized. This control of the conditions of lease or sale was embodied in the Gold Coast Concessions Ordinance of 1900 and applied in the other three colonies—notably in the Southern Nigerian Land Acquisition Ordinance of 1903. In Northern Nigeria concessions were a Crown prerogative; and alienation was prohibited altogether by the Land Proclamation of 1902. High Commissioner Girouard's radical policy of 'nationalization' of African tenure was not applied in full (C. 37), though his plans for a land tax were accepted by the Northern Nigerian Lands Committee in 1908 and made law in the Native Rights Proclamation of 1910.

In the absence of a complete study of land tenure, the most numerous concessions seem to have been made on the Gold Coast. Mining 'royalties' were introduced, after clarification with the Treasury in 1902 (C. 28, 32). But the Ashanti Goldfields Corporation kept its special conditions arranged in 1897. Palm oil concessions were sought by Lever Brothers in 1913, and were granted, after considerable resistance from the Gold Coast administration, though the full rights were not taken up (C. 39-44).

A. TRADE AND TARIFFS

1

THOMAS BROWN TO LORD CARNARVON: GAMBIA EXCHANGE, 24 SEPTEMBER 1875[1]

[The Gambia has a fine harbour and provides access for several hundred miles into the interior of Africa.]

... COMMERCIALLY, this transfer will soon annihilate British trade in the Gambia, for we know from past experience that all Treaty stipulations will not save us: the Treaty which restored Goree and Senegal to France after the war was carried out in a way that soon made it imperative for the British to retire from those Settlements and remove to the Gambia to carry on their trade.

I inclose for your Lordship's information a copy of some questions addressed by the Governor of Senegal to the merchants thereof upon the trade of that river, with their reply thereto, which was forwarded to the Minister for the Colonies in Paris, as lately as July last, by which your Lordship will see that these merchants seek to put differential duties on foreign goods in addition to the duty now paid by them, and also an additional exceptional duty of 25 centimes per metre on the manufactured blue bafts (guinées) of Manchester; this amounts to 3 fr. on a piece of goods costing 7 fr., which is, in fact, a prohibitory duty; their object being, as they admit, to encourage their own manufactures of Pondichery, to the exclusion of those of Manchester.[2] Beyond this, these merchants also seek to put a differential duty on foreign ships importing ground-nuts into Marseilles from the Gambia and Sierra Leone, without which they allege they cannot cope with the merchants in the British colonies on the coast.

If the Gambia be ceded to France, and if it adopts the system of prohibitions and protective duties recommended by the merchants of

---

[1] *Parl. Papers*, 1876, lii [C. 1409], pp. 56-7. *Thomas Brown*, Gambia trader and member of the Legislative Council.
[2] Encl. questionnaire to French firms in Senegal and the Gambia; Manchester Chamber of Commerce to C.O., 13 October 1875. For the guinea cloth tariff, C. W. Newbury, 'The Protectionist Revival in French Colonial Trade: the Case of Senegal', *The Economic History Review*, 2nd Series, vol. xxi, no. 2 (1968), pp. 337-48.

Senegal, it will be impossible for British merchants to carry on trade in the Gambia under such a state of things; as well might Her Majesty's Government confiscate all British property in the Gambia.

Your Lordship must be aware that there is a strong party in France in favour of prohibitory and protective Tariffs.

Morally and socially, it cannot, I submit, redound to the credit of a nation like Great Britain, so justly proud of the liberty of her subjects, that she should by force transfer a community of them and their property to a nation alien in blood, language, and religion, and whose laws and institutions are so different to their own.

The liberated Africans and their descendants on the Gambia ask why England should have taken so much pains and spent so much money, as they did, to redeem them from slavery and to educate and civilize them, if they meant afterwards only to deal with them as goods and chattels to be transferred from one owner to another at their pleasure; they say, with truth, that no native King or Chief ever exchanged or sold a whole community, even in the worst days of slavery, except in cases of conquest by war.

His Excellency C. H. Kortright, when introducing a new Tariff of duties to increase the revenue of the Colony, assured us that the Government had no intention of reopening the question of the cession of the Gambia to France. My Lord Kimberley is understood to have previously given a similar assurance, so that the present revival of these negotiations has taken the community by surprise.

In conclusion, I have to bring under your Lordship's notice that I have been connected with the trade of the Gambia for the last forty-four years, having resided there upwards of forty years; that I have a considerable amount of capital invested there in lands, houses, machinery, and vessels suited to the trade of the river, as also a large amount in debts, goods, and produce, which must inevitably suffer great depreciation if this transfer be made—the French laws on freehold property and inheritance differ very materially from the English . . .

2

ACTING CONSUL WILLIAM A. McKELLAR TO LORD DERBY: PROTECTION ON THE NIGER, 17 JUNE 1876[1]

[Miller Bros. vessel, the *Sultan of Sockotoo*, has been]attacked by African traders from Brass.]

THE operations of those Merchants who send trading steamers up the Niger have always been regarded with extreme jealousy by the

[1] F.O. 84/1456. See also I.D. no. 2, p. 94.

Agents trading in the Brass. Many of the markets from which the Brassmen procure their oil are situated on the banks of the Niger, and to a certain limited extent any development of the Niger trade is accompanied by a decrease in the exports from Brass. Hence the jealousy and suspicion to which I have referred.

But the point to which I wish to direct Your Lordship's attention in the most especial manner is that by these murderous attacks the lives of many British Subjects are seriously imperilled. The Merchants trading in the Niger have between them not less than four hundred British Subjects (Europeans, Accra men, and natives of Sierra Leone) in their employment. The large majority of these are cut off from all intercourse with Europeans now. They are living amongst a population that would not hesitate to murder them to gain possession of the valuable property of which they are the guardians. Hitherto their lives have only been spared, and their goods left untouched because of the conviction entertained that the trading steamers would return when the River rose and restitution [be] demanded for offences committed. But this conviction would be seriously shaken, if not overthrown, by the steamers being unable to ascend the River during our rainy season. In this matter I wholly agree with the gloomy views entertained by Captain Croft.[1]

In the opinion of those best acquainted with the Niger it is impossible to ascend the river this year by the route ordinarily followed. At present it is intended to obtain access to the interior by entering the Forcados River. But it is by no means certain that there is sufficient water in the upper part of that stream to permit vessels such as the 'Sultan of Sockotoo' or the 'King Massaba' to reach the main river. Moreover, it is but too probable that, in ascending the Forcados, steamers would be exposed to an attack similar to that reported by Mr. Hunter.[2] The hostility to Europeans of Alluma, the principal Chief of Benin, has long been known and he has already notified his intention to prevent (by force of arms if necessary) steamers from going up the Forcados. His objection may be overcome by a judicious expenditure of goods and money; and Mr. Croft is prepared to be liberal in such matters. But as matters now stand there is but little time to be lost. Relief to be effectual must be speedily rendered. I beg therefore most respectfully to suggest for Your Lordship's consideration that one of the smallest of Her Majesty's Gunboats be directed to ascend the Niger as far as the village of Agberi . . .

[1] *James A. Croft*, one of the directors of Goldie's United African Company, 1879. Encl. Croft to McKellar, 27 June 1876, ibid.
[2] Encl. J. Hunter to McKellar, 27 June 1876, ibid.

3

WILLIAM WYLDE, MINUTE:
PROTECTION ON THE NIGER,
6 AUGUST 1876[1]

I WOULD beg leave to observe with reference to the subject matter of this despatch that there are two courses open to us, either to give up entirely the Navigation of the Niger River which has for some years past been ascended regularly for a distance of upwards of 400 miles by our trading steamers, and where a valuable Trade is being developed, or else to take such steps as may be necessary to chastise the Natives who have attacked our vessels and to ensure that for the future they shall not be molested by the Brass Chiefs or People. As I have before pointed out the hostility of the Brass Chiefs and the People of the lower Delta is occasioned by their markets being what they call 'tapped' by the steamers passing above them and intercepting the produce which used to pass through their hands, and I am sorry to say that there can be but little doubt that the hostility of the Natives is fostered and encouraged by the European Merchants trading in the Brass River whose business is affected by the Steamers trading up the River.

Some years ago the Traders on the Afn. Coast were given to understand that if they chose to establish themselves up the Rivers where the Natives were hostile they must do so on their own responsibility and that they must take the consequences and not expect to be protected by our Cruisers. But where there is money to be made our Merchants will be certain to intrude themselves, and it is all very well to say that they will not be protected, but the fact is that if they establish a lucrative trade Public opinion in this country practically compels us to protect them, and a great outcry takes place if our Traders are attacked and murdered or their goods pillaged and no redress is obtained. In the case of the Niger we have spent a considerable sum of money on the opening of the River to our Merchants. As soon as the Delta is passed the Natives are all favourable to our Traders and in several instances have protected the Steamers for six or eight months when they have been caught by a falling River and have remained aground until the next season abandoned by their crews. We can hardly therefore allow these Brass pirates to put a stop to the navigation of a great River like the Niger, more especially as they are within easy reach of our Ships of War and there would be

---

[1] F.O. 84/1456. For naval expeditions on the Niger, see K. O. Diké, *Trade and Politics in The Niger Delta 1830–1885* (Oxford, 1956), p. 207. This opinion was referred to the Admiralty, 14 August 1876.

no great difficulty in punishing them if proper vessels drawing not more than 8 or 9 feet of water are employed.

I would propose to send copies of this letter & of its Enclosures to the Admty. and to express hope that the Commodore on the West African Station may be enabled to take such steps for punishing the Chiefs and People who attacked our Steamers as will prevent for the future a repetition of similar aggressions . . .

4

R. H. MEADE TO JAMES F. HUTTON: GAMBIA PROTECTION, 19 FEBRUARY 1877[1]

I AM directed by the Earl of Carnarvon to acknowledge the receipt of your letter of the 7th, calling attention to a circular recently issued by the Acting Administrator of the Gambia,[2] pointing out the limits of British jurisdiction on that river.

2. In reply I am to state that the circular in question has been issued in conformity with general instructions from Her Majesty's Government, and although somewhat loosely worded, and capable of conveying to persons unacquainted with the circumstances the impression that a new limit of jurisdiction was now being laid down, it is in reality only the reiteration of a public statement which has long ago been announced.[3]

3. McCarthy Island has always been considered as the extreme limit of British jurisdiction in the Gambia River, and traders have frequently been warned that in going beyond that point they do so at their own risk, and must not look for protection from the Colonial Government.

4. It appears to Lord Carnarvon that the fact of engagements having been concluded with native chiefs, under which they agreed to afford facilities to trade, cannot be held to bind the Government of the Gambia to seek redress for any trader who may suffer wrong or injury in the territories of such chiefs, and to enforce it by military or naval measures if refused; but there is no intention on the part of Her Majesty's Government to abandon any territory or any lawful jurisdiction which may belong to Great Britain on the West Coast of Africa . . .

[The treaty made by W. Hutton in 1829 with the King of Wuli has never been approved; so Fattatenda has never come under British jurisdiction.]

---

[1] *Parl. Papers*, 1877, lx [C. 1827], p. 21.
[2] Circular, 13 January 1877, ibid., p. 10.
[3] e.g. Carnarvon to Kortright, 24 November 1876 ibid., p. 5

5

GOVERNOR SIR SAMUEL ROWE TO SIR MICHAEL HICKS BEACH: SIERRA LEONE CARAVAN TRAFFIC, 18 JANUARY 1879[1]

I HAD the honour to forward in my Despatch No. 110, dated 5 July, a return furnished by the Government interpreter and protector of strangers, of the numbers of the caravans of Native traders who visited Freetown during the half year January 1st to June 30th, 1878, and a comparison between those numbers and the numbers of similar returns for previous half-years.[2]

2. He has now furnished me with the return for the last half of the year 1878, from which it will appear that the numbers visiting Freetown were somewhat less during that period than during the corresponding period of 1877. The addition of the two half-years still shows a greater number than that for 1877.

3. I have the honour to transmit also a copy of the report which he has furnished to me, giving some information as to the state of political relations between the interior tribes in trading communication with this Settlement, and I regret the unsatisfactory state of the relations between the Seracoulie tribe under Fodey Mohammedoo Daramy and the Falaba and Soolyma country. I fear these tribes are too distant from Freetown to permit of my exercising any satisfactory influence over them; and I also entertain a natural fear that Freetown trade will suffer to some extent from their animosity, as the Sangarahs contribute largely to the total number of the inland natives who come here. In my Despatch No. 37, dated 4th April 1878, I had the honour to mention having met with some 5,000 of them at Port Lokkoh.

[Enclosure.]

Return of Caravans or Strangers from the Interior, viz., Futtah, Harmana, Dangrarwie,[3] &c. to Freetown, for trading purposes, from 1st July to 31st December 1878

S. L. 4 January 1879

Time of Arrival	No. of Caravans
July to September	Nil
October	163
November	185
December	160
	508

[1] C.O. 879/15 no. 175.
[2] These valuable returns are in Lawson to Rowe, 4 July 1878: C.O. 267/335.
[3] Sic, Futa Jallon, Hamana (on the Didi–Falaba trade route), Dinguiray.

Recapitulation

From January to June 1878	9,587
From July to September	Nil
From October to December	508
Total number	10,095

Remarks. In consequence of the war reported to be now going on in the interior between a Sarakoolay Chief named Fodey Mohammedoo Daramy and the Sangarahs, no Muslim is allowed to pass through to Falaba and the Soolima country, either going up or coming down. This they assigned [sic] to prevent their country being overrun and taken by the Foulahs and other Mohammedan powers—the Falabahs and Solimas being looked upon by them as Infidels. This war is the great cause why so few strangers found their way down since October last.

It appears that the war is with the intention of subjugating the Sangarahs or Solimas to the Mohammedan faith. It is reported that Fodey Mohammadoo Daramy's war people captured and put to death almost the whole of the caravans [which] last left here for the Sangarah country. This is what alarmed the Falabahs and Solimas, and caused them to pass the law prohibiting any Mohammedan to pass through their countries.

The road from Port Lokkoh through Falaba to Sangarah is stopped; no Sangarah is permitted to pass through Falaba. There is a road from Port Lokkoh through the Limba country to Abal's country, and from there to any part to the interior countries, without passing through Falaba and Solima.

No hope of Sangarahs coming down just now, as the new road must be through Abal's country, who, it appears, joined Fodey Mohammadoo Daramy against the Sangarahs. There are two other branches of the war against the Sangarahs, viz., Sarmadoo's war and Cearay Brimah's war. Sarmadoo, a Mandingo Chief, seems to have joined Fodey Mohammedoo Daramy to fight the Sangarahs; and Cearay Brimah, also a Mandingo or Sarakoolay, seems to have brought war against the Kankahs and the Harmanahs. The Kankah tribe has received presents from this Government. They have a trade road with the Liberian country, but they have often visited Freetown.

Thos. G. Lawson,
Government Interpreter.

Caravans to Freetown

Months	1874	1875	1876	1877	1878
January to June	2,848	2,554	1,200	8,043	9,587
July to December	262	187		655	508
Total	3,110	2,741	1,200	8,698	10,095

6

A. W. L. HEMMING: MINUTE, TARIFF
EQUALIZATION, 17 NOVEMBER 1879[1]

... ALTHOUGH I do not in all points clearly follow Dr. Rowe's reasoning I think that on the whole it would be almost impossible to effect any tariff arrangements with the French Govt. which would not result in such a loss of revenue as the West African Settlements are in no position to afford. The facts and arguments which he adduces lead me to an entire modification of the opinion I expressed on 12293 in favour of offering to the French an equalization of tariffs as one of the bases of negotiation.

It is true that in para: 11 of his desp. and para. 53 of the memorandum enclosed Dr. Rowe says that if by an equalization of tariffs a satisfactory territorial arrangement with the French could be arrived at, he would consider it desirable to carry out such a scheme. But in the first place this is somewhat inconsistent with other parts of the desp. & memo. in which he shows that a reduction of duties would involve a considerable loss of revenue which even now is insufficient for the wants of the Colony, and, secondly, he assumes (para. 11) that the territorial arrangement would allow of the extension of British influence up to the Pongas, whereas the F.O. propose to make the Mahniah River the line of demarcation, & to give up to France the Isles de Los & consequently the Barga district.

I gather from the figures given by Dr. Rowe that the revenue of S. Leone would be affected by the various schemes of rearrangement which have been proposed, with & without reduction of duties as follows:

The present Customs Revenue of S. Leone may be taken at £60,000. If British jurisdiction, with the present rates of duties, were extended to the Pongas an increase might be expected of £24,000—making a total Revenue (Customs) of £84,000.

If the extension of jurisdiction with present rates stopped as proposed by the F.O. at the Mahniah R., the probable increase would be £12,000 less £3,000 now received at the Isles de Los which would be given up, = £9,000, making a total revenue of £69,000.

If the duties were reduced 25% (& a smaller reduction would hardly be accepted by the French), and British jurisdiction were extended to the Pongas, the probable Customs Revenue would be £45,000 (¾ the present amount) + £18,000 = £63,000.

[1] C.O. 267/338. On Rowe to Hicks Beach, 13 October 1879. Rowe was opposed to the suggestion of tariff equalization between French and British posts proposed in Hicks Beach to Rowe, 6 September 1879: C.O. 879/17, no. 206.

But if jurisdiction were only extended to the Mahniah River, giving up the Isles de Los & Barga district, the probable Revenue would be only £45,000 + £6,000 = £51,000, or very considerably less than the present Customs Revenue of the Settlement, with increased responsibilities & a greater cost of collection. This is a result which I think we could hardly face, more especially when we remember that under the present circs. of S. Leone, we should be obliged to consult the Treasury before taking any measures which would have the effect of reducing revenue—and it is not likely that they would consent to their adoption. Moreover it must not be forgotten that we cannot treat this question in connection with S. Leone only. The French would doubtless require that any arrangement for reduction of duties should include the Gambia, if not the G. Coast & Lagos. And at the Gambia there is no adjacent coastline over which our jurisdiction could be extended, as the French have already come close to the Settlement both on the North & South. Increase of Revenue could only come from a development of trade in the upper part of the River (see para. 20 of Dr. Rowe's memo), and to nourish & foster this, it would be urged (& with force) upon us that we ought to afford that protection to traders which it has been decided shall not now be given beyond McCarthy's Island.[1] And the Gambia could less afford even a temporary loss of revenue than Sierra Leone.

As for the G. Coast & Lagos we could hold out no sufficient prospect of future advantages to compensate for a large immediate sacrifice of revenue. Assinie & Grand Bassam do not now, I think, materially affect the G. Coast trade & revenue—& the value of Cootenoo is now so greatly discounted by the presence of the sharks & our acquisition of Katanu that it would be quite unnecessary to reduce the Lagos tariff with a view to inducing the French to levy equal duties there . . .

[It is unlikely the British Government would authorize extension of jurisdiction as far as the Rio Pongas.]

I think we must be content to try if the French will accept the Isles de Los in lieu of the Mellicourie district and consent to the Mahniah R. being made the boundary limit.[2] It will then be for the Govt. of S. Leone to adopt the best means in their power in developing the trade of the districts over which they will have undisturbed & undisputed influence.

---

[1] No. 4.
[2] Section II, nos. 8, 16. Other officials accepted Hemming's judgement: Minutes, Meade, 22 November; Herbert, 25 November; Hicks Beach, 26 November 1879.

7

CAPTAIN R. L. T. LONSDALE:
MISSION TO ASHANTI AND SALAGA,
18 MARCH 1882[1]

. . . THE leading traders, organisers of the caravans, invariably expressed the hope that the kola may once again be as plentiful in the Salagha market as during the time when the Ashantis controlled it. Primarily because of the increased distance for them to travel to Kuntampoh, and particularly on account of the loss they suffer on that extended portion of their journey through sickness and death among their horses, mules and donkeys, a large number of each of which accompany the caravans as beasts of burden, the horses being also for sale. A very small quantity of kola nuts find their way into the Salagha market and are disposed of at once without difficulty. These nuts are imported usually by Kwau traders from the forests of eastern Akim, but only in a casual way, not as a recognised fixed remunerative trade. I took every opportunity which presented itself of finding and speaking with Kwau traders relative to developing this branch of industry. There are to be found in Salagha at this season a number of traders, Accras, Fantees &c., from the coast. I also pointed out to them, as I did to all who might be likely to direct their attention to that line of business, the many advantages to themselves; in the first instance as importers, to the market of Salagha, which would again benefit them as the more trade developed in Salagha the greater the demand for coast and other produce and the consequent gradual enriching of themselves. It was with the object of developing this trade that I obtained from Jan Kweku of Atabubu a promise of making a thoroughly good road from his town to Kwau, and so to the Akim forest where the kola trees grow. At Kete (a young Salagha), half an hour from Kratshie and its trading place, there is a large Mahomedan population, the majority being Houssas. It contains about 4,050 houses and 7,000 to 8,000 inhabitants. I interviewed the chief men of these, and put before them my views on this point which they appeared to grasp at once, and promised to give this new idea a fair trial. I can only account for this trade not having become more active, and a recognised fact, through the want of some publicity being given to the existence of a road from Salagha to Eastern Akim over which all persons could travel with their goods without danger or fear of interference. Or it may be that the nuts are carried to the coast for shipment to Lagos; should they, however, not find their way

[1] *Parl. Papers*, 1882, xlvi [C. 3386]. For the development of the kola trade, see Nehemia Levtzion, 'Salaga—A Nineteenth Century Trading Town in Ghana', *Asian and African Studies*, vol. ii (1966), pp. 207–44.

out of the Protectorate by this channel, I am convinced that the more
the exportation of them to Salagha, or even Kete, is encouraged, the
more the existing trade of the Colony will be strengthened and increased. One hundred kola nuts purchased at Salagha for 1s., will
realise at Sokoto or Kano and other chief markets in Houssa land
from 14s. to 16s. per 100, that is, its equivalent in goods of various
kinds, which again bring a good profit at Salagha, and at Kuntampoh.
I found it impossible to trace the limit to which these nuts are carried
into the interior; possibly they find their way right across the
Continent . . .

8

J. A. CROWE TO LORD LYONS: FRENCH DIFFERENTIAL TARIFFS, 20 JUNE 1884[1]

[A new tariff has been decreed for Gabon, 8 June 1883, the effect of
which is to impose a differential duty on British trade to the extent of 20
per cent on imports by sea.]

. . . IN the Settlements of Senegal I find an 'octroi de mer' which
applies to St. Louis and Dakar, and gives no special privileges to
French over foreign merchandize. But Decrees, of which the earliest
is dated the 19th February, 1868, and the latest the 14th June, 1881,
establish, in addition to the 'octroi de mer' a Tariff of Customs
duties applicable to the whole of the coast from its northernmost
limit at the mouth of the Senegal to the mouth of the Saloum.
The charges of this Tariff are 15 per cent ad valorem for arms and
munitions of war, 10 per cent. ad valorem for tobacco, and 5 per cent.
ad valorem for all other merchandize except guinea cloths.
For guinea cloths the duty is differential, viz., 2½ centimes per
metre for those of French or French Colonial manufacture; 6½
centimes per metre for those of manufacture not French or Colonial.
This differential treatment of guinea cloths is made more stringent,
and extended indirectly to all other goods by anchorage dues, which
are levied at the rate of 1 fr. per measurement ton on foreign vessels,
whilst French vessels only pay 50 centimes per measurement ton.
The working of the system is favoured by the liberal rules of so-
called fictitious bonding, by which trading firms are allowed to keep
goods in their own stores for a year on bonding account.
Taking the statistics of 1880, we shall find that the imports of goods
of all kinds into St. Louis of Senegal were 9,817,031 fr., of which
3,472,401 fr. were French, 757,638 fr. French Colonial, 5,586,992 fr.

[1] F.O. Confidential Print, 4992 (1884). J. A. Crowe, commercial attaché in Paris,
1882–96.

foreign; but out of the total trade amounting to nearly 10,000,000 fr., only 366,795 fr. worth entered St. Louis in vessels that were not French.

Out of 5,500,000 fr. worth of foreign goods that entered St. Louis, 5,083,481 fr. came from French bonded warehouses, and only 136,356 fr. from foreign ports direct.

The trade in guinea cloths alone affords a similar illustration. The total import of guinea cloths into St. Louis in 1880 was 339,087 pieces, valued at 2,773,938 fr. Of these, 760 pieces were French Colonial; the rest were foreign. Yet not more than 4,200 pieces came direct from non-French ports. The rest were carried in French bottoms from French bonded warehouses.

The system on which the French work in Senegal thus results in bringing the bulk of the carrying trade for goods not made in France into French hands, and preventing the current of business from running directly through any but French houses. African traders alone can explain how it is that foreign guinea cloths pass through French bonded warehouses before they get to the French West African Settlements.

Goree and the small ports of the coast from St. Louis in the north to the mouth of the Saloum in the south are, to all intents and purposes, free ports. But, in the rivers north of the Mellacoree, an export duty of 5 per cent. *ad valorem* is levied, and in the Mellacoree itself, an export due of 2½ per cent. *ad valorem* is imposed.

Interesting as showing the method upon which the French proceed is the monopoly which they have established on the Senegal and other rivers. The navigation of the stream of the Senegal is closed to foreign vessels of all kinds, and the prohibition extends even to ships which have paid the duties called 'droits et actes de francisation'.

The same system applies, by recent Treaties, though in varying proportions, to the Rivers Mellacoree and Casamance, south of the Gambia, and north of Sierra Leone, and to the Ogoouwé, on which M. de Brazza's operations are carried on. The Ogoouwé is closed to foreign trade altogether.

In stipulating for the security of the Senegal frontier with Arab tribes on the north and negro Chiefs on the south bank of the stream, the French Government have naturally consulted their own interests. Clause 4 of the Treaty of the 2nd April, 1879, between France and the Trarza Moors, declares that French traders shall be free from the burden of dues, presents, and taxes of every kind.

The same stipulation in the Treaty of the 5th June, 1879, between France and the Bracknas Moors, are made more explicit by a specific allusion to the trade in gums and other natural produce, which is declared to be free to French merchants, leaving the matter in doubt as regards traders not of French nationality.

The same principle is apparent in the Treaties of the 16th January, 1883, with Cayor; of the 2nd February, 1883, with N'Diambour; and of the 8th March, 1883, with Baol, which are all native states bordering on the railway from Dakar to St. Louis. But, in N'Diambour, no person is allowed to establish himself or to undertake works of public utility without authority from the French Governor.

With Bafing, on the upper tributaries of the Senegal, a Treaty was signed on the 14th December, 1882, which declares that commerce shall be free on the footing of perfect equality between the Malinkés and French subjects 'or others' placed under French protection. By a series of Treaties of this kind, French establishments are brought into immediate proximity with those of Great Britain and Portugal, as a glance at the map of the Gambia and the Portuguese Settlements on the Rio Grande will show.

The tendency of this system is not only to enable France to hold supremacy on rivers which she has brought under her influence, but to make that influence paramount by monopolizing the course of the streams. On the head-waters of the Mellacoree she has obtained the Protectorate of Samo by a Treaty, dated the 3rd April, 1879, the 3rd clause of which is to the effect that commerce shall be carried on freely and on the footing of the most perfect equality between French subjects or others and the natives under the Protectorate of France. But a specific clause allows the French to levy anchorage dues at Benty. The Treaties of the 21st April, 1880, with Kaback, and of the 20th June, 1880, with Balé-Demba, repeat the above clauses of the Treaty with Samo. A different form will be found in the clauses of the Agreements which secure to France the monopoly of the course of the Casamance River. Three Treaties of suzerainty for the basis of the French claims in this region, i.e., the Treaty of the 11th April, 1882, between France and Pakao; the Treaty of the 7th April, 1882, between France, Balmadore, and Souna; and the Treaty of the 18th March, 1882, between France and Jacine. In all these Treaties a clause reserves commerce exclusively to the French, viz.:

First Treaty, Clause 5: 'Commerce in Pakao is exclusively reserved to the French'.

Second Treaty, Clause 4: 'Commerce in Balmadore and Souna is exclusively reserved to the French'.

Third Treaty, Clause 5: 'The right to commerce in Forguy and Jacine is exclusively reserved to the French'.

More recently, in an official Report published by the 'Revue Maritime et Coloniale' of 1884, Dr. Colin reports to the French Minister of Marine and Colonies 'that he has signed Treaties with the Tambaoura and Diébedougou tribes, situated south of Medine and west of Bafoulabé, on the Senegal, reserving to France the exclusive right of working gold mines, making roads, creating establishments, and obtaining concessions of land'.

Less authentic, or rather more obscure, are the negotiations of France with Fouta Djalon, where, it is said, Dr. Bayol, a French Agent, has made an arrangement with the Kings of Timbo, by which an assurance has been obtained from the late ruler and his successor that full freedom of commerce shall be enjoyed by France to the exclusion of the English at Sierra Leone and the Portuguese at Boulam.

The points which seem to be established in regard to the course followed by France in Western Africa are these:

They have established differential treatment at Gaboon to the extent of 20 per cent. in favour of French goods; they have done the same in another way at St. Louis and on the coast of Senegal. They are monopolizing, or have monopolized, the course of great rivers, and asserted their sole right to trade, to work mines, open roads, and obtain concessions of land at several points within the territories between the head waters of the Senegal and the West Coast. They have founded numerous Settlements that are wedged in between those of Great Britain on the one hand and those of Portugal on the other. The railway which they had planned to extend from the coast at St. Louis to Bamakou on the Niger is partly realized, though it will not so speedily be finished . . .

[Elsewhere, Guadeloupe will follow this system; Algeria will be assimilated to metropolitan tariffs; no other French colonies have differential duties, except St. Pierre and Miquelon.]

9

EARL GRANVILLE TO BARON PLESSEN:
FREE TRADE, 8 OCTOBER 1884[1]

. . . THE expression 'freedom of commerce' is commonly used in so many different senses, varying from a mere absence of prohibition to trade up to a complete exemption from all duties and charges, that Her Majesty's Government assume that the German Government agree with them, that duties should be moderate in amount, and that there should be complete equality of treatment for all foreign traders.

I observe also that your note proposes the establishment of freedom of commerce in the basin of the Congo, but only freedom of navigation in the River Niger, and I am therefore in some doubt as to whether it was intended to make a difference in the position of foreign traders in the two rivers. I need scarcely say that Her Majesty's

[1] F.O. Confidential Print, 2023 (1884). In reply to the German invitation to the Berlin West Africa Conference. Section II, nos. 23, 24, 26, 27.

Government would gladly see the fullest freedom both of navigation and commerce secured, not only for the Niger and Congo, but that they would also welcome the extension of the principle, as far as circumstances would permit, to other rivers in Africa.

The Regulations of the Congress of Vienna in 1815 for the navigation of rivers referred exclusively to such as ran through the well-defined territories of civilized States, whereas the Regulations to be made for the navigation of the Congo and Niger will have to deal with rivers whose course lies through the imperfectly known tracts occupied by savage tribes. The problem therefore to be solved is the application of the general principles of the Treaty of Vienna to the very different circumstances that present themselves in Africa, and upon the solution of this difficulty Her Majesty's Government would be glad to learn, as far as possible, the conclusions at which the German Government has arrived.

Upon the still larger question of the principles upon which annexations of unoccupied territory should be founded, Her Majesty's Government would also be glad to be favoured with the views of the general principle on which the German Government propose to base the agreement.

I need not assure you that it is with no desire to raise unnecessary difficulties or in anticipation of any difference of opinion that Her Majesty's Government seek for further information upon the abovementioned points, but as I have already said, the questions are asked only to facilitate the harmonious and speedy work of the Conference.

Her Majesty's Government observe with satisfaction that the German Government propose to invite all the Powers who have commercial or territorial interests on the Western Coast of Africa.

10

GOVERNOR SIR SAMUEL ROWE: MEMORANDUM, SIERRA LEONE TRADE AND TARIFFS, 29 APRIL 1886[1]

. . . 20. THE points, therefore, which in my opinion we have to consider are:

1. How we may best supplement our present revenue to the extent needed to carry on the present system of Government.
2. How we can do this with the least disturbance to trade.
3. If we can take advantage of present needful change in our traffic to replace duties which affect trade injuriously by those which will be less prejudicial.

[1] C.O. 879/24, no. 323. Encl. in Rowe to Granville, 29 April 1886 (recommending increased duties).

21. We may, I consider, take it as granted that the presence of ports easily accessible on our northern border where no import duties are collected has lessened considerably the trade of this place, that we cannot hope to bring it back so long as the existing differences continue between the duties charges in Freetown and in Mellicourie and elsewhere, and that in Freetown we cannot afford to reduce our tariff to that which prevails in those rivers; but it is still of vital importance to our trading interests that we do not by fresh imports injudiciously selected drive away trade more than we have already done.

22. Some difference of opinion prevails in the mercantile community as to the result of an ad valorem duty in thus driving away trade; by very far the majority consider that the resulting harm will be small, and that if by its imposition it be possible to remove the export an absolute benefit to trade will result.

23. In my despatch No. 81, dated 6th March, I had the honour to say that I had not bound myself to any fixed ideas as to the specific amounts which should be levied. The rates shown in the accompanying tariff are not those which have been chosen on account of any special fitness to this place, but the accompanying comparison between them and the rates paid in other British Colonies does not show them to be excessive, and there is no one of them which is peculiarly objectionable on account of the local condition of this place.

24. Then as regards the amount needed to provide that revenue which has already been found necessary for carrying on the government of the place on its present scale, it may be provided, even with present trade depression, by an ad valorem duty of five per cent. only, and I consider that if such a duty be imposed for this purpose it should be continued without any remission of other duties until a sufficient amount has been collected to make up the deficit on this and last year's revenue.

25. Next, if it be desired to make any addition to the existing scheme of Government, with a view to influencing the production and collection of the articles which we export, the means to do this are required, and the specific duties I have noted provide such a means; or if it be thought more desirable to devote the surplus to replacing in the first instance the export duties, they offer the means of doing this and subsequently of lessening port charges.

26. I consider also that the very first opportunity should be taken to remove the additional 2d. per lb. duty on tobacco imposed in 1883, and to reverting to the duty formerly in force, and to abolish also the additional import on guns.

27. The addition to the revenue which resulted after the first few months has been in my opinion more than compensated by a lessening of the volume of trade, and the disturbance of its routine which has

resulted in causing the intended buyer of a gun or case of guns to go to another market has been productive of more loss in other ways than has been compensated by the gain to the revenue.

28. I am inclined to consider that whatever may be the objections urged against the imposition of a general ad valorem import duty, which being imposed on cotton goods, amongst other articles, would according to its rate so far affect the sale of cotton goods to this place, and cause their purchasers to go to the northern rivers at which no import is imposed, that no such objection can weigh against the majority of the specific duties proposed; almost all the articles taxed are consumed by the dwellers in Freetown and other parts of Sierra Leone, they are most of them to a certain extent luxuries, and while the community objects to direct taxation in the shape of a poll tax or house or land tax, I believe that the great body of the people recognise that they may fairly be expected to contribute a little to the expenses of their Government, and that this is as fair a way of collecting such a contribution as can at present be devised.

29. The tax on salt may be considered objectionable for some reasons. I would remark here that the proposed tax of 26s. per ton is really a matter of exceeding smallness. Salt comes to this port generally in bags; 26 of these bags go to make up a ton. At 1s. per bag it amounts to less than one fifth of a penny per lb. Considering the length of time which is taken to consume 1 lb. of salt I cannot think that there will be any hardship experienced as a result of tax.

30. An ad valorem duty of five per cent. on those articles imported during 1884 which do not already pay specific duties would amount to approximately

	£12,500
The export dues gave in 1884	6,190
The wharfage	4,599
	10,789
The tonnage dues were	2,400
	13,189

31. I have already said that I doubt very much if freights will be lessened by the abolition of tonnage dues, or if competition for freights will result; so far no vessel, I am assured, thinks of coming to this place in search of a cargo except she be specially chartered. I do not think the so-called mail steamers can ask more than that they should pay dues only on the amount of cargo they discharge and load at this place.

32. I have the honour to transmit a number of statistical tables which have been compiled for me by Major Festing from the official records, and diagrams illustrating these, which show the commercial

movement of the Settlement for some years back, and also returns which have been prepared for me by the Collector of Customs. Instructive deductions may be made from their consideration.

33. I think from Table A. I am justified in concluding that the lessening in our imports and consequent Customs receipt is directly the result of the lessened quantity of our exports.

The returns of the quantities of the various articles exported show a considerable falling off in value also, and as there is a falling in the quantities exported and also on the value of the lessened quantity which was sent away the return which shows the change of value will show even a greater fluctuation than that of quantities. As our revenue is collected principally on imports, if we wish to continue to receive the same sums at the Treasury it will be necessary not only that we should collect an equal quantity of produce to that which has been previously exported, but that we should supplement the falling off in value by an increase in amount.

34. The purchasing power of the dutiable African produce exported which may be considered to represent the collection from the inland areas neighbouring the Settlement rose to 276,000 *l.* in 1879. Since that date there has been a steady fall until in 1885 the value is only 156,000 *l.*

35. I gather also from these tables that when produce is plentiful specie is not remitted to Europe. Thus in 1875, 4,896 *l.* in specie was remitted. The amount fell in 1879 to 370 *l.*, and it has risen to so much as 39,278 *l.* in 1884.

36. The value of the orders for money given by the Post Office is also an indication of our purchasing means, the amount of money orders and specie, as I have above stated, corresponding directly, in inverse ratio, with the amount of African produce; the money remaining here when African produce is plentiful, it being sent to England and elsewhere to buy manufactures when there is no produce.

37. The amount of money orders issued has risen from 7,209 *l.* in 1877, and 8,268 *l.* in 1880, to no less than 23,597 *l.* in 1885.

38. The necessity in any change of Customs tariff for considering the competition offered by the trading establishments in the northern rivers is, I consider, illustrated by tables H.

39. From 1853 to 1872 the duty on tobacco was 1½d., in 1872 it was raised to 4d. In 1869 the import of tobacco on which duty was paid was 1,051,664 lbs, and the duty was 1½d., in 1885 it was 591,578 lbs., and the duty had been raised to 6d. In 1872 the tobacco duty was raised to 4d. from 1½d., and the import fell to 664,179 lbs. in 1874 (that being the first year in which the change of tariff would affect the trade). In 1883 the duty was again raised from 4d. to 6d., and the import in 1885 has fallen to 591,578 lbs. and I am assured that I shall find a farther fall in 1886.

40. The amount received in 1884 may, I am told, be considered exceptional and not available for comparison because merchants had made arrangements and needed to meet the native buyer who was not yet aware of the change in the prices, and who consequently came to Freetown instead of going to Mellicourie.

41. I attach a statement showing the quantities of tobacco imported and the total duty paid.

Tobacco

	Duty	Quantity. Lbs.
1875	—	717,000
1876	10,594	595,000
1877	12,186	761,000
1878	13,881	848,000
1879	12,894	542,000
1880	15,036	939,000
1881	14,698	884,000
1882	13,234	798,000
1883	12,695	699,000
1884	17,074	687,000
1885	14,700	591,000

It will be seen that the tobacco duty in 1880 at 4d. per lb. produced 15,000 *l.* and in 1885 at 6d. only 14,700 *l.*

42. If we add together any three consecutive years of the above table it will be found that the years 1883-4-5 give a less quantity than any other three following years.

43. From these returns I also deduce an additional reason for the importance which I consider attaches to securing peace in the districts in which the African produce is grown which is exported from the ports of Sierra Leone, and safety to travellers passing along the trade routes which lead to them. I gather from these tables that our most important duty, if we wish to increase the revenue of Sierra Leone, is to increase the quantity of exports.

44. Table No. 7 shows that in 1879 at Sherbro' the total amount received at the Customs station, independent of that paid at Freetown on account of merchants trading at Sherbro' was no less than 21,291 *l.*, as compared with 6,747 *l.* in 1875, 10,002 *l.* in 1884, 9,217 *l.* in 1885, and that this result depends entirely on a corresponding rise in the export of palm oil and palm kernels. The cracking of the nuts which give the palm kernels is specially the industry of the women and children. In a time of war the women and children dare not go outside the fenced towns to collect the nuts, and the person carrying his load of palm kernels for sale is liable to be pounced on by the kidnapper. This industry requires even less preparation than the making of

palm oil, and is more immediately affected by the existence of peace or war.

45. In 1879, 3,561 *l.* export duty was collected at Sherbro', as compared with 2,075 *l.* in 1875 and with 1,833 *l.* in 1884 and 1,834 *l.* in 1885. In the same year the export from the Settlement of palm oil and palm kernels, which products are sent away almost exclusively from Sherbro', amounted to—

	Palm Oil.	Palm Kernel.
1875	716,505	378,007
1879	440,175	513,258
1884	261,305	319,750
1885	307,155	330,656

11

EDWARD STANHOPE TO ADMINISTRATOR J. S. HAY: GAMBIA TARIFFS AND TRADE, 30 OCTOBER 1886[1]

[The Gambia Mail Subsidy is ended.]

... IN considering the question of tariff revision, the first point to be settled is the amount of revenue required. In a place like the Gambia, where the revenue is liable to sudden and extensive fluctuations owing to the outbreak of disturbances in the interior, or a failure of the ground nut crop, the produce of which is the chief mainstay of the Settlement, it would be injudicious, even if it were possible, to impose a tariff sufficiently heavy to ensure that the ordinary expenditure of every year should be met from the revenue of that year. To effect this it would be necessary to place on the commerce of the Settlement burdens which, in view of the competition of the neighbouring French Settlements, it could not bear for any length of time, and would in the result prove disastrous to the Settlement. What should be aimed at is a tariff which would as far as possible be in harmony with the generally received principles of taxation, and would in ordinary years yield a small surplus to form a reserve to be drawn upon in years when from any of the causes mentioned the receipts fall below the expenditure.

The present invested reserve is sufficient to meet the deficit of the current year, and also to provide for the possibility of the revival of trade and revenue being less rapid than may fairly be expected.

I think, therefore, that the estimates of expenditure for the current year may be taken as showing the amount of revenue which will be required from taxation, and that for the maintenance of the reserve

[1] *Parl. Papers*, 1887 [C. 4978], pp. 59–60.

fund we must look to the expansion of trade which will, I trust, result from amendment of the tariff. I rely upon this hope with the more confidence as the estimates of revenue framed by Mr. Carter and Mr. Blackburn, of which I have availed myself, appear to be moderate, and likely to be more than realised in an average year.

The expenditure for 1886 is placed at 23,795 *l.*, and the abolition of the mail subsidy will reduce this to 22,595 *l.*, which may be taken as the average annual amount which will have to be raised for the future from customs and other sources. On the average of the last three years the receipts other than customs, with which it is not proposed to interfere, have amounted to a little over 4,200 *l.*, and deducting this from 22,595 *l.*, we arrive at 18,395 *l.* as the sum which will have to be provided from customs duties. The tariff proposed by the Council is estimated to bring in 22,812 *l.*, or nearly 4,500 *l.* more than is required, and, as I have already stated, more than it would be wise to levy, and I proceed therefore to suggest some modifications of the tariff, which I am disposed to think will tend to facilitate and stimulate the revival of the trade and revenue of the Settlement, which is at present so depressed.

The total removal of the tonnage dues appears to have met with general approval, not a single voice in the Settlement, so far as I am aware, having been raised in defence of this impost, the effect of which has been to give a monopoly of the carrying trade of the Colony to the British and African Navigation Company, who were exempted from payment of the dues under their mail contract.

The increase proposed in the duties on spirits, wine and tobacco also appear to have been accepted unanimously, and I see no reason to differ from the opinion of the Council that the trade will probably not be affected to any great extent by the increase.

With regard to the taxation of cola nuts, I am, however, unable to agree with the majority of the Council that the duty on this article should be doubled. It must be borne in mind that the removal of the subsidy to the British and African Steam Ship Company may probably for a time impair the facilities at present enjoyed for communicating with Sierra Leone, and to add to that disability by doubling the duty would probably result in so hampering the cola nut trade as to seriously diminish the yield of the duty, if it did not prove altogether fatal to it. As at present advised, therefore, I think it would be imprudent to add anything to the present duty of 1*d.* a lb. on colas. This will reduce the revenue estimated from the tariff proposed by the Council from 22,812 *l.* to 20,833 *l.*, leaving it still 2,438 *l.* more than the 18,395 *l.*, which I have shown to be necessary to raise from customs duties. This margin I propose to utilise for the purpose of sweeping away the export duty on ground nuts.

At present the Gambia trade depends almost solely on the ground nut export. Within the last few years the great development of railways in India, and the considerable fall in freights to that country which has taken place, have brought a formidable competitor in the ground nut trade into the field, and the price of ground nuts has fallen accordingly. In these circumstances it is obvious that the export duty of 4*d.* a cwt. at present levied at the Gambia must place the exporters of that Settlement at a serious disadvantage, as compared with those of India and other countries, where no such duty is imposed. This disadvantage is increased by the monopoly at present existing in favour of one shipping company, which has prevented the Gambia from sharing in the general reduction of freights . . .

12

GOVERNOR SIR W. B. GRIFFITH TO LORD KNUTSFORD: ASSINIE–GAMAN TRADE, 13 APRIL 1889[1]

. . . 5. A GOOD deal of trade appears to be carried on from Grand Bassam and Assinie, the imports being guns, lead bars, gin, rum, cotton goods (from Liverpool), and tobacco, the exports from Grand Bassam palm oil and palm kernels, from Assinie ivory, gold dust, and rubber, but no oil. The Grand Bassam Chiefs, I am informed, do not allow the Gaman people to come to the Coast, but buy the goods, take them to Gaman and sell them there, and the Chiefs at Assinie act in the same manner, trading with both Sehwi and Gaman. Mr. Sarbah, a member of the Legislative Council of this Colony is my informant on the above points, but Mr. Lethbridge also informs me that, during his recent mission he met Gaman traders passing to and from Kindjabo, which is not far from the coast. Mr. Sarbah is a native merchant at Cape Coast, but has recently established a branch business at Grand Bassam. Messrs. Swanzy & Co. also have a branch business there, as they have at Beh Beach at the other extreme of our frontier. Now that I have visited Apollonia and Wassaw, I think that there is very little doubt that a large smuggling trade is carried on from Grand Bassam into the Protectorate, and I shall do what I can to stop it, but there is a large field to cover for preventive purposes, and the difficulty is complicated by the protracted settlement of the boundary question.

6. Mr. Sarbah was of opinion that the cause of trade being so flourishing at these places was the cheaper rates which merchants were enabled to charge owing to no duty being levied. On the other hand, the surf, he said, was very dangerous, the French had no system of administration, . . .

[1] C.O. 879/28, no. 354.

[The French have a gunboat and five trading launches on the Grand Bassam River.]

... 8. I do not myself yet see what further steps this Government can take to divert this trade to Cape Coast, if it is to be carried on by middlemen, and fostered by the French merchants cultivating friendly relations with the Chiefs of the interior and giving them presents. The Cape Coast merchants do not adopt this plan, and I do not suppose that Her Majesty's Government would sanction the establishment of a Revenue Station in Sehwi, nor is it clear to me that, if established, it would be likely to be of much practical value, while it would probably be incentive of international disputes.

13

MAJOR C. M. MacDONALD: REPORT, THE NIGER AND OIL RIVERS, 13 JANUARY 1890[1]

Notes on Revenue and Customs

THERE are only two Custom-houses, properly so called, in the Niger Territories—one at Akassa and one at Lokojah.

The Regulations concerning these are that no vessel, boat, canoe or other craft entering the waters of the Niger Territories may touch, load or discharge at, from, or into any part of these Territories without having first entered and cleared at Akassa.

Again, no vessel, boat &c., coming from below Lokojah shall touch, load &c., from or into the port of Lokojah, or any port of entry above Lokojah without again entering and clearing at the said port of Lokojoh.

The import duties payable at Akassa are:

	s.	d.
Spirits of every kind, per imperial gallon	2	0
Tobacco of every kind, per lb.	0	6
Salt, per cwt.,	1	0
War material, including fire arms, gunpowder and explosives, *ad valorem*	100 per cent.	

The duties payable at Lokojah are, in addition to the above:—

	s.	d.
Spirits of every kind, per imperial gallon	2	0
Salt, per cwt.,	1	0
War material as above, *ad valorem*	100 per cent.	

[1] *F.O. Confidential Print*, 5913 (1890), pp. 82, 97.

Goods intended for places above Lokojah may be declared and duty paid at Akassa, in which case they need not be declared at Lokojah. As a matter of fact, no duties have ever been paid at Lokojah, the Company paying all their duties in London, and such foreigners as have traded above Lokojah have availed themselves of the Regulation I have mentioned, i.e. paying at Akassa. All import duties have to be paid in British currency.

The Regulation regarding export duties is as follows:

No vessel, canoe &c., shall receive on board any merchandize from any port of entry and export in the Niger Territories that has not passed the Export Custom-house of that port as attested by proper certificates from the Custom-house authorities.

The export duties are as follows:—

	s.	d.
Palm kernels, per cwt.	1	6
Palm oil, per old wine gallon . . .	0	1
Shea butter, per old wine gallon . . .	0	1
Ivory, per lb.	1	0

All other native produce, including lubi (potash), and country cloth, 20 per cent on local cost price.

The above duties have to be paid in British currency, or in an equivalent amount of produce exported.

To return to the subject of Custom-houses, I consider that the complaint of the traders in New Calabar and Brass River is a reasonable one, viz., that they have to take their goods from the above-mentioned localities to Akassa to declare them and pay customs. I have visited all these places, and have also questioned the officials of the Niger Company, and only wonder that the complaints have not been more pronounced than they have been . . .

General Conclusions

[There are no grounds for the majority of complaints from the German Government, Lagos, Benin, Brass, and New Calabar traders. But the whole system of regulating ports of entry is wrong and calls for abolition, as it leaves the Company open to the charge of monopoly.]

The question of 'markets' forms the basis of the grievances of all the native traders of Brass and New Calabar, and as soon as customs duties and the existing regulations of the Company regarding licences and ports of entry commence to be enforced in the newly opened-up regions of the Wari branch, the complaints from Benin will become considerably stronger than they now are. The facts briefly are that a large number of villages, from which for many years past the traders and middle-men Chiefs obtained their oil, are now closed by reason of, as is alleged, the prohibitive duties and licences; they are, however, much more effectually closed, as I have shown, by the regulations of the Company respecting ports of entry. As one instance of many, I may mention that at the village of Oagbi, situated near the Wari branch and well within the Niger Basin, I saw Benin men trading with the people: Oagbi is an oil-manufacturing centre. As soon as the Regulations of the Company come into force here this village will be closed for purposes of trade, and no one will be allowed to trade, even on payment of customs dues and licences. (*Vide* Chapter on Benin complaints). This does not tend to the development of trade. I see no reason, as I have stated above, why Oagbi as well as numerous other Oagbo villages (the Oagbos are oil-manufacturers) should not be made trading ports, not necessarily 'ports of entry'.

In the district of the Oil Rivers, by a circular of Lord Rosebery's, then (1886) Minister for Foreign Affairs, all markets have been declared free and open to natives and Europeans alike. By a Regulation of the Niger Company, in their vast territories, which march with the Oil River district, only forty places are open for trade.

These are what may be termed the real grievances of the traders, and they should be remedied without delay . . .

14

ALVAN MILLSON TO THE COLONIAL SECRETARY: TRADE IN THE LAGOS INTERIOR, 14 FEBRUARY 1890[1]

[The Ijebus are obstructing trade by interference and excessive duties and tolls; there are excellent palm oil and cotton resources in the Yoruba country; the use of cloth for clothing is widespread.]

12. THUS we see a market of 30,000,000 yards of cloth per annum entirely cut off from the coast by the interference of a weak and idle race, whose ill-merited good fortune has, for the time being, enabled them to control the trade of the Interior. The value of 30,000,000 yards of cloth at 4d. per yard, the present price of native cloths varying, as we have seen, from 3d. per yard for very inferior cloths, to 4d. per yard for those of finer texture, would represent the sum of 500,000 *l.* sterling. Assuming that Lagos were only able to supplant a fifth of the present supply of native cloths, we should see an annual increase of 100,000 *l.* to our imports of cotton goods, whilst one fifth, or 100,000, of the Yorubas now employed in cloth working, would be set free to trade and to cultivate their palm fields. If I calculate the total increase to our cotton trade at 100,000 *l.* per annum, I do so under the firm conviction that the estimate is one of extreme

[1] C.O. 879/33, no. 399. *Alvan Millson*, District Commissioner at Lagos, 1887, Assistant Colonial Secretary, 1889, special commissioner to the Yoruba, 1890, Deputy Governor, 1893.

moderation. To this amount must be added the consumption of English yarns, salt, tobacco, liquors, guns, powder, hardware, crockery, and fancy articles. The increase to our trade to be derived from these imports may be estimated without exaggeration at 50,000 *l*. per annum.

31. From the above considerations we are driven to conclude that an annual import market of at least 150,000 *l*. awaits development within a hundred miles from the water-ways of the Colony. The effect upon this market of opening up the Oshun river for canoe navigation, and of repairing the existing roads through the Jebu country would, in all probability be very important. The means of communication throughout the interior are so excellent, that no improvement to the roads would be necessary.

14. From consideration of the resources of the country which may be classed as—Bread-stuffs, Cam-wood, Dye stuffs, Gums, Fibres, Ivory, Live stock (horses, cattle, sheep, goats, poultry, &c.), Native cloths, Palm oil, Palm kernels, and Shea-butter, without counting the possibilities of future development in other directions, it appears certain that it would pay the natives handsomely to carry their produce to Lagos, or the intermediate markets by way of the Oshun river, which is navigable in canoes to a little below Iwo, of Owo-de, or of Ikorodu. When I mention that 11 gallons of palm oil are frequently sold at Ikirun for 2s. 6d.—the ordinary price is from 3s. 6d. to 4s.— and that miles of palm forests are entirely neglected by the natives, it becomes evident that the expenses of transit to Lagos would be well repaid by the price to be realised at that port. If it pays the natives to sell palm oil at their farms for 3s. 6d. per 11 gallons, and the load per carrier is estimated at 11 gallons, the journey to Lagos being calculated at not more than, at the outside, nine days, and the price obtained being not less than 9s., the profit would be 5s. 6d., or over 7d. a day for their journey, a state of affluence to people who have been accustomed to earn, by hard and uncongenial labour, an average of less than 2½d. a day.

15. The price of palm kernels at Ikirun is 9d. a load of five measures, the value of which would be 5s. and upwards in Lagos, giving a fair profit to those who cared to take them to that market. At present they are thrown away and left to rot in the palm-fields, or mixed with the clay with which the houses are built.

16. Camwood I find to be very plentiful throughout the country, and from samples in my possession, it appears to be of excellent quality. Large quantities of this could be conveyed to Lagos and sold at a great profit.

17. Elephants are frequently killed in the northern portion of Yoruba from Ikirun to beyond Ogbomosho. The tusks are now buried by the hunters and command a merely nominal price.

Considerable quantities of ivory would be available for the Lagos market were the road thrown open to commerce.

18. Shea-butter trees (Bassia Parkii) extend over many miles of otherwise uncultivated country, at a percentage of about 60 trees to the acre, and Ogea trees are plentiful. Examples of this frequency of Bassia trees are to be seen on the barren watershed which bounds the Odo Obba river valley between Ifeodan and Mashifa, and in the sterile tracts of upland country which form the northern water parting of the Oshun river in its upper course.

19. The local trade in indigo and other native dyes would doubtless be considerable, as well as that in live stock and breadstuffs, the supply of which appears to be practically unlimited.

[Horses, yams, corn, sweet potatoes, and eggs are cheap; the soil is fertile.]

20. Estimating the produce to be supplied by the Yorubas as equal in value to the estimated imports into their country through Lagos, it would appear that an increase of at least 300,000 *l*. would accrue to the annual commerce of Lagos without any further development of the resources of the land. Of the ultimate possibilities of future development it is difficult to speak with certainty. On the geology and mineral wealth of the country I am preparing a report, with specimens for scientific examination. The possible development of trade in improved growths of cotton, and other articles of commerce, should also be taken into consideration when estimating the future exports of so industrious a race as the Yorubas. Neglecting all such considerations, however, I am convinced that a very small number of years would see established between Lagos and this portion of the Interior a trade amounting to not less than half a million of pounds sterling. The people pray for it, the chiefs desire it, and the King is anxious to secure the advantages of free intercourse with Lagos. The difficulties put in the way of the realisation of this prosperity alike for Lagos and the land of the Yoruba lie solely at the doors of the King and people of Jebu . . .

[It is for Government to decide how to open up the country—by treaty, compensation or by force.]

15

GOVERNOR SIR W. B. GRIFFITH TO
LORD KNUTSFORD: GOLD COAST–TOGO
TRADE, 12 SEPTEMBER 1890[1]

I HAVE the honour to acknowledge the receipt of your Lordship's Despatches, No. 171, of the 1st, and No. 181, of the 16th of July,

[1] C.O. 879/31, no. 384.

'on the subject of smuggling from the Togo Protectorate', but in view of what is stated in the enclosure to the last Despatch from the Foreign Office, I trust I am not in error in assuming that your Lordship does not now wish for 'a full report upon the smuggling which took place from the German Protectorate of Togoland into the Gold Coast Colony, with such particulars and details as it is in my power to obtain.'

2. Before the receipt of Despatch, No. 181, of the 16th of July, I had intended to submit, for your Lordship's consideration, that it appeared to me unadvisable, from a circumstance which was not within your Lordship's knowledge at the date of the Despatch referred to, to make any representation to the German Government upon the subject of smuggling spirits from Togoland into the Protectorate of the Gold Coast. That such smuggling did take place does not admit of a doubt, because, by means of the preventive force at Danoe, and by its patrols, gin, rum, tobacco, and other merchandise coming from Togoland, were seized in very large quantities within the Protectorate. There can also be no doubt that the *German authorities in Togoland were well aware of the fact*, for Captain Lamb, the Commissioner of Kwitta, informed me in a confidential letter, dated the 21st of August, in reply to my inquiry, 'there is no doubt whatever that Natives prefer trading in the Protectorate. As for the German merchants, they *prefer carrying on business in their Protectorate, as there they direct the administration of the Colony*, elsewhere they are merchants.' And those were the men whose trade was supported by the introduction, by illicit means, of their low duty merchandise into this Protectorate. In short, as Deputy Richter is reported to have stated in the Reichstag on the 27th of November last, as quoted in the copy of your Lordship's letter of the 1st of July to the Foreign Office (Despatch No. 171), 'The increase of trade (in Togoland) which had been mentioned as a matter of congratulation was due to extensive smuggling operations.' Latterly the Hausa patrols at the frontier became so strict, and so many seizures were made, that smugglers refrained for some little time from going to Lomé and Bageida for their supplies of spirits, and began to obtain them latterly from Kwitta, which will account for the improvement of the Customs revenue there from January to April last. And this check told very sensibly upon the sales of the German merchants at Lomé. The Commander of one of the mail steamers, in whose ship I was a passenger sometime ago, informed me that, a short time previously, a Frenchman who was the agent of a firm at Lomé, told him that if Captain Lamb remained at Kwitta and continued such a strict watch upon smuggling on the frontier as that which he was carrying on, the trade of Lomé would be ruined, for that it mainly depended on successful smuggling into the Protectorate.

3. The circumstance alluded to in the preceding paragraph to which I stated your Lordship's attention had not yet been drawn, was the complete change which had been brought about by your Lordship's authorising that the tariff of Customs duties leviable throughout the Protectorate should, from the 1st of May last, be placed at Kwitta on a par with the duties imposed by the German Government in their Protectorate. The complete cessation of smuggling, and to admit of the substitution of a police guard of seven men at Danoe for the large detachment of Hausas which had been kept there, and its transference to the protection of the right bank of the Volta from smuggling, but the greater portion of the trade of Bageida and Lomé has been transferred to Kwitta, where the duties received have yielded very large sums, so that Kwitta is now sending money to, instead of receiving it from, Accra, and the trade in native produce has increased considerably. I will satisfy your Lordship of my accuracy upon these points by asking reference to the annexed statement showing the revenue and expenditure of Kwitta for the first six months of this year, and also its imports and exports. With regard to the former, your Lordship will observe that the Customs duties, from January to April,

	£	s.	d.	£	s.	d.
inclusive, produced . . .	1,346	10	2			
and for May and June . .	1,119	17	10			
or in the six months . . .				2,466	8	0
while the total sum received in the first six months of 1889 was .				597	3	5
showing an improvement in 1890 of				£1,869	4	7

The Customs duties in July and August were 1,235 *l.* 13s. 8d. against 193 *l.* 1s. 5d. in July and August 1889, showing a gain on the comparison of the two months of 1889 and 1890 of 1,042 *l.* 12s. 3d. in favour of 1890, and of 2,911 *l.* 16s. 10d. in Customs revenue in the first eight months of 1890 as compared with the same period in 1889. I would also draw your Lordship's attention to the comparatively enormous quantity of rum sold in Kwitta in May and June last, being 44,512 gallons in 1890, against 5,285 gallons in 1889. Yesterday an application was made to the treasurer from Kwitta for authority to bond 500 puncheons of rum (the duty on which would be 800 *l.*) by the firm of Regis Aîné, a French house, formerly doing business at Lomé and Bageida, but immediately on the duties being lowered they started a branch house at Kwitta, where their principal operations are now carried on. I am informed privately that the revenue of the Togoland Administration has fallen so low that it is short of funds to pay its employées, and that where formerly it received 100 *l.* in duties it now gets 10 *l.* But I am sorry to have to report that in order to support the trade at Lomé and Bageida the German authorities are insisting that Natives in their Protectorate, as well as in that which is to be transferred to them, shall take their produce to Lomé and Bageida, and purchase their requirements of merchandise at those places. This action appears to me to be in contravention of Chapter VI, Article 35, of the General Act of the Conference of Berlin; and, inferentially, of Chapter VII of the Anglo-German Agreement, and I am informed that it has had the effect of calling forth resistance from the Natives, some of whom are said to have had a conflict with a German force, in which some Natives and a German officer and some of his force were wounded . . .

16

R. L. ANTROBUS: MINUTE,
SIERRA LEONE TRADE, 20 MARCH 1891[1]

. . . THE increase of shipping on the abolition of tonnage dues is very satisfactory. The no. of steamers calling in is almost one a day— 353 steamers in 365 days. The expansion of the Sulymah trade is also satisfactory. The improvement in trade, both there and throughout the Colony has more than repaid the cost of the measures taken to encourage and protect it. If we had only spent a little money on making treaties with the countries at the back, and so prevented ourselves from being hemmed in by the French, S. Leone might have become a much more valuable possession than it is now . . .

17

SIR GEORGE GOLDIE TO
THE MARQUIS OF SALISBURY: MIZON'S
NIGER EXPEDITION, 12 OCTOBER 1891[2]

[Conditions of navigation in international law are not identical for the Congo and the Niger.]

THE confusion between the legal status established on the Congo and the Niger by the Berlin Conference has been so general as to give considerable probability to the belief that hence arises the erroneous view that the Riverain States on the Niger have, by Treaty, parted with their normal sovereign right to refuse transit to armed vessels of other States. It is not conceivable that the French Govern-

[1] C.O. 267/388.
[2] F.O. Confidential Print, 6352 (1893), p. 35. For the expedition, see Flint, Sir George Goldie, p. 169; and for the later expedition, 1892–3, pp. 174–5.

ment will admit this right of refusal in the case of armed vessels of a friendly State, and deny it in the case of irresponsible adventurers on the ground that these take with them a few bales of cotton goods, wherewith to purchase provisions and other necessaries from such natives as are not shot down by their machine-guns and their sharp-shooters. No trace has been found in any Treaty, from that of Vienna (1815) to that of Berlin (1885), of the creation of a right to utilize the newly-born principle of commercial free transit for the acquisition of territory by conquest or Treaty or even for scientific explorations. The theory of free transit is based on the principle that no State having possessions on the higher portions of a *mixed* river ought to have its commercial highway to the ocean blocked by the ill-will, cupidity, or caprice of a State having possessions on both banks of lower portions of that river. The Niger Navigation Act is very explicit on this point, and refers clearly to 'les navires marchands' and to no others. The Company did not, as the French Government implies, assert the militant character of Lieutenant Mizon's mission, on the simple ground of his being a naval officer, but on the following combination of facts given in my letter of the 9th May last:

'Lieutenant Mizon's expedition was brought to the Niger by a French man-of-war, it was officered by French naval and military officers, quarter-masters, and sergeants, it was manned by sharp-shooters, and armed, not only with rifles, but quick-firing cannon'. . . .

18

J. BRAMSTON (COLONIAL OFFICE) TO FOREIGN OFFICE: LAGOS–DAHOMEY TARIFFS, 27 JANUARY 1892[1]

I am directed by Lord Knutsford, with reference to the correspondence noted in the margin, to request you to call the attention of the Marquis of Salisbury to the position of the question with respect to the conclusion of an agreement between the Colony of Lagos and the French Settlement at Porto Novo, for the establishment of similar tariffs under section 5 of Article IV of the Agreement of 10th August 1889.

By that article it was agreed that the Lagos Government should not establish customs stations on the Ajarra Creek or in the Pokra District pending the conclusion of a tariff agreement.

It is perfectly clear from the correspondence which passed at the time, that the intention was that negotiations for such an agreement should be opened within a short period, and it was understood that

---

[1] C.O. 879/34, no. 409. By the end of 1892 it was clear the French would not agree to a common tariff, and posts were established on the boundary.

M. Bayol, who was then returning to West Africa would take up the matter on his arrival.

The trouble with Dahomey prevented him however from doing so.

More than two years have since elapsed, and nothing has been done, nor has any satisfactory reply been returned by the French Government to the representations which have been made to them on the subject.

In the meantime, as was pointed out in the letter from this Department of 18th September last, much injury has been inflicted on the trade and revenue of Lagos by the unchecked importation of goods into the Protectorate from Porto Novo through Pokra, and this still continues.

Lord Knutsford understands that M. Bayol has recently been appointed Governor of French Guinea, and he thinks that the opportunity should be taken to endeavour to come to a settlement of the question, and that the French Government should be asked to instruct M. Bayol to enter into negotiations with the Governor of Lagos for the conclusion of the proposed tariff agreement.

Lord Knutsford would further suggest that it should be intimated to the French Government that in the event of their being unable to accede to this request, or of the local authorities failing to come to an agreement, Her Majesty's Government will be compelled to consider whether the Lagos Government should not be authorised to establish customs posts on the Ajarra Creek and in the Pokra District, in order to prevent the passage of goods from Porto Novo into the British Protectorate; and in this case it would be still open to the French Government at a later date to resume the negotiations for a customs agreement should they desire to do so.

The injurious effects to the Colony of the present position of affairs justifies, in Lord Knutsford's opinion, a strong pressure being put upon the French Government to open negotiations.

19

THE MARQUIS OF SALISBURY TO
LORD DUFFERIN: FREE TRADE,
30 MARCH 1892[1]

[It will be the duty of Mr. Phipps and Sir Joseph Crowe in the Paris Embassy to keep informed on the progress of the Boundary Commissions demarcating the interior of the Gold Coast and Sierra Leone, according to the Anglo-French Agreement of 1891.]

I SHOULD wish your Excellency to draw . . . special attention to the importance of the British commercial interests involved in the various

[1] *Parl. Papers*, 1892, lvi [C. 6701], p. 4.

demarcation negotiations; this branch of the question was fully understood, and its value correctly estimated, by Mr. Egerton. It falls within the special province of Sir Joseph Crowe. Wherever, in West Africa, Great Britain has undertaken the task of developing and civilizing the interior, French trade profits equally with that of this country; but the tendency of French arrangements with the natives is to obtain exclusive commercial privileges for French commerce. Her Majesty's Government have no evidence that the trade of any of the British Colonies has as yet suffered from diversion of trade routes in consequence of Treaty obligations with France; they are aware that the Chiefs of the interior would not easily be compelled to abandon roads leading to favourable markets; but they cannot ignore the fact that British merchants are apprehensive that attempts may be made to exclude them from sources of trade in territories under French influence, and they observe that these apprehensions are to some extent justified by the stipulations of the VIIIth Article of the French Treaty with Samadu of 1889. No effort should, consequently, be spared to obtain an understanding that in territories under French, as in those under British influence there shall be no differential treatment; and, as far as possible, to secure agreements as to Tariffs. Such an arrangement was, as your Excellency will observe, contained, as regards the settlement of Assinie, in the Agreement of 1889. A similar arrangement was also, as will be seen from section 5 of Article IV of the Agreement, contemplated in the case of Lagos and Porto Novo. It has not as yet been carried into effect, but correspondence on the subject is still going on between the two Governments.

20

EDWARD WINGFIELD TO THE FOREIGN OFFICE: GOLD COAST–TOGO TARIFFS, 13 JANUARY 1893[1]

I AM directed by the Marquess of Ripon to acknowledge the receipt of your letter of 6th instant, forwarding a despatch from Her Majesty's Ambassador at Berlin, from which it appears that the German Government are desirous that the proposed agreement for a Customs Union between the Gold Coast Colony east of the Volta and Togoland should be concluded as soon as possible.

In reply I am to request to inform the Earl of Rosebery that Lord Ripon is not aware of any reason why the matter should be any longer delayed.

The provisions which have been agreed to in the correspondence

---

[1] C.O. 879/37, no. 434. The arrangement came into force from 1894.

between Her Majesty's Government and the German Government appear to be:

1. That the arrangement should be restricted to the territory east of the Volta, provision being made that any goods passing into the other portions of the Gold Coast Colony, wherever imported, shall pay the higher rates of duty which are in force there. (*See* Sir E. Malet's note of 11th December 1891, and Baron Marschall's reply of 19th December.)

2. That a duty of not less than 1s. a gallon, or 0·22 marks per litre, should be levied on spirits, irrespectively of their degree of strength. (*Vide* Baron Marschall's note of 4th June 1892 enclosed in Sir E. Malet's despatch No. 40 of 7th June.)

3. That an 'ad valorem' duty of 4 per cent. should be levied on all the articles mentioned in Part I. of the schedule to the Gold Coast Ordinance No. 25 of 1889. (*See* Colonial Office letter of 5th January 1892.)

4. That the duty on salt in the Togoland Protectorate should be abolished. (*See* Baron Marschall's note of 19th December 1891.)

5. That the duration of the agreement is to be limited in the same way as is provided in article 5 of the similar agreement between Germany and France. (Accepted by Baron Marschall in his note of 19th December 1891.)

6. That engagements shall be given on both sides that there shall be no unlawful influencing of the natives with regard to the choice of their localities for buying and selling. (*See also* Baron Marschall's note referred to above.)

Lord Ripon sees no reason why an agreement embodying these provisions should not now be concluded.

21

ROYAL NIGER COMPANY: NAVIGATION REGULATIONS, 19 APRIL 1894[1]

. . . THE following Regulation has been duly made by the Council, this 19th day of April, 1894:

(a) This Regulation may be cited as 'The Niger Navigation Regulation (1894),' or, numerically, as 'Regulation No. XL (1894).'

(b) Merchant vessels passing in transit from the sea to inland ports beyond the Niger Territories shall enter and clear in transit at one of the custom-houses, established from time to time for that purpose, at or near the seaboard of the Niger Territories.

---

[1] Hertslet, *Commercial Treaties*, vol. xviii (1893), pp. 166–9.

(c) Vessels returning to the sea in transit from inland places beyond the Niger Territories, shall enter and clear in transit at the nearest custom-house, established from time to time for that purpose, near the inland frontier of the Niger Territories.

(d) Merchant vessels in transit may, as heretofore, call for fuel, provisions, and other necessaries at the numerous ports of entry, and other wooding stations not being ports of entry, on the banks of the waterways of the Niger Territories, and the purchase of such necessaries shall, as heretofore, be held not to be loading or discharging of cargo under clause (e) of this Regulation.

(e) The transit certificate given to such merchant-vessels shall be shown to the authorities of the Company at all ports of entry, or wooding stations within the Niger Territories at which such vessels may call while in transit, and shall, as heretofore, free them from all further Customs formalities, so long as they do not load or discharge cargo within the Niger Territories or otherwise infringe the territorial Regulations of the Niger Territories.

(f) Persons in charge of merchant-vessels passing in transit shall, if they desire it, be furnished at the custom-house, where they enter and clear, with a collection of such of the territorial Regulations of the Niger Territories as are applicable to them, at a reasonable charge, which shall be the same for persons of all nationalities.

(g) Lists of the custom-houses, ports of entry, and other wooding stations shall be published from time to time in the 'Niger Gazette', and in newspapers of the neighbouring Colonies or Protectorates of every nation, or by notice to the Executive authorities of these Colonies or Protectorates. Until the publication of such lists, the custom-houses for merchant-vessels in transit shall be, as heretofore, Akassa, near the mouth of the Nun branch of the Niger; Gana-Gana, near the mouth of the Forcados branch; and Yola, on that affluent of the Niger known as the River Benué, and the ports of entry shall be as heretofore—

Leaba, Jebba, Rabba, Egbaji, Egga, Sokun, Lokoja, Mozum, Yola, Ibi, Abinsi, Amagedi, Idah, Illushi, Illah, Ogrugru, Igbaku, Asaba, Abutshi, Atani, Oguta, Gregiani, Munakor, Utshi, Aboh, Assay, Agberi, Sabergreia, Ekow, Gana-Gana, Akassa.

And the wooding stations, not being ports of entry, shall be as heretofore—

Odeni, Arago, Asibefu, Djen, and Due (on the River Benué) . . .

[Regulations for declaration of arms and ammunition, sealing.]

Aberdare,
George Taubman Goldie,
Scarborough.
Henry Morley, *Secretary.*

22

E. C. H. PHIPPS TO LORD DUFFERIN:
SIERRA LEONE–GUINEA TRADE,
21 DECEMBER 1894[1]

AT an interview which I had with Monsieur Haussmann[2] at the Colonial Office this morning, I questioned him more closely as to the commercial concessions to which his Department would be prepared to agree (should a Sierra Leone arrangement be concluded), with the following result:

1. Article VIII of the French Treaty with Samory would be regarded as inoperative, and no impediment placed in the way of British trade with the French Soudan and Fouta Djallon.

In the latter district, the roads would be kept open, according to the old arrangement made with the Chief by Her Majesty's Government.

2. An undertaking would be given that trade should not be diverted by French agents from the British to the French sphere.

3. As to import duties, it is not the intention of the French Government, owing to the difficulties of levying them, to impose any duties at present on British goods entering the French Soudan or Fouta Djallon from the British sphere. Such duties are levied on goods entering the northern portion of Senegal by the maritime frontier, but not on goods entering Casamance or the Rivières du Sud, and they amount altogether to 12 per cent., being 5 per cent. *ad valorem* on French goods and 7 per cent. additional on foreign goods. In any case, should import duties (not now contemplated) ever be imposed on the land frontiers, they would not exceed those levied on the maritime frontier.

In answer to my inquiries, Monsieur Haussmann said that in view of the present policy in vogue in France under Monsieur Méline's influence, the French Government could not bind themselves (without the consent of the Chambers) that at some time the general tariff might not be applied to imports into Senegal, &c., . . . as had been done in the case of Indo-China, where it had been productive of serious inconvenience.

4. In regard to duties on exports from the French Soudan and Fouta Djallon entering the British sphere, I understood Monsieur Haussmann to say that they would not exceed 7 per cent. *ad valorem*, the valuations being already established by the Chamber of Commerce at St. Louis. It would be understood that such duties would be levied

---

[1] C.O. 879/41, no. 472.
[2] *Jacques Haussmann*, Minister of Colonies.

at certain points to be agreed upon, and not only as at present at Benty, Mellacourie, &c., and I suggested one at Ouassou, one to the north of Kukunia, at Heremakuno, and possible at other points.

It will be remembered that during the negotiations in 1889 the French Government entirely declined to enter into any such commercial arrangements, so, if the intentions as above expressed are carried out, Monsieur Hanotaux's engagements would appear to be complied with . . .

23

SIR GEORGE GOLDIE TO THE
FOREIGN OFFICE: UPPER NIGER
TRADE, 27 JULY 1897[1]

. . . IF it is said that occupation of the east (or left) bank of the river would be sufficient, without occupying the vast regions behind it, I would point out that that bank would be of no value (a) if France were to occupy the country behind it, and (b) that one bank of the Middle Niger has no fiscal value (and therefore no value at all unless minerals are discovered on the bank itself) if the opposite bank is held by France. I wish to set forth the results of permitting France to hold the British territory of Boussa, and to have a port as proposed on the navigable Niger, for I cannot help feeling that if Her Majesty's Government were aware of the gravity of the proposed concession, they would insist on the British rights being respected.

If France were to remain in possession of the west bank of the Middle Niger and were allowed to obtain a port on the Lower Niger, say at Leaba, their vessels would, under the General Act of Berlin, be free from search for munitions of war, which they would undoubtedly pour into their new territory of Boussa, and thence smuggle, by canoes at night, across the river into the Sokoto Empire, for gift or sale to the Sultan and the Emirs of provinces. This would at once give France complete influence, as against England, over these potentates. England might, indeed, counteract French influence by pouring into Sokoto a larger quantity of rifles, machine-guns, and ammunition, but, in doing so, she would be assisting in destroying her own powers in those regions. No agreement between England and France, by which the latter Power engaged to respect British rights to the east of the Middle Niger, could have any effect in preventing the Foulah Princes, thus armed, from crushing out the British power; and when England had retired discomfited, the field would remain open to France, as no one would care to uphold British rights over a region where we could not penetrate. It was owing to Lieutenant

[1] C.O. 879/48, no. 529.

Mizon's distribution of machine-guns, rifles, and ammunition in Muri and Yola, notwithstanding the written assurance of his Government that he would not part with them, that he acquired such complete influence over the Sultans of those two provinces, until he was recalled by M. Ribot. This action of Lieutenant Mizon has already cost the Niger Company dearly, and it will not cease to have effect until the Company crushes Yola (Adamawa) as it has crushed Nupe and the lesser power of Ilorin.

Secondly, if France obtained a port on the Lower Niger, she could pour masses of spirits into that region, as she did into Nupe during the struggle of 1892–4; and as the Niger Company has precluded itself from so doing, French influence over the natives would become supreme, no matter what agreement may be made between France and England.

Thirdly, as regards general trade, France, if in possession of Boussa down to Leaba, could draw the bulk of the commerce of the British sphere to the east of the Niger down to the river bank, where it would be smuggled in canoes by night to the French or west bank, and thence through territory ceded to France down to Leaba for water carriage to the sea. In this way central Soudan commerce would entirely escape the import and export duties on which alone British power must rest, unless the Imperial Treasury is disposed to bear the entire cost; and as the Company has practically to provide out of its private income all deficiencies of public revenue, it would be ruined in a very brief period.

It is impracticable for England, if she holds only one bank of the Middle Niger, to establish a sufficiently effective coast-guard organisation along a distance of hundreds of miles in an uncivilised country and in such a climate. The whole of the canoes would, of course, be at once domiciled on the right or French bank, out of British jurisdiction.

I have only briefly indicated the three principal ways in which Nigeria (and, therefore, the company administering it) would be ruined. I could usefully fill a volume on the subject, which has occupied my unceasing attention since July 1884. It was to obviate these dangers that I so strongly and so successfully urged certain points on Her Majesty's Representatives at the Berlin Conference, 1884–85, and I cannot but express my concern at the prospect of the whole British success at that Conference being now thrown away. It was also to obviate the above dangers that, while at Berlin, I despatched Mr. Joseph Thomson in haste to Sokoto and Gandu for the Treaties of 1885, and also Lieutenant Hamilton and Mr. Green-shields to Boussa to procure the Treaty of 1885. The Niger Company would never have accepted the Charter of 1886, or, at any rate, it would never have extended its powers beyond Lokoja, if it had foreseen the possibility of these Treaties being made ineffective by France being conceded a port on the navigable Niger.

So completely and rapidly would the proposed cession to France ruin the administration of the British sphere, that I earnestly trust that Her Majesty's Government will carefully consider the alternative scheme of handing over to France, for an equivalent elsewhere, the entire Niger territories north of the Benue and of the Niger above the confluence at Lokoja—in short, the Sokoto Empire and Bornu . . .

24

ERNEST MANNHEIMER, TO THE COLONIAL SECRETARY, LAGOS: ILORIN–LAGOS TRADE, 27 SEPTEMBER 1897[1]

I HAVE the honour to request you to bring to the notice of his Excellency the Governor the following resolution which was passed at a General Meeting held on the 24th instant:

'That in the opinion of this Chamber a very considerable amount of trade in the more valuable manufactured goods of Europe and also in Native products is being lost to the Colony owing to the action of the Royal Niger Company in imposing prohibitive conditions upon caravans from the distant interior when wishing to proceed to Ilorin and/or Lagos, and that there is consequently grave cause for alarm with regard to the narrow outlet which has for some time back hampered the progress of the commerce of the Colony, and which now threatens to become a permanency. The Chamber respectfully urges his Excellency the Governor to use his influence in having the obstruction removed, so that the traders from the vast and well-populated country beyond the precincts of the Niger may have free and uninterrupted access to this Colony as formerly; to the mutual advantage of interior and Lagos merchants, to the proper development of that portion of Africa beyond the Niger which is under British protection, and for the benefit of home industries.'

I am also directed to ask if his Excellency will grant an early interview to a deputation of members of the Chamber who wish to lay before him certain facts which have come to their knowledge; should the Governor so desire, they are prepared to substantiate the statements made in the resolution by producing persons whose produce was recently seized when *en route* for Lagos.

[1] C.O. 879/45, no. 509. *Mannheimer* was secretary to the Lagos Chamber of Commerce. Encl. in McCallum to Chamberlain, 6 October 1897.

25

HENRY MORLEY (ROYAL NIGER COMPANY) TO FOREIGN OFFICE: ILORIN-LAGOS TRADE, 30 NOVEMBER 1897[1]

I AM directed by the Governor and Council to acknowledge receipt of the Foreign Office letter of the 19th instant, together with a copy of a letter from the Lagos Chamber of Commerce to the Colonial Secretary of that Colony, both of which have had most careful attention, and on which I am to offer the following observations for the information of the Marquess of Salisbury and of the Colonial Office.

The import duties levied by the Niger Company in the Central Soudan regions, including those behind the Hinterland of Lagos, are as follows:

	s.	d.	
Tobacco of every kind	0	6	per lb. weight
Salt	2	0	per cwt.

Flint-lock guns and trade powder (as permitted in Brussels Act), 200 per cent. *ad valorem.*

The export duties on the produce found in those regions are as follows:

	s.	d.	
Shea butter	0	1	per old wine gallon.
Ivory	1	0	per lb. weight.

All other native produce, including lubi [potash] and native cloth, 20 per cent. *ad valorem* on local cost price.

I am, however, to point out that the import duty on salt overland from Lagos is purely nominal, as this commodity cannot compete with water-borne salt. The import duties are therefore practically reduced to those on tobacco and war material.

I am also to point out specially that the 20 per cent. *ad valorem* duty on native produce, being only on the local cost price, which is very low, is really a very light duty.

It is hardly necessary to point out that in Central Africa the cost of produce has to be exceedingly low, and the gross barter profits have to be extremely large, to produce a net trade profit, in view of the heavy expenditure on account of commercial, as on all other, operations in those regions.

I am to state, further, that during the recent war with Nupe and

[1] C.O. 879/45, no. 509.

Ilorin, and for some little time afterwards, until the country settled down, it was impossible to allow caravans to pass through to Lagos and *vice versa*. But as soon as circumstances permitted, a system was established by which caravans could pay their duties on leaving and entering the Company's territories.

In reply to the inquiry in the second paragraph of the Foreign Office letter, I am to say that from 1877 and until the establishment of order in the Lagos Hinterland subsequent to the Jebu war, there was little or no trade passing overland from the Central Soudan to Lagos or *vice versa* . . .

Since the Hinterland of Lagos has been pacified, and the road thence to the Central Soudan opened, the flow of caravans to Lagos has largely increased, to the detriment both of the revenue of the Niger Company as a Government and of the Niger Company as a commercial body. Hence the necessity of charging the same duties on goods and produce passing from and to Lagos as are charged on goods and produce from and to other parts of the world.

The importation of spirits into those regions is absolutely prohibited, and the Emir of Ilorin has entered into a positive engagement with the Company to insist on the destroying of spirits found within the prohibited zone.

It is as yet too early to be able to give any return as to the amount of trade passing from Lagos into the Company's territories and *vice versa*.

With reference to the letter from the Lagos Chamber of Commerce, I am to point out that the removal of the 'obstruction'—or, in other words, the fiscal frontier—to which the Lagos Chamber takes exception, would mean that all merchandise passing into Nigeria or out of Nigeria would then at once take, as it has lately tended to take, the direction of Lagos, instead of passing up and down the Niger and paying duties to the Company.

26

MAJOR E. A. ALTHAM: NOTES ON THE NEUTRAL ZONE, [1898][1]

III.—TRADE AND TRADE ROUTES

THE value of the Neutral Zone lies in the fact that it includes the main trade routes of the Moshi caravans, who bring down from the north slaves, sheep, cattle, horses, leather-work, cloths, hats, salt, and swords, selling them in the south for kola nuts from Ashanti and European goods, such as clothes, powder, guns, rum, gin, brass,

[1] C.O. 879/54, no. 562.

and copper rods, flint, beads, and cotton goods. The traders carry their goods on donkeys and mules, and move generally in caravans of 50 to 60 men.

This trade has originated and settled into its present channels from three causes:

(I.) The demand for kola nut in the Western Soudan.

(II.) The fact that the nut can best be obtained from the Ashanti forest.

(III.) The fact that the Hausas, who are the great traders of West Africa, have hitherto found it convenient to meet the requirements of this trade by arranging that the year's supply of kola nuts should be collected at the markets of Salaga, Yegi, Attabubu, and Krachi.

The main staple of barter in exchange for the kola nut has been animal stock, the Ashanti, Gonja and Brong being largely dependent for their meat supplies on the Moshi caravans. This dependence in the case of the Brong and Gonja is probably due to laziness, but in the case of the Ashanti it would seem unavoidable, as the thick forest appears unsuited for rearing cattle. The profits of the trade would seem very good, but somewhat fluctuating. The following is an extract from a report of the French Resident of Wagadugu, recently published.

'The market of Wagadugu is attended by an increasing number of native merchants, and will attain its full development as soon as the Gourunsi robbers (Barbatu?) no longer cut the road to Salaga, whither numerous caravans are dispatched to obtain kola nuts in exchange for salt, cattle, country cloth, and tobacco. Excellent profits are realised by the merchants. A sheep, which costs from 3 to 5 francs at Mossi, is sold for about 15 francs (1,500 cowries) at Salaga; an ox costing from 35 to 40 francs sells at 120 francs (120,000 cowries). In Wagadugu long cloth (la guinée) is in but little demand; but Vosges linen (la toile des Vosges) is quickly cleared off, and cloth (les étoffes), for the most part of English production, sells well.'

The prices, however, above given as ruling at Salaga do not agree with those stated in Captain Kenney-Herbert's report of the 24th of June last, which records as 'fair samples' of Salaga prices:

	£	s.	d.
Bulls . . .	1	10	0 upwards.
Sheep . . .	0	5	0 upwards.

Captain Kenney-Herbert,[1] moreover, points out that a large portion of the merchandise is paid away in road dues to the local chiefs through whose territory the caravan passes, good roads and safe conduct being guaranteed in return.

[1] Report, 24 June 1898, in C.O. 879/52, no. 549.

There can, however, be no question that a remunerative trade has, and to a certain extent does still exist, and providing that the French in Moshi do not succeed in diverting it, this trade will develop considerably as soon as the Neutral Zone is in the hands of a Government which will protect the traders from pillage and exorbitant dues. Hitherto the trade has been much checked by the heavy tolls exacted by the Dagombas, the unsettled condition of that country, and the two destructions of Salaga already recorded. Salaga was undoubtedly the great centre on which all the trade routes formerly concentrated, and a glance at Ferguson's map and at Lieutenant Spicque's map of the 'Boucle du Niger' will show the remarkable number of roads which radiate from it. It is for this reason that the Germans made a deliberate attempt in 1896 to remove the remnant of its population to Kratye, with the hope that the trade would follow. Fortunately, however, the greater portion of the Hausas who formed the old trading community of Salaga had moved to Yegi after the first destruction of Salaga.

In the north, Gambaga forms another centre on which the majority of the routes concentrate, although a route branches off from Wale-wale into western Moshi. This route, however, is but of minor importance.

The following are the main trade routes referred to in recent reports, which may be taken as supplementing Mr. Ferguson's map (I.D. No. 1214 (d)).

(i.) Gambaga–Tamale–Donkolade–Salaga–Yegi. This route was traversed by Inspector Armitage from Yegi to Tamale; his traverse agrees generally with the route shown in Mr. Ferguson's map (I.D. No. 12. 14 (d)). Mr. Armitage appears to consider this the main trade route between Gambaga and Yegi, as he refers to it twice in his covering report as 'the Gambaga–Yegi' road, and does not allude to any other main trade route between those two points, although he states that 'a network of good paths cover the country, affording easy communication between the villages in any direction in the dry season.' Mr. Hodgson's telegram of 22nd June, 1898, states that the possession of this route is of 'essential importance,' and that 'the loss of the trade route means loss of trade.'

(ii.) Gambaga–Yendi–Turu–Donkokade–Salaga–Yegi. This road has been recently surveyed by Captain Kenney-Herbert from Yegi to Turu. So far north as Donkokade it is identical with (i.) It had previously been traversed by Mr. Ferguson so far north as Yendi.

(iii.) Gambaga–Yendi–Kratye (German).

Kratye (or Ketti) is a great market centre with a large population (including Haussa refugees brought from Salaga by the Germans). It at one time had a great caravan trade with the north, but this has ceased, owing to the hostilities between the Germans and the King of Yendi. For this reason the Germans are very anxious to acquire Yendi. They have started Kola plantations at Kratye, but as yet without decisive success (v. p. 10 of No. 474, Consular Reports, 'German Colonies, 1897').

(iv.) Gambaga–Wale-wale–Pigou–Savelegu–Yegi, referred to in Lieutenant-Colonel Northcott's telegram of the 1st of March last, and his report dated Yaboum, 9th March, 1898. Looking to Inspector Armitage's road report already above quoted, it appears certain that, although the terminus of the Moshi caravan trade has been temporarily transferred from Salaga to Yegi, yet the old road through Salaga is still used. This route must therefore be identical with (i). Colonel Northcott states that this road is largely used.

(v.) Gambaga–Patenga–Sogne–Zong–Salaga–Yegi, referred to in Colonel Northcott's telegram of the 13th March last, which stated 'that it is necessary to secure from German Empire this route in the interests of the Colony.' This road is also shown in Ferguson's map, and is stated by Mackworth to pass through Karaga. From Gambaga to Patenga it coincided with the Gambaga–Yendi road, and again further south at Zancum (v. I.D. map 1214 (d)) it joins the Yendi–Salaga road (route ii). This route is identical with that referred to in the footnote of the previous page.[1]

From the above reports, therefore, it may be concluded that there are two main caravan routes between Gambaga and Yegi, (i.) the western one through Wale-wale–Pigoo–Savelegu–Tamale–Dooko-kade–Salaga, and (ii.) the eastern through Karaga–Patenga–Sogne–Zong–Donkokade–Salaga; of these two, at the present time it would appear that the western one is certainly the more important.

The trade route from Gambaga to Kratye via Patenga and Yendi has been in the past of considerable importance, and would, no doubt, if the country were settled, form a great avenue of commerce between the north and German Togoland.

It has been conjectured as possible that if Salaga were handed over to the Germans, it could be cut out of the western of the two Gambaga–Yegi routes, but this conjecture does not appear very probable in the face of Captain Kenney-Herbert's report of the 9th February last, in which, after referring to the fact that the Haussa traders are returning to Salaga, and that the place is being rebuilt and the foundations of six mosques have already been constructed, he calls attention to 'the extreme conservative tendencies of the native mind, which will always incline him to obtain his supplies from the old accustomed sources,' and prognosticates that 'so long as security of property is assured by our presence, Salaga will rapidly recover its old prestige, and become again the most important market in this part of the Western Sudan.' It may be urged that the acts of violence

[1] Not printed.

committed by the Germans in the past will cause another exodus if they take over Salaga, but against this view must be weighed the fact that that violence was due to the deliberate policy of diverting the trade from the Neutral Zone into Togoland, and that this policy would be entirely changed if Salaga became German territory. The Governor of the Gold Coast is most emphatic in his recent telegram of 22/6/89 as to Salaga. He states: 'Possession of Salaga of great importance. Possessor of Salaga and trade route referred to (*i.e.*, western route) holds key to trade with interior.'

It is evident, therefore, that while the value of the Zone rests entirely on its trade, there are only two places within the Zone of real importance to that trade—Salaga and Yendi. If we surrender the latter to Germany, it will be most unreasonable of her to grudge us the former.

A discussion may possibly turn on the question of the navigation of the Volta. The trade routes by land through the Zone are impassable for six months in the year owing to the heavy rain which places the whole country under water. During those six months the Volta rises some 45 feet, and would become a main avenue for commerce, were it not for the rapids in the lower parts of its course at Tinkranku, Pejai, and Yegi. The improvement of the waterway would, no doubt, greatly develop the river traffic; the cost of water transport being far less than that of carrier transport. It is noticeable that in August last a native trader with two canoes pushed his way up the river from Yegi as far as Daboya. Captain Mackworth reports as to the upper course of the White Volta: 'It appears to me that the river would be navigable in flood, as the water rises high over all rocks, islands, etc., Captain Murray has since reported that the Volta is navigable by canoes from Addah to Daboya during the months of July, August, and September. Mr. Ferguson appears to have formed a similar opinion during his two journeys in the Hinterland.

There seems, therefore, reason to anticipate that, though the navigation of the Volta is at present somewhat impeded, it may in time become an important avenue of trade to the Hinterland.

27

JOSEPH CHAMBERLAIN TO ACTING GOVERNOR G. DENTON: SPIRITS TRADE, 8 DECEMBER 1899[1]

I HAVE the honour to inform you that, in a letter which was recently received by the Foreign Office from the Royal Niger Company, it was stated that, although the importation or sale of spirituous liquors

[1] C.O. 879/58, no. 586.

is totally prohibited in all parts of the Niger Territories north of the 7th parallel of latitude, this prohibition has lately become ineffective in consequence of the introduction of spirits from the Colony of Lagos.

2. It was further stated that the area over which this new influx of spirits extends is rapidly increasing, and that the Company has not the means of dealing with the question.

3. I therefore request that you will consider and report what steps can be taken by the Colonial Government to assist the Company in maintaining the prohibition.

4. When the administration of the Company's territories is transferred to the Crown, I propose that the prohibition should be maintained; and I attach much importance to steps being taken by the Colony and the Niger Coast Protectorate, as well as the Government of the Niger Territories, to make the prohibition effective.

28

ACTING GOVERNOR G. DENTON TO JOSEPH CHAMBERLAIN: SPIRITS TRADE, 23 FEBRUARY 1899[1]

I HAVE the honour to acknowledge the receipt of your despatch confidential of the 8th December last, on the subject of spirits imported through Lagos finding their way to the Niger territories north of the 7th parallel of latitude in which the importation and sale of spirituous liquors is totally prohibited.

2. No doubt some spirits from Lagos do find their way as far north as the Niger territories, but I am given to understand by those who are in a position to speak authoritatively on the subject that the quantity is small, owing to heavy cost of carriage, which causes the price of a small bottle of alcohol diluted to 20 per cent. below proof to be 5s.

3. It is, I submit, misleading to say the 'prohibition has lately become ineffective in consequence of the introduction of spirits from the Colony of Lagos.' Matters in this respect are very much what they have been all along, the import of spirits into Lagos being considerably less in 1896, 1897, and 1898, than it was in 1893, 1894, 1895. In support of this statement I attach a return which has been prepared for me by the Acting Collector of Customs, and in connection with it I would ask you to note the falling off which has arisen since the duty was increased from 1s. to 2s. per gallon at the latter end of 1895.

4. I notice that the Royal Niger Company do not touch on the

[1] Ibid.

fact that spirits in very large quantities are imported by them into the territory south of Asaba. As far as I can learn there is nothing to prevent these spirits finding their way by land into the prohibited area, and, as the distance is not so great as from Lagos to the seventh parallel, and there is no preventive force of any kind on the boundary of the two zones, it is probable that they do so. I am told that there are numerous creeks connected with the Niger, by which spirits could be conveyed to the territories north of the seventh parallel without coming under the observation of the Company's officers posted on the river.

5. But this is hardly the question, as in the present under-developed state of the Hinterland to the north of the seventh parallel, the class and origin of spirit that finds its way there, must, in the absence of Customs laws and proper supervision, be more or less a matter of opinion.

6. With regard to what steps can be taken by this Colony to assist the Company in maintaining the prohibition, I beg to express the opinion that, to be effective, the matter must be dealt with in the prohibited area. If natives found in possession of spirits were severely punished, they would, I believe, soon give up buying them, but whether we have either the power or the right to enforce such a drastic law in a sphere of influence is a point on which there may be a difference of opinion. If such course could be followed it would, I am sure, be a good thing in the end for the country though, when first introduced, it would, I fear, check trade for some little time.

7. The opening of the Railway from Lagos to Ibadan will un-doubtedly lessen the price of spirits in the Hinterland unless measures be taken to make the charges for carriage much higher in proportion for spirits than for other goods. An international increase in the import duty on spirits would also lessen the consumption, but all these are half-hearted measures, and would, I am convinced, be of but little service, the only really effective way of preventing spirits finding their way in certain area being in my opinion, as I have already said, the punishment of the persons found in possession of them.

29

R. L. ANTROBUS TO THE FOREIGN OFFICE: SPIRITS IMPORTS, 6 APRIL 1899[1]

I am directed by Mr. Secretary Chamberlain to acknowledge the receipt of your letter of the 27th March, enclosing the draft of a

[1] C.O. 879/58, no. 586.

Convention which Baron Lambermont has prepared for submission to the forthcoming Conference on the African Liquor Traffic.

2. Mr. Chamberlain has perused the draft, and shares the view of the Belgian Government that the second scheme for the 1st Article is preferable.

3. The draft deals with the raising of the duties on imported spirits, but the Marquess of Salisbury will have learnt, from the memorandum enclosed in the letter from this Department of the 23rd of March, that Mr. Chamberlain desires that the Convention should also deal, if possible, with the following matters:

1) The establishment of Prohibition Zones;

2) The method of calculating the duty on imported spirit, more especially with reference to over-proof spirit;

3) The prevention of the importation of spirit containing matter injurious to health.

4. Mr. Chamberlain considers that the last two matters are comparatively unimportant, and need not be pressed if the Conference is unwilling to deal with them. He would, however, suggest that Baron Lambermont should be asked to have two new Articles, dealing with the points in question, added to his draft.

5. With regard to the other point, Mr. Chamberlain is in favour of proposing to the Conference to settle the prohibition zones at once. But the other Powers having possessions in West Africa would probably be unwilling to commit themselves to the establishment of any such zones without first consulting their local officers; and, as these officers could be consulted by telegraph before the Conference meets, Mr. Chamberlain would suggest that Baron Lambermont should be asked to inform the Powers concerned that it is proposed to discuss the question of prohibition zones, so that their representatives may receive the necessary instructions before attending the Conference. If this is not done, he fears that the representatives will insist on referring the matter to their Governments for instructions, and that this will involve great delay.

6. As an alternative, Mr. Chamberlain suggests that it would be possible to add to the Convention an Article similar to the second part of Article XCI of the General Act of the Brussels Conference, 1889-90, leaving it to the Powers concerned to establish prohibition zones after the Convention had been signed; but it appears to him that there would be less chance of securing what is desired by adopting this course.

30

JOSEPH CHAMBERLAIN TO GOVERNOR F. M. HODGSON: SPIRITS IMPORTS, 11 AUGUST 1899[1]

You are aware that an International Conference recently met at Brussels for the purpose of dealing with the question of the Liquor Traffic in West and East Africa.

2. I transmit, for your information, a copy of the protocols of the sittings of the Conference, to the last of which is annexed a copy of the Convention which was signed by the Plenipotentiaries of the different Powers.

3. This Convention will have to be submitted to the Legislative Bodies of some of the signatory Powers for ratification, and it is improbable that it will be finally ratified before the beginning of next year.

4. You will observe that Article 1 of the Convention fixes a minimum duty of 70 fr. per hectolitre at 50° C. for the whole of the Liquor Zone, with an exception of 60 fr. per hectolitre at 50° C. for Togoland and Dahomey. These duties are equivalent to 3s. per proof gallon, and 2s. 7d. per proof gallon respectively.

5. You will also observe that all the signatory Powers which have possessions in the Liquor Zone are under an obligation to increase the duty on spirits proportionally for each degree of strength above 50° C., but that it is left to each of them to decide whether the duty shall be diminished proportionally for spirits below that strength.

6. In that part of the Colony which lies to the West of the Volta, the duty already exceeds the minimum prescribed by the Convention.

7. With regard to the district to the East of the Volta, it will be necessary, in consequence of the Customs Union with Togoland, to wait until the German Government has raised the duty in that possession; and, in this connexion, I should state that it has been agreed that arrangements shall be made, if necessary, between the administrations of the Gold Coast and Togoland for the purpose of preventing smuggling.

8. I am asking the Secretary of State for Foreign Affairs to ascertain when the French and German Governments propose to raise the duties in their West African possessions which adjoin the West African possessions of this country.

9. With a view to preventing the importation of concentrated alcohol, the British representatives suggested to the Conference the imposition of a duty, with triple proportionate increase for spirits

[1] C.O. 879/58, no. 586.

above the strength of 50° C. This proposal was not favourably received by the other representatives, and it was the general opinion that the difficulty would be best solved by giving greater facilities in the different possessions for diluting spirits when in bond. This is a matter to which I attach much importance, and I request that you will give it your consideration.

10. With regard to the Protocol of the Convention, Her Majesty's Government will endeavour to arrive at some arrangement with the French and German Governments for securing the Zone of Prohibition which it has been decided to establish in the Northern Territories of the Gold Coast against the importation of spirits from the surrounding foreign possessions. The necessary regulations to prevent the importation of spirits into those territories should be framed and brought into force without delay.

11. It would be of great service to the International Bureau at Brussels, if a return could be furnished as soon as possible after the beginning of each year, giving the quantities and strength of the spirits imported into the Gold Coast during the preceeding year; and I request that you will take the necessary steps to ensure that this shall be done.

12. The return should be made out in the accompanying form, the strengths of the spirits being given in the centesimal notation in use on the Continent, and the quantities being stated in hectolitres. The enclosed book (see pp. 126–131) explains the Continental method of calculating the strength of spirit, and I assume that the conversion from the British to the centesimal system of notation can be effected without difficulty by the Customs officials. In converting the quantities from gallons into hectolitres, 1 hectolitre may be taken as the equivalent of 22 gallons.

31

HIGH COMMISSIONER F. D. LUGARD TO JOSEPH CHAMBERLAIN: SPIRITS IMPORTS, 10 APRIL 1900[1]

I HAVE the honour to inform you that I have promulgated the Proclamation of which copy is attached. I submitted a Proclamation on this subject to the Colonial Office on September 9th, but I have not so far received a reply.

2. Under Clause 12 of the Order in Council of December 27th, 1899 for Northern Nigeria, the regulations of the Company remain in force until repealed, and these were embodied in my Proclamation No. 10.

[1] C.O. 879/58, no. 586.

3. Under these circumstances I was advised that it was illegal for the Company to sell liquor (as they have been doing) to Europeans. The Company therefore ceased the sale, and have since represented to me by letter and telegram that their business was seriously suffering by the restriction, while I found that great inconvenience and discontent was also being caused among the Europeans in the Protectorate who were now unable to purchase the wines and spirits which they had been accustomed to. I awaited the incoming mail, and finding that it contained no reply on this subject, I have promulgated the enclosed urgent Proclamation, which I trust will meet with your approval.

32

W. GEE: COMMERCIAL REPORT ON THE NIGERIAN RAILWAY SURVEY, 20 JULY 1901[1]

. . . 2. POLITICAL AND COMMERCIAL.

A. The town of Ilorin is a most important centre of trade and political influence, and covers an area of 6.65 square miles, and contains, according to Dr. Dwyer's estimate, 180,000 permanent inhabitants, principally Mohammedans, and 30,000 itinerant traders. The natives say that Ilorin has twice as large a population as Abeokuta and 1½ times larger than Ibadan. In a late fire, the Emir states that 10,000 houses were burnt in one quarter of the city; this on your estimate of five people to a house would mean 50,000 people in one quarter alone. On the other hand Sir Gilbert Carter's estimate in 1893 was 70,000 and Sir William MacGregor considers *that* in excess even now. That the cessation of the Ilorin wars and the settlement of the country under British rule has resulted in a large increase of population and cultivation in the district is an undoubted fact. This question of population will be dealt with in more detail in the final report. I subjoin a list of the estimated population of towns and villages in the Ilorin District, supplied by Dr. Dwyer.

B. The greater part of the trade with Ilorin comes via Shonga, Lafiagi, and Share, from Bida, Kano, Sokoto, and the Hausa country, and even from Morocco, Tunis, Khartum, Berber, and Suakim. Dr. Dwyer has himself met traders from these places.

We at one place met a party of Mohammedan Tuaregs with 30 pack animals (ponies and very good donkeys), with loads of merchandise, who told us they had come 60 days' journey from the country

---

[1] C.O. 879/67, no. 647. *Gee* was Chief Engineer for Messrs. Shelford & Son, Consulting Engineers to the Crown Agents.

north of Sokoto, and were going to Ejirin market on the Lagos Lagoon to return thence with European goods.

C. The chief imports into Ilorin from the south are kola nuts (principally from the Gold Coast), palm oil, salt, Manchester goods, Sheffield cutlery, gin, and gunpowder.

From the north they consist of antimony, potash, native ironwork and cloth, leather work (saddlery), goat skins, large quantities of rice from the Hausa country, horses, donkeys, sheep, rams, goats, 'Morocco' skins (red, blue, green and yellow), and ostriches in small numbers from the Central Soudan. Ostriches are worth £5 each and thrive well in Ilorin, and there is great demand for their feathers. From my knowledge of ostrich farming in South Africa, I should say this might soon become a profitable industry in the Ilorin District.

Cotton grows well, but is of short staple, and cannot be put on the Lagos market from this distance by human transport to compete with America and the East. Improved seed and cheap railway transport would soon create a supply. It might be expedient for the Government to erect cotton gins and bale presses at convenient stations on the railway, for the use of which a small charge to cover expenses might be made. In a country rich enough to supply all *actual* native wants, apathy towards new ideas and methods is the rule with native prince and peasant alike, and will only give way before the initiative of the white man.

The so-called 'Morocco' leather, which has been an important article of commerce with Europe for centuries, is in reality manufactured from goat skins in the Central Soudan. The bulk of it is carried by camel caravans to Morocco and Tunis. These caravans travel principally by two routes, occupying some 22 weeks on the journey north from Kano to the north coast of Africa. The first route is via Kuka on Lake Tchad, Ghat, Ghadames to Tripoli and Tunis. The second route is from Kano via Sinder to the Gulf of Gabes, and is conducted under French protection. A small portion of this valuable trade finds its way to Lagos by carriers and pack animals, and the skins are then worth 1s. to 1s. 3d. each, according to size and quality. In England and America the skins are split, the surface portion being stamped and used for bookbinding and kindred purposes and the soft inner portion is made into wash leathers and gloves. This information was supplied me by one of the leading Lagos merchants, who had himself been to Morocco and Tunis to to enquire into the subject. A railway to Ilorin, and even more so Kano, would tap and divert the greater part of this valuable trade to the British port of Lagos, to be exported thence in British bottoms.

D. The native manufactures of Ilorin are glass, armlets, inlaid wooden work, white metal jewellery, ornamental grass mats, Hausa swords, spears and ironwork, blue cotton cloth and dyes.

E. I cannot agree with Sir William MacGregor that Ilorin is such 'a dull and lifeless place' compared with other Yoruba towns (we saw more traders and larger markets there than at any other town we visited except Lagos, and, perhaps, Ibadan, now that the railway has awakened it to life), but I am quite in accord with him *that Kano and not Ilorin or Jebba is or should be the real objective of the Lagos Railway*. Anyone with imagination enough to gauge the possibilities of this enterprise by the experience of the development of other countries by similar means would be fired with enthusiasm at the prospect.

33

GOVERNOR SIR WILLIAM MacGREGOR TO COLONIAL OFFICE: EGBA TOLLS, DECEMBER 1902[1]

... I PUT before you briefly and succinctly my policy with regard to tolls. To not allow the imposition of new tolls; to not permit existing tolls to be increased; to abolish each toll as opportunity occurred ...

[Tolls in Egbaland and Ibadan cannot be abolished under existing treaties.]

I have consistently followed the policy I indicated at first with regard to tolls. They represent practically the only revenue or income of the principal chiefs. They can be set aside only by agreement that at Ibadan, Abeokuta and Oyo would mean compensation on a large scale. Probably the dues or tolls of the Egbas may be now nearly £10,000 a year. They depend on this for the means of carrying on their Government. Goods for Lagos can escape Egba tolls if they are carried by the railway which is not comprised within the Egba jurisdiction.

The tolls charged at other places other than the Egba territory are comparatively light ...

---

[1] C.O. 147/164. In reply to a deputation from the Aborigines Protection Society, received by MacGregor in London. For an account of Egba finances at this period, see E. Baillaud, *La Politique indigène de l'Angleterre en Afrique occidentale* (Paris, 1912), pp. 217–30. Despite this intention to abolish, revenues of the Egba authorities increased. See Newbury, *Western Slave Coast*, pp. 168–9.

34

GOVERNOR F. D. LUGARD TO LEWIS HARCOURT: NORTHERN NIGERIAN CUSTOMS, 29 MAY 1913[1]

. . . 8. I HAVE the honour, therefore, to request your sanction to close all the customs stations on the northern frontier of Nigeria between the fourth and fourteenth degrees of longitude. I may add that in this proposal my responsible officers concur.

9. It is, of course, unusual for administration to free entirely one of its borders from customs control, but I feel that, for the reasons stated above, it is a step which should be taken in regard to this frontier; and I am of opinion that it would tend to the encouragement of trade between the French possessions and Nigeria, and that it would remedy a state of affairs which is by no means a credit to the Administration.

10. In the event of your concurrence in my proposals, I would ask that His Majesty's Secretary for Foreign Affairs should be moved to press the French Government to offer reciprocal advantages by removing all restrictions on the export of live stock from French territory to Northern Nigeria between the same degrees of longitude, since our proposed action will no doubt greatly benefit their salt trade.

11. By closing the frontier stations and surrendering the duty on potash and the surtax on salt the revenue would, as explained in paragraph 6, lose the sum of £7,577 in addition to the £17,943 mentioned in paragraph 5, viz., a total sum of approximately £25,520 a year. To make this loss good, I propose the following increases in import duties:

	Estimated to produce.
1s. 3d. instead of 1s. per cwt. on salt imported by sea or elsewhere than between longitude 4° and 14° (As shown above this increase will in practice be collected almost entirely at the sea-board.)	say £10,000[2]
9d. instead of 6d. per 100 cigarettes, the increase producing	£10,000
	£20,000

---

[1] C.O. 879/113, no. 1005.
[2] (Lugard) Increase on existing imports £8,100. Increased imports due to reduction of duty in the North, say £1,900 (note to text).

The balance of £5,520 will be more than made good by the recent increase in the duty on spirits.

12. In selecting the articles which should bear increased duty, I have endeavoured to arrange that the increased taxes should, as far as possible, fall on those persons in Northern Nigeria who would be relieved of a portion of the duty on salt. The consumption of cigarettes amongst the natives of Northern Nigeria is enormous and apparently rapidly increasing. The total number of cigarettes imported into Nigeria has risen from 20 millions in 1908 to 115 millions in 1912, in spite of the fact that the duty was doubled in 1911, and it would appear that at least half of this quantity is consumed in Northern Nigeria. The small increase in the salt duty at the coast is estimated to cost the native of Southern Nigeria an extra ¼d. a year, which he can well afford to pay, while the native of Northern Nigeria will be benefited to the extent of 15s. a ton on imported salt, and the total abolition of duty on salt and potash entering across the northern frontier. The nett result is to cheapen this necessary commodity to the bulk of the people, and I trust that it may be found possible at a later date to steadily decrease the coast duty.

B. RAILWAYS, ROADS, HARBOURS

I

GOVERNOR SIR SAMUEL ROWE TO SIR MICHAEL HICKS BEACH: SIERRA LEONE ROADS, 14 FEBRUARY 1879[1]

[Roads in the Colony are in bad repair; the Ordinance of 1872 is to be repealed and the Ordinance of 4 December 1855 to be re-enacted.]

6. IT is true that the streets of Freetown as compared with the streets of the Native towns of Africa are magnificent, and the roads of the Settlement bad as some of them at present are, compared with the pathways outside its borders are equally so, but the whole of the funds at the present disposal of the Executive for the repair of Roads, Streets and Bridges is unequal to the repair of the Bridges alone.

7. I have been informed that the majority of the people were not unwilling formerly to work after their fashion on the roads, and I have a proof of this in Mr. Bridge's district—the 2nd Eastern. There through the personal influence of the Manager the work on the roads

[1] C.O. 267/337. Road Tax Ordinance, approved in Hicks Beach to Rowe, 30 September 1879.

has been done by the villages as though the old Road Tax was in operation. He appoints a day for certain villages to turn out and clear the paths between their own and the next village, and the inhabitants accede willingly to this request. He has thus made many miles of paths around Waterloo. The change however in stepping from his district to his neighbours is very marked.

8. I have found on the part of the villagers around Freetown a fair willingness to clear and repair their roads on being lent tools when I have myself been able to visit them; but the old men of two or three villages have often complained to me of the conduct of certain individuals who set at naught their authority and even deride the others when working.

9. They have asked that these persons should be punished for their contumacy, but at present there does not seem to be any law to meet their case. Among a less peaceable people the working majority would soon deal with the difficulty.

10. In the district of Freetown the roads are improving rapidly under the efforts of the past three years, but the cause is, that a very large proportion of the money spent on Roads, Streets and Bridges, has been spent on a few of the principal streets of Freetown.

11. It might be urged that as there are no beasts of burden here, footways are all that is required; but Streets are more than footways, they are main arteries of ventilation.

12. I cannot see that there is any hardship inflicted under this Ordinance; four days' work in a year from each householder is not very much . . .

2

GOVERNOR C. A. MOLONEY TO THE COLONIAL SECRETARY: LAGOS ROADS, 2 MARCH 1888[1]

By showing a continuous interest in their markets and means of communication, and by advice, encouragement and request I have brought about in the Northern District behind Ebutte Metta the road widening and clearing represented in the accompanying printed return.

The service has been effected, with their full will and consent, through the stipendiary Chiefs, Headmen, and people of the towns and villages named, and without cost to the Colony.

I wish to see what the Commissioners of the Eastern and Western Districts can do in a like direction. The importance of lagoon-side

---

[1] C.O. 147/64. Encl. in Moloney to Knutsford, 23 July 1888. And printed returns of roads cleared (Lagos District, 68 miles; Western District, 61 miles).

roads running parallel with the waterway is obvious, as also of roads to communicate from lagoon with sea beach. Main roads should be at least 12 feet: bye roads 6 feet.

A quarterly return will be made by each Commissioner of what he has been able to effect.

3

GOVERNOR SIR W. B. GRIFFITH TO THE MARQUIS OF RIPON: GOLD COAST RAILWAY, 24 OCTOBER 1892[1]

I HAVE the honour to acknowledge the receipt of Lord Knutsford's despatch, No. 105, of the 3rd of May relative to applications from

1.) Lord Gifford,
2.) The African Concessions Trust, and
3.) Mr. H. W. A. Cooper,

for various concessions to facilitate the construction of railways on the Gold Coast.[2]

2. In that despatch Lord Knutsford remarked, 'It appears to me that the Colony has nothing to gain from the intervention of any of these applicants. But while these particular proposals cannot be entertained, I think that the time has come when steps should be taken to decide upon the policy to be adopted by the Government with regard to the construction of railways.' And His Lordship continued, 'The first question to be determined is whether railways should be made at all, and for this purpose it is necessary to have such a preliminary survey made as will enable a trustworthy estimate of the cost to be prepared. Without this information the Government cannot deal with this question of construction in any form, whether by the Government or by private enterprise.'

3. When I was last in England, in one of the interviews which I was honoured with by the Secretary of State, while stating the projects I intended to submit for the consideration of Her Majesty's Government, Lord Knutsford remarked, 'What about railways?'; when I stated that they occupied a prominent position in my programme, and that I hoped their proposed construction would meet with his approval when my scheme was submitted to him; to which His Lordship replied that he was greatly in favour of developing the resources of the Colony so far as this could be promoted by means of railways at a reasonable cost. I then remarked that I thought they would advance the material interests of the Gold Coast beyond anything that could be contemplated, and that I considered Her

[1] C.O. 879/38, o. n451.　　　　[2] Knutsford to Griffith, 3 May 1892, ibid.

Majesty's Government would be fully justified in authorizing the borrowing of such amounts as might be necessary for laying down 300 to 350 miles of railway; that the money could probably be raised at 3½ per cent, and that Sir Frederick Ommanney had told me that he thought a sinking fund of one per cent would be sufficient if the repayment of loans was made to extend over a long period. I mention this conversation[1] because it will show to your Lordship that I am of opinion railways should be made, and that they would be productive of enormous advantage to the Colony. Besides, even if they simply paid their way and the provision for loans had therefore to come altogether out of the Revenue, I think the indirect benefits that would accrue to the Colony by means of railway communication would fully compensate for this outlay. Indeed, it would partly be met by the duties on additional imports which would be based on the increased shipments of produce,—such, for instance, as palm kernels and oil which are now wasted as it will not pay to transport them to the coast, but which, by means of railways, would be collected and brought to the seaboard for export.

4. In obedience to the instruction contained in Lord Knutsford's despatch, I have placed on the Estimates for 1893 the sum of 2,000 *l.* which I consider will be sufficient for distribution as follows for one year:

		£
The Chief Officer employed		1,000
Two Assistants, 250 *l.* to 300 *l.*		600
Passages, &c.		150
Transport and labour		250
Total		2,000 . . .

4

A. G. FOWLER TO ACTING GOVERNOR DENTON: LAGOS RAILWAYS, 6 MAY 1893[2]

As instructed by you on 5th May, I have the honour to report on the country lying between Lagos and the River Niger in regard to the best location for a line of railway between these termini.

[1] In early 1892. There had also been some correspondence with Acting Governor Hodgson in 1891 about a light railway from Axim, supported by the Tarkwa and Abosso Mining Company. As a result, Capt. Lang of the Royal Engineers was sent out in 1893 and made the first survey reports in April and May of that year. Lang and Messrs. Shelford & Son recommended a railway from Apam to Insuaim, which the Governor rejected. Later survey reports recommended a line Sekondi–Tarkwa, which Chamberlain approved in December 1897.

[2] C.O. 147/90. Encl. in Denton to Ripon, 11 May 1893. Fowler went with Carter on his treaty-making expedition in 1893. His survey report (and map) were commended by the Intelligence Division of the War Office: to C.O., 14 July 1893.

2. I hope you will accept these my superficial views for the present, as I have not yet plotted my plans or worked out my barometer heights, and will allow me to add a fuller report when the proposed line has been shown on the map.

3. The line I propose would start from Ebute Metta and touch the Ogun River 15 miles therefrom. Follow the Ogun to within three miles of Abeokuta, then cross the Ogun and turn easterly, crossing the Odo Omi River five miles to the south of Ibadan, still continuing east it would cross the Odo Oban River at the junction of the Odoje River, pass on to Ogbomosho, cross the watershed of the River Niger unto the Aza River, pass through Illorin, follow the Awon River to the Niger. The mouth of the Awon is five miles above the Ijibba Factory of the Royal Niger Company.

4. I have not travelled over the country between Abeokuta and Ibadan, but do not expect there would be difficult gradients on the summit between the Odo Omi and the Odo Oban Rivers. The third summit on the Niger watershed will most likely be the easiest of the three.

5. By this route the nearest point on the railway would be three miles from Abeokuta and five miles from Ibadan, but the line would pass close to Ogbomosho and Illorin.

6. The earthworks would be less than the average, but any cutting deeper than eight feet would meet hard junstone and gneiss rock. This latter would be used for the bridges, but would be costly for excavation.

7. The spans of the bridges, the length of the line, &c., I will leave for a further report.

5

M. F. OMMANNEY, MINUTE:
LAGOS RAILWAYS, 31 JULY 1893[1]

MR. MEADE,

I quite concur in your view. If this proposal is entertained, two consequences will follow. First the Syndicate will, at the expense of the Colony, make a handsome profit on the Survey, and, next, the Colony will find itself committed to the guarantee system, which, in plain English, means the use of the Government's credit for the enrichment of promoters and the same troubles and losses for the Government which other colonies have experienced.

If there is a prospect of a Railway in Lagos paying, the Government

---

should make the Survey. It will only pay the actual cost and will be able to ensure that it is a real Survey, made by competent engineers under the supervision of a Consultant Engineer, not a red line on a plan, intended to grace a Syndicate's Prospectus for the benefit of the railway investor. When the survey is made and some real knowledge is acquired of the probable cost of the line and its earning capacities, the question of how it should be built can be considered. If, with this fuller knowledge, the idea of giving a guarantee is still entertained it can be made a condition of the concession—as in the Indian Railway guarantee contracts—that the Company shall take over the survey at its cost to the Govt., and under a clause freeing the Govt. from responsibility for the accuracy of survey reports or estimates.

Possibly the survey party which is going out to Sierra Leone[1] this autumn might go on to Lagos the next season. Those of its members who survive will have acquired very useful West African experience.

6

ACTING GOVERNOR CARDEW TO THE MARQUIS OF RIPON: SIERRA LEONE TRANSPORT, 9 JUNE 1894[2]

... 4. THE interior must be naturally very productive; following the route taken, as far as Bandejuma, the oil-bearing palm and the rubber-vine abound; from about Waima to Bafodeya the former ceases to grow, but at the latter place it is found again, but becomes very abundant towards Samaiya and the coast. The rubber-vine and kola-nuts are abundant in the Konno, Kuanko, and Sulima districts, but owing to Sofa raids and the remoteness and inaccessibility of the country, trade has not penetrated into these districts, as is very apparent from the absence of European goods in the possession of the natives, with the exception of the flint-lock gun and trade-powder which may be seen in the remotest parts of the interior. Obviously the best way of developing the products of the country is to facilitate communication between the different districts of the interior by opening up routes and laying down railways. Schemes for the latter have already been projected at the instance, I am informed, of the Liverpool Chamber of Commerce, and a survey of a line carried out as far as Bumpan, and also one of another line in the Sherbro district, which I believe has been surveyed from the mouth of the Bum Kittam River, thence across the Upper Kittam River near Pujehun to

---

[1] Again, on C.O. initiative: Ripon to Crown Agents, 7 June 1893: C.O. 879/38, no. 451.
[2] C.O. 879/49, no. 533.

Bandasumah on the Sulima River, and thence to Gigbama, but it appears there are objections to both these lines. The former, owing to the hilly nature of the country, does not admit of extension further into the interior than Bumpan except at great cost, which is a disadvantage, and moreover it does not tap the richest part of the country; and the latter, though it passes through perhaps the most productive part of the interior, has the objection that it would divert a large portion of trade from Freetown, which is the capital and seat of Government of the Colony.

5. I am of opinion that in any project for a railway, it should start from Freetown, the capital, and from inquiries I have made, it appears feasible to lay a line from Freetown *viâ* Senahu and Mafwe to the valley of the Sulima River, tapping nearly the same districts as the line projected from the mouth of the Bum Kittam River, and as the Sulima River is a very large one, I am in hopes that the line might be extended along its course without meeting with severe gradients as far as Kanre Lahun. I am informed that the districts through which such a line would pass are undoubtedly the most productive of those of the interior, that the kamwood, the kouta, and other hardwood trees abound in most of these districts, and there is besides the fact to be taken into consideration that trade would be opened up with the *hinterland* of Liberia. If necessary hereafter, a branch line could be laid from say Mafwe to Bendu opposite Bonthe on the island of Sherbro or to the mouth of the Bum Kittam River. I trust I am not taking too sanguine a view when I record my opinion that the products of the interior alone if properly developed would make such an increase in the volume of trade as to largely swell the revenue. In the proposal I have made above, I am not speaking from personal knowledge of the country through which the line I have suggested would have to pass, but I think it would be advantageous for the officer who may be administering the Government of this Colony, to take a tour to Kanre Lahun next January, with a view of getting a knowledge of the country, and most desirable if he could be accompanied by a civil engineer, say Mr. Bradford,[1] who has already been employed for railway survey purposes, to report on this proposed line.

6. But for the proper development of trade it is essential that peace should prevail over the interior. I am happy to report that such is, generally speaking, the case, but there are still certain disturbed areas in which trade cannot thrive . . .

[A Protectorate should be declared over the interior.]

---

[1] An engineer engaged by Shelford & Son in July 1893. The C.O. had already decided that the terminus should be at Freetown and the survey made via Songo Town and Magbele to Bumban (not to Falaba, as originally proposed).

7

M. F. OMMANNEY (CROWN AGENTS) TO COLONIAL OFFICE: SIERRA LEONE RAILWAYS, 3 SEPTEMBER 1894[1]

WITH reference to your letter of the 7th June, 1893, and subsequent correspondence, relative to the preliminary survey of railways in Sierra Leone, I have the honour to forward a copy of the report of our consulting engineer, Mr. Shelford, together with a portfolio of the plans and section and an enlarged plan showing the route of the proposed railway through Freetown. This report deals with the preliminary surveys of two distinct lines of railway, one, which is referred to as the main line, running from Freetown through Songo Town to Bumban, the other traversing the Sulima District lying to the south east of Sherbro Island. The general results of the survey may be summarised as follows:

2. Neither line presents any considerable engineering difficulties or any features entailing works of exceptional magnitude and cost. The length of the main line will be 139 miles and of the Sulima line about 55 miles, which mileages may possibly be reduced by deviation when the more detailed surveys, which must precede construction, are made. Mr. Shelford has furnished estimates of the cost of these two lines, based on two different types of construction. For a metre gauge line, with moderate gradients and curves, and of the same standard of construction as governs the metre lines of India, the cost of the main line will be 637,038 *l.*, or 4,570 *l.* a mile. The Sulima line, if of a similar character, will cost 414,094 *l.*, or 6,495 *l.* a mile. The second type of line contemplated by Mr. Shelford will be one of 2 feet 6 inches gauge with considerably steeper gradients and sharper curves and, generally, of materially lighter construction than the Indian metre gauge standard. This line would, in fact, be essentially a light surface line, with a limited traffic capacity and low speed. Subject to these material distinctions, the saving of the cost of the two types of line is very considerable, being no less than 187,865 *l.*, or 1,347 *l.* per mile for the main line, and 146,222 *l.*, or 2,012 *l.* per mile for the Sulima.

3. One, however, of the most valuable characteristics of Mr. Shelford's very full and clear report is that it places in its proper light this much contested question of the saving to be effected in railway construction by diminution of gauge. He has been careful to point out that the comparatively large saving referred to in the last

[1] C.O. 879/40, no. 464. Both the War Office and the Manchester Chamber of Commerce favoured the light construction lines. The C.O. authorized the line to Songo Town.

paragraph, is due less to reduction in gauge than to fundamental differences in the character of the two lines, and he states in the later part of his report that the saving as between a metre gauge and a 2 feet 6 inch gauge of identical character in all other respects, would probably not exceed 10 per cent. This is practically the conclusion which was arrived at when questions of the gauge of the Trinidad Railways and the Ceylon Railway Extensions were under consideration, and it appears to us to be satisfactory to receive this confirmation of that conclusion from an engineer who has made narrow gauge railways his special study.

4. It is impossible to decide whether the standard metre gauge line or the light surface line would best meet the requirements of the case in Sierra Leone without carefully considering the question of the existing traffic to be dealt with and its probable development within a reasonable period of years. Mr. Shelford has, accordingly, at our request devoted his special attention to this point.

5. On pages 13 to 18 of his report he gives some useful figures relating to this branch of his subject. Dividing his main line into sections and taking from Freetown to Songo Town as his first section, he anticipates that the net traffic receipts shortly after the completion of that section will amount to 2,608 *l.* per annum. For the whole of the main line from Freetown to Bumban, he estimates the net receipts from existing traffic at 8,333 *l.* per annum. Taking the interest and sinking fund on the capital required for the light narrow gauge line at 5 per cent., these figures would give an annual deficit on the working of the railway, at the outset, of 14,126 *l.* In other words, as he points out, the traffic of the light line would require to be trebled before it could cover its working expenses and pay interest and sinking fund on the loan raised for its construction. The question upon which the decision as regards the construction of this railway appears to us to turn is, consequently, whether there is a reasonable prospect of this development of traffic occurring within so limited a number of years that the Colony will be able to recover the losses incurred on the undertaking within the period of the currency of the loan which may be taken at 47 to 50 years from the opening of the line. In dealing with the different sections into which Mr. Shelford proposes to divide that main line, he has given the grounds upon which he anticipates in certain districts and from certain sources a considerable development of traffic, and it appears to us desirable that the attention of the Governor should be specially directed to this branch of the subject. Mr. Shelford, in his estimate of probable earnings, has assumed for both types of railway a high rate of working expenses. This seems to us to be judicious, because even the light railway will, for some years to come, be working below its carrying capacity, and because the difficulties of railway administration in

such a climate as that of Sierra Leone must necessarily add greatly to expenditure. Mr. Shelford has not overlooked this point, but I am not sure that he is not perhaps too sanguine in his anticipations. He thinks that the construction of a railway to Songo Town will give ready access to much more salubrious districts, where the conditions of European residence are far more favourable than in Freetown. He thinks that the European officials would be able to reside in this district, for instance at the small township of Hastings, without unduly suffering from the ill-effects of the climate and also that it will be possible to train members of the native police for subordinate work on the railway. It appears to us, however, that, under the most favourable conditions, the superior European staff will always have to be more numerous than the importance of the railway would in itself justify, that they would have to be paid more liberally than elsewhere and that, however excellent the arrangements for the administration of the line might be, they would always be liable to disturbance from the absence of responsible officials from sickness, and the temporary employment of acting officials not specially conversant with the work of the different departments. It seems to us also that it is hardly probable that native policemen can be trained for such duties as foremen, either of workshops or plate-laying, or as engine drivers or guards. This question of administration is, perhaps, the greatest difficulty connected with the problem of railway construction in the West African Colonies.

6. In his general observations at pages 75 and following, Mr. Shelford summarises the principal arguments relating to the all-important question of the type of line to be adopted. He sums up strongly in favour of the light 2 feet 6 inches line, and his conclusions appear to us to be sound. He recommends that the section to Songo Town should first be constructed as a test of the possibility of solving the various difficulties which have been referred to. It is important that the first attempt at railway construction in the West African Colonies should be made in respect to the line which held out the greatest promise of success. We have no knowledge of the results of the surveys which we understand have been made for railway purposes in the neighbouring Colony of the Gold Coast, but, as far as Sierra Leone is concerned, it seems to us that this first section of the main line is more likely to secure, at an early date, a fairly remunerative traffic and to afford the means of judging to what extent and in what directions further extensions may be possible, than any other part of the route which has been surveyed.

7. As regards the Sulima line, the prospects of a remunerative return are even more remote and uncertain than on the main line, and it appears to us the consideration of the construction of a railway in that district should be postponed.

8. I have to suggest that, with a copy of Mr. Shelford's report, the portfolio of detailed plans and the plan of Freetown should be forwarded to the Governor, and that, in addition to the questions to which we have called attention in this letter, he should be requested to consider whether there are, in his opinion, any objections of a practical or local character to the arrangements which Mr. Shelford proposes to make for running a line from the town of Freetown. The portfolio and the plan of Freetown should be returned to us when convenient.

9. If the section from Freetown to Songo Town is to be completed by November, and the system under which the work of construction is to be carried out will require careful consideration.

8

M. F. OMMANNEY (CROWN AGENTS) TO
COLONIAL OFFICE: GOLD COAST
RAILWAYS, 19 MARCH 1895[1]

WITH reference to your letter of the 11th December, I have the honour to forward a copy of the report by Mr. Shelford, C.E., on Captain Lang's[2] surveys for a railway from Apam to Eusa, near Insuaim, on the Gold Coast. This report, which is very clear and complete, is illustrated by a map which gives in a graphic form the principal conditions affecting the scheme.

2. Mr. Shelford states his concurrence in the general line proposed by Captain Lang for the railway, and in the selection of Apam as the coast terminus, and he expresses the opinion that the very complete manner in which the survey has been carried out justifies its acceptance as a basis on which to deal with the question of railway construction on the Gold Coast. But he also explains that the line proposed by Captain Lang is of a much better and more expensive type than the traffic is likely to require for many years to come. The gradients and curves adopted permit of a comparatively high rate of speed over the greater part of the line, but at the cost of heavy earthworks and a high rate of expenditure.

3. Mr. Shelford proposes to limit the speed to 15 miles an hour, a condition which will enable him to introduce steeper gradients and sharper curves and, at the cost of some increase in the mileage, to effect great reductions of earthworks and expense. Captain Lang's

surveys are so complete that the necessary revision of the plans can be made without re-survey, and the sections which require to be re-adjusted on the ground can be dealt with when laying out the line.

4. The gauge of the line is to be either 3 ft. 6 ins. or metre, whichever may be considered most suitable on military grounds. As the traffic to be dealt with immediately exceeds by nearly four times that which is expected in the case of the 2 ft. 6 ins. line recommended for Sierra Leone, this increase of gauge seems to be necessary. The length of the line, as revised by Mr. Shelford, will be about 55 miles, and he estimates its cost, including the improvement of landing facilities at Apam, at 331,043 *l*., or 6,020 *l*. a mile.

5. In discussing the question of paying capacity of the line, Mr. Shelford deals first with the question of rates. He shows that, if the traffic were only 24,400 tons a year, a rate of 9·7d. per ton mile would have to be charged to cover working expenses and the charges of the debt. If the traffic increased to 55,000 tons a year the rate would fall to 3·76d. per ton mile, and he quotes Captain Lang's opinion that a 4d. rate would greatly foster and develop the palm-oil trade. He then proceeds to examine whether the statistics of existing trade would justify this rate, or one nearly approaching it, and at pp. 18 and 19 of his report he shows that a yearly tonnage of 40,363 tons may be expected from this trade. This is equivalent to a rate of 5·12d. per mile, a large reduction on the present cost of transport, and it may fairly be assumed that a very moderate development will bring this rate down to the 4d., which has been taken as the ideal rate. Mr. Shelford's conclusion that the line will be remunerative appears therefore to be sound, assuming that he has made sufficient allowance for the exceptional difficulty of maintaining an efficient railway staff in the Colony. He has taken this into account, and has allowed a very full percentage of gross receipts for working expenses, but experience alone can show whether his forecast is accurate in these respects.

6. Generally speaking, the line appears to hold out a better prospect of success than that at Sierra Leone. The existing traffic is much more considerable, the country greatly more populous and, apparently, possessed of more abundant and varied natural resources. If it should be determined to try, in this instance, the first experiment in railway construction on the West Coast of Africa, the mode of procedure recommended by Mr. Shelford at page 5 of his report seems to be that which should be adopted. It seems to us, however, to be very desirable to defer the decision until the results of the Lagos railway survey are known, as a failure at the outset would greatly retard the solution of the question of West African railway construction.

9

M. F. OMMANNEY (CROWN AGENTS) TO COLONIAL OFFICE: NIGERIAN RAILWAYS, 31 OCTOBER 1895[1]

. . . 3. In considering these different routes, it appears to us that no scheme can be entertained which does not provide for the accommodation of the traffic of both Abeokuta and Ibadan. The populations of these towns are estimated at 150,000 and 200,000 respectively, and it is clearly impossible to neglect either of two centres of so much importance. The schemes shown by diagrams 4 and 4 A can only fulfil this essential condition by two separate systems of railway, involving duplicate working organisation and equipment. Moreover, the adoption of either means the shipment of the whole of the Ibadan traffic at a lagoon port and its transport thence by water to Lagos, for a second transhipment, involving extra cost, delay, and risks. It seems, therefore, that these two routes may be dismissed from consideration.

4. Mr. Shelford estimates the total existing traffic derivable from the district served equally by all the remaining surveyed lines at 95,132 tons per annum, and he shows that two at least of these lines will earn, from this traffic, a considerable surplus over and above their working expenses and the annual charges of the capital borrowed for their construction, provided the traffic will bear a charge of 4d. per ton mile. He further assumes that the whole of the traffic now transported by river will come to the railway, a consideration of much importance in connexion with the section from Abeokuta to Lagos, which runs parallel, throughout its length, to two navigable rivers which are now, and have long been, the accustomed channels of trade. Both points require most careful investigation before the question of the best means serving the traffic of the whole district from Lagos to Abeokuta in one direction, and from Ilaro to Ijebu Ode in the other can be decided. The expenditure involved is considerable, varying from 800,000 l. to a million and a quarter, and it is clearly undesirable to adopt any one of the proposed schemes in its entirety until Mr. Shelford's estimates of traffic and his assumed tonnage rate have been confirmed by the Colonial Government.

5. There is, however, no present necessity for arriving at so far-reaching a decision. Mr. Shelford, in the last lines of his report, advocates the immediate construction of the short section of 22 miles from Lagos to Otta, and the proposal appears to us to have much to

[1] C.O. 879/40, no. 464. Chamberlain agreed with the Crown Agents and authorized the Lagos–Otta section: C.O. to Carter, 26 November 1895.

recommend it. Railway construction in Lagos, as elsewhere on the West Coast of Africa, will be attended with exceptional difficulties, towards the solution of which the experience gained on a short tentative section, such as that to Otta, will greatly contribute. It will enable us to deal, with some confidence, with the serious question of the necessity of a large importation of alien labour; it will show how far it is possible to carry on railway construction continuously throughout the change of seasons and under the condition of frequent leave of absence to members of the staff which is inevitable; it will test the possibility of working with some measure of economy and it will open up a district from which stone can be readily supplied to Lagos, where the prosecution of public works of the first importance has had to be abandoned owing to the entire absence of this material.

6. If, then it can be shown that the section from Lagos to Otta is a necessary link in any larger scheme which may hereafter be adopted and if, further, it appears that its construction is not likely to entail too great a financial risk on the Colony, the case for proceeding immediately with its construction would seem to be strong.

7. The condition stated at the outset of this letter as governing the whole question of route, namely that the traffic of both Abeokuta and Ibadan must be secured, is the answer to the first of the questions. A glance at the diagrams will show that either the whole of this traffic, or at all events, the very considerable portion of it coming from Abeokuta, must pass through Otta and that the Lagos–Otta section is an integral part of any practicable scheme intended to serve the whole district.

8. As regards the second question, Mr. Shelford, at page 15 of his report, gives an estimate of the probable initial goods and passengers traffic on this section, which shows a balance of 500 *l.* above working expenses. The estimated cost of the section is 174,000 *l.*, and the interest and sinking fund charges on this capital, assuming it to be raised by loan, may be taken at $4\frac{1}{2}$ per cent., making an annual charge of 7,830 *l.* a year. The burden which the construction of this section may possibly impose on the Colony until further extensions have opened up new sources of traffic, will thus be 7,830 *l.* less 500 *l.* of net earnings, or 7,330 *l.* a year. It may be observed, however, that Mr. Shelford's estimate of revenue from goods traffic is based solely on the limited goods traffic now passing between Otta and Lagos, carried at the rate of 9d. per ton mile. It does not seem unreasonable to suppose that the opening of the line will attract a considerable portion of the traffic of the country lying within a day's journey to the north of Otta, which is now carried to various points on the Ogun river, for canoe transport to Lagos. During the dry season, when the navigation of the river becomes difficult, much of even the traffic now going to Lagos, via Abeokuta, might be expected to be diverted

to Otta and, once so diverted, the chance of its reverting to canoe transport is small. There is the further possibility that the trade may be able to bear a higher rate than 9d. per ton mile. If, however, it is assumed, for the sake of safety, that 7,330 *l.* a year represents the price which the Colony of Lagos may have to pay, during a limited period, for the early commencement of its railroads, it may perhaps be held that the advantages to which we have referred in the fifth paragraph of this letter would not be too dearly purchased at that price.

9. If Mr. Secretary Chamberlain decides to authorise the commencement of the work during this dry season, it will be necessary for us to take immediate steps for sending out engineers and the necessary plant, equipment, and materials, so that work can be commenced before the end of the year . . .

10

EDWARD WINGFIELD (COLONIAL OFFICE)
TO WAR OFFICE: GOLD COAST
TELEGRAPH, 30 SEPTEMBER 1897[1]

I AM directed by the Secretary of State for the Colonies to acquaint you, for the information of the Marquess of Lansdowne, that he has been in communication with the Director of Military Intelligence as to the construction of telegraph lines in connection with the operations about to be undertaken in the hinterlands of the Gold Coast and Lagos, and that he has decided to construct a field telegraph line from Coomassie to Kintampo, in the Colony of the Gold Coast, and from Lagos to Rabba, in the Colony of Lagos, and I am to ask that Lord Lansdowne will, if possible, cause to be supplied from store the materials necessary for an air line of 130 miles in length for the Gold Coast, and for an air line 250 miles in length for Lagos. Poles should not be included in the material supplied, instructions having been given for their preparation in the two Colonies.

If Lord Lansdowne finds it possible to comply with this request, I am to ask that arrangements may be made with the Crown Agents for the Colonies for shipping the material, if possible, by the steamer leaving Liverpool on the 9th of October.

[1] C.O. 96/298.

11

GOVERNOR H. McCALLUM TO
JOSEPH CHAMBERLAIN: LAGOS
TELEGRAPH, 7 OCTOBER 1897[1]

IT is with much satisfaction that I learn from you that Her Majesty's Government are sending from England 250 miles of Field Telegraph, as, when this is erected, it will give us facilities such as the French now enjoy by the line of telegraph which they have constructed to Carnotville and which I understand they are now running from thence to the Niger.

2. From Lagos to Saki is about 200 miles, the town of Eruwa being about half way. As regards preparation of poles and holes which I am directed by you to get ready, I have telegraphed proposing that the first 100 miles to Eruwa shall be taken in hand by the labour parties of the Railway Department working simultaneously in each of five sections of 20 miles each, as this work will not long delay the railway proper.

3. I propose preparing the second 100 miles to Saki by officers of the Public Works Department, who will put all other work on one side and engage native working parties along the line of route.

4. This will leave 50 miles to spare for frontier work or for further advance, at the discretion of the officer commanding the troops, according to development of events.

5. I take this opportunity of strongly recommending that you will approve and give orders for 100 miles of more substantial telegraph material (less poles) for the use of this Colony, the same to be chargeable to surplus balances.

6. Advantage could then be taken, with the approval of the War Office, of the presence of the Royal Engineer detachments in the Colony in connection with the approved field telegraph to employ them in connecting Iseyhin (through which town the field telegraph will pass) with Oyo, Ogbomosho and Ibadan, as shown in marginal sketch.

7. Ogbomosho is near the boundary of territory belonging to the Royal Niger Company and on the direct road from Ibadan to Ilorin and Jebba. Her Majesty's Government may therefore probably find it of great service in view of possible eventualities in the Hinterland to construct a line from Jebba to Ogbomosho so that the Niger and Lagos can be brought into telegraphic communication with each other.

8. As the Consulting Engineer for Railways has included a

[1] C.O. 879/51, no. 545.

permanent telegraph line in his railway estimates from Lagos to Ibadan *viâ* Abeokuta, I also recommend that he be instructed to carry out this portion of the work as soon as the permanent way already opened and the new surveys will allow. Until this permanent line is completed and opened I trust that the field telegraph can be maintained in sufficiently good order to enable us to secure the necessary communication through Iseyhin.

12

GOVERNOR H. McCALLUM TO JOSEPH CHAMBERLAIN: LABOUR, 26 OCTOBER 1897[1]

OCTOBER 26.—Using utmost endeavours to obtain from Ekipi 500 labourers in order to enable Royal Engineers construct field telegraph on arrival of materials. Railway Department must prepare poles' holes as far as Eruwa in accordance with arrangement. Cannot manage otherwise. Other European staff or labour not available. With great difficulty after impressing carriers two companies of 2nd West India Regiment have been despatched to-day. Regret to report excessive unrest and scare throughout country. To meet requirements of Her Majesty's Government, I must make discreet use of such means as are at disposal, including Railway and Public Works Department. Will not interfere with Bridges. As regards operators, six telegraph stations will be required, two each station. Referring to your telegram of 6th October, on reconsideration send out as soon as possible six operators, also ask manager Telegraph Company six native operators.

13

E. HELM (MANCHESTER CHAMBER OF COMMERCE) TO COLONIAL OFFICE: GOLD COAST RAILWAY, 25 JULY 1898[2]

I AM instructed by the Board of Directors of this Chamber to acknowledge receipt of the letter addressed to me by your direction on the 15th instant, with reference to the projected Tarquah railway on the Gold Coast.

When the Chamber received, on the 4th instant, your courteous invitation to send representatives to confer with you on the 7th instant, upon the subject of a railway terminus in Takoradi Bay, it was assumed that the line referred to was the long contemplated

[1] Ibid.   [2] C.O. 879/49, no. 531.

railway to the interior. It is now learnt with surprise that another project was engaging your attention of which the Chamber was in ignorance until the receipt of the letter now under acknowledgment, although it appears to have been contemplated in February 1897, and to have been submitted about that time, together with a report upon it from Mr. Shelford, to the Castle Gold Exploration Company.

The Chamber is fully alive to the importance of carrying out any well devised railway project in the West African Colonies, having as far back as on February 20th, 1893, earnestly advocated the introduction of railways there, in a letter addressed to Lord Ripon. There are, however, in the opinion of the Chamber, some very serious objections to the construction of the Tarquah railway at the present time, which I am instructed respectfully to submit for your earnest consideration.

1. The Tarquah scheme is designed mainly if not exclusively in the interest of a particular industry, that of gold mining, and there is little likelihood that it can do much toward serving the general industrial and commercial interests of the Colony.

2. It must, therefore, be dependent for traffic upon one source, which, besides being uncertain in its duration, is very unlikely to furnish sufficient revenue to warrant the outlay.

3. The project, if carried out, can hardly fail to involve a heavy charge upon the Treasury of the Colony. In the first place a harbour has to be constructed, the cost of which is estimated at 88,500 *l.*, and will probably reach 100,000 *l.* If this harbour were made at a point which might become a central depôt for a large part of the colony, and so do away with the present dangerous and expensive landing of goods through the surf, the expenditure of even a larger sum might be justified, but it would be difficult if not impossible profitably to construct a railway connecting Takoradi Bay with Cape Coast and Accra, or to extend the proposed line into the interior. Secondly, the cost of the railway itself will be very great. Writing of this route, Captain Lang in his report on page 8 says: 'It is believed that the cost of a railway would be exceedingly high, if not prohibitive, without the aid of special appliances to overcome steep gradients. The traffic would consist of timber, wood for fuel, provisions, and gold for export, not, however, in sufficient quantities to make the line remunerative for some years. The hilly country north of the mining localities appear to prohibit the extension of such a line into the far interior.' In other parts of the colony Captain Lang estimates the cost of construction at 5,000 *l.* a mile, and in this case 7,500 *l.* a mile would probably not be an excessive estimate. At this latter rate the cost would be 300,000 *l.* making together with the outlay upon the harbour, a total expenditure of 400,000 *l.* in a part of the colony where there is at present very little trade.

4. It is greatly to be feared that the construction and working of this line will impose upon the colony for a long time to come, and perhaps permanently, a financial burden so serious as to deter the carrying out of the project, which has been under consideration for several years, of laying down a railway into the heart of the hinterland.[1] This object and its early accomplishment are, in the opinion of the Chamber, of paramount importance. The report of Captain Lang (page 7) says:

'The efforts of the Government should in the first instance be devoted to the development of the country, so as to increase the trade and foster manufacture, and to the enlightenment of the native population. These objects can only be obtained by the projection of lines into the interior.'

With these words the Chamber cordially agrees, and it is convinced that any postponement, or risk of postponement, of the original railway scheme, due to the prior construction of the Tarquah line, is earnestly to be deprecated in the interests of the Colony and its trade.

14

M. F. OMMANNEY (CROWN AGENTS) TO COLONIAL OFFICE: LAGOS HARBOUR, 25 JULY 1898[2]

. . . 5. THERE remains for consideration only the complete project for the removal of the bar. In Messrs. Coode Son and Matthews' report of the 21st April, 1892, they estimated the cost of these works at £830,000. They have been able, in the light of the more complete information now available as to the sources of supply of stone and the cost of its delivery at the works, to reduce this estimate by £30,000, and it stands at £800,000. They explain in their report the grounds upon which they find it impossible to effect a more material reduction, and it becomes necessary to consider whether Lagos would be justified in incurring the charge on her revenues for interest and sinking fund on this heavy capital expenditure, which will amount to from £28,000 to £32,000 a year, according to the terms upon which we may be able to raise the money. The full incidence of this charge will not be felt until the expiration of the twelve years which the work is expected to occupy in construction, and as the improvement of the

---

[1] i.e. through to Kumasi. In May 1898 the C.O. decided in favour of Takoradi, as the terminus for a railway, though the Admiralty was asked to survey Sekondi as well. See the excellent map of projected lines in Kwamina B. Dickson, *A Historical Geography of Ghana* (Cambridge, 1969), p. 231.

[2] C.O. 879/67, no. 647.

bar will not be effected until the works have advanced to near completion, it will not be possible, within that period, to impose upon the trade of the port harbour dues or other charges which might in a measure relieve the revenue of the Colony. Messrs. Coode Son and Matthews estimate that, when the works are completed, the benefit to the existing trade of Lagos from the removal of the bar will amount to £24,000 a year, and if a large development of that trade occurs it will be possible to meet, by some form of harbour dues, the greater proportion, if not the whole, of the charges of the debt. But we can perceive no means of lightening the burden on the finances of the Colony during the greater part of the period of construction unless the opening up of such a harbour as Lagos would possess when the bar is removed were considered a matter of sufficient Imperial importance to justify a contribution from Admiralty funds towards the cost of the work for a limited number of years. A contribution, for example, of £20,000 or even £15,000 a year for the next ten years, would go far towards justifying the immediate commencement of the scheme.

6. The question is, it appears to us, one which can only be decided on broad issues connected with the future development of this part of British West Africa. It seems inevitable that when once the Lagos Railway has reached Ibadan, the opening up of the whole of the Niger territory and of Sokoto must be by means of the extension of that railway across the Niger. To approach that problem from any other direction, as, for instance, by means of a railway from Forcados, would be to sacrifice the enormous advantage of the heavy expenditure which will have been incurred by the time the Lagos Railway reaches Ibadan, and it seems as though the necessity of serving the rich and populous districts through which the Lagos Railway will pass has already determined the line of future railway development and the destiny of Lagos as the port at which the great bulk of the trade of Nigeria will have to be dealt with. If this view be sound, there can be very little doubt as to the wisdom of commencing these works with the least possible delay and of pushing them vigorously forward. There is in this case every reason for anticipating with confidence the complete success of the scheme. The volume of water brought down for discharge through the proposed moles will place at the command of the engineers an unusually powerful means of dealing with the obstruction presented by the bar and it is seldom that consulting engineers can venture upon so confident a prediction of success as is contained in the 9th paragraph of Messrs. Coode Son and Matthews' report.

7. There is an additional argument in favour of the early removal of the Lagos bar, which appears to us to be of much weight. An open harbour at Lagos, combined with a largely developed trade, would

offer attractions to steamship owners which would inevitably result in the abolition of the monopoly which at present hampers in every direction the trade of the coast, and adds largely to the very serious difficulties and heavy expenses which are inevitable in the prosecution of large public works in such a climate. Any proposals for the improvement of the port of Lagos will, there is very little doubt, meet with the strenuous opposition of those who are already in possession of the field, and that opposition will be, in itself, an indication of the necessity for these works and a justification to the Colony for undertaking them. The demands of the railway, particularly if it is to receive the great extension to which we have referred, for materials and stores, and especially for coal, could only be met with much difficulty and at an exorbitant rate, if the present system were to continue in unabated force . . .

15

ASHANTI GOLDFIELDS CORPORATION, LIMITED, TO COLONIAL OFFICE: GOLD COAST RAILWAYS, AUGUST 1898[1]

PRIVATE.

HEARING with great satisfaction that Her Majesty's Government have begun the construction of a railway from Sekondi to Tarkwa, and that such railway may be considered the trunk line for a probable extension into Ashanti, we venture to submit a proposal, in the hope that, while primarily serving our own purpose, it may be also considered as eminently serviceable to the interests of the Gold Coast Government.

The proposal rests upon the assurance that a railway communication with Ashanti is in every way desirable; that the natural products of the country fully warrant such a development; that there is a reasonable prospect of such means of communication becoming a remunerative investment for the Colony; that the hinterland developments appear to demand such communication; that the evidences already gained afford sufficient warranty for an extension at least as far as Kumasi, and that the time is ripe.

Our immediate object is to secure railway communication to our extensive property, situated about half-way (or rather more) in an almost direct line between Tarkwa and Kumasi—a property from which, by actual milling tests and the best procurable expert evidence, we have information that would warrant our spending very large

---

[1] C.O. 879/49, no. 531. The C.O. agreed to a survey from Tarkwa to Kumasi, but would not guarantee the building of a line: C.O. to Ashanti Goldfields Corporation, 31 August 1898.

sums in its development once the question of transport has been settled.

Our evidence assures us that the field is not only of great richness, but that such riches exist over a large area, one capable of affording attactive and remunerative employment for an army of natives, and likely by royalty to greatly add to the revenue of the Colony.

It is of extreme importance to us that we secure this railway connexion, if possible, concurrently with that now in progress, and our information would lead us to believe that such joint construction could be arranged with great economy, always presuming that the intermediate country—as we are also advised—should be found suitable for the construction of a railway.

Our proposal is that you should kindly order a survey to be forthwith made between Tarkwa and Kumasi, passing as near as may be found reasonably possible to our property. Our estimate is that such survey, if well done, would not cost more than, say, 1,500 *l.* to 2,000 *l.*, and we respectfully offer to bear the cost of such survey up to, say, 5,000 *l.* (the fact of our so doing being, of course, known to the Colonial Office only, during the progress of the survey), on the assurance that the railway being found feasible may be at once proceeded with.

The evidence to which we have made reference we will gladly place at your disposal. The funds for the suggested development are already in our possession, and we are prepared to deposit 2,000 *l.* as proof of our good faith in respect of the offer we make.

If the railway extension is made so that we are able to get heavy machinery up to our mines, and develop our property, we have every reason to believe that the royalty we should be enabled to earn for the Government would give a handsome return on the cost of the railway from our mines alone, to say nothing of the traffic we should place upon the line.

Soliciting the favour of your obliging and early consideration.

16

GOVERNOR F. M. HODGSON TO JOSEPH CHAMBERLAIN: GOLD COAST RAILWAY, 31 AUGUST 1898[1]

REFERRING to your Despatch, No. 248, of the 1st July, I have carefully considered Mr. Shelford's Report on the railway surveys made in this Colony last year by Messrs. Foord and Day, as well as the enclosures which accompanied it, and I have the honour to submit to you the following observations.

[1] C.O. 879/49, no. 531.

2. In the first place, I must state at once—as it is the foundation of my opinion—that I entirely coincide in the view expressed by the late Governor Sir William Maxwell that the principal railways of the Colony should converge upon Accra as the seat of Government, and that at Accra should, as far as possible, be concentrated the rolling stock and stores, and all skilled and other supervision over them.

3. In Accra, which has been the seat of Government since 1877, a comparatively large amount of fixed capital has, from time to time, been sunk, and it would, I consider, be a mistaken policy, and certainly very expensive both as regards staff and buildings, to raise up another and a rival port, as would necessarily be the case if the suggestions which Mr. Shelford makes in favour of Appam were adopted.

4. The Crown Agents, in paragraph 7 of their letter of the 25th May, raise the question of the permanency of the location of the seat of Government at Accra, but I cannot conceive why there should be any doubt in the matter. If Appam, or any other port had been as good a commercial centre as Accra the annual trade statistics would have shown it, and I entirely disagree with the statement in paragraph 6 of their letter that 'Accra is not suited to be the terminus of a railway from Kumasi.' Again, Accra was selected as the seat of Government because of its having been reported to be the most healthy site for the residence of Europeans. I am not aware that the situation in this regard has in any way changed since that report was made.

5. Although I am at variance with Mr. Shelford as regards the question of making Accra the terminus of a railway to Kumasi, I am glad to find myself in agreement with him in almost all other essential points.

6. It is clear to me that, apart from the fact that the country through which it would pass is shown by Mr. Foord to be particularly unfavourable for railway construction, a direct line between Accra (I prefer to spell the name as it is always spelt) and Oda (Insuaim) would serve no good purpose; it would not pass through a single oil-producing district; it would collect no produce along the route; there would be no passenger traffic worth mentioning, and without an onwards extension to Kumasi it would be of little use in augmenting the Import trade. I have therefore no hesitation in concurring in the conclusion which Mr. Shelford comes to, namely, that the construction of the line in question, which is called the 'direct' line, is not desirable.

7. A line following the route surveyed by Captain Lang, namely, from Appam to Oda (Insuaim) is on an entirely different footing. It would pass through one of the richest oil-producing districts of the Colony, and that fact alone should ensure for it freights of palm oil and palm kernels, which there is no reason to suppose would not steadily increase in quantity and freight value.

8. Mr. Shelford, in paragraph 56 of his report, says: 'The whole

question of railway communication turns upon the position and character of the shipping places to be constructed.' In this I entirely agree, and, therefore, as I hold the opinion that Accra should be maintained as the seat of Government, and that in connexion with the construction of railways it should be made the port for the Eastern province of the Colony, it is necessary to examine the reasons for and against such an arrangement . . .

17

GOVERNOR SIR F. M. HODGSON TO JOSEPH CHAMBERLAIN: MOTOR TRANSPORT, 27 OCTOBER 1899[1]

. . . 10. AFTER passing out of Akim the track leads across the Kwahu range of hills, and some engineering work will probably be required at that point. Very little is known of this track by the Government, and before the work is taken in hand the route must, I submit, first be surveyed, and an estimate of cost obtained. I have no one in the Colony to detail for the work, and I regret extremely that is therefore not within my power to comply with your request to push on with the road as far as Attabubu and the Neutral Zone. I beg leave to ask that a competent surveyor be sent out to survey the country between Apedwa, to mark out the route for the road thence to Attabubu and right up to the Neutral Zone, through Prang. Then, as soon as the report and estimate of cost come in, three road constructors should be sent out; they must arrive at the beginning of September next year, when the rains will be coming to an end, to push on quickly with the work of construction.

11. Knowing this country as I do, I beg to state that I am not in favour of the employment of motor cars, and in this respect I am not by any means singular. Before, therefore, motor cars are introduced on a large scale, I suggest that one, or at most two, be tried in the first instance, and that the trial be on Colonel Northcott's road between Wuiyima and Gambaga, which he states is available for motor car traffic, if the cars can be got up there.

12. Colonel Northcott states that he has been making his roads in the Northern Territories of a width of 14 feet. In the Colony they have, as a rule, been 12 feet roads, but there is no objection, excepting in the matter of cost, to the road in question being made of the former width. If it is to be constructed for motor cars the surveyor selected must be advised, because a motor-car road should, in this

[1] C.O. 879/58, no. 585. See Dickson, *Historical Geography of Ghana*, pp. 218–29. The first motor car—a Gardner–Serpollet—arrived in 1902, for use by Governor Nathan.

country at any rate, be a road hardened with metal of some kind, the gradient must be such as a motor car can negotiate, and bridges of sufficient strength must be constructed. With regard to bridges the weight of the motor car, with its maximum load weight, must be ascertained and furnished. This information Colonel Northcott will no doubt have obtained . . .

18

F. S. B. GAFFNEY: TRAFFIC PROSPECTS, SIERRA LEONE RAILWAY [NOVEMBER 1899][1]

. . . THE prospect of goods traffic, however, appears to be much more satisfactory, because produce will continue to come down country, and it is impossible that it could, for any length of time, be carried on the heads of natives parallel to the railway. No doubt there is still remaining a large element of slavery, so that chiefs in the interior procure their carriers in exchange only for their nourishment, but even the chiefs will probably soon perceive that it will pay them better to dispose of their produce to the traders who will be established at the end of the railway. Apart from the fact that this system of slavery is rapidly disappearing, the value of rice and palm oil consumed by the natives, going and returning, would pay for the carriage of the produce on the railway. Take as an example Moyamba, which is 75 miles from Freetown. Between these two places a man's journey there and back occupies 10 days, and a carrier's support for that time on native diet costs at least 3d. per day. He has to carry his own rice, so that 50 lbs. of produce is the most he can deliver. This journey then costs 2s. 6d., equal to £5 12s. 6d. per ton, taking the worst form of slavery, and the loss to the master of the service of this man for ten days. There is a large amount of gum copal in the neighbourhood of Moyamba, and from here more is supplied than from any other place in Sierra Leone. The European traders I interviewed all told me the same, that in proportion as the natives grow more independent of their chiefs, the less the produces comes down, for not only the chiefs have more difficulty in procuring carriers, but also they are unable to get people to collect the material.

At such a distant place as this palm kernels are practically no use. They are only worth about £6 per ton on the coast, and therefore cannot bear the rate of £5 12s. 6d. per ton for transport to Freetown.

[NOTE—The palm kernels go to the coast ports where they form the principal export. See Colonial Secretary's Statistics, September 1899 (Appendix B), S. & S.[2]]

---

[1] C.O. 879/62, no. 612. F. S. B. Gaffney to Shelford & Son, encl. in Crown Agents to C.O., 15 November 1899.   [2] *Sic*, Shelford & Son.

Some 60 miles farther up country there is rubber, but all the native traders I spoke to said the trade in it was almost quite undeveloped.

In looking at the existing map of the country, it will be observed that there are large tracts shewn where apparently no roads or village exist, but this is quite deceptive. These are merely places as yet unexplored, and are probably as thickly inhabited as are the well-known places. This I gather from the fact that wherever our party passed through such places they were found to contain populations quite as numerous as those in the better known districts, though shewn on the map as if they were mere deserts. In all such places produce of some description is to be found, so that, in course of time, it will find its way to the railway. This appears obvious.

At present the natives have a custom of growing enough rice for their own consumption with a little more for the purpose of barter (in lieu of any currency), but were the railway to be near, and they found what a large price could be obtained for their labour by supplying Freetown, I think that that trade too would be soon developed . . . All such enterprise depends a good deal on the population, and as the country is so thickly inhabited, there is every reasonable prospect of a large goods traffic.

19

CROWN AGENTS: MEMORANDUM,
GOLD COAST RAILWAY, 6 MARCH 1900[1]

HEADS of Agreement between the Crown Agents for the Colonies, acting on behalf of the Government of the Gold Coast, and the Ashanti Gold Fields Corporation, Limited.

1) The Colonial Government undertakes to extend the railway at present under construction between Sekondi and Tarkwa from the latter place to the town of Kumasi, following generally by the line laid down in Messrs. Shelford and Son's report of the 12th of July, 1899.

2) The Colonial Government undertakes to commence the construction as soon as the rails reach Tarkwa, and to proceed with it with all due expedition as far as the northern boundary of the Ashanti Gold Fields Corporation's property so as to complete it to this point by the end of the dry season of 1901–2, unless delay should arise from causes beyond the control of the Colonial Government. Completion in this clause shall mean that the line shall be so far finished as to allow goods and passenger traffic to be conveyed over it up to the

[1] C.O. 879/57, no. 578, encl. in Crown Agents to C.O., 9 March 1900. Chamberlain approved this arrangement: C.O. to Crown Agents, 15 March 1900.

above point, although such work as complete ballasting, the substitution of permanent or temporary bridging and the completion of the stations, workshops and quarters may still remain to be executed.

3) The Ashanti Gold Fields Corporation undertake to make up the net earnings of the railway in each year to the amount of £30,000. In this connection, net earnings is to be understood to mean the difference between the gross earnings and the working expenses, which latter are to include only such expenditure as is usually and properly chargeable to revenue.

4) If in any year during the existence of the guarantee the net earnings of the railway shall exceed the sum of 4½ per cent. upon the capital expended on its construction and equipment, the excess shall be divided between the Corporation and the Government in the proportion of one-fifth to the Corporation and four-fifths to the Government.

5) A schedule of the rates to be charged for the different classes of import and export goods shall be agreed between the Government and the Corporation and shall from time to time be subject to revision, but the average rate for imports shall not, at the outset, be less than 1s. 6d. per ton per mile, nor shall the rate for exports be less than 1s. per ton per mile.

6) This agreement shall come into operation as soon as the railway reaches the property of the Corporation, and shall remain in force from that date for a period of 20 years.

7) The Corporation undertakes to obtain the signature of the Ashanti Consols Company, Limited, to an agreement supplementary to this agreement, under which £50,000 of subscribed but uncalled capital shall be hypothecated as a security for the due carrying out of this agreement.

20

SIR W. MacGREGOR TO JOSEPH CHAMBERLAIN: LAGOS RAILWAY, 9 AUGUST 1900[1]

... 6. IT appears to me that should you decide to extend the Lagos Railway to Ilorin the Colony of Lagos could, with careful financial management, pay the additional sum required to meet the interest on the cost of construction as far as its boundary on the north, assuming that the cost would be about £5,000 a mile. It may be doubted that the finances of Lagos could safely be looked to for anything beyond that.

[1] C.O. 879/67, no. 647. At this time, Lugard was pressing for a Kano–Kaduna railway survey. The C.O. agreed to survey as far as the Niger, but towards Jebba crossing.

7. I would, however, respectfully say that to me personally it does not appear that the Lagos Railway can terminate at Ilorin, but that it must be carried on at least to the heart of the Hausa country, probably to Kano, perhaps some day to the Nile. Recent experience in moving troops from Northern Nigeria to the Gold Coast has shown, in a striking manner, that water transport by the Niger is very uncertain and that transport by rail from Northern Nigeria to the coast will be indispensable. No doubt, alternative routes, having their terminus in Southern Nigeria, should be carefully considered. In this question, however, there are factors of a general nature that possess perhaps more weight than any that can be based on local or provincial considerations. The probabilities must appear very strong to one conversant with current French writings that a French railway will soon be built from the Mediterranean to the Niger or Lake Chad.[1] The political and strategic value to France of such a line would undoubtedly be great, more especially in view of the self-contained nature of the great French establishments in Algeria. It therefore becomes a grave question how the British provinces of Northern and Southern Nigeria and of Lagos can best protect themselves, commercially and otherwise, in the face of this projected French Railway.

In my humble opinion it will be found that the best protection in peace or war would be afforded by the extension of the Lagos railway to Kano or Lake Chad. It is, of course, a strong argument in favour of the Lagos line that in a few months 120 miles of it will be open to traffic. Its geographical position naturally puts on this line the duty of protection from invasion. To the Empire at large it must be a matter of indifference whether the produce of Northern Nigeria is carried by way of Lagos or of Forcados;[2] but the question of the best means of defending these provinces is a broad one of great importance that must present itself in considering the extension of the Lagos Railway . . .

21

SIR W. MacGREGOR TO JOSEPH CHAMBERLAIN: RAILWAY LABOUR, 25 MARCH 1901[3]

I HAVE the honour to inform you that it would not be wise for the neighbouring British Colonies to continue to look to Lagos for an additional supply of labourers for Railway purposes, or as recruits for their defence or Police Forces.

---

[1] On information received from F.O. to C.O., 14 January 1901 (from an unreliable report on the 1900 Algiers Conference of Geographers).
[2] As pressed for by Moor to F.O., 26 June 1897, ibid.   [3] C.O. 147/154.

2. A few days ago I had a request from the neighbouring French Colony of Dahomey for 1,000 labourers for the Railway now being built there. This was of course refused by me. No recruiting is allowed here for any foreign possession. A notice will be inserted in the Government Gazette to that effect.

3. But even with the cessation of recruiting for foreign possessions there is no longer any real available margin of the able-bodied population left for British Colonies. There are many complaints of the want of labourers here. Further emigration would retard internal development, by reducing the number of hands and inordinately raising wages for unskilled labour. Numerous farms have been neglected during the absence of the labourers on our own railway. This diminishes exports and damages trade. I am therefore not disposed to favour any further recruiting on a large scale here at present.

22

C. P. LUCAS (COLONIAL OFFICE) TO TREASURY: NIGERIAN RAILWAYS, 29 AUGUST 1901[1]

I AM directed by Mr. Secretary Chamberlain to state, for the information of the Lords Commissioners of the Treasury, that the question of railway construction in Nigeria has been engaging his serious attention for some time, as well as that of the Governor and High Commissioners of the territories concerned.

2. The present condition of affairs is that a railway, about 130 miles in length, from Lagos via Abeokuta to Ibadan, was completed in the early months of the present year, and was opened for public traffic in March last. The cost of its construction has been, roughly, one million sterling, and has been borne entirely by the Government of Lagos, which has borrowed £792,500 for the purpose from the Imperial Exchequer under the Colonial Loans Act, 1899, and the remainder from other sources. On the loan from the Treasury the Colony is paying at present, in respect of interest and charges for repayment, a yearly sum of £41,730. It is the unanimous opinion of all who are interested in railway construction in Nigeria, and who are most competent to express an opinion on the subject, that it is essential, on political no less than on financial grounds, to carry on the extension of the Lagos railway as far as the Niger with the least possible delay, and eventually to push it on as rapidly as circumstances will permit towards Kano, which is the chief commercial

[1] C.O. 879/67, no. 647. The Treasury agreed to cover the expense of the survey, but not as far as Kano. Treasury to C.O., 10 September 1901.

centre of the populous Hausa States. This has been recognised for some time, and in November last year a party was sent out to survey the country from Ibadan towards the Niger with a view to determining the best route for the extension of the railway. The cost of this survey was estimated at £5,100, and their Lordships consented to the inclusion of half this amount in the Estimates for Northern Nigeria for the current financial year. The party remained in the country while the season permitted the work to be carried on, and they have now returned to England. It was hoped that they would be able to complete the survey up to the Niger, but the engineer in charge, Mr. Gee,[1] to whose discretion the matter was left, decided not to go beyond Ilorin, which is at a distance of some 100 miles beyond Ibadan, and to examine two alternative routes for the railway between those towns. The operations of the survey party have established the fact that the extension to Ilorin is practicable, although the particulars collected have not yet been worked out sufficiently to determine the exact route. In the meantime, Messrs. Shelford and Son, the Consulting Engineers under whose supervision the present railway has been constructed, strongly recommend that another survey party should be sent out in October next, at an estimated cost of £5,628, to study the Niger River from Egbom to Jebba, with a view to ascertaining the most suitable crossing place for the railway, and to survey back from the place finally selected to Ilorin to join up with the survey already completed.

3. Mr. Chamberlain is in entire concurrence with the Governor of Lagos and the High Commissioners of Southern and Northern Nigeria in attaching the utmost importance to the pushing on as rapidly as possible of railway construction in Nigeria, and he does so on the following three main grounds:

(1) He is anxious that the territories contained by Lagos and the two Nigerias should be rendered self-supporting as early as possible, and it appears to him that the most effective way of achieving this end will be to advance the commercial development of the country by establishing railway communication with the interior, and bringing down to the British West African Coast and to England the undoubtedly vast trade which is carried on in Kano, Sokoto, and other parts of Hausaland.

(2) The activity of the Germans as regards railway construction in the adjacent Protectorate of the Cameroons, and of the French, not only in Dahomey but also in the regions between Lake Chad and the north and north-west coasts of Africa, indicates the existence of some danger that, if corresponding enterprise is not shown by the British, a large portion of the trade which should find its outlet

[1] W. Gee to Crown Agents (Interim Report), 20 July 1901.

in Lagos and the Niger delta, may be diverted permanently to foreign ports. The position in this matter may be realised by a perusal of the enclosed copies of memoranda which were drawn up a few months ago at His Majesty's Embassy in Paris, and at the Intelligence Division of the War Office respectively.

(3) Political and strategic considerations, and the importance of maintaining an efficient system of defence upon the frontiers of Northern Nigeria, add weight to the commercial and financial arguments in favour of advancing the railway. This aspect of the question is dealt with in the accompanying extract from a despatch from the High Commissioner, Sir Frederick Lugard.

4. In view of the last-mentioned consideration, and of the great benefits which must accrue to British merchants from the opening up of the Hausa markets to British trade, Mr. Chamberlain considers that the question of railway construction in Nigeria is one which may fairly be regarded as affecting Imperial as well as local interests.

5. The immediate proposal is, as stated above, to send out a second survey party next October to find a crossing place for the railway on the Niger, and to survey back from it to Ilorin. Their Lordships will see, from the second paragraph of this letter, that it has not yet been possible to come to any conclusion as to the actual construction of the line beyond Ibadan; but Mr. Chamberlain is strongly of opinion that the proposed continuation of the survey should not be delayed, for the following reasons:

(a) Because it is essential, as Sir F. Lugard has urged, that the general direction of the railway from Lagos towards Kano should be settled as soon as possible, so that such works as roads and surveys in Northern Nigeria may be carried out with due regard to the coming railway.

(b) Because the determination of the point at which the Niger is to be bridged is an all-important factor in fixing the general direction of the railway; and

(c) Because the Consulting Engineers have now available a staff of survey engineers who have acquired experience of the country and the work, and whose services will be lost if the survey is postponed.

6. The arguments which justified the division of the cost of the last section of the survey in equal parts between Northern Nigeria and Lagos, hold good, in Mr. Chamberlain's opinion, for this further section. One half of its cost will therefore be charged to Lagos, and I am to request you to move their Lordships to sanction the remainder, or £2,814, as at present estimated, being paid by Northern Nigeria.

7. In view of the urgency of the matter, Mr. Chamberlain has authorised the Crown Agents to proceed at once with the necessary

preparations, and I am to ask that their Lordships may give their consent to the sending out of the party on the proposed conditions at their earliest convenience.

23

SHELFORD & SON TO THE CROWN AGENTS: NIGERIAN RAILWAYS, 10 OCTOBER 1901[1]

. . . 18. WE finally arrived at the conclusion that the Western Route, via Fiditi, Oyo, and Ogbomosho is the one which we should recommend and which the railway should follow.

19. The first point which had our consideration in the selection of the two routes was, naturally, the ultimate length of the line, and as the reduced length of the railway on the Western Route, after taking into account the 10 per cent. extra on both routes, is no less than 27 miles, the adoption of this route will effect a very substantial economy of capital.

There is also the important fact that a shorter and more direct route is superior to a longer one if the railway is to be ultimately carried over the Niger to reach the great centres of trade in Northern Nigeria. Against this advantage to the Western Route there are several disadvantages, the chief being that the Western Route traverses a more broken country, probably involving the maximum gradients of 1 in 50 in various places. The approach to the summit is also difficult and may require a rock cutting. Further, the population along the Western Route is considerably smaller than on the other route.

20. The points just enumerated are the chief advantages and disadvantages of the Western Route, but there are others to which we would refer. Mr. Gee has stated in his report that the fertility of the country all along the Eastern Route is superior to that passed through on the Western. It must, however, be remembered that the Western Route was traversed at the end of the dry season when vegetation was at its lowest ebb, and that two months' difference at this time of the year, according to our experience of West Africa, affects the general aspect of the country. We are of opinion that if the Eastern Route had been surveyed first instead of the Western we might have been told the Western was the superior in this respect. We think it may be taken for granted that the countries are similar in this respect.

[1] C.O. 879/67, no. 647, encl. in Crown Agents to C.O., 30 October 1901. Governor MacGregor, on the other hand, recommended the 'eastern' route through Iwo, Oshogbo, and Ikirun. MacGregor to Chamberlain, 23 December 1901.

21. We note that the chief traffic from the North passes through Ilorin to Ibadan via the Western Route, and the waterways on this route are also less in number than the Eastern. We also find on consulting the plans that several bridges of moderate size would have to be constructed on the Eastern Route. Besides this, Mr. Gee informs us that along a large portion of the Eastern Route the railway would run through a dense tropical forest, an item which adds very materially to the cost of the line and which can be balanced against the possible rock cutting on the Western Route.

22. After weighing carefully all the considerations in favour of and against each route we have arrived at the conclusion that the Western Route should be the one adopted, chiefly on account of its shorter mileage and the consequent advantage obtained for through traffic when the railway is carried up to and over the Niger.

23. Estimate. Basing our estimate on our experience in the construction of the existing railway, we estimate that the extension of the line from Ibadan to Ilorin via the Western Route, a total of 115 miles, will be £747,500 on the basis of £6,500 per mile, to which must be added, for additional rolling stock and terminals, £52,500, making a total of £800,000 for which amount provision should be made although the survey when completed should show that it can be done for less.

24. Recommendation. As the construction work on the open line to Ibadan is now practically complete we would recommend that the location survey should be proceeded with this dry season. If this meets with your approval it will have some important advantages:

In the first place it will save the delay and cost due to the stoppage and renewal of the construction work, which may be considered as an economy equal to the cost of 6 months' administration at the least.

It will also lead to the formation of a depôt at Ibadan from which the working survey can be commenced and where stores can be forwarded for the construction, and it will afford an opportunity for consolidating the completion of the open line to Ibadan by drawing away the construction staff from the various minor works on the open lines, which will require attention for some little time and will thus be more conveniently and economically performed. In conclusion we therefore have the honour to recommend that a survey party should be sent out this dry season (in addition to the one recommended in our interim report for the survey of the Niger, and already sanctioned) to start the location of the line along the Western Route from Ibadan towards Ilorin.

24

SHELFORD & SON TO THE CROWN AGENTS: NIGERIA RAILWAY POLICY REPORT, 27 MARCH 1902[1]

... 7. DEALING first with the Western district in which a railway has already been constructed between Lagos and Ibadan for a length of 123½ miles by the Colonial Government we find that some difference of opinion exists in regard to the port of Lagos, and its suitability for development into a large depôt and terminus for a trunk railway. It is put forward by Sir R. Moor that Lagos is unsuitable for many reasons, of which the shallow depth of the bar, the unhealthy situation of the town, and its poor water supply, are the chief; and he proposes that a branch line should be constructed from another Port such as Warri or Sapele, to join an extension of the present railway at Oshogbo. Sir F. D. Lugard has also suggested that in place of costly harbour works at Lagos, a branch line from Sapele might be considered as an alternative, to join the existing railway at Ibadan, which is practically the same idea. These points will, no doubt, settle themselves by discussion in due course, but at the present moment the question is rather the extension of the existing Lagos Railway.

8. In dealing with this as a whole, the first consideration is the important fact that Lagos Colony has made, at its own expense, 123½ miles of railway, with a terminus at its port, the future effect of which upon the country it serves is fully appreciated in the Lagos Colonial Report for 1900–1901, and presented to Parliament last month (February, 1902).

It would not, in our opinion, be good policy at present to interfere with the rights thus acquired by constructing any other railway in the Western district except so far as it may contribute to the prosperity of Lagos.

9. It will be seen on reference to the Map that a railway starting from any one of the Western ports must cross the River Niger in order to reach the upper portion of Northern Nigeria, and the importance of establishing the position of this crossing is a matter which has been in our mind now for some considerable time, and has been fully recognised by Sir F. D. Lugard in nearly all his despatches relating to the Railway Extension into his territory.

If Jebba is selected, it may be regarded as certain that the Lagos Railway will be extended sooner or later to the Niger at that place, the more so because it may be laid so as to traverse a populous and productive country favourable to its construction by stages, which should be in themselves remunerative; and in the ultimate development

[1] C.O. 879/76, no. 695.

of the territory, the improvement of Lagos Harbour for navigation may become a reality. Last November an Expedition was sent out under our direction to examine the River with the object of fixing the point of crossing, and although the party has not at the time of writing returned, we apprehend from the cables and reports to hand that Jebba will be the most suitable, if not the only crossing possible without a heavy expenditure of capital.[1]

10. We fully concur with the remarks made by Sir F. D. Lugard in his Annual Colonial Report, dated May 1st last, under the head of 'Railways' in which he points out that surveys should be made to the Northward of the Niger, and that every yard of railway in that district would, by superseding the present caravan-transport tend greatly to promote the development of trade. The details of such surveys may be altered on the return of our Niger Expedition, but we are of opinion that:

(1.) A flying survey should be at once made up the Kaduna Valley, via Wushishi to Kano.

(2.) And a similar survey made from Jebba towards Sokoto.

The total estimated expenditure is £4,500 for each survey exclusive of such military escort as may be considered necessary.

The former of these would have for its object the examination of the country from the point of view of construction and traffic (actual in Colonial produce, and prospective in European commodities) to be served and obtained by establishing at once a small port on the Niger near the Kaduna River, and the construction of a railway up the Kaduna Valley, pending the making of a bridge over the Niger. The latter would have similar objects in the direction of Sokoto.

11. The exploitation of the Eastern district, which being a separate matter and much in arrear of Lagos, should be dealt with in the coming season by making an independent survey of a line from the seaport of Old Calabar up the valley of the Cross River, as far as the Military situation will permit, and at an estimated expense of £4,000. This would become a second trunk line to open up the Eastern part of Nigeria.

12. We quite agree that there are 'prima facie' reasons for selecting Old Calabar as the terminus for Eastern Nigeria. With the exception of Freetown, Old Calabar has, we think, been shown to be second to none for its harbour accommodation on the whole Coast Line of British West Africa, and is practically the only port at which a railway terminus and depôt could be made in this district (see our Report upon a 'General Scheme of Railways,' dated June 30th, 1900).

13. From Messrs. Coode, Son, and Matthew's Report, dated March, 1898, on the Protection of the River Frontage at Old Calabar,

[1] The Jebba crossing was still opposed by Lugard: Lugard to C.O., 1 March 1902, ibid.

we find that the town is situated about 40 miles above the bar at the mouth of the river. The depth over the bar at low water is 16 feet, and at high water about 24 feet, and the river is safely navigable for vessels drawing 18 feet. The width of the river opposite the town is nearly ½ a mile, with a depth in the centre at low water of between 30 and 35 feet. The West bank of the river is low-lying, but the East bank, on which the town is situated, is bordered for about 1½ miles by a sandy cliff varying in height from 50 to 150 feet, and on this cliff the chief Government offices are situated.

14. As mentioned in the Colonial Office letter (12th October, 1901), we understand the country to the North of Old Calabar in the Cross River district to be rich, and Sir R. Moor holds the opinion that a railway could be run with ease through this district, but we regret to say that owing to lack of reliable information we have little to add to what has been already written, and until a survey has been made it is impossible to make any definite statements.

15. The policy of constructing railways step by step is one which we take to be settled by the financial strength or otherwise of the Colonies concerned, unless strategic or other considerations should induce the Imperial Government to expedite the defence and development of Northern Nigeria. In the absence of an heroic scheme there is no better alternative in our opinion than that now pursued successfully in the treatment of our own British lines, viz., the occupation of the country by railways as and when each appears to be expedient or profitable . . .

25

GOVERNOR W. EGERTON: MEMORANDUM, RAILWAY AND MOTOR ROAD CONSTRUCTION IN NIGERIA, 26 JUNE 1906[1]

. . . 7. IN my humble opinion a great mistake has been made in yielding to the demands of the Imperial Treasury, and exacting from Southern Nigeria and Lagos large annual contributions from their revenues which might have been so much more profitably laid out—both for the inhabitants of those countries and for the Imperial taxpayer—in building railways and roads into the interior and thus hastening the development of the trade and with it the revenue.

8. In the correspondence on railway extension the immense possibilities for cotton production of Northern Nigeria are dilated on but it is nowhere pointed out with sufficient clearness that at

---

[1] C.O. 879/93, no. 845. The C.O. approved construction to Oshogbo and extension to Ilorin, 18 December 1906.

Ibadan a thickly-populated cotton-producing country has been reached which has so far supplied *all the existing cotton ginneries can deal with*, and has done this in the face of considerable uncertainty as to the price paid to the cultivators. From all the accounts given me by persons who know the countries, there is no portion of the route between Ibadan and Kano that is as thickly-populated as the portion between Ibadan and Oshogbo, and it is probable that the country between Ibadan and Ilorin is capable of producing as much cotton as any other portion of the Kano line. If this is so, this is the portion, Oshogbo to Jebba, that should be first built, because:

(a.) It is the nearest to the Port of Lagos, and, therefore, freight will be less.

(b.) It is well settled and peaceful, and interruptions to cultivation and losses from risings are unlikely to occur.

(c.) It is thickly populated by an agricultural race.

(d.) Its cotton-growing possibilities have been actually tested and have increased *pari-passu* with the ginning facilities.

(e.) The local Government can find the funds without assistance from the Imperial Government.

9. Ilorin is in Northern Nigeria. Endless trouble and friction will result if the whole line is not under one control. There will also be great economy in working it merely as an extension of the present Lagos line. Why not, in sanctioning the extension, transfer to Southern Nigeria all the territory to the south and west of the Niger, arranging at the same time that the £15,000 contribution now paid by (what was the Colony and Protectorate of Lagos) the Western Province of Southern Nigeria be cancelled in consideration of the Southern Administration assuming responsibility for the cost of administering this large portion of Northern Nigeria? If this were done, several very difficult questions could be easily solved, the cost to the Imperial Government of supporting Northern Nigeria could be at once lessened, and a step would be taken towards the desired goal of freeing it from pecuniary responsibility altogether.

10. The mercantile community of Lagos—native as well as European—is protesting—and, I must say, I sympathise with the protest—against the collection of tolls on goods taken from and to Lagos across the Northern Nigeria boundary. I am informed that the total realised by this vexatious tax at the toll stations on the boundary was only about £4,000 in 1905–6, and a portion of this (about ⅛th) has—in theory—been given up in 1906 as goods intended for export by sea are now allowed to be taken out of Northern Nigeria free. I say 'in theory' because I fear that native traders will find it difficult to convince native toll collectors that their goods are intended for such export . . .

26

GOVERNOR SIR WALTER EGERTON TO LORD ELGIN: WEST AFRICAN SHIPPING, 31 MARCH 1907[1]

I HAVE the honour to acknowledge the receipt of your Lordship's despatch circular of the 29th January last, requesting information as to the existence of shipping 'rings' or 'conferences' in the carrying trades to, from, or between ports in this Administration. I have communicated copies of your Lordship's circular to the Chamber of Commerce at Lagos and to the Chairman of Agents at Calabar, Opobo and Warri . . .

2. No rules or regulations have been passed for the purpose of regulating or suppressing such shipping rings or conferences, or in any way affecting such combinations, or the granting of rebates or discrimination to shippers.

Shipping rings, rebates, or discriminations are not illegal or prohibited, or even void as against public policy in this Colony or Protectorate, but I should much like to be authorised to propose legislation to prohibit or very much restrict all such combinations.

Shipping rings need not be registered in order to become legal in Lagos.

My replies to the questions are as follows:

(1) There is a combination or agreement or understanding between the shipping lines trading to West Africa, controlled by Sir Alfred Jones . . . and the Woermann Linie.[2] The detailed terms of this agreement are probably better known to the Crown Agents than to me, but it is the usual arrangement under which a merchant is compelled to ship all his goods by the lines forming the combination, the shipment of a single package by any outside ship entailing the loss of a whole year's rebates. This rebate is believed to be 10 per cent. on the freight originally paid, but there is some probability of an arrangement existing under which certain large firms obtain a higher rebate—at any rate as regards their shipments to certain ports—and it is believed that the Niger Company and Messrs. John Holt have certain favourable arrangements regarding their trade under which they receive rebates, although chartering certain special steamers for the Niger wet season transport. The only ships visiting Southern Nigeria ports are the ships of the companies mentioned above. They carry all the inter-port trade as well as the trade with ports in the

---

[1] *Parl. Papers*, xlvii, 1909 [Cd. 4669], vol. ii, part ii, p. 199.
[2] Including the African Steam Ship Company, British and African Steam Navigation Company, Ltd., Elder, Dempster Ltd., Compagnie Belge Maritime du Congo.

British Empire and foreign countries. It is very seldom indeed that any outside ship visits these ports, and such ships are generally specially chartered shallow-draught steamers for the high water season of the Niger River for visiting ports up that river.

(2) The shipping combination is believed to be the cause of the excessively high rates of freight now current to Southern Nigerian ports which are as set out in the enclosed list.[1] For unusually bulky or heavy articles very high rates are demanded.

(3) It is generally believed that 'tramp' steamers would visit these ports if it were not for the existence of the conference arrangement, and that even other regular lines might be established . . .

[(4) and (5): no instances of British shipping carrying foreign goods at lower rates than British or colonial goods can be given.]

(6) I understand that but for the rebate system special steamers would be occasionally chartered by merchants here.

(7) I am not aware of any [beneficial results], and the excessive rates charged are a heavy tax on the trade. It is only right to add that the class of vessels of the passenger service have been immensely improved within the last five years, but this would probably have taken place in any case owing to the large development of the passenger service, the increased amount of freight offering, and the competition or the German Woermann Line.

4. Your lordship is aware that the principal firms in the Protectorate of Southern Nigeria have an arrangement amongst themselves as to prices, the arrangement being designed to prevent new firms starting; and there is no doubt that an almost complete monopoly of the trade has been maintained at certain ports by these firms owing to this arrangement.

5. As pressed before upon your Lordship, I consider that outside legislation the best way of rendering any such combination unprofitable is to improve communications by rail, road, and river. When the entrance to the Lagos Harbour is deepened by dredging, it will be far easier for tramp steamers to visit our ports, and for new shipping lines to be established, but until the rebate system is made illegal merchants are practically compelled to ship by the Conference Lines.

[1]

	Liverpool	London	Hamburg
Palm kernels per ton gross weight	30s.	40s.	30s.
Palm oil per ton gross weight	40s.	47s. 6d.	40s.
Cotton per lb. net weight	¼d. (46s. 8d. per ton)	—	¼d.
Maize per ton gross weight	20s.	—	20s.
Cocoa per ton gross weight	45s.	—	45s.

27

SIR E. P. C. GIROUARD: REPORT ON TRANSPORT POLICY OF NIGERIA, 30 MAY 1907[1]

... V.—*Transport Policy of Nigeria.*

IN November, 1906, at the request of the Under-Secretary of State for the Colonies, I prepared a memorandum on this subject. After as thorough an examination as possible of the ports of Lagos and Forcados, the Lagos Government Railway and its reports, a comprehensive tour as between Baro and Kano, and full consultation with the local authorities, I see little or no reason to depart from the general conclusions then arrived at except in one respect. In England I could not consider the practicability of improving the Niger navigation as no data were available upon which to form an opinion. I am now fully persuaded that improvement both efficient and economical can be effected as required. This strengthens my view that the Niger is the best outlet for the development of the Niger and Benue valleys and the rich uplands of Northern Nigeria, but also alters the conclusion that Lokoja should at an early date become the railway centre based upon the Niger navigation. With river improvement Baro will amply fulfil this object for some years to come and can be unhesitatingly adopted as a railway base even in the present condition of navigation on the Niger. In an enclosure to this report will be found a detailed description and plans of the proposed Baro terminus.[2] (Appendix No. 1.[3])

The first and greatest factor which determines any general transport policy for Nigeria is the presence of a great natural transport route on the Niger River which with its main branch the Benue divides the country into three sections:

(1) the south-west;
(2) the south-east;
(3) the north and north-west.

The south-western portion is provided with the backbone of a railway system. The south-east has not begun railway construction. The north has a beginning in a 22-mile tramway connecting the nearest navigable point on the Niger waterway with the capital, Zungeru.

[1] C.O. 879/93, no. 845. Encl. in Girouard to C.O., 30 May 1907.
[2] A Baro–Zunguru line had been surveyed by Shelford & Son: Memorandum, 22 January 1907. But the Treasury would not approve the cost before 1911.
[3] Not printed.

(1) Roads.

In several parts of Nigeria, both north and south, a beginning has been made in road construction. The wisdom of such a policy seems somewhat doubtful. Throughout Southern Nigeria and the southern provinces of Northern Nigeria, owing to the prevalence of the tsetse fly and animal epidemic disease, animal or wheeled transport is economically impossible; the only portion of the country promising well for animal transport being the northern and north-western provinces of Northern Nigeria. It might be urged that motor-transport would be practicable, but bearing in mind the many climatic difficulties of this purely tropical belt of Nigeria, I have grave doubts of the success of motor transport on any useful scale. Where animal transport is not practicable it would appear to be best to clear the native bush tracks for ordinary trade or, where justifiable, build very cheap tram lines based upon railways or navigable waterways.

(2) Railways.

(a) South-West Nigeria.

The south-west, which includes all territory west of the Niger not ultimately to be served by that waterway, is being developed by means of a railway system based upon the port of Lagos. From this point a railway of 3 ft. 6 in. gauge of a fairly high standard of construction has been constructed to Ibadan (125 miles) at a cost of £7,800 per mile, is being actually extended to Illorin, and approved to Jebba situated on the Niger, the financial resources of the country permitting of such development at local expense. In so far as its construction to Illorin is considered the project appears economically sound, though the high standard of cost adopted would not appear to be justified.

It is proposed to extend the line from Illorin through Jebba to Zungeru, whence it would tap a main line leading on to Zaria and Kano. Such a line would pass through a country almost depopulated and incapable of affording much way traffic, therefore the remainder of the line to Lagos would have to support any loss in its working. The distance from Zungeru to Lagos would be about 400 miles, and, if cotton could be carried at three-pence per ton per mile, it could be landed at Lagos from Zungeru at about £5 a ton. This rate it should be remarked is considered unremunerative by the railway authorities. If a pioneer railway is constructed from the common competing point (Zungeru) to the Niger at Baro, there is no doubt in my mind that cotton will get to the sea at Forcados at £2 a ton or equal to a rate of about a penny a ton a mile on the Lagos Railway.

Personally, therefore, the policy of an extension through Jebba and the construction of a great bridge over the Niger appears to me ill-advised and unnecessary. The Lagos Railway may form the backbone of a considerable system for the south-western portion of Nigeria, but it is my firm conviction that in the economical development of Northern Nigeria we must place our reliance upon the existing waterways, supplemented by railway systems based upon them. The Lagos system should connect with them, at or opposite a common point on the River Niger, where, until a bridge was justified, a steam ferry service should suffice. The traffic it will secure will be mainly that of European or native passengers, mails and fast perishable or high class goods. The connection will, moreover, permit of the Lagos traders, a most enterprising community, reaching Northern Nigeria by a direct route. Should the common point be Baro, it would not appear that the Lagos system would be in any worse position to compete (if it can do so) than if it came to Zungeru, and any such connection would pass through country of higher potential value than exists from Illorin over Jebba.

It would appear more judicious to spend any further available funds of Southern Nigeria in the completion to Illorin and on branches from the main line through other productive areas.

(b) South-Eastern Nigeria.

Of this section I can have little to say. As in the south-western portion of Nigeria, it would appear that any railway policy should aim at local development and not at reaching points in the far interior, much more economically effected by a line based on the Niger or the Benue. Eventually in a similar manner to the south-east a connection might be made with the north at some point on the Benue.

(c) Northern Nigeria.

Northern Nigeria, and by this term I mean to convey from a transport policy point of view all the country east of the Niger and north of the Benue after their confluence at Lokoja, presents to my mind an entirely distinct problem. Its southern confines in all directions are bounded by two great open navigable rivers—rivers to-day affording an efficient navigation, rivers, moreover, which at any time and at the very small cost of the annual upkeep of a few river dredgers can be improved up to a very high standard. Under such circumstances it does not appear possible that any railway system could compete with water-borne traffic. The choice of a base from which to use railways in conjunction with these rivers for the development of the north-east is geographically dictated by the course of the Niger. Baro, situated at the point where the river bends to the west, must be the primary base. Fortunately, it is in every way suitable and is in point of fact the only possible site north of Lokoja.

From Baro a railway should be constructed by way of the prosperous Nupe Province through the Gwari country south of the

Kaduna River; thence a very rich part of the Zaria Province would be traversed extending to Zaria town; whence by way of Kudan, Rogo, and Yelwa, through a great agricultural country, Kano itself should be reached, a distance on the present surveys of about 400 miles. I do not think the presence of the Zungeru cantonment should influence the choice of route. Universally condemned as a capital now, though dictated in position at the time of its choice, it must eventually, for the sake of the health and well-being of the central Government, be moved to one of the higher and more healthy sites which will be found all along the new line of railway.

Moreover, the probable staple exports of Northern Nigeria will not bear heavy rates, and everything points to the necessity of securing as short a line as possible as between Baro and Zaria, the first of the great producing centres. The line will in fact be an improvement on the alignment laid down in 1904, but, generally speaking, closely follow the route then surveyed but now no longer traceable upon the ground.

Having traversed the possible routes from end to end, I have no doubt of the feasibility of constructing a cheap pioneer line on an alignment which can be improved as traffic justifies it. It will be a line of easy gradients through what I must call a very rich country, and, though too much must not be expected in the commencement owing to the underdeveloped nature of the inhabitants, its promise for the future would appear distinctly bright. The line can undoubtedly be built for, say, £1,200,000, or £3,000 per mile, and at such cost rates of carriage should be possible which will permit of the export of the staples of the country with profits remunerative to both producer and exporter.

The general railway policy to be aimed at for Northern Nigeria in my opinion should be:

(1) That the Northern Nigeria railway system must be based upon communication with an evacuation by the Niger and Benue navigation.

(2) That the eventual base may be Lokoja at the junction of the two rivers. This will not be necessary for some years, as dredging operations can be undertaken to render the river available above Lokoja.

(3) That its primary base might be either of the two most geographically suitable sites on the navigable Niger or Benue above Lokoja, whence a railway could be thrown towards Kano.

(4) That taking the existing administrative, agricultural, and mineral, development into account the Niger base is apparently the best to consider and operate on at first.

(5) That this base should be Baro.

(6) That the line or lines should be built and worked under local control, economy of construction being secured by a low standard in structures, buildings, &c., without sacrificing hauling capacity, and by utilising to their utmost the services of the civil, military, and marine, Departments of the Protectorate.

SUMMARY.

Summarising the policy for Nigeria as a whole there would be three railway systems:

1. South-west;
2. South-east;
3. North.

The South-west, based on Lagos and Sappeli or Warri, would confine itself to local development, and exchange with the north any goods its rates would permit by means of a steam-ferry at Baro.

The South-east, based on Calabar, would develop its local resources by river and rail and look eventually to a rail connection with the north at some point on the Benue.

The North, based on the Niger and Benue navigation, would develop its resources by one and eventually two great transport lines, the first viâ the Niger and Baro to Kano, the other viâ the Benue and north-eastwards to Bornu from a selected point where reasonable navigation could be secured at low cost. The second of these routes would not be required for some years.

Finally when joined together all would come under one control and management.

28

R. L. ANTROBUS: MINUTE, LAGOS HARBOUR, 22 SEPTEMBER 1908[1]

... THERE is no going back. It was recognized when the policy of extending the Lagos Railway up to and across the Niger was decided upon, that Lagos harbour must be made accessible for the ocean going steamers. Nor is there any difficulty about the cost: for the charges on the loan for the improvement of the harbour will be less than the expenses which the trade has now to bear through the transhipment of cargo from ocean-going steamers to the bar steamers and vice versa.

I think therefore that we are bound to sanction the preparations for the construction of the Western mole; while insisting, of course, on the desirability of not carrying out the complete scheme if the dredging will enable the object to be attained at less cost.

[1] C.O. 520/66. On Egerton to C.O., 22 September 1908. Lord Crewe agreed: Minute, 1 November 1908.

C. LAND, AGRICULTURE, MINING

I

ACTING ADMINISTRATOR C. A. MOLONEY
TO ADMINISTRATOR C. C. LEES:
LAGOS LANDS, 8 JANUARY 1879[1]

[Earlier efforts to bring order into the confused tenure system have broken down.]

4. AN Enquiry would be an easy matter were the land in possession of first holders, but such is far from the case.

Original whole grants have been cut up in a great measure and in some cases grants have been issued for portions thereof, the matter of the issue of the original whole grant being entirely forgotten. Grants in some cases have been cancelled but no record has been kept of such nor have such Grants been returned while fresh Grants have been issued for the same land.

5. In certain cases holders have lost their Grants and the investigation as to titles in such cases would from the absence of the necessary legal formalities be most difficult.

6. The question of Native holdings would have also to be gone into and will be found very complicated. The custom of the King has been never to give Grants. In fact I learn he could not, similarly with Kings on the Gold Coast. He himself possessed merely a life interest and accordingly was only able to bestow a similar interest on his people which as a rule was renewed in cases of succession the renewal on each occasion being recognized by a present from the occupant. True in the case of some European Firms and Natives of Sierra Leone Grants under the seal of Docemo have been issued by him prior to the cession of Lagos, but in general the greater portion of the Native population have [sic] been allowed, as it is customary, to settle. They or their descendants possessed no grant from former Kings, Docemo or the Government. To interfere with such people in their occupation would be unintelligible and unjust.

7. The difficulty to distinguish such cases from those of squatters and from occupations the result of squatting originally will be found very great.

8. In the case of squatters land is still retained by some of them. In such there will be no difficulty. In others the land has been sold, the buyers probably ignorant Natives or Emancipados from the

---

[1] C.O. 147/37. No thorough investigation was made at this date: instead two ordinances for compulsory registration and declaration were prepared: Hicks Beach to Lees, 23 May 1879, ibid.

Brazils having full confidence in the right of such persons to dispose of the land for which they have paid. Such land has in many cases passed from one to another, each, except for the first settler, believing in the right of the other to sell the same and to dispossess the present holders could not be understood by and would be most unfair to them.

9. These are a few of the difficulties that will have to be met in the matter of an Enquiry as contemplated by the Secretary of State for Colonies and should such a course be decided upon I would venture to suggest the desirability of having the boundary question of the Settlement gone into at the same time . . .

2

GOVERNOR SIR SAMUEL ROWE TO THE COLONIAL OFFICE: SIERRA LEONE LANDS, 22 DECEMBER 1880[1]

[Mr. Grant has applied for a concession of a thousand acres on the Peninsula.]

2. I THINK that the time has arrived when the Governt. may claim some rent for Crown lands and for cutting timber.

3. There is no direct taxation of any kind in Sierra Leone, and House property has considerable value in Freetown as well as land.

4. I have made allusion in reporting on Estimates for 1880 to two plots of land, one valued at £200 . . .

5. A similar plot in the best trading thoroughfare changed owners for £500. The Government paid Mr. Heddle £1,600 for land and buildings and Mr. Verminck has certainly paid several thousands for the plot near the Wharf which he has recently purchased.

6. Native traders not infrequently build houses which cost £1,500 to £2,000 or more.

7. They are anxious to have the water laid on to these houses and willing to pay for it.

8. Before anything practical can be done in collecting rents of Crown Lands, some help is needed in the Survey Department and I would ask that a Surveyor be temporarily employed to take up this matter.

9. In reference to the Land and Escheat Court I had the honor I believe to say that it appeared to me undesirable to attempt to decide titles to land without being able to lay accurate plans of such lands before the Court.

10. I would recommend that a fit person be especially employed in

---

[1] C.O. 267/343. The C.O. asked the Treasury, 7 January 1881, to pay for a surveyor for a two-year appointment.

making a survey of Crown lands, and that so soon as the necessary information is obtained an Ordinance should be proposed giving authority to collect rental at certain reasonable rates from the occupiers beginning with those tracts in the immediate neighbourhood of the Villages and high roads . . .

12. I doubt if the outlay and trouble will for some years be repaid by the return, but I think it time that some record should be attempted of the lands which belong to the Crown.

13. At present the more cunning and intelligent are buying and enclosing land with but little right and there will be much trouble resulting from these transactions hereafter.

3

GOVERNOR SIR J. S. HAY
TO LORD KNUTSFORD: SIERRA LEONE
LAND CONCESSIONS, 9 OCTOBER 1890[1]

HAVING been informed that Mr. J. M. Harris, from whom the Government purchased land at Sulymah and Manoh Silijah, had returned to the Colony for the purpose of obtaining concessions of land on behalf of some English companies from the Chiefs in the Sulymah District, I deemed it well to consider the conditions under which the Chiefs within the protected area, and with whom we are in constant and intimate relations, hold the land, and ascertain whether they have the right to rent or sell the same without the consent of their people. I may observe that this has always been considered a most difficult and delicate question, being one on which the Chiefs are most reticent.

2. I beg to transmit a copy of a Memorandum I prepared on the subject which I addressed to Mr. Samuel Lewis, Barrister-at-Law, and an Unofficial Member of the Legislative Council, and Mr. Parkes, Superintendent of the Aborigines Department, together with the replies of these gentlemen.[2] It will be observed that I assumed that the land is held by the Chiefs for the joint use of themselves and people, and that consequently the latter, who have a vested right, should be consulted, and their consent obtained before any alienation of land takes place. I may add that I directed attention to the necessity for protecting the farming rights of the people simply as a natural sequence to the above assumption, not that they would practically suffer by concessions being granted, as the population is sparse indeed in comparison to the extent of the land. The question of the

[1] C.O. 879/49, no. 533. The C.O. agreed, but requested registration of titles: C.O. to Hay, 10 November 1890.
[2] Encl. Lewis to Hay and Parkes to Hay, 8 October 1890.

share of compensation payable to the people was equally treated by me as a corollary to my view of the case.

3. The clear and full opinion with which I have, however, been favoured by Mr. Lewis, and which differs little from that expressed by Mr. Parkes, has shown me that the Chiefs have undoubtedly the right to sell and otherwise transfer unappropriated land in their country without the consent of the people, and that the latter have no such right as may interfere with the power of the Chiefs.

4. Having regard, therefore, to the fact that the Chiefs within the protected area are beyond the jurisdiction, are not amenable to our laws, but govern their people according to their native custom, none of their institutions being affected by the presence of the police in their country, I do not think it would be convenient for the Government to take any part, in or interfere with, the commercial transactions of the Chiefs further than that suggested by Mr. Parkes, viz., that should they at any time have any doubts as to any contract which may be put before them they may refer to the nearest Government Officer for information, but that it is to be distinctly understood that all contracts they make are *at their own risk*.

5. Having in view the present peculiar position of Government with regard to the Chiefs and people within the belt of land between the frontier road and the sea, I do not think it would be convenient to adopt the suggestion of Mr. Parkes that we should grant permits to British subjects who may be desirous of obtaining concessions of land. By so doing it would, I think lead to the impression that the Government control over the country is much more direct than it really is, and the question of protection would probably become embarrassing.

6. I venture here, my Lord, to remark that I conceive that our position with regard to the Chiefs and people within what I have designated as the 'protected area,' is in a *transition* state. At present we protect them from raids from without, and for that protection we expect them to obey all the orders of Government, and keep the peace amongst themselves. None of their institutions are interfered with and they administer their native laws as of yore. How long this condition of affairs may continue to exist is, to my mind, doubtful. It may be that the course of events in the next few years may compel us to assume further responsibilities in connection with them, and I respectfully beg to observe that it is a question that should not be lost sight of.

7. In the meanwhile I should be glad to receive the expression of your Lordship's views on my suggested course of action in connection with persons seeking to obtain concessions of land, as contained in the fourth paragraph of this Despatch.

4

J. T. HUTCHINSON TO GOVERNOR SIR W. B. GRIFFITH: GOLD COAST LANDS BILL, 7 APRIL 1891[1]

SIR,

. . . 3. Whatever shape the proposed legislation took, it would, I presume, not interfere with existing rights in land now actually occupied and not permanently abandoned (lying fallow, in short, according to the Native practice of letting land lie fallow for several years); so that the Crown would only actually appropriate and take immediate possession of the unoccupied, or, as I will call them, 'waste' lands; but at the same time the Crown would assume the ultimate lordship of all the land in the Colony and Protectorate.

4. The question is a very large one, and I feel that I am not yet fully master of it, and that I do not yet see all the good and evil that might result from legislation such as is suggested.

5. I believe that all the land in the Colony and the Protectorate, whether occupied or not, has according to Native law an owner. Some of it is stool land, some family land, and a very small part is private property. It can be alienated. The alienation may be absolute; but an absolute alienation of stool or family land can only be made under special circumstances, and for a particular object, as, for instance, to raise money for payment of a stool or family debt. Most commonly the alienation only gives a limited right: the right, namely, for the grantee and his family to occupy and live on or cultivate the land, upon the condition (often, but not always) of rendering or paying to the grantor and his representatives, as tribute, either part of the crops or an annual sum of money, and when the land ceases to be occupied it reverts to the grantor or his representatives. A money payment is sometimes made to the grantor before the grant is made; but in the case of limited grants such as I have described of stool or family land to Natives, there is usually no money payment down, but only a gift of rum, and, perhaps, a sheep or some cloth.

6. Native rules and practice as to right and mode of alienation of land, and as to rights of a squatter on it, vary in different districts; but I believe that what I have stated is generally true.

7. A Chief, therefore, has a substantial interest in the land attached to the stool; for on each fresh grant he receives some small gift; and the money rent or produce annually received in respect of the grants made by him and of former grants serves for the support of himself

---

[1] C.O. 879/46, no. 513. Encl. in Griffith to Ripon, 29 August 1894. For the background history of the Lands Bills of 1891 and 1894 from the viewpoint of the local opposition, see Kimble, *Political History of Ghana*, chap. ix.

and his officers. So with respect to family lands, the head of the family receives all tribute and payments from occupiers of the family land for the benefit of himself and the family. I use the word 'family' in the Native sense, which includes in the term all persons related by blood, however remotely, through females, and also all 'domestics,' that is, persons who were formerly house slaves, and still remain attached to the house.

8. Every member of the family has a right to live on the family land, and to have a portion of it assigned to him for habitation or cultivation. Similarly, every subject of a Chief is recognised as having a right to have a portion of the unoccupied stool land allotted to him if he needs it. The Chief can grant the stool land to one who is not subject to his stool, but only with the concurrence of his Council; and the head of a family can grant the family land to one who is not a member of the family, but only with the concurrence of the family council.

9. Natives appear to have a strong feeling of attachment for their stool or family lands. A large part of the litigation in the courts is about lands; and I have often been surprised at the pertinacity with which they fight about the right to possession of small pieces of land, sometimes land which has hardly any value except the sentimental value arising from connexion with the stool or the family, and perhaps from the fact of some Chiefs or members of the family having been buried in it, or from its association with some tribal or family fetish.

10. The above remarks apply to all the land in the country. The great tracts of unoccupied forest land, however, are probably a source of very little (if any) profit to their owners, and probably have less sentimental value also than the open lands.

11. Stool and family lands are thus a source of income and of dignity and power to the Chief or the head of the family; and they have also the further sentimental value which I have indicated.

12. The advantages to be gained from expropriation of the present owners by the Crown would be: 1) a possible increase of revenue from sales and leases of the land, and 2) a possible benefit to the community from the creation of indisputable titles derived from the Crown.

13. I presume that the Crown would pay compensation to the present owners of the land, although it is at present lying waste. And in the case of family or stool land, it would not be fair merely to compensate the present life owner, that is, the Chief or the head of the family: I doubt whether the people as a rule would, except on compulsion, part with the whole of their stool or family land to the Crown for any price; still, if a generous price were paid, they might reconcile themselves to the loss. When the amount paid for compensation

is set off against the profit to be made from sales and leases, it is not unlikely that the Crown might be the loser. For this is not a country into which immigrants are likely to pour and take up the waste lands at good prices, and the amount of unoccupied land is everywhere so large that, except in the neighbourhood of the towns, it is not likely to advance quickly in value. The expenses of surveys and plans which would be necessary when Crown grants were made must also be taken into consideration.

14. It would certainly be a great benefit to the community if indefeasible titles were created. At present an intending purchaser of land, or a merchant wishing to lend money on mortgage, has great difficulty in finding out who is the owner or person entitled to seal or mortgage; the greater part of the land in the country is stool or family land, to which a perfectly good title can seldom be made to a purchaser or mortgagee; and outside the towns there is the further difficulty of identification, owing to the absence of fences and boundary marks. The first step towards remedying this would be a survey of the whole country. But that is probably too large and costly an undertaking to be entered upon at present.

15. Perhaps the most important effect of expropriation by the Crown of the present owners of the waste lands would be that it would permanently lower the dignity and importance, and therefore the power, of the Chiefs and heads of families. At present the Chief or head is the life-owner of all the land, unoccupied or waste, belonging to his stool or family; it is he who has power to make grants of it upon the customary Native terms and tenure; and he receives the customary presents and tribute due from the grantees. If this power and these emoluments were taken from future Chiefs and heads of families it is impossible that their estimation in the eyes of their people should not be lowered. This consideration alone would, in my opinion, be enough to make us reject the proposed legislation, unless the reasons in favour of it are overwhelmingly strong.

16. I conclude that the gain to the Government from appropriation of the waste lands would be doubtful; and that the injurious effects of it in lowering the importance and influence of the Chiefs and heads of families, and in raising a sense of injustice and consequent hostility to the Government in the minds of the people, outweigh any probable gain that could accrue to the Government from it.

17. But I think there are good reasons why the Crown should take possession of the minerals and of the unused and unoccupied forest lands. Minerals in this country have not been a source of revenue, except to a very few owners; and I cannot imagine that any sentimental value can attach to their possession. There can, therefore, be no hardship, and no likelihood of rousing the hostility of the people in an appropriation of them by the Crown for the public benefit,

provided that mines now worked and concessions already made are not interfered with. The forest lands also have never been a source of profit to any one; and although they may belong to a stool or family, I doubt whether they have the same value in the eyes of the owners as the open lands have.

18. Concessions of mining and timber rights are now being made on a large scale to European companies. It would be a public misfortune if those rights over large tracts of country should get into the hands of persons, especially absentees, who could not or would not work them.

19. My present opinion is that it would be wise to enact a law vesting in the Crown all mines and minerals in and under any land within the Colony or the Protectorate, and also all waste forest land within the Colony or the Protectorate.

20. Mines now being worked, and all grants of mining or timber rights already made, should be exempted from the operation of this provision.

21. Full powers for working and getting minerals and timber should be given to the Crown and its grantees and lessees.

22. All grants of mining or timber rights already made, and all future grants, if unworked for (say) five years consecutively, should be made liable to forfeiture.

23. It may be a question whether, in the case of future grants by the Crown of rights or mining in certain districts in the neighbourhood of existing workings, some compensation should not be reserved to the present owners.

24. 'Forest land' would require careful definition and limitation.

25. Care should be taken not to impose any conditions which might discourage or hamper legitimate enterprise.

26. One immediate result of this legislation would be that persons wishing to take grants or leases of mining or timber rights could get an absolutely good title to them. At present I believe they often find great difficulty in acquiring a good title, and are subject to annoyance and loss in consequence.

5

COLONIAL OFFICE: MEMORANDUM,
BOTANICAL STATIONS, 12 SEPTEMBER 1893[1]

THE development of the Botanic Station System and of Technical Education in the Four West African Colonies.

At a conference of the four West African Governors, the Director, and Assistant Director of the Royal Gardens, Kew, which was held

[1] C.O. 879/65, no. 635.

at the Colonial Office on the 12th of September, 1893, it was decided that it was desirable that:

1. The Curator of a Botanic Station should be made a permanent official.

2. His salary should be £200 a year, rising by annual increments of £16 13s. 4d. to £250 a year.

3. He should receive travelling allowance according to his rating.

4. He should be entitled to the benefit of the Colonial Regulations regarding the leave, passages, pensions, &c., of West African officials.

As regards Training in Agriculture, it was agreed that the following course should be adopted, as far as possible:

(A) Training lads at Botanical Stations.—This might be regarded as a first step in the direction of teaching boys in agricultural pursuits. Intelligent boys should be attracted to the work under a definite arrangement made with the Government for their future career. The lads receive a small sum at first towards their maintenance, to be gradually increased year by year as they improved. The training should be thoroughly practical and suited to the circumstances of the Colony. Of these lads, the best might be selected for further training in the West Indies, or at Kew. When qualified the trained lads might be employed, (1) as officers in charge of branch Botanic Stations, (2) as managers of private plantations, (3) as instructors in agriculture in schools, (4) to replace the Curator when occasion may require. The number of lads in training should be regulated by the capacity of the Station. The Curator should not be burdened with board and lodging of the lads. The arrangements for training should be entirely in the hands of the Curator. It will probably be found best to place each lad singly under the training of one of the workmen, and move him from one kind of work to another as circumstances arise. The whole training should extend over four or five years at least.

(B) Branch Botanic Stations.—As circumstances demand branch stations might be started in various parts of the Colony. These could be placed under charge of trained natives, supervised by the Curator from headquarters. These branch stations would become in time valuable agencies for the diffusion of agricultural knowledge; they would act as depots for plants sent from the chief Botanic Station; and they might devote attention to the special kinds of products suited to the district in which they were placed.

W. Brandford Griffith.
F. Fleming.
G. C. Carter.
R. B. Llewelyn.

6

J. T. HUTCHINSON TO GOVERNOR SIR W. B. GRIFFITH: GOLD COAST LANDS BILL, 2 AUGUST 1894[1]

REFERRING to my letter to your Excellency, Confidential, No. 102, of the 26th of July last, on the subject of waste lands, forests, and mines, I understand that the Bill is to be forwarded to the Secretary of State. I should like therefore to make a few observations explanatory of my reasons for adopting the provisions embodied in the Bill.

2. I must refer to my confidential letter, No. 5, of the 7th of April 1891. In that letter, for reasons there given but which are too long to quote here, I gave my opinion against the proposed appropriation of the waste lands of the country by the Government. I still think that the statements of fact in that letter are, in the main, accurate and the reasons good. But the reservation contained in this Bill of Native rights of occupancy and user, and of permitting members of the family or tribe to occupy and use the family or stool land, removes the chief of the objections which I formerly felt to this appropriation by the Government.

3. In paragraphs 5 to 8 of my letter of the 7th April 1891 I described the rights now enjoyed by Natives in respect of their stool and family land, which two classes comprise the greater part of the land in the country. Those rights, so far as regards occupancy and user by members of the family, and the Chiefs and subjects of the stool, and the granting of permission so to occupy and use, will not be affected by the Bill, except to this extent, that they will not be exerciseable over land which the Crown has already occupied or has granted to some other person. And when we remember that the greater part of the land in this country, perhaps more than nine-tenths of it, is unoccupied and uncultivated, we may feel sure that in this respect the Natives will practically not suffer at all.

4. The right, if it exists, of making grants to strangers, particularly to Europeans, of waste land, and of minerals, and of concessions of forest land, will be taken away. The practice of making such grants and concessions is quite modern, and is probably illegal according to Native law and custom.

5. If the Bill becomes law:

i) all waste land and all mines and forests will be vested in the Crown, subject to certain reservations in favour of Native rights and

---

[1] C.O. 879/46, no. 513. Encl. in Griffith to Ripon, 29 August 1894; approved in Ripon to Griffith, 10 October 1894. And Kimble, *Political History of Ghana*, pp. 335-7.

of existing grants. 'Waste lands' means the same as 'Unoccupied lands' means in the Public Lands Ordinance. At present the Government, under that Ordinance, can acquire for the public service any 'Unoccupied land' without payment.

ii) all grants of waste land, and concessions of mining rights and forest land, and of rights of cutting timber, will in future be made by the Crown. At present mining and timber concessions are often made by rival Chiefs to different persons or companies, over vast and ill-defined tracts of country, subject to no conditions binding the grantee to work them, or to work them with reasonable skill; and the grantee seldom gets a safe title. In future the area affected by each grant will be defined, and the grantee will be put on terms to work his concession within a reasonable time and in a proper manner; he, on his part, will be able to bargain with the Government for improvement of roads and other means of access to his work, and—a matter of great moment —he will get an indefeasible title.

6. I propose that, before the Crown makes any grant, a procedure should be adopted similar to, but not quite so elaborate as, that which is adopted when the Government acquires land under the Public Lands Ordinance. This will secure the consideration of objections to the grant before it is made.

7

JOSEPH CHAMBERLAIN TO GOVERNOR W. E. MAXWELL: GOLD COAST LAND CONCESSIONS, 10 SEPTEMBER 1895[1]

I HAVE had under my consideration your Confidential Despatch of 9th May in which you submit the draft of a public notice which you propose should be issued, to the effect that no concessions purporting to be granted by Native Chiefs will be recognised unless approved by the Governor. I am disposed to think that the issue of such a notice would be desirable, and, further, you have my authority for issuing it.

It would, however, be well to omit the second recital from 'and whereas' down to 'protection.' The notification is itself a sufficient assertion of the authority of the Crown, without going so far as formally to declare that the Queen claims to interfere with the rights of property possessed by Native Chiefs. In the absence of any law for the purpose, the Crown has no right which the Courts would enforce to prevent the Chiefs from making concessions of Native territory.

---

[1] Ibid. This concessions notice served as a model for the Gambia, Sierra Leone, and Lagos: C.O. Circular to West African Governors, 11 December 1895, ibid.

The real value of the notice is that it will probably prevent speculators from taking advantage of the Natives by obtaining improvident concessions from them.

I would also suggest for your consideration whether the 'seal' of the Governor is necessary, as well as his 'signature.'

8

JOSEPH CHAMBERLAIN TO GOVERNOR W. E. MAXWELL: GOLD COAST LANDS BILL, 13 MARCH 1896[1]

IN my Despatch, No. 304, of the 10th of September last, upon the subject of waste lands, forests, and minerals, in the Gold Coast Protectorate, I informed you that I approved of your not proceeding further at that time with the Crown Lands Bill drafted by Sir Joseph Hutchinson; and in your Despatch, No. 412, of the 12th of October, you replied that you had, in consultation with the Attorney-General, drafted an entirely new Bill, which you hoped to transmit, for my consideration, in a few months, with a further report upon the position of affairs which calls for legislation.

2. In the meantime, various communications have been addressed to me by persons who have obtained, or propose to obtain, grants and concessions from Chiefs within the Protectorate, to which I have replied by referring to the notice which was issued by your direction on the 10th of October last.

3. I now propose to state, for your guidance in connexion with the draft Bill which you have before you, the main points which, in my opinion, the Government should secure in dealing with this question.

4. There are two kinds of concessions to be considered:

1.) Concessions of monopoly rights over a very large extent of country, where the concessionaries would be in the position of an Exploration Company, and would, no doubt, attempt to form subsidiary companies for developing the concession; and

2.) Concessions of a comparatively small estate, or a single mine, sufficient for the capital of a small company.

5. In the first case I think that the concessionaires should be required to pay a large sum of money, either in cash down or by instalments, which might be used by the Government in making roads or railways, and otherwise opening up the territory. There would also have to be conditions securing the working of the monopoly at an early date, as it would not be wise to lock up large tracts of country with no assurance that any early development would take

[1] C.O. 879/46, no. 513.

place. As an instance, the Government might recognise monopoly rights in the whole of one of the countries now under British protection, such as Bekwai or Adansi, giving power to explore and work minerals, timber, and all kinds of produce. In this case the Government should consider the best means of connecting the country with the coast by rail or roads, and should ask for a large contribution towards, or the whole of, the cost from such concessionaires as the price of the monopoly. A large stretch of country would thus be opened up on the line of the proposed road or railway.

6. In the other case, where the grant would be of a much more limited kind, it would not be possible to require a large sum for the concession, and the Government might be satisfied with guarantees that the particular development would be pushed forward together with a royalty of some kind on minerals or profits.

7. All arrangements with the Chiefs and people should be made by and through the Governor of the Gold Coast, and the sum to be paid for their consent (which should be, I think, in the shape of a moderate rent or annuity) should be paid through the Governor.

9

JOSEPH CHAMBERLAIN TO GOVERNOR
F. CARDEW: SIERRA LEONE LANDS
AND MINERALS, 9 DECEMBER 1896[1]

REFERRING to my telegram of the 5th instant in which I instructed you to repeal Part IV (Lands) of the Protectorate Ordinance, I have the honour to explain that such repeal is necessary, if any part of the Ordinance is to remain in force, for, as I have been unable to advise Her Majesty to sanction Part IV, the whole Ordinance must have been disallowed unless that Part were got out of the way by means of a repealing Ordinance.

2. The 34th Section of the Ordinance purports to vest in the Crown all minerals within the Protectorate, but, as Her Majesty does not claim any property in the soil of the territories which she takes under her protection, this section cannot be allowed to stand. It will, however, be necessary, in the interest of the public, that Her Majesty should have power to take and hold any portions of the territory which may be required for roads, railroads, and for other purposes of general utility. It will also be necessary to provide machinery for assigning to individuals the right to occupy specified portions of unoccupied land for mining or other industrial pursuits.

3. These subjects are being dealt with on the Gold Coast, and I shall defer giving you instructions upon them until the land system

[1] C.O. 879/49, no. 533.

of the Protectorate adjoining that Colony has been further worked out, so that the same principles may, as far as possible, be adopted in both places. I will only say that one essential provision will be the creation of some Board or Commission for investigating past concessions and deciding whether, and to what extent, they can be recognised by the Government.

4. It is obviously impossible that Her Majesty, who has taken the Native tribes under her protection, should, as the first result of that protection, allow, without inquiry, large tracts of land to pass into the hands of speculators, under the pretext that they have obtained from the Chiefs documents conveying these lands to them absolutely and in perpetuity. So far as I am aware, it has never been distinctly ascertained that the Chiefs of tribes possess the fee simple of the lands occupied by their tribes, or that they have the right to dispossess the Native families living on those lands, and to make them over to strangers. Experience also shows that in some instances Chiefs are induced to sign documents, of whose effect they are ignorant, at any rate, according to the English law, by which the nominal grantees will seek to interpret those documents. Further, the inadequate nature of the consideration expressed in the documents is frequently of itself evidence that the nominal grantors must have been unaware of what they were doing.

5. These questions do not now come before the Colonial Office for the first time. A special court was created in Bechuanaland for examining and reporting on the numerous concessions claimed in that country; a somewhat similar course is being followed at the Gold Coast, and in due time will have to be taken at Sierra Leone.

6. I had thought that the matter might have waited till the return of the Attorney General from leave, for I had no definite knowledge of any existing concessions of land; and, as you had not referred to me for instructions before inserting in the Ordinance a provision validating as against the Crown, all past concessions, I concluded that you also were not aware of the existence of concessions of any magnitude. But rumours have recently reached me respecting concessions purporting to convey thousands of square miles of protected territories, and, as I perceived that the matter did not admit of delay, I telegraphed to you on the 5th instant to repeal Part IV of the Ordinance.

7. It would also seem that the provision validating concessions, as against the Crown, has been supposed to have the effect of making them valid for all purposes; but I am unable to admit this view. If the Crown does not claim the land or minerals as its own property, such a provision is meaningless. In any case, however, it would not touch the question of the validity of the concessions as against the Native grantors, or obviate the necessity of full investigation into the

circumstances under which they were obtained. For, even if the land and minerals were vested in the Crown, it would still be the duty of the Crown, on behalf of the public, to satisfy itself that its rights were not being infringed by concessions of questionable value—questionable, that is to say, by reason of having been signed by persons who were not competent to grant them, or who, if competent, had been led to make the grants in ignorance of their contents or for trivial and unfair consideration, or by direct fraud.

10

ACTING GOVERNOR DENTON TO JOSEPH CHAMBERLAIN: LAGOS FORESTRY, 9 FEBRUARY 1897[1]

I HAVE the honour to report that I left Lagos on the 16th ultimo, and reached Odo Otin on the 3rd instant.

2. I stayed one day at Epe, one day at Jebu Ode, four days at Ibadan, one day at Iwo, and one day at Oshogbo. I also passed nights at the Omi River, Olowa, Odo Ona Kekere, Lalupon, and Ede.

3. I found matters at Epe in a very satisfactory condition, no complaints of any kind being made to me.

4. At Jebu Ode I went into the recent trouble upon which I have reported, and was able to settle matters satisfactorily with the Awujale, I am glad to say. The only question independent of this raised by the Awujale was as to whether he was allowed to impose a royalty on rubber collected in his country. I informed him that I considered he might properly do so, provided rubber made in other territories, but passing through the Jebu country to Lagos, was not taxed. He promised to be very careful on this point, and, following the precedent established in Ibadan, the royalty was fixed at 2s. the 60 lbs.

5. On my way from Jebu Ode to Ibadan I regret to say I saw very many rubber trees which appeared to be dead; some also had been cut down, and the felling of trees in the forest generally struck me as being carried out in a most dangerous manner. No doubt the unusually dry season has a good deal to do with the unhealthy appearance of the rubber trees, and some may perhaps recover when the rains come, but, however this may be, I am convinced that the present system of allowing persons to collect rubber and cut down trees wherever and whenever they please cannot but prove most injurious to the industries of the country.

6. I think myself that a Forest Department established on somewhat similar lines to that in India, but, of course, limited in its

---

[1] C.O. 879/65, no. 635. Referred to Kew Gardens. Already there were stations at Kotu (Gambia) and Aburi (Gold Coast).

dimensions, is an urgent need, and I would recommend that the Director of the Royal Gardens, Kew, be consulted on the subject. Both Mr. Thiselton Dyer[1] and Dr. Morris have given us valuable assistance in the past, and take a great interest in Lagos, and I feel sure that they will do their best to suggest to us a practical way out of the difficulty. As a temporary measure I have caused Messrs. Leigh and Dawodu, who went through courses of botanical and agricultural training in Jamaica and at Kew, to be sent to Ibadan, and I have directed the Acting Resident to employ them to instruct the people engaged in the rubber industry in the proper methods of collecting rubber, and they will also use their best endeavours to prevent the wholesale destruction of the forests which is at present going on. I am glad to say that the different Chiefs have promised to give us every assistance, and in this way I hope to minimise the danger until a proper Department can be established.

11

GOVERNOR W. E. MAXWELL TO THE LEGISLATIVE COUNCIL: GOLD COAST LANDS BILL, 10 MARCH 1897[2]

Rights of Chiefs.

. . . THE rights of the people to help themselves to such public land as they require for their actual use are only exerciseable where native custom permits this to be done without the express authority of a Chief. Custom probably varies according to locality, and there are perhaps parts of the Colony where the permission of a headman is a necessary preliminary to the occupation of land by a native in his district.

Recognised Chiefs will continue to have this power of giving out to their people, for occupation, cultivation, and improvement, allotments of public land not being town land. They may also allot land for shifting cultivation.

But if they have, by native custom, any power to deal with public land otherwise than in the manner provided for in the two sections last quoted, such power will only be exerciseable in future with the written consent of the Governor thereto first obtained.

[1] (Sir) William Turner Thiselton-Dyer, botanist, Director of Kew Gardens, 1885–1905.
[2] C.O. 879/49, no. 531. The message was read by the Colonial Secretary. Encl. in Maxwell to Chamberlain, 11 March 1897. For the formation of the Aborigines' Rights Protection Society and opposition in England to the 5 per cent Royalty, see Kimble, Political History of Ghana, pp. 340–5. The Bill was at first approved in Chamberlain to Maxwell, 29 April 1897; and in May it was agreed to defer its passage through the Legislative Council.

Legal effect is given in this way to the declaration announced in the notification of the 10th October 1895, which has already been quoted in full.

Powers of the Governor in respect of Public Land.

In the interests of good government and for the greater security of persons (especially those who are not natives) who may desire to acquire rights over public land, it is necessary that the paramount power should exercise, concurrently with local Chiefs where necessary, the power of allotting land and interests in land to applicants. Power is therefore given to the Governor to authorise (by a document called a Land Certificate) the occupation of public land for any purpose by such person or persons and on such terms and conditions and for such consideration and either in perpetuity or for a term of years, absolute, conditional or defeasible, as he shall think fit. The bed of a river or lagoon is declared to be 'public land,' so the right of dredging for gold may be the subject of a Land Certificate or a licence.

It must not be supposed that the enforcement in future by the Governor of powers which have sometimes been exercised by persons claiming to be Chiefs or native authorities will be injurious to the latter. The Governor will, where necessary, consult with recognised native Chiefs before creating private rights over public land in the districts of the latter respectively, and it may be accepted as quite certain that the Governor will ordinarily secure for the Colony at the hands of investors better terms and more appropriate conditions than natives would get for themselves. Allusion has already been made to the intention of the Governor to secure for native Chiefs a 'proper share' of the revenue arising from land disposed of in their districts. Payments to Chiefs, which will take the shape of a moderate rent or annuity, will be paid to them by the Government, and direct dealings between them and the holders of concessions will not be permitted.

All necessary rules for giving effect to this policy will be made hereafter and power to make rules for various purposes is given to the Governor in Council.

Land in respect of which a Land Certificate is issued will be subject to English law exclusively and as this tenure will probably become popular, because land so held will be more readily marketable than land under the native tenure, it is provided that a recognised proprietor may exchange his native title, whatever it is, for a Land Certificate. But this can only be done where there has been preliminary survey and on proper conditions (which may include a small quit-rent).

Allusion must also be made to the powers given to the Governor to set apart portions of public land for public purposes merely by a proclamation in the 'Government Gazette' containing the necessary description.

General.

These, then are the rights and powers of the Governor, the Chiefs, and the people, respectively, and it is believed that Part II of the Bill provides a simple form of tenure and a system of procedure which are suited to the state of things at present existing in the Gold Coast Colony.

There are grounds for hoping that the removal of the uncertainty which has been allowed for so long to surround all incidents of tenure in this Colony will give an impulse to industry of all kinds.

Two subjects, not mentioned under previous headings, may be briefly alluded to. One is the prohibition directed to public officers against acquiring land beyond a block of land, not to exceed 50 acres, intended for actual residence or cultivation. This regulation exists in various forms in other Crown Colonies, and it is essential to forbid anything like land-jobbing in the public service. The other is the power given to the Supreme Court to order a partition under certain circumstances. Native customs in regard to family property must not be allowed to act prejudicially upon the just claims of persons interested (including perhaps judgment-creditors) and legislation to this end seems to be required.

Constitution of a Concessions Court.

The Governor desires to remind the Legislative Council of an announcement on the subject of the policy to be pursued in respect of concessions which he made in July 1896, when addressing at their request, the African Section of the Liverpool Chamber of Commerce on the affairs of the Gold Coast and Ashanti. Though not official, it is not perhaps unknown to them. It was then stated that—'The recognition of mining and timber concessions must be accompanied by a condition that a substantial payment, either in cash or in the shape of royalties, shall be secured to the Government, the native chief or tribal representative getting a share.'

'Concessions upon which no *bonâ fide* work is being done or upon which there is no reasonable prospect of *bonâ fide* work being done within reasonable time (say five years from the passing of the Ordinance) must be liable to cancellation.' . . .

'All dealings with and payments to native authorities in respect of lands must be conducted through the Colonial Government.'

The possession of a good title is the first condition of any enterprise based upon a concession of rights in land. It has been already shown that the right of native Chiefs to make alienations for their own benefit is at least doubtful; Government recognition has not been given and no title to mining land or to forest land, though possession may have been taken and work commenced, is really safe. The claims and pretensions founded upon documents which ignorant natives may have been induced to sign are in many cases inadmissible, and it has been finally determined, with the sanction of the Secretary of State, that there shall be a very thorough examination of claims, that the recognition of concessions shall carry with it the obligation to make certain payments to the Government of the Colony, and that all alleged rights will be subject to forfeiture in default of the performance of certain conditions, among which may be mentioned abandonment or cessation to carry on *bonâ fide* operations.

Part III of the Bill provides for the establishment of a Concessions Court, which will be composed of one or more Commissioners sitting together or separately, and will conduct its proceedings on the model of those of the Supreme Court. All claims will have to be filed within a time to be fixed by the Governor, ample notice of which will be given, and those which are not filed with the Secretary of the Concessions Court within the fixed time, or within an extended time, if any is allowed, are *ipso facto* void.

The Court will have before it the Chiefs whose alleged concessions are brought forward, if they choose to attend in pursuance of notice which will be given to them.

The proceedings will be public and witnesses may be summoned and examined on oath in the same manner as in the Supreme Court, and with the like penal liability if perjury is committed.

The Concessions Court will decide whether any person claiming to be, or claimed by others to be, a Chief really had any right to grant land or make concessions.

The object of the Government must necessarily be that land shall be taken up, that mines shall be worked and timber exported and that everything shall be done whereby the development of the Colony shall be facilitated and accelerated. Those, therefore, whose claims may be rejected by the Concessions Court, on one or other of the grounds now to be alluded to, can apply to the Government for a fresh concession upon equitable terms if they really contemplate *bonâ fide* operations.

The Concessions Court is not to recognise any grant or concession:

1.) If it is found to have been made by a Chief without the express consent or concurrence of the councillors (if any) whose consent may be necessary by native custom;

2.) If made by a Chief in respect of land regarding which the concurrence of another Chief and his councillors, if this is necessary by native custom, has not been obtained;

3.) If it is found to have been made by fraud or without adequate consideration;

4.) If conditions have not been performed; or

5.) If the Concessions Court is not satisfied of the authenticity of the documents or that the parties fully understood their meaning.

The Concessions Court will have power to reduce immoderate claims, to modify the terms, conditions or scope of any grant to impose equitable limitations, restrictions, and conditions.

Where a grant or concession is recognised by the Concessions Court, recognition will only be accorded subject to certain statutory conditions, which will include the payment of a small quit-rent, if the land is a town-lot or agricultural land, or the payment of a royalty on the gross output in the case of minerals, timber, rubber, &c.

There will be an appeal to the Privy Council subject to a reasonable time limitation.

Fees of court will be payable and will be taxed in the usual manner.

The jurisdiction of the Supreme Court is taken away in respect of matters which fall within the scope of the duties of the Concessions Court.

The sooner that the Concessions Court can be organised and can commence its sittings, the sooner will there be a possibility of confirming to grantees and concessionaires a marketable title for reasonable areas on equitable terms. The terms, it will be observed, include a payment to the Government over and above the sum (if any) which the grantee may have bound himself to pay periodically to the native Chief.

The Government is being called upon to provide railways and roads for the development of the mining districts, but it is idle to suppose that this can be done if the minerals and timber which are the chief wealth of the Colony are allowed to be taken out of it without contributing in any way to the public revenue. Those who have lived in a mining district know that its success is dependent upon the provision of good and reasonably cheap means of transport; and the Governor believes that those who are interested in gold-mining in the western districts of the Colony will willingly pay the royalty which will be demanded, knowing, as they must, that the saving in transport when roads and a railway have been constructed, and the increase in value of property when made easily accessible, will cover again and again the contribution which they are required to make to the revenue.

The Governor earnestly trusts that the deliberations of the Legislative Council upon the important Bill which will be submitted to them will result in the adoption of a measure which will settle in a satisfactory manner the numerous important questions involved. The preparation of the Lands Bill, 1897, has been approached, after a period of some controversy, in the most conciliatory spirit and with the utmost desire to act fairly and justly with all classes of interests. It is impossible to leave matters as they are. Public rights have been invaded and are being daily invaded, and the Government has finally determined that the administration of the public domain for the public benefit shall be ensured by efficient State machinery. The Native Chief, who will receive through the Government a reasonable share of the land revenue, will not be unduly prejudiced, the native peasant who is offered legal proprietorship will be a gainer, and the holders of concessions who intend to turn them to account will have an opportunity of obtaining a safe and marketable title on fair conditions.

These are the classes whom it must be the object of the Government to encourage. For those who, by the enforcement of a fixed system of land administration, lose the chance of irregular profits enjoyed under the old state of things, the Legislative Council is not likely to have any sympathy.

12

JAMES H. BREW TO THE
COLONIAL OFFICE: GOLD COAST
LANDS BILL, 10 JUNE 1897[1]

... THE present Bill, however, goes further in certain directions than the previous one that was withdrawn, and needs closer analysis; so much so, that I have deemed it necessary in this communication to address myself to the principal objections to the new Bill, reserving for a subsequent letter anything like detailed criticism of its numerous sections.

First.—The preamble of the Bill assumes that the Government possess *the right* to deal with the lands of the Protectorate as it may deem proper.

To this I most humbly, but most emphatically, say it does not possess any such right—

a.) Because the country has not been acquired by contest [*sic*; conquest], treaty, or cession.

b.) Because the Government have, up to now, not claimed any such right, as the country is a Protectorate.

c.) Because the Government have hitherto (not that recognition by them was necessary to the validity of the exercise of any such right) recognised, and not interfered with, *the right* of the Kings and Chiefs and others to deal with their lands as they deem fit.

d.) Because there are judicial decisions of the British courts of the Colony upholding the right of the Kings, Chiefs, and others so to deal with their lands, and querying the authority of the Government to issue grants of land in the Protectorate.

e.) Because the Government have acquired lands by purchase from some of the Kings, Chiefs, and other individuals of the Protectorate.

f.) Because the circular letter (leaving aside for the present other documentary evidence which may be brought forward in support of this contention later on) from Governor Griffith, dated Accra, 22nd December 1890, and that addressed 'To all District Commissioners,' by the Colonial Secretary, from Accra, 22nd August 1891, regarding 'concessions and grants of land by natives, Kings, and Chiefs,' directly admit the right of the Kings and Chiefs to deal with their lands as they think fit.

g.) Because, for the past 20 years, the Government have recognised such right, by merely making provision for the payment of stamp duties and registration fees on all grants of land, whereby individuals and companies have been led to acquire concessions and other rights in land, and thus invest their moneys.

This much at present on this head . . .

13

GOVERNOR SIR W. E. MAXWELL TO JOSEPH CHAMBERLAIN: GOLD COAST LANDS BILL, 15 JULY 1897[1]

. . . Now, it is intelligible that native Chiefs should be vaguely uneasy when they hear that a law affecting stool-lands is under contemplation. But the persons likely to be anxious regarding the constitution of the tribunal, which is to investigate the transactions of the past few years, are not, I venture to think, the native Chiefs, but the native middlemen, who have been the brokers in negotiations between native Chiefs and European speculators, and to whom a really searching investigation is likely to be unwelcome. I regard the agitation which has been got up in the windward districts as being entirely the work of people of this class. It is a remarkable fact that where the native land-broker does not exist, there is no remonstrance on the part of Chiefs. East of the region where traders in concessions are to be found there is no agitation, no protest, and no petitioning . . .

[1] C.O. 879/48, no. 531. The Bill was forced through the Legislative Council in July and published in August 1897. In 1898 Chamberlain allowed the Bill to be withdrawn in favour of the Concessions Ordinance, no. 19.

14

F. E. R. LEIGH AND T. B. DAWODU: REPORT ON NIGERIAN FORESTS, 28 JULY 1897[1]

W E found the forests of all these countries abound, more or less, in Ire rubber trees, but we discovered, most unfortunately, that all rubber working had practically ceased even in these far off countries, a consequence due entirely to the same overworking of the trees.

As far as we could inspect them, all the trees had been overtapped, and consequently many of them were dying, as in the case with the Jebu and Ibadan forests.

We therefore thought it our best plan, seeing the condition of their forests, to call together the Kings, Bales, Chiefs, and townspeople of the different towns we visited, and conveyed to them the wishes of the Lagos Government with regard to the rubber industry.

We called their attention to the ruined condition of all the rubber trees in their forests, and pointed out to them the folly and short-sightedness of the system of 'killing the goose for the golden eggs.'

We made them to understand that it is the earnest wish of the Lagos Government to make the rubber industry permanent, and to improve the working of it, and that for this purpose we had been sent up to them, at great expense, but that it is impossible for the industry to last another five years with the present system of working the trees, and that we would strongly advise them, therefore, in accordance with the wishes of the Government, to stop all rubber working in their forests for the next two or three years, so that the survived trees might have sufficient time to recover themselves with bark, and to allow young ones (of which their forests abound) to attain tappable sizes. After this period of time every proprietor of forests should then begin afresh to work his bush on quite a different system. That in this way the industry would be permanent, and they would derive yearly income from their forests.

We pointed out to them the great commercial value of this tree, and its financial superiority over kola and palm trees, and therefore strongly urged them to devote as much, if not greater, attention to the rearing and cultivation of this tree, as they do to the latter ones.

They were made to understand that by doing this they would not only be carrying out the wishes of the Lagos Government, which is an incumbent duty on them, but that they would also be promoting the interest of trade and be benefiting themselves and children substantially.

[1] C.O. 879/65, no. 635. *Leigh* and *Dawodu* were Assistant Curators at the Botanical Station, Ebute Metta. Encl. in Denton to Chamberlain, 28 June 1898.

Finally, we told them that they are not at liberty, and it is their duty, to stop all intruders in their forests, as it was strangers who had ruined their forests more than the inhabitants themselves . . .

15

GOVERNOR H. McCALLUM TO JOSEPH CHAMBERLAIN: NIGERIAN FORESTS, 19 AUGUST 1897[1]

IN continuation of my despatch, No. 195, dated 24th June, enclosing circular relative to local timbers, I beg to bring to your notice that I am now constantly being informed of good timber and valuable bush produce in different parts of the country, but the Botanical Staff being limited, I am unable to have such enquiries made by an expert as would enable me to know whether or not the reports made are of commercial importance or not.

2. I am very anxious that the exports of Lagos should not be practically confined to palm oil and palm kernels (now that rubber has received such a check), and I believe I am only carrying out your wishes in using such means as are at my disposal to develop the resources of the Colony and of its hinterland. The export of timber has, I am glad to say, made a start, thirty logs of Mahogany having been shipped last week.

3. One of the best collections of timber arranged botanically which I have as yet received has been made by Mr. Cyril Punch,[2] Manager of the Ilaro Coffee Estate, which post he is leaving on termination of his agreement. With his West African experience, botanical and planting knowledge, and with the excellent character which he has for activity, honesty, and steadiness, he is just the sort of officer which the Government requires as an Inspector of Forests, including the conduct of the enquiries referred to in paragraph 1 of this despatch, and the conservation of forest produce.

4. I sounded Mr. Punch as to whether he would care for such an appointment, and upon his answering in the affirmative, I directed him to submit an application for your consideration. This I now enclose, and ask for your approval to employ him on probation for one year on the provisional and temporary establishment as Inspector of Forests, at a salary of £20 per mensem, or £240 per annum.

5. As regards the cultivation of tropical products, I am sorry to say that the result of my enquiries in the best-informed quarters is a

---

[1] C.O. 879/65, no. 635.
[2] Encl. Punch to McCallum, 14 August 1897. The C.O. agreed to appoint Punch as Inspector of Forests: Chamberlain to McCallum, 13 October 1897.

general opinion that we shall be unable to get the natives to take up anything of commercial importance until they actually see plantations of the same growing, and in some cases yielding returns under Government control and supervision. At present they are as a rule content with forest produce, and with planting fast-growing food stuffs for immediate consumption.

6. A few trees, plants, and shrubs in a Botanical Garden gives them no idea of how the same should be worked and cultivated, and when they do purchase coffee or cocoa plants they generally soon lose them from sheer neglect.

7. I propose, for your consideration, that in 1898, we should select well-watered fertile tract of ground in a conveniently central situation, and that we should establish there an experimental model farm, at which there should be blocks of from two to four acres each of such crops as different sorts of rubber, tobacco, coffee, tea, pepper, gambier, kola nuts, tapioca, cotton and indigo. Such a farm would not only be the object lesson for the instruction of the natives, but would be the distributing centre for plants and seeds for extension and development of such agricultural enterprises as might be found suitable and successful.

8. I have also not failed to notice your despatches, No. 187, of 12th October, 1893, and No. 235, of 6th December, 1894, and of Sir Gilbert Carter's reply, No. 7, of 10th January, 1895. The impressions which I received when reading them have been fully corroborated by enquiry and observation. The natives, as represented in those despatches, require close parental control and guidance on the part of the Government. Their ignorance and inexperience of new products and commodities cannot be met by private enterprise, for neither Europeans nor natives in this Colony seem to have the means or the inclination to leave the present well-beaten path and to bring the means of improvement or development to the doors of the native.

9. At the same time, Yorubas are such keen traders, that I am of opinion, if we only show them how anything ought to be done and how it can be made to pay, that they will readily follow the lead which has been given them, and will rapidly develop any enterprise out of which money can be made.

10. In this part of West Africa, at all events, Government, and nobody but Government, can show them practically how copra must be dried and prepared for the home markets; how coffee must be pulped and cured; how valuable fibre, which is indigenous and growing at their doors, must be extracted and cleaned; how silk cotton must be selected and pressed; how palm kernels can be mechanically decorticated, and so on. Such instruction will include very possibly the erection of simple but suitable machinery, which can be disposed

of as soon as the native has been sufficiently trained to undertake the work himself.

11. It will also possibly entail in some instances the purchase of raw materials or crops from the native Collectors or producers, and the sale of the finished articles to the merchants, but some small risk is necessary on the part of Government if Lagos is ever to become an agricultural Colony, and be developed in the way I should like to see it.

12. I respectfully beg that you will be good enough to give the matters which I have brought forward in this despatch your earnest consideration, and, if you agree with me in the conclusions which I have formed, that you will authorize me to include in the Annual Estimates, 1898, the following two items for the approval of the Legislative Council:

(A) Expenses connected with model farm, £2,000.

(B) Encouragement of agricultural enterprise, £2,000.

16

GOVERNOR H. McCALLUM TO JOSEPH CHAMBERLAIN: NIGERIAN FORESTRY BILL, 2 DECEMBER 1897[1]

YOUR despatch, No. 278, of 19th August last, was laid by me on 11th October before the Executive Council, together with other papers relative to destruction of rubber trees and the desirability of protecting the newly-developed timber industry.

2. The result of the discussion which ensued was to the effect that it would be inadvisable to attempt to give effect to the suggestion contained in paragraph 3 of your despatch, seeing that the public forests within the limits of the Colony and the Protectorate are comparatively small in area, the boundaries moreover at the present time in the absence of survey being unknown and undefined, whilst practically all the rubber trees contained within those boundaries have already been destroyed.

3. In the Native States, where forests are under the control of the Kings and Chiefs, any such arrangement as that proposed would be extremely unpalatable, and would interfere with well-defined native rights in respect to royalties, &c. These Kings and Chiefs have suffered heavily in a pecuniary sense from our interference with their country, as their former lucrative pursuits of war, looting and

---

[1] C.O. 879/65, no. 635. The Bill was withdrawn during the difficulty over the Gold Coast Land Bill and revived in the Forestry Ordinances for Southern Nigeria, 1901 and 1902, which created reserves.

slave-raiding are now denied them, and it would be impolitic at the present time to make them feel still more acutely the change which has been made in their condition.

4. Looking, moreover, at the climate, the nature of the country, and the character of the people, I am doubtful whether any material advantage would be gained by granting exclusive rights to Europeans over moderate areas, even if they were willing to compensate the Native Chiefs concerned for loss of income and prestige.

5. The Executive Council, however, advised that, although the Colony proper would be but little affected by any legislation which would have for its object the protection from destruction of forest produce, yet we should give the Native States a lead in the matter, and provide them with materials upon which they could, under our advice, base their own rules and regulations.

6. A Bill dealing with forest produce generally was therefore prepared (copy enclosed), having for its object the establishment of a Forest Department, the issue of licences, the payment of fees and royalties, and the control of the operations under proper regulations. The Bill was introduced on 3rd November, and passed the second reading on November 11th without any serious criticism. I had been careful to impress on the Queen's Advocate the desirability of so framing the Bill that no exception could be taken to it on the pleas that it dealt with matters of land tenure. I found, however, that in spite of this some such idea was excited in the minds of a large section of the native community, who were much disturbed by its provisions.

7. At the present juncture I am very desirous that the grave unrest which has just been tided over should not again be resuscitated at a time when foreign politics are so much more important than domestic politics, especially as the Government is in such matters so dependent upon the active assistance of the natives in the way of carriers, &c. I considered, moreover, that it would be unsound policy at the closing meeting of the Council to push through a Bill which particularly affected a large illiterate class, who, by excitement displayed, had evidently not had the time to properly understand its provisions, but were ready to listen to any mischievous explanations.

8. Reviewing the circumstances of the moment, therefore, I determined not to close the session of the Legislative Council, but to adjourn *sine die* until a more convenient opportunity is afforded for considering the Bill in Committee.

9. I have thus time to send you the proposed Bill for any remarks which you may have to make thereon. As regards licences, I propose that a nominal fee only shall be charged. The collection of royalty or percentage will, I am afraid, be attended with much difficulty if such royalty has to be collected from the woodcutter or rubber

collector. The simplest plan would be to collect it from the purchasing merchant prior to export, if you have no objections to such a course.

10. As regards your approval in despatch No. 351, of 13th October, that Mr. Cyril Punch be appointed Conservator of Forests, I have informed that gentlemen that under the circumstances I am temporarily holding back his appointment. Mr. Punch is at present acting as my Private Secretary, and quite concurs in this arrangement.

17

LAGOS COLONIAL SECRETARIAT: FORESTRY RULES, 10 DECEMBER 1898[1]

It having become urgently necessary that steps should be taken for the protection of the Timber and Rubber industries in the Countries immediately adjacent to and under the influence of Lagos the Acting Governor desires Travelling and District Commissioners to take the following suggestions as a guide in dealing with the question.

Both the industries named, are to be regarded as specially belonging to the people of the Country and their development must therefore be carried out only with the permission and under the direction of the Native Authorities who are entitled to require fees from those persons who may collect and manufacture rubber or cut trees within the territory under their jurisdiction.

A Commissioner of Woods and Forests, whose special duty it is to conserve the Forests and to provide for reafforestation when requisite, having been appointed by the Government, Travelling and District Commissioners will use their best endeavours to induce the Native Authorities to carry out any suggestions he may from time to time make.

In the case of rubber no persons should be allowed to work this industry except under a Licence to be granted him by the Authorities of the Country; as the conditions of such Licences will no doubt differ in the various Districts it is impossible to lay down definite instructions with regard to them in this memorandum but the principal points to be observed may be taken to be,

1. The prevention of injury to the trees by too frequent tapping;
2. The prohibition of the collection of juice from immature trees;
3. The cutting down of Rubber trees on any pretext whatever; and
4. The preparation of the Rubber on approved principles which preclude adulteration of the product.

So far it has been admitted that the imposition of a royalty on every

[1] C.O. 879/65, no. 635. Encl. in Denton to Chamberlain, 6 January 1899. Approved by the C.O., 24 March 1899.

load of Rubber sent to Lagos is a legitimate means of obtaining revenue for local uses in the Native States and it follows therefore that the payment of a reasonable fee for a Licence may be regarded in the same light. This being so the Native Authorities should be given to understand that they are at liberty to enact regulations to protect their interests and also that they may punish by fine or imprisonment any persons who may infringe such regulations.

The time product will also be governed by regulations to be passed by the Native Authorities and in its case the guiding principle should be the payment of a fair and just sum for every tree cut down and the planting of a young tree of the same species in the place of such tree so cut down.

The fees to be paid for felling must be governed by local circumstances but the Acting Governor considers that the fine for cutting down a tree without authority should be at least ten times the established fee.

Attached are draft rules which it is hoped will be found of use in framing the regulations to be enacted by the Native Authorities.[1]

18

GOVERNOR SIR F. M. HODGSON TO JOSEPH CHAMBERLAIN: GOLD COAST CONCESSIONS, 12 AUGUST 1899[2]

. . . 2. I SHALL have to refer to five concessionaires, namely:

a.) Mr. F. W. Ensor, about whom nothing of any value is known, as no enquiry appears to have been made as to whether he was working for himself or representing a syndicate or company;

b.) Mr. Claude Beddington, who was accredited to the Acting Governor in your despatch, No. 12, of the 11th January.

c.) Captain Kenneth Campbell, who came to the Colony on behalf of a syndicate comprising among others Mr. Alfred Jones, the Chairman of the African Lines of Steamers, as advised in your despatch, No. 478, of the 23rd December, 1898;

d.) Mr. N. B. Walker, acting for the Obuassi Gold Mining Syndicate, and referred to in your confidential despatch of the 21st February; and

e.) Mr. David, acting for an Anglo-Belgian Syndicate, got up by Mr. Walford, of Antwerp, and others (the money I believe is almost entirely subscribed by Belgians).

3. In your confidential despatch of the 8th December, 1898, you defined very clearly, as I think, the lines on which the provisional

---

[1] Not printed.   [2] C.O. 879/57, no. 578.

recognition of this Government may be given to concessions, and the reasons for such action. I interpret your instructions as meaning that in cases in which the Government is satisfied, as far as it can be, that the concessionaire has obtained his concession in a manner which meets the approval of this Government, and upon lines which include the due provision of remuneration to the native chiefs conceding the mining or other rights, and where it may reasonably be assumed that the concessionaire means bona fide business, and is not concession-mongering, the Government may by letter provisionally recognise the claim subject to the conditions set forth in the despatch.

4. Mr. Low has not so interpreted your letter. He has taken it as meaning that in cases in which he was satisfied that action by the Government might be taken, such action should take the form of a formal agreement between the Government and the concessionaire, on the lines of the agreement made with the Ashanti Gold Fields Corporation, and with Mr. H. B. W. Russell (this latter agreement is not a goldmining agreement). He has made a formal agreement with Mr. Ensor and as you are aware two agreements with Captain Kenneth Campbell; but in not one of them has any saving clause been inserted providing that the agreement is made subject to the provisions of any Ordinance which may be passed, dealing with concessions, and to any order of the Concessions Court, and, further, as I shall, I regret, have to show they have been made with an unaccountable disregard of your instructions, and with a want of care which cannot fail to cause serious embarrassment to the Government.

5. I am advised that the agreements made with Mr. Ensor and Captain Kenneth Campbell place them, excepting as regards the payment of royalties, which I shall refer to later, in almost the same position towards the Government as the Ashanti Gold Fields Corporation. But even if it be possible for the Concessions Bill to sweep in these agreements as having been made after the 1st January, 1898, or whatever may be the date fixed, there must be embarrassment, because, upon the strength of the agreements, if they are not set aside, companies will be formed and action taken, which the Concessions Court will find it difficult to ignore . . .

19

JOSEPH CHAMBERLAIN TO GOVERNOR SIR F. M. HODGSON: GOLD COAST LAND CONCESSIONS, 22 DECEMBER 1899[1]

WHEN you were last in this country advantage was taken of your presence to discuss with you the subject of the legislation required

[1] C.O. 879/57, no. 578. The Bill did not apply to the Ashanti Gold Fields

for regulating concessions of rights relating to land by natives of the Gold Coast.

2. I have now the honour to transmit to you the draft of an Ordinance which is the outcome of these discussions.

3. As the basis of this draft is materially different from that of the Lands Bill which was under consideration during the administration of Sir William Maxwell, I do not think it necessary to refer to that Bill, beyond observing that in considering this question I have had regard to the representations made by the deputation which came to this country in 1898. While I consider it absolutely necessary for the Colonial Government to supervise grants of land, so as to protect all parties against fraud or misrepresentation, to secure to them the rights given or reserved, to guard against results prejudicial to the public interests, and to obtain for the Government a reasonable income from profitable operations, at the same time I do not wish to make any 'fundamental alteration in the rights of the natives' such as was apprehended by the deputation. The draft accordingly does not purport to confer on any Government authority the right of claiming or making grants of any land whatsoever which is owned by natives of the Gold Coast, and the idea of vesting any unoccupied land in the Governor as public land has been abandoned. The native owner is left free, as now, to make his own bargain if he wishes to sell to a European; and the benefit of his bargain is not interfered with, but on the contrary more effectually secured to him by the conditions which the Bill imposes on the grantee. I should be glad if you would take an opportunity of explaining this character of the Bill.

4. The draft provides for the establishment of a Concessions Court in the Colony to which every concession granted by a native will have to be notified, together with particulars of the concession and the documents on which the claimant relies in support of his claim. The Court will have power to certify the concession to be valid or invalid, except that any concession dated before the 10th of October, 1895, duly registered, and undisputed, would be certified as of course to be valid if the Court be satisfied that the rights granted under such concession have been in fact exercised, and that the natives resident in the locality have known of and acquiesced in the exercise of such rights.

5. The Ordinance provides that the term of a concession is not to exceed 99 years, nor that of a prospecting licence three years.

6. The Ordinance restricts the area of single concessions to five square miles in the case of mining rights, and 20 square miles in the

Corporation agreement with Maxwell in June 1897, nor to the agreement with the Castle Gold Exploration Syndicate. The Ordinance was passed with some C.O. amendments in February 1900. See no. 28.

case of rights to take timber or rubber or other products of the soil. No one person or corporation is to be allowed to hold at one time concessions the aggregate area of which exceeds 20 square miles in the case of mining rights or 40 square miles in the case of rights relating to timber, rubber, or other products of the soil. The provisions of this and the preceding paragraph do not, however, apply to any concession dated before the 10th of October, 1895.

7. The Ordinance provides for the levying of a tax of 5 per cent. on all profits made by the holder of a concession from the date on which the Ordinance comes into force. Prospecting licences are to be subject to a stamp duty of £1 per square mile.

8. The draft was communicated to the Chambers of Commerce of London, Liverpool, and Manchester, and also to certain other persons who were known to be interested in the subject, and they were invited to furnish me with their observations on it. A considerable number of criticisms not specially invited have also been received. I transmit herewith copies of letters which have been addressed to this Department on the subject, and I have to refer you for others to my despatch, No. 499, of the 30th of November last relating to the Castle Gold Exploration Syndicate.

London Chamber of Commerce,	23 Sep.
Liverpool ,, ,, ,,	29 ,,
Manchester ,, ,, ,,	28 ,,
West African Trade Association,	26 ,,
Messrs. Ashurst, Morris, Crisp & Co.,	18 ,,
Mr. Irvine,	15 ,,
Mr. Tarbutt,	14 ,,
Mr. Perks,	29 ,,
Mr. Kempf,	27 ,,
,,	9 Oct.
,,	2 Nov.
Castle Gold Expl. Syndic.,	25 Sep.
West African Mahogany and Petroleum Co.,	20 Oct.
African Estates Co.	1 Dec.

9. The draft Ordinance as now transmitted to you represents the printed draft which was submitted to the Chambers of Commerce and other persons, with the amendments suggested by the resulting criticisms. These amendments are noted by hand on the margin, and 20 copies of the draft as so amended are enclosed.

10. The substantial objections to the draft Ordinance were, as you will observe, mainly directed against the following points:

1.) The retrospective character of the Ordinance, under which it would be necessary that all concessions, however old, should be referred to the Concessions Court, and under which restrictions of area would be applied to concessions not dated prior to the 10th of October, 1895.

2.) The requirements of clause 12 as originally printed in regard to the proof of consent, of adequate consideration, and of other matters.

3.) The limitations of area in clause 19 to which I have referred in the sixth paragraph of this despatch.

4.) The tax of 5 per cent. on profits.

5.) The provisions of clause 14 of the printed draft (now struck out) under which it was proposed to confer on the Court wide powers of modifying the terms of any concession.

11. With regard to 1.), I think that it would be impossible to accept the objections without validating numerous vicious claims. You will observe that possible cases of hardship are met by special provisions.

12. With regard to 2.), it will be seen that amendments making the provisions of the Ordinance considerably less stringent in these respects have been introduced into the draft.

13. With regard to 3.), I have to draw your attention to what is said in the enclosed letters as to the limitation of the areas of concessions, and to suggest that you should take into consideration the question of taking power in the Ordinance to allow larger areas in special cases. I am, however, at present of opinion that this power, if taken at all, should be confined to existing concessions. As the limitation of areas is a provision which was not in the Lands Bill of 1897, and is therefore new to concessionaires, some hardship might result from its being made retrospective, but there is no such objection to applying it to future grants.

14. With regard to 4.), it is urged that the tax will fall entirely on the share-holders, and that the debenture-holders will escape. The objections to a tax on gross output are, however, more serious, and I see no advantage in re-opening the matter.

15. With regard to 5.), considerable alarm was manifested at the wide powers which, by clause 14 as printed, it was proposed to confer on the Concessions Court. On considering the point I have come to the conclusion that the clause would confer too much power on the Court, and it has accordingly been struck out. Any regulations as to gold mining which may prove necessary will be better made by subsequent legislation than by the action of the Concessions Court under that clause.

16. I request that you will cause to be added, in regard to certain clauses of the Ordinance which impose penalties for infractions of its provisions (Nos. 9 (2), 28, 35, and 41), a statement of the Courts in which the penalties are to be recovered.

17. I have further to transmit to you, in original, a memorandum upon the Bill submitted by Sir Brandford Griffith, which I request

that you will take into consideration when the Bill is being dealt with by the Legislative Council. I request that you will return this memorandum, or a copy of it, when submitting the Bill for my further consideration.

18. With reference, however, to this memorandum and other criticisms of the draft, I trust that it will not be found necessary to modify the main principles of the Ordinance, though with regard to the details of the measure I desire to leave you a free hand to adopt amendments which will tend to make the measure more complete and to facilitate the practical working of its provisions.

19. I approve of your introducing the draft Ordinance into the Legislative Council without further reference to me, but, inasmuch as it is possible that considerable amendments may be found necessary, it would be desirable that I should be consulted after the Bill has been considered in committee; and I therefore request that, when that stage has passed, you will have the Bill reprinted so as to show by means (if possible) of deleted type and italics the manner in which the Bill as originally introduced has been altered by the Legislative Council, and that you will also submit to me a report on the amendments which have been made, with your recommendations thereupon.

20

HIGH COMMISSIONER SIR RALPH MOOR TO JOSEPH CHAMBERLAIN: NIGERIAN TIMBER CONCESSIONS, 29 JANUARY 1900[1]

I HAVE the honour to forward enclosed one copy of Proclamation No. 1 of 1900, issued in accordance with instructions contained in your telegram of 8th December; further copies will follow on my return to headquarters.

2. As the Niger Company are working timber in areas which were formerly the property of the Royal Niger Company, and which have now passed into the hands of Her Majesty's Government, also in other areas which are not the private property of the Company, and it would not, in my opinion, be advisable or just to cause the Company to stop work and disband the large number of labourers engaged in same, I have sanctioned that the work be carried on, subject as from 1st January to such terms, conditions, and restrictions as it may be deemed advisable to impose on Timber Concessions.

3. I have drawn up a form for Timber Concession—copy enclosed —giving the terms, conditions, and restrictions on which I propose to

---

[1] C.O. 879/65, no. 635. Approved in C.O. to Moor, 14 March 1900.

grant such Concessions. In drawing up this instrument, in the absence of any information as to the regulations and systems in force in West African Colonies, I have been guided by what seem to me to be the local requirements and terms, conditions and restrictions imposed are not such as to unnecessarily interfere with the industry in any way, or to hamper its development; at the same time the interests of all concerned are reasonably safeguarded and provision is made for re-afforesting the areas deforested.

4. The Niger Company has been directed to obtain Concessions without delay for the areas which they are now working, and other applicants now applying for Timber Concessions are informed of the terms, &c. On my return to headquarters a supply of the forms for such Concessions will be printed and forwarded to all District Headquarters, with definite instructions to the District Commissioners on the subject.

5. I have communicated with the Governor of Lagos and the High Commissioner, Northern Nigeria, on the subject, forwarding copies of the proclamation and draft form of Timber Concession.

21

JOSEPH CHAMBERLAIN TO GOVERNOR
SIR F. M. HODGSON: ASHANTI LAND
CONCESSIONS, 20 FEBRUARY 1900[1]

I HAVE the honour to acknowledge the receipt of your confidential despatches of the 9th of September and 23rd of October, upon the subject of concessions of mining rights and the position held by the Government in respect of land in Ashanti.

2. I have deferred writing to you on this subject until I had consulted the Law Officers of the Crown with regard to the exercise of Her Majesty's jurisdiction in the territories near or adjacent to the Gold Coast, as to which I have now addressed you in my confidential despatch of the 19th instant.

3. You advise, and I entirely agree with you, that, in any legislation as to land, no distinction should be made between Coomassie and the rest of Ashanti; that the Concessions Ordinance, the draft of which has recently been sent to you, should be applied to Ashanti; but that, as under native rule no king or chief had power to give away any of his tribal land or to enter into any agreement with foreigners without the consent of the paramount king, and as the British Government

---

[1] C.O. 879/57, no. 578.

is now recognised by the Ashantis as standing in the place of the paramount king, the Ashanti kings and chiefs should not be allowed to grant concessions with the same freedom from control as those of the old Protectorate.

4. There do not appear to be any difficulties in the way of giving effect to these views. In the instructions to the Resident dated the 10th of February, 1896, Sir William Maxwell gave instructions that no concession of land in any part of Ashanti, whether dated before or after the 20th of January, 1896 (the date of the deposition of Prempeh) was to be recognised in any way by the Resident, but that every concession to be valid must be sanctioned by the Governor, and he caused all the kings of Ashanti to be warned that they must not grant any rights without the Governor's authority. He is also stated by Captain Stewart, in his letter of the 30th of March, 1899 (a copy of which is enclosed in your despatch of the 9th of September), to have given instructions that every demand for a concession in Ashanti was to be filed in the Resident's Office, and there enquired into to see whether the chiefs who signed the agreement were the real owners of the property, and thoroughly understood what they were signing. These instructions have, I understand, been carried out without any objection either from the natives or from the seekers for concessions, although some concessionaires have failed to comply with them, and the printed rules drawn up by you and dated the 7th of August, 1899 (copies of which were enclosed in your despatch of the 9th of September) are based upon them.

5. I agree with you in thinking it very important that the procedure prescribed in these rules should continue to be followed. From a legal point of view, these rules at present take their sanction only from the fact that the Governor will not recognise concessions obtained or rights required otherwise than in accordance with the rules, and that without such recognition any concessions or rights in Ashanti will be unmarketable, and have no commercial value. But as soon as an Order in Council has been passed authorizing the Governor of the Gold Coast to legislate by proclamation for Ashanti, as proposed in my confidential despatch of the 19th instant, the rules should be embodied in a legislative proclamation applying the Concessions Ordinance to Ashanti, and making the Ordinance and the rules part of the law of the Ashanti Protectorate, and I have to request that you will have the draft of such a proclamation prepared for my consideration.

22

GOLD COAST LANDS:
DRAFT PROCLAMATION [JULY 1900][1]

WHEREAS it is expedient to make provision with regard to the grant by natives of concessions whereby any right interest or property or the option of acquiring any right interest or property is conferred in or over land in Ashanti with respect to minerals precious stones timber rubber or other products of the soil or whereby any licence is given to prospect for the same:

Now therefore I, Frederick Mitchell Hodgson, Governor of the Gold Coast Colony &c. proclaim as follows:

The provisions of the Ordinance of the Gold Coast Colony entitled the Concessions Ordinance 1900 shall subject to the provisions hereinafter contained apply to Ashanti and for the purposes of such Ordinance the Concessions Court established in the Gold Coast Colony under the provisions of the said Ordinance shall within the limits of Ashanti have jurisdiction in all matters relating to the aforesaid concessions and licences in the same manner and to the same extent as if Ashanti formed part of the Colony.

Provided that no concession within the meaning of the said Ordinance shall be certified as valid by the said Court unless the following additional provisions have been complied with:

1. Any person desiring to obtain a concession in Ashanti must in the first instance apply to the Governor through the Colonial Secretary of the Gold Coast at Accra for permission to obtain a prospecting licence.

2. The Governor if the application appears to him to be one which should be granted will so acquaint the Resident at Coomassie and will so advise the applicant.

3. The applicant must present his letter of advice to the Resident at Kumasi who if he is unaware of any local objection to the application will issue a licence to prospect in the locality named by the applicant and will at the same time acquaint the Chief or Chiefs concerned and instruct them to give the necessary facilities.

4. In the case of a licence to prospect for minerals within the meaning of the Concessions Ordinance the licence fee prescribed by the said Ordinance and in the case of a licence to prospect for timber rubber or any other product of the soil a licence fee of £10 must be paid by the applicant upon the issue of the licence for the payment of which he will be given a receipt.

5. A licence may be issued to different prospectors for the same locality.

6. The holder of a prospector's licence may remove from the locality in which he has prospected a sufficient quantity of quartz or alluvial gold or of timber rubber or other product of the soil to serve as specimens but he must declare them to the Resident and state the name or position of the place or places from which they were taken.

7. The holder of a prospector's licence may apply to the native Chief or Chiefs concerned for a concession of gold mining or other rights over land in the locality in which he was licensed to prospect and the native Chief or Chiefs concerned may grant the concession if they are willing to do so but no such application or grant may be made in respect of any land which has not been prospected under a licence granted by the Resident.

8. Every application for a concession of mining or other rights must be notified to the Resident who will instruct the native Chief or Chiefs concerned to appear before him and will ascertain from them in the presence of the applicant whether they are willing to grant the concession applied for and are prepared to co-operate in the supply of labour and so forth. He will arrange with the applicant in the presence of the native Chief or Chiefs concerned the sum which they should receive annually in consideration of the concession.

9. The terms of the agreement made between the applicant and the native Chief or Chiefs concerned are to be embodied by the former in a deed of agreement which is to be signed by the interested parties in the presence of the Resident. The deed is to contain full particulars of boundaries and a suitable plan showing the same.

10. No concession or licence or interest therein may be assigned without the consent of the Governor.

11. Every notification of application for a concession which must be accompanied by the prospector's licence will upon receipt by the Resident be marked by him with the date and time of receipt and applications for concessions in the same locality will be considered and dealt with in the order of their receipt.

12. Where there is any variance between the Concession Ordinance and these provisions the latter shall prevail.

23

COLONIAL OFFICE TO FOREIGN OFFICE: NIGERIAN FOREST RESERVES, 20 DECEMBER 1900[1]

I am directed by the Secretary of State for the Colonies to acknowledge the receipt of your letter of the 24th of September, asking, on behalf of the Government of the Soudan, to be furnished with

[1] C.O. 879/65, no. 635.

information as to the policy adopted in regard to the india rubber industry in the West African Colonies, and in transmitting to you, to be laid before the Secretary of State for Foreign Affairs, copies of the regulations as to india rubber in force in Lagos, and of draft regulations for the Gold Coast, I am to state that at present the subject must be considered as still in an experimental stage in West Africa.

2. In Lagos it has been thought necessary to adopt the policy of Government Reserves, and an area of about fifty square miles in Ibadan, containing rubber trees, amongst others, has been set aside for public purposes, and vested in the native authorities of the place. A model farm has also been started adjacent to the reserve, in order to serve as an object lesson to the natives, and to furnish a supply of saplings for the replanting of denuded areas. It will be observed from the enclosed regulations (Forestry Rules) that the plan is adopted of inducing the native authorities to prescribe the provisions necessary for the preservation of india rubber plants.

3. On the Gold Coast it is also in contemplation to establish Government Reserves. The Curator of the Gold Coast Botanical Station makes tours in the Colony from time to time for the purpose of giving information to the natives on botanical matters, and amongst others as to the tapping and planting of india rubber trees and vines. Young plants are distributed from the Botanical Station, and as far as the staff permits, instruction is given there to natives sent for the purpose by the Kings and Chiefs—With reference to the regulations, of which a copy is enclosed, I am to point out that they are only in draft, and appear to need some amendment.

4. In order to check the wasteful exploitation of india rubber in Southern Nigeria by too frequent tapping, the High Commissioner has suggested that, in addition to the prohibition against collecting rubber during the dry season of the year, which is insisted upon as far as possible in certain parts of the Protectorate, the exportation of rubber should similarly be prohibited during a corresponding season. This suggestion is still under consideration.

5. As far as the Secretary of State is aware, there are no contracts specially relating to rubber to which the Governments of the West African Colonies are parties . . .

24

JOSEPH CHAMBERLAIN TO GOVERNOR SIR W. MacGREGOR: NIGERIAN LAND CONCESSIONS, 4 JUNE 1901[1]

I HAVE the honour to acknowledge the receipt of Sir Geo. Denton's despatch, No. 281, of the 31st of October last, transmitting draft

[1] C.O. 879/67, no. 654.

regulations consolidating the notices and rules which have been issued on the subject of concessions of land, together with the draft of an Ordinance to give legislative force to the regulations.

As the Order by Her Majesty in Council of the 27th of December, 1899, has not yet been published in the Lagos Government Gazette and has, therefore, not come into operation, I am advised that the Legislative Council of Lagos has no power as yet to legislate for the Protectorate. When such power has been conferred by the new Order in Council which it will now be necessary to issue, it appears to me that it will be sufficient for the present to pass a law providing that no person other than a native shall acquire any interest in, or right over, land without the consent of the Governor, and to issue a notice that the consent of the Governor will only be given in the circumstances specified in the draft regulations, forwarded by Sir George Denton. I enclose a copy of the Northern Nigeria Proclamation, No. 8, of 1900,[1] which might be followed with the necessary formal alterations. I may add that a precisely similar law has been passed in Southern Nigeria. Elaborate legislation on the lines of the Gold Coast Concessions Ordinance, 1900, will not be necessary until the country has been opened up and concessions are being largely acquired . . .

25

GOVERNOR M. NATHAN TO THE COMMANDANT NORTHERN TERRITORIES: LAND CONCESSIONS, 1 JULY 1901[2]

. . . 6. You will observe that the procedure it involves differs very considerably from that adopted in the Colony and in Ashanti, and is briefly as follows:

A person applies for, and is granted for 6 months, an exclusive licence to prospect over an area of which the limits are approximately defined, and pays for that licence on the basis of the area it covers. During the term of the licence its holder can apply and be granted rights of option over the whole or part of the area included in it, the area for such rights being somewhat more definitely defined in the description, and on the ground. The rights are to last one, two, or three years, and each year a payment is to be made to the Government on the basis of the area, and if in the opinion of the Chief Commissioner (which title I have suggested should in future be given to your office) native chiefs should receive payment on account of the rights given over their lands a further sum also calculated on the basis of

---

[1] Encl. Proclamation, 1 January 1900 (by F. D. Lugard).
[2] C.O. 879/67, no. 652.

area is to be paid to Government for distribution to these chiefs. During the term of the rights of option their holder can apply for and be granted a lease over the whole or part of the area over which those rights extended, the area included in the lease being accurately defined by description and survey, and marked on the ground by boundary pillars. The lease will be a valid title for a period not exceeding 90 years, and each year a payment will be made for it to Government on the basis of area as well as a payment for disbursement to native chiefs on similar conditions to the payment to them in the case of rights of option.

7. The draft proclamation also provides for payment to Government of a duty of 5 per cent. on net mining profits similar and to be similarly collected to the duty imposed by the Concessions Ordinance on mining operations in the Colony. It further embodies clauses empowering the Chief Commissioner to make rules and to settle disputes as to areas, restricting the use of lands leased to defined purposes, preserving the existing rights of natives in them, giving the Governor certain powers over lands leased, preventing their being assigned or underlet without the Governor's consent, providing for the determination of leases if conditions are not fulfilled, and laying down penalties for offences.

8. The main point in which the draft proclamation is at variance with the legislation that has been adopted for the Gold Coast and Ashanti is that the concession is granted direct by the Government and not by the native chiefs with subsequent declaration of validity by a Concessions Court. Large tracts of the Northern Territories appear to be uninhabited or sparsely populated by rude savages without recognized headchiefs or central forms of government, and the Gold Coast system would be quite inapplicable to such tracts. Further, it seems right that the main part of the rental for unoccupied lands should go to the paramount power which, by a very large expenditure on administration, has made it possible to utilize those lands. At the same time where native chiefs have rights by native custom over minerals and produce got from the soil, they should derive some advantage from the work of European Companies in this direction, and also the existing rights of individual natives must be preserved to them. These matters are in the draft proclamation left largely to the Chief Commissioner, who is in the best position for seeing that the natives have justice done to them.

9. The system by which rights of option and lease are to be granted by the Government and not concessions by the native chiefs obviates the necessity for extending the operation of the concessions court to the Northern Territories.

10. Another fundamental point in which the proposed legislation for the Northern Territories differs from that which has been adopted

on the Gold Coast and in Ashanti is that no restriction is placed on
the area for which a lease may be granted to one individual . . .

26

ACTING HIGH COMMISSIONER PROBYN TO JOSEPH CHAMBERLAIN: NIGERIAN AGRICULTURE, 6 SEPTEMBER 1901[1]

. . . 7. I ALSO believe that it will be found that the best way of
advancing agriculture in the Protectorate will be to take advantage of
the Native Councils. The head of the Agricultural Department, whose
qualifications I have referred to above, would be able to visit the
several Districts in the Protectorate, and to determine in each case
what particular class of cultivation would be most likely to be successful. Under the head of the Agricultural Department there should be
two highly qualified agricultural instructors of proved experience in
the cultivation of tropical produce. When the head of the Department
has decided that a district will grow produce of a particular kind,
he would issue instructions to one of these instructors to go to the
district. The Divisional Commissioner would then introduce the
instructor to the most enterprising members of the Native Council,
and would use his influence to persuade those members to carry out
the advice of the instructor. At first a system of grants-in-aid might
be introduced to induce the natives to make the necessary experiments. The Native Councils are already alive, in many cases, to the
fact that they are responsible for taking whatever steps may be
necessary for the advancement of their districts, and I do not think
that there would be any difficulty in getting the advice of the instructor
acted upon, on a practical scale, in any district recommended by
the head of the Department as being suitable for the experiment.

8. If this system were carried out it would not be necessary to have
a central Botanical Station on a very extensive scale, and the grants-
in-aid, which I have suggested, would amount to a much smaller
sum than the cost of maintaining an extensive Botanical Station.

9. I have seen cocoa trees in many Districts which are badly
pruned and cared for; I have also seen the appliances for curing cocoa,
and I am convinced that at the present moment there is scattered
throughout the Protectorate a great deal of undeveloped wealth.

10. I respectfully beg to suggest, therefore, that advantage should
be taken of the presence of the High Commissioner in England to
settle, with a view to immediate action, the organization of the
Botanic Department.

[1] C.O. 879/69, no. 661. *L. Probyn,* Acting High Commissioner, Protectorate of
Southern Nigeria, 1901–3.

27

GOVERNOR M. NATHAN TO JOSEPH CHAMBERLAIN: GOLD COAST AGRICULTURE, 21 DECEMBER 1901[1]

I HAVE the honour to report that at a meeting of the Legislative Council, held at Government House, on the 10th instant, a sum of £150 was voted to meet expenditure in connection with the creation of a Government cocoa-nut plantation.

2. Since 1898, Messrs. Elder, Dempster & Company have constantly urged on this Government the desirability of giving encouragement to the planting of cocoa-nut palms for the production of copra on a large scale. The matter was brought before me immediately on my arrival in the Colony, and I caused a letter to be written to the Chambers of Commerce at Cape Coast and Accra, asking for their assistance and advice, and instructions to be sent to District Commissioners to draw the attention of cultivators to the advisability of extending the planting of cocoa-nut trees. I also decided to form a Government plantation in the neighbourhood of Accra, which might ultimately, by being carefully looked after and worked, teach the natives that a profit can be made from the growth of these trees, and the manufacture of copra from the nuts. At present, though there are considerable areas covered by cocoa-nut trees in the east of the Colony, the natives rarely take the trouble to collect the nuts and prepare copra for them.

3. About 16,000 nuts were purchased at Ada and Kwitta. Of these, about 14,000 were found suitable for planting, and were planted in a nursery in the gardens of Christiansborg Castle. Some 9,000 germinated, and of these 1,000 have been planted out on an open plot of land between the road from Christiansborg to Labady and the sea, just outside the municipal boundary. This plot is being acquired under 'The Public Lands Ordinance, 1876,' and surrounded by a live fence. The young palms already planted out are doing well, and it is proposed to plant out the remainder as soon as the rains recommence.

4. The expenditure to the end of the present month is estimated at £150, and it is for this sum that the vote was taken in the Legislative Council, for which your approval is now asked.

[1] C.O. 96/384.

28

R. L. ANTROBUS (COLONIAL OFFICE) TO THE TREASURY: NIGERIAN MINING ROYALTIES, 31 JANUARY 1902[1]

I AM directed by Mr. Secretary Chamberlain to acknowledge the receipt of your letter of the 3rd of December, on the subject of the agreement with the Royal Niger Company in respect of royalties on minerals in Northern Nigeria.

2. It is clear that, under the terms of the Treasury Minute of the 30th of June, 1899, and the letter addressed to the Company on the 1st of July, which constitute the agreement between the Government and the Company, the Government is bound to impose a royalty on all minerals which may be worked in a certain portion of Northern Nigeria provided that such minerals are exported from a British port or pass through a British Custom House, and to pay to the Company half of the receipts from any royalty so imposed; and that the term 'royalty' must be held to cover any profit made by the Government by sale or by the issue of licences in connection with the working of minerals.

3. It is not, however, clear to Mr. Chamberlain that the term 'royalty' must be held to cover a tax on profits, although in your letter 'royalty' and 'tax on profits' appear to be regarded as convertible terms.

4. In its primary and natural sense 'royalties' is merely the English translation or equivalent of 'regalitates', 'jura regia.' In its secondary senses the word 'royalties' signifies, in mining leases, that part of the reddendum which is variable and depends upon the quantity of minerals gotten (Attorney-General of Ontario versus Mercer, 52, L.J.P.C. 89, quoted in Stroud's Judicial Dictionary); or the agreed payment to a patentee on every article made according to the patent.

5. It is possible that there may be instances in which the term 'royalty' has been used to denote a percentage or tax on profits, but in the Treasury Minute of the 30th of June, 1899, the word is clearly used to denote a proportion of the minerals actually worked in a particular portion of Northern Nigeria, and exported in a specified way. In other words, it denotes a tax, not on the profits of persons working the minerals, but on the gross value of the minerals gotten; and, although by the Treasury letter of the 1st July the meaning of the term is expressly extended so as to include for the purposes of the agreement any profit made by sale or by the issue of licences, there is nothing which would, in Mr. Chamberlain's opinion, justify the Company in contending that it includes a tax on profits.

[1] C.O. 879/76, no. 701.

6. This view is confirmed by the provision in the agreement with regard to specific taxation. It is provided that 'no specific taxation shall be imposed on the mining interest, as such, which would prevent the imposition of such an amount of royalty as may be compatible with the development of that industry in the territories in question.' The provision is not very clearly worded, but it is obviously intended, while reserving power to the Government to impose specific taxation on the mining industry as such, to guard the Company against the risk that the Government might impose such heavy taxation as to prevent the imposition of an adequate royalty. Such a provision would have been quite unnecessary if it had been intended that the Company should be entitled to share in the proceeds of any specific taxation.

7. It is unfortunate that the amount of royalty to be imposed was not specified in the agreement. The interests of the Government and the Company in regard to the amount are conflicting, and the only stipulation in the agreement is that it must be compatible with the development of the industry.

8. The subject of taxation and royalties has recently occupied Mr. Chamberlain's attention in connexion with the development of gold-mining on the Gold Coast. It was at first proposed to impose a royalty on the gross value of the minerals gotten, and in two special agreements, which were made with the Ashanti Gold Fields Corporation and the Castle Gold Exploration Syndicate respectively, before the enactment of the Gold Coast Concessions Ordinance, 1900, this course was adopted. Upon further consideration, however, Mr. Chamberlain came to the conclusion that a royalty or tax on output would be unfair in its incidence, and when the Ordinance of 1900 was passed a tax of 5 per cent. on profits was imposed in place of the royalty, which, in the case of the Ashanti Gold Fields Corporation, had been fixed at 5 per cent., and in that of the Castle Gold Exploration Syndicate at $2\frac{1}{2}$ per cent. on the gross value of the minerals gotten.[1]

9. In the case of Northern Nigeria, it is necessary to impose a royalty in order that the profit derived from it may be divided equally between the Company and the Government, unless the Company should be willing to accept a share of the profit derived from a tax on profits instead of a royalty, in which case, of course, the Company's share would be less than one-half. But, as a preliminary to any such arrangement with the Company, the amount of the royalty to be imposed under the Treasury Minute of the 30th of June, 1899, must be settled.

10. Mr. Chamberlain is of opinion that high royalties are not compatible with the development of the mining industry, as royalties are unequal in their incidence, and press most heavily on the mines

[1] See above, no. 16, pp. 391–4.

which are poorest, and in which the working expenses are consequently heaviest. He is not prepared, therefore, to impose a higher royalty than 2 per cent. on the gross value of the minerals gotten. He does not suppose that anything much higher than that can have been contemplated by the Company when the agreement embodied in the Treasury Minute of 30th June, 1899, was made; and under the terms of the letter of the 1st July, 1899, the Company will also have half the profit from sales or the issue of licences.

11. If the Company understand that the Government will decline in any case to impose more than a moderate royalty, such as 2 per cent., it should not be difficult to come to an arrangement with them, under which the Government would agree to impose a tax on profits instead of a royalty, and to pay to the Company a certain proportion of the profit from such a tax.

12. It is not proposed that any attempt should be made to alter the arrangement under which the Company are entitled to one-half of any profit derived from the sale of mines or the issue of licences in connexion with the working of minerals, but, as the Company are only entitled to one-half of the profit in connexion 'with the working of minerals,' it is presumed that the Government would keep the whole of any profit derived from the issue of licences to prospect as distinguished from licences to mine.

13. I am to call special attention to the term 'profit', which is used in the Treasury letter of the 1st of July, 1899, but not in the Treasury Minute of the 30th of June, in which the word used is 'receipts.' It is presumed that the Government will be entitled to deduct from the proceeds of royalties, sales, or licences, any charges of Government which have been incurred or made necessary by the working of the mines, and that the balance only will have to be shared with the Company. These charges would include such items as the expenses of sending Government officers to make arrangements with the native rulers with regard to the opening of mines, the cost of special police or soldiers to guard the miners, and of assessing and collecting the taxes, and the salaries, &c., of a Mining Department, if one should be instituted.

14. If the Lords Commissioners concur in the views expressed in this letter, Mr. Chamberlain would propose to explain to the Company, that, while the Government are prepared to impose both a moderate royalty and a tax on profits, in which case the Company would receive one-half of the profit from the royalty, but no part of the profit from the tax, they consider that it would be much more convenient to all concerned, and better calculated to promote the development of the industry, that one tax only should be imposed, namely, a tax on profits, and that of the profits derived from that tax the Company should receive a proportion, but not so much as one-half.

15. With regard to the rate at which the tax on profits should be levied, I am to explain that the circumstances in Northern Nigeria differ from those on the Gold Coast. The right to minerals on the Gold Coast is vested in the natives, and all persons engaging in mining have to pay rents to the native chiefs in addition to the taxation imposed by the Government. In Northern Nigeria, on the contrary, it is claimed that all mineral rights are vested in the Government in virtue of treaties, which were concluded by the Royal Niger Company, and the benefit of which was transferred to the Government on the revocation of the Company's Charter. The Government is, therefore, in a position to impose higher taxation on the mining industry in Northern Nigeria than on the Gold Coast, and it is proposed that the tax on profits to be imposed in Northern Nigeria should be a graduated one, beginning at $2\frac{1}{2}$ per cent. on the net profits, when these exceed 5 per cent., but are under 10 per cent., and going up to 50 per cent. (one-half) when the net profits exceed 100 per cent. The Government would, however, be under no obligation either to the Company or to the mining industry, not to reduce or raise the tax, but the scale would be open to revision from time to time, as in the case of any other tax, if circumstances made it desirable.

29

GOVERNOR M. NATHAN TO JOSEPH CHAMBERLAIN: GOLD COAST AGRICULTURE, 17 MARCH 1902[1]

. . . 2. I HAVE already explained to you in my despatch, No. 594, dated December 21st, 1901, the reasons for starting the *cocoa nut* plantation at Christiansborg, which so far promises well.

3. The report of the Curator on the *rubber* trees grown in the gardens at Aburi is satisfactory, and it seems possible that at some future time, when the available labour of the country is not mainly required in connection with the mining industry and with public works for its development, large rubber plantations properly managed under European supervision may take the place of the scattered wild trees and vines in producing this staple for the European markets. The loss of a great part of the area from which rubber from these trees formerly came to Gold Coast ports, the destruction of many trees in the remaining part by injudicious treatment, and the small profits to be gained by bringing rubber to the coast compared to those that accrue from connection with the gold mines of the Colony

[1] C.O. 879/69, no. 661.

have temporarily reduced the export of rubber from the Gold Coast to a relatively small amount, as will be seen from the annexed statement.

4. In spite of the fairly encouraging reports on the *fruits* sent to England from Aburi, I am doubtful whether the coarse shaddock and somewhat insipid grape fruit would ever be largely consumed in Europe. I see no reason why bananas from the Gold Coast should be able to compete with the same fruit grown under equally favourable conditions in countries to which European markets are more easily accessible.

5. The *cocoa* industry, which has grown in a short time to such considerable dimensions, is threatened with a fate similar to that which a few years ago caused the coffee farms that had been made in the Eastern part of the Colony to go out of cultivation. The natives are not satisfied with the price they get, and the merchants say that this price is the biggest they can pay consistent with getting a small profit from the transaction. I annex, with regard to this serious matter, copies of two reports from the Curator, dated the 30th January and the 6th March of this year, dealing with the complaints of the growers in Akwapim and Krobo, and of a letter in which the first of these reports was sent to the Accra Chamber of Commerce for their remarks. These have not yet been received. I suggest that these communications should be sent to the Liverpool Chamber of Commerce for their views. I am disinclined to revert to the former system so strongly objected to at the time by the West African Trade Association, and described in paragraph 33 of the Report on the Blue Book for 1898, of Government advancing money on the produce to the growers, selling it in England, and then paying to the growers the balance of the receipts after deducting expenses. It is in principle unsound for the Government to endeavour to regulate prices by underbuying the merchants, who may be assumed to have interests in the industry being maintained in the future as well as in making profits in the present. At the same time I realize that if the cocoa industry once dies away it will probably be many years before it could be reintroduced, and that in these circumstances exceptional action by the Government may be justified to avert what may really be called an agricultural calamity to the Colony. Before taking such action I should like, however, to have the views of the Liverpool West African merchants in the matter. No doubt the best and most legitimate course for the Government to pursue to assist the cocoa industry would be by the early construction of the Accra–Kpong Railway, which, passing through the principal cocoa-growing districts, would lessen the cost to the natives of bringing their produce to market, and so increase their profits without diminishing those of the merchants. This railway, with the harbour works at Accra, which is

the complement to it, and the Accra Water Supply Works, which will be essential when the Railway brings more people to the town, will cost not much under three-quarters of a million sterling. Such an expenditure could, no doubt, be faced, but if the works were entered upon at once, it could not but be to the detriment of the mining interests, as a large part of the available labour in the Colony would be deflected from the Sekondi–Kumasi Railway and other enterprises in the West and centre.

6. There appears to be no doubt that valuable *fibres* could be grown in the Colony. The only questions are whether it would be profitable to grow them, and if so, who will do it. With regard to the first point it seems very doubtful whether any large profits are to be made on products requiring much cultivation or local preparation. I have given my reasons for this view at length in my despatch, No. 562, dated the 26th November last, which dealt specially with the cultivation of cotton. With regard to the second point the mercantile firms in West Africa adhere to the general principle of leaving the cultivation, collection, and preparation of products to the natives, and making what profit they can on their disposal in the European market. This principle answered well in the old times, when the producing areas were unrestricted by foreign neighbours, and when labour was largely unpaid for, and competition for it not so keen. The native now looks for high profits and quick returns, and if he cannot get these by cultivating the soil or collecting its produce he will go as a labourer or do nothing. If the cocoa industry fails for the reasons already indicated it will be very difficult to get the natives to take up any new one, such as fibre planting on a large scale. Possibly the best solution of the question of increasing the agricultural resources of this Colony in the future is for the Government, while continuing to do all it can to encourage native enterprise by the distribution and sale of industrial plants and seeds to native growers and to missionaries to expend annually sums of money in taking up and planting waste lands with economic plants, eventually either selling the farms or itself shipping and disposing of the produce. A start in this direction has been made in the Christianborg Cocoanut plantation, and I shall be prepared if you approve, and if the financial condition of the Colony at the time justifies it, to start some other large Government plantation for fibre, rubber, or cotton, in 1903 . . . .

30

JOSEPH CHAMBERLAIN TO HIGH COMMISSIONER SIR RALPH MOOR: NIGERIAN MINING REGULATIONS, 26 AUGUST 1902[1]

I HAVE the honour to acknowledge the receipt of your confidential despatch, No. 11, of the 30th of May, and of your telegram, No. 46, of the 27th of June.

2. I am advised that Proclamation No. 1. of 1900 does not give the High Commissioner power to make regulations with regard to prospecting for minerals and mining. It would be possible to regard the proposed regulations as the conditions under which the High Commissioner will give his consent to the holding of land from a native; but this would not be wholly satisfactory and might lead to difficulties in the enforcement of penalties. I consider it far preferable, therefore, to enact a fresh Proclamation empowering the High Commissioner to prescribe by regulations the terms and conditions on which land may, with the consent of the High Commissioner, be acquired from natives by persons other than natives for the purposes of prospecting for minerals or mineral products or of mining for the same. All regulations should then be issued under this Proclamation.

3. I have considered the draft regulations enclosed in your despatch, and approve generally of them, except as regards the limits imposed for the area of concessions in paragraphs 19 and 20. In the 11th paragraph of my confidential despatch of the 23rd of January, I stated that I should not object to promising to take up on behalf of Messrs Lake and Currie's clients concessions recommended by them up to a total area of 100 square miles; but that was only intended in connexion with the special circumstances of the case in question. Apart from that case, I consider that five square miles is an ample maximum limit for a single mining concession, and 20 square miles for the aggregate area which may be held by any one individual or syndicate. These are the limits which I have approved in the case of Northern Nigeria, as you will see from section 10 of the Northern Nigeria Minerals Proclamation, 1902, a copy of which is enclosed. When minerals of the kinds prospected for have been found within ten miles of the area, the corresponding limits should be one and three squares respectively. I regard it as very undesirable to give preferential treatment to syndicates in the form of increased areas of mining concessions, as such a course would tend to encourage speculative formation of subsidiary companies of the kind which has done so much mischief in the early days of other mining markets.

[1] C.O. 879/67, no. 654.

4. I observe that you propose to make no charge for prospecting licenses. In Northern Nigeria, as you will see on reference to the Proclamation, two kinds of prospecting licenses, general and exclusive, the cost of the former being nominal, while a charge is made for the latter at the rate of £1 per square mile per annum. I gather that you do not propose to issue exclusive licenses at all. There is, however, much to be said in favour of them, not only as supplying an additional source of revenue, but also as encouraging the right kind of persons to prospect. If general licenses are freely issued, and no exclusive licenses are given, there may be a rush of all sorts of prospectors, and the sounder concerns may hold aloof, while they might be more likely to come in if they were able to secure, even by a comparatively large payment, an area within which they could prospect at leisure undisturbed by adventurer competitors. If, however, you are convinced that the interests of Southern Nigeria will be better served by the system you propose, I do not wish to press this point upon you.

5. The draft regulations are entitled 'Regulations regarding prospecting for minerals or mineral products in Southern Nigeria'; but as they also deal with concessions for mining and working the minerals, the title is not quite complete.

6. In the 4th paragraph of the 'Memorandum of terms for Government negotiations,' which forms the second enclosure to your despatch, the term 'royalty', is used to denote the tax on profits payable under the regulations. The term has a special meaning in connexion with mining, and, for reasons connected with certain correspondence with the Niger Company in reference to Northern Nigeria, it is desirable to avoid its use in the sense of a tax on profits. . . .

31

THE LONDON CHAMBER OF COMMERCE TO THE COLONIAL OFFICE: GOLD COAST AGRICULTURE, 16 JANUARY 1903[1]

YOUR letter of the 11th June last (13583/1902), together with copy of correspondence received from the Governor of the Gold Coast on the subject of cocoa cultivation in that Colony, has been circulated to all the members of the West African Section of this Chamber, and the replies received have been carefully considered by a Special Committee of the Section, nominated for that purpose, by whom I

---

[1] C.O. 879/69, no. 661.

am now instructed to forward you the following observations on the question at issue.

From enquiries made in the London market it appears that the lowest quotation for Gold Coast cocoa in January, 1902, was 54s. per hundredweight ex quay, Liverpool; while at the present time it is 48s. The lowest quotation for Trinidad cocoa, which stood at 70s. per hundredweight in January, 1902, has declined to 60s. at the present time, a drop of 10s. during the year.

The dropping quotations for cocoa from all districts are said to be due to the large general supplies, and although the consumption in Great Britain and the Continent has increased to the extent of ten per cent. in the last four years, the world's supply has apparently more than kept pace with the demand. It is impossible to compute at present what this season's crop will amount to, but about one thousand tons has already been marketed, and there is probably still a good deal to be forwarded. Whilst this crop is probably superior in condition to any previous one, it is by no means equal in condition to that from St. Thomé, Trinidad, or other places. It is suggested that more care should be taken in dealing with this produce before shipment, especially in the matter of fermentation and cleaning, so as to render it a more saleable article, and the committee consider that the natives could be easily shown how to do this, and thus improve the quality. The size of the grain will increase with the age of the trees, and so add to the market value.

At the present time, the bulk of the crop from the Gold Coast goes direct to Hamburg, as that has been found to be the better market for it, but a small proportion is still sent to Liverpool, and with an improvement in quality the demand will increase in this country and other markets.

The Section recognises that the Government did well to encourage the cocoa industry and to realise on behalf of the planters the first parcels shipped. The production, however, is now of such magnitude that in the natural course of supply and demand the planters can depend upon realising a proper price for their produce. It has been pointed out that if, instead of selling through middlemen, the natives brought their crop direct to the factories of the English merchants, they would save the middlemen's commission, and so obtain higher prices for their produce.

32

C. P. LUCAS (COLONIAL OFFICE) TO THE NIGER COMPANY, LIMITED: MINING ROYALTIES, 14 APRIL 1903[1]

WITH reference to your letter of the 24th of March and previous correspondence relating to the agreement between the Royal Niger Company and Her late Majesty's Government on the subject of royalties on minerals in Northern Nigeria, I am directed by Mr. Secretary Chamberlain to inform you that, upon further consideration with the Lords Commissioners of the Treasury, and after consulting the Law Officers of the Crown, he is satisfied that, although the wording of the Treasury Minute of the 30th of June, 1899, and of the Treasury letter of the 1st of July, 1899, is not free from doubt, the intention both of the then Chancellor of the Exchequer and of the Governor of the Royal Niger Company was that the Company should receive one half of the revenue derived from the mining industry by the imposition of (1) a royalty or percentage on the gross value of the minerals gotten and exported as provided by the Treasury Minute, or (2) of a tax on profits or (3) of fees for the granting of licences to prospect or mine, and that this share should be paid to the Company without deduction of any charges or expenses incurred by the Government for protection, or otherwise, on behalf of the mines and the persons prospecting for or working the minerals.

2. I am accordingly to state that the High Commissioner will be instructed to pay over to the Company one half of the fees received for licences to prospect which have been or may hereafter be granted under the provisions of the Minerals Proclamation, 1902, and that it is not proposed to impose any royalty or percentage on the gross value of minerals gotten, but that a tax or percentage will be levied (as contemplated in Section 19 of the Minerals Proclamation) 'on the annual amount of all profits made on the capital employed in or about the exercise of the rights conferred by such licence,' i.e. by a licence to mine; and that Mr. Chamberlain will be prepared to consider with the Company what the amount of this tax or percentage should be.

---

[1] C.O. 879/76, no. 701. The Company suggested a reduced scale of tax, but the Treasury would not agree. The level was kept at 5 per cent.

33

SIR RALPH MOOR TO THE
COLONIAL OFFICE: NIGERIAN
MINING SURVEY, 30 JUNE 1903[1]

I HAVE the honour to forward enclosed copy of proposals prepared by Professor Dunstan, after consulting with me, for a mineral survey of Southern Nigeria—with which it is suggested to include a systematic botany survey for possible economic vegetable products now undeveloped.

2. The question of a mineral survey has already been raised on previous papers and I am strongly in favour of its being at once undertaken. The practical utility of such work in developing the resources of the territories as expeditiously as possible is self-evident and it is in my opinion one of the obvious duties of the Local Government to undertake it. From past experience it is clear that no advance in this direction is likely to be made by enterprise, or rather the want of enterprise, of commercial firms having interests locally, and the information obtained from such a survey will very probably result in the establishment of fresh industries which will considerably augment the revenues of the Administration. On the other hand, the knowledge obtained by it will probably enable the Government to effect considerable savings in public works and perhaps other directions which will more than compensate the cost. Take, for instance, the heavy expense in all building operations now experienced owing to the want of lime for making mortar, which would be minimised by the discovery of a good limestone. The saving which would result from this discovery alone will cover probably the entire expense of the survey during its actual progress, not to mention the saving that will result in future years.

3. The scheme proposed in Professor Dunstan's minute[2] is, in my opinion, a thoroughly practical one, and such as is likely to give sound and valuable results. The question of expense is, as in all such matters, a serious one, but the approximate figures of revenue and expenditure for 1902–3, which I have received by mail just in, show that ample funds are available.

The figures are:

Revenue, approximate, 1902–3 . . £441,500
Expenditure, approx., 1902–3 . . 467,000

as against figures shown in estimates, 1902–3:

[1] C.O. 879/67, no. 654. Approved in C.O. to Dunstan, 11 September 1903. (*Sir*) *Wyndham R. Dunstan*, Chemist and Director of the Imperial Institute, 1903–24.
[2] Encl. Dunstan, Memorandum, 24 June 1903.

Revenue, estimated, 1902–3   .   .   £400,000
Expenditure, estimated 1902–3 .   .   449,613

The approximate figures which may be taken as accurate show, therefore, that the financial position is better than estimated by about £24,500, so that on the 31st March last the excess of assets over liabilities amounted to, approximately, £153,000. It must be borne in mind that the expenditure in excess of revenue during past year 1902–3 amounting to £25,000 was due to exceptional circumstances— payment of expenses properly chargeable to 1901–2 having, owing to peculiar circumstances, been made during the year 1902–3, and that taking the revenue and expenditure for the two years together the revenue has exceeded the expenditure by, approximately £5,000. The figures are:

Revenue 1901–2   .   .   .   .   £361,815
  „   1902–3   441,500
                                 Total
                                 £803,315
Expenditure 1901–2 .   .   .   .   £331,396
  „   1902–3   467,000
                                 Total
                                 £798,396

Also that though the expenditure for current year is shown in estimate at £432,075 as against estimated revenue of £400,000, there is now every reason to suppose that the results of the Aro expedition on the volume of trade are assured and permanent and that the revenue for current year will fully meet the expenditure, but should this not be the case there is an available surplus, exclusive of 'funds', amounting to, approximately, £16,000, of £137,000 to meet any deficit.

The annual cost of scheme proposed amounts to, approximately, £2,000. The work should be carried out in about three years, entailing a total expenditure of £6,000 which I consider may be reasonably undertaken, and there is every probability of the results justifying and giving a sound return for the outlay.

4. With regard to the economic botanist portion of the scheme which is merely suggested as a slight elaboration of it, I think perhaps the Inspector of Forests might first be consulted, as in discussing his work with him on his arrival shortly before I left West Africa it was understood that the forest economic products would come within the scope of his work, which would naturally include the work of a botanist to a great extent. At the same time I am inclined to think that the services of an economic botanist would be exceedingly valuable

and probably the Inspector of Forests will recommend the employment of such an officer in connection with the mineral survey scheme
when he is made fully acquainted with it.

34

H. M. HULL: MEMORANDUM, GOLD COAST AGRICULTURE, 20 APRIL 1905[1]

... FORTUNATELY, it is not the way of West African Governments
to be discouraged by the difficulties which have to be faced daily
when inducing the natives to regard matters from a different point
of view from that of themselves and their fathers before them, and
much has been, and is being, done to make them see the advantage of
re-afforesting their lands with different kinds of rubber-producing
trees.

With this object in view, the Director of Agriculture, in the year
1900, interviewed 13 chiefs in the neighbourhood of Aburi, when
plants and instruction were offered free of charge. As a result of this
6,544 rubber plants were distributed, although, in consequence of
promises which the chiefs gave at the time, arrangements were made
to supply some 50,000 more. Two years later, 15,000 of these young
trees were planted out on a plot of land some 35 acres in extent
acquired for the purpose, and adjoining the Aburi Botanic Gardens,
and this is now a thriving plantation.

In 1901 a plot in the same gardens was planted with 200 trees of
para rubber, and towards the end of 1902, the Director of Agriculture
visited Ceylon with the primary object of studying the cultivation of
this species, owing to its general superiority over other kinds.

In 1903, a second Botanical Station was opened at Tarkwa, in
Lower Wassaw; another will be opened in Ashanti next year, and it
is proposed to establish a 4th in the Central Province during 1907.
Six thousand seeds of para rubber have been sown at Tarkwa for the
purpose of distribution; the conditions of soil and climate being more
favourable to their growth there than in the Aburi Gardens. In the
course of the same year the Director of Agriculture was travelling for
132 days in Eastern and Western Krobo, in the Ada, Keta, Winneba,
Saltpond and Cape Coast Districts as well as in Eastern and Western
Akyem, interviewing and instructing the chiefs and people with a view
to encourage the cultivation of rubber, cocoa, cotton, &c.

An effort made by the District Commissioner to induce the inhabitants of the Winneba District to cultivate rubber failed through
their not possessing sufficient energy to fetch the plants from Aburi,

[1] C.O. 879/88, no. 785. Encl. in Rodgers to Lyttelton, 27 April 1905. *H. M. Hull*,
Secretary of Native Affairs.

and, although the Director of Agriculture shortly afterwards went through this district, with the same object in view, his efforts met with no greater success.

Whilst it has been attempted to improve the primitive agricultural methods employed by the farmers and planters in the Colony by practice and precept preached by the Director of Agriculture and his European Assistants, in particular, and by every travelling official, from the Governor downwards, it has also been sought to inculcate a taste for agriculture in the minds of the schoolboys, and to eradicate the prevailing belief that manual labour is derogatory to their dignity. Prizes for agriculture are offered annually to a large number of schools, and to the teachers employed there; a limited number of agricultural-paid apprentices are received at the Aburi Botanic Gardens, and notices have been published in the Government Gazette, and in the local papers, setting forth these prizes, and the Government appointments in the Department, for which natives are eligible.

Under the administration of the present Governor a great deal has been done to further encourage economic agriculture. His Excellency has visited many parts of the Colony in the past 12 months, and has never failed to impress on the chiefs through whose divisions he travelled, the great need which existed of increasing the areas under cultivation, and the acquiring of improved methods of agriculture by sending their young men to Aburi for instruction. Special instructions have been issued to provincial Commissioners to lose no opportunity of endeavouring to give an impetus to the planting of rubber, cotton, cocoa, kola, coffee, sugar-cane, &c., &c., by informing the chiefs and people in their provinces that the best kinds of seeds and plants available can be obtained on application to the Director of Agriculture at Aburi, with printed instructions in English and in the native languages as to the best methods of cultivating these and preparing the resultant produce for the market, and arrangements have also been made to hold an Agricultural Show at Accra in November next.

Fifty thousand para rubber seeds were recently disposed of before they had even arrived in the Colony; and the expected arrival of 100,000 more of these in September has been advertised in all the local papers. The suggestion made by the Secretary of the London Chamber of Commerce that cocoa growers should plant rubber trees to form shade for their young cocoa has long been anticipated, and is recommended in the printed instructions already referred to. Moreover, it has also been sought to induce the people to plant up their disused vegetable farms with similar trees. It will, however, be understood from what has been written in the early part of this statement, that the native planter will not devote trouble, money, and time to rubber from which he cannot hope to obtain any return for some 10 years when the same energy spent in rearing cocoa, kola, and, perhaps, cotton, will give him a speedier and more constant means of acquiring wealth.

35

W. H. JOHNSON TO THE SECRETARY FOR NATIVE AFFAIRS: GOLD COAST AGRICULTURE, 14 SEPTEMBER 1905[1]

I HAVE the honour to inform you with reference to the subject of the correspondence mentioned in the margin that I held a meeting of farmers at Odumase on the 21st August, at Akropong on the 28th August, and at Aburi, on the 1st instant, and explained the measures which the Accra Chamber of Commerce is of opinion should be enacted for the purpose of improving the quality of cocoa and other agricultural and forest products in the Gold Coast. Each meeting was well attended by the principal chiefs and farmers in the snrroundiug districts; 600 were present at Odumase, 300 at Akropong, and about 300 at Aburi. The subjects which I brought before them were keenly discussed, and I attach copy of letters embodying the opinions of the respective meetings.

2. The salient points in these letters are:

The cause for so much inferior cocoa being offered for sale is more due to the fact that one price is paid for all qualities than to the reasons put forward by the Accra Chamber of Commerce; and it is suggested as a remedy that improperly prepared cocoa should not be purchased. The introduction of laws to improve the cultivation and preparation of cocoa is calculated to do more harm than good. The compulsory sale of produce at fixed market places would prove of serious inconvenience to farmers unable to provide transport. The present system of brokerage was introduced by European merchants, and it is suggested that their native clerks are now commissioned to carry on this business.

3. In order to thoroughly appreciate the present condition of the Gold Coast cocoa industry, it is necessary to review the course of its history since its establishment. The cocoa tree appears to have been grown in the Gold Coast as early as 1857, but as it commences to bear fruit when four years old, and no cocoa was exported until 1885, when about 1 cwt. was shipped, it is assumed that most of the first plantations were neglected, and consequently vanished. Six years later (1891) only about half cwt. of cocoa was exported.

[1] C.O. 879/88, no. 785. Encl. in Rodgers to Lyttelton, 1 December 1905. *W. H. Johnson*, Director of Agriculture.

In 1890 the Government established the Botanic Garden at Aburi, and introduced large quantities of cocoa seeds both for planting experimental plots with a view to instruct the native farmers in the cultivation of this product, and to provide plants and seeds for distribution. It is reported that in the same year the Basel Mission imported cocoa pods to sell to the natives.

In 1898 the exports had risen to 3,698 cwts., but the quality of the produce was very inferior as the farmers were unacquainted with the curing of cocoa. Cocoa curing experiments, which cocoa farmers watched with much interest, had, however, been in progress at the Botanic Garden; the cured article realized 70s. per cwt. (whereas that prepared by the farmers sold for 50s. per cwt.), and was reported upon by London cocoa brokers as well prepared and similar to Ceylon cocoa. The Curator accordingly suggested to Government the advisability of his visiting the cocoa-growing districts for the purpose of instructing the farmers in the preparation and cultivation of cocoa, and provision was made to relieve him of his duties at Aburi for this purpose. A pamphlet giving simple instructions for the cultivation and preparation of this product was also prepared by him, and this was printed by Government and freely distributed.

At this period many of the farmers experienced great difficulties in finding a market for their produce, so arrangements were made for all cocoa cured in the manner recommended by the Curator to be accepted at the Botanic Garden and shipped to the English market by the Government on their behalf. This scheme was highly appreciated by the farmers, for they were able to dispose of their produce in a satisfactory manner, and it has proved one of the primary factors in developing this industry; moreover, they benefited by the opportunity thus afforded them to learn how cocoa was cultivated and prepared for market at the Botanic Garden. New plantations commenced to spring up in all directions, and within three years, i.e., 1901, the exports had increased to 19,602 cwts., or more than 500 per cent. The principal object for which the scheme had been instituted being attained, and various European merchants having complained that it was interfering with their business, it was suspended at the end of 1901.

Large sums of money were advanced by many of the European merchants to farmers and native traders or brokers who contracted to supply cocoa to the value of the advance. Many of these contracts are unfulfilled at the present day, while in other cases the contractors, not obtaining sufficient cocoa from their own trees, purchased the remainder regardless of quality, and at the lowest possible price. At the principal buying centres the merchants arranged amongst themselves to pay a fixed price for cocoa, and latterly, at several of the largest markets, such as Accra and Akuse, all cocoa bought is pooled and divided, *pro rata*, amongst the various merchants, thereby destroying all chance of competition. By these arrangements the inexperienced, or careless farmers, receive the same price for their produce as those who, by long experience and industry, are able to produce a far superior article. The inevitable result is endless dissatisfaction, especially as the market price has fallen considerably during recent years, and many farmers, who at one time took great pains in the preparation of their produce are now not only neglectful in this matter but in the management of their plantations.

4. I have spoken to several of the Basel Missionaries with regard to the suggestion that they should be appointed Inspectors of cocoa farms, and I learn that they would not be willing to act in this capacity.

5. The establishment of fixed produce markets would doubtlessly be of great convenience to both farmers and merchants, but at the same time a farmer should have the option of selling his produce elsewhere. Many farmers live three or four days' journey from any of the suggested market places, and some are not in a position to provide for the transport of their produce, and consequently would either be compelled to abandon their farms or illegally dispose of their produce to the various itinerant traders or brokers who swarm to the cocoa-growing districts during the cocoa harvest. I am dubious whether it would be just to tax and limit the profits of this class of traders any more than their European confrères, as the latter could employ their own clerks to explain to farmers the price and weight of cocoa brought for sale.

6. Legislation on the lines suggested by the Accra Chamber of Commerce is, in my opinion, more likely to injure than to improve present conditions, especially while the present system of purchase obtains, and should not be adopted until less drastic measures have been given a fair trial.

7. I have mentioned in previous reports that many of the farmers, and more particularly those who have commenced cocoa planting within the last few years, are ignorant of the proper methods to adopt in the cultivation and preparation of cocoa, and I submit that it would materially improve the present condition of cocoa and other agricultural industries in the Colony if provision were made for agricultural instructors to visit the different agricultural districts for the purpose of advising farmers.

36

C. A. BIRTWISTLE: REPORT,
NORTHERN NIGERIAN AGRICULTURE,
27 APRIL 1907[1]

. . . 22. CONCERNING cultivated crops for export other than cotton, I am inclined to think that ground-nuts will take second place, provided the trade is not strangled by over-high freights. All along the road from Ilorin to Kano, wherever there was a small market ground-nuts were, almost without exception, to be seen on sale, and the finest I noticed were being gathered so far north as Kudon, beyond Zaria. I am not quite certain of it, but believe I have read in some cotton publication that ground-nuts make a most suitable crop for growing in rotation with cotton, in which event one would think a free market for the nuts would be doubly appreciated. In addition to cotton and ground-nuts a considerably diversified range of crops is grown in the various districts along the route Ilorin to Kano, viz., guinea corn, millet, rice, 'Alkama' (a species of wheat), sweet potatoes, koko yams, cassava, sugar cane, onions, peppers, tobacco and dye plants, but I doubt if any, excepting perhaps peppers and dyestuffs, could be profitably exported to Europe, although doubtless a local trade per rail to Ilorin, Abeokuta, Ibadan and Lagos could be worked up in some of them, rice in particular. The fine tobacco farms in the Katsena sub-province are worthy of mention, and one would think that, if properly cured, an important coast trade could be established. Strange to say, I saw no maize further north than Bida.

23. Although I believe that cotton will prove to be the principal 'down' freight for the proposed railway, this report would be incomplete without some reference to the prospective business in the produce of the shea tree, which is to be found in many parts of Northern Nigeria. Whilst it is an exaggeration to say that the tree abounds along the whole route of the suggested railway, there is no doubt that there are vast numbers of them on the road referred to, and that in course of time, given cheap transport, shipments of the shea nuts or 'butter' will figure largely in our export list. From the country below Ilorin up to so far north as Kano, one sees great numbers of these trees in many of the districts traversed, which, however, away from the river, are contributing nothing to the trade of the Protectorate, and even near the Niger very little owing to the lack of European competition. So far north as between Zaria and Kano, or, to be more exact, between Kudon and Karia, there is a fine belt of shea, and

---

[1] C.O. 879/93, no. 845. *C. A. Birtwistle*, Commercial Intelligence Officer for Southern Nigeria.

from the number of blossoms when I passed (February, 1907), I conclude that the trees in that part must be extraordinarily prolific. One point struck me in travelling through the length of the Zaria province (where many of the shea trees are at present stunted, owing presumably to the annual bush fires underneath), namely, that when this district is being repopulated and farm clearings made, it should be rendered illegal to cut down the shea tree, which in course of time will, I am certain, be a valuable asset to the farmers, and a source of much revenue to the railway . . .

37

HIGH COMMISSIONER E. P. C. GIROUARD: MEMORANDA ON LAND TENURE, NORTHERN NIGERIA, 2 NOVEMBER 1907[1]

IV.—Conclusions.

1. FROM the reports which have been rendered as to the conditions of land tenure both in the Pagan and Mohammedan States, there would appear to be little doubt on one most important point, and that is the non-existence in Northern Nigeria of any system approaching the English position as to land tenure, viz., the proprietary rights of individuals.

2. Moreover, it would appear that in the Mohammedan States a system of nationalisation does exist. Here, unlike India, there were no Zemindars, Taluqdars, or Rajahs claiming private or landlord's rights, but a species of fief holder resembling in position the original grantees of William the Conqueror, holders of estates by pleasure and at will, for which in the past they had to render certain services to the Crown, and notably to collect, on a percentage basis, the Crown Rents from the agricultural population. To-day the fief holders, not necessarily the persons who formerly occupied the positions, have become District Heads appointed by the State, frequently, but not necessarily, on the advice of the Emirs, and carrying on purely administrative functions as native administrators, amongst others the collection for Government of the rentals fixed on the farms held by the agriculturists. Nor is it to be assumed that the fief holders in former times occupied any different position with regard to the people. They certainly at times exercised arbitrary powers both as to confiscation and alienation of land, but such action was entirely subject to the approval of the reigning Emir, and indicated in no way a proprietary right in land on the part of the fief holder.

The agriculturists apparently held their land at pleasure, but were

[1] C.O. 879/98, no. 906.

ordinarily granted continuous occupation and the right of user unless they seriously misbehaved, or fell under the great displeasure of their ruler. In the taking up of new land, the custom obtained of what is called the 'buying' of a farm, amounting in reality to the grant of a licence to farm.

If the above general description of the condition of land tenure in the Mohammedan Provinces is accurate, there would appear to be no difficulty, and without change of legislation, in establishing the 'Economic' theory of land tenure. On one point I would desire as much further information as possible, and that is the law or custom of inheritance in land, which would appear to have a considerable bearing on the subject of the rights in land.

3. In the Pagan states the question of land tenure would not appear to be any less clearly defined. Leaving aside all idea of right by conquest, and dealing with it simply on the basis of the good of the peoples, it would appear to me, more particularly after consideration of the results which have accrued on the coast, that the legitimate and best trustee for the people in their dealings with aliens is the Governor of the Protectorate, acting for the King. There would, therefore, seem to be no reason why these lands, apparently held in patriarchal tenure, should be treated in a different manner to the lands held under the more progressive Mohammedan tenures.

4. Now, though there is no individual right in land, there is undoubtedly in existence a common claim as to village boundaries, embracing not only the agricultural lands in the occupation of individuals, but considerable areas outside the cultivated ground, these areas being utilised either for a change of soil after a farm has been tilled for some years, for pasturage, for the collection of sylvan produce, where it exists, and for the provision of construction materials or firewood. So long as the country does not witness European immigration, there will be no impediment to the maintenance of existing rights over these areas of so-called waste or forest land. With the advent of Europeans, and probably demands for the use of agricultural lands, the position will be otherwise. There would, however, appear to be no difficulty in dealing with the newcomers without any loss to the native population if the lands are to be considered as national. Should land be required for agricultural purposes, which was standing as waste or forest land, not bearing sylvan produce, a licence to farm might be granted to an applicant on a lease for a term of years subject to (1) the payment of Crown Rents after the lapse of three years, on a settlement extending over a period of years; (2) the right of Government in all minerals; (3) a reversionary right to Government of the land should it remain in an uncultivated condition on the expiry of the three years, or for a settled period in the duration of the lease. Should the land so acquired by a newcomer

contain sylvan produce, the licence to farm the land or exploit the natural products should be of higher value, and cover compensation to the village community for any mutually agreed deprivation of the present value of such sylvan produce, pasturage rights, &c.

5. If leases in perpetuity are unknown, and a landlord class does not exist, which certainly appears to be the case in the Mohammedan States of Northern Nigeria—if, in dealing with Pagan tribes, the issue is not confused by the importation of British law, tending to upset an appreciation of patriarchal systems which can even more readily assimilate an economic or people's system of tenure, and from which British Land Law is divorced by a thousand years of private rights, laws, and litigation—why introduce a system of tenure which modern nations are spending untold millions to bring more into accord with an economic system, securing to the nation for all time the full rental values of the land?

6. If lands were nationalised, and alienation in fee simple made impossible, they would, for the time being, be best described, in my opinion, as 'Native Lands,' the description 'National Lands,' which might suggest itself, being, to-day, for obvious reasons, a misnomer. As the native or national lands would include the requirements of their government, there would appear to be no necessity for the term 'Crown Lands.'

7. By a method such as the one outlined, or one analogous to it, the people could apparently secure (1) recognition and registration by the State of their rights of occupation; (2) through Government expenditure the full benefits of any rentals in land and rentals of any subsequent newcomers; (3) compensation for disturbance in any rights, and immunity from disturbance except by mutual agreement; (4) that as the leases fell in, succeeding generations would benefit by any rise in the value of the land due to the progress of society, all increases being retained in the hands of the State; (5) the exclusion of the land speculator and the usurer.

38

COLONIAL OFFICE: MEMORANDUM, GOLD COAST LAND CONCESSIONS, 22 NOVEMBER 1910[1]

. . . When Europeans first began to wish to acquire land—in any quantity—in the Gold Coast, about the year 1897, Sir William Maxwell, the then Governor, decided to pass an Ordinance by which all the land of the Colony should be vested in the Crown, as trustee

[1] C.O. 879/109, no. 977.

for the people—practically the settlement now made in Northern Nigeria.

There was infinite debate and correspondence over this proposed Ordinance, but eventually it was defeated, mainly because not only were the would-be concessionaires against it but so also was the native opinion in the Colony, at least all the opinion that was articulate, i.e. the native chiefs and native lawyers. In the face of this opposition Mr. Chamberlain felt obliged to approve the withdrawal of the Ordinance.

In its stead was substituted the Concessions Ordinance, No. 14 of 1900, which (with unimportant amendments) has governed, with certain exceptions, the grant of land by natives of the Gold Coast Colony ever since.

The Ordinance is of considerable length, but the main principles may be summarized as follows:—

(1) The land of the Colony is acknowledged to be the property of the Natives; the Crown claims no land in the Colony except what it has purchased or acquired for public purposes.[1]

(2) No grant of rights in or over land shall be valid unless its validity has been certified by the Supreme Court.

(3) The Court must satisfy itself that—

(a) The grant was made in writing;

(b) That the proper persons were parties to the concession and that they understood the terms of it;

(c) That it was not obtained by fraud, &c.;

(d) That it was not made without adequate consideration;

(e) That all the terms and conditions of the grant have been performed;

(f) *That the customary rights of natives are reasonably protected in respect of shifting cultivation, collection of firewood, and hunting and snaring game.*

(4) A concession cannot be for more than 99 years, or be of larger area than 5 square miles for mining or 20 square miles for other purposes.

These provisions seem very fair and reasonable, but their administration by the Supreme Court has, perhaps, not been wholly satisfactory, for the following reasons:—

(1) One, at least, of the judges has been lax in giving effect to the provisions.

(2) It is very difficult to ascertain who really has the right to give grants of the lands; the chiefs and heads of families may have only fiduciary rights. In the absence of a Doomsday Survey of

---

[1] 'This is assumed, not expressly stated in the Ordinance.' Note in text.

the Colony it is almost impossible for the judges to go behind the evidence brought before them by the chiefs who are anxious to sell their supposed rights. On this point *see* the memorandum by one of the Provincial Commissioners (No. 20727). It is a question of protecting the native common people, and especially their posterity, against their chiefs and the native lawyers.

(3) When the Ordinance was drawn up it was practically a question of mining concessions only (though the Ordinance included in its purview other concessions). Now, people are acquiring land for growing rubber and cocoa; and it is difficult to see how the native rights as to snaring game, shifting cultivation, &c., are to be protected on such concessions.

(4) The clause restricting area is readily evaded by people getting grants in different names and then amalgamating; nor is it easy to see a remedy.

The late Governor[1]—a man of great ability and experience— suggested (28754/10)—

(1) More rigid restriction of area.

(2) As to native customary rights; the standardizing of the rights which should be reserved to natives; and their enforcement by the District Commissioners.

(3) More stringent provisions as to forfeiture of concessions for non-working.

(4) Arrangements by which the rents, &c., paid by the concessionaires should be used for the benefit of the tribe and not pocketed by the native chiefs.

Another suggestion of value is that one of the Law Officers should attend all enquiries into concessions, and watch them in the general public interest.

Speaking generally, it seems . . . that the policy of granting concessions is one of degree.

It is certainly not desirable that any large proportion of the land of the Colony should pass into private lands, destroying the tribal system, and the authority of the chiefs, and reducing the natives to the position of day labourers. On the other hand, it is in the interests of all that a reasonable field should be offered for European enterprise.

The area of the Gold Coast is about 24,200 square miles, and population about a million. There should be room easily for five millions, so that there is plenty of land to spare at present.

According to the best information we have, the total area granted under the Concessions Ordinance in ten years is 970[2] square miles.

---

[1] Sir John P. Rodger.
[2] Acting Governor Bryan to C.O., 9 November 1910: C.O. 96/500.

This does not seem alarming, especially as the grants cannot be for more than 99 years, and the period included two booms. But the accuracy and meaning of these figures requires, and is receiving, further investigation.

39

GOVERNOR H. CLIFFORD TO LEWIS HARCOURT: GOLD COAST PALM OIL CONCESSIONS, 29 JANUARY 1913[1]

. . . 6. SINCE the abandonment of that Bill the Government has, in certain instances,—as, for example, in the case of the recent Forestry Ordinance, which, as you are aware, has not yet received the Royal Assent or come into operation—assumed the right of legislating in matters which affect, not the ownership, but the management of land. It has been maintained that the Government, being *in loco parentis*, owes it as a duty to the native population to take such steps as may be possible to prevent the land, which is the property of the people, from being wantonly injured through ignorance or carelessness. It is at least open to argument how far the assumption of such responsibility is compatible with the admission that all land is the property of the natives, since ownership, as ordinarily understood, would seem to carry with it the right to make such use of the land possessed as the owners may see fit. It is not, however, necessary to discuss this matter at length in the present connexion.

7. If, however, all land is to be recognized as the property of the natives, and if Government is to restrict its interference with land to such regulation of its management as may be dictated by a higher appreciation of the common interest than is possessed by the native land-owners, I can see no justification for introducing legislation one of the effects of which will be to prohibit native land-owners from adopting improved methods for treating their own produce. Yet such, I submit, is the nature of the Palm Oil Bill now before the Legislative Council.

8. Section 3 of the Bill will give to the Governor of this Colony power to grant to any person over an extensive area and for a period not exceeding twenty-one years 'the exclusive right to construct and work mills to be operated by mechanical power for expressing or extracting oil from the pericarp of palm fruits.' The ownership of the

[1] C.O. 879/116, no. 1023. (*Sir*) *Hugh Clifford*, Governor of the Gold Coast 1912–19; Governor of Nigeria, 1919–25. The Sierra Leone Bill approving concessions was passed, 28 February 1913; on the Gold Coast, Unofficial Members voted against a similar Bill, 4 July 1913, but the C.O. allowed it to stand.

palms is not in dispute: they are the property of the native inhabitants. Concessionaires who have obtained exclusive rights under this section will naturally select for their operations districts where these palms are now growing in abundance; and the effect of this Bill, should it become law, will be to prohibit the owners of these palm-trees, during a period which may extend to twenty-one years, from employing mechanical power for the extraction of oil from the pericarp yielded by their own trees.

9. It may be maintained that the natives of the palm-bearing districts of this Colony will not in the near future be in a position to erect such machinery on their own account, and this may conceivably be true. No one, however, can foresee with certainty what the next few years may bring. It is impossible that efficient and comparatively cheap machines for the purpose may ere long be put upon the market, and prove to be within the means of a single native palmland owner, or of a combination of such owners. The growing wealth of the native population, consequent upon the profits now being made from cocoa, renders it necessary to recognize that such a possibility exists; but if exclusive rights to erect and work machinery for extracting oil from the pericarp is conferred upon any person for a period of one-and-twenty years the native land-owner will, during that term, be definitely prohibited from working his property to the best advantage, even though he be able and willing to expend the necessary money on machinery.

10. To amend Section 3, however, so as to give to the concession holder exclusive rights as against rival European capitalists only would not, I think, be possible, and would, in any event, be likely to have no practical effect, as a European competitor would probably experience little difficulty in evading such a provision with the aid of native land-owners. In these circumstances, the question resolves itself into whether or no the Government of this Colony can grant to any person exclusive rights to employ the most efficient means of utilizing the produce of palm plantations which belong neither to Government nor to the person seeking these exclusive rights.

11. It appears to me that in the answer which is to be given to this question a principle of grave moment is involved, and that, by comparison, the practical considerations touched upon in paragraph 9 of this despatch may be regarded as of minor importance. I venture, moreover, to doubt whether legislation the effect of which—at any rate in theory, and quite conceivably in practice—will be to prohibit the owners of land and of crops growing thereon from employing the most economical methods of extracting their produce during the space of two decades has ever been approved in any other British Colony.

12. To pass such legislation would, I submit, constitute a serious

encroachment upon the rights of the natives, and as this aspect of the matter does not seem hitherto to have received consideration, and as it was placed before the Legislative Council with much force and logic by the Honourable Mr. Grey, and was endorsed by the Honourable Mr. Hutton-Mills and Chief Mate Kole, I have felt it to be my duty to represent it fully to you, and to delay further action on the Bill until I receive your reply to this despatch. In the event of it being held that the objection now raised to the principle of the Bill is not valid, I shall be greatly obliged if you will instruct me as to the line of argument whereby it is to be met.

40

LEWIS HARCOURT TO GOVERNOR H. CLIFFORD: GOLD COAST PALM OIL CONCESSIONS, 3 MARCH 1913[1]

I HAVE the honour to acknowledge the receipt of your Confidential despatch of the 29th of January, in which you enunciate certain objections to the principle embodied in the draft Palm Oil Ordinance, which, you state, are shared by some of the Unofficial Members of the Legislative Council.

2. It does not seem to me at all probable that any individual native will, in the near future, have sufficient palm fruit of his own growing to render it economically advisable (even if he could obtain sufficient capital) to establish a factory operated by mechanical power for the treatment of his fruit. There is nothing to prevent a native or any one else working a hand mill within the exclusive area.

3. The position, as I understand it, is that there are large quantities of palm fruit growing in scattered places, more or less difficult of access, which are allowed to be wasted owing to the difficulty of transport: while even those which are gathered do not yield as large or as valuable a product as they might, owing to the imperfect methods of extraction in use. In this connexion, I may refer you to page 384 of Volume VII of the Bulletin of the Imperial Institute, where it is stated: 'The preparation of palm oil as practised by the natives throughout West Africa is managed in a crude and wasteful manner—133 lbs. of fruit containing 30 lbs. of oil yielded in practice 8·85, equivalent to a loss of two-thirds of the oil'—and to page 388, where the writer states the oil 'is generally very rancid when it reaches the European market.'

4. Messrs. Lever have proposed to remedy this state of affairs by establishing a central factory, and by improving the means of conveyance of the fruit to the factory. The only special privilege which they

[1] C.O. 879/116, no. 1023.

are now asking is that, in view of the large amount of capital required for the enterprise, no other factory shall be established within this area for 21 years; and, in spite of the criticism to which the proposed grant has been subjected no one has come forward with a proposal to erect a similar factory without such a privilege.

5. It is true, as you observe, that no exactly similar legislation, so far as I am aware, has been passed in any other British Colony: but the reason is that similar conditions have not arisen, and I need not remind you that in the case of excise legislation and private railway legislation the right of individuals to deal with their own produce and their land has been, for special reasons, no doubt, even more seriously curtailed than by the proposed Ordinance. The principle of the Ordinance seems to me sufficiently analogous to that of the patent laws: by which in all civilized countries, the inventors of improved methods of manufacture are rewarded by a limited monopoly of the use of their inventions.

6. With regard to the natives, I would observe that there will be no compulsion on them to grant the site for the factory or other rights and wayleaves which will be necessary to give to Messrs. Lever's scheme, if they are advised that their interests will be prejudiced by such action; nor, again, is there anything in the Ordinance to prevent the natives in a palm oil area combining together to obtain a grant under the provisions of the Ordinance.

7. I trust that, in view of these considerations, you will be able to induce the Unofficial Members to reconsider their opposition to the Ordinance; but, if not, it must be carried by the use of the official vote, as I cannot withdraw from my pledge to Messrs. Lever to pass the Ordinance substantially in the form which it has now taken.

41

GOVERNOR H. CLIFFORD TO LEWIS HARCOURT: GOLD COAST PALM OIL CONCESSIONS, 24 MARCH 1913[1]

[In Sierra Leone tribal authorities are required to assent first to palm oil concessions. The Gold Coast Bill has been amended in this sense.]

... 18. THE effect of the amendment is to make the Clause read as follows:—

'Subject as in this Ordinance provided it shall be lawful for the Governor *with the consent of the owners of the land* to grant to any person within such area not exceeding a circle with a ten mile radius and for such period not exceeding twenty-one years from the

[1] C.O. 879/116, no. 1023.

date of the grant and upon such terms and subject to such conditions as the Governor may think fit the exclusive right to construct and work mills to be operated by mechanical power for expressing or extracting oil from the pericarp of palm fruits; provided that no such grant shall be made in respect of any area as aforesaid which includes a town containing more than 10,000 inhabitants.

'The Governor may at the expiration of any such grant renew the same for such period not exceeding twenty-one years from the date of renewal and upon such terms and subject to such conditions as he may think fit.

'No exclusive right or renewal thereof under this section shall be granted by the Governor unless the terms of such exclusive right or renewal shall have been published in the *Gazette* at least three months prior to ratification.'

19. The rejection of this proposed amendment by the use of the official vote, summarily and without full consideration, appeared to me to be impossible, in spite of the instructions contained in the concluding paragraph of your despatch under reply;[1] and I accordingly allowed this Clause to stand over to be dealt with at a subsequent sitting of the Committee.

20. I fully realize the grave responsibility which, by adopting this action, I individually incurred: but I must very respectfully submit that the peremptory use of the official vote on this occasion, and in the circumstances described, would be calculated to result in very serious consequences. It appeared to me to be my duty, both to you and to the people of this Colony, to afford sufficient time for careful consideration of all that our action would entail before committing the Government to a course from which retreat would be undignified, if not impossible.

21. The grave principle which, it appears to me, is in danger of being violated by this Bill is placed before us by means of this amendment in a concrete, and no longer in merely an academical, form. Konor Mate Kole[2] asks, with the support of his brother Unofficial Members that the exclusive right to extract oil from the pericarp of the palm (by the only means which, in the near future, may continue to be remunerative) be not granted to persons who have at present no rights over the trees in question by the Governor, who is similarly situated, without the consent of the owners of the land, to whom these trees belong.

22. The request is, I would submit, at once modest and reasonable. It is in accordance with the principle which the Government of this

---

[1] Document 40.
[2] *Mate Kole*, Konor of Manya Krobo, Unofficial Member of Legislative Council.

Colony, by the direction of the then Secretary of State, adopted, and adhesion to which it has publicly proclaimed ever since Sir William Maxwell's Land Bill of 1897 was dropped. To refuse it entails an immediate and public abandonment of the position which the Government has taken up with regard to native rights in land, and, in justification of such action, I would submit, no argument touching the question of principle involved has, up to the present time, been brought forward by the Government . . .

42

LEWIS HARCOURT TO GOVERNOR H. CLIFFORD: GOLD COAST PALM OIL CONCESSIONS, 24 MAY 1913[1]

. . . MUCH of your despatch is devoted to the question of the interference by the provisions of the measure with the rights of private property. Such interference is not unknown where public interests are involved. I cannot but think that you take an exaggerated view of the extent of this interference. No right at present enjoyed will be interfered with, and the contingency of a wealthy and enterprising native within a protected area finding himself precluded from introducing competitive machinery is not one of practical politics.

You are aware that arrangements are already in progress for the establishment of depericarping mills in other palm-producing territories, and with protection far more effective than that proposed to be given on the Gold Coast. If the result of that should be, as it well may, such an increase of the production of these places as to cause a substantial fall in the price of palm oil, the result to the natives of the Gold Coast would be far more serious than any interference with the remotely possible exercise of private rights which you view with so much apprehension.

To remove, however, any objection to the measure on this ground, I am prepared to agree to the insertion in Clause 3 after the word 'Governor,' of the words 'if he is satisfied that the consent of the tribal authorities or a majority of them has been obtained.'

I do not find myself able to accept the amendment excluding trading stations from the prohibition against the creation of machinery within the area granted, as I imagine, though you afford me no guidance on the subject, that these stations are so numerous that their exclusion would render the Ordinance nugatory. I would, however, point out that ample notice of any application for an area is required by Clause 3, so that any person interested may make representations against any particular grant.

[1] C.O. 879/116, no. 1023.

I concur with you in thinking that amendments reducing the area of the grant to a radius of one mile and excluding towns with a population of more than 500 cannot be entertained, as they would destroy the effect of the Ordinance. I enclose a copy of correspondence with Messrs. Lever, from which it would appear that they do not object to a provision for securing the consent of the natives, but would regard the three amendments just specified as negativing the value of their proposed grant . . .

43

LEWIS HARCOURT TO GOVERNOR F. D. LUGARD: NIGERIAN PALM OIL CONCESSIONS, 18 AUGUST 1913[1]

. . . 3. You will observe that the requirements of the firm are stated, in their letter of the 21st of October, 1910, to be only 'that no other firm should be allowed to erect and establish machinery for the treatment of the whole fruit within twenty miles of our location.' In the letter from this Office of the 24th of February, 1911, I informed Messrs. Lever that I was prepared to authorize the Governor to grant the desired facilities within one area for a period of twenty years, subject to certain conditions:—(1) the 'radius' or distance within which similar machinery was not to be erected was reduced from twenty to five miles; (2) the site for the 'mills' was to be approved by the Colonial Government; (3) the prohibition to other firms was to apply to power machinery only, and (4) should the approved site be within five miles of an existing station of any European trading firm, that firm would not be debarred from establishing similar machinery within half a mile of its present premises.

4. In their letter of 20th June, 1911, Messrs. Lever expressed regret that their original proposal had not been approved, and the correspondence then ceased for some months. I may observe that the reference in this letter to Messrs. Lever's previous application of the 31st of October, 1908, must have been made in error, as that letter referred only to their application in respect of Sierra Leone, which was of a different character.

5. On the 9th of January, 1912, Messrs. Lever expressed their willingness to accept the conditions offered in the Colonial Office letter of the 24th of February, but asked that the 'radius' should be fixed at ten miles, and this was agreed to 'provided that a suitable area could be found.'

[1] Ibid. Lever Bros. had asked for a concession on the Cross River. This was refused by the Colonial Office in January 1914. The company had mills at Opobo and Apapa.

6. You will perceive from this summary of the correspondence that the requirements of the firm, quoted in paragraph 3 above, have not been modified, except that 'ten miles' has been substituted for 'twenty miles' as the distance from the site of the mills within which (under the conditions specified) machinery for the treatment of the whole fruit may not be installed.

7. It is evident, therefore, that, before taking any further steps in the matter, the site of the mills—without which the 'area' cannot exist—must first be determined and approved by the Government.

8. I do not propose to depart in any way from the agreement already arrived at with Messrs. Lever. The proposals contained in their letter to you of the 17th June, and illustrated by the map enclosed in your despatch of the 19th of that month, appear to involve a complete departure from that agreement. If the site of the mills is within the area shown on the map, considerable portions of the area must be more than ten miles from the mills, wherever they are situated. If, on the other hand, the mills are outside the area (as seems to be contemplated) Messrs. Lever would have no right to object if a similar mill were erected by another firm alongside their own, and as that firm would have equal rights of collecting fruit within the area it is difficult to see what advantage Messrs. Lever would obtain.

9. I entirely concur in your view that any agreements with chiefs which may be necessary to give effect to the arrangement with Messrs. Lever should be negotiated by Government officers, and no other system was ever contemplated by me. The site for the mills would be acquired in the usual way under the Native Lands Acquisition Ordinance, and in any agreements with chiefs within the ten mile radius the procedure laid down in that Ordinance should be followed as closely as possible.

10. Until the misunderstanding which appears to exist on the part of Messrs. Lever as to the interpretation of the agreement arrived at has been cleared up, it is unnecessary to consider the form which the agreement or agreements with the chiefs should take. I may mention, however, that it has been suggested that a simple way out of the difficulty would be for the Government to take power to forbid the erection of power machinery for the treatment of the whole fruit of the palm except under licence. Licence for erection at any point within ten miles of Messrs. Lever's mills would not be given, and the necessity for any agreements with the chiefs (except for the site of the mills under the Native Lands Acquisition Ordinance) would be obviated.

44

GOVERNOR E. M. MEREWETHER TO LEWIS HARCOURT: SIERRA LEONE PALM OIL CONCESSIONS, 6 JULY 1914[1]

. . . 6. As regards the four applications made by Mr. Milligan,[2] I have no objections to offer those mentioned in my despatch No. 268, of the 13th May, with regard to the applications of Mr. Ivor Bevan and the Sierra Leone Palm Oil Manufacturing Company. In the former case, the boundary of the area applied for must be moved to the northward, so as to exclude the area of 6,000 acres applied for by Copra Finance, Limited (Copra and Palm Oil Company, Limited), which they have now selected in preference to the other area applied for by them. In the latter case, the boundary must be moved so as to exclude Kambui Forest Reserve, or another area must be selected.

7. The establishment of manufacturing centres in the Northern Sherbro District, and the development of trade which will ensue, cannot fail to have a civilizing effect upon the people, and will, I believe, do more to check the activities and lessen the power of unlawful societies than any repressive measures. I am therefore of opinion that every encouragement should be given to persons and firms wishing to obtain planting concessions or grants of exclusive rights under the Palm Oil Ordinance, provided that you are satisfied of their *bona fides* and financial ability to carry out the undertaking.

8. I note that you consider it desirable to give applications for planting concessions preference over applications for grants of the nature contemplated in the Palm Oil Ordinance, and I fully concur in this view.

9. A notice to the four applications submitted by Mr. Milligan will be inserted in the Government *Gazette* after the expiration of a fortnight from this date.

[1] C.O. 879/116, no. 1023.
[2] *F. Milligan*, who had applied on behalf of the Peripalm Syndicate Ltd. Lever Bros. had a factory at Yoni which was transferred to a subsidiary, West African Oils, in 1913.

45

GOLD COAST LAND CONCESSIONS, 1900–1913[1]

Character and Extent of Alienation under the Concessions Ordinance.

... 157. BY successive returns furnished by the Gold Coast Administration in response to requests from this Committee, it transpires that in the first ten years of the operation of the Ordinance, *i.e.*, from 1900 to 1910, the native authorities of the Gold Coast alienated, according to notifications in the Gazette, 23,606 square miles of land (23,151 square miles for mining purposes and 455 square miles for 'agricultural and arboricultural purposes'). Within the same period the courts struck out concessions aggregating 8,673 square miles. From the end of 1910 to the end of 1913, a further 1,502 square miles have been alienated, a feature of these more recent alienations being that they are for the most part alienations of surface rights. It will thus be observed that of their own volition, and acting in ignorance—we must assume—of the character and extent of the public rights with which they were parting, in the vast majority of cases for one year only short of a century, the chiefs of the Gold Coast have in the past thirteen years alienated an area which actually exceeds the total area of the colony itself. This does not take into account the alienations to which they have consented in the last two or three years, and which have not been notified in the Government Gazettes . . .

... The position at the close of 1913 may therefore be summed up as follows:—

	Square Miles.
Total area of the Gold Coast	24,335
Total alienation of land by native authorities of the Gold Coast which have been notified in the Government Gazette from 1900 to 31st December 1913 . .	25,108
Total area of alienation struck out by the courts from 1900 to end of 1913 (Telegram 22nd April 1914) . .	10,279
Total area remaining alienated on 31st December 1913 .	14,829
Total area (being part of the last-mentioned area) whose alienation has been validated by the courts up to 31st December 1913 (Despatch 6th 1914) . . .	1,084

158. The situation set out above cannot be defended on any ground. The most serious feature, in our view which it connotes, is the failure of the Government to protect the present and future generations of natives in their public rights . . .

[1] C.O. 879/116, no. 1046. Cf. Kimble, *Political History of Ghana*, p. 21. The West African Lands Committee was appointed in 1912 and sat till 1914. The Report had no influence on land policy till after 1917.

V

STATISTICAL APPENDICES

1800–1914

TABLE I

Exports of British Goods and Manufactures to Western Africa: 1812–1854[1]

Declared and Real Values. £

	1812	*1813*[2]	*1814*	*1815*
Senegal	7,262	..	..	..
Sierra Leone (Gambia)	3,724	..	..	..
Western Coast of Africa	92,840	?	94,984	89,466

	1816	*1817*	*1818*	*1819*
Western Coast of Africa	98,637	123,907	158,399	122,956

	1820	*1821*	*1822*	*1823*
Western Coast of Africa	129,315	184,845	193,151	163,008

	1824	*1825*	*1826*	
Western Coast of Africa	156,518	183,123	120,556	

	1827[3]	*1828*	*1829*	*1830*
Senegal	718	nil	nil	nil
Gambia–Sierra Leone	75,454	62,099	85,699	87,143
Windward Coast	9,014	12,008	7,690	9,648
Gold Coast	22,413	41,985	46,961	52,888
Volta to Cape of Good Hope	47,743	75,358	103,851	102,442

	1831	*1832*	*1833*	*1834*
Western Coast of Africa	234,768	290,061	329,210	326,483

	1835	*1836*	*1837*	*1838*
Western Coast of Africa	292,540	467,186	312,938	413,354

	1839	*1840*	*1841*	*1842*
Western Coast of Africa	468,370	492,128	410,798	459,685

[1] Customs 8/1–79 (1812–54); *Accounts and Papers: Tables of Revenue Population and Trade . . . 1820–1852* (compiled by G. R. Porter (1820–44) and A. W. Fonblanque (1844–52) for the Board of Trade): 1840, Part X; *Tables of Trade and Navigation of the United Kingdom* (Annual Accounts from 1853), Customs and Excise Library. The Cape is excluded. 'Western Coast' includes British possessions.

[2] Customs records for 1813 'destroyed by fire': *Parl. Papers*, 1816, vii (506), Appendix 24, p. 219.

[3] See also *Parl. Papers*, 1842, xi (551), Part II, for tables of exports 1827–41, by area.

TABLE I *(cont.)*:

	1843	*1844*	*1845*	*1846*
Western Coast of Africa	590,609	458,414	532,028	421,620

	1847	*1848*		
Western Coast of Africa	518,420	571,022		

	1849	*1850*	*1851*	*1852*
Gambia	35,770	43,700	47,197	50,784
Sierra Leone	60,290	70,230	94,546	103,609
Gold Coast	134,591	87,871	107,653	47,566
Fernando Po	3,197	3,668	31,535	18,018
French Possessions	9,096	2,545	4,361	2,633
Western Africa[1]	377,425	433,960	373,642	313,748

	1853	*1854*		
Gambia	52,106	55,365		
Sierra Leone	126,192	93,042		
Gold Coast	55,862	117,419		
Fernando Po	49,478	46,115		
French Possessions	1,725	8,125		
Western Africa	617,764	646,868		

[1] i.e. all undesignated ports, mainly Volta to the Congo.

TABLE II

Exports of Foreign and Colonial Goods and Merchandise to Western Africa: 1809–1854[1]

Official Values: £

	1809	*1810*	*1811*	*1812*
Senegal	8,837	11,687	8,388	4,651
Sierra Leone	8,030	3,288	4,837	3,791
West Africa General	58,035	36,813	51,554	29,124

	1813[2]
Senegal	..
Sierra Leone	..
West Africa General	?

	1814	*1815*	*1816*	*1817*
Coast of Africa[3]	86,625	92,532	60,168	83,247

	1818	*1819*	*1820*	*1821*
Coast of Africa	105,972	84,634	113,367	139,055

	1822	*1823*	*1824*	*1825*
Coast of Africa	150,782	119,742	176,000	137,663

	1826	*1827*
Coast of Africa	82,222	121,549

	1828	*1829*	*1830*
Senegal	4,555	nil	nil
Gambia–Sierra Leone–Mesurada	71,617	94,047	60,113
Windward Coast	878	510	797
Gold Coast	26,867	23,324	37,777
Volta–Cape of Good Hope	26,964	43,551	35,082

	1831	*1832*	*1833*
Western Coast of Africa	155,276	..	..
Senegal	..	1,749	nil
Gambia–Sierra Leone–Mesurada	..	64,402	66,065
Windward Coast	..	1,169	449
Gold Coast	..	39,598	37,834
Volta–Cape of Good Hope	..	53,916	75,258

	1834	*1835*	*1836*	*1837*
Senegal	175	914	1,234	190
Gambia–Sierra Leone–Mesurada	97,426	65,307	72,747	94,994
Windward Coast	736	nil	nil	566
Gold Goast	33,052	29,636	57,597	27,564
Volta–Cape of Good Hope	42,427	42,161	53,894	34,980

[1] Customs 10/1–45 (1809–54). And printed sources in Table I, p. 595, n. 1.
[2] See Table I, p. 595, n. 2.   [3] Western Africa including British possessions.

TABLE II (cont.):

	1838	1839	1840	1841
Senegal	93	303	262	29
Gambia–Sierra Leone– Mesurada	76,758	86,970	74,492	75,995
Windward Coast	1,156	1,135	458	nil
Gold Coast	37,413	28,170	36,238	29,462
Volta–Cape of Good Hope	60,516	75,994	114,423	118,541

	1842	1843	1844	1845
Senegal	858	1,446	nil	715
Gambia–Sierra Leone– Mesurada	71,415	83,582	86,500	93,771
Windward Coast	2,029	7,340	851	647
Gold Coast	22,561	48,777	33,621	42,949
Volta–Cape of Good Hope	127,450	178,937	161,191	170,200

	1846	1847	1848
Gambia	36,637	12,103	7,990
Sierra Leone	84,795	97,965	70,419
Gold Coast	34,626	29,674	31,085
Fernando Po	2,113	1,946	1,442
French Possessions	206	5,432	414
Western Africa[1]	143,753	188,659	186,491

	1849	1850	1851
Gambia	14,295	18,309	27,798
Sierra Leone	68,016	58,255	91,625
Gold Coast	51,894	33,691	50,248
Fernando Po	2,764	705	24,296
French Possessions	1,418	nil	173
Western Africa	197,072	189,100	193,161

	1852	1853	1854 (Real Values £)
Gambia	26,301	30,508	19,942
Sierra Leone	78,941	61,713	37,772
Gold Coast	18,416	23,234	17,466
Fernando Po	11,568	59,557	14,878
French Possessions	622	4,230	1,016
Western Africa	185,428	235,848	174,073

[1] i.e. all undesignated ports, mainly Volta to the Congo.

TABLE III

Exports of British and Foreign Merchandise and Manufactures from the United Kingdom to Western Africa: 1855–1914[1]

Total Declared or Real Values: £

	Total	(United Kingdom)	Total	(United Kingdom)
	1855		*1856*	
Gambia	76,062	(47,641)	65,205	(46,580)
Sierra Leone	177,000	(147,271)	198,456	(165,444)
Gold Coast	128,306	(111,182)	118,751	(93,445)
Fernando Po	54,527	(38,816)	17,806	(13,492)
French Possessions	11,380	(11,270)	5,463	(5,424)
Western Africa	1,059,658	(839,831)	890,416	(666,374)
	1857		*1858*	
Gambia	78,511	(55,576)	70,759	(49,398)
Sierra Leone	258,119	(223,495)	142,204	(119,395)
Gold Coast	114,364	(91,473)	105,906	(94,932)
Fernando Po	17,716	(10,816)	12,257	(10,765)
French Possessions	10,500	(10,187)	15,845	(13,353)
Western Africa	1,017,575	(766,517)	841,755	(667,287)
	1859		*1860*	
Gambia	59,747	(43,206)	41,994	(27,774)
Sierra Leone	184,963	(169,860)	238,793	(215,523)
Gold Coast	75,103	(65,905)	106,069	(97,069)
Fernando Po	6,858	(5,422)	24,574	(20,166)
French Possessions	10,891	(10,740)	877	(862)
Western Africa	906,091	(696,027)	1,145,434	(951,295)
	1861		*1862*	
Gambia	81,901	(56,872)	90,730	(52,537)
Sierra Leone	203,305	(180,065)	190,602	(170,354)
Gold Coast and Lagos	157,893	(144,194)	140,149	(126,728)
Fernando Po	15,049	(8,371)	17,802	(14,574)
Portuguese Possessions	20,833	(20,829)	28,551	(28,372)
French Possessions	4,017	(3,638)	11,389	(7,669)
Western Africa	1,076,452	(841,259)	1,146,955	(888,593)
	1863		*1864*	
Gambia	101,870	(69,037)	45,462	(28,200)
Sierra Leone	221,450	(178,726)	179,967	(158,978)
Gold Coast and Lagos	101,503	(80,849)	134,131	(85,718)
Fernando Po	32,314	(28,617)	19,005	(12,263)

[1] Customs 8/81–141 (1855–99); Customs 10/46–90; C.O. 442/2—Colonial Statistical Tables; *Trade and Navigation of the United Kingdom*: Annual Accounts, 1853–1914, Customs and Excise Library. Export values of United Kingdom produce and manufactures are given in parenthesis. Bullion is excluded from these totals.

TABLE III (*cont.*):

	Total	(*United Kingdom*)	Total	(*United Kingdom*)
		1863		*1864*
Portuguese Possessions	34,347	(34,162)	51,398	(47,949)
French Possessions	5,031	(3,517)	7,462	(7,234)
Western Africa	778,762	(590,111)	664,714	(498,516)
		1865		*1866*
Gambia	61,012	(43,949)	75,947	(51,268)
Sierra Leone	221,810	(187,316)	239,287	(210,475)
Gold Coast and Lagos	198,152	(171,704)	301,486	(271,832)
Fernando Po	11,208	(8,198)	14,500	(11,089)
Portuguese Possessions	76,819	(73,034)	57,297	(54,873)
French Possessions	11,134	(10,965)	11,045	(8,045)
Western Africa	747,056	(548,236)	676,454	(528,525)
		1867		*1868*
Gambia	107,095	(75,700)	89,522	(63,192)
Sierra Leone	254,987	(225,655)	250,893	(222,148)
Gold Coast and Lagos	362,342	(328,702)	376,209	(347,796)
Fernando Po	19,219	(15,253)	23,366	(17,279)
Portuguese Possessions	10,949	(6,811)	61,773	(59,033)
French Possessions	345	(313)	790	(700)
Western Africa	981,061	(794,073)	1,033,804	(827,068)
		1869		*1870*
Gambia	48,809	(33,620)	57,488	(40,465)
Sierra Leone	230,176	(198,029)	252,596	(217,612)
Gold Coast and Lagos	425,080	(392,254)	421,072	(401,429)
Fernando Po	20,896	(16,241)	23,012	(19,379)
Portuguese Possessions	136,184	(128,051)	138,351	(136,696)
Western Africa	880,983	(682,399)	1,024,954	(780,141)
		1871		*1872*
Gambia	59,067	(35,176)	65,651	(46,332)
Sierra Leone	232,055	(200,585)	332,916	(294,339)
Gold Coast and Lagos	477,168	(442,870)	446,612	(417,882)
Portuguese Possessions	113,536	(109,323)	134,882	(128,273)
Fernando Po	16,376	(13,970)	19,151	(16,806)
Western Africa	1,095,453	(896,360)	1,194,813	(941,132)
		1873		*1874*
Gambia and Sierra Leone	359,836	(315,276)	420,296	(372,860)
Gold Coast and Lagos	420,573	(386,310)	512,000	(480,228)
French Possessions	18,450	(18,297)	21,613	(17,965)
Portuguese Possessions	132,301	(128,484)	146,380	(143,872)
Fernando Po	30,324	(24,978)	16,491	(13,122)
Western Africa	1,237,410	(953,176)	1,030,405	(761,932)

	Total	(United Kingdom)[1]	Total	(United Kingdom)
		1875		*1876*
Gambia and Sierra Leone	327,928	(275,086)	249,366	(203,776)
Gold Coast and Lagos	524,604	(483,045)	554,083	(515,713)
French Possessions	19,641	(16,514)	19,882	(19,401)
Portuguese Possessions	86,075	(81,508)	115,279	(103,396)
Fernando Po	7,813	(4,373)	12,992	(8,825)
Western Africa	941,345	(692,418)	1,120,643	(867,360)
		1877		*1878*
Gambia and Sierra Leone	322,429	(281,962)	414,070	(360,742)
Gold Coast and Lagos	569,756	(528,316)	557,707	(511,618)
French Possessions	33,195	(28,254)	33,878	(29,055)
Portuguese Possessions	117,369	(112,590)	104,665	(100,818)
Fernando Po	15,047	(10,045)	9,093	(6,493)
Western Africa	1,310,883	(1,026,717)	1,285,145	(1,038,971)
		1879		*1880*
Gambia and Sierra Leone	371,025	(313,880)	388,654	(328,961)
Gold Coast and Lagos	475,330	(430,280)	502,223	(461,014)
French Possessions	51,988	(44,261)	56,444	(47,569)
Portuguese Possessions	137,856	(127,572)	194,587	(187,153)
Fernando Po	9,844	(7,689)	8,429	(6,414)
Western Africa	857,176	(656,902)	964,354	(752,601)
		1881		*1882*
Gambia and Sierra Leone	317,711	(281,402)	361,085	(319,127)
Gold Coast and Lagos	394,524	(361,612)	514,683	(473,963)
French Possessions	78,032	(65,448)	72,880	(63,357)
Portuguese Possessions	229,177	(225,484)	281,048	(275,597)
Fernando Po	12,738	(9,544)	11,258	(7,840)
Western Africa	1,006,296	(824,337)	1,078,794	(879,525)
		1883		*1884*
Gambia and Sierra Leone	415,801	(372,858)	405,845	(366,161)
Gold Coast and Lagos	510,213	(482,628)	594,852	(557,850)
French Possessions	93,048	(84,787)	213,687	(209,033)
Portuguese Possessions	305,025	(299,398)	680,522	(677,220)
Fernando Po	10,507	(7,395)	13,723	(10,034)
Western Africa	1,493,017	(1,247,853)	1,320,338	(1,112,640)

[1] Cf. William Page, *Commerce and Industry*, vol. ii (London, 1919). The total export values to non-British West Africa given in Page for 1881–1891, are less than the total of exports given here, as they omit French possessions and Fernando Po, in some years, and Portuguese possessions in others.

TABLE III (cont.):

	Total	(United Kingdom)	Tota	(United Kingdom)
		1885		1886
Gambia and Sierra Leone	249,146	(213,917)	422,760	(393,207)
Gold Coast and Lagos	504,165	(452,086)	435,321	(393,925)
French Possessions	201,104	(196,833)	62,098	(56,985)
Portuguese Possessions	311,593	(308,840)	318,667	(315,779)
Fernando Po	11,653	(8,637)	11,263	(8,083)
Western Africa	984,521	(779,263)	870,617	(716,002)
		1887		1888
Gambia and Sierra Leone	289,454	(262,621)	316,374	(286,739)
Gold Coast and Lagos	443,763	(405,136)	509,922	(464,622)
French Possessions	91,096	(84,946)	114,319	(99,676)
Portuguese Possessions	363,499	(360,358)	227,548	(273,379)
Fernando Po	12,092	(9,103)	7,820	(5,694)
Western Africa	772,807	(639,909)	915,749	(768,925)
		1889		1890
Gambia and Sierra Leone	342,304	(308,424)	402,009	(362,962)
Gold Coast and Lagos	519,565	(474,230)	539,343	(489,340)
French Possessions	105,683	(99,653)	119,292	(110,350)
Portuguese Possessions	583,745	(575,937)	532,765	(520,705)
Fernando Po	8,294	(6,522)	11,346	(7,778)
Western Africa	903,221	(769,740)	1,126,313	(971,259)
		1891		1892
Gambia	70,874	(52,541)	57,943	(43,368)
Sierra Leone	367,105	(344,116)	317,984	(291,471)
Gold Coast	392,341	(354,614)	379,579	(340,245)
Lagos	353,812	(337,425)	234,837	(212,098)
Niger Coast Protectorate	674,897	(589,494)	611,366	(501,790)
French Possessions	144,637	(130,262)	477,896	(465,020)
Portuguese Possessions	470,549	(458,845)	334,536	(317,908)
Spanish Possessions	11,680	(8,380)	10,796	(7,158)
Congo Free State	94,847	(89,260)	72,011	(65,795)
Western Coast	413,299	(339,270)	267,974	(221,793)
		1893		1894
Gambia	74,451	(58,373)	55,115	(35,814)
Sierra Leone	346,064	(320,897)	360,012	(333,714)
Gold Coast	420,464	(385,925)	472,187	(431,494)
Lagos	372,284	(350,521)	411,542	(380,089)
Niger Coast Protectorate	624,017	(508,303)	629,179	(514,892)
French Possessions	174,580	(153,122)	196,331	(172,934)
Portuguese Possessions	389,652	(373,040)	400,804	(387,065)

	Total	(United Kingdom)	Total	(United Kingdom)
		1893		1894
Spanish Possessions	12,662	(8,201)	13,367	(9,189)
Congo Free State	114,025	(103,662)	101,983	(91,890)
Western Coast	251,414	(214,911)	261,579	(228,265)
		1895		1896
Gambia	37,722	(25,903)	47,437	(38,183)
Sierra Leone	269,114	(245,283)	334,497	(307,747)
Gold Coast	471,501	(420,791)	501,884	(449,488)
Lagos	418,884	(391,356)	562,130	(526,484)
Niger Coast Protectorate	564,984	(475,471)	607,229	(506,493)
German Possessions	76,557	(66,418)	77,161	(68,355)
French Possessions	308,017	(282,727)	376,314	(348,258)
Portuguese Possessions	418,945	(406,473)	414,759	(402,445)
Spanish Possessions	15,137	(10,008)	15,046	(40,415)
Congo Free State	106,079	(99,882)	98,559	(91,816)
Western Coast	68,931	(53,729)	59,768	(48,847)
		1897		1898
Gambia	81,969	(70,803)	91,376	(69,510)
Sierra Leone	305,759	(278,894)	322,177	(285,878)
Gold Coast	482,378	(432,442)	550,463	(487,456)
Lagos	521,204	(476,160)	578,196	(528,586)
Niger Coast Protectorate	608,193	(505,162)	746,206	(628,075)
German Possessions	101,109	(91,320)	119,862	(109,580)
French Possessions	428,958	(401,224)	573,003	(531,848)
Portuguese Possessions	371,185	(360,121)	439,485	(428,320)
Spanish Possessions	16,228	(13,253)	16,502	(28,738)
Congo Free State	99,102	(91,867)	126,338	(117,628)
Liberia	38,888	(32,048)	46,505	(36,343)
Western Coast	16,867	(14,802)	18,109	(13,789)
		1899		1900
Gambia	82,851	(70,194)	91,124	(77,798)
Sierra Leone	386,095	(336,705)	324,100	(282,568)
Gold Coast	690,107	(615,738)	689,136	(576,456)
Lagos	546,738	(485,577)	595,928	(530,166)
Niger Coast Protectorate	714,455	(607,866)	808,567	(681,161)
German Possessions	137,913	(126,047)	138,922	(120,910)
French Possessions	742,428	(693,255)	751,896	(709,900)
Portuguese Possessions	514,945	(503,788)	1,097,609	(1,084,072)
Spanish Possessions	18,492	(39,956)	24,824	(31,086?)
Congo Free State	112,934	(105,545)	162,308	(151,753)
Liberia	51,797	(39,480)	61,297	(45,563)
Western Coast	13,507	(10,268)	16,958	(14,859)
		1901		1902
Gambia	76,007	(58,294)	100,678	(93,865)
Sierra Leone	338,767	(308,719)	374,644	(349,402)
Gold Coast	999,484	(855,438)	1,174,290	(1,029,236)
Lagos	518,399	(473,447)	611,731	(574,263)

TABLE III (*cont.*):

	Total	(*United Kingdom*)	Total	(*United Kingdom*)
		1901		*1902*
Southern Nigeria Protectorate	783,842	(651,421)	829,504	(690,720)
German Possessions	90,137	(76,868)	127,652	(110,571)
French Possessions	565,024	(529,879)	582,931	(553,689)
Portuguese Possessions	499,619	(488,914)	304,604	(286,919)
Spanish Possessions	24,580	(19,281)	19,088	(15,472)
Congo Free State	138,510	(125,751)	108,705	(102,000)
Liberia	76,650	(57,012)	67,829	(52,235)
Western Coast	12,576	(11,348)	14,161	(12,052)
		1903		*1904*
Gambia	98,133	(90,637)	96,628	(86,596)
Sierra Leone	406,928	(384,253)	368,759	(343,516)
Gold Coast	1,137,717	(1,054,194)	1,035,333	(951,224)
Lagos	536,662	(509,704)	532,488	(499,807)
Southern Nigeria Protectorate	949,150	(809,801)	1,002,210	(871,564)
German Possessions	134,830	(121,873)	129,223	(118,593)
French Possessions	824,280	(799,426)	741,868	(713,965)
Portuguese Possessions	351,875	(345,645)	464,475	(455,722)
Spanish Possessions	19,245	(16,917)	18,364	(14,814)
Congo Free State	111,823	(107,680)	123,210	(117,610)
Liberia	77,777	(71,610)	60,350	(50,069)
Western Africa	18,981	(18,004)	14,989	(12,820)
		1905		*1906*
Gambia	85,063	(79,175)	121,741	(114,084)
Sierra Leone	344,663	(315,829)	407,960	(370,650)
Gold Coast	819,981	(762,340)	1,028,258	(970,142)
Lagos	723,581	(690,597)	692,684	(662,640)
Nigerian Protectorates	1,063,622	(948,706)	1,027,242	(920,103)
German Possessions	186,716	(175,666)	220,305	(205,207)
French Possessions	850,992	(827,631)	909,958	(884,409)
Portuguese Possessions	458,135	(447,169)	901,418	(886,474)
Spanish Possessions	15,857	(12,636)	17,841	(14,494)
Congo Free State	136,245	(129,559)	142,521	(134,308)
Liberia	63,523	(54,059)	85,047	(71,755)
		1907		
Gambia	135,993	(114,516)		
Sierra Leone	474,498	(436,262)		
Gold Coast	1,209,184	(1,144,297)		
Lagos	1,019,566	(975,351)		
Nigerian Protectorates	1,474,834	(1,300,844)		
German Possessions	273,292	(257,548)		
French Possessions	836,917	(803,174)		
Portuguese Possessions	736,565	(717,384)		

	Total	(United Kingdom)	Total	(United Kingdom)
		1907		
Spanish Possessions	22,220	(17,938)		
Congo Free State	115,630	(107,758)		
Liberia	109,109	(95,907)		

		1908		*1909*
Gambia	106,947	(95,892)	108,798	(100,824)
Sierra Leone	428,582	(396,157)	469,456	(431,618)
Gold Coast	1,148,554	(1,076,282)	1,213,568	(1,141,344)
Colony and Protectorate, S. Nigeria	2,511,431	(2,279,584)	2,604,435	(2,388,529)
Protectorate, N. Nigeria	262,995	(258,025)	323,679	(317,429)
German Possessions	190,609	(172,323)	229,166	(210,634)
French Possessions	822,607	(782,362)	1,039,671	(1,008,478)
Portuguese Possessions	501,455	(486,780)	438,103	(423,816)
Spanish Possessions	26,227	(21,005)	18,996	(15,780)
Congo Free State	111,084	(103,448)	101,281	(91,995)
Liberia	74,348	(61,279)	69,511	(57,620)

		1910		*1911*
Gambia	162,356	(150,907)	177,428	(163,370)
Sierra Leone	604,994	(538,076)	606,655	(548,355)
Gold Coast	1,792,183	(1,674,378)	1,783,103	(1,652,424)
Colony and Protectorate, S. Nigeria	2,940,841	(2,701,186)	3,063,937	(2,807,032)
Protectorate, N. Nigeria	191,717	(187,042)	257,677	(252,807)
German Possessions	429,107	(412,035)	476,095	(455,489)
French Possessions	1,493,793	(1,448,168)	1,356,962	(1,307,330)
Portuguese Possessions	1,107,751	(1,094,821)	652,324	(640,059)
Spanish Possessions	22,110	(18,936)	28,261	(24,604)
Congo Free State	153,139	(142,151)	269,218	(256,551)
Liberia	81,266	(67,348)	102,058	(88,087)

		1912		*1913*
Gambia	191,664	(173,454)	247,751	(235,036)
Sierra Leone	734,571	(669,373)	829,412	(755,506)
Gold Coast	1,923,027	(1,735,480)	2,144,960	(1,876,940)
Colony and Protectorate, S. Nigeria	3,616,537	(3,332,134)	3,679,741	(3,410,184)
Protectorate, N. Nigeria	254,262	(246,755)	331,757	(323,693)
German Possessions	496,022	(472,097)	415,410	(385,697)
French Possessions	1,322,618	(1,260,013)	1,542,964	(1,479,321)
Portuguese Possessions	595,131	(583,126)	554,521	(543,347)
Spanish Possessions	40,448	(34,654)	39,557	(34,728)
Congo Free State	382,417	(367,063)	304,564	(288,699)
Liberia	110,837	(92,977)	101,466	(90,258)

TABLE III (*cont.*):

	Total	(United Kingdom)
		1914
Gambia	144,461	(136,849)
Sierra Leone	730,401	(667,162)
Gold Coast	2,232,982	(1,964,543)
Nigeria	4,230,464	(3,955,102)
German Possessions	259,403	(239,621)
French Possessions	930,156	(888,307)
Portuguese Possessions	403,542	(393,313)
Spanish Possessions	32,789	(29,002)
Congo Free State	191,526	(175,844)
Liberia	89,246	(79,410)

TABLE IV

Imports of West African Produce into the United Kingdom: 1812–1914[1]

Official Values (£): 1812–1853
Declared or
Real Values (£): 1854–1914

	1812	*1813*[2]	*1814*	*1815*
Senegal	5,602	..	..	..
Sierra Leone (Gambia)	11,203	?	..	..
West Africa General	92,297	..	..	..
Coast of Africa[3]	..	..	149,663	197,475

	1816	*1817*	*1818*	*1819*
Coast of Africa	127,323	122,353	110,281	153,620

	1820	*1821*	*1822*	*1823*
Coast of Africa	63,282	164,077	114,971	133,515

	1824	*1825*	*1826*	
Coast of Africa	151,910	154,756	167,019	

	1827	*1828*	*1829*	*1830*
Senegal	nil?	nil	nil	nil
Gambia–Sierra Leone– Mesurada	57,122	47,240	57,781	50,076
Windward Coast	435	1,589	404	4,398
Gold Coast	9,200	10,451	11,387	18,819
Volta–Cape of Good Hope	96,674	123,255	188,674	239,318

	1831	*1832*	*1833*	*1834*
Senegal	13,157	8,050	20,779	19,468
Gambia–Sierra Leone– Mesurada	53,988	66,415	45,568	84,405
Windward Coast	1,664	?	2,920	2,730
Gold Coast	39,558	20,595	38,072	46,182
Volta–Cape of Good Hope	203,700	234,908	282,376	322,699

	1835	*1836*	*1837*	*1838*
Senegal	4,694	24,337	22,481	43,973
Gambia–Sierra Leone– Mesurada	75,816	65,968	89,504	77,642
Windward Coast	57	2,460	8,659	6,414
Gold Coast	32,530	44,849	39,937	60,878
Volta–Cape of Good Hope	328,144	290,557	246,343	277,851

	1839	*1840*	*1841*	*1842*
Senegal	79,190	27,681	12,116	27,036
Gambia–Sierra Leone– Mesurada	74,621	71,545	102,336	89,834

[1] Customs 4/8–94 (1812–99); *Trade and Navigation of the United Kingdom*: Annual Accounts, 1853–1914, Customs and Excise Library.
[2] See Table I, p. 595, n. 2.   [3] Western Africa including British possessions.

Table IV (cont.):

	1839	1840	1841	1842
Windward Coast	6,742	5,270	2,320	7,020
Gold Coast	55,382	67,682	59,467	61,174
Volta–Cape of Good Hope	308,419	285,107	426,711	469,312

	1843	1844	1845
Senegal	13,531	?	30,820
Gambia–Sierra Leone–Mesurada	69,886	84,225	79,146
Windward Coast	11,083	3,358	98
Gold Coast	80,438	60,410	64,521
Volta–Cape of Good Hope	368,916	1,163,566	2,607,258

	1846	1847
Senegal	?	(no totals)
Gambia	39,057	
Sierra Leone	44,802	
Windward Coast	?	
Gold Coast	22,112	
Fernando Po	8,416	
Western Coast	479,269	

	1848	1849	1850	1851
French Senegambia	12,644	12,120	nil	95
Gambia	18,225	24,366	28,306	23,665
Sierra Leone	33,007	28,774	26,350	35,443
Gold Coast	47,424	44,542	40,180	49,150
Fernando Po	11,708	13,322	6,814	14,717
Western Coast	498,807	539,875	504,308	671,835

	1852	1853
French Senegambia	nil	nil
Gambia	19,727	18,830
Sierra Leone	39,319	44,353
Gold Coast	24,573	27,903
Fernando Po	40,461	113,507
Western Coast	583,004	537,780

Declared or Real Values

	1854	1855	1856	(Official)
French Senegambia	401	nil	nil	(nil)
Gambia	28,002	29,326	19,522	(12,457)
Sierra Leone	153,559	141,167	99,982	(35,239)
Gold Coast	71,253	113,287	75,531	(38,030)
Fernando Po	125,801	158,136	11,169	(6,351)
Western Coast	1,528,896	1,516,279	1,657,375	(846,216)

	1857	1858	1859	1860
French Senegambia	7	1,417	nil	nil
Gambia	23,273	31,368	22,555	26,300
Sierra Leone	107,062	145,050	98,728	63,261
Gold Coast	86,509	31,829	42,763	51,577
Fernando Po	23,182	3,199	8,767	24,054
Western Coast	1,822,162	1,563,085	1,517,177	1,776,565

	1861	1862	1863	1864
Gambia	47,015	45,246	37,252	41,720
Sierra Leone	72,732	97,692	64,666	54,860
Gold Coast and Lagos	74,466	91,836	89,288	198,806
French Possessions	nil	2	6	nil
Portuguese Possessions	21,834	45,511	36,971	52,226
Fernando Po	25,607	14,030	22,325	26,248
Western Africa	1,467,992	1,655,983	1,352,982	985,694

	1865	1866	1867	1868
Gambia	30,852	42,615	36,055	49,929
Sierra Leone	76,221	82,617	72,063	105,916
Gold Coast and Lagos	295,619	388,500	290,933	382,996
French Possessions	nil	nil	nil	nil
Portuguese Possessions	78,521	71,308	136,999	136,807
Fernando Po	28,648	34,237	41,251	24,560
Western Africa	1,239,816	1,351,629	1,340,744	1,748,031

	1869	1870	1871	1872
Gambia	39,748	33,352	34,988	20,161
Sierra Leone	81,356	68,124	107,278	69,438
Gold Coast and Lagos	488,194	300,469	399,654	386,746
French Possessions	nil	nil	nil	nil
Portuguese Possessions	165,855	151,344	125,795	109,961
Fernando Po	31,293	36,905	20,681	22,947
Western Africa	1,446,770	1,569,437	1,816,419	1,895,656

	1873	1874	1875
Gambia	18,109	37,524	Gambia and } 139,851
Sierra Leone	68,442	92,360	Sierra Leone }
Gold Coast and Lagos	386,854	468,605	469,955
French Possessions	nil	nil	nil
Portuguese Possessions	148,101	121,646	76,694
Fernando Po	54,898	19,138	27,567
Western Africa	1,760,508	1,824,367	1,651,071

	1876	1877	1878	1879
Gambia and Sierra Leone	132,328	176,111	128,540	118,124
Gold Coast and Lagos	548,639	591,958	492,682	462,026
French Possessions	nil	nil	340	nil
Portuguese Possessions	81,996	94,353	72,544	72,528
Fernando Po	16,177	21,207	18,504	14,771
Western Africa	1,597,764	1,531,250	1,213,270	1,386,217

	1880	1881	1882	1883
Gambia and Sierra Leone	157,964	160,730	263,885	241,509
Gold Coast and Lagos	621,284	349,464	368,958	488,106
French Possessions	6,119	4,030	15,389	16,394
Portuguese Possessions	185,072	136,257	142,442	121,049
Fernando Po	13,923	5,604	7,126	7,301
Western Africa	1,705,527	1,449,116	1,582,933	1,617,318

	1884	1885	1886	1887
Gambia and Sierra Leone	254,932	141,271	156,454	205,536
Gold Coast and Lagos	844,324	738,538	670,394	558,370
French Possessions	17,808	13,237	15,788	21,206
Portuguese Possessions	117,251	101,552	90,461	147,587
Fernando Po	12,307	10,435	6,620	5,960
Western Africa	1,360,408	1,131,097	973,165	951,125

TABLE IV (*cont.*):

	1888	*1889*	*1890*
Gambia and Sierra Leone	192,030	183,829	258,839
Gold Coast and Lagos	647,430	742,754	816,933
French Possessions	25,009	14,515	36,132
Portuguese Possessions	94,504	107,424	86,072
Fernando Po	3,883	6,427	8,839
Western Africa	851,942	908,545	971,051

	1891	*1892*	*1893*
Gambia	43,526	21,395	21,012
Sierra Leone	233,808	206,993	271,674
Gold Coast	313,752	265,020	338,794
Lagos	733,250	1,025,334	1,235,098
Niger Coast Protectorate	452,026	268,248	295,669
French Possessions	73,726	44,328	68,437
Portuguese Possessions	88,883	26,692	36,511
Spanish Possessions	7,943	3,390	6,758
Congo Free State	12,503	3,908	16,286
Western Coast	411,043	338,718	227,847

	1894	*1895*	*1896*
Gambia	27,652	37,193	50,404
Sierra Leone	218,712	219,509	241,186
Gold Coast	379,261	394,189	361,402
Lagos	952,165	1,034,650	1,256,717
Niger Coast Protectorate	396,345	428,963	314,216
German Possessions	—	48,431	42,001
French Possessions	222,198	221,704	203,442
Portuguese Possessions	56,845	88,875	33,937
Spanish Possessions	4,964	1,020	387
Congo Free State	11,164	21,064	12,985
Western Coast	116,184	52,123	41,051

	1897	*1898*	*1899*
Gambia	49,238	54,229	30,597
Sierra Leone	191,483	124,268	150,960
Gold Coast	460,131	664,494	706,047
Lagos	1,100,943	1,128,193	1,133,646
Niger Coast Protectorate	351,617	372,918	406,696
German Possessions	68,194	35,007	48,736
French Possessions	312,430	431,159	461,267
Portuguese Possessions	116,554	82,274	68,021
Spanish Possessions	969	2,353	3,113
Congo Free State	13,859	10,632	5,679
Liberia	36,434	43,303	49,284
Western Coast	4,690	7,441	15,943

	1900	*1901*	*1902*
Gambia	22,372	24,624	18,589
Sierra Leone	138,258	127,909	129,426
Gold Coast	621,045	373,168	298,387
Lagos	367,631	264,257	380,866
Southern Nigeria Protectorate	987,717	1,164,622	1,164,303
German Possessions	94,681	111,915	114,881
French Possessions	534,727	406,385	420,257
Portuguese Possessions	75,037	53,635	59,509
Spanish Possessions	6,246	7,352	6,274

	1900	*1901*	*1902*
Congo Free State	17,619	18,114	15,198
Liberia	57,403	67,936	77,749
Western Africa	20,364	20,079	4,455

	1903	*1904*	*1905*
Gambia	15,158	20,305	16,831
Sierra Leone	152,967	159,313	189,397
Gold Coast	430,424	524,665	520,492
Lagos	337,659	322,918	301,360
Nigerian Protectorates	1,206,742	1,429,781	1,340,562
German Possessions	96,572	187,679	68,833
French Possessions	622,120	813,498	755,139
Portuguese Possessions	47,892	66,630	50,000
Spanish Possessions	8,369	7,430	9,290
Congo Free State	21,143	17,428	16,432
Liberia	75,745	62,710	58,247
Western Africa	857	1,843	—

	1906	*1907*	*1908*
Gambia	27,241	35,154	34,742
Sierra Leone	199,056	204,238	119,955
Gold Coast	581,831	761,278	665,550
Lagos	375,219	475,764	S. Nigeria 2,097,247
Nigerian Protectorates	1,556,111	1,955,352	N. Nigeria 11,847
German Possessions	125,413	154,520	158,693
French Possessions	793,661	842,958	605,955
Portuguese Possessions	38,336	46,410	44,497
Spanish Possessions	8,414	7,046	3,090
Congo Free State	29,365	71,232	61,597
Liberia	72,814	76,215	73,954

	1909	*1910*	*1911*	*1912*
Gambia	34,394	53,190	39,704	48,406
Sierra Leone	173,774	197,133	242,691	229,418
Gold Coast	693,672	1,065,314	890,354	836,760
Colony and Protectorate, S. Nigeria	2,280,905	3,238,401	2,796,540	3,052,810
Protectorate N. Nigeria	11,435	4,541	12,067	182,386
German Possessions	174,684	265,044	229,517	238,375
French Possessions	719,055	962,929	772,787	901,992
Portuguese Possessions	109,165	121,660	90,688	148,976
Spanish Possessions	5,027	5,656	4,431	7,750
Congo Free State	22,713	53,417	35,891	22,897
Liberia	63,509	66,440	59,320	45,000

	1913	*1914*
Gambia	54,270	58,194
Sierra Leone	243,156	313,784
Gold Coast	985,689	876,330
Colony and Protectorate, S. Nigeria	3,314,979	}Nigeria 4,742,423
Protectorate N. Nigeria	575,459	
German Possessions	228,776	94,576
French Possessions	888,631	682,698
Portuguese Possessions	171,421	133,080
Spanish Possessions	4,452	7,277
Congo Free State	43,733	Belgian Congo 342,023
Liberia	56,709	53,450

TABLE V

Import and Export Values (£) of British West Africa: 1817–1914[1]

(a)

	Gambia		Sierra Leone	
	Imports	*Exports*	*Imports*	*Exports*
1817			72,516	
1818			94,800	
1819			80,863	
1820			66,725	
1821			105,061	
1822			85,351	
1823		57,651	121,443	
1824		?	77,838	65,261
1825		49,347	77,974	58,965
1826		?	56,190	44,513
1827		?	?	?
1828	50,269	60,302	79,648	41,442
1829	43,081	65,130	109,686	57,854
1830	32,527	50,765	87,251	71,076
1831	39,255	38,434	104,639	81,280
1832	50,522	92,860	90,261[2]	58,920[2]
1833	37,702	66,221	73,264	57,164
1834	63,455	74,033	100,454	58,174
1835	75,502	91,368	69,311	66,903
1836	114,772[2]	147,732[2]	98,856	71,927
1837	99,763	138,226	112,132	98,934
1838	105,625	129,498	91,198	64,996
1839	153,903	162,789	103,384	58,440
1840	105,397	124,669[3]	125,818[3]	65,888[3]
1841	96,708[3]	144,610	100,879	75,939
1842	111,153	146,939	95,617	87,553
1843	85,827	108,404	96,538	104,608
1844	96,152	136,753	83,049	91,444
1845	119,187	154,801	111,474	103,382
1846	95,403	164,805	105,368	125,875
1847	90,706	178,090	116,689	100,818
1848	68,960	152,082[4]	89,173[4]	95,615[4]
1849	73,410	107,802	102,885[4]	111,904[4]
1850	86,036	142,366	97,890[4]	115,139
1851	107,611	186,404	103,477	80,366
1852	217,856	217,856	87,536	117,759
1853	105,896	185,825	98,781[5]	135,808[5]

[1] Where not otherwise stated, statistics are from *Blue Books* and C.O. 442 (Colonial Statistical Tables, 1834–1912). See also, R. Montgomery Martin, *History of the British Colonies* (4 vols., London, 1835), vol. iv, 603; and for Sierra Leone imports, 1817–24, *Parl. Papers*, 1825 (520), p. 5 (exports for those years are given in quantities only).

[2] Also R. Montgomery Martin, *Statistics of the Colonies of the British Empire* (London, 1839), pp. 542–3; *Parl. Papers*, xxxvii, 1847 (696); *Accounts and Papers* (Colonial Reports), 1848, p. 289; 1850, pp. 167–8. It is clear from tables for the Gambia that much of the import values consisted of goods for re-export along the coast: for example the values of goods re-exported from the Gambia in these years were: 1836: £44,865; 1837: £44,221; 1838: £38,283; 1839: £57,980; 1840: £31,750.

[3] These differ from the totals in Colonial Reports, 1850, p. 167.

[4] C.O. 879/2 (26), 1856, tables for 1848–51.

[5] *Accounts and Papers*, xlvi, 1874 [C. 941].

	Gambia		Sierra Leone	
	Imports	*Exports*	*Imports*	*Exports*
1854	124,047	173,882	110,813	154,126
1855	126,454[1]	215,803[1]	114,910	170,548
1856	108,852	176,577	152,907	180,385
1857	118,620	201,628	172,315	288,728
1858	118,693	227,460	139,805	225,349
1859	76,149	110,764	169,727	247,261
1860	73,138	109,137	172,726	304,394
1861	109,581	136,837	168,070	213,204
1862	99,825	154,443	144,269	268,814
1863	172,965	141,673	209,106	295,853
1864	135,777	148,157	190,441	201,808
1865	128,808	138,693	368,545	237,240
1866	108,298	158,368	373,269	259,719
1867	193,420	214,389	284,766	296,718
1868	144,524	187,357	295,826	296,466
1869	94,027	109,312	289,779	404,862
1870	91,996[2]	142,517[2]	280,864[2]	349,488[2]
1871	102,064	153,100	305,850	440,469
1872	123,088	127,225	411,936	436,750
1873	114,404	110,816	490,994	465,113
1874	130,300	180,094	418,009	481,894
1875	142,754	147,465	326,011	350,202
1876	89,356	86,216	288,183	297,035
1877	93,058	125,057	392,134	388,530
1878	147,441	204,299	526,208	391,646
1879	190,167	207,364	409,642	391,081
1880	191,580	138,983	491,993	375,985
1881	142,589	140,423	374,375	365,862
1882	173,890[3]	254,711[3]	398,815	420,017
1883	212,647	208,120	433,581	442,373
1884	184,684	199,483	455,424	377,055
1885	97,168	119,385	318,505	326,932
1886	69,019	79,516	264,886	325,352
1887	78,334	86,933	335,168	333,517
1888	99,850	118,188	301,665	339,043
1889	137,919	167,599	315,881	319,719
1890	148,039	164,374	374,558	349,319
1891	172,118	180,052	444,690	477,656
1892	169,973	172,197	413,117	420,451
1893	166,509	204,721	417,466	398,664
1894	130,349[3]	149,143	478,025	426,499
1895	97,399	93,537	427,338	452,604
1896	110,324	116,981	494,688	449,033
1897	176,327	165,894	457,389	400,748
1898	246,092	247,832	606,349	290,991
1899	240,907	241,936	689,806	336,011
1900	277,659	281,976	558,271	362,471
1901	252,647	233,667	548,286	304,010
1902	303,615	248,140	625,935	403,518
1903	341,063	334,017	700,827	418,631
1904	306,149	311,283	717,236	484,870
1905	305,181	280,272	702,648	563,150

[1] *Accounts and Papers* xlvi 1874 [C. 941].
[2] *Statistical Abstracts*, 1885, no. 22 [C. 4521]; no. 31 [C. 7526]. Including bullion and specie. Totals for Sierra Leone imports, 1870-3, are 'Imports for consumption only'.
[3] Imports for consumption only.

Table V (*cont.*):

	Gambia		Sierra Leone	
	Imports	Exports	Imports	Exports
1906	447,657	428,678	885,851	716,623
1907	445,359	408,476	988,022	831,259
1908	390,740	374,138	813,700	736,755
1909	404,560	477,964	978,807	981,466
1910	578,983	535,447	1,162,470	1,249,367
1911	807,118	682,037	1,267,231	1,300,238
1912	756,854	735,172	1,424,864	1,540,754
1913	1,091,129	867,187	1,750,303	1,731,252
1914	688,007	926,127	1,405,049	1,250,478

Import and Export Values (£) of British West Africa: 1831–1914[1]

(b)

	Gold Coast (Cape Coast Castle)		Lagos Colony	
	Imports	Exports	Imports	Exports
1831	130,851	90,282		
1832	188,067	181,104		
1833	151,439	124,147		
1834	181,263	182,737		
1835	175,985	171,705		
1836	243,023	174,832		
1837	264,990	122,703		
1838	159,405	124,207		
1839	354,460	194,576		
1840	423,170	325,008		
1841	no returns			
1842	,,	,,		
1843	,,	,,		
1844	,,	,,		
1845	,,	,,		
1846	,,	,,		
1847	79,400	148,030		
1848	no returns			
1849	,,	,,		
1850	88,656	263,932		
1851	84,880	219,050[2]		
1852	71,635	159,250[2]		
1853	60,000	115,000		
1854	107,200	200,002		
1855	149,587	140,697		
1856	105,634	120,999		
1857	118,270	124,394		
1858	122,457	154,136		
1859	114,596	118,563		
1860	112,454	110,457		
1861	162,970	145,819		
1862	145,900	102,086		
1863	76,955	53,764	171,138[3]	158,341[3]
1864	no returns		120,796	166,309

[1] Computed from *Blue Books*; Martin, *Statistics of the Colonies*, p. 555 (table of exports valued in trade ounces); *Parl. Papers*, 1842, xi (551), Part II, 1831–40.
[2] C.O. 879/2 (1856) has £218,500 (1851) and £115,300 (1852).
[3] Manuscript returns in Nigerian Records have slight differences from the *Blue Books* sent to England: e.g. [*cont. opposite*]

| | Gold Coast | | Lagos Colony | |
	Imports	Exports	Imports	Exports
1865	no returns		114,284	175,636
1866	,,	,,	220,766	262,699
1867	206,920	160,291[1]	321,997	531,157
1868	140,226	148,909	340,815	517,253
1869	213,491	281,913	416,895	669,598
1870	253,398	378,239	400,558	515,366
1871	250,672	295,208	391,653	589,802
1872	260,102	385,281	366,256	444,848
1873	225,525	330,624	258,884	406,986
1874	no returns		348,636	486,328
1875	364,672	327,012	459,737	517,536
1876	446,088	465,268	476,813	619,260
1877	327,274	387,002	614,359	734,708
1878	394,153	393,457	483,623	577,336
1879	323,039	428,811	527,872	654,380
1880	337,248	482,058	407,370	576,510
1881	398,125	373,258	333,659	460,007
1882	392,975	340,019	428,883	581,064
1883	382,582	363,868	515,394	594,136
1884	527,339	467,228	538,221	672,414
1885	466,424	496,318	542,564	614,181
1886	376,530	406,539	357,831	538,980
1887	363,716	372,446	415,343	491,469
1888	432,112	381,619	442,063	508,238
1889	440,868	415,926	464,260	457,649
1890	562,103	601,348	500,827[2]	595,193
			(see also Protectorate of Southern Nigeria, and Royal Niger Company)	
1891	665,781	684,305	650,192	717,643
1892	597,095	665,064	522,041	577,083
1893	718,353	722,107	749,027	836,295
1894	811,634[3]	850,344	744,561	821,682
1895	924,419	877,804	815,815	985,595
1896	905,135	792,111	901,475	975,263
1897	907,670	857,793	770,511	810,975
1898	1,095,864	992,998[4]	908,351	882,329
1899	1,314,922	1,111,738	966,595	915,934
1900	1,289,343[5]	885,446	830,470	885,112
1901	1,795,187	559,733	737,285	909,232
1902	2,120,433	774,186	930,745	1,337,865
1903	2,082,544	980,942	864,147	1,146,323
1904	2,001,857	1,340,026	919,824	1,210,721
1905	1,486,068	1,646,145	1,222,765	1,139,271

	Imports	Exports	
1863	171,147	153,341	
1864	120,796	166,093	(misprint?)
1867	321,977	513,158	

Where there are differences, *Blue Book* and *Statistical Abstracts* totals have been given.

[1] Excluding Dixcove.
[2] Nigerian Records have £485,502 (1878).
[3] Metcalfe, *Great Britain and Ghana*, p. 751, has £812,830.
[4] Ibid., has £1,992,998.
[5] Ibid., has £1,283,343.

TABLE V (*cont.*):

	Gold Coast	
	Imports	*Exports*
1906	2,058,939	1,996,412
1907	2,366,195	2,641,674
1908	2,029,447	2,525,171
1909	2,394,412	2,655,573
1910	3,439,831	2,697,706
1911	3,784,260	3,792,454
1912	4,023,322	4,307,802
1913	4,952,494	5,427,106
1914	4,456,968	4,942,656

Import and Export Values (£) of British West Africa: 1887–1914

(c)

	Protectorate of Southern Nigeria		Royal Niger Company[1]	
	Imports	*Exports*	*Imports*	*Exports*
1887			73,819	223,450
1888			120,878	230,073
1889			139,465	260,846
1890			180,692	286,200
1891			224,729	335,000
1892			181,012	341,800
1893	726,916[2]	843,501[2]	159,989	405,935
1894	929,333[2]	1,014,088[2]		
1895	730,864[2]	825,099[2]		
1896	750,975[2]	844,333[2]		
1897	655,978[2]	785,605[2]		
1898	639,699[2]	750,223[2]		
1899	732,640[2]	774,648[2]		
1900	725,798[2]	888,955[2]	*Northern Nigeria*	
	(1,115,583)	(1,133,605)		
1901	1,297,116	1,253,706	207,865	73,273
1902	1,246,481	1,254,696	238,110	68,442
1903	1,492,748	1,431,984	264,697	103,863
1904	1,793,460	1,718,717	344,844	152,821
1905	1,753,536	1,710,941	no returns	148,258
	Southern Nigeria (and Lagos)			
1906	3,148,268	3,151,417	no returns	
1907	4,438,907	4,202,704	539,120	235,488
	Southern Nigeria		*Northern Nigeria*	
1908	4,284,830	3,409,288	793,620	314,198
1909	4,962,544	4,169,161	1,215,084	406,722

[1] *Statistical Abstracts* no. 31 [C. 7526].
[2] For twelve months ending 31 March of the year stated. The total in parenthesis for 1900 is for twelve months.

1910	5,857,335	5,304,186	1,374,433	352,981
1911	5,680,981	5,319,467	886,463	836,268
1912	6,430,601	6,089,706	799,275	974,241
1913	7,201,819	7,352,377	105,718	?

	Nigeria	
	Imports	Exports
1914	6,901,072	6,610,046

TABLE VI

Imports and Exports of Bullion and Specie (£): 1870-1914[1]

		Gambia	Sierra Leone	Gold Coast	Lagos
1870	Imports	—	—	—	—
	Exports	—	768	131,776	—
1871	Imports	—	20,265	—	—
	Exports	—	20,827	66,760	—
1872	Imports	—	22,587	2,032	—
	Exports	—	21,186	57,759	50
1873	Imports	—	12,420	—	—
	Exports	—	9,170	—	—
1874	Imports	—	3,332	—	—
	Exports	—	16,051	—	—
1875	Imports	—	90	17,266	5,650
	Exports	—	4,938	46,427	—
1876	Imports	—	40	33,428	2,637
	Exports	—	7,242	65,584	—
1877	Imports	—	—	23,748	5,896
	Exports	—	1,524	39,817	—
1878	Imports	—	1,461	39,574	30,026
	Exports	—	3,630	40,762	—
1879	Imports	28,404	—	22,693	21,741
	Exports	1,400	1,370	79,859	1,903
1880	Imports	21,889	17,634	19,168	15,628
	Exports	4,332	12,128	52,537	14,647
1881	Imports	18,039	12,489	34,846	12,274
	Exports	1,517	20,557	74,989	7,797
1882	Imports	15,757	9,262	24,370	37,581
	Exports	5,035	16,331	84,673	2,721
1883	Imports	21,532	8,741	37,624	28,471
	Exports	3,633	20,537	70,597	2,761
1884	Imports	12,538	25,706	67,941	39,987
	Exports	6,054	39,075	73,830	227
1885	Imports	4,661	6,018	38,680	18,867
	Exports	3,984	42,976	110,208	199
1886	Imports	5,486	6,063	14,824	4,951
	Exports	2,737	27,977	110,531	3,974
1887	Imports	7,136	7,562	20,495	13,412
	Exports	12,148	23,358	104,406	770
1888	Imports	9,768	7,553	24,488	25,595
	Exports	17,383	25,859	95,839	450
1889	Imports	24,266	7,558	40,296	55,715
	Exports	10,375	23,685	114,089	1,456
1890	Imports	27,101	18,537	119,415	61,108
	Exports	9,887	27,926	98,085	9,106
1891	Imports	27,058	15,040	86,479	80,123
	Exports	8,846	38,432	125,605	16,284
1892	Imports	38,101	5,753	48,025	72,515
	Exports	6,724	43,154	128,329	59,283
1893	Imports	20,393	6,696	91,876	120,273
	Exports	6,677	29,067	102,197	35,133
1894	Imports	11,177	14,666	43,255	43,609
	Exports	7,226	42,598	112,855	87,287
1895	Imports	13,432	8,966	78,751	182,648
	Exports	4,490	28,906	133,079	100,789
1896	Imports	19,262	22,389	98,416	138,337
	Exports	543	33,646	152,773	68,870

[1] *Statistical Abstracts*, no. 42, 1890-1904 [Cd. 2679].

		Gambia	Sierra Leone	Gold Coast	Lagos
1897	Imports	36,515	6,045	95,412	69,293
	Exports	2,272	39,054	108,720	69,791
1898	Imports	59,030	45,154	238,684	148,800
	Exports	2,722	24,185	91,025	61,218
1899	Imports	69,335	32,818	248,419	160,351
	Exports	7,439	28,082	79,980	81,576
1900	Imports	83,251	5,129	190,302	75,510
	Exports	41,271	44,491	59,128	131,814
1901	Imports	67,552	1,752	199,823	12,416
	Exports	39,212	38,587	33,007	111,201
1902	Imports	115,376	30,140	287,576	35,431
	Exports	37,790	77,341	143,511	78,182
1903	Imports	126,273	36,068	252,966	332
	Exports	43,277	77,337	310,923	221,374
1904	Imports	108,719	83,086	275,850	51,648
	Exports	61,994	77,888	438,633	148,145
1905	Imports	123,456	83,330	105,407	68,617
	Exports	95,876	87,275	788,229	175,917
					Southern Nigeria
1906	Imports	167,168	145,310	426,999	300,951
	Exports	129,426	121,441	910,383	201,026
1907	Imports	149,656	122,566	436,992	599,566
	Exports	117,828	96,827	1,258,663	339,372
1908	Imports	145,290	83,660	160,789	238,258
	Exports	102,480	147,049	1,314,362	73,377
1909	Imports	146,620	196,650	389,217	432,940
	Exports	126,745	139,163	1,179,134	54,924
1910	Imports	209,077	190,280	656,365	730,075
	Exports	112,194	199,210	874,070	45,734
1911	Imports	384,784	217,832	881,092	432,808
	Exports	215,473	190,475	1,378,837	37,360
1912	Imports	285,223	205,461	720,978	478,624
	Exports	196,429	190,582	1,741,672	316,217
					Nigeria
1913	Imports	471,835	312,268	1,442,189	872,202
	Exports	204,781	240,964	2,028,796	254,731
1914	Imports	299,668	238,298	871,616	612,564
	Exports	232,469	208,571	2,131,845	189,586

TABLE VII

British West Africa. Summary of Revenue and Expenditure (£): 1800–1914 (a)

	Gambia Annual Grants to the Committee of the Company of Merchants Trading to Africa[1]	Gold Coast Annual Grants for Management of the Gold Coast Forts[2]
1800	13,000	40,000
1801	20,000	20,000
1802	20,000	18,000
1803	18,000	16,000
1804	16,000	18,000
1805	18,000	20,054
1806	18,000	20,138
1807	18,000	18,000
1808	—	23,000
1809	—	23,000

	Gambia		Gold Coast	
	Revenue	Expenditure	Revenue[3]	Expenditure
1810			23,500	
1811			no returns	
1812			35,000	no returns
1813			25,000	
1814			25,000	26,939
1815			30,000	31,033
1816			23,000	24,715
1817			23,000	
1818	no returns		28,000	
1819			28,000	
1820			25,000	
1821			25,800	
1822			26,742	
1823			15,500	
1824			52,354	
1825			29,500	
1826			36,996	
1827			41,000	
1828			12,000	
1829	4,276[4]	2,733[4]	4,000	

[1] *Parl. Papers*, 1816, vii (506), p. 109. Prior to this period, the annual grants were:

1750–54: £10,000 annually	1765–70: £13,000 annually
1755: £16,000	1771–81: £15,000
1756–60: £10,000	1782–95: £13,000
1761–3: £13,000	1796–7: £20,000
1764: £10,000	1798–1800: £13,000

[2] *Parl. Papers*, 1827, vii (312); C.O. 267/91–3 (for manuscript reports of the Commissioners of Inquiry); and a summary in Martin, *Statistics of the Colonies*, p. 197.

[3] Annual Parliamentary Grants. By 1831 this had been reduced to £4,000; 1832–9, £3,500; 1840–51, £4,000.

[4] Gross revenue, including Parliamentary Grants for salaries.

	Gambia		Gold Coast	
	Revenue	Expenditure	Revenue	Expenditure
1830	4,493	3,401	4,000	
1831	4,574	4,104		
1832	no returns	5,616		
1833	4,840	3,982	returns of Parliamentary grants only	
1834	no returns	5,158		
1835	5,211	5,436		
1836	6,487	5,356		
1837	5,526	no returns		
1838	4,294	no returns		
1839	7,754[1]	18,589[1]	,,	,,
1840	6,038[1]	3,698[1]		
1841	4,616[1]	2,800[1]		
1842	6,895			
1843	9,322	no returns	,,	,,
1844	7,741			
1845	9,746			
1846	8,737		4,876[3]	4,127[3]
1847	8,889		5,603	4,617
1848	8,948	8,171	4,773	4,344
1849	5,638[2]	11,094[2]	5,579	4,346
1850	7,130	12,292	no returns	
1851	11,345	16,102	5,551	5,770
1852	8,927	13,263	6,740	6,402
1853	11,622[4]	15,127[4]	13,249[7]	6,178[7]
1854	10,412[4]	18,868[4]	10,211	9,376
1855	11,063[4]	14,753[4]	9,830	8,501
1856	17,375	14,097	12,917	10,772
1857	16,434	17,737	7,410	10,087
1858	15,920	15,457	7,062	7,855
1859	15,599	16,962	8,286	
1860	14,154	15,274	7,948	9,558
1861	16,162[5]	16,492[5]	9,334	9,195
1862	15,169	15,178	9,154	9,204
1863	17,263	19,325	8,547	9,409
1864	17,204	17,662	no returns	
1865	14,758	17,151	,,	
1866	19,079	17,681	11,053	11,589
1867	22,415	18,664	10,839	10,993
1868	22,088	17,082	15,404	11,651
1869	15,518	20,236	24,127	18,836
1870	18,969[6]	21,937[6]	30,852[6]	35,609[6]
1871	17,490	16,662	28,609	29,094
1872	17,249	17,783	40,165	42,786

[1] *Blue Books*; cf. *Parl. Papers*, 1843, xxvii (622), which gives different totals for these years.

[2] And C.O. 879/2 (26): 'Memorandum on the British Settlements on the West Coast of Africa', 1856.

[3] Consisting almost entirely of Parliamentary Grants for civil expenditure.

[4] Later accounts in C.O. 879/2 (26) give:

1853	£14,583	£15,127
1854	£16,103	£18,686
1855	£15,353	£15,210.

[5] C.O. 879/3 (124) has Expenditure 1861: £16,563; 1863: £19,004.

[6] *Blue Books* and *Statistical Abstracts*, 1870–84, no. 22 [C. 4521].

[7] *Blue Books*, and C.O. 879/2 (40). Including Parliamentary Grants.

TABLE VII (*a*) (*cont.*):

	Gambia		Gold Coast	
	Revenue	Expenditure	Revenue	Expenditure
1873	19,335	24,068	65,706[1]	61,207
1874	21,380	20,787	74,868	47,796
1875	22,700	19,565	67,368	71,644
1876	19,787	21,489	64,788	93,994
1877	26,585	21,381	93,347	82,742
1878	25,731	19,807	105,092[2]	68,411
1879	28,505	20,639	90,432	98,064
1880	24,553	19,926	119,500	86,957
1881	24,451	22,116	116,424	134,776
1882	26,625	22,964	104,817	116,501
1883	28,866	23,982	105,648	99,289
1884	24,959	29,482	125,956	112,957
1885	20,236	26,595	130,457	112,698
1886	14,233	23,353	122,531	133,294
1887	13,377	23,920	122,351	139,443
1888	20,986	21,335	97,807	133,468
1889	26,281	21,566	111,388	125,003
1890	30,573	22,759	156,499	117,899
1891	31,038	27,697	186,022	133,407
1892	30,978	28,740	183,075	158,104
1893	31,899	38,143	201,783	178,935
1894	23,798	31,640	218,761	226,932
1895	20,561	28,867	230,076	265,289
1896	26,172	25,301	237,460	282,278
1897	39,415	27,059	237,857	406,370
1898	46,718	29,035	258,822[3]	377,976
1899	46,840	30,405	322,796	309,658
1900	49,161	29,818	333,283	515,657
1901	43,726	48,518	471,193	469,459
1902	51,016	51,536	491,755	522,608
1903	55,564	67,504	554,553	593,956
1904	54,180	52,301	682,193	622,377
1905	51,868	72,297	572,462	596,119
1906	65,430	56,900	673,102	602,307
1907	65,892	57,729	703,718	602,124
1908	57,898	61,097	752,142	667,292
1909	72,676	56,237	778,552	709,367
1910	82,880	63,301	1,006,633	775,482
1911	86,454	71,390	1,111,632	889,501
1912	96,222	81,340	1,230,850	1,020,518
1913	124,995	95,210	1,301,566	1,257,540
1914	86,071	120,921	1,331,713	1,572,333

[1] Including a Parliamentary Grant of £40,000.
[2] Higher revenues because of increased customs returns which doubled from 1875 (£59,525) to 1884 (£110,854).
[3] Excluding Imperial Grants in aid, 1898–1901: £195,000 for the Northern Territories, £399,300 for Ashanti disturbances.

Summary of Revenue and Expenditure (£): 1807–1914 (b)

	Sierra Leone	
	Revenue[1]	Expenditure
1807	14,000	
1808	16,310	
1809	17,360	
1810	15,710	
1811	14,416	
1812	14,020	16,002[2]
1813	14,102	23,788
1814	14,102	29,693
1815	15,760	28,725
1816	15,660	41,444
1817	15,814	45,947
1818	15,450	55,336
1819	16,688	68,684
1820	22,358	71,045
1821	22,444	75,032
1822	22,177	74,980
1823	22,817	94,951
1824	53,729[3]	76,682
1825	32,761[4]	39,504
1826	33,078[4]	no returns
1827	16,200[4]	17,809
1828	14,891[4]	17,125
1829	incomplete returns	14,047
1830	16,751[5]	13,910[6]
1831	22,239[7]	22,717[7]
1832	24,156	26,143
1833	23,135	25,032
1834	22,663	23,487
1835	28,050	27,089
1836	26,285	27,195
1837	incomplete returns	30,854
1838	,,	30,184
1839	,,	30,668
1840	17,332[8]	21,979

[1] Total grants for civil expenditure. For military and naval expenditure, see N. A. Cox-George, *Finance and Development in West Africa. The Sierra Leone Experience* (London, 1961), pp. 156–7. *Parl. Papers*, 1830, xxi (57); C.O. 267/91–3.

[2] *Parl. Papers*, 1830, xxi (57). Including expenditure for the settlement of Liberated Africans, 1812–28. After 1812, revenues were derived also from modest customs, rising to £4,656 in 1819.

[3] Including grants for the Liberated African Department.

[4] Grants and net revenues (customs, courts, etc.), 1825–8.

[5] Including a Parliamentary grant.

[6] Martin, *Statistics of the Colonies*; Cox-George, *Finance and Development in West Africa*, p. 156, has £13,951.

[7] *Blue Book*, 1836, including expenditure for the militia and the Liberated African Department, 1831–6.

[8] Revenue from 1840 to 1852 excludes grants in aid of civil government. Cox-George, *Finance and Development in West Africa*, p. 156, for civil grants:

1840	£13,684	1843	£13,340	1846	£17,448	1849	£8,564
1841	£14,300	1844	£13,120	1847	£12,112	1850	£8,197
1842	£14,386	1845	£14,745	1848	£14,533	1851	£7,853
						1852	£6,710

TABLE VII (b) (cont.):

	Sierra Leone		Lagos	
	Revenue	Expenditure	Revenue	Expenditure
1841	11,137	26,963		
1842	9,779	26,209		
1843	12,603	25,214		
1844	16,842	28,880		
1845	20,953	34,755		
1846	20,695	23,680		
1847	24,180	40,831		
1848	21,910	37,584		
1849	20,399	29,451		
1850	17,836	27,908		
1851	20,858	28,002		
1852	17,914	26,430		
1853	26,659[1]	25,043		
1854	29,225	27,585		
1855	28,778	32,418		
1856	35,601	34,457		
1857	33,068	30,582		
1858	30,681	28,931		
1859	31,433	29,147		
1860	34,734	31,136		
1861	36,461	36,243		
1862	37,355	44,265	7,130[4]	6,511[4]
1863	47,334[2]	47,051	16,708	15,837
1864	49,113	51,061[3]	21,335	22,805
1865	46,405	59,042[3]	24,081	24,095
1866	58,889	60,539	23,823	23,602
1867	55,808	69,062	29,974	30,195
1868	56,907	55,694	33,896	33,712
1869	69,005	70,465	40,438	39,431
1870	67,135[5]	68,033[5]	41,684[5]	42,379[5]
1871	80,486	76,131	45,116	45,611
1872	94,436	86,783	41,346	41,346
1873	92,103	103,629	52,240	52,225
1874	92,970	91,290	39,336	37,296
1875	116,217	113,652	43,367	44,380
1876	57,721	72,295	46,448	45,170
1877	94,460	87,987	59,390	42,305
1878	69,142	57,113	50,889	49,736
1879	75,790	60,808	54,940	45,935
1880	76,008	87,775	47,987	55,476
1881	69,814	71,530	42,422	45,462
1882	65,537	62,913	44,636	44,039

[1] Gross revenues from 1853, including Parliamentary Grants: *Blue Books*; C.O. 879/2 (26); *Parl. Papers*, 1874, xlvi [C. 941].
[2] Slightly different totals are given in *Parl. Papers*, 1874, xlvi [C. 941]:

1863	£47,136	1866	£62,161
1864	£48,692	1867	£64,871
1865	£46,934	1868	£59,272
		1869	£69,617

[3] Cox-George, *Finance and Development in West Africa*, p. 156, has £51,510 (1864), £48,490 (1865), for expenditure.
[4] *Blue Books: Parl. Papers*, 1874, xlvi [C. 941].
[5] *Statistical Abstracts*, no. 51, 1915 [Cd. 7786].

	Sierra Leone		Lagos	
	Revenue	Expenditure	Revenue	Expenditure
1883	65,491	76,762	50,559	37,879
1884	76,210	85,259	57,932	44,684
1885	67,760	70,917	63,505	40,314
1886	62,935	63,482	53,507	55,383
1887	59,094	58,334	51,347	78,610
1888	63,035	63,288	57,058	60,840
1889	68,336	64,271	57,633	57,488
1890	73,708	63,056	56,341	63,600

			Lagos (and Southern Nigeria)	
1891	89,869	69,511	78,625	66,388
1892	86,866	83,852	68,421	86,513
1893	92,769	84,691	115,317	101,251
1894	98,838	93,100	137,017	124,829
1895	97,852	96,690	142,049	144,484
1896	96,109	115,183	179,745	168,445
1897	106,009	111,678	177,421	182,669
1898	117,682	121,112	196,444[1]	203,803
1899	168,382	145,089	192,792	223,289
1900	168,668	156,421	211,467[2]	187,125[2]
1901	192,138	173,457	275,022[2]	235,495[2]
1902	205,765	184,940	359,960[2]	254,331[2]
1903	237,730	206,464	334,696[2]	303,086[2]
1904	240,472	237,892	410,251[2]	354,254[2]
1905	281,523	295,490	292,924[3]	303,336[3]
1906	305,074	285,661	404,608	450,383
1907	359,104	345,567		
1908	321,000	341,871		
1909	361,326	336,746		
1910	424,215	360,799		
1911	457,759	387,142		
1912	559,855	450,664		
1913	618,383	556,646		
1914	675,689	680,146		

	Niger Coast Protectorate	
	[For years ending 31 March]	
1893	97,749	98,611
1894	173,606	138,539
1895	127,353	176,331
1896	155,513	145,044
1897	112,441	128,411[4]
1898	153,181	121,901
1899	169,568	146,752
1900	164,108	176,140

[1] Excluding £10,000 Parliamentary Grant for telegraphs.
[2] For twelve months ending 31 March for the year indicated.
[3] For nine months ending 31 December 1905.
[4] Including £20,000 paid to the Royal Niger Company for losses in the Akassa raid.

TABLE VII (b) (cont.):

| | Niger Coast Protectorate | | Northern Nigeria Protectorate | |
	Revenue	Expenditure	Revenue[2]	Expenditure
	Southern Nigeria Protectorate			
1901	380,894	306,193	335,730	241,857
1902	361,815	331,397	318,424	298,519
1903	440,809	455,294	357,009	389,391
1904	470,606	477,756	508,727	498,986
1905	550,233	516,395	185,545[3]	520,546
1906	⎰556,780	⎰580,731	217,087	498,260
	⎱659,809[1]	⎱605,907[1]		
	Colony and Protectorate of Southern Nigeria			
1907	1,459,553	1,217,337	213,005	498,848
1908	1,387,975	1,357,763	248,444	540,644
1909	1,361,891	1,648,680	283,436	566,843
1910	1,933,235	1,592,282	344,989	565,760
1911	1,956,176	1,717,259	615,291	827,939
1912	2,235,412	2,110,498	528,993	710,532
1913	2,668,198	2,096,311	749,310	830,490
	Nigeria			
1914	2,948,381	3,596,764		

[1] For twelve months, 1906.
[2] For years ending 31 March. The totals include Imperial grants in aid—about £300,000 every year, contributions from Southern Nigeria (£40,000 a year), and small amounts of ordinary revenue.
[3] Excluding Imperial grants.

TABLE VIII

Public Debt and Expenditure (£) from Loans on Public Works:
1871–1914[1]

	1871	1872	1873	1874	1875
Lagos					
Public debt	14,443	18,628	18,453	21,517	11,517
Sierra Leone					
Public debt	26,580	27,581	52,879	53,594	80,335

	1876	1877	1878	1879	
Lagos					
Public debt	288	288	288	288	
Sierra Leone					
Public debt	74,392	50,000	66,000	104,000	

	1880	1881	1882	1883	1884
Lagos					
Public debt	288	716	..	..	..
Sierra Leone					
Public debt	83,000	73,000	73,000	63,000	58,000

	1885	1886	1887	1888	
Lagos					
Public debt	..	..	..	..	
Sierra Leone					
Public debt	58,000	58,000	58,000	58,000	

	1889	1890	1891	1892	
Lagos					
Public debt	..	..	..	..	
Sierra Leone					
Public debt	58,454	58,454	50,000	50,000	

	1893	1894	1895	1896	
Southern Nigeria					
Public debt	..	..	..	..	
Loan expenditure	..	..	7,723	69,173	
Sierra Leone					
Public debt	..	..	..	25,000	

	1897	1898	1899	
Southern Nigeria				
Public debt	..	..	..	
Loan expenditure	128,985	141,767	317,691	
Sierra Leone				
Public debt	25,000	..	..	

	1900	1901	1902	1903
Southern Nigeria				
Public debt	972,902	1,066,124	1,081,024	1,248,329
Loan expenditure	294,370	111,043	139,976	77,453
Sierra Leone				
Public debt	..	457,665	589,448	783,369
Loan expenditure	..	492,422	150,378	218,698
Gold Coast				
Public debt	..	1,330,020	2,082,718	2,252,975
Loan expenditure	..	..	..	1,049,338

[1] *Statistical Abstracts*, 1885 [C. 4251]; 1924 [Cmd. 2224].

TABLE VIII (cont.):

Southern Nigeria	1904	1905	1906	1907
Public debt	1,140,341	2,000,000	2,000,000	2,000,000
Loan expenditure	583,536	495,088	192,512	296,872
Sierra Leone				
Public debt	1,274,420	1,277,129	1,279,243	1,208,137
Loan expenditure	170,794	52,198	50,110	32,214
Gold Coast				
Public debt	2,272,501	2,248,159	2,252,743	2,206,965
Loan expenditure	675,602	..	44,617	112,387

Southern Nigeria	1908	1909	1910	1911
Public debt	5,000,000	5,000,000	5,000,000	10,000,000
Loan expenditure	852,517	611,490	1,023,867	589,790
Sierra Leone				
Public debt	1,376,447	1,271,027	1,262,501	1,255,101
Loan expenditure	13,844	5,694	3,333	46,005
Gold Coast				
Public debt	2,207,164	2,663,448	2,514,118	2,489,118
Loan expenditure	99,348	293,570	271,799	143,041

Southern Nigeria	1912	1913	1914
Public debt	8,267,655	8,267,569	8,267,569
Loan expenditure	307,083	566,161	335,753
Sierra Leone			
Public debt	1,248,048	1,295,676	1,730,648
Loan expenditure	74,741	75,794	91,424
Gold Coast			
Public debt	2,469,118	2,449,118	3,464,118
Loan expenditure	117,725	232,547	247,788

TABLE IX

Prices at Liverpool for West African Produce, 1815[1]

	Unit	£	s.	d.		Unit	£	s.	d.
Palm Oil	ton	35	0	0	Ebony	ton	15	0	0
Ivory	cwt.	19	0	0	Beeswax	ton	140	0	0
Pepper	cwt.	17	0	0	Gum copal	lb.		1	6
Guinea grains	cwt.	5	0	0	Gum senegal	lb.		2	0
Barwood	ton	8	0	0	Hides	piece		2	0
Camwood	ton	21	0	0	Gold	oz.	3	18	0

[1] *Parl. Papers*, 1816, vii (506), p. 12.

TABLE X

Prices of goods shipped by the African Committee to Sierra Leone: 1808–1815[1]

	Unit	Prices of the African Committee			Prices at Sierra Leone		
		£	s.	d.	£	s.	d.
Gunpowder	barrel	6	6	0	12	7	0
Beef	tierce	10	0	0	15	3	6
Pork	barrel	6	12	0	10	9	0
Flour	cask	3	1	0	4	3	8
Bejutapauts	piece	1	0	3	{ 1	18	6
					{ 2	1	7
Niccanees	,,		13	6	1	7	7
Romals	,,		12	5	1	5	8
,,	,,		12	5	1	4	0
Sustracundees	,,		14	0	1	8	9
Cushtees	,,		13	4	1	0	1
Chelloes	,,	1	1	4	1	12	0
Cordage	cwt.	6	9	6	18	12	5
Canvas	bolt	4	10	0	8	0	0
Linseed oil	gall.		9	6	{	17	6
					{ 1	0	0
Rum	,,		5	2		8	6
Iron bars	each		1	10		6	6
,, ,,	cwt.		?		{	18	6
					{ 1	1	0
Tar	barrel	'none shipped'			3	0	0
Lead bars	cwt.	1	16	6	3	7	2
White lead	,,	3	14	3	{ 6	9	0
					{ 7	1	11
Black paint	?	6	6	0	{ 11	4	0
					{ 11	10	8
Yellow paint	?	3	3	0	{ 5	12	0
					{ 8	12	0
Bright red	?	2	12	0	{ 5	12	0
					{ 4	17	0

[1] *Parl. Papers*, 1816, vii (506), p. 6; see also p. 113 for an identical list.

TABLE XI

Official values of British imports from Africa and exports to Africa:
1825[1]

Imports		Unit	£	s.	d.
Dye and Hardwoods:	Fustic	per ton	9	o	o
	Logwood	,,	12	o	o
	Mahogany	,,	8	o	o
Elephants' teeth		per cwt.	6	o	o
Gum arabic, senegal		,,	2	2	6
Palm Oil		,,	1	o	o

Exports	Unit	£	s.	d.
Foreign and Colonial merchandise				
Cotton manufactures of Europe	per yard		1	8
Dyed calicoes (various)	,,		1	8
Brandy	per gal.		5	o
Geneva	,,		5	o
Rum	,,		6	o
Tobacco	per pound			4½
British and Irish manufactures				
Calicoes, white or plain	per yard		1	3
,, printed	,,		1	6
Earthenware	per 100 pieces		5	o
Gunpowder	per pound			7¼
Guns	each		15	o
Hardwares and cutlery	per cwt.	2	15	o
Bar iron	per ton		10	6
Salt	per bushel			8
British spirits	per gal.		3	o

[1] *Parl. Papers*, 1826 (385), p. 22.

INDEX

Abeokuta (Abbeokuta), 101, 122, 128, 150, 479, 488; *see also* Egba; Yoruba
Abomey, *see* Dahomey
Aborigines Protection Society, 473, 453
Acts, colonial, and Ordinances, 362; Public Lands (1876), 561; Supreme Court (1876), 248; Native Jurisdiction (1882), 249; British Settlements (1887), 292, 293; Foreign Jurisdiction (1890), 243, 251, 256, 260, 272, 274; Gambia Protectorate (1894), 279; Gold Coast Concessions (1900), 558, 563, 583, 585–6, 594; Sierra Leone Concessions (1900), 585; Forestry (1901, 1902), 544; Nigerian Courts (1913), 359; *see also* Orders in Council
Adansi, 68, 85
administration, in West Africa, 2, 242–371; The Gambia, 3, 4–6, 7–16, 201–2, 270–2, 279–80; Gold Coast, 49–50, 91, 295–6, 321, 324–32; Northern Nigeria, 311, 334–5, 339–40, 344–5, 366, 398–401; Northern Territories, 308–9, 390; Sierra Leone, 41–8, 246, 257, 275, 284–5, 312–18, 388–9; Yorubaland, 138–9, 243, 302, 345–6; *see also* civil service; protectorates; courts; taxation
Admiralty, 6; *see also* Navy
African Aid Society, 128
African Association, 138
agriculture, 420, 560–1, 565–70, 574–80; *see also* coffee; cotton; cocoa; groundnuts; palm-oil; plantations
Akassa, 3, 182, 288–90
Altham, E. A., 461
Amakiri (Amachree), Chief of New Calabar, 104
amalgamation, in Nigeria, 351–3, 361–71
ammunition, 85, 122, 232, 431, 455, 460; used against Burmi, 156
Anderson, H. P., 179, 185
Anderson, J., 383
annexation, in West Africa, 158–241, 275; Baro, 516–17
Ansa, John Owusu (Ansah), 68, 80, 84, 90
Antrobus, Sir R., 309, 450, 467, 518
Appa, 184
Aqua (Akwa), *see* Cameroons
arms, trade in, 84–5, 276–7, 344, 446, 455, 460–1; *see also* guns; gunpowder; muskets; ammunition
Armstrong, W. Cairns, 138

army, *see* West African Frontier Force; West India Regiment
Aro, 341
Asantehene (King of Ashanti), 2–3, 56, 59–68
Ashanti, 2–3, 50–6, 59–61, 295–6, 321, 324–32, 430
Ashanti Goldfields Corporation Ltd., 326, 392–3, 420, 421, 495–6, 500, 548–9, 563
Assin, 50

Badibu (Baddibu), 216, 222, 234
bafts, blue (*guinées*), 421, 431–2, 462
Bank of British West Africa, 244, 385
Barnett, Assistant Inspector, 56
Barra, 5, 12
Barrow, Capt., 53
bars, *see* currencies
Bathurst, 4–16
Beach, Sir Michael Edward Hicks, 18, 99, 166, 168, 171, 246, 376, 426, 475
Bell, Sir Henry Hesketh, 402
Benin, 95, 129, 141, 147, 183
Berkeley, George, 373
Berlin (West Africa) Conference, 185–7, 189–90
Bickersteth, E. R., 133, 134
Bida, 148, 336–8; *see also* Nupe
Birtwistle, C. A., 579
Blake, E. E., 401
Bokari, Alimamy, 30, 31
Bokari Sardu, 4, 7
Bondu, 2, 4, 7, 194
Bonnat, J., 329 and n.
Bonny, 95, 102–3, 182, 340
Borgu, 208, 213, 215, 227–33, 236
botanical stations, 526–7, 577; *see also* agriculture
Bower, R. L., 146
Brackenburg, Commander J. W., 50, 194
Bramston, 120, 125, 292
Brass, 94
Brazza, Pierre Savorgnan de, 178, 180, 432
Brew, James H., 84, 539
British and African Steamship Company, 381–2, 385, 441, 512
British subjects, 60, 61, 99, 108, 114, 116, 130, 174, 245, 251, 423
Brown, Thomas, 421
Brussels Conference, 467–8, 469–70
Buaké, Prince, 51
budgets, colonial, 375, 381; *see also* finance

Newbury, Colin W
British policy towards West Africa; select
documents ...   Oxford, Clarendon Press, 1965-

    v.   illus., maps (part fold.)   23cm.

    Bibliographical footnotes.
    Contents.-[v.1] 1786-1874.-[v.2] 1875-1914,
with statistical appendices, 1800-1914.

1.Africa, West-Hist.-Sources.   2.British in West Africa.
I.Title.